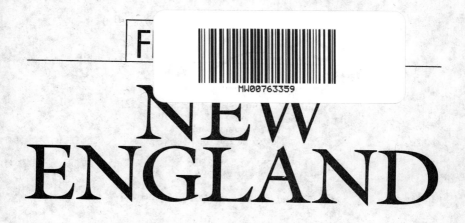

NEW
ENGLAND

TOM BROSNAHAN

1990

PRENTICE HALL

New York □ London □ Toronto □ Sydney □ Tokyo □ Singapore

Published by Prentice Hall Trade Division
A Division of Simon & Schuster Inc.
15 Columbus Circle
New York, NY 10023

ISBN 0-13-218355-2
ISSN 1044-2286

Manufactured in the United States of America

CONTENTS

MAPS

For Jane
Thanks to Kim Grant for her help.

INTRODUCING NEW ENGLAND

1. THE REASON WHY

2. FROMMER'S DOLLARWISE TRAVEL CLUB—HOW TO SAVE MONEY ON ALL YOUR TRAVELS

1. The Reason Why

When it comes to American history and culture, New England is where it all began.

Certainly history is not the only thing to attract you to the six states that make up the region: Connecticut, Rhode Island, Massachusetts, Maine, New Hampshire, and Vermont. Each state has natural beauties worth bragging about, like the beaches of Rhode Island, the windswept dunes of Cape Cod, the rugged coasts of Maine, or the Green Mountains of Vermont. And there's the local cuisine, particularly the seafood: lobster, the freshest you can get; clam chowder, easily the best in the world; Vermont cheddar cheese; hotcakes with New Hampshire's maple syrup.

New England is not all cities and civilization, either—despite all the talk about the Eastern megalopolis. The Appalachian Trail has its beginnings here; the sandy shores of Cape Cod are over 100 miles long; Vermont alone has over two dozen challenging ski areas; and if even these places are too busy for you, head for the un-tracked wilderness forests of northern Maine. In fact, it's not really the big cities such as Hartford, Providence, and Boston that set the tone of New England community life, but rather the small New England villages—Litchfield, Conn.; Newfane, Vt.; Kennebunkport, Me.—each with its village green surrounded by the church, school, library, and town hall, each village separated from its neighbor by rolling pastureland, lush woodland, and glacial lakes.

Although New England is not *just* history, one soon discovers that New Englanders love the region *because* of its history, because it is unique. Only here can you see Plymouth Rock, climb Bunker Hill, visit the site of the very first Thanksgiving feast. At Connecticut's Mystic Seaport you can see a New England maritime town out of the past, re-created and in full operation; and at Sturbridge Village and Plimoth Plantation the crafts of the colonial period are performed as they were centuries ago.

Even in modern Boston the history of New England is everywhere, for you'll come across charming colonial buildings nestled between sleek skyscrapers, and cobblestone streets lit by gas on Beacon Hill; you can even trace America's ethnic history by exploring the neighborhoods that tenaciously hold to their native culture: Italian, Irish, Chinese, Afro-American.

You might say that the lifeblood of New England is tradition. And out of this very tradition spring so many new ideas and ways of doing things. Harvard is an excellent example of the particular relationship of old to new in New England. Harvard, the oldest college in the United States and so tradition-bound, is one of the great institutions to which we look for innovation in research and progress in education.

THE GOALS OF THIS GUIDE: This is a complete guidebook, containing everything you'll need to know about New England at a price lower than that of any comparable guidebook on the shelf. I've searched through the cities, towns, and villages looking for quaint, charming bed-and-breakfast guesthouses, the small places other guides can't afford to uncover. I've sampled the restaurants that local people enjoy, and I keep track of the chefs and the management. I've described these establishments in enough detail that you'll know what you're getting, and what makes one place different from another. There's plenty of information on how to get from here to there, by every possible means, and I've kept in mind both the traveler with a car, and the one without. Every major attraction in New England is thoroughly described in this book, plus many of the charming, lesser-known sights off the beaten track.

If all this sounds sensible and self-evident, think again. These days, some guidebooks are written by committees of editors, others are done entirely through the mail, still others charge money (under one scheme or another) for the "privilege" of being included in their pages, or for stickers saying "Featured in Such-and-such Guide," or for signs to hang out front, or for membership in an "association." The only person who pays me anything is you, the reader—by buying this book. I'm working for *you*.

INFORMATION IN NEW YORK CITY: Residents and visitors to New York City are lucky, because they can benefit from the services of the **New England Vacation Center,** 630 Fifth Ave., Rockefeller Center Concourse Shop No. 2, New York, NY 10111 (tel. 212/307-5780); it's located in Rockefeller Center, between 50th and 51st Streets.

SOME DISCLAIMERS: When I travel around New England looking for the best hotels, bed-and-breakfast guesthouses, country inns, restaurants, and places of amusement, I do my best to keep a secret of what I'm up to, hoping to be treated as any newly arrived customer would be treated, and thus find out firsthand how an establishment is run. Sometimes it's necessary to confess I'm preparing a guidebook —better that than be mistaken for the Mad Bomber as I peer into kitchens, facilities, and rooms. And so the recommendations found in this book are strictly personal, unaffected by reputations or the blandishments of managers. No establishment in this book has paid to appear in these pages, which means that if I get a lot of complaint letters from readers (which I read and answer personally), I can remove any establishment without qualm.

But I hasten to add that if you do not find a favorite place of yours listed in these pages, it's because this is not an exhaustive guide, but rather a selection of some of the best, most convenient, unique, quiet, friendly—in short, *satisfying*—places in New England. They were chosen not according to some inflexible checklist of facilities and luxuries, but with the practical day-to-day needs of discerning travelers in mind.

Prices and Inflation

Remember as you use this book that inflation is a fact of life today, and although I tried to present the most complete, inclusive, and accurate price information of any guidebook, prices may change between the time the book goes to press and when you use it. Check prices when you arrive to avoid confusion.

The prices of rooms, meals, and other expenses given with my recommendations are as accurate as I could make them; if I determined that a price rise was likely between the time of my visit and the time of yours, I figured the rise into the quoted prices. No establishment promised me to keep the prices I quote, and therefore you cannot demand of any establishment that they charge you exactly what is quoted here. When in doubt, a quick telephone call is the best way to determine whether or not prices have changed.

Safety

Whenever you're traveling in an unfamiliar city or region, stay alert. Be aware of your immediate surroundings. Wear a moneybelt and don't sling your camera or purse over your shoulder; wear the strap diagonally across your body. This will minimize the possibility of your becoming a victim of crime. Every society has its criminals. It's your responsibility to be aware and be alert even in the most heavily touristed areas.

THE FOUR SEASONS: Weather in New England is a much-discussed topic, but it is always surrounded by a certain fatalism, not so much because there's a lot of bad weather, but because it's so unpredictable. My rough, personal survey of weather reports has revealed that the weather forecasters are wrong a surprising 60% of the time for Boston! But, after all, Boston does seem to have its own weather: a snowfall may cover all New England, but stop short at Rte. 128, Boston's ring road; or a summer downpour may drench the city while the sun shines everywhere else. However, there are some generalizations that seem to hold true from year to year, and these will affect your plans on when to visit New England.

Spring

Coming very late and staying very briefly, spring tends to be a disappointment. The week or two of spring days in the normal year are a delight, with cool temperatures in the evening and just the perfect degree of warmth during the day, in bright, clear sun. In the countryside the thaw brings "Mud Time," the period between frost and spring planting. Mud Time is the slowest season for tourist facilities, coming after ski season and before summer warmth and school vacations bring out the city folk. Thus many country inns, resorts, and amusements close for a few weeks in April or thereabouts.

Summer

By mid-June, summer is well established and despite the region's northerly and coastal location, it can be pretty hot and sometimes quite humid. When it's 85° (or even up to 95°) and humid, as it often is through mid-September, head for the beaches, the islands, mountains, lakes, and riverbanks. Sailing, along the coast or on the rivers, is choice activity, as is a hike to the top of Mount Washington, or a week at a beach on Narragansett Bay. But a drive through the Berkshires or along the Connecticut coast can also be very satisfying.

Autumn

This is undoubtedly New England's glory and its finest season, and if you have a choice of vacation times this is the one to pick. Although you may have to forsake swimming, the famous fall foliage is a worthy substitute; it's at its peak usually in late September and early October, starting in northern Maine, New Hampshire, and Vermont and moving southward as the weeks pass. Days are still warm and very pleasant, nights cool but comfortable. City people load their bikes into the car and head for the country, picking up fresh apple cider, pumpkins, and squash on the way home. Fresh cranberries are on sale in the markets all autumn, and although the blueberry-picking season is past, many apple orchards open on a "pick-your-own" basis to provide the energetic with the freshest fruit possible at a very low price. *Everybody* wants to get away for the weekend, no matter where they live. Those who don't want to tangle in the traffic on weekends can take special bus and rail **foliage tours** from the major cities. Tourist resorts and inns stay open, mostly, through September and often to Columbus Day. Those that stay open all year sometimes close for two weeks or so from mid-October to early December to give the staff a break before the advent of the ski season. By Thanksgiving, everyone's getting in shape for the ski season and shopping for the holidays.

Winter

Winter, as they say, depends: in the winter of 1976–1977, the region had six inches of snow in November, which is very early, for the first flurries usually come in mid-December, when hopes are high that the accumulation will be sufficient for good skiing during the holiday season. Sometimes snow wishes are too well answered, as in the Great Blizzard of 1978, which piled six feet of snow on Boston, closing the city for a week. Ski reports appear in newspapers and the broadcast media, and the special ski condition phones go into operation. January through March is cold and snowy, and the skiing may be quite good through April; gray snowy days alternate with brilliant, crisp, sunny days when the air's very cold but the sun's warmth makes it pleasant. Those who aren't skiing take advantage of the cities' cultural season, perhaps escaping to an inn somewhere in the snow-clad mountains for a weekend.

Mount Washington Weather

None of this applies to Mount Washington in New Hampshire, of course. This "highest peak in New England" is said to have the worst weather in all the U.S., and New Englanders delight in exchanging horror stories of the latest report: winds of 150 mph (the record is 211 mph!), temperatures of minus 40° Fahrenheit, wind-chill factors that don't seem earthly. Regional news media often carry the reports even though they don't really affect anyone but the forlorn weather forecasters who have to sit through the storm on the mountaintop.

A NOTE ON LODGINGS: In my lodging recommendations, you'll find the full mailing address, with the ZIP Code, so that you can write ahead for reservations. Telephone numbers, and a toll-free reservation number if the hotel has one, are included. The hotel or motel room you rent (but not bed-and-breakfast or country-inn rooms) will normally be air-conditioned and will have a private bath and a TV, usually color. The room may have either one or two double beds in it (single beds are rare), and note that prices are for the *room,* not each bed. To make your life easier, I've figured in the tax as well.

Tips for Families: The most economical way to travel is for several people to stay in the same room, and normally a party of five or even six can use the same room. Here's how it works: Two people are charged the regular room rate. Then there is usually a per-person charge for each extra person, but the charge is low. There is also a low cost for rollaway beds. For families there's an extra bonus, because most modern hotels and motels allow children to stay for free with their parents if the parents pay the normal two-person rate and the children use the room's existing beds. So in a room with two double beds, a family of four can stay as cheaply as two. If there are three children and a rollaway bed is necessary, there'll be a small charge (about $10) for it. The age permissible for children under the "family plan" varies.

Weekend Specials: Sometimes there are other special rates, especially at big-city hotels. Many of the more expensive places try to fill rooms on weekends, when business travelers are gone, by offering special mini-vacation rates for two nights (Friday and Saturday), plus some credit toward meals and drinks in the hotel's restaurants and bars. A $120-a-night double might be $85 per night for the two-day period from 5 p.m. Friday to check-out time on Sunday, with perhaps $20 credit toward drinks and dinners, or maybe a free sightseeing tour of the city. These mini-vacation programs and rates vary from year to year and from hotel to hotel, so it's best to call or write ahead for full details.

Some hotels and motels offer a discount to senior citizens who have proper identification, such as a membership card in the American Association of Retired Persons (AARP). Ask about this if you qualify.

Bed-and-Breakfast Guest Houses: The bed-and-breakfast house, long popular in Europe, is sweeping America as travelers discover that they can get charming accommodations at a "B&B." Some houses have half a dozen rooms, others only one or two; some serve a full, hearty sausage-and-eggs breakfast, others provide home-baked muffins and rolls; some guesthouses provide no breakfast. Rooms can be large or small, with a view or without—in short, nothing is standard. I've given special attention to B&Bs. Though I can describe hotel, motel, and inn rooms, which are usually of a certain standard, the only sure way to know what you're getting at a B&B is to look at the room yourself. I've chosen the houses recommended below on grounds of general cleanliness, friendliness, price, location, and charm.

Country Inns: New England is famous for its country inns, delightfully cozy and hospitable places to stay, often with very fine food. You should realize, however, that country inns are no longer the informal roadside "guesthouses" that they were a generation ago. Prices tend to be fairly hefty, and requirements for a stay can be complex, very much like those at a resort. For instance, one inn charges $75 for a double room with bath in summer on Monday through Wednesday nights, but $120 for the same room on Thursday through Sunday. To these rates you must add 9.7% room tax, $3 for the maid's tip (required), and $8 if you use the fireplace in the room. All in, that comes to over $94 for the "$75" Monday-through-Wednesday room, or $144 for the "$120" Thursday-through-Sunday room.

You may have to reserve well ahead for a country-inn room, particularly if you wish to stay during foliage season or when there's some big event nearby.

City hotels offer weekend packages, as the business trade disappears on weekends. But for country inns, weekends are the busy time. What you want to do is plan your city visits for weekends (or at least partly so), and spend Monday through Thursday out in the country.

Pets: By far, pets are not allowed in the majority of hotels, inns, motels, and guesthouses recommended in this book. Although I've done my best to find highway homes for pets, most places just don't allow them. If a hotel or inn does accept pets, I've mentioned this in the text. No mention of pets means that no pets are accepted.

ADVANCE RESERVATIONS: At certain times of year, rooms in New England's hotels and inns are in high demand, and you may not be able to get the room you want in the establishment you want unless you reserve it well in advance. The busiest periods are high summer (mid-July through Labor Day), foliage season (mid-September through Columbus Day), Christmas and New Year's Eve, and ski season (late January through March). Low seasons, when business is slack and many inns may be closed, are April, May, and late October through late December.

POINTS TO WATCH: Inn brochures paint rosy pictures of the warm welcome you're bound to receive, and of the friendliness and hospitality of your hosts. But innkeepers are in the lodging business in a sellers' market, and they must make a profit, so they make certain stipulations that you must know about. If you make a reservation and put down a deposit, and the inn or hotel accepts your deposit and confirms your reservation, you have made a legal contract. However, it is usually the inn that spells out the terms of the contract, and this can lead to unpleasant surprises. Though you both want the contract to work out as anticipated, one or the other of you may lose a substantial amount of money if it doesn't, so you must know what to expect. When making reservations, you can avoid hassles and disappointments by asking some of the following questions. These questions are the distilled wisdom of my experiences with inns, and also that of generations of readers of this guide.

Is smoking allowed in the inn? Are children welcome? What age? What about pets?

Is there a requirement for a minimum stay of two, three, or four nights?

Can you reserve a precise room or sort of room ("with antiques," "in the main inn and not in the annex," "with a canopy bed and full bath") or must you take whatever the innkeeper gives you? How many beds does the room have? Real beds or sofa beds? Can you get all this in writing?

Are meals included or required? If breakfast is included, is it store-bought doughnuts and instant coffee, or freshly made French pastries and brewed café au lait? If the inn has no dining room, how close is the nearest restaurant?

Is there a service charge? Is there tax? How much? Are there any other charges, such as for activities or use of a fireplace? They might not tell you if you don't ask.

Are credit cards accepted? *Never assume that they are!* Many of the most popular inns refuse to accept credit cards, preferring not to pay the 4% to 6% service charge to the credit-card company. They require cash, traveler's checks, or an approved personal check, sometimes for the full amount of your reservation, which might approach $1,000. Be prepared.

How much deposit must you send, and how soon? Under what circumstances can you ask for, and get, a refund of your deposit? What if you are delayed in transit by car problems, a late train or ferry, or weather conditions impossible for flying?

Does the deposit guarantee you a room at the inn absolutely, or does the innkeeper have the option of finding you "equivalent lodgings nearby"?

If your deposit is to be returned, will a "service charge" of 10% to 25% be deducted? What is the deadline for the innkeeper's return of the deposit? Two weeks? Two years?

A REAL NEW ENGLAND CLAMBAKE: Whether on the beach around a driftwood fire, at a backyard cookout, or in a restaurant, chances are you'll encounter the traditional clambake during your stay in New England. The true clambake takes place on the beach, starting with the digging of the clams, but the backyard and restaurant versions are good substitutes provided you observe the rituals properly.

The three essential courses are steamed soft-shell clams, corn on the cob, and lobsters. Here's a recipe: take one very large pot, fill with clean seawater, and place on the fire to boil. Put live lobsters in the bottom, then a layer of seaweed, then ears of corn, more seaweed, and finally a layer of "steamers" (soft-shell clams for steaming). When the clams open, they're ready.

How to Eat Steamers

Take a clam, open it completely, and lift out the meat. The "neck" is black and covered with a wrinkled black membrane. Shuck the membrane off (you pick up the knack for this by about the fifth clam), hold the clam by the neck, and dip it in "clam broth" (seawater that has had clams steamed in it—even in a restaurant you'll be provided with it). The "broth" is strictly for dipping, not for drinking; the dip washes any sand off the clam. Next, dip in the melted butter provided, and then enjoy.

When you've had your fill of clams, it's on to the buttered ears of corn, and finally to the lobsters. Eating a lobster is an art in itself.

How to Eat a Lobster

Restaurants will prepare lobsters in any number of elaborate ways, but to a true New Englander there are but two ways to cook a lobster: you boil it or you broil it.

To broil, take a live lobster, make a straight cut underneath from head to tail, and place cut-upward under the broiler.

Boiling is even easier. Plunge live lobsters in boiling seawater, and let them cook until they turn bright red (10 to 15 minutes). When you take them out they'll be very hot, and full of hot water too. Give the lobster a few minutes to cool, and you're ready to begin.

Hold the body in one hand and the tail in the other, and twist the tail off. Stick a fork into the tail meat and pull—the whole delicious morsel should come right out. The tail is the largest meaty portion of the lobster, but there's lots more.

Each claw should be broken (claw-crackers are always provided) and the meat taken out, even from the joints that connect the claw to the body. This is the most delicious part, a real delicacy. Lobsters molt each year, shedding their hard shells to reveal a new, temporarily soft shell underneath. If you dine on lobster in late July or August, it will have just molted and the soft shell can easily be broken with your fingers. At other times of the year, particularly in May and June, you're certain to need claw-crackers to deal with the old rock-hard shell.

In the larger lobsters (1½ pounds and over), you'll find tender little bites in other places too. Twist the four "flippers" off the end of the tail and chew out the delicate meat inside. Twist off each small leg: in the knuckle next to the body there's a nugget, and you can chew tender meat out of each segment in a leg.

Diehard lobster-lovers (I'm one) go even farther. Take the body apart, and behind where each leg was attached there is a good bit of meat. Of the innards, the gray-colored liver (called "tomalley") is edible—chefs sometimes use it in sauces. If you find a waxy red substance, that's roe (eggs), edible but not choice.

By now you will have discovered that eating lobster is not a refined pastime. The image of the lobster as an item in haute cuisine is justified by its delicious flavor. But simple boiled lobster cannot be improved by even the most creative chef, and eating it should not be an exercise in etiquette. A picnic table, with a newspaper covering to catch the shells, is the perfect setting; a seaside lobster shack is the best location.

AN INVITATION TO READERS: Like the other books in the Frommer series, *Frommer's New England* hopes to list the establishments that offer the best value-for-money. In achieving this goal, your comments and suggestions can be of tremendous help. Therefore, if you come across a particularly appealing lodging, restaurant, store, even a sightseeing attraction, please don't keep it to yourself. In fact, I encourage you to write to me on any matter dealing with this book. Every now and then a change of management, staff, or ownership will affect the quality of an establishment, and if you find that this is the case with any recommended place, let me know so I can look it over extra carefully for the following edition. And if you found a suggestion of mine particularly good, or found the book helpful in general, I don't mind hearing that either! Finally, you might want to share your extraordinary experiences with other readers: "Go to this museum on weekdays only, it's less crowded and admission is half price."

You have my word that every letter will be read by me personally, and answered as soon as possible in almost every case. Send your notes to Tom Brosnahan, c/o Prentice Hall Travel, 15 Columbus Circle, New York, NY 10023.

2. Frommer's Dollarwise Travel Club—How to Save Money On All Your Travels

In this book we'll be looking at how to get your money's worth in New England, but there is a "device" for saving money and determining value on *all* your trips. It's the popular, international Frommer's Dollarwise Travel Club, now in its 29th successful year of operation. The club was formed at the urging of numerous readers of the $-A-Day and Frommer Guides, who felt that such an organization could provide continuing travel information and a sense of community to value-minded travelers in all parts of the world. And so it does!

In keeping with the budget concept, the annual membership fee is low and is immediately exceeded by the value of your benefits. Upon receipt of $18 (U.S. residents), or $20 U.S. by check drawn on a U.S. bank or via international postal money order in U.S. funds (Canadian, Mexican, and other foreign residents) to cover one year's membership, we will send all new members the following items.

(1) Any *two* of the following books

Please designate in your letter which two you wish to receive:

Frommer $-A-Day© Guides

Australia on $30 a Day
Eastern Europe on $25 a Day
England on $50 a Day
Europe on $40 a Day
Greece on $30 a Day
Hawaii on $60 a Day
India on $25 a Day
Ireland on $35 a Day
Israel on $40 a Day
Mexico (plus Belize and Guatemala) on $35 a Day
New York on $60 a Day
New Zealand on $45 a Day
Scandinavia on $60 a Day
Scotland and Wales on $40 a Day
South America on $35 a Day
Spain and Morocco (plus the Canary Is.) on $40 a Day
Turkey on $30 a Day
Washington, D.C. & Historic Virginia on $40 a Day

($-A-Day Guides document hundreds of budget accommodations and facilities, helping you get the most for your travel dollars.)

Frommer Guides

Alaska
Australia
Austria and Hungary
Belgium, Holland, and Luxembourg
Bermuda and The Bahamas
Brazil
California and Las Vegas
Canada
Caribbean
Egypt
England and Scotland
Florida
France
Germany
Italy
Japan and Hong Kong
Mid-Atlantic States
New England
New York State

Northwest
Portugal, Madeira, and the Azores
Skiing USA—East
Skiing USA—West
South Pacific
Southeast Asia
Southern Atlantic States
Southwest
Switzerland and Liechtenstein
Texas
USA

(Frommer Guides discuss accommodations and facilities in all price ranges, with emphasis on the medium-priced.)

Frommer Touring Guides

Australia
Egypt
Florence
London
Paris
Scotland
Thailand
Venice

(These new, color illustrated guides include walking tours, cultural and historic sites, and other vital travel information.)

Gault Millau

Chicago
France
Hong Kong
Italy
London
Los Angeles
New England
New York
San Francisco
Washington, D.C.

(Irreverent, savvy, and comprehensive, each of these renowned guides candidly reviews over 1,000 restaurants, hotels, shops, nightspots, museums, and sights.)

Serious Shopper's Guides

Italy
London
Los Angeles
Paris

(Practical and comprehensive, each of these handsomely illustrated guides lists hundreds of stores, selling everything from antiques to wine, conveniently organized alphabetically by category.)

A Shopper's Guide to the Caribbean

(Two experienced Caribbean hands guide you through this shopper's paradise, offering witty insights and helpful tips on the wares and emporia of more than 25 islands.)

Beat the High Cost of Travel

(This practical guide details how to save money on absolutely all travel items—

accommodations, transportation, dining, sightseeing, shopping, taxes, and more. Includes special budget information for seniors, students, singles, and families.)

Bed & Breakfast—North America
(This guide contains a directory of over 150 organizations that offer bed-and-breakfast referrals and reservations throughout North America. The scenic attractions, and major schools and universities near the homes of each are also listed.)

California with Kids
(A must for parents traveling in California, providing key information on selecting the best accommodations, restaurants, and sightseeing attractions for the particular needs of the family, whether the kids are toddlers, school-age, pre-teens, or teens.)

Caribbean Hideaways
(Well-known travel author Ian Keown describes the most romantic, alluring places to stay in the Caribbean, rating each establishment on romantic ambience, food, sports opportunities, and price.)

Frommer's Belgium
(Arthur Frommer unlocks the treasures of a country overlooked by most travelers to Europe. Discover the medieval charm, modern sophistication, and natural beauty of this quintessentially European country.)

Frommer's Cruises
(This complete guide covers all the basics of cruising—ports of call, costs, fly-cruise package bargains, cabin selection booking, embarkation and debarkation—and describes in detail over 60 or so ships cruising the waters of Alaska, the Caribbean, Mexico, Hawaii, Panama, Canada, and the United States.)

Frommer's Skiing Europe
(Describes top ski resorts in Austria, France, Italy, and Switzerland. Illustrated with maps of each resort area. Includes supplement on Argentinian resorts.)

Guide to Honeymoon Destinations
(A special guide for that most romantic trip of your life, with full details on planning and choosing the destination that will be just right in the U.S. [California, New England, Hawaii, Florida, New York, South Carolina, etc.], Canada, Mexico, and the Caribbean.)

Marilyn Wood's Wonderful Weekends
(This very selective guide covers the best mini-vacation destinations within a 200-mile radius of New York City. It describes special country inns and other accommodations, restaurants, picnic spots, sights, and activities—all the information needed for a two- or three-day stay.)

Manhattan's Outdoor Sculpture
(A total guide, fully illustrated with black-and-white photos, to more than 300 sculptures and monuments that grace Manhattan's plazas, parks, and other public spaces.)

Motorist's Phrase Book
(A practical phrase book in French, German, and Spanish designed specifically for the English-speaking motorist touring abroad.)

Paris Rendez-Vous
(An amusing and *au courant* guide to the best meeting places in Paris, organized for

hour-to-hour use: from power breakfasts and fun brunches, through tea at four or cocktails at five, to romantic dinners and dancing till dawn.)

Swap and Go—Home Exchanging Made Easy

(Two veteran home exchangers explain in detail all the money-saving benefits of a home exchange, and then describe precisely how to do it. Also includes information on home rentals and many tips on low-cost travel.)

The Candy Apple: New York with Kids

(A spirited guide to the wonders of the Big Apple by a savvy New York grandmother with a kid's-eye view to fun. Indispensable for visitors and residents alike.)

The New World of Travel

(From America's #1 travel expert, Arthur Frommer, an annual sourcebook with the hottest news and latest trends that's guaranteed to change the way you travel—and save you hundreds of dollars. Jam-packed with alternative new modes of travel that will lead you to vacations that cater to the mind, the spirit, and a sense of thrift.)

Travel Diary and Record Book

(A 96-page diary for personal travel notes plus a section for such vital data as passport and traveler's check numbers, itinerary, postcard list, special people and places to visit, and a reference section with temperature and conversion charts, and world maps with distance zones.)

Where to Stay USA

(By the Council on International Educational Exchange, this extraordinary guide is the first to list accommodations in all 50 states that cost anywhere from $3 to $30 per night.)

(2) Any *one* of the Frommer City Guides

    Amsterdam
    Athens
    Atlantic City and Cape May
    Boston
    Cancún, Cozumel, and the Yucatán
    Chicago
    Dublin and Ireland
    Hawaii
    Las Vegas
    Lisbon, Madrid, and Costa del Sol
    London
    Los Angeles
    Mexico City and Acapulco
    Minneapolis and St. Paul
    Montréal and Québec City
    New Orleans
    New York
    Orlando, Disney World, and EPCOT
    Paris
    Philadelphia
    Rio
    Rome
    San Francisco
    Santa Fe, Taos, and Albuquerque
    Sydney
    Washington, D.C.

(Pocket-size guides to hotels, restaurants, nightspots, and sightseeing attractions covering all price ranges.)

(3) A one-year subscription to *The Dollarwise Traveler*

This quarterly eight-page tabloid newspaper keeps you up to date on fastbreaking developments in low-cost travel in all parts of the world, bringing you the latest money-saving information—the kind of information you'd have to pay $35 a year to obtain elsewhere. This consumer-conscious publication also features columns of special interest to readers: **Hospitality Exchange** (members all over the world who are willing to provide hospitality to other members as they pass through their home cities); **Share-a-Trip** (offers and requests from members for travel companions who can share costs and help avoid the burdensome single supplement); and **Readers Ask . . . Readers Reply** (travel questions from members to which other members reply with authentic firsthand information).

(4) Your personal membership card

Membership entitles you to purchase through the club all Frommer publications for a third to a half off their regular retail prices during the term of your membership.

So why not join this hardy band of international budgeteers and participate in its exchange of travel information and hospitality? Simply send your name and address, together with your annual membership fee of $18 (U.S. residents) or $20 U.S. (Canadian, Mexican, and other foreign residents), by check drawn on a U.S. bank or via international postal money order in U.S. funds to: Frommer's Dollarwise Travel Club, Inc., 15 Columbus Circle, New York, NY 10023. And please remember to specify which *two* of the books in section (1) and which *one* in section (2) you wish to receive in your initial package of members' benefits. Or, if you prefer, use the order form at the end of the book and enclose $18 or $20 in U.S. currency.

Once you are a member, there is no obligation to buy additional books. No books will be mailed to you without your specific order.

GETTING THERE

How you travel to New England depends on several things: the time you have to spend, the thickness of your vacation wallet, the distance you must travel, and whether you're coming alone, with a partner, family, or group. Although you may already have decided how you'll travel to New England, I'd suggest you look through these pages in any case—perhaps some of the facts and figures will prove useful. If you're planning to go by some kind of public transport, check the appropriate chapter of this book which deals with your chosen destination to see what local transport to that spot is like. Remember also that airlines, bus lines, and the Amtrak rail network all have special excursion and family plans which can save you a good deal of money. But you must call them for current details and schedules—a special fare offered during the busy summer months may not be available in the spring or autumn; a discount on a ticket may be offered only if you travel late in the evening, or on a weekday, and this applies to all means of travel: air, bus, or rail.

1. Getting to New England

BY AIR: For the person with a limited amount of time (the normal two-week vacation) who is traveling alone, flying to New England has obvious advantages: it's the quickest way to go and is not all that much more expensive than other means, and it may be cheaper than some. When planning for a flight, be sure to ask about the special fares that may be applicable. For instance, you save nothing by buying a regular round-trip ticket over buying two regular one-way tickets (the round-trip fare is exactly twice the one-way fare), but you save a considerable amount by buying a round-trip excursion ticket good for a certain amount of time (usually a weekend or a 30-day period). You may have to fly at certain times to qualify for these tickets, perhaps early in the morning, late at night, or on certain days of the week. Check on these requirements when you go to buy your ticket. Remember that Night Coach fares (for planes that depart late in the evening) are lower than normal fares, and you can save money by flying Night Coach both ways, although you won't save as much as by buying an excursion ticket.

These days, air fares are so complicated and they change so frequently that only by calling your travel agent can you get an idea of the fare structure. Besides the basic regular one-way fare, you're sure to find half a dozen bargain, special-interest, or excursion fares, and you will almost certainly qualify for one of them.

BY RAIL: Trains are often looked upon as the poorer cousins of the airplane and the automobile, and they do have their disadvantages: they are slower than a plane, often more expensive than taking the car. But there are advantages to train travel as well. You see the cities and the countryside from a train, while an airplane shows you only clouds. There's room to get up and walk around on a train—much more room than in a bus, car, or plane—and on the long-distance trains restaurant and bar cars, and even sleeping cars, can turn the vehicle into a hotel-on-wheels. Trains can give you a sense of ease, and of being in limbo for a while, which might be just the way to start your vacation. Here are some facts and figures on getting to New England by train:

First, Amtrak offers a **U.S.A. Rail Pass,** similar to the popular Eurailpass, which for a set amount allows you unlimited train travel for a certain period of time. The passes are good on all Amtrak and Southern railway lines and on some lines in Canada as well. Travel is by coach class, but by paying the appropriate surcharge (which any passenger with a normal ticket would also have to pay) you can travel first class, using the Metroliner trains, parlor cars, and sleeping cars. Amtrak ticket agents or any travel agent can give you details on how to buy a U.S.A. Rail Pass.

In addition to the U.S.A. Rail Pass, Amtrak offers special reduced-rate round-trip excursion fares to various points and for seasonal and special reductions. Call them for details. Information given below is subject to change, so be sure to check with Amtrak (tel. toll free 800/872-7245, which is 800/USA-RAIL).

Sample Rail Fares	
To Boston from:	**Coach Fare**
	One-way
Atlanta	$182
Chicago	$117
Dallas	$259
New Orleans	$192
New York	$49.50
San Francisco	$309
Washington, D.C.	$88

Remember that meals are *not* included in these prices; you must pay for meals on the train when you receive them, or carry your own food.

BY BUS: Virtually all cities and towns of any size have public transport connections with New England; every major U.S. city seems to have at least one bus a day that heads off for New York City, from which connections can be made for Boston or other points in New England. Many are through buses, meaning that you won't have to change until you get to New York. The bus has advantages: it's a bit faster than the train, often cheaper than the plane, and has great flexibility as there are buses to practically everywhere. Disadvantages are that buses are as cramped as planes, meals are at rest stops (unless you pack food), and even on through buses you'll find yourself heading frequently into the stop-and-go of city traffic— transcontinental buses may pull into 20 or more cities.

Greyhound/Trailways offers a time-travel pass, good for unlimited travel.

From New York's Port Authority Bus Terminal, Eighth Avenue and 41st Street (tel. 212/564-8484), various lines run to the different parts of New England:

Bonanza Bus Lines (tel. 212/564-8484, or toll free 800/556-3815): Bonanza's routes go to Albany, N.Y., via the Berkshires (Great Barrington, Stockbridge, Lee, Lenox, and Pittsfield) from New York City; and from New York City to Cape Cod (Falmouth, Woods Hole, and Hyannis) via Hartford and Providence. During the winter months, service to Falmouth and Woods Hole (for the ferries to Martha's Vineyard and Nantucket) is via connection at Buzzard's Bay, Massachusetts. Bonanza also operates in conjunction with Greyhound Trailways between New York City and Providence and Newport, R.I., and New Bedford, Mass. Buy your tickets in New York's Port Authority Bus Terminal at the Greyhound Trailways Ticket Plaza.

Greyhound/Trailways Lines (tel. 212/635-0800): Greyhound/Trailways operates buses from New York City to Hartford, Springfield, Worcester, New Haven, New London, and Providence. Service to Cape Cod is provided in conjunction with Bonanza. The Boston service has a few buses daily. The direct trip to Boston takes about 4¾ hours. From Boston, connections are made to points in Maine, New Hampshire, and Vermont.

Vermont Transit Lines (tel. 212/594-2000, or toll free 800/451-3292; toll free in Vermont 800/642-3133): Vermont Transit operates in conjunction with Greyhound/Trailways to serve Vermont's ski and vacation regions as well as Montréal, P.Q., and several points in New Hampshire.

Sample Bus Fares

To Boston from:	One-way Fare	To Boston from:	One-way Fare
Chicago	$148	Toronto	US$109
Montréal	US$60	Washington, D.C.	$71
New York	$37		

Round-trip fares, by the way, are in some cases only 40% more than one-way fares.

BY CAR: Coming to New England by car obviously has lots of advantages, but few people think of the disadvantages of car travel when they plan their vacation: costs including gas, tolls, and parking fees, etc., plus the expenses you'll have for lodging en route. If you still decide to take the car, here are some useful tips on getting to New England.

If you don't plan to visit New York, the best way to skirt it is on Interstate 84 from Pennsylvania. This connects with I-87 (New York State Thruway, a toll road), and also with the Taconic State Parkway, a very beautiful highway which goes north to the western end of the Massachusetts Turnpike (I-90, a toll road). I-84 itself goes east after these intersections, straight to Hartford and Boston. You can branch off from I-84, on Conn. 34, to get to New Haven, and then I-95 will take you straight to New London, Newport, Providence, and Cape Cod.

---

2. Getting Around New England

Good public transportation and a network of Interstate highways make getting around New England very easy. The region, like Europe, is compact, and visitors from the wide-open spaces out west may be surprised to find that no two points in New England are more than a comfortable day's drive apart: for example, from New Haven, Conn., to Montpelier, Vt., is a mere 200 miles. A train from New Haven to Boston takes only about three hours.

Details of available public transportation will be given along with lodging, restaurant, and sightseeing recommendations in each chapter, but here are some guidelines:

BY AIR: The large cities (Boston, Providence, Hartford, etc.) all have good air service provided by the larger domestic airlines. Deregulation of the airline industry has brought about the birth of numerous regional "feeder" airlines in New England, and it is now possible to fly between most of the larger cities, even in this small region. There are also many connections by regional carrier to New York City.

Almost all of the small regional airlines operate in conjunction with larger national and international airlines. The regional airlines' flights are included in the flight schedules of the larger airlines, including American, Continental, Delta, Eastern, Pan American, and USAir. Call these airlines for information on flights, fares, and cities served.

BY RAIL: Amtrak operates trains connecting Boston with Springfield, Mass., Pittsfield, Mass., and Albany, N.Y.; Hartford, New Haven, New London, and Mystic, Conn.; Providence, R.I.; and (via Springfield) Brattleboro, White River Junction, and Montpelier, Vt., and Montréal, Québec. There is no interstate train service northeast of Boston, but there are connecting buses from Boston's South Station to Portsmouth, N.H., and major cities and towns in eastern Maine. Trains on routes between Boston and points south and west are fast and frequent; but to get to points in Vermont from Boston, connections are not good, and service is infrequent.

BY BUS: Bus service is quite good in New England. Here are some of the major companies, their Boston phone numbers, the terminal from which they operate in Boston, and the areas they serve:

American Eagle (tel. 508/990-0000), Peter Pan Terminal, operates frequent buses daily between Boston and New Bedford.

Bonanza Bus Lines (tel. 617/423-5810), Greyhound/Trailways Terminal, runs from Boston to Cape Cod (Falmouth and Woods Hole), and Newport and Providence, R.I. Other routes run from Providence to central and western Connecticut and the Berkshires of Massachusetts, and from Providence to Cape Cod.

Cape Cod Bus Lines (tel. 508/775-5524), Hyannis, operates routes serving towns between Hyannis and Provincetown, on Cape Cod.

Concord Trailways (tel. 617/482-6620, or toll free 800/258-3722, 800/852-3317 in New Hampshire). Concord Trailways is the line to take to New Hampshire. Buses start at Logan Airport and the Peter Pan Terminal in Boston, then head north to Concord, Laconia and North Conway, Plymouth, Waterville Valley, and Franconia. Another route goes to Alton and Wolfboro.

Englander Bus Lines (tel. 617/423-5810), Greyhound/Trailways Terminal, runs its buses from Boston along Mass. 2 all the way to Williamstown, in the northwest corner of the state.

Greyhound/Trailways (tel. 617/423-5810), with its terminal at 10 St. James Ave. in Boston (any Green Line subway car to Arlington), operates many of the long-distance routes in New England, and connects the region with the rest of the country. Greyhound/Trailways buses operate from Boston via Hartford and New Haven to New York City; from New York City via New Haven and Hartford to Springfield, Mass., connecting with Vermont Transit buses for points in Vermont, and Montréal, Québec.

Another Greyhound/Trailways route is from Boston via Portsmouth, N.H., to the Maine coast, stopping at Portland, Freeport, Brunswick, Bath, Wiscasset, Camden, and Bangor (with connecting service to Ellsworth for Bar Harbor); this route connects with Canadian SMT buses headed for New Brunswick and Nova Scotia.

Greyhound/Trailways also connects New York City via New Haven and New London, Conn., with Providence, R.I., and with connecting service to Hyannis and Provincetown on Cape Cod.

Another route is between Islip, N.Y. (on Long Island), via New Haven and Hartford, Conn., and Boston.

Greyhound/Trailways also operates buses heading due west from Boston, stopping at Worcester, Springfield, Lee, Lenox, and Pittsfield, Mass.; and Albany, N.Y.; with connecting service to points west in both the United States and Canada.

Peter Pan Bus Lines (tel. 617/426-7838, or toll free 800/628-8468, 800/332-8995 in Massachusetts), at the Peter Pan (formerly Trailways) Terminal in Dewey Square, opposite Amtrak's South Station, runs between Boston and Albany, Amherst, Bridgeport, Danbury, Hartford, Holyoke, Lee, Middletown, New Britain, New Haven, New York City, Northampton, Norwalk, Pittsfield, Springfield, Sturbridge, Waterbury, and Worcester. Other routes connect Springfield, Mass., with Bradley International Airport and Hartford, Conn. Trailways Bus Lines terminated all of its service in New England in 1987, and Peter Pan Bus Lines took over those routes.

Plymouth & Brockton Street Railway Co. (tel. 508/746-0378 or toll free 800/328-9997 in Massachusetts), Greyhound/Trailways Terminal, is the one to take from Boston to Plymouth, Sagamore, Barnstable, Hyannis, and Provincetown on Cape Cod. P&B also runs from Hyannis to Chatham on Cape Cod. Many P&B runs start at Logan Airport, then head into Boston for stops at the Greyhound/Trailways Terminal, the Peter Pan Terminal, and South Station. You can take any P&B bus from Logan Airport, and transfer to another one downtown.

Vermont Transit Lines (tel. 617/423-5810, or 802/864-6811 in Vermont), Greyhound/Trailways Terminal, in collaboration with Greyhound/Trailways Lines, operates from New York City via Albany to Bennington, Manchester, East Dorset, Rutland (with connecting service to Killington, Woodstock, and White River Junction), Middlebury, and Burlington. Connecting service from Burlington goes on to Montréal.

Another service is from Boston via Manchester, Concord, Mount Sunapee, and Hanover, N.H.; to White River Junction (with connecting service to Woodstock, Killington, and Rutland), then to Barre, Montpelier, Burlington, and Montréal.

Vermont Transit also runs buses between Portland, Me., Burlington, Vt., and Montréal, stopping at North Conway and Bretton Woods, N.H.; and St. Johnsbury, White River Junction, and Montpelier, Vt.

Another route takes travelers from New York City or Boston to White River Junction for connections to St. Johnsbury and Newport, Vt., and Sherbrooke and Québec City.

To get to Stowe, Vt., you must first go to Burlington or Newport, Vt.

NEW ENGLAND

AIRPORT ✈

0 _____ 50
Miles

N →

Map labels

ATLANTIC OCEAN

MAINE

Auburn
North Conway
Sebago Lake
Bath
Brunswick
Yarmouth
Casco Bay
Portland
Biddeford
Kennebunk
Ogunquit
Boothbay Harbor

NEW HAMPSHIRE

Bretton Woods
Lake Winnipesaukee
Concord
Manchester
Portsmouth
Hampton
Hanover
Keene

VERMONT

Green Mountains
Woodstock
Rutland
Bennington
Williamstown
Brattleboro
Montpelier
Connecticut R.
Champlain

MASSACHUSETTS

Lexington
Concord
Cambridge
Boston
Salem
Lynn
Gloucester
Rockport
Massachusetts Bay
Worcester
Amherst
Springfield
Northampton
Pittsfield
Great Barrington
Sturbridge
MASS TPKE
Provincetown
Wellfleet
Cape Cod
Cape Cod Bay
Plymouth
Hyannis
New Bedford
Woods Hole
Fall River
Martha's Vineyard
Nantucket

RHODE ISLAND
R.I.
Providence
Newport
Narragansett Bay
Rhode Island Sound
Block I.
Westerly

CONNECTICUT

Hartford
Middletown
Norwich
New London
New Haven
Bridgeport
Danbury
Westport
Norwalk
Candlewood Lake
Long Island

NEW YORK

MAINE TPKE

Route markers: 95, 93, 89, 9, 7, 495, 91, 90, 84, 8, 87, 195

Sebago Lake

BOSTON: THE HUB

"Boston is the Hub of the Universe," or at least that's what many people remembered Dr. Oliver Wendell Holmes as saying. Actually, his statement about his beloved city was less ambitious: "The Boston State House is the Hub of the Solar System." No matter, because to Bostonians their city is still The Hub, the center of the world. And though outsiders may quibble about its being the Hub of the Universe, they must accept the fact that Boston is and always has been the capital of New England. The Pilgrims settled on the shores of Massachusetts Bay in the 1620s, and the other great cities of the six-state region were offshoots from this early colony: Thomas Hooker, the man who founded Hartford, went there from Cambridge in 1636, and about the same time Roger Williams fled the area to found Providence. The pattern of arriving in Boston and then pushing on into the hills beyond was to be a permanent feature of New England life, and consequently, today the city is a rich mixture of ethnic neighborhoods, almost a little United Nations. Immigrants from all over the world arrived at Boston's docks, and later established communities of their own within the city. From these communities second-generation immigrants would then move out across the state and across the nation.

What gives Bostonians the idea they're special? Well, theirs was the first large town in the region, first in resistance to British measures that brought on the Revolution, and first in science and culture during the 19th and early 20th centuries. And in 1960 their favorite son became president of the United States. Their city is the home of the Celtics, the Bruins, the Red Sox, as well as the Boston Pops and countless other types, famous and infamous.

Although Greater Boston today is home for over half of the 6,000,000 people of Massachusetts, the city of Boston itself is a fairly small area with a population of something over 600,000. But if one adds in the populations of the neighboring cities such as Cambridge, Somerville, Charlestown, Chelsea, Brookline, and so on, the total comes to about 3,000,000. And yet Boston is one of the most "livable" and manageable cities in the world, with the economic and cultural advantages of a great city, but with some of the spirit and ease of a small town. It's a delightful place, and Bostonians know it.

1. Arrival and Orientation

As major American cities go, Boston is eminently approachable. The airport is less than a 15-minute taxi or subway ride from the center of the city. The train station is right downtown, as are the two bus terminals. But once you get here, Boston's famous twisty colonial streets take over, and Boston's notoriously sloppy drivers threaten, so read the sections below carefully.

ARRIVAL BY AIR: Boston's **Logan International Airport** (tel. toll free 800/235-6426) is one of the busiest in the country, but it is well organized, and has the advantage of being very near the center of the city, as airports go. After you get your bags, look for the signs to buses, taxis, and "limo," and after a few steps you'll see the stops.

Downtown by Subway
The **Massport Shuttle Bus** (run by the Massachusetts Port Authority) runs the airport loop, and is free of charge. The bus goes to all the terminals and to the MBTA "Airport" subway stop, where you can take a Blue Line train downtown. The subway into town costs 75¢, and a person in a booth will make change for you except during late-night hours. The ride takes only ten minutes once you board the train. Some of the hotels recommended in this book are within a few blocks of the Government Center stop, but for most places you'll have to change from the Blue Line at Government Center to Green Line trains bound for Boston College, Cleveland Circle, Riverside, or Arborway (all of which pass near the hotels recommended). For Cambridge, take the Green Line one stop from Government Center to Park Street and change to the Red Line for Harvard or Alewife. It's a fairly long haul to Cambridge, with two subway transfers.

Downtown by Water Shuttle
Vehicular traffic through the tunnels connecting the airport to Boston has become very heavy in recent years. One innovative solution to the problem is a water-shuttle service between the airport's own dock and Rowe's Wharf, on Atlantic Avenue. A one-way ticket for the ten-minute shuttle boat costs $6 for adults, half price for children. Trips run on the hour and half hour during peak morning and evening rush hours, less frequently at other times between 6 a.m. and 8 p.m. From Rowe's Wharf it's only a few steps to South Station's train, subway, and bus stations.

Downtown by Limo
The **Airways Transportation Company's** minibuses (10 Gainsboro St.; tel. 442-2700) will take you from the airport (all terminals) to any downtown hotel for $5.50 per person. The minibuses operate every day from 7 a.m. to 7 p.m., running every half hour, 7 p.m. to 10 p.m. running on the hour, and stopping at the stops marked Bus Stops outside each terminal.
The **Hudson Bus Lines and Hudson Limousine Service** (tel. 395-8080) have scheduled service to downtown Boston.
The Westin Hotel in Copley Square has its own limo service. Call 426-8800.

Downtown by Taxi

A taxi from Logan Airport to downtown Boston will cost between $8 and $10 for the ride, plus 60¢ toll, plus excess baggage charge (if any), plus tip. Figure $9 to $12 all together.

Beyond Boston

Chances are good that you won't be roaring straight through Boston on your way north, west, or south. But in case you are, you should know about these services:

Share-a-Cab: In principle it works like this: you call the Massport Dispatcher (tel. toll free 800/235-6426), or simply pick up one of the special Share-a-Cab phones near the baggage-claim areas. You give your name and destination (any suburban community, but not Boston itself) to the dispatcher, and within 15 minutes you're on your way, sharing the expense of the cab with several other passengers going to, or near, the same destination. In practice this excellent idea has been languishing of late due to competition from suburban limo companies. You may or may not find that Share-a-Cab works for you. Best time to try is at rush hour, of course.

Limousines to Eastern Massachusetts: To Lexington, call Hudson Bus Lines or Hudson Limo Service at 395-8080; to Concord, call Townsend Limousine Service at 597-6296; to Plymouth or Hyannis, call the Plymouth & Brockton Street Railway Co. at 773-9400, or South Shore & Cape Cod Airport Limo at 451-1410 or toll free (in Massachusetts only) 800/343-7450.

Buses to Rhode Island: Bonanza Bus Lines (tel. 423-5810) goes from Logan Airport right to Providence, a 1½-hour trip, daily every hour on the half hour between 8:30 a.m. and 10:30 p.m., with a final trip at 11:45 p.m.

Buses to New Hampshire: Concord Trailways (tel. 482-6620, or toll free 800/258-3722) will take you to Manchester, Concord, Lake Winnipesaukee, North Conway, Jackson, Glen, and Hanover, right from the airport.

Buses to Vermont: Vermont Transit (tel. 423-5810, or toll free 800/451-3292) operates from the airport to New Hampshire, Vermont, and Montréal.

ARRIVAL BY TRAIN: All Amtrak trains operate into and out of Boston's **South Station** (tel. 617/482-3660), the terminus for Boston. If you plan to stay downtown or in Cambridge, go to South Station, the end of the line, and transfer to the Red Line subway inbound, "Alewife." In two stops you'll be at Park Street for downtown hotels, and if you stay on the Red Line you'll get to Harvard Square.

ARRIVAL BY BUS: Boston's masterplan calls for all bus and train terminals soon to be located in a grand South Station Transportation Center, at Amtrak's South Station. Many local, commuter, and regional bus lines already operate from South Station, and **Peter Pan Bus Lines,** 555 Atlantic Ave. (tel. 426-7838), is located in its own terminal in Dewey Square, just across the street from South Station. They offer service to and from Maine, New Hampshire, Connecticut, Rhode Island, and Massachusetts. Want to find your way there from downtown? Look for the towering silver Federal Reserve Bank building, which resembles mightily an enormous truck radiator. Washboard? Cigarette machine? Anyway, it's right in Dewey Square.

Greyhound/Trailways Lines has its own terminal at 10 St. James Ave. (tel. 423-5810), near Park Square, the theater district, and the Public Garden. Information on service to Portland, Me., can be obtained by dialing 542-3520; to New York City, 542-2380; to Hartford, 542-2991. At the Greyhound/Trailways Terminal, you're only two blocks from the Arlington (Green Line) subway station.

ARRIVAL BY CAR: The easiest and fastest way to enter Boston by car from the west is via the **Massachusetts Turnpike** ("Mass Pike"), which goes right through the Back Bay to the center of the city; then it connects with the **John F. Fitzgerald ("Southeast") Expressway.** There are exits at Prudential Center and Chinatown (Kneeland Street).

The Southeast Expressway (few people call it the Fitzgerald Expressway) is also Rte. 3 as it comes up from the South Shore (Cape Cod and Plymouth). It's the main commuter route from everywhere south of Boston, and is traveled very heavily; at rush hours there are frequent tie-ups. When it gets right into Boston around Haymarket, the road is sometimes called the "Central Artery." The Central Artery is subject to frequent attacks of arteriosclerosis.

Two divided highways skirt the Charles River toward Cambridge, the faster and busier one being **Storrow Drive** on the southern bank, the more scenic being **Memorial Drive** in Cambridge on the northern bank of the Charles. Take either one to go between Boston and Harvard Square, and go all the way to the Larz Andersen Bridge and Cambridge's John F. Kennedy Street (which used to be named Boylston Street), then turn right (north) for Harvard Square.

Coming from the north, enter Boston on I-93 or U.S. 1 (from I-95), both of which converge on the Mystic River Bridge (also called Tobin Bridge; toll inbound), and at the southern end of the bridge the Central Artery/Southeast Expressway begins. Follow signs on the bridge to get to Storrow Drive for the Back Bay or Harvard Square.

Once downtown, Boston's warren of winding, confusing streets, most of them one way, will try your patience, but once you make your way to a hotel, park the car and try to forget it for the rest of your visit. Driving downtown makes little sense, and driving to Harvard Square even less sense (the parking problem there is worse). Take the car out to go to Lexington, Concord, or the North Shore, but otherwise leave it parked.

ORIENTATION: In its earliest days Boston was called "Trimountain," for the three hills around which the settlement was built. At that time Trimountain was almost an island, connected to the mainland only by the narrow natural causeway called "Boston Neck."

In the 19th century an ambitious development plan resulted in the leveling of two of the hills and the moving of the dirt to fill in around Boston Neck; the marsh and bogs that were filled in to make the Back Bay quarter soon became a prime residential district with a Manhattan-style grid of streets and a wide, shady central boulevard called Commonwealth Avenue.

From the time when Trimountain had only a few winding pathways, the city has grown to be a maze of twisty streets difficult to get through in a car, easy to get lost in on foot. I'll try to make the maze more comprehensible for you by describing the city's more important sections and what you'll find in them when you stroll through.

The North End

Starting at the very northeastern tip of Boston's peninsula, the North End is one of the city's oldest quarters. The graves in **Copp's Hill** burying ground go back to the 1600s, and **Old North Church,** from the tower of which Paul Revere got his famous two-lantern signal, dates back to 1723. Many other sights on the **Freedom Trail** (described below) are here. In successive centuries the North End has been the first landing point for many waves of immigrants, and today the four- and five-story brick buildings packed close around the North End's narrow streets are occupied mainly by Italian families who have made the North End their own. **Salem Street** is the quarter's shopping street, with several Italian groceries featuring all the imported products necessary to the old country's cuisine, as well as a half dozen Italian butcher shops and vegetable stands. The street is always lively, and on Saturday it's closed to traffic so pedestrians can enjoy the stroll up and down it, perhaps with a

SOUTHWESTERN NEW ENGLAND

NEW HAMPSHIRE

VERMONT

NEW YORK

MASSACHUSETTS

CONNECTICUT

RHODE ISLAND

6

84

202

2

9

8

44

202

2

91

Saxtons River

Brattleboro

W. Dover

Newfane

Mt. Snow

Wilmington

Marlboro

Bennington

Williamstown

North Adams

Mount Greylock

Adams

Charlemont

Windsor

Windsor St. Forest

Greenfield

Deerfield

Cummington

Amherst

S. Hadley

Northampton

Holyoke

Springfield

Connecticut R.

MASSACHUSETTS

Brimfield

Sturbridge

TURNPIKE

Lanesboro

Shafer Village

Pittsfield St. Forest

Dalton

Pittsfield

Lenox

Lee

October St. Forest

Stockbridge

Stockbridge Bowl

Great Barrington

S. Egremont

Sheffield

Norfolk

Riverton

Winsted

Hillsdale

N. Egremont

Bash Bish Falls

Mt. Everett St. Pk.

Salisbury

Lime Rock

Sharon

stop for a glass of wine and a meal at the small restaurant with a few tables on the sidewalk. **Hanover Street,** one block southeast and parallel to Salem, is the North End's main street, always dotted with groups of men standing on corners and passing the latest news—all in Italian, of course. The best and most authentic espresso and cappuccino in Boston is served in the Italian cafés that line the street, and if you plan to have a cup, stop first at one of the delectable bakeries or pastry shops on the street for a treat to go with it.

Haymarket

Most of the costermongers in Haymarket's Friday and Saturday open-air produce market are oldtimers from the North End, and no wonder—a three-minute walk under the Central Artery via a special passage unites the two areas. The pushcarts and stalls in the market are heirlooms passed down from father to son, or sold at a very high price, because the market is so profitable that a family can live all week from the money made on the two market days.

Faneuil Hall Marketplace

Haymarket's open-air stalls may be packed on Friday and Saturday but across the street at Faneuil Hall Marketplace, shops and vendors are hard put to serve the crowds every day of the week. This phenomenally successful restoration of Boston's historic Quincy Market, North Market, and South Market buildings is not only beautiful and historically important, but also just plain fun. The Marketplace deserves its own restaurant guide for the dozens of places to buy the snacks, lunches, or elegant dinners that are housed here; you can buy sausage, cheese, pastries, Turkish figs, freshly baked French or Italian bread, wine, and on and on for your own picnic as well. Go to buy, or to eat, or just to look.

Waterfront

East of Faneuil Hall Marketplace and south of the North End is Boston's Waterfront, another area in which restoration has brought new life and vitality. The solid old brick and granite buildings which once served as warehouses for India and China traders have been modernized and converted to offices, shops, and apartments, and a fine waterfront park brings picnickers, Frisbee-throwers, kids on bikes, and anyone out for a walk. Lewis Wharf, Commercial Wharf, Long Wharf, Rowe's Wharf, and all the rest are well worth a stroll. The New England Aquarium and Marriott Long Wharf hotel are at the southern end of the "new" Waterfront.

Government Center

All of the quarters mentioned above touch on Government Center, a bureaucrats' corral surrounded by striking modern buildings housing city, state, and federal offices and dominated by the **City Hall,** placed in the midst of a brick-paved plaza which covers several acres. The plaza, with its sunken fountain, is a focus of outdoor activities in summer—free concerts, plays, and exhibits. This used to be Scollay Square, the city's tenderloin section close to the rundown waterfront and peopled by sailors and students out for a good time in the burlesque houses and bars which were planted thick as mushrooms.

South of Government Center is the city's **financial and commercial heart,** centered on State Street, Milk Street, Devonshire Street, and the surrounding ways.

Beacon Hill

Due west of Government Center is Beacon Hill, last of the three hills of Trimountain and now the very exclusive residential section with a surprisingly European ambience. The crown of the hill is Bulfinch's great **State House,** topped by its gold dome; the building is the home of the "Great and General Court of Massachusetts Bay" (the state legislature). Be sure to take a walk around Beacon Hill and its famous **Louisburg Square,** where some of the most attractive houses are situ-

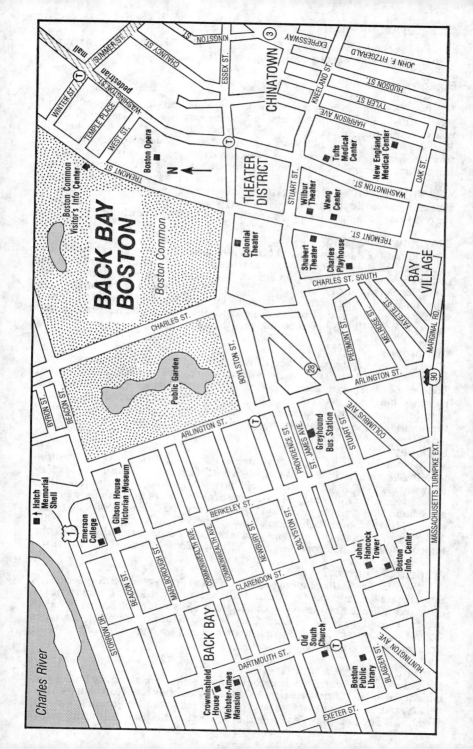

ated. Today, besides Boston's Old Money, Beacon Hill is home for a good number of students and young professional people as well.

Boston Common

South of Beacon Hill is Boston Common, the city's "central park," with a Frog Pond—filled with splashing children in summer and skaters in winter—statues and monuments, walkways, and benches. Park Street Station, at the Common's southeastern corner (intersection of Park and Tremont Streets), is the heart of the "T," Boston's subway system, and also a gathering place for soapbox orators, one-man bands, religious zealots, panhandlers, mimes, and hawkers who will want you to join fringe political groups. The grass on the Common may look pretty worn in late summer, but not so the grass in the **Public Garden,** right next to the Common to the west. The Public Garden's flower beds and lawns are kept with meticulous care, and the famous **Swan Boats** (run by pedal-power) which slowly cruise sightseers around the pond may be aging, but they get a fresh coat of white paint each spring.

Downtown Crossing

Southeast of the Common is the city's downtown shopping district, a pedestrian zone called Downtown Crossing; take the subway to Washington Station at the corner of Winter and Washington Streets, and you can enter either of the two big stores, **Jordan Marsh** or **Filene's,** without even leaving the subway station. But walk south on Washington Street and soon you'll be in the **Combat Zone,** dead during the day but roaring in the evening and on into the night, its nudie bars and peep shows doing a brisk business most nights of the week.

Chinatown

The jumble and juxtaposition of Boston's neighborhoods is surprising, and perhaps most of all when one discovers Chinatown right on the edge of the Combat Zone, east of Washington Street. Dozens of very presentable Oriental restaurants, groceries, businesses, and churches are packed into the area around Beach Street, Tyler Street, and Harrison Avenue. Like the North End, Chinatown is a place where the language of the old country may greet your ears more frequently than English.

Back Bay

West of the Public Garden is the large section called Back Bay, with **Commonwealth Avenue** as its residential axis, **Boylston Street** its axis of business and pleasure with office buildings, restaurants, clubs, and shops. Walking west on Boylston Street in Back Bay will bring you to **Copley Square,** one of Boston's most genteel areas, bounded by the classic **Boston Public Library,** the elegant **Copley Plaza Hotel,** and Henry Hobson Richardson's famous **Trinity Church** built in the late 1800s. Modern intruders on this gentility are the striking mirror-glass shaft of the **John Hancock Tower** and the sprawling complex called **Copley Place.**

Prudential Center

Even farther west along Boylston Street is the **Prudential Center,** Back Bay's first large-scale redevelopment scheme, with the Prudential Tower ("the Pru") as its centerpiece, flanked by the mammoth **Sheraton Boston Hotel,** several blocks of luxury flats, and stores such as Lord & Taylor. Also in the Pru complex is the **Hynes Convention Center,** now extensively renovated and again the scene of everything from rock concerts to the boat show.

Huntington Avenue and the Fens

After the Pru Center, Huntington Avenue (which runs along the Pru's southern side) passes the **Christian Science Center, Symphony Hall, Northeastern University,** and the **Museum of Fine Arts** on what might be called Boston's "Cultural Highway." The **Back Bay Fens** sound uninviting, but actually this unappetizing

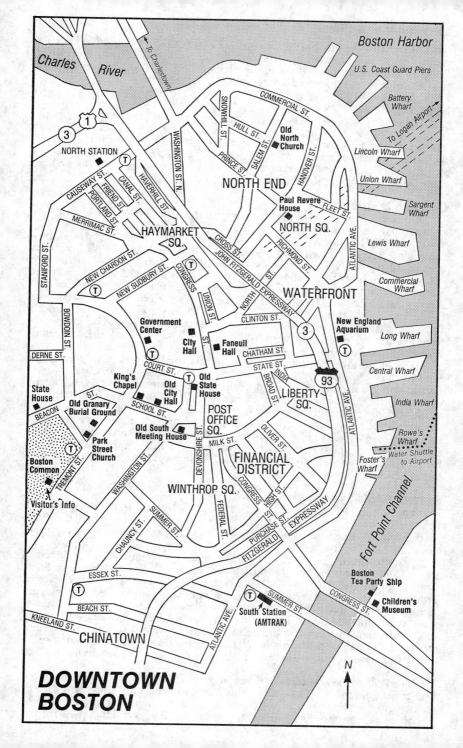

name designates the first links in Frederick Law Olmsted's "Green Necklace," a chain of green parks, copses, and waterways for the residential districts of Back Bay, Roxbury, Jamaica Plain, and Brookline, stretching for miles from the green banks of the Charles River to the **Arnold Arboretum** way to the south.

Kenmore Square

The westernmost part of Boston proper is centered on Kenmore Square, at the intersection of Commonwealth Avenue, Beacon Street, and Brookline Avenue; **Boston University** is just a block or two west from the square, and thus Kenmore's life is dominated by its student denizens, who flock to its cafeterias, book and record stores, movies, and clubs. On the Boston skyline at night, you can always locate Kenmore Square by the huge red Citgo delta.

Outlying Districts

Although the city of Boston is fairly large, it is dwarfed by Greater Boston, officially termed the Metropolitan District, which consists of a dozen other cities as well as some outlying sections of Boston proper. **Charlestown,** north of the tip of Boston peninsula, is dominated by the **Bunker Hill Monument** obelisk; *Old Ironsides* is berthed nearby in the old Boston Navy Yard. **East Boston,** to the northeast, is reached by two tunnels: **Callahan Tunnel** runs north (outbound, no toll), **Sumner Tunnel** runs south (inbound, toll), and the big industry here is Logan International Airport. **South Boston,** southeast of downtown, is separated from the city proper by the Fort Point Channel. "Southie" is the city's Irish bastion, and here St. Patrick's Day is the national holiday. (*Note:* If someone mentions the South End, they're referring to the residential district just south of Back Bay. The South End and South Boston are, confusingly, completely separate places.)

West of Boston is **Brookline,** a large, mostly residential city and the former hometown of the Kennedy family. On the northern banks of the Charles River, **Cambridge** got most of the riverfront land, while **Somerville** had to be content with a mere foothold. The banks of the Charles from the Charles River Dam (topped by the Museum of Science) all the way to Harvard are covered in grass and trees, and in summer the grass is covered with sunbathers, picnickers, readers of paperbacks, and listeners to portable radios. The **Charles River Esplanade** is the river's edge of Beacon Hill, and is perhaps the loveliest part of the Charles's banks, with its marina for small sailboats, the **Hatch Memorial Shell** for summer concerts, a bikepath, and lots of benches.

Several Bird's-Eye Views

The best way to become familiar with Boston's layout is to hover above it in a helicopter. The next best way is to climb to the top of one of the city's tall buildings for the view. Whereas a helicopter ride might be expensive, the skyscraper observatories won't bust your budget.

Take the Green Line (any car you see except "North Station" or "Lechmere") to the Copley Station for the **John Hancock Observatory,** 200 Clarendon St. at Copley Square (tel. 572-6429). The ticket office entrance is on the corner of Trinity Place and St. James Avenue. This, the tallest building in New England, has landmarks picked out for visitors with special telescope-like viewers. Several audiovisual shows outline Boston history and the makeup of the modern cityscape. Hours are Monday through Saturday from 9 a.m. to 11 p.m., year round. On Sunday, summer (May through October) hours are 10 a.m. to 11 p.m.; in winter, noon to 11 p.m. Last tickets are sold at 10:15 p.m. Adults pay $2.25; seniors, $2; children 5 to 15, $1.50.

The **Prudential Tower,** 800 Boylston St. (tel. 236-3318), centerpiece of the Prudential Center, has a **Skywalk** on the 50th floor with a full-circle panorama of the city. It's open from 10 a.m. to 10 p.m. Monday through Saturday, and noon to 10 p.m. on Sunday. Admission is $2.50 for adults, $1.50 for children (5 to 15) and seniors. Two floors above is the Top of the Hub restaurant and cocktail lounge, and you can see the city for free when you buy a drink or a meal. To get to the Pru, take a Green Line "Arborway" car to Prudential Station, or "Boston College," "Cleveland Circle," or "Riverside" cars to Auditorium Station or Copley Station.

VISITORS' INFORMATION: Before coming to Boston, call 617/536-4100, or toll free 800/858-0200, or write the **Greater Boston Convention & Visitors Bureau,** Prudential Plaza West (P.O. Box 490), Boston, MA 02199, and they'll send you an information packet.

If you call the Massachusetts Division of Tourism at 617/727-3201 or (outside Massachusetts) toll free 800/623-8038, and leave your name and address, they'll send you a Massachusetts **Vacation Kit.**

Much of Boston's historic downtown area is now part of the Boston National Historical Park, and so the National Park Service maintains a **Visitor Center** at 15 State St. (tel. 617/242-5642). Free guided Freedom Trail tours are available in the spring and summer. The Information Center is open daily from 9 a.m. to 5 p.m. You'll see park rangers here and there at historic spots, ready to help with directions or information.

On Boston Common (Green Line or Red Line to Park Street Station), at the intersection of Tremont and Winter Streets just a few steps from Park Street Station, there's the **Boston Common Visitor Information Center** (tel. 617/536-4100), open year round from 9 a.m. to 5 p.m. Come here to get maps and booklets describing the Freedom Trail and other visitor information.

Publications

The best calendar of current happenings for free is *Where* magazine, available at visitors' information desks and in hotel lobbies. It's a complete listing of the best plays, sports events, concerts, special exhibits, and programs. Another way to get current news of current offerings is to buy a copy of one of the city's alternative weekly tabloid newspapers, such as the *Boston Phoenix.* These routinely have theater, concert, cinema, and lecture listings, as well as information on poetry readings and performances at coffeehouses, jam sessions, and some of the most fascinating "Personals" ads in the country. These weekly tabloids can be bought at any newsstand or from street hawkers. If you are near a university, go to the student center where the newspapers are often distributed at no charge.

Guided Tours

A guided bus tour is the easiest way of all to get acquainted with the city and its landmarks, and the price for such an introduction is reasonable. The **Gray Line,** at Park Square (tel. 426-8805), offers 16 tours of New England, one a tour of Boston and Cambridge. Their Tour No. 1 takes three hours, covers 18 miles, and includes many Freedom Trail sights, Beacon Hill, Bunker Hill, and *Old Ironsides.* Harvard and MIT Tours leave every day at various times and cost $14 for people 13 years and older; free if you're 12 or under. Contact them by phone or at the sightseeing desk of one of the larger hotels.

Boat Excursions: A novel way to get acquainted with Boston is by taking a cruise in the harbor and Massachusetts Bay. **Bay State Provincetown Cruises** (tel. 723-7800) operates vessels that tour the waters of Boston. Cruises take 1½ hours (three cruises a day); the price is $4 for adults, $2 for children under 12. A 55-minute cruise of Boston's Inner Harbor is also available with the option of going ashore at the Charlestown Navy Yard. There's also a cruise to Nantasket Beach and whale watches. In addition to these cruises, short trips at lunchtime (12:15 to 12:45 p.m.) are a refreshing break from city life and cost only $1 per person. Sandwiches and beverages are for sale on board. Call for exact schedules. These boats depart from the red ticket office at 20 Long Wharf, opposite the Chart House Restaurant, near the Aquarium (Blue Line) subway station. Offices are at 66 Long Wharf.

The M/V *Provincetown II,* also operated by Bay State, journeys to Provincetown from Boston daily in late June, and throughout July and August, with one trip a day sailing from Boston about 9:30 a.m., arriving Provincetown at about 12:30 p.m., then departing P-town at about 3:30 p.m. to arrive back in Boston before 6:30 p.m. The M/V *Provincetown* also makes the voyage on weekends in May, early June, September, and October. For more details, see Chapter VII, Section 11, "Provincetown."

---

2. Getting Around

THE T: Boston's subway and bus system, one of the oldest in the country, has been revitalized and improved. You'll find the T (short for Massachusetts Bay Transportation Authority, or MBTA) the best way to get around downtown and Back Bay. At this writing, fares are 50¢ on most buses and 75¢ on the subway, but note this: on several lines (most notably the Green Line) the cars surface and serve as trolleys after they leave the central part of the city. When a car emerges, passengers boarding above ground ride for free. If you catch a Green Line trolley inbound, however, you pay the entire fare to your destination (which may cost up to $1.75) when you get on, and then there's nothing to pay later. Children five to 11 pay half fare, seniors pay 10¢ for any ride. Buses that go to outlying communities (Salem, Marblehead, etc.) charge up to $2.50 one way for the ride. All fares are on an *exact-change* basis: on buses and trolleys you *must* have the exact fare; at subway stations there are change booths open during service hours.

Subway lines are color-coded: the **Red Line** goes from Alewife in Cambridge via Harvard Square through the central station at Park Street and then on to the suburbs of Quincy, Braintree, Dorchester, and Mattapan; the **Green Line** goes from Lechmere Square in East Cambridge through Park Street and downtown and then out to the western suburbs. I'll mention the line—Red, Green, Blue, or Orange—and the appropriate station for most of the sights mentioned in this book, and thus speed your way to your destination.

The **MBTA Information Booth** is in Park Street Station. For information by telephone, call these numbers: for Lost and Found, 617/722-5000; for route information, 722-3200 or toll free 800/392-6100; for MBTA commuter railroad schedules to places north and west of Boston, 617/227-5070 or toll free 800/392-6099. To points south, 617/482-4400 or toll free 800/882-1220. When in doubt, the central MBTA switchboard number is 617/722-5000.

Hours of Operation

Times on subway and bus lines vary, but you're pretty sure of being able to take the T any day from 5 a.m. up to 12:30 a.m. (and up to 1 a.m. on some lines). After that, be prepared to take a cab, unless you get the final trip time from an officer of the line, and meet the schedule. Hours may vary on Sunday.

Subway Pickpockets

Any big-city transportation system has its pickpockets, and Boston is no exception. The *modus operandi* is for a group of four or five such types to ride the trains or buses together so the stolen wallet or purse can be passed from one to the other, thus protecting the one who actually lifted it. Watch for people who continually bump people and crowd toward the doors at a stop, and then "decide this must not be the place," and move back in; they'll be carrying coats or raincoats (whatever the weather) to conceal a light-fingered hand and also any prizes they may take. If you see one in action and challenge him or her, the reaction will be aggressive defense—"Who are you calling a pickpocket?"—and then a quick exit.

If you should be so unlucky as to have your pocket or purse picked, call one of the numbers listed in the white pages under "Mass. Bay Transportation Authority, Lost and Found" (the number will depend on the subway line or bus you were on); try a few days later as well, as wallets are often found, minus cash, and turned in.

BOSTON MBTA RAPID TRANSIT Ⓣ

TAXIS: An ad which runs perpetually in the *Boston Globe*'s "Job Opportunities" classifieds begins, "Sooner or later you'll be a cab driver." There are many long-time professional drivers, of course, but there are also many part-time, out-of-town students, and beginning drivers who may or may not know their way around. There are also those who may know their way around but who will get "lost" because you're paying them by the mile. Such is life in a big city. It could be worse: you could be driving your own car, watching its fenders being bent, battling for parking places. There's no charge for normal luggage, but there is a surcharge for trunks. If you've got a complaint against a driver, get his hackney carriage medallion number, and his name and number (from his permit, posted in the cab), record the date and time of the occurrence, and call the Boston Police Department's Hackney Carriage office at 247-4475. Medallions, or permits to operate cabs, cost in the tens of thousands of dollars, and drivers or companies will do a lot not to lose one.

DRIVING: Boston drivers are famed for being slow of wit and heavy of foot. Traffic control is often minimal, leaving each to fend for her- or himself. It's not so much that Boston drivers are aggressive as that they're thoughtless and inconsiderate. There is a widespread belief that stop signs have no meaning, and that red lights, especially late at night, are mere bagatelles. Although there is a required state vehicle inspection, you may run into five or six cars with inoperative brake lights during even a short drive across town. Horror statistics: A fairly expensive late-model car with full collision insurance can cost its owner over $2,000 a year in insurance premiums alone. One reason is that Boston is the stolen-car capital of the U.S.

Parking is definitely a problem if you want to do it on the cheap. Downtown parking can cost $8 for the first half hour. For the visitor unfamiliar with the city, I'd suggest the large **Boston Common Underground Garage,** entered from Charles Street between the Common and the Public Garden. Here the rates are moderate, and there's a free shuttle bus to take you to nearby points. If you stay for some time in Boston, do not accumulate a backlog of unpaid parking tickets: cars are towed and held hostage until the tickets are paid. By the way, you will see every No Parking zone in the city parked solid almost all the time. It's done, here and in Cambridge, but a few of the scofflaws come back to find their cars towed away or securely locked in place by the big yellow "Denver Boot" (so named after the city that originated its use). The price to get the car back is about $80 plus the cost of overdue tickets.

BIKES: Boston is a good town for bicycling: the hills are gentle, the views are better from a bike, and there are marked bike paths and a new bikeway running from near the center of town along the beautiful Esplanade and the south bank of the Charles River all the way to Harvard Square. Bring a strong lock or heavy chain to prevent theft, especially if you have a ten-speed. Perhaps the greatest advantage of biking in Boston and Cambridge is the ease and cheapness of parking: any lamppost will do, and it's free. You can rent bikes in Boston or Cambridge. Rental shops are listed in the Yellow Pages under "Bicycles—Renting." You can also rent mopeds, but these cost about three times as much as a bike, require a hefty deposit, and have more potential for problems than a simple bicycle.

---

3. Hotels

The best way to get to know Boston is to stay right downtown, where the action is. Boston has a very fine selection of downtown hotels, and each one seems to have something special to recommend it.

Note that the room tax of 9.7% is a significant amount; it will be added to your total hotel bill.

You can get more lodging value for your money if you follow these suggestions:
Visit on a Weekend: First of all, if you want to stay right downtown, by all means *plan your visit for a weekend!* A double room at any luxury hotel right in downtown Boston may cost a *minimum* of $150 during the week. But if you sign up for a two-night stay on Friday and Saturday, you may get that same room for just over half price, plus a bottle of champagne, breakfast in bed, the morning's newspaper, and free parking. These "weekend specials" are offered by all of the city's luxury hotels, and many are even lower in price. It even makes sense to detour out of town—to Salem and the North Shore, to Cape Cod, or to Old Sturbridge Village—in order to arrive in Boston on Friday afternoon or evening. (By the way, country inns and resorts are most crowded, and highest in price, on weekends; so it makes sense to visit the country places during the week.)

Try a Bed-and-Breakfast: Another way to save money is to try a bed-and-breakfast room. Several agencies will make reservations and arrangements for you, and they're all listed below. By staying in a bed-and-breakfast room, you can pay a half or even a third of the downtown hotel price, and make new Bostonian friends in the bargain.

Stay on the Outskirts: Finally, there are the hostelries on the outskirts of town. If you have a car and are willing to stay in Salem, Lexington, Concord, or some other suburban location, you can save 25% to 50% of the cost of a downtown room.

Here, then, are descriptions of Boston's hotels. I'll describe a few of the luxurious, grand old places you might want to patronize as a treat. Following these are details on the city's very comfortable, moderately priced establishments. Finally, you'll find some hints on lower-priced lodgings, just in case you're running over your budget.

THE TOP HOTELS (Doubles for $160 and up): My favorite of the grand old Boston hotels is the **Copley Plaza,** right on Copley Square, Boston, MA 02116 (tel. 617/267-5300, or toll free 800/826-7539). The attractions are the hotel's grand style and original touches: a quiet cocktail lounge which is in fact a comfy club library complete with oil portraits and brass-nailed leather chairs; the striking, ornate, elegant Plaza dining room, in which the ceilings are heavily gilded, the mantelpieces are marble, and the maître d' a soft-spoken and very suave man in a tuxedo; and Copley's, a mirror-laden brass-rail bar serving drinks and sandwiches, with trompe l'oeil paintings on the mirrors and doors. Single rooms are $150 to $190; double or twin rooms run $160 to $210; suites run $300 to $750. Valet parking is $20; nearby parking is $14.

Anyone who's ever come to Boston has considered staying at the **Omni Parker House,** School and Tremont Streets, Boston, MA 02108 (tel. 617/227-8600, or toll free 800/843-6664), a traditional beauty which capitalizes on its antiquity, showing off its wood paneling, ornate gilded ceilings, and leather-upholstered furniture. The rooms, although fairly small, are decorated very tastefully with reproductions of antiques. The dining room, Parker's, is a haven of quiet, shining crystal and silver, heavy mirrors, and thick carpets. Lunch here might be $20 to $30, and dinner about $40 to $50 per person. Downstairs from the lobby is The Last Hurrah, an eye-catching collection of Tiffany-style lamps, 1890s bars and booths, brass globe-top lamps, pictures of turn-of-the-century prize fighters, and the like. The Last Hurrah is where many office workers in the nearby government and financial districts come for lunch or after-five cocktails that are served with hot and cold hors d'oeuvres (on the house). The 535 rooms at the Omni Parker House are priced at $145 to $265 single, $160 to $280 double.

"What a perfect place for a hotel!" That's how the **Bostonian Hotel,** Faneuil Hall Marketplace, Boston, MA 02109 (tel. 617/523-3600, or toll free 800/343-0922), introduces itself. It's true: next to Faneuil Hall, Government Center, the weekend open fruit-and-vegetable market, the North End's Italian shops and restaurants, the Bostonian is in the midst of the action. Modern with colonial accents, the hotel boasts tiny balconies overlooking Faneuil Hall on most rooms. It's a small, low-rise (four-floor) luxury hotel with 155 rooms priced at $170 to $210 single, $190 to $220 double. Honeymoon rooms with Jacuzzi tubs and fireplaces cost somewhat more. Kids under 12 stay free.

Four Seasons hotels are noted for their quiet whispering of elegance and status, and the 288-room **Four Seasons Hotel Boston,** 200 Boylston St., Boston, MA 02116 (tel. 617/338-4400, or toll free 800/268-6282), is no exception. This is an impressive addition to Boston's lineup of luxury hotels, and opened in June 1985. Facing the Public Garden, near Back Bay and its chic shopping, a block from the theater district, and a short walk across Boston Common to the central shopping and financial districts, the Four Seasons couldn't have a better location. Facilities are extremely well-thought-out for guests' comfort, and very plush in an up-to-date style inspired by tradition. Rates are $175 to $215 single, $195 to $235 double, with suites costing up to $1,000 a day. Many rooms, by the way, have views of the Public Garden.

Boston's newest luxury hotel is the **Boston Harbor Hotel,** 70 Rowe's Wharf, Boston, MA 02110 (tel. 617/439-7000, or toll free 800/752-7077), on Atlantic Avenue near the intersection of High Street (from the Central Artery, take the "South Station" exit). Opened in September of 1987, the hotel is part of a landmark redevelopment plan which restored the dramatic old buildings at Rowe's Wharf into a complex which includes the hotel, offices, condominiums, shops, restaurants, a yacht marina, and a ferryboat terminal. You can spot the striking flat-domed main portal easily if you're driving on the Central Artery.

The hotel is wonderfully luxurious, with 230 rooms that are almost junior suites, each with its own sitting area separate from the sleeping area, plus a mini-bar and remote-control television. There are bathrobes, hair dryers, 24-hour room service, free shoeshine service, fresh flowers, maid service twice daily, windows you can open to let in the sea breezes, and top-class luxury furnishings in classic style. Besides the standard rooms, the hotel has 96 deluxe rooms with harbor or city views, and 28 luxury suites.

The public spaces are classic, conservative, beautiful, and suggest wealth and richness, from the lavish use of colored marble to the crystal chandeliers, the thick patterned carpets, and the displays of antique maps and charts of Boston and New England. Classical music murmurs in the background, or a piano tinkles in the spacious sea-view lounge. Hotel services include a 60-foot lap pool, a large whirlpool, a sauna, steambaths, massage rooms, exercise equipment, and spa-treatment facilities. There are classes in aerobics and weight-training instruction. The restaurant features New England seafood and other regional American cuisine, and has a sweeping view of Boston harbor.

Single rooms cost $175 to $245, doubles range from $195 to $265, though weekend packages can bring the cost of a room, single or double, down to $145 per night. By the way, the interesting stone pavilion with a copper-clad dome, perched out by the wharf, is the terminus for ferryboats.

A Glance at the Luxury Line-up

The aforementioned are by no means Boston's only luxury hotels, they're just the ones that I think convey a special spirit of the city. In the range of $150 to $200 per night for a double room, you'll also find these excellent places:

The **Hotel Meridien Boston,** 250 Franklin St., Boston, MA 02110 (tel. 617/451-1900, or toll free 800/223-9918) is Air France's elegant hostelry housed in the handsome former headquarters of the Federal Reserve Bank of Boston, in the heart of the financial district.

The **Boston Marriott Hotel Long Wharf,** 296 State St., Boston, MA 02109 (tel. 617/227-0800, or toll free 800/228-9290), is a new luxury hotel with traditional lines, right on the waterfront next to Faneuil Hall Marketplace.

The **Ritz-Carlton Hotel,** 15 Arlington St., Boston, MA 02117 (tel. 617/536-5700, or toll free 800/241-3333), is Boston's *grande dame* in the luxury class, with careful service and a prime location right next to the Public Garden.

The modern 500-room **Lafayette Swissôtel,** 1 Avenue de Lafayette, Boston, MA 02111 (tel. 617/451-2600, or toll free 800/992-0124, 800/325-2531 in Massachusetts), one of Boston's newest hotels, is right at Downtown Crossing, in the heart of the shopping district, part of the Lafayette Place complex.

The **Colonnade Hotel,** 120 Huntington Ave., Boston, MA 02116 (tel. 617/424-7000, or toll free 800/962-3030), concentrates on modern luxuries and European-style service in a location near Symphony Hall, Copley Place, the Hynes Convention Center, and the Prudential Center.

The **Sheraton-Boston Hotel and Towers,** 39 Dalton St., Boston, MA 02199 (tel. 617/236-2000, or toll free 800/325-3535), the enormous lodging right in the Prudential Center, has two hotels in one: the convention-oriented Sheraton Boston, and the more genteel and select Sheraton Towers.

The **Back Bay Hilton,** 40 Dalton St., Boston, MA 02115 (tel. 617/236-1100) and the **Westin Hotel Copley Place,** 10 Huntington Ave., Boston, MA 02116 (tel. 617/262-9600, or toll free 800/228-3000) are two other additions to the luxury line-up, in an ultramodern complex built right next to traditional Copley Square in the Back Bay.

The **Royal Sonesta Hotel,** 5 Cambridge Parkway, Cambridge, MA 02142 (tel. 617/491-3600), is actually closer to downtown Boston than to Harvard Square. A short trundle from the hotel across the Charles River Dam by the Museum of Science brings you right to Beacon Hill. The Sonesta has 400 modern rooms with views of the river and of Beacon Hill. Rooms are priced at $150 to $190 single, $170 to $210 double.

THE UPPER BRACKET (Doubles for $110 to $175): Lower in price than the luxury hotels, these "Upper Bracket" places still offer all the services, such as air conditioning, parking garages, color television, room service, restaurants and bars, and downtown locations. Many also have those marvelous weekend special rates. Be sure to ask about them when you call for information or reservations.

A well-located, upper-range hotel in downtown Boston is the **57 Park Plaza Hotel–Howard Johnson,** 200 Stuart St., Boston, MA 02116 (tel. 617/482-1800, or toll free 800/654-2000). The 350-room hotel is only two blocks from Boston Common and the Public Garden, and right near the Greyhound/Trailways bus terminal, in a multipurpose complex of buildings which includes a parking garage, two cinemas, two lounges, and two restaurants. This is one of the more luxurious establishments in the Howard Johnson chain, and it even boasts a year-round swimming pool and a sauna. Business meetings provide a big part of its clientele, both because of the new facilities and because of its very central location. A single person pays $105 to $150; two in a double bed pay $115 to $165; two persons in two double beds pay $115 to $165. Charge for an extra person is $15. Children under 18 can stay for free if their parents pay the normal two-person rate; the hotel gives discounts to AARP senior citizens with ID cards.

Enjoy the pleasures of the Prudential Center and Copley Place by staying at the **Lenox Hotel,** 710 Boylston St., corner of Exeter, Boston, MA 02116 (tel. 617/536-5300, or toll free 800/225-7676 outside Massachusetts). Here you're right in the same block as the Pru, and rooms cost $100 to $180 single, $120 to $200 double; an extra person pays $20, and children under 18 stay free with their parents. An English-style pub is open for lunch, supper, and late-night snacks (till 2 a.m.). The Lenox provides its rooms with Provincial, Oriental, or Colonial decor, individually controlled air conditioning, color TV, coffee makers, and soundproofed walls; some rooms have fireplaces. Besides being right in the Prudential Center, the Lenox is right next to the Boston Public Library, and only a block from Copley Square.

The **Holiday Inn** at Government Center, 5 Blossom St., Boston, MA 02114 (tel. 617/742-7630), just off Cambridge Street, between Government Center and the Longfellow Bridge over the Charles River, is a high-rise haven slightly out of the center of things. It's several blocks from Government Center, and then several blocks again from Government Center to the Boston Common. But prices are not too bad in this modern building, and facilities are good: swimming pool (summer months only), free covered parking, and a penthouse restaurant. Rooms cost $100 single, $145 double. Within the same complex as the 300-room hotel are two cinemas, a supermarket, and rows of shops. Children under 18 stay free with their parents.

Boston's famous Statler Hilton is no more, but in its place—actually, in the very same building—you'll find the **Boston Park Plaza Hotel and Towers,** 50 Park Plaza, on Arlington Street, Boston, MA 02117 (tel. 617/426-2000, or toll free 800/225-2008). The new management performed a complete renovation of all the 977 rooms. At the far end of the lobby from the entry is a great fireplace, now hidden in a café. The hotel has a restaurant, piano bar, garden lounge, and 30 of the airline offices in Boston; it's near the Greyhound/Trailways bus terminal, a scant block from Boston Common, and 15 minutes from Logan. Prices are: $99 to $159 for single rooms, $115 to $176 for double rooms. Children stay for free with their parents. All rooms have air conditioning, color TV, AM-FM radio. The Boston Park Plaza Hotel and Towers is easily within walking distance of most attractions. The nearest T stop is Arlington.

The **Howard Johnson Hotel Kenmore Square,** at 575 Commonwealth Ave., Boston, MA 02215 (tel. 617/267-3100, or toll free 800/654-2000), is perfectly situated if you're visiting Boston University and well placed for most everything else. A modern 179-room hotel with indoor swimming pool, Profiles Café, and Box Seat Lounge, its location allows you to hop right on a Green Line train for the short ride to Park Street Station on Boston Common. Room prices are $100 to $125 single, $112 to $138 double. Kids up to 18 stay free, seniors get discounts, and lots of special money-saving package plans are offered. Call for details.

MODERATELY PRICED HOTELS (Doubles for $100 to $125):

Perhaps the best bargain in the area of the Prudential Center, Symphony Hall, and the Christian Science Center is the **Copley Square Hotel,** 47 Huntington Ave. at the corner of Exeter Street, Boston, MA 02116 (tel. 617/536-9000, or toll free 800/225-7062). Like most of the older hotels in Boston, its rooms have been carefully refurbished and maintained, and are very comfortable. The hotel's management divides its rooms into three categories: standard ($86 single, $98 double), superior ($96 single, $108 double), and deluxe ($106 single, $118 double, $145 for family suites suitable for two, three, or four persons). All rooms are equipped with a TV, a coffee maker, and air conditioning. All rooms also have private bath. This is a full-service hotel with a bar, restaurant, and coffeeshop; $12 overnight parking; limousine service from the airport at $5.50 per person; and a family plan (children under 18 stay free). In the winter months when trade is down the people at the Copley Square Hotel are liable to offer special package rates—write and ask about them, detailing your plans. The hotel is a short block from Copley Square, the Prudential Center, and Boylston Street.

The **Howard Johnson Lodge Fenway,** 1271 Boylston St., Boston, MA 02215 (tel. 617/267-8300, or toll free 800/654-2000), is a 94-room hotel near Fenway Park, home of the Boston Red Sox during baseball season. The Museum of Fine Arts and the Gardner Museum are also close by, and public transportation easily gets you to the city's other sights. Prices are moderate for a city hotel: $100 single, $115 double. As usual at Hojo's, kids under 18 stay for free, senior citizens get discounts, and package plans bring the price down on numerous occasions.

The **TraveLodge Boston** is actually in the neighboring city of Brookline, at 1200 Beacon St., Brookline, MA 02146 (tel. 617/277-1200, or toll free 800/255-3050). The 190 rooms in this residential neighborhood are clean and fairly quiet, with clock-radios and color television sets. Public transportation will take you the several miles into town fairly easily. Single rooms are priced at $88, and doubles at $99.

BUDGET LODGINGS (Doubles for $45 to $90): It's no simple task to find a truly inexpensive, respectable room in Boston, but still it can be done. You'd be well advised to reserve your room in advance, to make sure you can nail down that low price.

A Hotel

The **Chandler Inn,** 20 Chandler St., Boston, MA 02116 (tel. 617/482-3450, or toll free 800/842-3450), at Berkeley Street, only about three blocks from the Greyhound/Trailways bus terminal, just across the Massachusetts Turnpike from the busy Back Bay commercial district, is a real find. An older hotel, the Chandler has 56 quite small, very simple rooms with renovated bathrooms (including tub and shower), and either a double bed or twin beds. The cost for a room is only $76 single, $87 double, and includes a continental breakfast. Children under 12 can occupy their parents' room for free. Most rooms have only one window and no view, but the corner rooms have two windows and some views; best of all is Room 808, on the top floor (there's an elevator) in the corner. The neighborhood here is undergoing renovation, so ignore its partially rundown appearance.

Bed-and-Breakfast Services

An interesting alternative to commercial lodgings is the bed-and-breakfast room. These are spare rooms or even apartments in private homes, rented to travelers at moderate rates. Bed-and-breakfast services will take your reservation, describe accommodations and prices, and give directions to your lodging. All this is best done in advance, but don't be afraid to call one of the following services if you arrive in town without a reservation.

New England Bed and Breakfast, Inc., 1045 Centre St., Newton Centre, MA 02159 (tel. 617/244-2112) will find you a room in a private home for $36 to $45 single, $46 to $60 double, with a small breakfast included.

A similar service is operated by **Bed and Breakfast Associates Bay Colony, Inc.,** P.O. Box 57166, Babson Park Branch, Boston, MA 02157 (tel. 617/449-5302 from 10 a.m. to 12:30 p.m. and 1:30 to 5 p.m.). For $2.50 they'll send you a directory describing hundreds of rooms, studios, suites, and apartments hosted by the service. Prices range from $45 to $80 single, $55 to $125 double, continental breakfast included.

Host Homes of Boston, P.O. Box 117, Waban Branch, Boston, MA 02168 (tel. 617/244-1308), will find you a room in Newton, Brookline, Cambridge, Boston, or another community for about $45 to $80 single, $48 to $90 double, breakfast included. They take credit cards, and using your card number you can call, make reservations, and get a confirmation the same day.

Greater Boston Hospitality, P.O. Box 1142, Brookline, MA 02146 (tel. 617/277-5430), makes reservations for private homes, private city clubs, small inns, and condominiums in Boston, Brookline, Cambridge, Needham, Newton, Wellesley, Quincy, Scituate, Gloucester, and Marblehead. You can write, or call 24 hours a day.

Room Rentals

Beacon Guest House, 248 Newbury St., Boston, MA 02116 (tel. 617/262-1771 or 266-7276), will arrange a daily or weekly room rental for you, with private bath and kitchenette with utensils, for $55 per day, $300 per week single; $65 per day, $275 per week double. All of their rooms are in brownstone apartment buildings located in Back Bay, on Newbury Street near the Prudential Center, the new auditorium, and public transportation.

Guesthouses

These tend to be plain rather than fancy. Boston's neighbor city of Brookline has several guesthouses, all reachable by going along Beacon Street from Boston. The street keeps the same name in Brookline. In fact, if you don't keep a sharp eye out, you'll miss the signs announcing that you've entered Brookline.

You can get to the following guesthouse by taking a Green Line subway train ("Cleveland Circle"). The guesthouses are right on the subway route.

Anthony's Town House, 1085 Beacon St., Brookline, MA 02146 (tel. 617/ 566-3972), is a turn-of-the-century brownstone town house with various rooms (private bath or shared bath) for $30 to $40 single, $40 to $55 double.

BUDGET MOTELS ON THE OUTSKIRTS: Although it's preferable to stay downtown and not get snarled in city traffic, you may want to know that Boston has several representatives of the budget-priced **Susse Chalet** motel chain. For reservations, call toll free 800/258-1980 (800/572-1880 in New Hampshire, 800/858-5008 in Canada).

Nearest to the center of Boston are the two motels in Dorchester. Both are on Morrissey Boulevard at Exit 12 or 13 off the Southeast Expressway (Rte. 3), five miles from Boston Common. The Susse Chalet at 800 Morrissey Blvd., Boston, MA 02122 (tel. 617/287-9100), charges $35.70 single, $39.70 double. Nearby, the Susse Chalet at 900 Morrissey Blvd., Boston, MA 02122 (tel. 617/287-9200), charges $46.70 single, $50.70 double.

There is a similar place in Cambridge as well. It's the Susse Chalet, Rte. 2, Cambridge, MA 02140 (tel. 617/661-7800), not far past the Alewife MBTA subway terminus, on the inbound side of the highway. Rooms here cost $46.70 single, $50.70 double. It's about a 15-minute walk to the Alewife station on the MBTA subway's Red Line, which goes directly to Harvard Square in Cambridge and Park Street (for Boston Common) in Boston.

The city of Braintree is due south of Boston. Take Exit 17 from the Southeast Expressway (Rte. 3, Southbound) for the Susse Chalet, Union Street, Braintree, MA 02184 (tel. 617/848-7890), which charges $41.70 single, $45.70 double for a room, and is very near the Braintree MBTA subway station, so you can catch a train directly into Boston.

Due north of Boston is the Susse Chalet, at the intersection of I-95 (Rte. 128) and I-93, Woburn, MA 01801 (tel. 617/938-7575), near an MBTA subway station. Rates are $46.70 single, $50.70 double.

4. Restaurants

Dining possibilities in Boston are virtually limitless. The city's array of restaurants includes at least one representative of every notable cuisine in the world, and usually more than one—in the Boston area there are over 150 Chinese restaurants alone. Most of Boston's restaurants take advantage of the fresh seafood that comes to the docks daily, whether the specialty is seafood or not.

For my recommendations, I've tried to help you choose from this bewildering array by sticking to restaurants in Boston proper and excluding the many fine places in the suburbs on the notion that you won't want to fight your way to an unfamiliar town and unfamiliar streets, but would rather spend your time in Boston. Also, I've chosen favorites, places that I've found satisfactory in every way, every time I've been there, and in which I've always felt I've gotten my money's worth. Remember that the many very fine hotel restaurants, lounges, and coffeeshops are covered along with the hotel itself in the preceding section; the good restaurants and coffeehouses in Cambridge are described in the chapter on Cambridge, but it's good to remember that most of them are within walking distance of the Red Line's Harvard subway station, and the trip can be made from central Boston in 10 or 15 minutes. The good restaurant in the Museum of Fine Arts, the best place for lunch if you're seeing the MFA or the Gardner Museum, is described along with the museum itself in the sightseeing section.

In the more expensive establishments, it's good to call ahead for reservations if they'll take them—many Boston places do not. This is true especially on weekends and holidays, of course. And when you call, ask whether they honor your credit card, and what parking arrangements there are.

Massachusetts has a meal tax of 5.7% added to every meal check over a minimal amount.

THE TOP RESTAURANTS ($50 and up): Any dispute over a city's "best" restaurant is likely to be hot and lengthy, for the simple reason that personal preferences favor certain types of surroundings, service, and cuisine.

Many Bostonians would agree that the best restaurant in town is **L'Espalier,** 30 Gloucester St. (tel. 262-3023), and for the city's ultimate dining experience, it may be equalled but can't be beat. This small, elegant restaurant in an old Back Bay town house serves only dinner, every night except Monday, and you must have reservations, which are sometimes difficult to get. A valet will park your car, and you enter through a vestibule and walk up a flight of stairs to reach the grand high-ceilinged dining room, which is quite nice but not really very "decorated." Waiters in black and white attend to you immediately, and are professional, polished, and friendly in their work. The menu lists the chef's latest creations of French nouvelle cuisine, which, though sometimes exotic, are really inspired and delicious. The wine list is long, good, and fairly pricey. You must be prepared to spend $150 on dinner for two here if you intend not to scrimp, and if you go all out, the tab might come to $200. Whether it does or not, you won't soon forget the meal.

Pride of place on Beacon Hill must go to **Another Season,** 97 Mt. Vernon St., between Charles Street and Louisburg Square (tel. 367-0880). Small and friendly, with a marvelous feeling of informal elegance, Another Season is one of those places where the chef puts her personal touch on classic recipes, then makes the rounds of the tables to see how diners have liked them. The wine list is very fine, the cuisine even finer, the service just as good. Get a reservation, then go with about $50 or so to spend for each diner, and you'll find the experience worth far more. Lunch is served from noon to 2 p.m. Tuesday through Friday, and dinner is from 6 to 10 p.m. Monday through Saturday.

Among Boston's restaurants of longstanding high quality, few can equal the record of **Maison Robert,** in the old Boston City Hall building at 45 School St., behind King's Chapel (tel. 227-3370). The restaurant shares this wonderful old building, fronted by a statue of Benjamin Franklin, with a bank. In summer, tables are set outside for Ben's Café, where you can have a large salad, cold plate, or entree for lunch, and the total bill might be $22 or so. But dinner is the main event here.

The cuisine in the dining room at Maison Robert is French, modern, and very appealing. You might start on oysters with raspberry vinegar, or pâté of leeks; go on to lobster with champagne sauce, or sliced breast of duck with apples and blueberries, or perhaps flamed rib of beef for two. Desserts are, of course, sumptuous, from crêpes suzettes through the house gâteau (chocolate), to various soufflés. Surroundings are formal and attractive; the service is impeccable. The bill, with wine, tax, and tip, will be in the range of $45 to $60 per person. Hours are 11:30 a.m. to 2:30 p.m. and 5:30 to 10 p.m. Monday through Friday, 6 to 10:30 p.m. on Saturday; closed Sunday. Have reservations.

Several years ago a group of Boston businessmen organized an exclusive club, called the Bay Club, in an aerie atop the Sheraton World Headquarters at 60 State St., right next to Boston's Old State House. At lunchtime it's the Bay Club, open to members only, but in the evenings the multilevel dining room and lounge with the three-story-high glass wall becomes the **Bay Tower Room** (tel. 723-1666), open to all. On the mezzanine level is a cocktail lounge (open at 4:30 p.m., with last call at midnight every day except Sunday) with a band for dancing (Monday through Saturday from 8 p.m. to midnight). Dining is on two levels below, and every table has the same marvelous view of the Customs House Tower, the bay, Logan Airport, and the hills beyond.

Dinner is served from 6 to 9:30 p.m. every evening but Sunday, and a jacket-and-tie dress code is in force. The food is very good, but the service surpasses it. As to the menu: it's long and inclusive, expensive but not outrageous. You can start with fresh caviar or with a simple soup. Fish and shellfish, fowl, and grilled meats are all featured; specialties are braised sweetbreads with goose liver and asparagus, roast duckling with broiled apples, and breast of chicken with foie gras in a madeira sauce. The bill, per person—tax, tip, and wine included—will be about $60 to $75. Have reservations.

The genteel atmosphere of the **Ritz-Carlton Hotel** (tel. 536-5700) is a good place to spend money on a fine lunch or dinner. From its location at 15 Arlington St. (at the beginning of Newbury), the second-floor dining room of the Ritz looks out over the Public Garden and its trees and beds of flowers, or snow scenes, as the case may be. Elegance is all around: gold tracery on the cream-colored ceiling, lofty many-paned windows surrounded by blue-and-white print drapes, crystal chandeliers, and sconces, potted plants, a tinkling piano, and the most refined service imaginable. The menu changes (and is reprinted on heavy stock) daily, but a typical luncheon menu might offer you roast duckling with cherries, médaillons of beef with mushrooms, a thin veal cutlet in chive butter, or perhaps a selection from the cold buffet, or an omelet. At dinner the selection is even more extensive: start with the lobster bisque with cognac, or Louisiana shrimp with a cocktail sauce, and then go on to a roast leg of spring lamb, or lobster prepared with whisky, or medallions of venison, cranberries, and chestnuts. For dessert, have one of the several dessert soufflés which are first a dream, then ambrosia, then a fond memory. Such a repast will cost $65 to $75 per person, with wine. You can have lunch at the Ritz daily from noon to 2:30 p.m.; dinner from 5:30 to 10 p.m. weekdays and Sundays, and to 11 p.m. on Friday and Saturday; Sunday brunch is from 10:45 a.m. to 3 p.m. The dress code is enforced at all times, of course.

Cornucopia, 15 West St. (tel. 338-4600), is a very fine restaurant in an odd but convenient place. West Street is a short street which runs from Tremont Street near the Boston Common Visitor Information Center to Washington Street at Lafayette Place. The restaurant is right next to the famous old Brattle Bookstore. Its location makes it convenient for anyone seeing the sights around Boston Common, or on Beacon Hill, or anyone shopping at Downtown Crossing. You enter a small, refined, up-to-date room done in soft muted colors, lighted by hanging lamps with diamond-shaped stained-glass shades. There's an enclosed terrace at the rear, and an attractive upstairs room as well. Original art hangs on the walls, and several black marble café tables with intricate white veining stand waiting near the sidewalk window. The cuisine is new American, the menu changes monthly, and a meal might begin with chicken ravioli in consommé with wild mushrooms, or salmon marinated in champagne with tropical fruit and kiwi vinaigrette, then go on to a main course of veal loin stuffed with Maine lobster and yellow chanterelle mushrooms, or red snapper sautéed with crushed black pepper and baby clams. The dessert selection changes daily, but is as wonderful as the heartier fare. Lunch should cost $20 to $28 per person; dinner, $30 to $40. Hours for dining are Monday through Friday from noon to 2:30 p.m. and Tuesday through Saturday from 5:30 to 9:30 p.m.; the lighter café menu, and drinks, are served Tuesday through Friday from 2 to 10 p.m., on Saturday from 5:30 to 10 p.m. Remember the café if you need a pick-me-up after shopping or before a night at the opera.

Boston's most famous restaurant is surely the **Hampshire House,** 84 Beacon St. (tel. 227-9605), facing the Public Garden between Arlington Street and Charles Street. While the restaurant is noted for its location in a fine early 20th-century

Georgian Revival mansion, its elegant decoration and its good cuisine, it is far more famous for its Bull & Finch Pub in the basement, which inspired the setting for the television comedy show called "Cheers." Every day countless visitors pose by the entrance to the pub and have their pictures taken, then descend the stairs to take a look inside, and perhaps to buy a Cheers T-shirt. Let me prepare you for the shock: the pub looks nothing like the set for the show—it is not spacious but rather cozy and crowded, and Sam and Rebecca are not behind the bar. The comfy booths are always crowded with a lively, happy, young, attractive crowd taking in the very English pub atmosphere. If the front room is too busy, wander down the long passageway to a similarly cozy room in back. The drink to order here is Samuel Adams lager, Boston's own top-quality beer, or Harpoon ale, brewed only a mile or two away on Northern Avenue.

Upstairs in the Hampshire House proper is another bar in the Oak Room, as sedate and Beacon Hill-ish as you could imagine. Tall arched windows framed by formal drapes let lots of light into the high-ceilinged room, bringing a glint to the polished glasses and a shine to the grand piano. Dignified gents and ladies, properly dressed, murmur quietly to one another while sipping classic concoctions and munching free hors d'oeuvres. The separate Library and Georgian dining rooms are also classic Beacon Hill, with graceful stemware, heavy napery, and polite service. Dinner is served nightly from 5:30 to 10:30 p.m. The menu is interesting without being overly exotic, with some classics such as fettuccine Alfredo, New England clam chowder, and French onion soup gratiné as first courses, then lots of steaks, and also chicken. Selected main-course dishes are low in fat, cholesterol, and sodium. Expect to pay about $45 to $60 per person for dinner. Lunch, for about $16 or so, can be had Monday through Friday from 11:45 a.m. to 2:30 p.m. Sunday brunch, by the way, is a Hampshire House tradition of many years, served from 10:30 a.m. to 2:30 p.m.

MODERATELY PRICED RESTAURANTS ($35 and up):
Because the largest number of recommended restaurants are in this price bracket, I've divided them up according to location and specialty. Here, then, is the best of the mid-range dining establishments:

On Beacon Hill
Rebecca's, 21 Charles St. (tel. 742-9747), has lots of strong points. A favorite of the young and beautiful, up-and-coming Beacon Hill set, it is also convenient for visitors to downtown shopping areas and tourist attractions. The food is continental, upbeat, and carefully prepared, interesting without being excessively exotic. Rebecca's serves lunch Monday through Saturday from 11:30 a.m. to 4 p.m., and dinner daily: on Monday from 5 to 10 p.m., Tuesday through Saturday from 5:30 p.m. to midnight, and on Sunday from 5:30 to 10 p.m. Lunch costs about $20 per person, and dinner runs about $32 to $45, wine, tax, and tip included. There's paella valenciana, fresh ravioli with spinach and cheese in a cream sauce with shrimp, and roast sea bass with mushrooms cooked with balsamic vinegar, white wine, fresh thyme, bacon, and garlic. You can see the luscious dessert cakes and pastries in the cold cases through the front window as you pass by.

Faneuil Hall Marketplace and the Waterfront
One of several Boston restaurants which have resisted change over the years is the venerable **Durgin-Park Market Dining Room** (tel. 227-2038), in the South Market building of Faneuil Hall Marketplace. Durgin-Park boasts that it was "established before you were born," and adds, somewhat unnecessarily, that "Your grandfather and great-grandfather may have dined with us, too." As you mount the stairs to the dining room, it crosses your mind that you must have taken the wrong stairway and entered some "employees only" door, for there before you is all the dishwashing machinery and hardworking kitchen help, and right next to this, the

kitchen itself with cooks and waitresses scurrying here and there. To left and right are large, plain rooms with steam pipes running about on the ceiling, and several sets of long tables covered with white or red checkered cloths. The menu, plainly printed with notices of daily specials stapled to it, bears pithy reminders and warnings such as "washroom downstairs" and "We are not responsible for any steak ordered well done." The prices have changed since the old days, but the dining room's decor and its food have stayed the same: the prime rib (while it lasts, for this is the specialty) is huge, and costs $20. *Fresh* lobster stew (emphasis theirs) is $12, a roast stuffed duck costs $10, and lowly "frankfort and beans" is $4.50. Clams, oysters, and fish are in the $8 to $14 range. Remember, gigantic portions are the rule here, and doggy bags are available. Oh, yes: you can have cocktails at the dinner table. Be warned that on weekends for dinner the restaurant is usually very busy, and no reservations are accepted. Perhaps the best time to go is at lunch, referred to as the "dinner bill," when prices are considerably lower (for smaller luncheon portions, of course) and the tables not so crowded. But be sure you get to the restaurant between 11:30 a.m. and 2:30 p.m. for the low-priced lunches. By the way, there's an oyster bar in the basement.

Also in the Faneuil Hall Marketplace, and a good place to dine outdoors, is the **Café at Lily's** (tel. 227-3434), in Quincy Market. Actually, there are two Lily's establishments in Quincy Market, the **Piano Bar at Lily's** (a major gathering place for the young and single) and, on the other side of Quincy Market, the Café. In warm weather, tables are set out in the promenades on either side of Quincy Market, and the glass "walls" are lifted into the glass roof to produce a spacious sidewalk-café atmosphere. Luncheon sandwiches run $5 to $8; a hearty plate of Boston baked beans and knockwurst is in the same range; or an elegant scallop dish named coquilles chablis costs only slightly more. For a very light, diet-conscious lunch, there are salads as well. Lily's is extremely pleasant in summer if it's not too busy (try a late lunch to avoid the jam); in winter the tables can't be put outside, but the greenhouse —like the main dining area—is almost as good under its glass roof.

Seaside Restaurant and Bar, 188 South Market Building (tel. 742-8728), is at the seaside end of the South Market Building. Lunch is the prime time for dining, seeing, and being seen, although in fact Seaside stays busy all day. Sandwiches built on elaborate recipes, complex and delicious salads, omelets, and quiches make up the midday bill of fare, with prices ranging from $5 to $10. Besides the natural-wood tables, Seaside has a bar at which you can sit to have a drink, or a sandwich, or both. At dinnertime, Seaside features prime steaks, lots of seafood, the chef's specialties for the day, and on some nights, live entertainment. On Wednesday, for instance, it's jazz from 8:30 p.m. till closing, and on Thursday it's a cappella oldies. Expect to spend about $30 to $45 per person for dinner here. Lunch is served Monday through Saturday from 11:30 a.m. to 5 p.m.; dinner is served every night from 5 to 10 p.m. (an hour later on Friday and Saturday). On Sunday there's brunch from 11:30 a.m. to 4:30 p.m.

MONEY-SAVING MEALS ($15 to $30): Among Boston's most interesting restaurants is the **Commonwealth Brewing Company,** 138 Portland St. (tel. 523-8383), a brewery and restaurant all rolled into one. It's located near North Station and Boston Garden, at the intersection of Portland and Merrimac Streets and Valenti Way. Even before you enter, you'll have noticed, through the huge windows, the gleaming copper antique brewing equipment. In the high-ceilinged main dining room, long brass-clad tables are everywhere, and a long stand-up bar runs the length of the back wall. There's a spirit of conviviality in the air, inspired by the decor but forcefully encouraged by the Commonwealth's forte: freshly brewed golden ale, amber ale, bitter, and stout. The beer is brewed right here and served live, and if you descend to the basement floor (where there are more tables, and another long bar), you can actually witness the brewing going on behind a glass wall. The menu is long and satisfying, filled with many familiar American light-meal dishes such as an open-face steak sandwich, shrimp salad, baby back pork ribs, and a smoked seafood sampler. You'll find something you like for sure, and the price is surprisingly moderate. For a glass of beer and virtually any dish, the bill will be less than $15. Come for lunch, dinner, a late-night snack, or just a glass or two of real beer, seven days a week, from 11:30 a.m. to midnight Sunday through Thursday, till 1 a.m. on Friday and Saturday.

Back Bay: Newbury and Boylston Streets

The two principal shopping and business streets in the Back Bay have a tremendous number of places to nosh, snack, eat, lunch, or dine. Keep this section in mind when you make the rounds of Newbury Street galleries.

Newbury Street holds a French restaurant of long standing. It's the **Du Barry French Restaurant,** 159 Newbury (tel. 262-2445), between Dartmouth and Exeter Streets (Green Line to Copley). Dinner entrees usually include filet of sole grenobloise and daube of beef bourguignon, frogs' legs are to be had, as are even less frequently seen delicacies such as rabbit sautéed in white wine, and beef tongue in a madeira sauce. Expect to spend $25 to $35 per person at dinner. At lunch the several platters are priced below $10. In good weather the outdoor patio and enclosed terrace are the choice places to dine—walk through the restaurant to reach them.

Perhaps the best all-around café on Newbury Street—and certainly the nearest thing to an authentic European café in Boston—is the **Café Florian,** 85 Newbury St. (tel. 247-7603), where you can sit at sidewalk tables or in the air-conditioned rooms down one flight and have a glass of wine ($3.25), imported beer ($3.25), or a cup of truly excellent Viennese coffee ("Kaffee Wien mit Schlag"); for a snack, add on a pastry from their pastry tray, a sandwich or a bowl of soup, a plate of cheese and bread or an antipasto and cheese plate, or even a full meal. Service is quick and friendly; coffee comes in ten different varieties, priced from $1.40 to $3. There are several kinds of tea, and a select wine list. The Florian opens at 9 a.m., and stays open until 6 p.m. Monday, 10:30 p.m. Tuesday and Wednesday; with live music on Thursday, Friday and Saturday nights it stays open until midnight, and on Sunday it's open for brunch from noon till 6 p.m. On Newbury Street, this is my favorite.

A good place for lunch, dinner, or an evening's sipping and prowling is **Friday's,** 26 Exeter St. at the corner of Newbury (tel. 266-9040), just a block from the Boston Public Library, and two blocks from Copley Square or the Prudential Center. The space next to the sidewalk has been covered by a greenhouse-like shaded glass canopy. The decor is upscale and attractive, and the menu is very eclectic, with dishes from a dozen different cuisines. Have mahi mahi fish from Hawaii, or blackened Cajun chicken, or Oriental, Mexican, and American appetizers, or any of a dozen brunch dishes. There are many steaks, sandwiches, and burgers. The drink menu is equally fascinating, with every conceivable concoction, plus such pleasant surprises as good champagne at retail-store prices. One might spend $12 to $16 for a light meal, $20 to $28 for a hearty tuck-in. Friday's is open from 11:30 a.m. daily; to midnight on weekdays, to 1 a.m. on weekends.

The **Harvard Bookstore Café,** 190 Newbury St. (tel. 536-0095), at the corner of Exeter, has one of the nicest locations in the Back Bay, a shady streetcorner with lots of interesting sidewalk and street activity. If you can grab a sidewalk table, do so; then settle in with coffee and pastry, or order from their menu of fairly substantial luncheon fare: minestrone soup, perhaps, and broiled bluefish with a Pommery mustard sauce, or maybe a portion of hearty cassoulet. With a glass of wine and dessert, a three-course lunch might cost $25 per person, with all that excellent people-watching at no extra charge. The café is open every day for lunch and early supper.

For Seafood

Legal Seafoods (tel. 426-4444) is a Boston institution, a no-nonsense operation which prides itself on freshness and reasonable prices. The restaurant in the Boston Park Plaza Hotel off Park Square (subway to Arlington) is big but nicely broken up, light and attractive. The menu is encyclopedic, listing close to 100 items, but this is for reference: when fresh stocks run out, that's it for any particular fish. Start with a shrimp cocktail or oysters on the half shell, go on to scrod, bluefish, Mako shark, sea trout, etc. Have a glass or two of wine, and you can expect to pay about $30 for your dinner. Choose carefully and you can spend $22 or so; have lobster, salmon, or scallops, and your bill will be more like $36. Hours are Monday through Thursday from 11 a.m. to 10 p.m., on Friday and Saturday to 11 p.m., on Sunday from noon to 10 p.m. Note that there is often a waiting line, especially long on weekends. No reservations accepted.

Several Boston seafood restaurants are legendary by this time, and none is more so than **Jimmy's Harborside** (tel. 423-1000), on Fish Pier, which is at the end of Northern Avenue (no. 242), due east of downtown Boston across the Fort Point Channel (Red Line to South Station, then a no. 7 bus, "City Point–South Station"). Enter the place, and pass a sign that announces "Proper Dress Required," and you come to a realm of nautical memorabilia, plush carpets and chairs, a boat-shaped bar surrounded by little cocktail tables. The menu for lunch always has a daily special which includes chowder (fish or clam) or lobster bisque, entree, salad, potato, dessert, and coffee, all for about $15; luncheon entrees alone cost $6 (for the cheapest sandwich) to about $15. At dinnertime you might be offered *two* fresh "chicken" lobsters (the small females, weighing about a pound apiece), with french fries and salad, for $26.75, or jumbo shrimp for $16.75, or perhaps a swordfish shish kebab for $13.75. The menu carries some delicious pasta specialties as well. The wine list runs to almost 115 items. Jimmy's Harborside, "Home of the Chowder King," is open from 11:30 a.m. to 9:30 p.m. every day but Sunday.

Chinese Dim Sum

The **Imperial Tea House,** at 70 Beach St. in the heart of Boston's small Chinatown (tel. 426-8439), has been around for a long time, but has only recently been recognized for what it is: the best place in town for dim sum yum chai. The classic meal of Chinese hors d'oeuvres is served every day of the week from 9 a.m. to 3 p.m. The best time to go is between 10 and 11 a.m., or after 1:30 p.m. on weekdays. Other times the crowd is dense. Most of the patrons here are Chinese Bostonians who know a good thing or, rather, things: spareribs, water chestnuts in gelatin, pork dumplings, tofu (soybean cake), green sugarcane leaves stuffed with sweet rice, pork and quail eggs, even fried duck feet. Sit in the upstairs room for dim sum. The à la carte restaurant downstairs is not as good. The system is this: you pick what you like from the carts which appear in a steady stream throughout the morning and afternoon. Each plate on the cart has about three portions of the item (so it's good to do dim summing with two friends). When you've had enough, the waiter counts up the plates and gives you the bill, which will be very low (about $10 or $15 per person) considering the amount and quality of the food.

Thai

"Last time I was in Bangkok, I ate at this great little restaurant. . . ." That may not be an often-heard phrase in your circle. Few Americans have a close familiarity with Thai cuisine, but anyone in Boston can rectify that lamentable situation with a trip to **Bangkok Cuisine,** 177a Massachusetts Ave., just down from the corner of Boylston Street, near Prudential Center (tel. 262-5377). Clear soups made with scallions, shrimp, and hot peppers; savory dishes of duck with pineapple, spices, and Oriental vegetables and mushrooms—once you've tried the food here, you may indeed want to take off for Bangkok. The restaurant is small, long and narrow, always busy, not romantic but bustling. Have soup or an appetizer, a main course based on seafood, pork, beef, or chicken, a dessert, and a bottle of Thai beer, and you'll pay about $20. A warning: Soups are marked "moderately hot," but in my experience they are very spicy-hot (and very good). Bangkok is open for lunch (11:30 a.m. to 3 p.m.) and dinner (5 to 10:30 p.m.) Monday through Friday, for dinner only on Saturday and Sunday.

Mexican

Since the **Sol Azteca** (tel. 262-0909) opened, crowds have flocked to its door at 914a Beacon St. in Boston, very near the Brookline town line. The word got around quickly among devotees of Mexican food that the guacamole, enchiladas (rojas, verdes, or Suizas), the tacos, and tostadas were authentic, delicious, and moderately priced. Dinner starts with a basket of tortilla chips and a hot sauce dip and perhaps a bottle of Dos Equis or Superior Mexican beer. The combination plates are the best buys, bringing you a little of everything, to the point where you will probably have no capacity left for dessert. When I last dined here with four friends, the total bill for a no-holds-barred feast came to $160, or $32 per person, tax, tip, and many bottles of cerveza included. On Friday and Saturday, especially during college term, it's really crowded, and no reservations are accepted. Dinner, daily except Monday from 6 to 10 p.m., is the only meal served. Get there early. By T, take a "Cleveland Circle" car on the Green Line, and get off at the first stop above ground.

Mexican food on Newbury Street? Yes, at **Acapulco**, 266 Newbury St. (tel. 247-9126), an attractive little restaurant done in brick, butcher block, and Mexican crafts. A typical meal might consist of gazpacho, a tostada, flan for dessert, and a glass of guava juice to drink, all for about $15. Or you could order taquitos, crispy buñuelos for dessert, and drink Dos Equis Mexican beer, and pay somewhat more. Have just a combination plate, very filling, for only $8.50. You can order meatless meals, or dishes put up to take out. Acapulco serves Monday through Saturday from 11:30 a.m. to 11 p.m., on Sunday from 2 to 11 p.m. In summer, enjoy the outdoor patio tables.

BUDGET RESTAURANTS (Meals about $10):

It's not difficult to dine inexpensively in Boston. The variety and cuisine make it possible to eat pleasantly for $10 per day, or less. But the restaurants recommended below are not just for those on a very slim budget. No one wants haute cuisine at every meal—few people's livers can stand it, in any case. For those times when you just want a quick and inexpensive meal, but one that's wholesome and delicious, try one of these places, arranged below according to location:

Along Newbury Street

On fashionable Newbury Street at no. 135 is the **Travis Restaurant** (tel. 267-6388), where a slice of pie à la mode and a cup of coffee, or a hamburger, or perhaps a large salad plate (with tuna, ham, etc.) costs only $4 to $7. The small tables on the sidewalk out front are not fitted with umbrellas, and the interior is the familiar lunch counter and stools (with some tables as well), and it's serve yourself, inside and out. The Travis is open Monday through Saturday from about 7 a.m. to 4:30 p.m., so it's not the place to plan to go for dinner or a late snack.

In the North End

Boston's most famous pizza place is **Pizzeria Regina**, 11½ Thacher St., at the corner of Thacher and North Margin Streets (tel. 227-0765)—if you have trouble finding it, just ask anyone in the North End, for the pizzeria is a center of community life here. Old dark-wood booths with Formica tables, and a small bar for the solitary lunchers make up the interior, which is anything but fancy. The pizzas, however, are very fancy, for the cooks know the secret of making a good one: the best imported cheese and tomato sauce, and a few dashes of real olive oil. All pizzas come in small or large sizes, and a small pie will feed two moderately hungry people for lunch for as little as $8. That price is for a small cheese pizza, but others come with mushrooms, anchovies, sausage, and the like. The top price is for the Regina

Special, everything on a large pizza for $13, and this should easily feed a party of four. Beer and wine are served.

In Faneuil Hall Marketplace

Good seafood in simple, small surroundings is the formula at **The Salty Dog,** in the basement of Quincy Market (tel. 742-2094; Green or Blue Lines to Government Center). The tiny restaurant is a bit hard to find: facing the front of Quincy Market, with your back to Faneuil Hall, walk to the right of the market façade and just under the southwest corner of the market is the stairway down to the Salty Dog. It's a seafood bar and grill where you can have fish and chips, clams on the half shell, or any one of several fried or baked fish plates for about $9. Service is hardly elegant, for your food comes in paper containers and you eat with plastic utensils, but the food is very good. The oyster stew seems expensive, but you'll find at least a half dozen whole, succulent oysters in each bowlful. Liquor is served. This tiny place is open from 11:30 a.m. to 11 p.m. daily.

Along the Freedom Trail

You're tromping along the Freedom Trail, trying to do it in a few hours, and you just want a quick bite for lunch? Join the be-suited business types grabbing a snack at the **Steaming Kettle,** corner of Cambridge (or Tremont) and Court Streets, very near the Government Center Station (also at 235 Washington St. and 100 Summer St.). The huge kettle over the door has been belching steam for years and years, and inside the waitresses dispense steaming coffee or tea, lemonade or milk, and sandwiches such as hot roast beef, frankfurter and beans, or bologna at prices between $3 and $5 to stand-up customers at the shelf-like hardwood counters that line the walls. If it's breakfast or seating you're after, the coffeeshop upstairs is open from 7:30 a.m. to 3:30 p.m.

---

5. Sights

THE FREEDOM TRAIL: The sights of Revolutionary Boston are linked together by the Freedom Trail, an ingenious idea that makes it easy for any visitor to find all the important colonial and revolutionary landmarks. Starting from the Park Street MBTA station on Boston Common, a red line painted on the sidewalk or a double row of bricks laid in the sidewalk leads past the **Massachusetts State House, Park Street Church,** the **Old Granary Burying Ground, King's Chapel,** the **Old State House,** the **Paul Revere House, Old North Church,** and *Old Ironsides* (U.S.S. *Constitution*), as well as other sights. Except for *Old Ironsides,* the trail passes all the important things to see in a mile and a half; *Old Ironsides* is across Boston's Inner Harbor in Charlestown, 2½ miles away, best reached by bus or car.

There is a bus that follows the Freedom Trail: the **Beantown Trolley** (tel. 287-1900). Arrangements for the bus vary with time of year, summer being the time when service is best and most frequent. Fare is $7.50 per adult ($4.50 per child 12 or under) for a day pass entitling you to hop on and off the buses as often as you like; buses run about every 45 minutes from 9 a.m. to 5 p.m. Buy your tickets right near the **Boston Common Visitor Information Center** (tel. 617/267-6446). The Information Center, on Boston Common near the Park Street Station, also hands out maps of the trail and brochures with facts about the sights. Here's a quick rundown so you'll know what there is to see (numbers are keyed to our map):

Boston Common (12)

This park in the center of Boston was the colonial town's "common pasture land," to which any citizen's cows could be brought. The pasture ordinance is still in

effect, so they say, but no one seems to take advantage of it—as though with all the picnickers, sunbathers, soapbox orators, street buskers, and pitchmen there'd be any room left for a cow quietly to graze!

State House and Archives (13)

The Massachusetts State House dominates Beacon Hill and the Boston Common, its gold dome shining and visible for miles. It was designed by Charles Bulfinch, Boston's most famous and best-loved architect, and built at the end of the 1700s. This is where the Massachusetts General Court (legislature) sits today; in its Archives (which you can visit) are curious and famous documents relating to the history of the colony of Massachusetts Bay and the early republic.

While you're up here on **Beacon Hill,** take a detour off the Freedom Trail and explore the back streets of what was once (and in many ways still is) Boston's wealthiest and prettiest residential neighborhood. Wander down the little "mews" (lanes behind the houses) where once the horses and carriages were kept, and don't miss **Louisburg Square,** a tiny private park which is Beacon Hill's gem. The beautiful old colonial and Federal houses extend to the base of the hill at Charles Street, and down toward the 19th-century developments of Back Bay.

Park Street Church (11)

Right next to Park Street Station is this tall-steepled, graceful church designed by Peter Banner and built in 1809. Take a look inside, so you can compare this early–19th-century church with the earlier churches farther along the Freedom Trail.

Old Granary Burying Ground (10)

Some of the American Revolution's most famous figures, from John Hancock to Crispus Attucks, are buried in this cemetery which took its name from a nearby granary, now long gone. Take a walk through—you'll constantly be surprised and delighted by the names, dates, and mottoes on the finely carved headstones.

King's Chapel (14)

The building dates from 1754, and in its interesting career changed from being an Episcopal church to a Unitarian meetinghouse. Services are held here, as are lectures and concerts as well.

Site of the First Public School (9)

Established in 1635, this is where it was.

Statue of Benjamin Franklin (8)

Most people remember the story of Franklin getting off the boat in Philadelphia with very little money and two loaves of bread for sustenance to begin his famous career, but some people forget that he was coming from Boston, his birthplace and childhood home. This statue by Richard Greenough (1856), in front of the city's old headquarters, pays tribute to Boston's famous son.

Old Corner Bookstore (7)

The *Boston Globe* bought and restored this famous house, and it's now a bookstore. The house itself dates from the early 1700s, but its fame began when it became a gathering place for famous American authors in the 19th century. At that time bookstores were also publishers, and Messrs. Ticknor & Fields, who ran the Old Corner Bookstore, published and drank coffee with the outstanding literary men of the age, including Longfellow, Hawthorne, and Whittier.

Old South Meeting House (6)

New England churches frequently call their buildings meetinghouses rather than churches, and it's from this that the Old South Meeting House gets its name, although it was used for town meetings as well. (Old North Church, from which the lanterns hung to signal Paul Revere, is a different building farther along the Freedom Trail.) Built in 1729, the meetinghouse saw its most famous meeting on December 16, 1773, when a group of colonials in Indian dress set out from here to throw the Boston Tea Party. Of the exhibits—old documents, currency, furniture—perhaps the most interesting is a plaster-and-wood scale model of the Town of Boston in 1775, which gives you a very clear idea of the size and layout of the town, and helps your imagination recast the events of the Revolution in their proper setting.

The Old State House (4)

The charming brick building at 206 Washington St. dates from 1713, and was built to house the colonial government; after the Revolution it was known as the State House, and after the present State House was built in 1795, this one became the Old State House. Washington addressed the citizens of Boston from its balcony. Now that it's hemmed in by giant buildings on all sides, much of the dignity it must have held for colonial and revolutionary Americans is lost. Inside, a museum holds military and domestic artifacts, portraits, and a good selection of nautical artifacts, from antique sextants to eight very fine scale models of ships and some dramatic paintings of great ships as well. Historical talks are given on the hour. There's an entry fee to the museum (tel. 720-3290) of $1.25 for adults, 75¢ for senior citizens, 50¢ for children. Summer hours are 9:30 a.m. to 5 p.m. every day.

Boston Massacre Site (3)

Here, near the Old State House, British soldiers fired into a crowd of colonials protesting what they saw as excesses by the British government. The incident must have happened much as the tragic killings happened at Kent State University during the Vietnam War protests: unarmed civilians expressing their resentment by throwing curses and stones at armed soldiers who were confused as to how they should respond.

Faneuil Hall (1)

Faneuil Hall (pronounced *fan*-yool or *fan*-l) was built by the Town of Boston in 1742 with money given by Peter Faneuil; designed by John Simbert, it was later enlarged by Bulfinch (1805). The ground floor has been devoted to shops since the building was built; the second floor was—and is—used for public meetings; and the third floor houses the headquarters of Boston's most famous chowder-and-marching society, the Ancient and Honorable Artillery Company. Entrance to the second-floor meeting hall is from the east side; National Park Service guides are on hand to tell you all about the building: the huge painting dominating the front of the hall, they will tell you, is of Daniel Webster speaking on the virtues of a close union of states (as opposed to states' rights). The speech was given in Washington in 1830, not in Faneuil Hall, but the painting must have inspired hundreds of less talented, although perhaps equally long-winded, orators. Entrance to the hall is free.

The area around Faneuil Hall has recently been rebuilt and restored, and it is a nice change from the boldly modern buildings nearby. (For details on shopping in Quincy Market, next to Faneuil Hall, see the separate Shopping section.)

While you're here in Faneuil Hall Marketplace, be sure to stop by the **Bostix** kiosk (tel. 617/723-5181 for a recording), right next to Faneuil Hall, to see what shows, concerts, and theater performances are on sale at half price. Usually the half-price seats are for today's (or tonight's) performances.

Paul Revere House (16)

A small clapboard dwelling in Boston's North End, surrounded by crooked cobbled streets, the Paul Revere House, 19 North Square (tel. 523-2338), is the only house left in Boston that was built in the 1600s. Paul Revere moved in about a century after the house was built, and he lived here during the Revolutionary period. The house would be interesting even if the great patriot had never set foot in it, with its quaint weathered exterior, small windows, and wide floorboards. But furnished in colonial style and equipped with an ingenious handrail/barrier which guides you through the house and gives you information on Revere's life at the same time, the house is worth more than an hour's lecture on Revolutionary history. Admission costs $2 for adults, $1.50 for seniors and students, 50¢ for children 17 and under. No photography is allowed inside the house. Hours are 9:30 a.m. to 4:15 p.m. in winter, to 5:15 p.m. in summer. Take a look around North Square, the small cobbled-and-gaslit space near the Revere House, and perhaps rest from your walk on one of its benches. This part of town, the North End, is now very Italian in character —you can hear the local dialect of the mother tongue in the surrounding streets.

Old North Church (18)

You can see by the church's location why it was a good place from which to give a signal. The code, as every schoolchild knows, was "one if by land, two if by sea," and it was two lanterns hung in the tower that started Paul Revere and William Dawes on their fateful night rides to warn the Colonials that British troops were heading out from Boston to search for hidden arms. On April 18, 1975, exactly 200 years from that historic day, President Ford inaugurated the American Revolutionary Bicentennial in Old North Church by lighting a third lantern (hanging at the front of the church). The church is the oldest church building in Boston (1723), and is today officially known as Christ Church, Episcopal. A walk around inside turns up many curiosities that bear on the history of Boston and the United States; memorial plaques to famous men, nameplates on the very high pews. The tall graceful windows of Old North Church are exceptionally fine. After your visit, it's good to drop the requested (not required) donation in the box near the door. Visitors are also welcome for Sunday services at 9:30 a.m., 11 a.m., and 4 p.m.

Although it's hemmed in by houses and shops on all sides, Old North Church does have a set of tiny terraces and gardens on its north side, open to the public. The small formal garden and the fountain are good to refresh your spirit on a hot day, and the memorial plaques set into the walls are, in some cases, delightful. One reads:

1757–1923
Here on September 13, 1757
"John Childs who had given public notice of his intention to
Fly from the steeple of Dr. Cutler's church, performed it to
The satisfaction of a great number of spectators"
In 1923 the year of the first continuous flight across
The continent this tablet has been placed here by
The Massachusetts Society of the Colonial Dames of America
To commemorate the two events.

The question that comes to mind: would it not have been faster to dispatch John Childs from the steeple to Lexington and Concord by air, rather than Dawes and Revere by land, on that historic night in 1775?

U.S.S. Constitution (22)

The *Constitution (Old Ironsides)* is still commissioned in the service of the U.S. Navy and could in theory be called to the defense of the country should the need arise. She still gets under way once a year, on the Fourth of July, when she's taken a short distance out into the harbor to fire a 21-gun salute. The dock here is right on a former navy base; sailors in 1812 period uniforms will take you through the ship and explain her workings to you free of charge. But the ship is not the only exhibit here: the nearby **Museum** ($2.50 for adults, $1.50 for seniors, $1 for kids 6 to 16; under 6, free) houses many artifacts dealing with the *Constitution*'s history and her 40 battles at sea (all won), besides a "Life at Sea" exhibit, showing what shipboard life was like in 1812. The Boston Navy Yard National Historic Site also offers programs on the yard and the American Revolution every hour in Building No. 5 (between the ship and the museum).

To get to these attractions, and to Bunker Hill with its monument, cross the Mystic River (Tobin) Bridge (toll) or the Charlestown Bridge (free) nearby and follow the signs to the U.S.S. *Constitution*. Bus 93 ("Sullivan Square via Bunker Hill") from Haymarket Square will take you fairly close to Bunker Hill and Boston Navy Yard; it runs about every half hour, more frequently during rush hours. You can walk to *Old Ironsides* from Haymarket in about 25 minutes, using the Charlestown Bridge.

Boston Tea Party Ship and Museum (20)

Strictly speaking, this is not on the Freedom Trail, but on a separate excursion called Harborwalk. The events it recalls are very much a part of colonial Boston's struggle for independence. Take the Red Line to South Station, walk north on Atlantic Avenue one block past the Federal Reserve Bank (which looks like a mammoth space-age radiator), turn right onto Congress Street and walk a block to the water, and there's the ship at Congress Street Bridge. A shuttle bus operates daily May through October from the rear of the Old State House on the Freedom Trail (corner of Devonshire and State Streets). What you see here is the brig *Beaver II*, a full-size replica of one of the merchant ships looted by the "Indians" on the night of the tea party raid, and a museum with exhibits outlining the "tea party." At the nearby Tea Party Store you can buy some tea and throw it over the side of the *Beaver* into Fort Point Channel, although I doubt that this will make the water any more potable. The ship and museum (tel. 338-1773) are open from 9 a.m. to dusk (about 8 p.m. in summer, 5 p.m. in winter) every day except three major holidays, at $3.75 for adults, $2.75 for children 5 to 14; under-5s are free, and special family rates are available. Complimentary tea is served—iced tea in summer, hot tea in winter.

MUSEUM OF FINE ARTS: The great Greek temple at 465 Huntington Ave. houses one of the world's finest collections of artworks, second in the country only to New York's Metropolitan. Boston's Museum of Fine Arts (tel. 267-9300) is a wonder, a vast collection of beautiful things in a beautiful building. Many pictures you may have admired for years through prints and photos in art books are here: Gilbert Stuart's *Athenaeum Head* portrait of George Washington; Renoir's *Le Bal à Bougival;* Burne-Jones's *The Love Song;* Whistler's *Girl in a White Dress;* works by Van Gogh, Gauguin, Degas, lots of Monets; *Death of Maximilian* by Manet; and works by Japanese, Chinese, European, medieval, Renaissance, and baroque masters are all well represented. A fine collection of Paul Revere silver, several rooms taken from French châteaux, full-size Japanese temples, a 9th-century Spanish chapel, Egyptian mummies, Assyrian seals—the list goes on to the treasures of almost 200 galleries. The way to find what you want is to pick up a floor plan as you enter; you can't possibly see even a fraction of it all, so pick out a few areas or rooms to concentrate on, and enjoy. Before you go, call 267-9377 (or A-N-S-W-E-R-S) for a recording of current special exhibits. If you need the help of a person, call 267-9300, ext. 363.

The entire museum is normally open Tuesday through Sunday from 10 a.m. to 5 p.m. (closed Monday), Wednesday evening till 10 p.m. On Thursday and Friday the main building closes at 5 p.m. but the west wing stays open till 10 p.m. Admission is $5 for adults, free for those under 16 years, $4 for seniors. If you come on Saturday from 10 a.m. till noon, you can get in for free; if you visit when only the new West Wing is open, the fee is $4.

The museum's restaurant is located in the west wing. Lunch is served daily from 11:30 a.m. to 2:30 p.m. (except Monday); dinner, on Wednesday, Thursday, and Friday from 5:30 to 8:30 p.m. Surrounded by glass, the dining room is ultramodern and attractive. The menu is often keyed to special exhibits—Chinese dishes predominated when the impressive Chinese bronzes were on display—and the prices are moderate. You can figure $10 to $12 for lunch, $18 to $22 for dinner. The wine list is short, good, and fairly priced.

For snacks and pick-me-ups, head for the café below the restaurant.

To get to the museum, take a Green Line "E" train ("Arborway" or "Huntington Avenue") and get off at the second stop above ground.

ISABELLA STEWART GARDNER MUSEUM: If you have a full day when you visit the Museum of Fine Arts, plan to spend at least a few hours of it at the Isabella Stewart Gardner Museum nearby (tel. 566-1401), at 280 The Fenway (walk west from the Museum of Fine Arts around its parking lot to the Fenway; turn left and walk two short blocks). "Mrs. Jack" Gardner early developed a love of art, and with her considerable wealth and the services of Bernard Berenson she set about to build an outstanding collection which now includes almost 300 paintings, almost as many pieces of sculpture, close to 500 pieces of furniture, and hundreds of works in textiles, ceramics, and glass. Most of the holdings are from the great periods of European art, but classical and Oriental civilizations are also represented. Not the least of the exhibits is the house itself, which she had built to hold the collection in 1902. "Fenway Court" is not much to look at from the outside, but inside it is Mrs. Gardner's vision of a 15th-century Venetian palace, with many doors, columns, windows, and the like, which were brought from Europe and assembled around an open court topped by a glass canopy. The court is always planted with flowers, in bloom summer and winter, and several fountains bubble merrily at one end. Upstairs in one room is a dramatic portrait of "Mrs. Jack" herself, displayed with various masterpieces above a floor covered in tiles from Henry Mercer's Moravian tile and pottery works in Pennsylvania. Along a corridor nearby, look for mementos of Mrs. Gardner's years, including letters from many of the great and famous of the turn of the century. Admission costs $5 ($2.50 for students and seniors); on Wednesday, admission is free. It's open Tuesday from noon to 6:30 p.m., Wednesday through Sunday from noon to 5 p.m., closed Monday. Except for July and August, free concerts of chamber music are given on Thursday at 12:15 p.m., on Sunday at 3 p.m., and Tuesday evening at 6 p.m.; they're usually very well attended, so go early and claim a seat (for information, call 734-1359). The museum has a nice café serving light meals as well.

OTHER GALLERIES: Perhaps it's the amalgam of college faculty, art-conscious Old Guard families, and artists themselves that makes Boston such a good place to go browsing in galleries. Whatever the cause, Boston is rich in exhibitions of painting, sculpture, and the more recent vehicles of artistic expression such as textiles and welded metal.

Prime among Boston galleries is the **Institute of Contemporary Art,** 955 Boylston St. (tel. 266-5151 for a recording, 266-5152 for a person), across the street from the Prudential Center (Green Line's "Boston College," "Riverside," or "Cleveland Circle" cars to Auditorium Station). The institute is a beautifully modern place inside a historic Richardsonian structure. Shows may be anything from an exhibit of New England photographers' work to works in various media by British artists, or perhaps a show of the outstanding works by modern artists that are in Boston private collections. Special events include video programs, musical concerts, and evening lectures. All exhibitions change about every six to ten weeks. The ICA is open Tuesday through Sunday from 11 a.m. to 5 p.m. (and on Thursday and Friday also from 5 to 8 p.m.). Admission is $4 for adults, $1.50 for senior citizens and children under 14, and $2.50 for students. Free admission on Friday evenings. There is never an admission charge for members except for evening events.

The institute never has works for sale. Those interested in browsing and perhaps buying—without any obligation to do so, of course—should pick a day to stroll down **Newbury Street,** where a good many of Boston's better galleries are located. Highlights and dining possibilities for such a stroll are covered in a separate section on "Newbury Street" in this same chapter. Other streets with galleries and antique shops are **Charles Street** at the base of Beacon Hill, and **Boylston Street.**

Boston City Hall, the Boston Public Library in Copley Square, and other public organizations and private corporations sponsor shows from time to time. See the tabloid weeklies such as the *Boston Phoenix* for full listings of what's currently available, or contact the Department of Public Relations (tel. 266-5152) with your questions.

There's often an interesting exhibit in the lobby of the **Boston Architectural Center,** 320 Newbury St. (tel. 536-3170), at the corner of Hereford Street (Green Line to Auditorium). The show will be connected in some way with architecture, whether it be the life and work of Henry Mercer, the turn-of-the-century Pennsylvania tile maker, or a collection of neon signs from many cities and many decades. Hours are Monday through Thursday from 9 a.m. to 9 p.m., on Friday and Saturday to 5 p.m. (on Sunday from 11 a.m. to 5 p.m. only in the winter season). Shows are always free, and if you're strolling along this part of Newbury Street, at least take a look through the windows to see what's on.

MUSEUM OF SCIENCE: Nobody ever has a bad time when they visit Boston's famous Museum of Science, Science Park (tel. 523-6664), because there are so many things to see and do, and of such a variety, that each person's tastes and expectations can be gratified. Children are especially delighted here, for they can walk into a full-size model of the Apollo Command Module; they can play with a Wang computer, see themselves on closed-circuit TV, and push buttons to start dozens of various exhibits and demonstrations ranging from fluid dynamics to the human circulatory system. Stand next to a replica of America's first rocket launcher built by Dr. Robert Goddard of Auburn, Mass., in 1926; or walk around a tremendous replica of *Tyrannosaurus rex.* See how baseball pitchers throw a curve ball, and hear them explain their techniques; watch the counter on the World Population Meter click off another birth every second or so; or learn how to make herbal textile dyes from common plants and weeds. Special exhibits include the Hayden Planetarium with celestial shows on various themes daily. The Museum of Science costs $6 for adults, $4 for children or senior citizens. There is an extra charge for the planetarium (buy your ticket early for this, when you enter the museum), and for the exciting new OMNIMAX theater. Hours September through April are Saturday through Thursday from 9 a.m. to 5 p.m., on Friday to 9 p.m. Hours May 1 through Labor Day are Monday through Thursday from 9 a.m. to 5 p.m., on Friday to 9 p.m., on Saturday to 5 p.m., and on Sunday from 10 a.m. to 5 p.m. During school months, open on Monday holidays and vacation weeks. Parking in the museum's own garage costs several dollars. Besides the rooftop Skyline Cafeteria, there's a Friendly's sandwich shop within the museum.

To get to the Museum of Science, take the Green Line toward Lechmere to the Science Park Station.

THE KENNEDY LIBRARY: The nation's memorial to JFK is the museum at the **John F. Kennedy Library.** This dramatic chalk-white building, designed by the distinguished architect I. M. Pei, sits on a peninsula on Dorchester Bay. The landscaping of Cape Cod roses, sea grass, and weeping willows serves to harmonize the building with the peninsula, harbor islands, and sea. The library features an exhibition which is introduced by a 30-minute movie on the late president's life. Then, arranged in chronological order, it displays JFK memorabilia from his christening dress, *PT-109* uniform and flight jacket worn when president, to papers relating to the Bay of Pigs and Cuban Missile Crisis. There is a re-creation of the Oval Office as it was when he was president, and his desk and rocking chair. The library is open daily from 9 a.m. to 5 p.m. except Thanksgiving, Christmas, and New Year's Day. Admission costs $3.50 for adults and $2.00 for seniors; those under 16 get in free. Take the MBTA Red Line to JFK/U Mass Station. For additional information, contact the John F. Kennedy Library at Columbia Point, Dorchester, MA 02125 (tel. 617/929-4523).

OTHER MUSEUMS: Boston has a score of other museums, each very rich in its presentations, and the best of these are outlined below:

Boston Children's Museum
Children's Museum is located at Museum Wharf, 300 Congress St. (tel. 426-8855), on Boston's waterfront near the Boston Tea Party ship, a short walk from Faneuil Hall Marketplace. The museum, an old brick-and-timber warehouse, is a kid's delight, for this is where the whole idea of "hands-on" exhibits began. Kids can clamber through sculptures; celebrate Japanese festivals in Japanese House; and challenge the computer to a game of tic-tac-toe. On Giant's Desktop everything is 12 times normal size. On Friday evenings and during Boston school vacations and holidays the museum presents the best in local entertainment for children—jugglers, musicians, magicians, and mime. From mid-June to Labor Day the museum is open daily from 10 a.m. to 5 p.m., on Friday till 9 p.m. During the rest of the year the museum is open Tuesday to Sunday from 10 a.m. to 5 p.m., on Friday till 9 p.m.; closed Monday except Boston school vacations and holidays. Closed Thanksgiving, Christmas, and New Year's. Admission is $5 for adults, $4 for children 2 to 15 and senior citizens. Friday from 5 to 9 p.m. admission is $1. By public transportation, take the Red Line to South Station.

The Computer Museum
"What?" you may say, "Computers aren't old enough to have a museum!" But they are. The computing devices on display at the Computer Museum on Museum Wharf (tel. 423-6758 for information read by a computerized voice, or 426-2800 for a human) go back centuries. It seems that we've always had a passion for number-crunching, but have been unable fully to realize that passion until today. The abacus has been used in China for a millennium; Scottish mathematician John Napier (1550–1617), inventor of the logarithm, came up with a calculator called "Napier's Bones"; French army officer Amedée Mannheim invented the slide rule in 1850. In 1893, in Zurich, a "direct-multiplying machine" called The Millionaire came on the market, and sold 4,655 units in the years following.

It was World War II and the Atomic Age that began the rush to truly awesome computing power. Nowadays the Whirlwind computer (1951) looks like a dinosaur: hundreds of vacuum tubes, electrical consumption of 150,000 watts, and less computing power than an Apple II. The first fully transistorized machine, the TX-O (1956) required a full-time staff of top-level scientists just to turn it on and get it ready to compute. But it was a mere calculator compared to the 20-ton monster known as SAGE, built for the U.S. Air Force in the 1960s.

Besides the historical exhibits, there are hands-on treats: you can try out any of the latest personal computers or (by simulation) fly an airplane, launch a rocket, or design the car of the future.

The Computer Museum is right next door to the Children's Museum, and just across Fort Point Channel from the Boston Tea Party Ship. Take the subway (Red Line to South Station), or drive, and visit from 10 a.m. to 5 p.m. any day in summer (till 9 p.m. on Friday); closed Monday in winter. Admission costs $5 for adults, $4 for students and seniors; admission is half price after 5 p.m. on Friday.

The Athenaeum

Tucked away atop Beacon Hill, facing the State House, is the Boston Athenaeum, 10½ Beacon St., off School Street (tel. 227-0270). It is that rarest of things, a private subscription library, but it is a museum of Boston culture open to the public as well. You needn't pay the $100 or so to become a subscriber unless you want to withdraw books. Pay a visit from 9 a.m. to 5 p.m. Monday through Friday (also 9 a.m. to 4 p.m. on Saturday from October through May), ask for a pass, and you can wander around the two lower floors of this grand old Boston institution, admiring the paintings and sculpture (some by Sargent and Saint-Gaudens), and the rich 19th-century neoclassical decor. For a full tour of the place (Tuesday and Thursday afternoons), call in advance.

Black Heritage Trail

You can take a Black Heritage Trail walking tour. Pick up a free walking-tour folder at the National Park Service Visitor Center, 15 State St.

NEW ENGLAND AQUARIUM: It seems fitting that a sea-conscious city such as Boston should have a major aquarium, and it has exactly that in the New England Aquarium (tel. 742-8870), on Central Wharf off Atlantic Avenue and two blocks from Faneuil Hall Market in the newly redeveloped waterfront area (look for the twin Harbor Towers apartment buildings, or take the Blue Line to Aquarium Station). Pride of the aquarium is the largest cylindrical glass-enclosed saltwater tank in the world, and this and other exhibit tanks are stocked with over 600 species of marine life, from electric eels to sharks. In the ship *Discovery,* moored next door, dolphin shows are put on daily for aquarium visitors (call for current show times). The variety of fishes is truly astounding, and the shapes, colors, and forms that evolution and adaptation have produced in these creatures really give one a sense of the richness of the marine environment. The price of admission includes all exhibits, including the dolphin shows, plus daily films, multimedia presentations, and audio tours on aquatic subjects; it's $7 for adults, $3.50 for children 4 through 15. For senior citizens, servicemen, and college students with IDs, it's $5. On Friday from 4 to 8 p.m. the charge is $1 off regular admission for everyone. Hours are Monday through Thursday from 9 a.m. to 6 p.m., on Friday to 8 p.m., on weekends to 7 p.m., but these may change a bit from season to season.

ARNOLD ARBORETUM: Ever since this 265-acre park was given to the city by Harvard, Bostonians have been going here to enjoy the peacefulness of the park and the more than 14,000 trees, plants, and shrubs from various parts of the world that make up the Arboretum's "living collection." Spring is a fine time to catch the first blossoms like the lilacs, early summer brings the rhododendrons, and all through the warm months the scents here will bring back any nose dulled by the city air.

The Arnold Arboretum of Harvard University, designed by Charles Sprague Sargent and Frederick Law Olmsted, is maintained jointly by Boston's parks department and Harvard, which uses it as an open-air classroom in botany. It's open to all and sundry from sunrise to sunset every day, free of charge. You can get there easily by taking the Orange Line to Forest Hills, or the Green Line to Arborway (the Orange Line's probably faster). For 24-hour recorded information, call 524-1717.

THE CHRISTIAN SCIENCE CHURCH CENTER: In 1866 a devout New England woman experienced quick recovery from a severe accident, attributing her cure to a glimpse of God's healing power as taught and lived by Jesus. Thereafter Mary Baker Eddy devoted the remainder of her long life (1821–1910) to better understanding, practicing, and teaching Christian healing; to founding the Church of

Christ, Scientist; and establishing the church's periodicals, including the renowned international daily newspaper, the *Christian Science Monitor.*

Today the Christian Science religion has branch churches in some 57 countries with headquarters in Boston, site of the denomination's Mother Church, built in 1894. Next to the church stands the Christian Science Publishing Society, home of the *Monitor* and other Christian Science publications. Two new church office buildings and the Sunday School complete the Church Center. The whole complex, near Symphony Hall at the intersection of Huntington and Massachusetts Avenues (MBTA: Auditorium or Symphony), is a new Boston landmark, and it's right between two other landmarks, Symphony Hall and the Prudential Center. Tours are arranged for free, or you can visit the various buildings on your own: the Mother Church is open Monday through Saturday from 9 a.m. to 4:15 p.m., on Sunday from noon to 4:15 p.m. The Publishing Society building is open Monday through Friday from 8 a.m. to 4 p.m., on Saturday and holidays from 9 a.m. to 4 p.m., on Sunday from noon to 4:45 p.m.; and tours are given weekdays at 9:30 and 11 a.m., and 1:30 and 3 p.m. (tour takes 45 minutes). You can inspect the bold architecture of the Sunday School building from 12:15 to 3 p.m. on Sunday, but tours on other days are at 10:30 a.m. and 1:45 p.m. only. During the winter (November to April) the hours are slightly shortened. For exact times and tours call 450-2000. Free parking is available while visiting the Church Center.

The main points of interest are the plaza and reflecting pool, the exterior of the Mother Church and its grand extension where services are held, and the Publishing Society's Mapparium and elegant Reading Room. You can take a tour which lasts 15 to 25 minutes through the Mother Church, or just take the elevator up to see the auditorium. This huge chamber is the main inner space of the church, which is built on the plan of a Byzantine church with its great dome and two semidomes.

The church's newest addition is a multimedia Bible Exhibit, located in the Colonnade Building, displaying rare Bibles and a giant Plexiglas map. This is open Monday through Saturday from 10 a.m. to 5 p.m. and on Sunday from noon to 5 p.m. (closed Tuesday).

---

6. Shopping

Like New York, Washington, and other great American cities, Boston has its special places to buy things, whether you're in the market for the mundane or the exotic. Here are some of the prime locales for getting rid of money.

DOWNTOWN CROSSING: The two Boston giants are **Jordan Marsh Company** and **Filene's,** located cheek-by-jowl in the downtown pedestrian shopping district on Washington Street (Red Line or Orange Line to Washington) called Downtown Crossing. Jordan's is a large department store with a vast assortment of items for sale, everything from baubles to bar stools. "Jordan's Great Basement Store" is admittedly great in terms of size, but it is outdone in popularity by neighboring Filene's Basement, which has become a New England legend. Stories circulate about women changing clothes right between the dress racks to try things on, of the crowds one must fight, of the "automatic reduction" policy which dictates that if an item is not sold in a certain amount of time, it is simply given away just to get rid of it.

Well, the basement has become a bit more refined now that it's famous, and the prices in many cases are similar to those in any of the big new suburban discount stores. As for the automatic reductions, they're still in operation, but few items reach the date when they're given away, and if they do it's usually because they're too torn or ugly or useless to be bought, and even so they're given away to charity (Goodwill

Industries, for example) as a tax write-off, and not to you. But the basement is still busy, often crowded, and it's because people know that there's a *good chance* they'll run into something that suits them at a very good price. Don't "go to Filene's Basement to buy a pair of shoes," but rather go dig around in the shoe bins and see what there is in your size, and at a good price—you may find something which it makes good sense to buy. And look through the other clothes departments, accessory counters, and various sections—a $400 outfit with a marked-down $40 price tag could very well be waiting there for you.

Surplus merchandise from famous stores such as Lou Lattimer's in Houston and Saks in New York comes frequently to Filene's Basement, with such classy labels as I. Magnin and Yves Saint Laurent. Don't be disappointed if you don't find anything. Come back in a few days, for the stock moves incredibly fast and new shipments arrive daily.

Also here at Downtown Crossing is **Lafayette Place,** a vast shopping mall with a central courtyard for sipping and dining, a 500-room hotel, and hundreds of shops.

Washington Street, the pedestrian thoroughfare of Downtown Crossing, has its own line-up of shops. Across from Filene's, at 333 and 387 Washington St., for instance, are entrances to the **Jewelers' Building,** a warren of little shops in a homely building. The building may not look like much, but the display cases in each shop are laden with fortunes in gold, diamonds, rubies, and emeralds. If you're at all interested in jewelry, take a stroll through here. Prices can be very good.

FANEUIL HALL MARKETPLACE: The Faneuil Hall Marketplace is a whole complex of buildings including **Faneuil Hall** and **Quincy Market,** flanked by the **North and South Markets** on either side.

Quincy Market is the centerpiece of this imaginative and fantastically successful redevelopment venture by the Rouse company with the guidance of Cambridge architect Benjamin Thompson. For years the area was a rundown waterfront slum, with only the 19th-century-style butchers' shops and provisioners to provide life. The early plan was to have the buildings razed to the ground and replaced with a modern shopping center, but architect Thompson changed the thinking to conservation, and the result is a beauty. Behind Faneuil Hall, the market is busy with crowds of customers from sunrise to sundown every day of the week. A granite block pavement is spread between Faneuil Hall and the market's pillared classic Greek façade, and inside, the long main hall stretches for a city block on two floors. Downstairs the shops sell food, from a carry-out snack to a full picnic-style meal, to a pound of camembert for the kitchen at home. On a recent stroll through Quincy Market I noted the following items for sale (partial list): a dozen kinds of bagels right out of the oven on the premises, an infinite array of deli sandwiches, southern fried chicken, shish kebab, subgum chow mein, Baby Watson cheesecake, German blutwurst, French brie, Châteauneuf-du-Pape, live lobsters, mixed nuts, cold cuts (domestic and imported), rumpsteak, fresh doughnuts, and, at the clam bar, half a dozen cherrystone clams opened and ready to eat. The wings of the market are of glass, and shelter restaurants, drinking places, and singles hangouts patronized by the good-looking and well-to-do from the business, financial, and government offices nearby. In the basement are various shops selling fish, meat, health foods, imported delicacies. On the second floor the emphasis is on crafts and exotic imports—rugs from Persia, jewelry from India, baskets from China and Mexico. There's a fine flower shop in a very handsome all-glass building in front, on the granite pavement, and benches set out under the trees between the market and the adjoining buildings.

About the best purchase you can make here at Faneuil Hall Marketplace is tickets to the theater, concerts, ballet, shows, etc. **Bostix** (tel. 723-5181) in a kiosk right next to Faneuil Hall itself, sells half-price seats for today's performances, and this is the only place in the city where you can buy them. Plan your nightlife while you're here, rather than coming all the way back. Cash only for same-day, half-price seats—that's the policy.

Street buskers and musicians are always on hand to entertain in the market promenades, and a genial mounted police officer draws scores of children, all wanting to pat his mount's nose. The whole complex is an all-year, day-and-night carnival you shouldn't miss, open for free. For restaurant details, see the restaurant section, above. To get to Faneuil Hall Marketplace, take the Green or Blue Line to Government Center, or the Blue or Red Line to State Street.

NEWBURY STREET: Boston's famous street of boutiques, galleries, and cafés runs from fashion to funk. It starts at the intersection of Arlington and Newbury, right next to Burberrys' and the Ritz-Carlton Hotel, and the shoppers' and strollers' delights continue for half a dozen blocks. Shops sell everything from the sublime (and expensive) to the ridiculous (and expensive); galleries can be chic or somewhat traditional. Cafés are good and bad, expensive and cheap, and all possible permutations of those four qualities. Serious shoppers and gallery goers should pick up two useful brochures, available at information booths (City Hall, Boston Common, Boston Public Library) entitled *The Newbury Street League Map,* which gives a list of most of the shops and some of the cafés along the street, their specialties, addresses, and phone numbers; and *Map of the Newbury Street Art Galleries,* which gives brief descriptions of the 30 galleries on the street, times of operation, special services, etc.

Newbury Street starts at the Ritz, and the shops in the first two blocks are, naturally, the most expensive. Furs, jewelry, art objects, and the like predominate. **Emmanuel Church,** just down from the Ritz in the same block, lends a cool note of English Gothic and ivy to the polished-brass-and-marble of some of the shops. By the way, the church sponsors a variety of musical and theatrical programs—jazz, chamber music, choral recitals, puppet shows—and advertises current offerings on a wooden signboard in the side doorway.

Streets in the Back Bay were laid out in a grid and the cross streets which run north-south were given names with initial letters running from A to H—Arlington, Berkeley, Clarendon, Dartmouth, etc.—so it's easy to know how far you are from the start of Newbury Street at Arlington Street. The second cross street, then, is Berkeley, and in the block between Berkeley and Clarendon is still more Gothic church architecture, this time in the form of the **Church of the Covenant** (Presbyterian), a bit plainer than the nearby Emmanuel. Organ recitals are held regularly at the Church of the Covenant, and usually a sign in the glass case will give the time: "Tuesday at 12:15," or whatever's current when you pass by. Two of the most famous stores on Newbury Street are located in this area, **Brooks Brothers** for men's wear, and **Bonwit Teller's** (in the old Boston Museum of Natural History Building) for women's fashions. **F.A.O. Schwarz,** the famous New York toy store, has a branch in Boston, at 40 Newbury and also in the Prudential Center.

COPLEY PLACE: Just off Copley Square is the vast new Copley Place, an ultramodern shopping, dining, lodging, and entertainment complex. **Neiman-Marcus** is the big store here, but there are dozens of shops as well. Ralph Lauren, Williams-Sonoma, Saint Laurent Rive Gauche, Jaeger, Gucci, and Godiva all have outlets, among others. Hours are normally 10 a.m. to 9 p.m. Monday through Friday, to 7 p.m. on Saturday, and noon to 5 p.m. on Sunday. The hotels in the complex are the Boston Marriott Copley Place and the Westin Hotel, Copley Place.

7. Nightlife

Forget everything you've ever heard about things being "banned in Boston," for at night in this big city it seems as though anything goes. The opportunities for evening activities are bewildering in their variety, and because of all the students in town, nightlife is very active, available, and—in many cases—not all that expensive. This section will give you some idea of what's going on, with details on a selection of the better things to see and do.

Bostonians have been known to call their city "The Athens of America"—they did this even before the city had a sizable Greek population. The reason, of course, is Boston's lively cultural and artistic life. It could fairly be said that on any given day of the year one could take a pick of a dozen or more lectures, concerts, or dance and theater offerings, and at least a few of these would be free of charge.

The best way to find out what's on tonight is to look in the listings: *Boston By Week* (a brochure arts schedule at information booths, hotel desks, and depots), or the tabloid "alternative" weekly newspapers: the *Boston Phoenix* is most easily available. Each one has an arts and entertainment section with reviews and advertisements for the current hot topics, and also a listings portion (classifieds and notices in the back of the arts section) which gives the latest information on the club and coffeehouse scene, poetry readings, and so forth. Look under headings such as "Music," "Lectures," "Theater," "Poetry," and "Lounges." When in session (fall and spring semesters), Harvard publishes its own *Gazette,* available for free from the Harvard University Information Office, Holyoke Center, Harvard Square. The paper includes listings of a great many films, lectures, discussions, gallery shows, plays, and concerts taking place at Harvard, many of which are open to the general public. The other great universities in the area also publish similar calendars, yours for the asking.

NIGHTCLUBS AND SINGLES BARS: The Boston area has over 75 colleges and universities, which give downtown nightlife a particularly lively character; a lot of graduates get to like the town so much they settle down here, and so Boston's crew of "young professionals" is also very large and very conspicuous in the clubs.

The Department of Commerce says that Boston is the most expensive city in the country except for Anchorage, and yet a night on the town won't kill your budget: drinks are mostly $4 to $6; beer or a glass of wine, $3 to $4.

Boston is covered with clubs, from the North End waterfront to Kenmore Square, but if I were asked to choose the top ones, here's what I'd pick:

The **Top of the Hub Lounge** (tel. 536-1775) is at the top of the lofty Prudential Tower in Prudential Center (subway: Green Line to Auditorium or Prudential). The view is panoramic, breathtaking, wonderful. The combo is cool, as are the drinks, as are the patrons. If you don't succeed in meeting someone interesting here, no matter—the view is worth it.

The **Profiles Café** and **Box Seat Lounge** (tel. 267-6059) are at the top of the Howard Johnson Hotel at 575 Commonwealth Ave., just past Kenmore Square going west (MBTA: Green Line "Boston College" cars to the Sherborn Street stop). The hotel is no skyscraper, but still the views of the Charles River, and of the lights and activity in Kenmore Square, are entertaining enough to keep you interested when you've stopped dancing. Live music nightly, some of the best in town.

The music at **Friday's,** 26 Exeter St. (tel. 266-9040), is recorded, but the people are very much alive and sociable. You can have a full meal here, a sandwich, or just a drink in the sumptuous Victorian atmosphere. The routine is to cluster at the small bar under the glass canopy—which will be pretty crowded—and when you inevitably bump into someone interesting, move on to one of the small tables in the dusky interior. Friday's stays open till midnight weeknights, till 1 a.m. on Friday and Saturday.

Boston's all-time success story, the **Faneuil Hall Marketplace** (MBTA: Green Line or Blue Line to Government Center) is a riot of activity morning, afternoon, and evening, with buskers and street musicians outside (in good weather), and a host of clubs and restaurants. For happy hour, you can't beat the crowd that gathers at the **Piano Bar at Lily's** (tel. 227-4242), in the Quincy Market Building: beautiful, young, well dressed, smooth, and with some money to burn. Sometimes it's hard to find a place at the bar or at one of the tables, but then again, asking to share a table is the perfect ice-breaker. Happy hour (5 to 7 p.m.) and after is the time when Lily's is most closely packed, with a piano player to provide accompaniment for the social action.

Daisy Buchanan's, 240a Newbury St. (tel. 247-8516), at Fairfield (MBTA: Green Line to Copley or Auditorium), is a favorite with the professional sports set and young Newbury Street sophisticates, making for an interesting mixture in the closely packed room. The music is recorded, the action is live. Drinks and light meals.

OPERA AND THE SYMPHONY: Although Boston does not have a proper opera house, the indefatigable Sarah Caldwell arranges for her **Opera Company of Boston** to perform in a downtown theater, and she and her company have gained fame nationwide for their ability to overcome all sorts of obstacles and stage memorable performances. Big-city opera companies are undergoing a period of great instability, mostly financial, and so I will not predict that you'll be able to see this-or-that opera in this-or-that hall; rather, call the Opera Company of Boston, 539 Washington St. (tel. 426-5300), to see what's up, or watch for the ads in the newspapers. Seats may be expensive, but usually there are cut-price student tickets for sale within two weeks of any performance; get to the office the first day they go on sale, and be prepared to wait in line.

Often the Metropolitan Opera Company comes up from New York for several performances; watch the newspapers for an announcement.

Boston's universities have been known to put on operas. Again, watch for such special one-time events in the newspaper listings.

Among the most successful opera seasons in Boston is that of the **Boston Concert Opera** (tel. 536-1166). Performances are held during the traditional opera season in Symphony Hall. Though the old favorites appear on the program, there are many lesser-known and rarely performed works—a real treat for true opera fans. Last-minute seats at moderate prices are often available. Note that this is "concert" opera: no sets, no costumes, but excellent conductor, soloists, chorus, and orchestra who give you a superb opera experience at an unbeatable price.

The **Boston Symphony Orchestra** preserves a reputation for excellence and innovation which it has had for over a century. The formal symphony season runs from September through April, with performances in Symphony Hall (tel. 266-1492). The hall was designed (1900) by McKim, Mead, and White, who carried out one of the earliest-known scientific acoustical studies for such a structure, and their careful work has been an outstanding success for over three-quarters of a century.

Symphony tickets are sometimes difficult to get, but the following tips will make the task much easier. First of all, normal ticket sales begin 28 days before any specific concert at the Symphony Hall Box Office, open from 10 a.m. to 6 p.m. Monday through Saturday. If you have no luck with these, try to get rush-seat tickets, which go on sale for only a few dollars, one to a customer, for Friday and Saturday concerts. Ticket sales begin in the Huntington Avenue Lobby of the hall at 10 a.m. on Friday and at 5:30 p.m. on Saturday. Failing that, you can loiter outside the door on the night of the concert and try to buy any "extras" that others have bought in advance, but that they can't use. Otherwise, Wednesday-evening Open Rehearsals at 7:30 p.m. are almost as good as concerts. Tickets are inexpensive, and include an informal discussion of the pieces to be rehearsed (usually that weekend's concert works) which begins at 6:45 p.m. in the Cabot-Cahners Room at Symphony Hall.

The Boston Pops

Many members of the BSO stay on for the **Boston Pops**. At Pops, the music is just that: the most popular and lighter pieces in the symphonic repertoire performed in a café atmosphere. The floor in Symphony Hall is cleared of seats, and café tables and chairs are brought in, the hall is festooned with boughs and garlands of flowers, and champagne and hors d'oeuvres are served at the tables. The program is always a full and varied one, with a major work and lots of "Pops Extras," unlisted numbers thrown in for fun, many of them catchy orchestral arrangements of current hit tunes. Pops season starts when the symphony's season ends in the spring, and goes through late July. As this is graduation season, many Pops performances are bought up *en bloc* by colleges; call Symphony Hall. An easier way to spend an "Evening at Pops" is by going early to one of the several summer concerts given for free by the Boston Pops in the Hatch Memorial Shell, on the Charles River Esplanade (Red Line to Charles Station). The finale to the Esplanade season is the traditional Fourth of July performance, which always ends with Tchaikovsky's *1812 Overture,* accompanied by a battery of cannons and followed by a mammoth display of fireworks over the river.

Tanglewood

After Pops season, the indefatigable members of the orchestra move out to the Berkshire hills in western Massachusetts for the **Berkshire Music Festival** at Tanglewood in Lenox, Mass. (tel. 413/637-1600 for administration, 413/637-1940 for tickets). Again, these performances are very heavily attended, and it's best to go early to get a good seat (you can sit inside the "Music Shed" or on the lawn outside, depending on how much you want to spend for a ticket); even more important than going early to the concert is to get a room reservation nearby, unless you plan to drive out and back (over three hours one way) the same day.

Other Concerts

Two well-known music schools offer frequent concerts by students, faculty, and visiting groups of performers. The **New England Conservatory of Music,** 290 Huntington Ave. (tel. 262-1120, ext. 257), has frequent concerts, many of them free, in its performance halls which include Jordon Hall. The conservatory is located one block from Symphony Hall, on Huntington Avenue at Gainsborough Street, close to the Boston YMCA and Northeastern University (Green Line's "Arborway" or "Northeastern U" cars to Symphony Station, or to the first stop above ground). A monthly calendar of events is available on request.

The other school is the **Berklee College of Music** (tel. 266-7455 for a recorded schedule, or 266-1400 for a human being), which has a Recital Hall at 1140 Boylston St. for small ensembles, and the Berklee Performance Center at 136 Massachusetts Ave. (near the corner of Massachusetts Avenue and Boylston Street) for larger groups. There's also the Berklee Concert Pavilion, an urban amphitheater, for outdoors events. Take the Green Line's "Boston College," "Cleveland Circle," or "Riverside" cars to Auditorium Station for both places. Both halls are fairly near the Prudential Center.

Few Boston institutions predate the venerable **Handel and Haydn Society,** which has been giving choral concerts in Boston since 1815. The society's season runs from September to May, with all performances in Symphony Hall. The society, older even than the Boston Symphony Orchestra, has a closely guarded reputation for high excellence in its performances. For information on its concerts, call the Symphony Hall box office (tel. 266-1492) or the Handel and Haydn Society, 158 Newbury St. (tel. 266-3605).

Concert Music Cruises

Young Bostonians are crazy for both boats and serious music, and a firm called **Water Music, Inc.,** 12 Arrow St., Cambridge (tel. 876-7777), has put the two together to make the "Concert Cruise." Twice each evening boats leave for a twilight tour of Boston Harbor and Massachusetts Bay, with its own prominent local or national musical group on board. Cruises operate in summer only, and the musical group is different each week. Food such as quiches, pâté, salads, and sandwiches can be purchased on board, as can wine, beer, and cocktails. Call for current schedules, musical programs, prices, and boarding information.

Cheap Seats

An outfit called **Bostix** (tel. 723-5181 for a recording) sells all kinds of tickets to all sorts of events in Boston and beyond. Buy a ticket to almost anything in eastern Massachusetts here. You'll pay the regular price plus a small service charge. This is a useful service.

But the real excitement at Bostix is the sale of tickets at half price on the day of performance. Theater, concerts, shows, etc., are put on a "daily list" of half-price offerings, and you must stop by the Bostix kiosk next to Faneuil Hall in Faneuil Hall Marketplace (subway to Government Center, Green Line or Blue Line) to read the list—they won't give you the list over the telephone. For same-day, half-price seats you must pay in cash, no refunds or exchanges; for advance bookings you may pay with a check drawn on a Massachusetts bank. No credit cards are accepted at all.

JAZZ, FOLK, ROCK: Modern music is all over Boston, but except for a few clubs downtown and a few coffeehouses in Cambridge, performers do a gig here or there and then disappear. The very big names usually play in the **Wang Center** (tel. 542-3600), 270 Tremont (Green Line to Boylston); in the **Hynes Convention Center** (tel. 262-8000) at the Prudential Center (Green Line to Auditorium), presently closed for renovation; in the **Boston Garden** (tel. 227-3200), below North Station (Green Line to North Station); or in one of the university halls.

The Jazzboat

Besides operating a concert music cruise, **Water Music, Inc.** (tel. 876-7777), has come up with weekly cruises featuring jazz musicians ("the Jazzboat") and various other groups from swing bands to a Caribbean steel band. Call for the latest information, and then get your tickets by mail from Water Music, Inc., 12 Arrow St., Cambridge, MA 02138, or pick them up from one of the outlets they'll tell you about.

THEATER: Boston's taste in theater runs the gamut from previews of Broadway musicals to the most experimental of experimental. The offering is so rich and varied it would be impossible in this small space even to give an idea of the range available: groups will pop up here and there, struggle to survive, and in the meantime put on fine performances, and then fail financially and disperse, having left many theatergoers with a lasting impression. I would stress that people interested in the theater should not limit themselves to the possibilities outlined below, but should take the trouble to seek out the new groups performing in odd places, for they're often at the frontier.

Nevertheless, if you have only a little time to spend in Boston and you'd like to take in a play or a musical, here are some hints:

The **Next Move Theater,** 1 Boylston Pl. (tel. 423-5572), is perhaps the city's most interesting and talented theater group. For all its technical excellence, it's a homey sort of place where the actors stand near the door as you enter and as you leave, greeting the audience and exchanging comments on the plays. Boylston Place is a tiny alley off Boylston Street, midway between Tremont and Charles Streets, across from Boston Common. By subway, take the Green Line to Boylston.

The old-line theaters with musicals and plays slated for Broadway are all downtown near the Green Line's Boylston Station: the **Colonial Theater,** 106 Boylston St. right near the station (tel. 426-9366); the **Shubert Theater,** 265 Tremont St. (tel. 426-4520), and the **Wilbur Theater,** 246 Tremont St. (tel. 423-4008), are both two blocks south along Tremont Street from the Boylston Station.

Good drama is the rule at the **Charles Playhouse,** 74 Warrenton St. (tel. 426-6912), right down behind the Shubert and Wilbur Theaters and the Bradford Hotel

(Green Line to Boylston; Warrenton is parallel to Tremont one block west, but it's only a block long). Comedians perform nightly in the **Comedy Connection;** and the **Charles Cabaret,** in the same building, has set the record for the longest run of *Shear Madness.*

Besides these, the universities have a great many drama offerings, usually at fairly low prices; and during the summer the city of Boston and other organizations sponsor outdoor performances in City Hall Plaza, other public squares, and along the Charles River Esplanade. (See also the section on **Cambridge.**)

DANCE: Dance is not quite as prominent in Boston's arts scene as, say, theater or music, but the energetic **Boston Ballet Company** (tel. 964-4070), is active all year. In spring, fall, and winter there is the regular ballet season at the Wang Center, 270 Tremont St.; in summer the troupe seems to be everywhere, putting on performances in the city's squares and parks, and along the riverbank. Watch for notices and times in the papers.

CINEMA: Movies are a big part of Boston's nighttime entertainment picture, and the hot-topic big releases are always crowded during the first few weeks. But besides major releases, silent movies, golden oldies, and bestsellers of the recent past are always available. Prices range from $7 per seat to free admission.

The local listings will let you know what's on tonight. What you may find of help is directions on how to get to the principal movie theaters. Remember to check out Cambridge movies as well, listed separately in the Cambridge section. Here are the prime movie houses in Boston:

Beacon Hill, 1 Beacon St., at Tremont St. (tel. 723-8110), near King's Chapel and the Parker House Hotel; Green or Red Lines to Park Street, or Green or Blue Lines to Government Center.

Charles, 195a Cambridge St. (tel. 227-1330), next to the Holiday Inn near the corner of Cambridge and Blossom Street; Green Line to Government Center, or Red Line to Charles.

Cheri, 50 Dalton St. (tel. 536-2870), next to Hynes Convention Center in the Prudential Center complex; Green Line's "Boston College," "Cleveland Circle," or "Riverside" cars to Auditorium, turn left out of the station, left again down Boylston, and look right.

Cinema 57, 200 Stuart St. (tel. 482-1222), in the tall 57 Park Plaza Hotel–Howard Johnson, in Park Square; Green Line to Boylston Station, then walk along the edge of the Common on Boylston Street to the intersection with Charles Street and turn left—it's right in front of you in the middle distance.

Coolidge Corner, 290 Harvard St., in suburban Brookline (tel. 734-2500); take the Green Line's "Cleveland Circle" car along Beacon Street to the junction with Harvard Street, called Coolidge Corner.

Copley Place, 100 Huntington Ave. (tel. 266-1300), in the new Copley Place complex next to Copley Square and the Prudential Center. Take a Green Line subway car to Copley or Prudential.

Nickelodeon Cinemas, 606 Commonwealth Ave. near Kenmore Square (tel. 424-1500), is actually slightly off Commonwealth at 34 Cummington St., behind Boston University's School of Public Communications, but you'll see the cinema's big sign as you walk west along Commonwealth from Kenmore Square.

Paris Cinema, 841 Boylston St. (tel. 267-8181), very near Prudential Center; Green Line to Copley, Auditorium, or Prudential.

The **Opera House** (tel. 426-5300) has two entrances: 163 Tremont St. (Green Line to Boylston, and the Tremont entrance is across the street from the subway station, a few doors down), or 539 Washington St. (Red or Orange Line to Washington, enter two blocks down on the right across from Lafayette Place).

Wang Center, 270 Tremont St. (tel. 482-9393), near Stuart Street in the Theater District; this is often booked with concert groups or plays rather than movies;

Green Line to Boylston, then south (away from the Common) on Tremont Street right into the honky-tonk for two blocks, and the Wang Center is on the left.

In addition, the **Museum of Fine Arts,** 465 Huntington Ave., has a film series with screenings most Thursday and Friday evenings. Call 267-9300, extension 290 or 300, for details, times, and prices.

Free Movies

Lots of films are shown for free in Boston, or very nearly for free—the college film series at many Boston colleges often charge as little as $1 for admission. Newspaper listings may or may not have information about college film series, and indeed the movie to be shown, place of screening, and even date and time may change without notice except for a few mimeographed flyers stuck up here and there on the campus. Still, try calling one of the college switchboards and asking about "the film series." For Harvard, check the *Gazette,* a weekly information sheet about the university available for free in the University Information Office, Holyoke Center, Harvard Square.

More dependable and predictable than the college film series are the films shown fairly regularly by these institutions, all for free:

Boston Public Library (tel. 536-5400), various films shown in the lecture hall and at the library's branches throughout the city. Take the Green Line to Copley.

Institute of Contemporary Art, 955 Boylston St. (tel. 266-5151), showing various films usually having to do with modern art or artists; see "Other Galleries" for transportation details.

SPORTS: Especially in summer, Boston is alive with outdoor activities: the Charles River is dotted with sailboats every day the breeze comes up, joggers and bikers huff and puff along the Esplanade, the roar of the Red Sox fans rises from Fenway Park. Every autumn, tickets to the Harvard-Yale game are grabbed up like passes into heaven, and while the aristocrats are urging Harvard to fight fiercely, the Boston Bruins and their opponents for the day are probably doing just that with their hockey sticks. Hockey is such a part of Boston's cold-weather life that in winter you may see a lot of kids with schoolbooks in their hands, but you'll see a lot more with hockey sticks. Here's a rundown on the major sports; parking is tough to find and expensive on game nights.

Baseball

The **Red Sox** play at Fenway Park (Green Line's "Riverside" car to Fenway Station, then follow the crowd!), and if you buy your tickets a few days before the game, you can get them at the nearest ticket agency (Ticketron, Bostix, and the like). Call 267-2525 for Red Sox information.

Basketball

The famous **Boston Celtics** play in Boston Garden (Green Line to North Station), a large hall that has nothing to do with Boston's Public Garden. Call 523-6050 for the latest info.

Football

The **New England Patriots,** affectionately called "The Pats" in these "pahts," play at Schaefer Stadium, Rte. 1 in Foxboro, Mass., some 30 miles southwest of Boston. Several Boston bus companies run special buses to the games; try calling Bonanza (tel. 423-5810) or Peter Pan (tel. 482-6620); for information on Patriots games, call 262-1776.

Hockey

The famed **Boston Bruins** battle it out with all comers at Boston Garden (same as basketball, above), and tickets are often sold out very early. Catch 'em when they take on Montréal and you've got a spectacle. Call 227-3200 for information.

Horseracing
Suffolk Downs is New England's only thoroughbred track. The track is located in East Boston on McClellan Hwy. (Rte. 1A) about two miles from Logan International Airport. Take the Callahan Tunnel if you're driving, or take the Blue Line subway to Suffolk Downs Station. Admission is $2 for both the clubhouse and grandstand. Post time is 1 p.m. (during the summer) every day except Tuesday and Thursday. Call 567-3900.

THE COMBAT ZONE: Police hate it, politicians want to get rid of it, some citizens revel in it—the several blocks of Washington Street between West Street and Stuart Street (Green Line to Boylston or Orange Line to Essex) are perhaps the most "un-Bostonlike" part of Boston. No grand old traditions are here except that of "the oldest profession"; no lofty artistry unless one can call nude dancing art. The Combat Zone, as it is known to all, is Boston's tenderloin: several blocks of prime downtown real estate full of strip shows, "naked college girl revues," porno films, and generally sleazy diversions.

Despite its sinister name and gamy appearance, the Combat Zone is not a wildly dangerous place to stroll through, and many of the bars and clubs and movie houses are safe enough to enter if you follow a few simple rules. First, don't go late at night; things are hopping by early evening, and you might as well see this part of the world around 8 or 8:30 p.m. rather than later. It's brightly lit and there are lots of police around. Second, don't go alone; anything's better than being a loner, whether you go with a date, a threesome, or a small group. In most places women are as welcome as men. Third, watch your wallet or purse. And finally, if you want to try out a place, go by gut feeling: some places are fairly attractive and seem safe enough; others look pretty bad, with all sorts of types hanging around. Walk around for a while until you find an acceptable place. And if all this seems terrifying, remember that the people who own the Combat Zone places are interested in selling you movie tickets, drinks, and not in ripping you off so you never come back again; they'd rather not have any trouble that'll bring the police.

ACROSS THE CHARLES

As Paul Revere sped through the countryside along another road, William Dawes made a famous midnight ride which took him from the banks of the Charles through the communities of Cambridge (once called Newtown), Lexington, and Concord. Boston's expansion, like America's, was westward toward the mountains, and these important communities west of the city were large enough to play a significant role in the Revolution.

Today the cities of Cambridge, Lexington, and Concord are linked by Battle Road, a designation given by the National Park Service, which harks back to that historic day when Revere and Dawes rode out, followed by troops of Redcoats. The story of Battle Road and the events of that day in 1775 are clearly told in the exhibits at Minuteman National Historic Park in Lexington and Concord, but before looking at revolutionary history, let's take a look at the home city of Harvard College, which is much older than the Revolution.

1. Cambridge

Cambridge means Harvard to most visitors who come to Boston, and although Harvard is not the only thing in the city of Cambridge (MIT's there too, after all), it is certainly the city's most important institution. Harvard Square, at the intersection of Massachusetts Avenue and John F. Kennedy Street (formerly called Boylston Street), is a crossroads which teems with evidence of a hundred lifestyles, from the stuffily academic to the loosest in dropouts.

Cambridge has its own collection of hotels, restaurants, and sights to see, examined below. The MBTA's Red Line subway connects Harvard Square to Park Street Station on Boston Common. Service is the fastest, most frequent, and most comfortable in the system, and the journey normally takes about 15 minutes from turnstile to turnstile. Going from Harvard Square into Boston, take any "Inbound" train; all trains stop at Park Street Station. From Boston to Harvard Square, take trains marked "Alewife" or "Harvard."

Those staying in Boston's Back Bay section might find it easier to walk to Massachusetts Avenue and catch a no. 1 bus ("Harvard-Dudley"), which goes past MIT, through Central Square directly to Harvard Square, the last stop.

INFORMATION: There's an information kiosk right in the center of Harvard Square maintained and staffed by **Cambridge Discovery, Inc.** (tel. 617/497-1630), open Monday through Saturday from 9 a.m. to 6 p.m. and on Sunday from 1 to 5 p.m.

WHERE TO STAY: Guidelines for Cambridge hotels are similar to those mentioned for Boston. There is no reason why you shouldn't plan to stay in Cambridge during the length of your Boston visit. Remember to consider your means of transportation when you choose a hotel in Cambridge.

Remember also that bed-and-breakfast organizations serving the Boston area serve Cambridge too. See the Boston hotel section for details.

Unrivaled queen of Cambridge hotels, and perhaps the most dramatic hotel in all of Boston, is the Aztec-pyramid **Hyatt Regency Cambridge,** 575 Memorial Dr., Cambridge, MA 02139 (tel. 617/492-1234, or toll free 800/228-9000). True to the dramatic design tradition begun by the first Hyatt hotel in Atlanta, the Hyatt in Cambridge has a central atrium, a grand interior space rising from ground floor to top floor, planted with trees and hanging vines and surrounded with mezzanine walkways to the rooms. Of the several restaurants in the hotel, Jonah's on the Terrace is on the mezzanine one flight up from ground level, and diners thus can enjoy the atmosphere of the central atrium, with its greenery and fountains. The Pallysadoe Bar, just off this mezzanine, has a good view of the Charles River.

But the most spectacular feature of the hotel is right at the top. Take one of the crystal-shaped glass elevators that slide up the wall of the central atrium to the restaurant on the top floor. Open for lunch and dinner, the restaurant affords a panoramic view of Boston, Cambridge, and the Charles. Once you're seated on a plush sofa with your table before you and plants all around, take in the view at once, because it will change quickly: the entire dining area is on a revolving disc which moves very slowly so that the perspective is always changing. Rooms cost $197 to $207 single, $219 to $230 double.

Newest of Harvard Square hotels is the luxurious **Charles Hotel** at Harvard Square, in the complex called Charles Square off Mount Auburn Street and Brattle Square, only steps from Harvard Square (tel. 617/864-1200), 1 Bennett St. at Eliot St., Cambridge, MA 02138. The Charles is independently run, beautifully decorated, and luxuriously furnished, with 300 guest rooms fully equipped: cable color TV, refrigerated bar, two telephones, and 24-hour room service. As you might expect, the hotel has its own indoor swimming pool, sauna, whirlpool, and exercise room. The restaurant, called Rarities, is elegant, epicurean, and pricey. The Regattabar is among the Boston area's best jazz clubs, with top-name artists. Prices? Here they are: $186 to $246 single or double. On weekends you can get a room (double or single) for $135, valet parking included.

The **Guest Quarters Suite Hotel,** 400 Soldiers Field Rd., Boston, MA 02134 (tel. 617/783-0090, or toll free 800/362-2779), is a good choice for families or anyone else in search of more room and features for the same money. Though the address is Boston, this 15-story, 310-room building is actually as close—or closer —to Harvard Square and MIT as it is to Boston University and downtown Boston. Each suite consists of a bedroom with king-size bed, color TV, AM-FM radio, writing desk, and telephone; full bath (with tub/shower and phone); refrigerator and wet bar; living room with full-size sofa bed, another color TV, dining table, and yet another phone. In addition to all this, the price includes a full American breakfast and an evening cocktail reception every day, free parking in the hotel's adjoining covered lot, use of the indoor swimming pool, sauna, and whirlpool bath, and a courtesy van to Cambridge and/or Boston. So what's the price? Not bad at all: $160 to $192 single or double. Packages and weekend specials bring prices down, though. Currently the weekend rate is $120 per night double.

The **Howard Johnson Hotel,** 777 Memorial Dr., Cambridge, MA 02139 (tel. 617/492-7777, or toll free 800/654-2000), is a 14-story, 205-room establishment. Here, the floor your room is on determines its price. Furnishings are clean and modern, and some rooms have small balconies, but otherwise the difference in the rooms is what you can see from them: Boston and the Charles, straight across the Charles, up the Charles River to Harvard (this is the prettiest view, in my opinion), and a city view of Cambridge. Pick your view: on the higher floors and with a river view, the prices are $88 single, $98 double, $108 triple, and $118 quadruple. Reserve a week in advance for a weekend date and you can sometimes get a room for $80. The hotel is quite comfortable and well run, and has as special offerings a swimming pool (mid-June to Labor Day), a paddle-tennis court (year round), all color TVs, free parking, a restaurant and bar, and a pleasant brick-and-dark-wood interior. Note that around the time of any Harvard special events (freshmen registration, Harvard-Yale game, Homecoming, graduation, and the like) rooms here are at a premium and should be reserved well in advance. Car or taxi must be used to get to and from Harvard Square or downtown Boston.

Without a doubt, the most convenient hotel to Harvard and Harvard Square is the **Harvard Motor House,** 110 Mount Auburn St., Cambridge, MA 02138 (tel. 617/864-5200). Note that this hostelry is not really a hotel but actually a motel, with only the facilities of a motel: air conditioning, ice machine, vending machines, and free continental breakfast served in the lobby. Parking is free, and a parking place—any parking place—near Harvard Square is a very good thing to have, so this is one of the Harvard Motor House's main advantages. Rooms are modern, all have TV, and are rented for $88 single, $98 double, $108 triple. Rooms for four cost $118; children under 16 stay free. Some rooms have views of Brattle and Harvard Squares.

At 1234 Soldiers' Field Rd., Boston (Brighton, MA 02135 (tel. 617/254-1234), is the local **Ramada Inn.** For $94 to $104 single, $105 to $126 double, midweek, you get a small swimming pool (open from Memorial Day to Labor Day) and a large restaurant, besides a selection of rooms with views of the river and the steeples and cupolas of Harvard in the middle distance. In fact, room prices are computed on the basis of the view, the front river-view rooms on the higher floors of the building being the most expensive. Children under 18 stay for free; an extra person costs $20; an extra bed, $20. On weekends room prices are lower.

The **Charles River Motel,** 1800 Soldiers' Field Rd., Boston (Brighton), MA 02135 (tel. 617/254-0200), is not in Cambridge, strictly speaking, but it offers advantages to visitors to Cambridge who have their own cars. Fairly quiet atmosphere, larger-than-average rooms, and lots of free parking are among the advantages, but the prices are the biggest advantage of all: $72 single, $82 double for an air-conditioned room and bath with color TV. The motel has no pool and no restaurant, but there are several restaurants within walking distance. It does have a cocktail lounge. If you're driving, get to the south bank of the Charles River and go west to Soldiers' Field Road, which is in a way the extension of Storrow Drive. Follow signs to Newton, dip down for an underpass, and then a mile or so later look to your left for the pillared southern mansion-style façade of the red-brick motel. You can get to the motel by bus from Central Square in Cambridge: take a no. 64 ("Oak Square") bus. Although the Charles River Motel is several miles from Harvard Square, Soldiers' Field Road allows you to speed to the center of town in only ten minutes. By the way, children under 12 stay for free here.

A newly renovated and historically preserved hotel not far from Harvard Square is the **Sheraton Commander,** 16 Garden St., Cambridge, MA 02238 (tel. 617/547-4800, or toll free 800/325-3535). Garden Street runs from Harvard Square past Cambridge Common to Radcliffe, and the Commander is just about equidistant (a ten-minute walk) from either campus. The decor in the public rooms tends to the high-brow colonial—the "commander" for whom the hotel was named is George Washington; a bronze statue of General Washington stands in the entry garden, to the right of the doors. Rooms cost $141 to $175 for one, $153 to $175 for two; children under 18 stay for free. Although there is free parking at the hotel, the lot is small and you may have to leave your keys at the desk so the doorman can jockey the cars around to best advantage.

The **Cambridge Quality Inn,** 1651 Massachusetts Ave., Cambridge, MA 02139 (tel. 617/491-1000), is a 15-minute walk from Harvard Square along busy Massachusetts Avenue. Recently renovated, it is functional, even comfortable, with 135 guest rooms, a small swimming pool for the warm months, a homey restaurant off the lobby, and, of course, free parking. If you stay here, you can walk to the subway and be in downtown Boston within 30 minutes from when you close your room door. A room with one double bed costs $72 to $80; with two double beds, $88 to $98. Kids under 16 stay for free; extra persons are charged $8 each.

WHERE TO DINE: Cambridge, in its woolly way, is even more cosmopolitan than Boston, and this is well demonstrated in its restaurants. Cannelloni to couscous, wonton to weisswurst, Cambridge has it. Some of the best places to have a good, inexpensive lunch or a light supper are Cambridge's coffeehouses, almost all of which serve food as well as coffee, tea, and hot chocolate. And finally, there are the ice cream shops of Harvard Square, worthy of a list unto themselves.

The Top Restaurants

The **Bennett St. Café** in the Charles Hotel, in the Charles Square complex just out of Brattle Square (tel. 864-1200), is among the area's most attractive and interesting restaurants. In fair weather you can dine outdoors in the court; otherwise, the indoor dining room is plush and attractive. The selection of luncheon salads, sandwiches, and light entrees (the menu changes constantly) is among the finest and most interesting I've seen among Harvard Square's plethora of upscale dining places. Expect to pay about $15 to $18 total for lunch, and that includes a drink or glass of wine. At dinner you can spend twice that much. The café is open for breakfast, Sunday brunch, lunch, and dinner every day.

Of the several good restaurants in the top price range in Harvard Square, first place goes to **Harvest,** 44 Brattle St. (tel. 492-1115), for its food, service, location, and ambience. Harvest is hidden away down the tunnel that penetrates the four-story glass building that houses Crate and Barrel on Brattle Street, and its location allows it to have the most pleasant outdoor luncheon area in all Cambridge. Open for lunch and dinner every day from 11:30 a.m. to 2:30 p.m. and 6 to 10 p.m., until 10:30 p.m. on weekends (Sunday brunch from 11 a.m. to 3 p.m.), Harvest offers a good selection of very interesting and meticulously prepared dishes: at lunch, a vegetable mosaïque pâté to start, then poached sole with oysters and caviar, and for dessert a chocolate marquise, for example. For dinner you might find mousseline of three fishes, breast of pheasant with black currants and cassis, and fresh pastry; the extravagant can order lobster and sweetbreads with sorrel. The price-conscious will be able to dine very well for $20 at lunch, for $35 to $40 in the evening, though you can easily spend more.

Matsu-ya has the best Japanese and Korean cuisine in Cambridge, and perhaps in all of Boston. An unpretentious place at 1790 Massachusetts Ave. (tel. 491-5091), about ten blocks north of Harvard Square, Matsu-ya has room for about seven dozen diners, and you can sit in booths or at low Japanese-style tables on a raised platform. Decoration is traditional but subdued, depending on simplicity for a harmonious effect; waitresses wear beautifully patterned Korean dresses. Pleasant as the surroundings are, they are outshone by the food, which has a subtlety of flavor too seldom found in any restaurant, Eastern or Western, and rarely found in Asian restaurants where MSG and garlic are used lavishly. If you like steak tartare, you'll love yukhae, morsels of choice raw beef flavored with sesame seeds and oil; more familiar dishes, such as pork sukiyaki ($10), are prepared right at your table and cooked to your specifications (nothing theatrical about this, no flaming braziers and such, and the food is served exactly when it is *à point*). Cheaper, but equally delicious, is sweet-and-sour beef ($9). Tea, rice, and chopsticks are served automatically. Other drinks (they now serve wine and beer) and Western eating utensils are available. A filling and very delicious meal for two, with tax and tip included, may come to $25 or $30 per person, complete. This is one of the best restaurants in Boston in my opinion: pleasant and restful decor, attentive service, delicate food, and moderate prices. Matsu-ya is open for dinner every evening from 5 to 10 p.m., to 11 p.m. on Friday and Saturday.

Favorite Cambridge Hangouts

The **Border Café,** 32 Church St. (tel. 864-6100), is a mock-stark Mexican cantina with rough wood tables and naïve murals of favorite Mexican bottles, but also a chic black-clad hostess to seat you (she'd never survive in a real cantina). The café is popular partly because of its tongue-in-cheek decor, but more because the food is surprisingly inexpensive. The cuisine here borrows from Mexican, Cajun, fajita, and mesquite-grill cooking, and you'll love it. Not only that, but you can have a sandwich and Corona (beer) for as little as $6 or $8, or more elaborate and delicious plates of shrimp, fajitas (shredded fried meat or chicken), or blackened redfish, and end up paying only $15 to $18 for a meal, with drinks, tax, and tip included. The Border Café is open daily for lunch and dinner.

The wurst restaurant in Harvard Square is of course the **Wursthaus,** at 4 Boylston St., right in Harvard Square (tel. 491-7110). Inside, a long bar and several rooms of booths and tables provide a nearly German atmosphere, and prices for the wursts—knackwurst, bratwurst, blutwurst—are moderate, mostly in the $8 to $12 range, and that includes sauerkraut, black bread, and butter. World travelers craving the exotic beer of some far-off land will probably find it here, as the Wursthaus tries hard to include on its "beerlist" just about every foreign beer you've ever heard of and dozens you never knew existed; they're priced from $3 to $8 a bottle. Hearty sandwiches are made here ($4.50 to $8.50). Lunch is served from 11 a.m. to 3 p.m., and dinner from 4 to 9 p.m. every day but Sunday, when the dinner menu is offered all day, from 11:30 a.m. on.

Every college freshman reads about Grendel, the dragon which threatens the hero of the ancient English epic *Beowulf,* but anyone in Harvard Square—freshman or not—can frequent **Grendel's Den,** 89 Winthrop St. (tel. 491-1160), a restaurant noted for its reasonable prices and large portions. Grendel's is behind a tiny patch of grass off John F. Kennedy Street at Mount Auburn Street, one block south of Harvard Square toward the Charles River: a huge sign on the roof leads the way. The cellar of the red-brick building is the bar, furnished with a fireplace for cold winter nights, and dark-wood tables. Upstairs is the restaurant, with two fireplaces and a glassed-in terrace overlooking busy John F. Kennedy Street. The menu tells of international specialties such as spinach pie, fettuccine, chicken curry, shish kebab, quiche, omelets, burgers, and sandwiches priced from $8 to $18. There's a good salad bar. Alcoholic beverages are served. As for the desserts, they're a list in themselves, but suffice it to say that they include chocolate fondue. Grendel's is open every day for lunch and dinner.

Among Cambridge's newer hangouts is the **Cottonwood Café,** 1815 Massachusetts Ave. (tel. 661-7440), in the renovated Sears, Roebuck building at Porter Square (take the Red Line subway in the direction of Alewife, one stop from Harvard Square). The Cottonwood is upscale Mexican, a cozy, attractive place with an inventive menu that might best be described as "New Latin American Cuisine": although Mexican-inspired, the dishes are original creations. Many are pretty spicy, so ask. Authentic, carefully chosen crafts enliven the decor. Prices are moderate at lunch, about $12 to $16 per person, and quite a bit more expensive at dinner.

They're open every day from 11:45 a.m. to 3:30 p.m. for lunch and 5:45 p.m. to 10 p.m. (till 11 p.m. on Friday and Saturday) for dinner.

Iruña, entered by a passageway between 54 and 56 John F. Kennedy St. (tel. 868-5633), is Harvard Square's best-kept secret. Though it's been here for years, only locals know about Iruña's good, hearty Spanish food, low prices, and pretty outdoor patio in the rear (summer only). Come for lunch and you can have soup, carne guisada (chunks of beef in a sauce of wine, mushrooms, and carrots), and salad for less than $12, tax and tip included! Arroz con pollo (chicken and rice) is the same price. You can spend even less by ordering only the main course. Prices at dinner are similarly pleasant. Wine and beer are served. Iruña is open from noon to 2 p.m. Monday through Friday, from 6 to 9 p.m. Monday through Thursday, to 9 p.m. on Friday, and from 1:30 to 10 p.m. on Saturday; closed Sunday.

Dolphin Seafood, on Massachusetts Avenue between Remington and Trowbridge Streets (tel. 354-9332), near where Massachusetts Avenue intersects Mount Auburn Street, is only six blocks east of the square. Upstairs in a split-level complex of shops, the Dolphin's decor is plain and functional, with the seafood being given all the attention. A big plate of steamers (steamed clams) with butter makes a substantial appetizer. Fried squid is a specialty (the chef is Portuguese), but there are always alternatives such as bluefish and whatever else is fresh that day, with potato, salad, rolls, and butter included. If you're lobster-happy, order twin lobsters with steamers or mussels. A whole dinner might cost $15 to $20 here, lunch even less. Wine and beer are served at reasonable prices. The Dolphin is good, and thus it's busy—go for an early or late lunch or dinner till 10 p.m.

Budget Meals

Many places in Harvard Square serve hamburgers and other sandwiches, but undoubtedly the best value-for-money is to be had at **Elsie's,** 71a Mount Auburn St. (tel. 864-0461), at the corner of Holyoke and Mount Auburn Streets, a block from the square. Elsie's is nothing fancy, but the prices, for quantity and quality received, have never been rivaled in Harvard Square: mainstay is the roast beef special, which comes with Bermuda onion and "Elsie's Special Russian Dressing," the turkey deluxe, the Elsieburger (a double hamburger), and the thick-cut Rumanian pastrami-filled landsman are other features, each for only $3.25 to $4.75.

Taking its name from Harvard's famous Yenching Library, the **Yenching Restaurant,** 1326 Massachusetts Ave., at the corner of Massachusetts Avenue and Holyoke Street (tel. 547-1130), has the best Chinese food in the square. Furnishings are simple but bright and tasteful, and the food is authentic and good. If you are not very familiar with Chinese cuisine, be sure to ask the waiter how a certain dish is prepared so as to avoid surprises such as too much garlic or red pepper. Most of the surprises here are very pleasant, however, the greatest being the price of the daily luncheon buffet—only about $7—which attracts a large crowd about 12:15 each afternoon. A hearty bowl of soup is brought to you after you're seated, and when it's finished the buffet line is next. The dinner menu is long but not encyclopedic, offering Szechuan shredded pork, Mandarin sweet-and-sour fish, and a whole Peking duck (order in advance). The average evening meal might come to $16 to $20. Service is quick and attentive. The Yenching is open for lunch and dinner every day, but the special luncheon buffet is served Monday through Saturday till 2:30 p.m. only.

The half-dozen restaurants in the **Harvard Square Marketplace,** a sort of mall bounded by Kennedy, Mount Auburn, and Dunster Streets, are all moderate to inexpensive in price. **Souper Salad** is an attractive lunch or light-supper place, with interesting spaces in which to sit, an upbeat menu, and prices to suit any appetite or budget. Nearby is **Baby Watson,** noted above all for its desserts. Baby Watson cheesecake is Boston's best known.

COFFEEHOUSES: An intellectual center will have its coffeehouses, dedicated to serving that beverage which stimulates thought and aids conversation. Harvard

Square has a good selection of coffeehouses, all of which serve light meals, desserts, ice cream, and beverages beside coffee. Each draws a special clientele, and you can spend a very pleasant day or two hopping from one to another of these, testing them out to find the one that suits you best. Here is a rundown of the best places:

It is generally agreed that the finest and most delicious coffee in Harvard Square —and the widest selection—is to be had at the **Coffee Connection,** 36 John F. Kennedy St., in the complex called Harvard Square Marketplace, at the corner of Kennedy and Mount Auburn Streets, one block from the MBTA station. Although light meals are served here, such as a breakfast of fresh-squeezed juice, croissant, and coffee ($3.90), or lunch/supper dishes of quiche, salad, soup, yogurt, and the like, the star of the show is the coffee. Why is it so different here? Because the approach to the brew is similar to that taken with fine wine: green (unroasted) coffees are ordered from the finest bean-growing areas of the world, are carefully stored, roasted twice a week, ground, and brewed to bring out the best qualities in each coffee or blend of coffees, right at your table. The different characteristics of the various brews are described in the menu. Note that some coffees are very strong and hearty, others are smooth and mild—but the flavor in both is delicate, well rounded, and delicious. The cheapest way to have good coffee here is to order the coffee of the day, at $1.25; cappuccino and other coffee specialty drinks go up to $3.50. Black and herbal teas are also available. Surroundings here are modern and attractive, light and airy, with a raised sitting area and a nearby counter where coffee beans and teas can be bought in bulk to take home. By the way, there's an entrance to the building at the corner of Dunster and Mount Auburn Streets as well.

Harvard Square's most obvious café is **Au Bon Pain,** 1360 Massachusetts Ave. (tel. 491-1523), in the Holyoke Center building next to the Cambridge Savings Bank. In summer the little square in front of the café is filled with tables and chairs; in winter you can see all the tasty croissants, baguette sandwiches, and pastries through the huge plate-glass windows. Buy your breakfast, lunch, or supper at the counter, and then find an unoccupied table. Croissants cost $1.25 (plain) to $3 (ham and cheese). Sandwiches such as roast beef or brie cost under $5.

Another coffeehouse in the square to feature live entertainment is **Passim,** 47 Palmer St. (an alley running between the two buildings of the Harvard Coop). You can stop into Passim for a cup of coffee (varieties priced from $1.25 to $3), pie, cake, or a cheese sampler as a light lunch for about $8. Spend some time at the small gallery which displays the work of local artists, or look for a bauble among the glass cases of interesting objets d'art from all over the world which are on sale here. But the big attraction at Passim is undoubtedly the evening performances by folk, blues, and jazz musicians of greater or lesser fame. Passim opens for business at noon, and shows begin somewhere around 7:30 p.m. Call 492-7679 for more information.

The crowd at **Algiers,** 40 Brattle St., in the complex of shops called Truc under the Brattle Theater, is usually lively and unorthodox, bright-eyed and interesting. The two subterranean rooms are often full, and when the weather's nice there's service at a tiny outdoor area along a passage at the side of the theater. Many people come just for coffee and conversation, or to meet new people. Lunches tend to the Arabic, of course: a selection of sandwiches made up with flat Arab bread is offered at $4 to $6 apiece, and there are soups, iced drinks, and desserts as well. Coffee costs $1.50 (espresso) to $2.10 (mocha espresso with whipped cream), and is served from 8 a.m. to 12:30 a.m. The morning hours make Algiers the place to come for a midmorning cup of coffee and a break to read the newspaper or to plan the day's activities. Enter either by a door and stairway to the left of the Brattle Theater entrance or through the theater entrance itself: from the vestibule of the theater, another stairway descends to the Truc complex, and the Algiers.

It is said that Longfellow, who lived only six blocks away, wrote his famous poem about a Cambridge blacksmith whose shop was on Brattle Street: "Under the spreading chestnut tree/The village smithy stands/The smith, a mighty man is he,/With large and sinewy hands." The spot the smithy occupied is now taken by the **Blacksmith House,** 56 Brattle St., a café and bakery. In summer the large terrace in front of the house is set with tables; in winter the coffee lovers have to settle for a nice upstairs room in the house furnished with small wood tables and spindle-back chairs. Coffee costs 90¢ (free refill), but the stars of the show are the German- and Austrian-style pastries such as Wiener torte, Sacher torte, Mozart torte, Linzer torte, apple torte, each one $2.95 a slice. Other types of *kuchen,* and also brioche and croissants, are made daily too. The Blacksmith House does as big a business selling cakes and pastries to go as it does selling coffee to stay.

Harvard Square's wooliest of intellectual coffeehouses is the **Café Pamplona,** at 12 Bow St., five short blocks east from the MBTA station along Massachusetts Avenue. Nothing disturbs the current of conversation here, for there's no telephone, no music, no live entertainment. Various kinds of coffee are served ($1 to $2.75), from the inexpensive espresso to the mocha, a rich coffee-and-chocolate topped with real whipped cream. Most coffees start from a very dark-roast bean, and are therefore quite strong. From 11 a.m. to 3 p.m., gazpacho, toasted sandwiches, and other light lunch items are prepared, and in summer the tiny terrace beside the Pamplona's entrance stairway is furnished with tables, chairs, and umbrellas (the indoor café is in a basement). In winter the atmosphere is that of a group of high-brow troglodytes, and invariably the table next to yours will be occupied by someone writing a poem, or music, or translating some abstruse language. The Pamplona is tiny, and you may have to wait for a seat. It's open from 11 a.m. (from 2 p.m. on Sunday) to midnight or 1 a.m.

ICE CREAM: From a short study of Harvard Square shops, it might appear that the two most valued commodities hereabouts are the Xerox copy and the ice cream cone. Ice cream, at $1.65 to $2.25 for a "small" (actually, huge) cone, is almost a cult object in Cambridge, and the virtues of the various shops and their selections of flavors are a frequent topic of debate, and even fierce loyalty. The eating of ice cream is by no means limited to the summer months, and in fact only one or two people thought it unusual that cones should be seen along Massachusetts Avenue during the bitter days of the winter of 1976–1977. Herewith, a guide for the discriminating cone-oisseur:

Once upon a time, a local fellow decided to open an ice cream parlor that served only ice cream made from cream and things like vanilla beans, fruits, and other natural ingredients. He set up shop in Somerville, and the lines of passionate devotees soon stretched around the block.

That's the legend behind the legendary Steve Herrell, founder of Steve's Ice Cream. He later sold the business and retired to the mountains for a breather, but then returned to franchise a new line of stores called **Herrell's,** with one at 15 Dunster St. (tel. 497-2179), along similar lines. Just around the corner from the Cambridge Savings Bank in Harvard Square, Herrell's is the ultimate of local ice cream shops. It's located in a former bank building, and you can devour your cone or dish in the vault, now walled with mirrors. Flavors change somewhat from day to day, and all cost the same. Take special note of Chocolate Pudding, a supercharged chocolate ice cream so rich you won't believe it. Herrell's is open until 1 a.m. on Friday and Saturday during the summer months.

As for **Steve's Ice Cream,** at 31 Church St. (tel. 497-1067), it is now famous from coast to coast, still producing top-quality treats, still attracting hordes of faithful devotees. The Harvard Square location has been added to the original shop at 191 Elm St. (Davis Square) in neighboring Somerville. The solution to unhappiness on any hot summer day is a cone from Steve's; winter days too, for that matter.

Another challenger to come into the field in a large way is **Baskin-Robbins,** 1230 Massachusetts Ave. at the corner of Bow Street and Massachusetts Avenue, several blocks east along Massachusetts Avenue from Harvard Square proper. Thirty-one flavors are sold. They'll make you an ice cream cake, sundaes, shakes, banana splits, freezes, and ice cream sandwiches.

WHAT TO SEE AND DO: Harvard Square is the heartbeat of Cambridge, a place where all styles of life commingle in a wild, busy carnival atmosphere. When you arrive at Harvard subway station on your Red Line train from Boston, you'll walk up the station's dingy stairs and out into a funky and fertile world right at the center of America's most staid and most prestigious institution of higher learning.

Harvard

The first college founded in the British colonies, Harvard was established in 1636 by the Great and General Court of Massachusetts Bay, the colonists' assembly. John Harvard, a clergyman, gave his library and a sum of money to the fledgling college, a generous gesture which has earned for his name worldwide fame. From that early beginning Harvard College grew into Harvard University, a huge educational establishment with an endowment of over $4.2 billion.

The university sponsors tours of its most historic sections during the summer, and during the school year when school is in session (that is, no tours during Christmas recess, spring vacation, etc.). Most of the tours depart from the **Harvard University Information Center,** 1350 Massachusetts Ave., in the Holyoke Center building, the tallest building in the square. During the months when school is in session, tours depart Monday to Friday at 11 a.m. and 3 p.m. from Byerly Hall, across Garden Street from Cambridge Common, in the Radcliffe Yard. Additionally, both the University Admissions Office and Information Center conduct tours daily. Saturday tours leave from the Information Center at 2 p.m. Summer tours are at 10 a.m. and 2 p.m. Monday through Saturday, all from the Information Center. The tours last about one hour and are free.

Harvard University Museums of Natural History

On Oxford Street, this is the largest and most varied of the museums at Harvard. To get there, ask your way to the Science Center and Memorial Hall, then walk between these buildings to get to Oxford Street; walk north on Oxford, and the third building on your right is the University Museum, identified by a sign. Actually, the huge and rambling building houses four museums in one. Here are the high points of each:

Botanical Museum: The world-famous collection of glass flowers is the big attraction here. The incredibly delicate and detailed glass replicas of flowers which grow all over the world were made in the days before color photography allowed a botanist to make teaching aids easily and cheaply with only a camera. The variety of "flowers" on view and the craftsmanship that it took to make them are truly amazing.

The Botanical Museum has other displays and dioramas on the stair landing as you enter the University Museum. These change from time to time, but may include such things as an exhibit of cross-breeding in the cultivation of corn, or the various narcotic substances used by primitive peoples in different parts of the world.

Museum of Comparative Zoology: Despite its forbidding name, this museum is a favorite with children, for it's loaded with stuffed animals of all kinds, from a tiny hummingbird to a towering giraffe. Sharks, ostriches, hippopotami, and zebras abound, as do the exotic beasts from exotic places: tapirs, lemurs, quetzals, and aardvarks. The museum is a product of that 19th-century rage for natural history which sent Harvard men all over the world in search of specimens to use in scientific teaching. Don't miss the full-size whale skeletons, in the same high-ceilinged room that houses the giraffe.

Peabody Museum of Archeology and Ethnology: The collection is very impressive indeed. Statues (authentic as well as fiberglass copies) from the Indian civilizations of Central and South America are accented by wall-size photographs of jungle scenes. Copies of the giant stelae and zoomorphs from Quirigua, Guatemala, and Copan, Honduras, dominate the exhibit, but some of the most interesting arti-

HARVARD SQUARE AREA

facts are the items of gold jewelry and household artifacts in the glassed-in wall displays. Notes and extracts from diaries posted here and there give you an idea of what it was like being one of the first archeologists to discover and study these fascinating works of art.

Although the Central American display is the grandest, the Peabody has several other displays—on China, the American Southwest, Polynesia—which are worth seeing. At this writing, the museum is undergoing renovation, so some exhibits may be closed.

By the way, the Peabody Museum Shop is one of Cambridge's most fascinating places. Handcrafts and folk art from all over the world are on display and on sale, at reasonable prices. Don't miss a look through, at least.

Geological and Mineralogical Museum: This museum, one of the four scientific museums located in the University Museum building, houses an internationally important collection of rocks, minerals, ores, and meteorites. Exhibits include an unusually comprehensive systematic mineral collection, minerals from New England, gems, and meteorites.

All of the different museums in the University Museum (tel. 495-1910) are open from 9 a.m. to 4:30 p.m. Monday through Saturday, and 1 to 4:30 p.m. on Sunday. Admission is $2 for adults, 50¢ for children 5 to 15.

Harvard Art Museums

Harvard University has three major art museums: the Busch-Reisinger, the Fogg, and the Arthur M. Sackler. All three are on Quincy Street, all are open from 10 a.m. to 5 p.m. every day except Monday; closed on Monday and major holidays. If you visit the museums on Saturday morning, admission is free. Otherwise you pay $3 ($1.50 for students and seniors) for a ticket which admits you to all three museums on that day. Kids up to 18 get in anytime for free. You can get recorded information on current offerings by dialing 495-9400.

The **Busch-Reisinger Museum** (tel. 495-9400) of central and northern European art used to be housed in Adolphus Busch Hall, a little Teutonic gem of a building complete with clock tower, just north of Memorial Hall, at the corner of Quincy and Kirkland Streets. However, as of this writing a brand-new museum, Berner Otto Hall, is being constructed adjoining the Fogg Art Museum (see below), with completion foreseen by 1992. Adolphus Busch Hall is open occasionally while it undergoes restoration. It continues as a gallery for medieval sculpture, plaster casts, and architectural fragments. The museum's famous Flentrop organ will remain in the building's Romanesque Hall, as will the full-size replica of the "Golden Gate," or main portal, of the cathedral of Freiburg, but the collections of the Busch-Reisinger Museum will be moved to the new building.

While the new museum building is under construction, major works from the Busch-Reisinger collection will be on view in a special gallery in the Fogg. Go here to see the museum's famous works by Kokoschka, Klimt, Kandinsky, Klee, Max Beckmann, and others.

The **Fogg Art Museum** ranks as one of the more important collections of painting and sculpture in the Boston area. Founded in 1891, the Fogg has long served as the center of art study at Harvard. The Fogg is on Quincy Street between Harvard Street and Broadway, east of Harvard Yard. As you enter, the mood for your visit to the galleries is set by the interior court, copied in Italian Travertine from an Italian building. Sometimes exhibits are set up in the court; during the academic year concerts are given here most Tuesday afternoons—ask at the desk for a schedule. The museum's permanent collections include a fine collection of English silver, drawings, photographs; Italian, Dutch, and American art; and 19th- and 20th-century Parisian art. Shows of other works from the museum's holdings are set up periodically, and are very well done.

The **Arthur M. Sackler Museum** is Harvard's newest art museum, opened late in 1985. Housed here are the university's collections of ancient, Oriental, and Islamic art, including the world's most extensive collection of ancient Chinese jades, plus important collections of Persian miniatures and Japanese prints.

A Walking Tour

The Cambridge Historical Commission and Cambridge Discovery put out a fine little brochure called the *Old Cambridge Walking Guide*, available for $1 from **Cambridge Discovery** (tel. 491-6278), which operates the information booth in Harvard Square. The brochure has a map and a description of the 30 sights and buildings to be seen along the walk, each marked with a sign giving the place's name and the number corresponding to that in the brochure. You could walk through the tour route in about an hour if you didn't stop to look closely at any one place, but it's best to plan at least a few hours, for you'll want to visit some of the buildings.

The Longfellow House

Those interested in 19th-century Cambridge will want to see this house at 105 Brattle St., which is now a National Historic Site (open from 10 a.m. to 4:30 p.m. daily, $2 admission; kids 16 and under, free). Although the house was built by one Maj. John Vassall in 1759, and was for a time Washington's headquarters (he and Martha celebrated their 17th wedding anniversary here), most of the furnishings are left from the time of Longfellow. Henry Wadsworth Longfellow lived here for 45 years, first as a boarder—the house had by this time been turned into a boarding house—and then as its master. Soon after he and Fanny Appleton were married, Fanny's father bought the house for the young married couple. From 1837, when Longfellow moved in as a boarder, until his death in 1882, this was his home. Virtually all of his belongings and furnishings are still here, as he left them when he died, for the house was occupied by his descendants until the early 1970s. It's an elegant and beautiful house, and yet still warm and homey, a treat to walk through. The National Park Service guides who take you through are friendly and very knowledgeable.

Longfellow House sponsors a concert series in the summer months. Concerts are held every two weeks on Sunday afternoons on the lawn, and are free and open to the public. Other special events include the annual February birthday anniversary celebration, and the annual Christmas open house. For exact information on dates, times, and programs, call 876-4491.

Theater

Touchstone of theater in Cambridge is Harvard's **Loeb Drama Center,** 64 Brattle St., corner of Hilliard (tel. 547-8300), home of the American Repertory Theater. This resident professional company performs a variety of works year round in a rotating repertory. For six weeks in the autumn and spring, the ART steps aside as Harvard/Radcliffe undergraduates take the stage.

The **Tufts Arena Theater** (tel. 381-3493), on the Tufts University campus in Medford, has lots and lots of plays both winter and summer. From Harvard Square, take a no. 96 ("Medford Square") bus, and get off at Talbot Avenue; walk up Talbot about a block, and the theater is on the left, behind the chemistry building.

The other outstanding college theater in the area is not really in either Cambridge or Boston. It's the **Spingold Theater** (tel. 894-4343), on the campus of Brandeis University in suburban Waltham. It's best to have a car for this one, as it's a long haul by public transport unless you catch the MBTA Commuter Rail train from North Station in Boston or Porter Square in Cambridge to Roberts Station/Brandeis University.

Cinema

Although Boston has a lively movie nightlife, Cambridge has its own group of theaters, many of which tend to be slightly more "far out" than some of the mass-market houses downtown. If you're staying in Boston but want to go to a cinema in

Cambridge, the Red Line to Central (for Central Square) or Harvard (for Harvard Square) will take you within an easy walk of the house you're looking for. Here are Cambridge's major film houses:

Brattle Theater, 40 Brattle St. (tel. 876-6837), one longish block from the Harvard subway station, specializes in nostalgia and American and foreign classics.

Central, 425 Massachusetts Ave. near Central Square (tel. 864-0426), features a mixed bag for the MIT clientele so near at hand.

Janus, 57 John F. Kennedy St. (tel. 661-3737), two blocks from the Harvard subway station down toward the river, usually has one of the hotter big films of the season, playing to a packed house until it gives out (the film, not the house).

Harvard Square, 10 Church St. (tel. 864-4580), is right in the square. The most popular films with the college crowd that have been released in the past few years are repeated at intervals of a few weeks; this is where you go to see it if you missed it two or three years ago, or didn't want to pay the high price when it was a hit. Seats are low-priced, especially before 6 p.m. (call for exact times). There are also two other auditoriums for first-run showings.

Free Films: Get hold of a copy of the Harvard *Gazette* (free) from the Harvard University Information Office (tel. 495-1000), Holyoke Center, just across the street from the subway station in Harvard Square. The *Gazette,* published only when Harvard is in its fall and spring semesters, lists all the university activities, including quite a few films for free or for a very low price.

Jazz Clubs

The big names show up in the plush atmosphere of the **Regattabar** at the Charles Hotel (tel. 864-1200), in the complex called Charles Square, off Eliot and Mount Auburn Streets just steps from Harvard Square. The club has hosted Stephane Grappelli, Ahmad Jamal, the Ritz, and many other big names, at prices ranging from $8 to $20, parking in the hotel's garage included. You can book through CONCERTIX (tel. 617/876-7777) for an additional fee.

---

2. Lexington

Lexington was the home of the first Minutemen to die from British bullets in the Revolutionary War. Although they were not the first Americans to die for their country (victims of the Boston Massacre hold that honor), nor even the first to offer spirited resistance as the Minutemen of Concord did, the eight Lexington Minutemen who fell on Lexington Green served their country well. For without the battle at Lexington, the Concord Minutemen might not have been determined to offer strong resistance to the British force.

Americans in the colonies had always had virtually total control over their own destinies, and so when the government in London tried to levy taxes of which the colonists did not approve, the colonists' anger was aroused. To show who was boss, troops were sent from England and quartered in the homes of the colonists, further stirring up their anger. As it looked more and more that a head-on collision might occur, the colonists, led by Samuel Adams and John Hancock, began stockpiling arms and ammunition, especially cannons. Hearing rumors of these stockpiles, General Gage, the British commander in Boston, prepared to send out a body of troops to scour the countryside and destroy the stockpiles so as to nip any armed resistance to London in the bud. But the colonists' spy network found out about the plan, and as the troops mustered late at night in preparation for the expedition, Paul Revere and William Dawes galloped through the darkness to alert the patriots.

The "alarm system" was so efficient that the Lexington Minutemen, led by Capt. John Parker, turned out shortly after Revere arrived at midnight, but there were no British troops in sight. The patriots returned home or retired to the

Buckman Tavern near Lexington Green, ready to appear again the minute they heard the sound of the drum.

About daybreak the British column finally arrived in Lexington, and the 100-or-so Minutemen drew themselves up in soldierly order on the Green. Nobody knew what would happen. The Minutemen knew only that a much larger force of some 600 soldiers was coming to search their homes, and although it would have been folly to try to stop them, they could still show that they didn't like it and perhaps worry the British a little; the British soldiers knew only that men with rifles were waiting in a position of defiance to keep the soldiers from doing their duty. When the forces finally came face to face at Lexington Green, officers on both sides seemed to think it would be just as well if everybody kept calm—everybody had a lot to lose—and not to fire a shot. Captain Parker, perhaps fearing capture of his men, ordered them to disperse peaceably; but this only encouraged the British to try and round them up, and some of the soldiers took after the Minutemen. Somehow the running added a sense of alarm to the situation, and a shot rang out. Whether it was a patriot defending himself and his friends, or a British soldier "out to get the rebels" and excited by the chase, the identity of the man who fired the first shot is still a mystery. But other shots followed, of course, and soon eight Minutemen lay dead, and ten others were wounded.

The "battle" was more like a troop riot, and once the British officers regained control of their troops, they started marching them out of town. The Minutemen took their wounded to Buckman Tavern to treat them. It all took less than a half hour. Word was rushed to Concord, where Minutemen assembled for the later events of the day knowing that they might be the next martyrs.

GETTING THERE: The National Park Service has organized most of the interesting historical sites in Lexington and Concord into **Minuteman National Historical Park,** and those with their own car can pick up the Park Service's *Minute Man* brochure which has a sketch map of Battle Road and most of the sights to see. Coming from Boston in a car, take U.S. 3 to Mass. 2, then a road with two route numbers, 4/225, into the center of Lexington. An alternative route subject to tolls is to take the Mass. Pike west to Rte. 128, exiting at Exit 44, "Bedford Street," for Lexington.

Public transportation to Lexington is good, but note that it is not possible to go directly from Lexington to Concord by public transportation. To Lexington, the easiest way is bus 528, "Hanscom Field–Harvard," which leaves Harvard Square on the 45-minute ride every hour during the day, every half hour during rush periods; no night or Sunday service. An alternative route is a commuter train from North Station to Waltham (every 20 minutes during rush hours, every 1¼ hours during the day, every hour in the evening, every two hours or more on weekends), and then bus 525, "Lexington-Waltham," to your destination—buses run every hour during the day, no evening or Sunday service.

WHERE TO STAY: Although Lexington will most likely be a day trip for you, here is a lodging suggestion in case your itinerary indicates a night in the Minutemen's town.

Whether driving or busing, the **Battle Green Motor Inn** is a convenient place to stay, only a few blocks from Lexington Green at 1720 Massachusetts Ave., Lexington, MA 02173 (tel. 617/862-6100, or toll free 800/343-0235, 800/322-1066 in Massachusetts). The 96 units here are modern and comfortable, grouped around a long central court dotted with young trees and potted plants. Rooms have color TV, HBO, and air conditioning, and you can park your car in a covered lot free of charge. Rates are $62 to $65 for a double or queen-size bed (one or two persons), $71 for two beds. From the inn you can easily walk to the Green and to all the historic sites.

WHERE TO DINE: Lexington has a small selection of restaurants, many good for

BOSTON AND ENVIRONS

breakfast or a sandwich. **Brigham's,** about three blocks from the Green on Massachusetts Avenue in the main shopping district, is the local incarnation of the chain that has stores all over Boston and Cambridge. Ice cream, breakfasts, and sandwiches are their forte; either item will be in the $3 to $5 range. **Baskin-Robbins,** an ice cream and sandwich place, has similar values.

The best value in a full restaurant is, believe it or not, Chinese. It's the **Peking Garden,** 27 Waltham St., several doors down from the intersection of Massachusetts Avenue and Waltham Street (tel. 617/862-1051), again right in the main shopping district. The cuisine is Mandarin and Szechuan; the hours are Sunday through Thursday from 11:30 a.m. to 9:30 p.m., on Friday and Saturday to 10:30 p.m.; and the special bonus is the Chinese buffet served Monday through Thursday evening from 6 to 9 p.m.—all you can eat for $9.95 (children under 10, $5.50), and the food is delicious and varied. Two or more can order the Special House Dinner at other times ($10.75 per person), and receive a varied and bounteous selection of dishes. Besides the evening buffet, the Peking Garden hosts a luncheon buffet Monday through Friday from 11:30 a.m. to 2:30 p.m.—all you can eat for an astoundingly low $5. Wine, beer, and drinks are served. Special Mandarin dim sum is served every Saturday and Sunday from 11:30 a.m. to 2 p.m., and prices range from 75¢ to $5.25.

Cory's, 20 Waltham St. (tel. 617/861-7549), is only a few steps from the traffic lights on Massachusetts Avenue. Its colonial decor is the setting for lunch service Monday through Friday and dinner every day of the week. Filling sandwich plates at lunchtime range from $6.50 to $9; full dinners (till 9:30 p.m.) can be had for $30 to $40 for three courses, with drink, tax, and tip included.

WHAT TO SEE: When you approach Battle Green and come up to the Minuteman statue (erected in 1900), you'll feel the great historic significance of the spot. Battle Green is really where it all began: the ivy-covered monument on the southwest part of the green marks the burial spot of seven of the eight Minutemen killed on the memorable day, April 19, 1775. The boulder that sits incongruously on the soft grass of the Green marks the place where the Minutemen drew up in a double rank to face the British grenadiers.

The Lexington Village Green looked much different then than it does today. The meetinghouse, or town church, was located near where the Minuteman statue stands; as it was mid-April, and the Green was in the center of town traffic, it may have been pretty muddy rather than "green." The best time to visit Lexington's historic sights is, of course, on April 19, when the townfolk reenact the famous confrontation with festivities, musketry drill, and fife-and-drum corps. But any day after April 19, until the end of October, will do instead. Note that most of the happenings and places mentioned below are closed November 1 and April 18.

First thing to do is to go to the **Chamber of Commerce Visitors' Center,** 1875 Massachusetts Ave. (tel. 617/862-1450), just off the Green near the Minuteman statue and next door to Buckman Tavern. Here, every day between the hours of 9 a.m. and 5 p.m. (10 a.m. and 4 p.m. in winter), you can pick up a sketch map of the town, and brochures and information on the sights. More important, you can inspect the diorama, or scale model, of the Battle Green and the events of April 19, 1775: the Minutemen in their farmers' clothes scattering before the long files of crack troops dressed in brilliant colors. The diorama is well worth seeing (it's free, too); historical accounts and explanations of the battle accompany the display.

Besides the Battle Green, several early buildings figured significantly in the battle, and they are today maintained by the Lexington Historical Society, P.O. Box 514, Lexington, MA 02173 (tel. 617/861-0928). All three are open mid-April through October 31, and each tour costs $2 for adults, 50¢ for children 6 to 16 (children under 6 enter for free); an adult combination ticket good for all three houses is on sale at Buckman Tavern gift shop for $4.50.

Of the houses, **Buckman Tavern** (1709) is the most important. Here, in the taproom, many of the Minutemen waited out the time between that first midnight call to muster and the final arrival of the British forces at daybreak. After the battle, the wounded were brought here and laid out on the tables for treatment. The tours are given by young ladies well versed in their subject, which encompasses not only the events of the battle, but ranges much more widely, covering a great number of topics on life in the colonies at the time of the Revolution. They'll tell you about the construction of the tavern, about the people who came there to stay, or to have a drink, or for a reception or tea; what and how they ate and drank, how they cooked, slept, and kept warm in unheated rooms. The tavern has an excellent collection of utensils, tools, and implements from the period, "time- and labor-saving devices" which show a good deal of Yankee ingenuity. The tour is well worth the price of admission. The tavern is located opposite the Common, has a gift shop, and is open from 10 a.m. to 5 p.m. daily except Sunday, when the hours are 1 to 5 p.m.; in high summer, the hours are extended to 8 p.m.

The **Munroe Tavern** (1695) was to the British what Buckman Tavern was to the Colonials: a headquarters and a place to care for the wounded after the battle. Today it's furnished with antiques and battle mementoes, and is open to the public on the same basis as Buckman Tavern. It's a walk (or a short drive) from Battle Green, southeast along Massachusetts Avenue at no. 1332, about seven blocks; the tavern will be on your right.

The third significant house is the **Hancock-Clarke House** (1698), which was the parsonage of the Rev. Jonas Clarke at the time of the battle, and it was with Clarke that John Hancock and Sam Adams, the two "rabble-rousers" most wanted by the British authorities, hid themselves during the uncertain days before the battle. Clarke's house was the first place Paul Revere headed for when he heard of the British plan to march out into the countryside. Revere actually came to Clarke's house twice to warn Adams and Hancock: on April 15, just after hearing that the British were about to do something, and again on April 18, the night the British troops moved out. Hancock-Clarke House is open at the same times and with the same admission fees as Buckman Tavern. It's located at 36 Hancock St., only about a block north of Battle Green.

Several other sights in Lexington are worth a look. Gravestone-rubbers will want to head for **Ye Olde Burying Ground,** just off Battle Green by the church, on its western side. The oldest stone dates from 1690. Another way to get into the spirit of the day of battle is to visit **Cary Memorial Hall,** several blocks southeast of the Green along Massachusetts Avenue, between the town offices and the police station. Here you can see Sandham's famous painting *The Battle of Lexington,* and also statues of John Hancock and Samuel Adams.

Lexington has an ultramodern gallery for historical displays of Americana, the **Museum of Our National Heritage.** Built by the Scottish Rite Masons in 1975, there are four galleries exhibiting photograph collections, documents, artifacts, and works of art and industry. Lectures and films are scheduled frequently as well, and many deal with anything from Benjamin Franklin or early racing cars to early maps of the New World. Call for current offerings and details. The museum is at 33 Marrett Rd. (tel. 617/861-6559), near the intersection of Rtes. 2A and 4/225, a short way from the center of Lexington on the road to Boston. It's open Monday through Saturday from 10 a.m. to 5 p.m., on Sunday from noon to 5 p.m. Admission and parking are free.

3. Concord

Concord today is a Boston suburb. It is a beautiful town filled with tall, old trees, graceful houses and mansions, and a rich history that goes beyond the events of the Revolution. Besides the historical sites encompassed by Minuteman National

Historical Park, Concord offers a look at the lives and times of America's great 19th-century writers and philosophers: Emerson, Thoreau, Hawthorne, and Louisa May and Bronson Alcott.

GETTING THERE: Those with their own cars should come via Lexington along Rte. 2A, following the signs reading "Battle Road." Along this route passed the British troops going out to Concord to search for arms stockpiled illegally by the colonials. A Visitors' Center has been set up a short distance past the intersection of Rtes. 2A and 128, and this is the place to get a map and brochure of Battle Road.

By public transportation, there's no way to go along Battle Road unless you're in a sightseeing tour bus. But train service between Boston and Concord is quite good.

By Train

On weekdays, 20 trains a day leave Boston's North Station for the 40-minute trip to Concord, and on Saturday there are 12 trains; on Sunday, 8. The train can also be boarded at Porter Square in Cambridge (go north on Massachusetts Avenue from Harvard Square for about a mile, and the station is next to the shopping center, under the iron bridge). Call 617/722-3200 for the latest detailed schedule information. The train arrives at Concord's Depot, which is about five blocks from Monument Square.

WHERE TO STAY: What there is to see in Concord can be seen in a day, but the town is very fine, and you may want to spend the night.

The nicest place to stay is the **Hawthorne Inn,** 462 Lexington Rd., Concord, MA 01742 (tel. 508/369-5610), directly across the road from "The Wayside," Nathaniel Hawthorne's house. The location, although a mile or two from the town center, is convenient to Orchard House, the Alcotts' home, as well. Single rooms cost $75 to $95, and doubles are $95 to $150, tax and continental breakfast (with home-baked goods and fresh fruit) included. An extra person costs $21. The inn has pleasant gardens with a tiny fountain, and rooms decorated with period pieces, antique beds, original works of art, and nice homey touches like hooked rugs. Only seven rooms here, so reserve early—it's extremely nice.

Right on the town green in Concord is the **Colonial Inn,** 48 Monument Square, Concord, MA 01742 (tel. 508/369-9200). Although the main building of the inn dates back to 1716, and is therefore a smallish, colonial-size hostelry, several new and modern additions have been unobtrusively added, giving the inn a total of 60 rooms. Only 12 original rooms are available to guests, and these are the ones most in demand. If you call or write ahead for reservations, you might ask for one of these, and the manager will do his best to put you in one, but he cannot guarantee any given room to any given guest. Rooms in the main inn, mostly with bath, cost $99 to $121 single or double; in the Prescott Wing, where rooms have bath and individually controlled air conditioning, prices are $110 to $137 single or double for some rooms, more for a suite with parlor. A special weekend rate of $87 is sometimes offered. Housekeeping rooms are also available should you be planning to stay a while.

WHERE TO DINE: Everybody can find a suitable place to have a meal in Concord, no matter what his or her budget.

For my taste, the nicest place to dine in Concord is at **A Different Drummer,** 86 Thoreau St. (tel. 508/369-8700), upstairs in the Concord train depot about five blocks from the town green (Monument Square). The decor is modern, Scandinavian inspired, with primary colors matched by plain white, and accents in smooth-finished wood and rough boards. Lunch is always a good value, while dinner is more elegant and moderately expensive. The daily luncheon specials might include a seafood quiche with salad ($9), or even veal piccata with salad ($10.50). At dinner, feast on freshly shucked clams or oysters for an appetizer, then have sautéed veal marsala perhaps, or scallops, or a steak. With dessert, coffee, tax, and tip, a four-course meal will be about $30 per person. Add a few dollars for wine. A Different Drummer is open every day in summer for lunch and dinner (11:30 a.m. to 3 p.m. and 5 to 9:30 p.m.). On Sunday, brunch replaces lunch, and dinner is served from 4:30 to 8:30 p.m.

WHAT TO SEE: Begin your walk around Concord at the town green, officially called Monument Square, complete with obelisk inscribed "Faithful Unto Death." The little church facing Main Street, **St. Bernard's** (Roman Catholic), is particularly pretty when seen from a short distance down Main Street. Of the other buildings on the green, the most historically noteworthy is the **Wright Tavern** which, being right on the road in from Boston, was one of the first places the British stopped to search for arms. Several shops and firms' offices are located in the tavern today, and you're welcome to walk in and look around during business hours. The **Concord Chamber of Commerce** (tel. 508/369-3120) maintains an office in the basement (enter from Main Street), open from 9 a.m. to noon Monday through Friday; free brochures, information, and maps are available. Another office is a few blocks away on Heywood Street (off Rte. 2A). Also, you can take questions to the front desk of the Colonial Inn.

Minuteman National Historic Park

The park encompasses many of the most important sites having to do with the first Revolutionary War battle at Concord. There's a Visitors Center located in the Buttrick Mansion, north of the center of Concord, on the other side of North Bridge. A large parking lot near North Bridge is often full during the summer, and if you have a good parking spot in town, and a few extra minutes, walk the half mile to the bridge and admire Concord's lovely old houses as you go.

After the events in Lexington, the British officers headed their men quickly off to Concord, afraid—no, certain—that since shots had been fired and men killed, there'd be a great deal more trouble coming. Of course, the Minutemen in Concord knew of the Lexington battle shortly after it happened and long before the British troops arrived at 7 a.m. The Minutemen kept an eye on the British as they entered the town, waiting for whatever was to happen. When a force of Regulars was sent to stand guard over Concord's North Bridge, the Minutemen retreated before them, crossing the bridge and taking up a position on a hilltop nearby, where they awaited reinforcements from nearby towns.

Meanwhile, in Concord a polite and not-too-thorough search was being carried out; some arms were found, in particular a number of gun carriages, which were brought out and burned. The Minutemen saw the smoke, assumed the British were burning the town, and began to advance in revenge. The Regulars retreated across the bridge and began firing at the Minutemen, who fired back and pursued them until they fled. It was here at the North Bridge, then, that the Minutemen fired the "shot heard 'round the world."

Soon afterward the British troops began the return to Boston, but Minutemen kept up a constant sniper fire on them all the way back to Boston, which enraged the Regulars and goaded them to murder some of the innocent persons they met along the way of their march. The bitterness left on both sides by the events of April 19, 1775, would soon bring war to all the British colonies in North America.

Walk across the placid Concord River on the Old North Bridge (a modern reproduction of the kind of bridge which spanned the river in colonial times), and it is easy to imagine, even to half see, the way things happened on the day of the battle. At the far (western) end of the bridge is Daniel Chester French's famous Minuteman statue, the pediment inscribed with Emerson's famous poem. On the near (east) side of the bridge, take a look also at the plaque on the stone wall commemorating the British soldiers who died in the Revolutionary War.

The Old Manse

After visiting the bridge and the Visitor Center on the far side, turn back toward town. Right next to North Bridge, slightly nearer to the center of town, is the Old Manse (tel. 508/369-3909), Concord's most famous house. It was built in 1769 by the Rev. William Emerson and was lived in by his descendants for 169 years, except for a three-year period when young Nathaniel Hawthorne and his bride, Sophia, lived here. Hawthorne's residence here gave him material for several later stories. The house today is filled with the spirit and the mementoes of their short stay, and those of the Emerson clan. Admission costs $3 for adults, $2.50 for seniors, $1.50 for ages 6 to 16, but this includes a guided tour. The Old Manse is open June 1 to October 31 every day except Tuesday and Wednesday from 10 a.m. to 4:30 p.m. (on Sunday and holidays from 1 to 4:30 p.m.). Open weekends only, mid-April to June.

Transcendentalist Associations

Concord was the center of a philosophical and social movement which, although small in scope, had important effects on American thought and literature. Emerson, Thoreau, Bronson Alcott, and others were all friends living in Concord during the period from about 1836 to 1860. They were aware of the philosophical upheaval going on in Europe at this time, and were encouraged to break away from the Unitarianism that had been their belief. Although they never published a manifesto detailing their beliefs, their creed at this time was that each man has a part of God within himself, and by being sensitive to the dictates of that part, can do what is good and right. Nature had a large share in this belief as well, for the Transcendentalists thought true harmony in life could only be achieved by communing closely with nature and coming to understand it. This, perhaps, was the basis for Thoreau's period of retreat at Walden Pond.

The Transcendentalists got together and tried out their beliefs by buying a farm and living with nature there (1841–1847). The Brook Farm experiment, although it failed, has been an example down to our own times. (The farm was in West Roxbury, now a posh suburb of Boston.) Hawthorne lived on Brook Farm for a while, and he and his friend, Herman Melville, were both affected by Transcendentalism.

The best way to learn about the Transcendentalist movement is to read Ralph Waldo Emerson's works. While you're here in Concord, you can visit his house and those in which other adherents of the movement lived, and also go out to Walden Pond and see the place where Thoreau's famous cabin stood. Here, then, are the sights of Transcendentalist Concord:

On your way back from the Old Manse, by Old North Bridge, take a detour up the hill, east off Monument Street before you reach the town green, to get to **Sleepy Hollow Cemetery.** Author's Ridge, on top of the hill, has the graves of Hawthorne, Thoreau, the Alcotts, and Emerson. Emerson's grave, you'll notice, is marked by a great uncarved boulder, very natural and without religious symbolism.

Starting from the town green, most of the Transcendentalists' homes are east along the Lexington Road (Rte. 2A); Thoreau sites and memorabilia are, appropriately, off by themselves, in another direction.

The **House of Ralph Waldo Emerson,** 28 Cambridge Turnpike, is at the intersection of Lexington Road and Cambridge Turnpike, a ten-minute walk from the green. The house was a center for meetings of Emerson and his friends, and still contains original furniture and Emerson's memorabilia. It's open Thursday through Saturday from 10 a.m. to 4:30 p.m., on Sunday from 2 to 4:30 p.m., from mid-April through October; open Wednesday also during July and August. Cost is $3 for adults, $1.50 for children 6 to 17 (children under 6, free).

Across the street from Emerson's house is the **Concord Museum** (tel. 508/369-9609), which transports the visitor back in time to the early 17th century, when the town of Concord was founded. The museum contains 15 period rooms and galleries arranged in sequence from the 17th to the mid-19th centuries and vividly depicts the growth and evolution of Concord. The collections of documented decorative arts and domestic artifacts were either owned by Concord-area residents or made by Concord-area craftspeople.

Permanent exhibits include the lantern that hung in the spire of the Old North Church in Boston on the night of Revere's famous ride, Ralph Waldo Emerson's study, Henry David Thoreau's belongings used at Walden Pond, and a collection of early powderhorns including the one worn by the model for Daniel Chester French's Minuteman Statue at the Old North Bridge. There are changing exhibitions in the French gallery throughout the year.

The museum is open year round on weekdays and Saturday from 10 a.m. to 4:30 p.m., and on Sunday from 1 to 4:30 p.m. A guided tour lasts about 45 minutes; phone to arrange a group tour. Admission is $4 for adults, $3 for senior citizens, and $1.50 for children 15 and under.

Continuing east along the Lexington Road, a short drive will bring you to **Orchard House** (tel. 508/369-4118), home of the Alcotts during the period from 1858 to 1877. Bronson Alcott, while he started life as an itinerant gizmo salesman, had as his life's passion the reform of traditional education methods. His open and natural approach to education was not appreciated in cosmopolitan centers like Boston, but was perfectly congenial to transcendentalist Concord. Here he was ultimately commissioned as superintendent of schools, and he opened a "School of Philosophy" in a building in his backyard. The house itself is a must for anyone, especially a child who has read Louisa May Alcott's *Little Women.* It's open early April through October from 10 a.m. to 4:30 p.m. (on Sunday, holidays, and after September 15, from 1 to 4:30 p.m.). Admission (and the requisite tour) costs $3.50 for adults, $3 for senior citizens, and $2 for kids.

The **Wayside,** just a few steps east of Orchard House, is actually the house described by Louisa May Alcott in her famous book, although today most of the furnishings are those of Margaret Sidney, who wrote *Five Little Peppers.* Hawthorne also lived here. You can visit the house Friday through Tuesday (*not* on Wednesday or Thursday) April through October, on a 30-minute guided tour from 10 a.m. to 5:30 p.m. (last tour starts at 5 p.m.). Admission is $2 for adults, free for children under 16. Tours are limited to ten persons.

Sights dealing with Thoreau's life are west and south of Concord's town green. The **Thoreau Lyceum** (tel. 508/369-5912) is a Thoreau "learning center" which includes a library, museum with artifacts dealing with his life, and a replica of Thoreau's Walden cabin. There is also a bookstore carrying old as well as new books by or about Thoreau. It's at 156 Belknap (pronounced *bell*-nap) St., and is open from 10 a.m. to 5 p.m. weekdays, from 2 to 5 p.m. on Sunday; closed on national holidays (on Mondays, January through March). Admission is $2.50 for adults, $1 for students, and 50¢ for those in Grades 1 through 8.

You can visit **Walden Pond,** where Thoreau had his hut from 1845 to 1847, by driving out Walden Street (Rte. 126), which leaves the center of Concord from Main Street near the Green. After crossing Rte. 2, look for signs on the right not far from the intersection; park and walk to the site of his hut, marked by a pile of stones. The path circling the lake provides an interesting and refreshing walk; fires and alcoholic beverages are not permitted at any time. The main parking lot by the public beach costs several dollars per carload in summer; the beach itself is free.

In a Canoe on the Concord River

After you've taken the standard walking tour of Concord, see the town again, adventurously, by renting a canoe for a paddle up the Concord River. The **South Bridge Boat House** (tel. 508/369-9438), west of the center of town at 496–502 Main St. (Rte. 62), will rent you a canoe for $5.70 per hour, $24 per day on weekdays, or $7 per hour, $35 per day on weekends (students get lower rates). In two hours or so you should be able to make your way down to Concord North Bridge and back, depending on the strength of your paddling arms. The grand houses and gardens that grace the riverbanks alternate with patches of field and wild shrubbery to make a serene and lovely landscape. The boathouse is open from the beginning of April into November until the first snowstorm.

A Visit to a Winery

You've heard of Concord grapes, a variety developed here by Ephraim Bull and now used for grape juice and jelly. You might think the **Nashoba Valley Winery,** 100 Wattaquadoc Hill Rd., Bolton, MA 01740 (tel. 508/779-5521), would use Concord grapes. But you're in for a delightful surprise. Nashoba pursues the old New England tradition of making delicious quality wines from fruits other than grapes: apples, peaches, pears, blueberries, cranberries. I can attest that the wines are intriguing, satisfying, and delightful. The tart, dry cranberry-apple goes especially well with Thanksgiving turkey, and the peach (labeled "semi-sweet") is not sugary, but has an exquisite sweet-dryness like good sauterne. Clear your palate and drop in for a free tasting any day of the week, until 6 p.m. Winery tours are conducted on Friday, Saturday, and Sunday from 11 a.m. to 6 p.m.

To get there, find your way to the town of Bolton, just west of I-495 (Exit 27). Take Rte. 117 west to the blinking yellow light in the center of Bolton. Turn left onto Wattaquadoc Hill Road; the winery is a quarter of a mile up the hill, on the left-hand side.

A Side Trip to Longfellow's Wayside Inn

Thirteen miles along the Sudbury Road (which starts from Main Street in Concord) and U.S. 20 West will bring you to the Wayside Inn (1700), South Sudbury, MA 01776 (tel. 508/443-8846). The inn was made famous by Longfellow's poems telling *Tales from a Wayside Inn,* and now boasts of being the oldest operating inn in the country. Bought by Henry Ford in the early 1920s, it is now a private, nonprofit operation, and all proceeds from the guest rooms and restaurant are put toward its upkeep and restoration. The inn has ten rooms with bath and air conditioning (but no radio or TV), eight twins and two doubles, which rent for $58 single, $63 double. Rooms 1 through 8 are of modern construction and traditional decor; rooms 9 and 10 are in the old, original part of the inn, and are very quaint. These two are the most in demand, particularly from April to December. Should you want to stay at the inn, it's wise to make reservations as far in advance as possible, even a month or two; but if you can't make them, call up in any case and see what vacancies they might have.

There was a fire in the inn around 1955 and it was heavily damaged (as you can see in the old kitchen), but restoration work was done well and the rooms are worth seeing even if you don't plan to stay for the night. A short tour of the inn is available for 50¢ per person, for free if you drop in for a meal. Lunch is served from 11:30 a.m. to 3 p.m.; dinner, from 5:30 to 9 p.m.; Sunday dinner, from noon to 8 p.m.

Besides the inn itself, you should explore the grounds and surroundings: the beautiful formal garden near the inn, the reconstructed barn across the road, and the **Grist Mill,** a short (15-minute) walk away, farther down the road. The Grist Mill, a pretty and romantic stone building, is a replica of the mills that used to dot the New England rivers and streams. It is in a beautiful spot, with a copse of pines nearby, and although it's not 100% authentic (the mill wheel is made of heavy-gauge steel), it is worth a look and a walk around. The flour ground here is used in the Wayside Inn's kitchens, and is for sale at the inn's shop. By the way, the Martha-Mary Chapel, on the road between the inn and the Grist Mill, is a typically New England meeting-house which Ford had built to be rented out for weddings. The chapel and the Wayside Inn are very popular with wedding parties and honeymooners.

THE MASSACHUSETTS NORTH SHORE

North of Boston are many of the towns that brought great wealth to the Massachusetts Bay area in the 18th and 19th centuries. Ships from these Essex County towns would sail to China and Africa, and return several years later with cargoes so rich that everyone involved in the voyage became wealthy overnight.

The gracious houses and public buildings constructed during this era are still here to be seen, and Salem's museums hold a treasure of mementoes and artifacts from the maritime boom. Marblehead and Rockport are still important as yacht harbors and excursion points, but all three towns now make their living primarily from the land: as "bedroom" communities for Boston, and as vacation stops for Bostonians and those who come from farther away.

TELEPHONE NOTES: All the North Shore towns covered in this chapter, including Salem, Gloucester, Rockport, and all of Cape Ann, *except Marblehead,* use the 508 area code. Marblehead is part of the Greater Boston calling area, and uses the Greater Boston area code, 617.

---

1. Salem

Think of Salem, think of witches. Although the fame of Salem's witch trials has spread around the world, the town's place in New England history comes from its maritime industries—shipbuilding, warehousing, chandlery, and trade. In the late 1700s, ships from Salem sailed the world, many dealing in trade from the Orient, especially spices, silks, and other luxury goods. The wealth of the Indies brought great prosperity to the town, enabling its citizens to build and decorate fine mansions and impressive museums.

As for the witches, it has never been proved that there were any in Salem! The witch-hunt took place in only one year (1692), and the score of people executed met that fate because they would *not* admit to being witches—many of the less courageous "admitted" being witches so that they wouldn't be executed. The whole affair reached a point of absurdity at which everyone was calling everyone else a witch, and then it fizzled out. Salem would like to forget it all, no doubt, but the rest of the world enjoys remembering this bizarre episode.

Salem today is a pretty town, with many of its old houses (dating back to the 1600s) and 19th-century mansions intact and in good repair. Part of the downtown section has been restored and closed to traffic as a fine pedestrian mall, and more restoration work is in progress. The **Peabody Museum,** the **Custom House** (National Maritime Historic Site), and the **Essex Institute** have brilliant displays of Salem's (and America's) maritime history. And painters, writers, and patrons add an active artistic element to this very cultured city, well worth a day-trip or even an overnight stop.

GETTING THERE: Driving, the best way to Salem (and neighboring Marblehead) is to take the Mystic River Bridge (also called Tobin Bridge) and U.S. 1; when it intersects with Rte. 16, follow 16 toward Revere Bridge and Rte. 1A. Route 1A North becomes Lafayette Street in Salem. (For Marblehead, take Rte. 129 off 1A in Swampscott, and follow it right into Old Town, Marblehead.)

Note: It's only fair to warn you that street and highway signing on the North Shore seems to be particularly bad. Routes are filled with turns, and signs are confusing or missing—you will probably find yourself lost more than once. Resign yourself to stopping and asking the way, not once but several times.

By Bus

Salem is served by MBTA bus 450, which leaves from the parking garage next to Haymarket subway station; the trip, under good traffic conditions, takes 40 minutes. Buses leave every 15 minutes during rush hours, every hour during the day Monday through Saturday, every 90 minutes on Sunday.

By Train

Commuter trains run from Boston's North Station to Salem, Beverly, Gloucester, and Rockport. The trip to Salem takes about 30 minutes; trains run about every 20 minutes during rush hours, every half hour during the day, every hour at night and on weekends. Call, toll free, 800/392-6099 for schedules.

Tourist Information

The **Salem Chamber of Commerce** (tel. 508/744-0004) maintains several information booths around the city. The main one is in Riley Plaza, near the station for commuter trains from Boston, open Monday through Saturday from 9 a.m. to 5 p.m., on Sunday from noon to 5 p.m. The National Park Service maintains a **Visitor Information Center** in the Central Wharf Warehouse on Derby Wharf, in the Salem Maritime National Historic Site. This is open every day from 10 a.m. to 4:30 p.m. Derby Wharf is just east of Pickering Wharf.

WHERE TO STAY: Luckily for travelers wanting to spend a night in Salem, the town has several excellent, moderately priced hotels right in the center of town.

The **Salem Inn,** 7 Summer St., Salem, MA 01970 (tel. 508/741-0680), is on Summer Street near the intersection with Essex Street, only a half block from the Witch House and two blocks from the Peabody Museum. It's a lovely old restored brick mansion with 23 nice-size, beautiful, and comfortable rooms priced at $75 to $85 double, or $90 to $95 for a two-room suite with kitchenette; an extra person pays $10 per night. Rooms have queen- or king-size beds, antique fireplaces, and telephones. The price differential for rooms depends on plumbing: all rooms have private bathrooms, but the baths for the less expensive rooms are across the hallway from the room itself.

The **Hawthorne Hotel,** "on the Common," 18 Washington Square West, Salem, MA 01970 (tel. 508/744-4080 or toll free 800/833-2008), at the corner of Essex Street and Hawthorne Boulevard, is easy walking distance to all the sights in town. It's a good-size hotel, restored with lots of fine wood paneling, brass chandeliers, and new paint. The lobby and public rooms (including the Tavern and the restaurant, called Nathaniel's) use these elements to achieve a simple but very elegant decor; it's echoed in the rooms with the use of smaller brass chandeliers and wing-back chairs, but otherwise the rooms are modern and decorated in solid colors to keep them bright and cheerful. Rates are moderate: $87 to $140 single or double, suites for $180; $20 for each additional person; children under 12 free in their parents' room. In the restaurant (open for breakfast, lunch, and dinner daily), luncheon plates cost about $8 to $12, dinner, about $30 to $40. The hotel serves the traditional Sunday brunch until 2:30 p.m.; there's live entertainment in the Tavern Friday and Saturday from 9 p.m.

Guesthouses

Other than these, Salem has several guesthouses charging somewhat less than the inns, but without the inns' central location. One is located on Lafayette Street, three-quarters of a mile from the center of town. The **Coach House Inn,** 284 Lafayette St., Salem, MA 01970 (tel. 508/744-4092), has rooms decorated in 19th-century style. Doubles here range from $60 to $82, the higher prices being for rooms with baths.

For those who are traveling in a group of four or six, this place is especially ideal, though not to the exclusion of smaller parties. The **Stephen Daniels House,** 1 Daniels St., Salem, MA 01970 (tel. 508/744-5709), was built in 1667, with a wing added in 1756. It is owned today by Mrs. Katherine Gill, who has furnished it in antiques of the period and virtually turned it into a time machine which takes you back to the Salem of witch-hunting and sea-captain days. Canopied four-poster beds, walk-in fireplaces hung with pots and kettles, low beamed ceilings, and a delightful little terrace garden make it a real showpiece. Prices for the rooms are $60 to $82 single, $88 to $93 double, or $137 (if you show Mrs. Gill this guidebook) for four in the two adjoining rooms. All rooms have private bath, and continental breakfast is included. Be sure to call or write ahead for reservations.

WHERE TO DINE: Salem has lots of interesting restaurants, large and small. The **Lyceum,** 43 Church St., near the corner of Church and Washington (tel. 508/745-7665), manages to be both large and small at once. The building, as its name implies, was once at the center of the city's cultural life, and Alexander Graham Bell, who once lived in Salem, gave the first public demonstration of the telephone in its halls. Today the various halls and chambers are all part of the restaurant, but each has been given a distinctive character, and so the Lyceum seems more a collection of restaurants than one large one. In the main room downstairs (to the left as you enter), the menu is continental, with local seafood; the variety of dishes available borders on profusion: steamed mussels, baked brie, onion soup, veal marsala, roast duckling, fettuccine, frogs' legs, and beef Wellington. Dinner here will cost $28 to $40 per person. Sunday brunch (10 a.m. to 3 p.m.) is a buffet which has its own special menu.

In the Pub, the menu includes the dining room's main courses, as well as lots of lighter fare. In good weather, find your way to the terrace out back in the courtyard.

For Waterfront Dining

The **Chase House,** on Pickering Wharf (tel. 508/744-0000), offers lunch and dinner from 11:30 a.m. to 11 p.m. Wednesday through Saturday, and until 10 p.m. Sunday through Tuesday, in summer. All the air-conditioned dining rooms share a nautical motif and a view of the waterfront activity; a nice protected outdoor deck is good for cocktails and light meals. Seafood is the heavy on the Chase's menu, as one might expect. At lunch a filet of fish is $7.50, and I would figure you'd spend $12 to $15 for the full meal. Dinner is fancier, and the oysters, scallops, lobster, and varieties of fish will probably tempt you to spend $20 to $28 per person. Kids and seniors get a price cut on some items.

WHAT TO SEE: A number of houses in Salem have been preserved from the 1600s, and are furnished with antiques and open to public view. But before you visit them, go to the **Salem Witch Museum,** 19½ Washington Square North (tel. 508/744-1692), next to Salem Common at the intersection of Brown Street, Hawthorne Boulevard, and Washington Square North. The Witch Museum is not really a museum—there are no artifacts on display—but rather a sound-and-light show relating the history of the infamous witch trials of 1692. It's open seven days a week from 10 a.m. to 5 p.m. (to 7 p.m. in July and August). Admission is $3 for adults, $2.50 for seniors, $1.75 for kids 6 to 14, free for kids 5 and under. Shows every 30 minutes.

17th-Century Houses

Visit one or more of these, as you have the time, to see what life was like in one of the earliest towns in the United States.

Witch House (tel. 508/744-0180), the home of Magistrate Jonathan Corwin, the judge in many of the witch trials, stands at 310½ Essex St., corner of Essex and North Streets, and is open July 1 through Labor Day from 10 a.m. to 6 p.m. daily; the rest of the year it is open until 4:30 p.m. Adults pay $3; children 5 to 16 years, $1.50.

The House of the Seven Gables, 54 Turner St. (tel. 508/744-0991), which served as the setting for Hawthorne's novel of the same name, is the centerpiece of a historic site with period gardens on Salem Harbor. The four sites—House of the Seven Gables (1668), Hooper-Hathaway House (1682), Hawthorne's Birthplace (c. 1750), and Retire Becket House (1655)—are open July 1 through Labor Day from 9:30 a.m. to 5:30 p.m. Guided tours of the Gables and Hawthorne's Birthplace cost $5 for adults, $2.50 for those 6 to 17 years old. During the rest of the year you can visit the House of the Seven Gables from 10 a.m. to 4:30 p.m. daily (the Garden Coffee Shop is open from May to October). Ample free parking.

The Essex Institute

The institute is a museum and historical society dedicated to the preservation, study, and exhibition of historical works and artifacts dealing with Essex County. The collection of artifacts ranges from rare early newspapers to entire houses, restored and furnished with authentic antiques. Just about anyone who comes to Salem finds something of interest here: the historian of American trade and culture uses the library, nautical buffs want to see the relics of the China trade, those interested in architecture and decoration take the tour through one or more of the institute's half-dozen Salem houses which date as far back as 1684. Children are fascinated by the unique collection of dolls, doll furniture, and toys from earlier times.

There's a lot more here than one can see on a day-trip to Salem, but an hour spent in one of the institute's 13 buildings, particularly in the main building at 132–134 Essex St. (tel. 508/744-3390) and the adjoining houses, is a must for any Salem visitor. Here is a list of some of the special collections you can look over: clocks, ceramics, military uniforms and weapons, dolls and toys, glassware, buttons, silver and pewter, lamps and lanterns, sculpture, tools, costumes from earlier centuries, and bits and pieces from the China trade, as well as a very good collection of Massachusetts works of art including paintings and furniture. Several galleries and exhibition rooms have changing shows, so the return visitor should check to see what's new.

The Essex Institute is open in winter on Tuesday through Saturday from 9 a.m. to 5 p.m. (November 1 to May 31), on Sunday and holidays from 1 to 5 p.m. From June 1 to October 31 the Institute is open on Monday also. Admission for adults to the museum and library is $3, and $2 to each of the institute's houses; children from 6 to 16 get into the museum for $1.50 and into the houses for $1, seniors for a slight discount. A combination ticket, good for all the buildings, can be bought at $5 for adults, $4 for seniors, $2.50 for children.

Peabody Museum

When a group of Salem sea captains and world travelers formed the East India Marine Society in 1799, their charter included provisions for "a museum in which to house the natural and artificial curiosities" brought back from their worldwide travels. This was the genesis of the Peabody Museum, America's oldest museum in continuous operation.

In 1824 the society and its collections moved to grand new headquarters in East India Marine Hall. Since then, four annexes have been added. The most recent, a bright and modern climate-controlled wing, was opened in 1976 and is used primarily for special temporary exhibitions. The Peabody has a research library and a photograph library of one *million* pictures.

The museum's major collections are in New England maritime history; the practical arts and crafts of the East Asian, Pacific Islands, and Native American peoples; and the natural history of Essex County. Maritime collections include portraits of captains, pictures of ships, scale models, figureheads, old navigation instruments and tools, scrimshaw, prints, and gear from the whaling era, plus porcelain, paintings, furniture, and silver from Salem's China trade. There's even a reproduction of the saloon (main cabin) of America's first ocean-going yacht, *Cleopatra's Barge,* built in 1816 by a member of the East India Marine Society. The Ethnology Department has superb collections of objects from everyday life in primitive Polynesia, Micronesia, and Melanesia. A similar collection from pre-industrial Japan is rated the best in the world.

The Peabody charges adults $3 for admission, half price for children 6 to 16, $2 for senior citizens and students with an ID card. It's open daily from 10 a.m. to 5 p.m., on Sunday from 1 to 5 p.m., with a free guided tour at 2 p.m. daily. Look for the Peabody on the Essex Street pedestrian mall, at the corner of Liberty Street.

Salem Maritime National Historic Site

In 1937 the National Park Service took over the **Custom House** (tel. 508/ 744-4323), where Nathaniel Hawthorne once worked, and nearby Derby Wharf, one of the city's busiest trade centers, as a basis for the Maritime Site. First thing to do is to pick up free copies of the National Park Service's materials about the site, which have a sketch map and directory of the buildings as well as short histories of the prominent Derby merchant family and of the adventures of several famous Salem vessels, both merchantmen and privateers. These accounts are very well written, and are just the thing to get you in the mood for a tour of the Custom House, wharves, and warehouses. The Custom House is open from 8:30 a.m. to 5 p.m. every day (except Thanksgiving, Christmas, and New Year's Day). Admission is free.

The National Park Service guides are very well informed, as usual, and daily in July and August will take you on a tour back to the Bonded Warehouse to show you what cargoes were like and how they were handled, measured, and weighed. **Derby House,** built for the shipping magnate Elias Derby by his father, Capt. Richard Derby, in 1762, is shown by a free guided tour April through December between 11 a.m. and 1 p.m. Wharf Walks, also offered in July and August, are of high quality, limited to eight people at a time, last about 30 minutes, and cover Derby family and Salem maritime history. The West India Goods Store, right next to Derby House, is again open for business and selling teas, coffee (beans and brew), spices, and other treasures from the East.

Whale-Watch Trips

You can take a boat out of Salem Harbor on a harbor tour or whale-watching expedition. **Barnegat Transportation Co.**, Pickering Wharf (tel. 508/745-6070), will take you out aboard the *New England Star*, Tuesday through Sunday, on either of two daily trips. Snacks, soft drinks, beer, and mixed drinks are available on board. The *Island Star* goes on harbor tours.

For the Children

Something for the children? Follow the signs out of the center of town to **Salem Willows Amusement Park**, northeast of downtown. If you have less time, take the **Salem Trolley**, a re-created oldtime vehicle which makes tours of the town and stop at Salem Willows every day between 10 a.m. and 4 p.m. on the half hour. Tours leave from Riley Plaza, you can buy tickets on board the trolley.

The aforementioned Witch Museum is a sure favorite with kids, but the witch industry is more elaborate, as you might guess. There's also the **Witch Dungeon**, 16 Lynde St., near Washington Street (tel. 508/744-9812), just half a block from the western end of East India Mall. Reenactments of a witch trial, a re-created dungeon, and a replica of Old Salem Village are among the exhibits. It's open daily from 10 a.m. to 5 p.m.

---

2. Marblehead

What Salem was to merchantmen a century ago, Marblehead is to yachts today. Summer and winter her beautiful perfectly sheltered harbor is full of white boats bobbing on the water, or in drydock, or heading out to sea. But it's not only yachters who come to Marblehead. This is without doubt one of the prettiest and best-kept towns in the country, and people love to come up from Boston on the weekend just to walk the streets and windowshop, or have a bowl of chowder in one of the several good restaurants. They also come for a look at *The Spirit of '76,* the famous painting made even more famous during the Bicentennial celebrations, which is hung in Abbot Hall, Marblehead's Town Hall. If you plan to go to Salem, make the detour to Marblehead for at least an hour or two, or for a meal or even overnight.

GETTING THERE: The trip by bus between Marblehead and Boston means a transfer at Lynn. The commuter trains between Boston and Salem (see Section 1, on Salem) stop at Lynn, and buses 441 and 442 run between Marblehead and Lynn's Central Square about every half hour during rush hours, every hour other times, but note that only no. 442 runs in the evening and on Sunday. The bus trip between Lynn and Marblehead takes about 25 minutes.

WHERE TO STAY: Should you really want to get into the spirit and soul of this beautiful seacoast town, you'll have to spend the night. Possibilities are limited, but very attractive. I suggest that you try to plan your visit for a weekday, and that you call ahead for reservations, especially in July and August.

Foremost place to stay is the **Harbor Light Inn**, 58 Washington St., Marblehead, MA 01945 (tel. 617/631-2186), between Pearl and Pickett Streets, a historic 18th-century Marblehead house right in the center of the historic district. The house is pretty from the outside, but even better inside, where the ten guest rooms are all different. Each has either a four-poster or a canopy queen-size bed; some have views of the harbor, some have television sets, one has its own large private deck with a fine view, others have working fireplaces, and all have antique furniture and modern private baths. The three suites are large, with canopy bed, fireplace, and Jacuzzi. Prices range from $75 to $110, with suites renting for $135 to $160, plus tax. Free morning coffee is included. There's a beautiful formal parlor, and an observation deck on the roof. The manager is a wonderfully friendly lady, with a smile for all. The location is very good, only steps from shopping and two blocks from the waterfront. To find the inn, drive along Washington Street all the way into the historic district, until you see the yellow Old Town Hall perched on its own little "island" in the middle of the road. Just behind the town hall is the corner of State Street, and just beyond that, on Washington, is the inn.

Another of Marblehead's good places to stay is the **Pleasant Manor Inn,** 264 Pleasant St. (Rte. 114), Marblehead, MA 01945 (tel. 617/631-5843). This grand Victorian mansion has been converted into a charming inn with a nice lawn, lots of parking, and a tennis court for guests' use. The high-ceilinged rooms are furnished in many cases with four-poster beds and dark-wood trim, and many have air-conditioners and beautiful marble fireplaces which, alas, can't be used (for insurance reasons). The inn can accommodate about 35 people in 14 rooms, all with private bath. Although rooms do not have TV or air conditioning, the antique charm and high ceilings make up for the lack of them, along with other extra touches, such as coffee makers in each room and a hall refrigerator for beverages. Rates are $55 single, $68 double in a room with bath; cots for another person cost $10; an extended continental breakfast is included. By the way, Dick and Takami Phelan, who keep the inn, will be glad to show you the room where Amelia Earhart slept when she visited Marblehead—it's on the third floor.

There is a recommendable guesthouse right downtown in Marblehead. It's **The Nautilus,** 68 Front St., Marblehead, MA 01945 (tel. 617/631-1703), run by Mrs. Ethel Dermody. This typically small Marblehead house is in great demand because of its waterfront location, and so it's advisable to call ahead for reservations, particularly on weekends in summer. Rooms are very cozy and homey, and cost $55 or $60 double and $40 single per night; a cot for an additional person costs $6. Bathrooms are not in the rooms but nearby, and a small fridge is in the hall for guests' use. One or two rooms have sea views, and are in great demand. Parking is a problem downtown, but Mrs. Dermody will recommend places without danger of towing or tickets. The Nautilus is right across the street from the Driftwood Restaurant, which is by the Municipal Parking Lot on the water at the end of State Street.

WHERE TO DINE: Marblehead is not particularly rich in good dining places, but you will certainly find a tasty and enjoyable meal here, perhaps even with a view of the harbor.

Without a doubt, Marblehead's most popular and famous place to dine is **Rosalie's,** 18 Sewall St. (tel. 617/631-5353), at the corner of School Street, directly behind the National Grand Bank and not far from the Talbots clothing store and the YMCA. Rosalie's is an unprepossessing three-story brick factory building on a back street. Enter the front door and you will see a long flight of steps. A third of the way up on the left is a door that seems to lead only into a small bar with some booths, but behind the booths is a large, high-ceilinged dining room where polite and friendly waiters glide professionally among the small tables. The decorations are eclectic, from 19th-century touches to Roman columns, but the overall effect is upbeat elegant. This is not the only dining room, however. There's another one at the top of the stairs, with its own kitchen visible at the back, and yet another one in the basement; but the maître d' is near the bar, so go there first. He will direct you to your table, then hand you a menu with the short-but-sweet list of Italian dishes: various antipasti such as snails and garlic butter in mushroom caps, or shrimp with prosciutto in a mustard-butter sauce. Then comes the pasta (manufactured on the premises) including lobster ravioli, canneloni, and fettuccine pomodoro (fettuccine noodles in a light tomato sauce sweetened with onion, and seasoned with fresh basil and garlic). Main-course dishes include Italian favorites of veal, chicken, and shrimp prepared in interesting ways. There's pollo Francesca, a boneless breast of chicken sautéed in a light egg batter and served with mushrooms in a Grand Marnier sauce; veal with eggplant, prosciutto, mozzarella, and marinara sauce; and the seafood posillipo of shrimp, mussels, Littleneck clams, and fish poached in marinara-clam sauce, served on a bed of linguine. Expect to spend $30 to $40 per person for dinner, $10 or $15 for lunch. Rosalie's is open for dinner daily, and Sunday brunch.

About the largest and most elaborate of Marblehead's restaurants is **The Landing,** on Clark's Landing, off Front Street, down on the water (tel. 617/631-1878). Here you'll find an English-style pub, and dining rooms with a view of yacht-filled Marblehead Harbor. Catering to the boating crowd—which includes early-morning amateur scallop and lobster hunters—the Landing is open for lunch and dinner, every day. Come for a simple lunch of fish and chips ($8), or something fancier if you prefer. At dinnertime there's mesquite-smoked duck, lobsters cooked with Pernod, and (in season) mahi mahi fish; full dinners cost from $30 to $45 per person. The setting, a semi-formal dining room right over the water, is excellent. The Landing also has a Pub section popular with the younger boating set with a taste for burgers and beer.

The literary-minded who have a free hour in Marblehead in the evening spend it at the **King's Rook,** a very European-style coffeehouse and wine bar at 12 State St., not far from the intersection with Washington (tel. 617/631-9838). Coffee is in the $1 to $3 range, depending on the type, of course, and the atmosphere—provided by captain's chairs, small wood-plank tables, low-beam ceiling, tin lamps, and watercolors on the walls—is yours at no extra charge. Beers (imported and domestic), wines by the glass, sandwiches, and a long list of desserts are also served. Many couples find it a romantic place.

The Driftwood Restaurant, 63 Front St. (tel. 617/631-1145), next to the Municipal Parking Lot near the intersection of State and Front Streets, on the water, is right out of a storybook about hearty New England fishermen and boatbuilders. Its barn-red clapboard exterior is matched inside with red-and-white checked tablecloths and a long lunch counter. At 5:30 a.m., when it opens, the fishermen troop in for coffee, eggs, and ham, and for talk of the day's weather and prospects for the catch; later in the day they may return for a bowl of chowder or a portion of "fried dough," a Driftwood specialty served with butter and maple syrup. Breakfast, clam chowder, sandwiches, and fish or seafood plates are the hot items here, priced from $3.50 to $7. The Driftwood's a piece of the real Marblehead. *Note:* Although it opens very early in the morning, it closes for the day around 5 p.m. in summer, 2 p.m. in winter.

WHAT TO SEE AND DO: Walking around, window-shopping, and admiring the buildings and the rugged coast are the best things to do in Marblehead's "Old Town" section. Here are some landmarks to seek out as you go:

Abbot Hall (tel. 617/631-4056) dominates the town from a hilltop, readily visible as you ride into Marblehead—you can hardly miss its brick clock tower. Go to the hall and ask the way to the Selectmen's Meeting Room (town council) to find that marvelous patriotic painting, *The Spirit of '76.* While you're there, take a look at the deed by which the Indians transferred ownership of the land to the European newcomers in 1684. Abbot Hall is open year round during business hours; in summer the hours are 8 a.m. to 9 p.m. weekdays, 9 a.m. to 6 p.m. on Saturday, and 11 a.m. to 6 p.m. on Sunday and holidays.

Down in the center of Old Town, near the intersection of Washington and Hooper Streets, are two old Marblehead mansions open to the public for a fee. The **Jeremiah Lee Mansion** (tel. 617/631-1069), owned by the Marblehead Historical Society, was built by a wealthy maritime merchant and furnished with the best things money could buy in 1768—before the Revolution. The style is Georgian, of course, and the furnishings are from all over the world. Admission charge is $2.50

for adults, half price for children 9 to 16, younger children free; it's open for visits from mid-May to mid-October, Monday through Saturday from 10 a.m. to 4 p.m.

The **King Hooper Mansion,** 8 Hooper St. (tel. 617/631-2608), more or less across the street from the Lee Mansion, is a smaller house and older, having been built in 1728, with a Georgian extension added in 1745. Now owned by the Marblehead Arts Association, it offers tours of four floors for $1 per adult, 50¢ per child; it's open from 1 to 4 p.m. every day but Monday. Art exhibits change each month.

After a walk in the "downtown" part of Old Town, make your way down to the waterfront and **Crocker Park,** on a hill at the western end of Front Street. Relax on one of the benches and admire the panoramic view of the harbor and the town. Bring a sandwich, or buy one in the Sandwich Shop, and have a picnic here. The view is unforgettable.

From Crocker Park walk east along Front Street, past its little restaurants, boat-yards, and houses built on the rocks, to **Fort Sewall.** The fort is an earthwork fortification first built in the 1600s and later "modernized" in the late 1700s to include barracks and half-buried buildings which still remain. The fort is right at the mouth of the harbor, and offers a commanding view of the water and of Marblehead Neck, at the other side of the harbor's mouth, dominated by a light. This is another good picnic place, especially for those with children, who will love playing within the fort with little risk of falling into the water.

When you're ready to leave Fort Sewall, walk back along Front Street, turn right on Franklin, then right again on Orne Street to get to **Fountain Park** and **Old Burial Hill,** where the town's first meetinghouse (church) was built (it's gone now) and where ancient gravestones mark the places of many of Marblehead's earliest inhabitants and Revolutionary War dead. Orne Street east of Fountain Park leads to the beach.

---

3. Introducing Cape Ann

When Bostonians tell you they're taking a trip to the Cape, they mean they're heading south to Cape Cod. But there is another cape that attracts weekend and summer visitors from the metropolis: Cape Ann, just over an hour's drive or train ride north of the city.

Though few out-of-towners are familiar with Cape Ann, many have heard of Gloucester and Rockport, the picturesque seaport towns with a fascinating, almost legendary, history of struggle and communion with the sea. Gloucester and Rockport both lie on Cape Ann, Cape Cod's less dramatic cousin to the north.

If you look closely at the map, you'll notice that Cape Ann is in fact an island connected by bridges to the mainland, as is Cape Cod (since construction of the Cape Cod Canal). The bays, inlets, harbors, and coves of Cape Ann lend a variety to the landscape and shoreline which has long attracted vacationers, especially in the summertime.

GETTING THERE: For a visit to Cape Ann, I'd suggest you tour by private car, using Rockport as your base. The drive up the coast from Salem is of exceptional beauty. Don't worry, though, if you have no car. There's train service to Gloucester and Rockport, and Cape Ann has its own Cape Ann Transportation Authority (CATA; tel. 508/283-7916) local buses which run among the towns and villages.

By Car

I'll describe the coastal road, Rte. 127, from Salem through Beverly, Magnolia, Gloucester, and Rockport. Starting from Marblehead, you must first go via Rte. 114 to Salem. Leaving from Boston and heading directly for Cape Ann, you'll save time by taking Interstate 93 north to I-95/Rte. 128. Follow I-95 North/Rte. 128 East, and when the highway divides, stay on Rte. 128 (I-95 will head north, toward Maine). For the coastal drive, follow Rte. 128 until you see signs for **Manchester.** This town is right on the water, and on the coast road, Rte. 127. Head for Manchester.

If you stay on Rte. 128, it will deposit you, quickly, right in downtown Gloucester. Between Gloucester and Rockport are two loop roads. Route 127 takes you to Rockport through the middle of Cape Ann, then loops around the northern and western shores to return to Gloucester. Route 127A, on the other hand, takes you up the eastern shore of the cape before reaching Rockport. If you get lost, don't worry. In a short while some loop will bring you back to one or the other town.

By Train

Boston's MBTA trains (tel. 617/722-3200), operated by the Boston and Maine Corporation, leave the downtown North Station 12 times a day (eight a day on weekends) for Manchester, Harbor Station, Gloucester, and Rockport. The ride takes about 1¼ hours to Rockport. Children's, seniors', and family fares can save you money, as can travel during off-peak hours (basically, that's before 4:30 p.m. from Boston, and after 8 a.m. from Rockport, on weekdays; all weekend trains are off-peak).

ALONG THE COAST: Manchester is a tidy little North Shore town peopled by old New England types and many professionals who commute into Boston by train. Should you visit during the summer, you can take advantage of **Singing Beach,** half a mile from the train station (center of town) along Beach Street. If you drive, you'll have to pay a parking fee. If you walk, you swim for free. **White Beach,** off Ocean Street, has the same arrangement and the same facilities: bathhouse and snackbar.

MAGNOLIA: Three miles northeast of Manchester along Rte. 127 brings you to Magnolia. Once a humble fishing village, Magnolia is now a lush and wealthy town. Lavish "summer cottages" built by the rich during the 19th century have been insulated, and heating installed, so that they can be used as year-round principal residences. The scenery is wonderful.

The town center is quite pretty, and less than a mile past it lie Rafe's Chasm and Norman's Woe, two natural features you may want to inspect. **Rafe's Chasm,** a dramatic cleft in the shoreline rock, is just opposite the reef of **Norman's Woe,** which figured in Longfellow's poem "The Wreck of the Hesperus." Should you want to spend some time in this lovely setting, there's a good place to stay the night.

An Inn

The **White House,** 18 Norman Ave., Magnolia, MA 01930 (tel. 508/525-3521), is a fine old Magnolia Victorian house with an unobtrusive residential wing attached. In the house are six charming rooms, three with private bath; in the wing are ten motel-style rooms with complete facilities: private bath, television set, air conditioning. Guests receive passes for the use of a private beach; Rafe's Chasm, Norman's Woe, and Hammond Castle (see below) are all close by. Right across Rte. 127 is Lexington Avenue, a short and interesting street of shops, ice cream parlors, and small café-restaurants. Rooms at the White House cost $77 to $88 double in high season, continental breakfast included.

Hammond Castle Museum

Just after heading out from Magnolia along Rte. 127, signs will point to the right, down Hesperus Avenue, to the Hammond Castle Museum, 80 Hesperus Ave. (tel. 508/283-2080 for a recording; 283-7673 for a person). The castle-mansion was built by inventor, electrical engineer, and collector Dr. John Hays Hammond, Jr. (1888–1965), whose creations included radio remote control, and aspects of radar and sonar, including torpedo guidance systems. Despite his name and his interest in things electric, J. H. Hammond, Jr., was not related to Laurens Hammond, inventor of the electric organ.

The castle-builder's father, John Hays Hammond (1855–1936), was a mining engineer who helped Cecil Rhodes to open up South Africa's hugely rich gold mines. He took part in the Boer War, was captured, ransomed, and returned to the United States.

His son grew up in a cosmopolitan and wealthy household, and did a lot of traveling himself, as you will see from exhibits in the castle. He grew rich on government defense contracts and the proceeds from his inventions, became a director of RCA, and spent his wealth on his obsession: European history. His castle is built in four sections, each made to epitomize a distinct period of European architecture. The Great Hall is Romanesque, the interior courtyard is fitted out as a medieval town square, and the living quarters are Gothic and Renaissance French. The guide who takes you on the obligatory 45-minute tour will explain Dr. Hammond's passion for collecting, and his macabre sense of humor. You come away from the tour marveling at the house's lovely setting, amused by its half-treasure-chest-half-gimcrack planning and construction, and puzzled by Hammond's genius, romanticism, and sheer weirdness. In any case, you don't want to miss it.

While you're waiting for the tour, you can explore the Tower Galleries, with various exhibits and artifacts, and you can pick up a flyer listing the museum's many concerts, lectures, and special programs. There are recitals on the Great Hall's fabulous 8,200-pipe organ, which got a brand-new console in 1987. Other concerts have included Scott Joplin, chamber music, and guitar music. There are special theme evenings as well.

Hammond Castle Museum is open daily from 10 a.m. to 4 p.m. (till 9 p.m. on Wednesday in July and August—that's for the candlelight tour). Admission costs $4 for adults, $3.50 for seniors, $2.50 for children aged 6 through 12.

---

4. Gloucester

After Hammond Castle, it's only three miles to Gloucester along Rte. 127. Hesperus Avenue rejoins the highway and takes you into town through West Gloucester and across the little drawbridge. Just before the drawbridge, however, you may want to stop for some . . .

TOURIST INFORMATION: The **Cape Ann Chamber of Commerce** (tel. 508/283-1601) provides information at two locations. Their downtown headquarters at 33 Commercial St., Gloucester, MA 01930, has a spacious information center furnishing maps, brochures, information on special events, listings of accommodations, restrooms, and a rack of restaurant menus. Not far from the statue of the Gloucester Fisherman, across the drawbridge, at the intersection of Rtes. 127 and 133, is their little **tourist information booth.** At either of these locations, they'll be happy to provide information on any town on Cape Ann.

GLOUCESTER'S HISTORY: The Pilgrims founded Plymouth in 1620, and three years later fishermen founded Gloucester (1623). The marvelous natural harbor and the plentiful fishing grounds made that early settlement a fisherman's paradise. Almost four centuries later, it still is.

Gloucester prides itself on being the birthplace of the schooner (1713). At one time it was an important shipbuilding town. Like many others on the New England coast, it profited from the wealth of forests inland, the plentiful fish, and the richness of trade. Over the years Gloucester lost so many of its sons to the ravages of the sea that the town thought it fitting to set up a memorial to them. The **Gloucester Fisherman** (also known as "The Man at the Wheel") is one of New England's most famous statues, with its plaque which reads "They That Go Down to the Sea in Ships, 1623–1923."

The sea is still Gloucester's provider, and the "fishing boats out of Gloucester" still head for open water early each morning. You'll see some of these sturdy little boats, festooned with all sorts of nets and rigging, down in the harbor. Fish-packing plants at quayside process the catch as soon as it's brought in.

Another maritime industry has become important in recent years: whale-watch tours. You might want to take yours from here (see below).

WHERE TO STAY: Motels dot the roadsides around Gloucester. East Gloucester, on a peninsula southeast of Gloucester proper, has numerous little old inns and summer rental places, but most of them are not up to snuff. Much of this area is an artists' colony, and interesting to drive through. But except for the few good places described below, the lodging possibilities in Rockport are infinitely better. Here are Gloucester's choice places to stay:

First choice, without a doubt, is the **Twin Light Manor,** Atlantic Road, Gloucester, MA 01930 (tel. 508/283-7500, or call Best Western toll free 800/528-1234). Atlantic Road is the shore road on the eastern side of the East Gloucester peninsula, and part of the ring road around the peninsula. Twin Light Manor is a complex of buildings centered on an attractive English Tudor mansion, set on a highland overlooking the ocean. The setting is fine, the mansion is wonderful, the seven acres of grounds are well kept, and the whole resort is a delight. Six buildings hold the 73 guest rooms, which come in all shapes and sizes. The most delightful ones are in the ivy-covered, granite, stucco, and half-timbered mansion with its gracious large public rooms, big fireplaces, dark wood, and even a Victorian billiards room. All guest rooms have modern private bath, climate control, direct-dial telephone, and color television. The vast original mansion bedrooms each have a king-size bed or two double beds, and some have fireplaces; they go for $150 in high season. The smaller "guest" bedrooms have king-size beds and rent for $120 double in high season. The other buildings have modern motel-style rooms, most with either king-size beds or two double beds, all with ocean views, many with private balconies overlooking the grounds and the sea. Prices for these rooms range from $115 to $140 in high summer.

The Twin Light Manor has numerous facilities and services, including the dining room in the mansion which serves breakfast and dinner daily to inn guests only (no meals are included in the room price). Besides that delightful billiard room, the living room in the mansion has a wide-screen television set on which movies are shown frequently. Badminton, volleyball, croquet, and shuffleboard courts are scattered around the grounds, and there are two swimming pools (one is heated). As guests at the manor, you can take a harbor cruise, or play 18 holes at the Bass Rocks Golf Club, at no extra charge. Twin Light is the perfect place to get away from it all.

If you plan to stay at least a week, try the **Blue Shutters Inn,** 1 Nautilus Rd., Gloucester, MA 01930 (tel. 508/281-2706), directly opposite Good Harbor Beach. This big white house with blue shutters is right in the curve of the road, only a block off Alternate Rte. 127, and just a few steps from the beach. Many of its guest rooms have beach and ocean views. Decorations are homey, neat, and comfortable. The inn has guest rooms with shared or private bath, and beach apartments completely equipped with linens, kitchen utensils, barbecue grills, and television sets, capable of lodging four people. For a guest room with shared bath, the rate for two is $70 per night; with a private bath, it's $85 per night. Continental breakfast is included in the rates. The Blue Shutters is open from May through October.

Up the hill behind the Blue Shutters is the **Gray Manor,** 14 Atlantic Rd. (Bass Rocks), East Gloucester, MA 01930 (tel. 508/283-5409). A nice big summer house has been converted to a guesthouse only a few minutes' walk from Good Harbor Beach. Most of the lodging places in East Gloucester cater to weekly and monthly guests, and Gray Manor is no exception. You'll find various efficiency apartments renting by the week, but also some guest rooms which go for $50 to $55 double per day. Late May through late June, and Labor Day through the end of October, off-season rates are in effect. Gray Manor closes for the winter.

WHERE TO DINE: Gloucester is plentiful in restaurants, most specializing in seafood, of course. Those who do not care for seafood can rest assured that any seafood restaurant always has a few meat, chicken, or vegetarian dishes to satisfy their unmaritime appetites.

Gloucester's fanciest and best is the **White Rainbow Restaurant,** 65 Main St. (tel. 508/281-0017), in the basement of a 19th-century brick office building on West Main Street (go by the street numbers, as the sign is small and difficult to spot). There are two places to dine here: the formal dining room and the less formal café. Both have dusky brick walls, low lights, and modern paintings. Waiters and waitresses are in black and white, friendly but professional, and after you've been seated they will take your order for things like lobster stew, grilled shrimp or baked Brie; then you can go on to roast duck, tournedos of beef, or a grilled prime veal chop. Desserts are heavily biased in favor of chocolate. The wine list gives you plenty of room for making your selection, and bottles are just slightly higher than the moderate range. Dinner is the only meal served, from 5:30 to 9:30 p.m. Tuesday through Friday, and Sunday; on Saturday, hours are 6 to 10 p.m. You can expect to spend about $35 to $50 per person here. It's a good idea to call for reservations.

For seafood in an informal atmosphere, at moderate prices, right next to the water, I'd head for the **Harbor Deck Restaurant,** 17 Rogers St. (tel. 508/281-4811), in the same building as the Imperial Marina Chinese restaurant, and right next door to Captain Courageous, another seafood place. Choose a table in the light and airy room with large windows or on the outside deck looking out over the docks and the boats. Chairs and tables of bright wood add a cheery note. The menu lists American and Italian dishes, many based on the seafood that comes in on the boats right next door. There's shrimp primavera, a baked sea scallop casserole, lobster tortellini Alfredo, and the interesting seafood chicken (chicken breast stuffed with crab meat and scallops, topped with Hollandaise sauce). As always in seafood restaurants, the freshest items are the daily specials listed on the blackboard menu. House wines are on order by the carafe or the glass; there's a full bar. Come for lunch any day from 11:30 a.m. to 3 p.m., for dinner from 4 to 9 p.m.; on Sunday, brunch is served from 11:30 a.m. to 3 p.m., dinner from 11:30 a.m. to 9 p.m.

Gloucester has a good Chinese restaurant, the **Imperial Marina,** 17 Rogers St. (tel. 508/281-6573), serving lunch and dinner every day from 11:30 a.m. to 9:30 p.m. (till 10:30 p.m. on weekends). Service is fast and attentive, cocktails are served, and prices are moderate. The hot-and-sour soup is very hot and very good, the beef with mushrooms delightful. You can expect to spend $6 to $8 per person for lunch or $15 to $20 for dinner. Liquor is served.

Among my favorite dining places in Gloucester is **The Gull Restaurant,** 75 Essex Ave. (tel. 508/283-6565), at the Cape Ann Marina on Route 133, a mile or so from the center of town right next to where the Yankee Whale Watch boats depart. The Gull is a big, friendly, fairly simple but attractive restaurant overlooking the Annisquam River, usually packed with boaters, whale watchers, families, couples, and sailors. All three meals are served; the Gull opens at 5:30 a.m. and closes at 9 p.m. Seafood is the forté here, and you can have the huge, succulent lobster sandwich or a full clambake with steamers, corn-on-the-cob, cole slaw, and a lobster, or settle for fish and chips. The Gull has a bar and serves alcoholic beverages. Lunch or dinner can cost from $8 to $18 per person, slightly more if you order a full lobster dinner.

Halibut Point is the name of a state park near Rockport, and also of a restaurant at 289 Main St. (tel. 508/281-1900) in Gloucester, not far from the A & P supermarket. The atmosphere is of a friendly neighborhood pub, not fancy but fun. The menu is short and to the point, with sandwiches, salads, burgers, and several popular seafood items, but the blackboard always bears interesting special dishes. Swordfish for lunch can be as low as $8. The soup-and-sandwich special, with a mug of beer, is even less. Open every day for lunch and dinner till midnight.

WHAT TO SEE AND DO: Signs direct motorists along Gloucester's **Scenic Tour,** covering the Harbor Cove, Inner Harbor, and Fish Pier, as well as to the famous statue of the **Gloucester Fisherman** by Leonard Craske.

If you're lucky enough to be in Gloucester late in June, ask about the **Festival of St. Peter,** the highpoint of which is the Blessing of the Fleet. Several hundred boats make up Gloucester's important fishing fleet, and the blessing pays tribute to them.

A great "summer cottage" turned museum, **Beauport,** the Sleeper-McCann House, is at 75 Eastern Point Blvd. (tel. 508/283-0800), on Eastern Point, the peninsula across the bay from downtown Gloucester. The house, now under the care of the Society for the Preservation of New England Antiquities, was built by Henry Davis Sleeper, a prominent interior decorator and antiquarian of the 1920s. Sleeper worked for 27 years to make Beauport a showplace. It still is. You can take the hour-long tour Monday through Friday, May 15 to October 15, from 10 a.m. to 4 p.m.; also on weekends from mid-September through mid-October, 1 to 4 p.m. Admission costs $5 per adult, $2.50 for children 6 to 12, $4.50 for seniors.

On your excursion down to Beauport, you'll want to stroll through East Gloucester's **Rocky Neck Art Colony.** The winding streets offer interesting glimpses of the harbor, and every other house seems to be an artist's studio. You'll see signs asking you to park *before* you enter the narrow streets. Take advantage of the lot next to the signs.

Beaches

Gloucester's favored place for a hot summer afternoon is **Good Harbor Beach** in East Gloucester, on Rte. 127A toward Rockport. It may be crowded if the day is really hot, and parking will be tight. Alternatives are **Long Beach** and **Pebble Beach,** just a bit farther along 127A, within the boundaries of Rockport. **Wingaersheek Beach** is on Ipswich Bay to the northwest (head back down Rte. 128 south and watch for signs). **Coffin Beach** is just northwest of Wingaersheek.

Whale-Watch Cruises

Motoring out to hunt for whales with camera and binoculars is a favorite New England sport, and Gloucester has its share of good whale-watch cruise boats. Cruises usually last between four and five hours, and thus take up a full morning or afternoon. Bring warm clothing, even on a warm day, because the maritime breezes out on the water will make the ambient temperature at least ten degrees cooler than on land, and the wind-chill factor might make it feel even colder. Also remember your sunglasses to ward off the glare from the water; and sunscreen, because that same glare, combined with the bright sun, can really give you a burn. Wear rubber-soled shoes on board if you have them. Whale-watch boats have snackbars where you can buy soft drinks and snacks.

Once out on the water, keep your eyes peeled for humpback whales, 30-ton creatures usually about 50 feet long which seem to love their briny habitat, breeching and playing for hours, accompanying themselves with their own curious songs. A cousin of the humpback is the finback, about twice as heavy and up to 80 feet long, making it the second-largest type of whale. Long and slender, it's a super-fast swimmer, propelling its great bulk through the deep at speeds of 20 knots or even more. The minke whale is "small," weighing only 11 tons, and growing to 30 feet in length. Minke whales have a well-developed sense of curiosity, and may snoop around your boat just to see what's up. In addition, you may see right whales, dolphins, pilot whales, seals, sharks, and seabirds such as petrels, shearwaters, gannets, and gulls.

Capt. Fred Douglass and his sons pioneered whale-watch cruises out of Gloucester with their Daunty Fleet of boats, and now they operate **Cape Ann Whale Watch,** Rose's Wharf (tel. 508/283-5110), with daily departures at 8 a.m. and 1:30 p.m. from Rose's Wharf, at 415 Main St., across from the Old Colony gas station. On Saturday and Sunday evenings during July and August there are additional sunset whale-watch cruises departing at 6 p.m., returning at 10 p.m., with a cash bar on board. Reservations are requested, and tickets can be purchased from the ticket office on Rose's Wharf daily from 7 a.m. to 6 p.m. If you plan to cruise on a weekday, and if you buy your ticket a day in advance, you'll be granted a discount of $1 per ticket. Tickets for the daytime cruises cost $18 per adult, $10 for children under 16, $14 for seniors over 60.

Seven Seas Whale Watch, Seven Seas Wharf (tel. 508/283-1776), operates daily cruises at similar prices. Continental breakfast is available on board ship. In high summer, there are also sunset cruises with entertainment.

---

5. Rockport

North of Gloucester is the small seacoast town of Rockport, famed as an artists' colony and, well, just as a very picturesque place. It's been a long time now since Rockport was a village of hearty, independent fishermen and their wives, living by their daily struggle with the sea, and today you're likely to see ten times as many daytrippers as you are to see colorful village types. But Rockport's popularity means that there are now lots of good places to stay and to dine, and if you decide to stay overnight here, you'll notice that as the evening wears on, the streets become calmer and the village takes on something of its slow, antique pace.

If you drive to Rockport, parking conditions downtown are sure to be very tight anytime in summer, so find a nice back street, or use the town-supported parking lot rather than getting snarled in the press of traffic downtown. The town lots charge several dollars per day for parking, but offer a free shuttle bus from the lot to downtown Rockport. This isn't a bad deal, considering the gasoline and frustration you'll waste trying to find a legal spot to park downtown.

INFORMATION: The **Rockport Chamber of Commerce** (tel. 508/546-6575) maintains an information booth on Upper Main Street (Rte. 127) on the outskirts of town, coming from Gloucester. In season, they'll help you find a room for the night—if there's a room available. Stop at the booth for this free service.

WHERE TO STAY: Though Rockport has several motels, most of its guest beds are in old houses, and that's part of the town's considerable charm. Here's the rundown on Rockport's hostelries, first the inns and guesthouses, then a motel or two. Note that many of these establishments do not accept credit cards. Ask about payment when you make reservations, or when you register.

Inns in Town

For my money, Rockport's finest place to stay is the **Addison Choate Inn,** 49 Broadway, Rockport, MA 01966 (tel. 508/546-7543). Rooms in the tidy old house (built in 1851) have been meticulously restored, and are equally well maintained. There's a feeling of authenticity bred of fine taste; nothing in the decor is overdone, but neither is it spare. It is not "chock full of antiques," it's tastefully furnished with them. With your room here ($68 to $75 double, private bath) you get continental breakfast and use of a pretty swimming pool. There is also a three-person suite for $105 and a stable house for $95 for two. The center of town is within easy walking distance.

The **Linden Tree Inn,** 26 King St., Rockport, MA 01966 (tel. 508/546-2494), is a tidy inn on a quiet street. The yard is shaded by an enormous old linden tree, as you'd expect. The inn has 18 rooms in various sizes and styles, priced from $48 to $72 double, continental breakfast included. Some rooms can take a folding bed ($10) as well; all rooms have a private bath; half have air conditioning. There's even a single room for $48. This is a nice place, homey, convenient, and friendly.

The **Inn on Cove Hill,** 37 Mount Pleasant St., Rockport, MA 01966 (tel. 508/546-2701), is only a few steps from the center of town on Rte. 127A. The charming house was built in 1791 with the proceeds (so they say) from cashing in some pirate gold found on Cape Ann. Today the house is as neat as a pin, old-fashioned in feel but modern in comforts. The double rooms have television sets, private baths, and prices from $42 to $83. Continental breakfast, served to your room or by the garden if you like, is included in the rates.

For many years now the **Peg Leg Inn,** 2 King St., Rockport, MA 01966 (tel. 508/546-2352), has been a haven for visitors to Rockport, and the original inn has now expanded to include five buildings with 33 rooms altogether, many with views of the water. The decor varies from room to room and building to building, but as the houses of the inn are a century or two old, emphasis is on Early American, with such modern luxuries as private bath and TV added. The rooms are kept as neat as the white clapboard houses they're in, and cost $65 to $90 double ($5 for an extra person) in high season, mid-June through October; off-season, the rates are lower; closed mid-December through mid-February. The difference in price depends on the size of the room, and the view it has of the water. The Peg Leg Inn is a short walk from the center of the town, but is also a good deal quieter, because of this location, than it might otherwise be. To get to the Peg Leg, drive to the center of Rockport and then north, staying as close to the water as possible, and you'll end up on Beach Street.

Lantana House, 22 Broadway, Rockport, MA 01966 (tel. 508/546-3535), is close to the center and moderately priced. It offers efficiency apartments as well as guest rooms. Doubles go for $55 to $70, continental breakfast included.

On the Outskirts

The **Yankee Clipper Inn,** P.O. Box 2399, Rockport, MA 01966 (tel. 508/546-3407), is on Rte. 127 toward Pigeon Cove, on the outskirts of town. Two of the inn's three buildings occupy a very fine waterfront site, with excellent views. The third is a fine old house designed by none other than Charles Bulfinch, architect of the Massachusetts State House in Boston, and (in part) of the Capitol in Washington. Grounds include several shady nooks, and a heated saltwater swimming pool. Most rooms are rented with breakfast and dinner in summer, and so a double room with sea view and meals, tax and 15% service charge included, can cost anywhere from $196 to $260 total per day for two people. In the Bulfinch House, however, you're up the hill a bit and across the road, and the only meal you absolutely must take is breakfast, so rates are more moderate: $116 to $127 double, all in. The ocean-front dining room is open to the public.

Among the best things about the **Ralph Waldo Emerson Inn,** Pigeon Cove, Rockport, MA 01966 (tel. 508/546-6321), is its location: a block in from the road, on a bluff overlooking the sea. The grand white inn actually did host Emerson at one time. Since then a new section has been added (1912), but the porch is still fine for sitting and taking in the view. The gracious and airy public rooms hold lots of good paintings. For fun, there's a heated saltwater pool, whirlpool bath, sauna, and recreation room. Room alone in summer costs $60 to $107 single, $86 to $122 double, tax and 10% service charge included; if you'd like breakfast and dinner, add about $25 per person. To get to the inn, follow Rte. 127 north and west from Rockport for a mile or two.

North and west of Pigeon Cove is Folly Cove, on the way to Annisquam, and it's here you'll find the **Old Farm Inn,** 291 Granite St., Pigeon Cove, MA 01966 (tel. 508/546-3237). It may be old but it is kept pretty as a picture. Set on five acres of grounds very near Halibut Point State Park, the farmhouse has three rooms, and there are another four rooms in the Barn Guesthouse. All have private bath, and such country touches as craft decoration and homey quilts. Rooms cost $75 to $100, the highest is that of a two-room suite, which sleeps four.

The **Seven South Street Inn,** 7 South St., Rockport, MA 01966 (tel. 508/546-6708), is a tidy six-room inn renting single rooms for $35 to $38. Doubles are priced at $60 to $80, depending partly on whether you have private bath or shared bath. All these prices include continental breakfast. South Street, by the way, is Rte. 127A east of town, so if you're coming up 127A from Gloucester, you'll go right by the inn.

Motels

The **Captain's Bounty Motor Inn,** 1 Beach St. (P.O. Box 430), Rockport, MA 01966 (tel. 508/546-9557), is right on the beach near the center of town, with 24 modern rooms and efficiencies facing the sea, on two levels. In season, rates for the double rooms are $87; for the efficiencies, $90 to $105.

For a modern motel on the outskirts, try the **Sandy Bay Motor Inn** (tel. 508/546-7155), on the road into town (the official address is 173 Main St., Rockport, MA 01966). The modern, colorful rooms here, equipped with color TV, air conditioning, and all the luxury features, are only the beginning of the story. Besides these the motel has an indoor swimming pool, a whirlpool bath, saunas, tennis courts, and Michael's Restaurant. Rates are $90 to $101 per room from late June through Labor Day, $64 to $82 from Labor Day through October, and $53 to $70 from November through the end of March. It might be good to make reservations in the busy summer months.

WHERE TO DINE: The first thing you should know is that Rockport is a *dry town.* No liquor, wine, or beer is served in its restaurants or sold in its inns or shops. You can drink in Rockport if you BYO, and the restaurants will provide set-ups, corkscrews, ice buckets, etc. But you must plan ahead and buy your booze in Gloucester, or in Lanesville, on Rte. 127 west of Rockport.

This all came about in 1856 when one Hannah Jumper, an outspoken leader of the temperance movement in Rockport, led a raid on the town's liquor supplies. In the four preceding years, sale of ardent spirits in Rockport had more than doubled, and many a fisherman and quarry worker spent wages on rum which should have gone for family needs.

The town's Fourth of July bash in 1856 had gotten out of hand as usual, and on July 8, Hannah and other good citizens went to work. Casks and bottles stored in shops and warehouses—and even private homes—were breached and broken, and though some people cried "Foul!" most people supported this radical solution. Hannah's early-morning direct action changed the history of Rockport, and it has been dry, by the active consent of a majority of its citizens, ever since.

Bearskin Neck, the center of Rockport's tourist industry, has numerous restaurants. One is named **The Hannah Jumper,** on Tuna Wharf, Bearskin Neck (tel. 508/546-3600). Its sign bears a huge axe—in gold leaf, no less—such as Hannah used to break casks during her noble endeavors to rid the town of Demon Rum. Though you can't get a glass of wine here, you can bring your own, and get a table with one of the best views of the harbor, especially good at sunset. Come for a lunch of sandwiches, chowder, salads, or seafood plates, or return in the evening for dinner. The chef offers baby gulf shrimp, fried for just a few seconds to retain their delicate flavor; and chicken Kiev, the breast wrapped around a luscious stuffing of butter and flavorings. Of course, there's boiled lobster. The dinner bill, not including your BYO drinks, will be about $15 to $20 per person. You can sit in the narrow dining room with its simulated rough-board walls, brick floor, and hanging ferns, or out on the shaded Harbor Deck, with the best harbor view of all. The restaurant is open every day from Memorial Day to Labor Day from 11:30 a.m. to 8:30 p.m. In the spring and fall it's open every day for lunch only.

Out at the end of Bearskin Neck where the cars turn around is **My Place,** 68 Bearskin Neck (tel. 508/546-9667), a typical small cedar-shingled building with several tiny dining rooms, a shaded patio, and wooden decks right down among the granite riprap overlooking the north bay. The blackboard is the menu here, and it changes daily, featuring home-style cooking. Lunch and dinner often depend largely on what's fresh in the way of seafood. Last time I visited it was oysters Rockefeller, stuffed wolf fish, and halibut baked in lime and butter. They also offered pork Florentine for the landlubbers. My Place has the nicest homey "feel" to it of any Rockport restaurant. It's open for lunch and dinner daily from 11:30 a.m. to 9:30 p.m. April through October.

Right at the landward beginning of Bearskin Neck, not far from Dock Square on the left-hand side of the street, is the **Galley Restaurant** (tel. 508/546-3721), a longtime favorite of Rockport residents and visitors. The granite-fronted building turns to frame in back, and that's where there are windows with nice harbor views. Dining rooms, as everywhere on Bearskin Neck, are small but cozy, and the fare is from the sea: a bowl of lobster stew is a meal in itself, or you can order baked swordfish, or a cold lobster-and-avocado salad plate (their salads are particularly interesting). Desserts are a strong suit, with many people going for the pecan pie with freshly whipped cream, but there's cheesecake and chocolate cream pie as well. Lunch is on from 11 a.m. to 5 p.m.; dinner, from 5 to 8:30 p.m. The dinner bill might be $16 to $22. No credit cards are accepted here, and the restaurant is closed on Tuesday. Remember to bring your own alcoholic beverages, if you want them.

Just want a bowl of chowder? The place to go is the **Portside Chowder House,** Bearskin Neck (tel. 508/546-7045), to the left off the main street on the Neck, a tiny hole-in-the-wall of a place with low ceilings, narrow passageways, and a few tables with partial views of the water. Chowder made from various seafoods is the specialty here, and it comes by the cup, the bowl, or the quart. Salads of lobster and crab, and fish sandwiches are served, and there are also a few beefy items from the grill. A quick and hearty lunch should cost something like $6 to $10 per person, all in. The Chowder House is open daily in summer from 11 a.m. to 8 p.m., in September and October to 4 p.m., in winter for lunch on weekends only.

The **Blacksmith Shop Restaurant,** 23 Mount Pleasant St. (tel. 508/546-6301), just off Dock Square, has something that Bearskin Neck restaurants don't have: lots of space. And yet the views of the harbor and of Motif No. 1 from the Blacksmith Shop are as good as any in town, and better than most. There is so much space here that you enter through various oldtime kitchen exhibits and memorabilia, then step down into the spacious waterside dining rooms to order from a menu heavy in seafood and traditional American favorites. Long hours are another advantage here, for the restaurant is open daily from 11 a.m. to 10 p.m. You can expect to pay anywhere from $22 to $38 per person for dinner.

Ellen's Harborside, a tiny, crowded but pleasant place just off Dock Square on T-Wharf (tel. 508/546-2512), specializes in budget seafood and homemade desserts, and packs 'em in every night of the summer. Ellen's is especially popular with thrifty seniors, who like the seafood, its freshness, the hardworking waitresses, and the delicious and abundant desserts. The dining room and lunch counter are simple and functional, and the hours of service are long enough to please anyone: Ellen's opens for breakfast at 5:30 a.m. and closes when things calm down after dinner. One person can have a full three-course seafood repast here for as little as $12 or $15. No credit cards are accepted.

One more popular Rockport restaurant is on Main Street, up the hill from Dock Square. For many years the standby in Rockport for dining has been **Oleana-by-the-Sea,** 27 Main St. (tel. 508/546-2049), not far from the center of town. With a tinge of Norwegian atmosphere, Oleana emphasizes the seafood of the area. The decor is simple but attractive, as though the decorators wanted you to concentrate on the views of the Atlantic to be had from most of the tables. The soup is homemade, and is quite good; seafood entrees generally run about $10 to $14, but the daily special will always save you money, and may be haddock in a cheese sauce, with potato and vegetable for about $10. For dessert, a Norwegian pastry with strawberries and custard is a good choice. Oleana is open April through November: in June, July, and August they're in service seven days a week from 11:30 a.m. to 8 p.m.

On the Outskirts

Let's face it: when you're on Cape Ann, you should order fresh seafood. If you wander out of town by bike or car, you'll find it at every turn.

Just down the hill from the Old Farm Inn on Rte. 127 in Folly Cove is the **Lobster Pool** (tel. 508/546-7808), known locally as Tommy's. The food is simple and good, the surroundings spare but cheery. Order a lobster roll of solid lobster meat (Tommy's doesn't use celery as filler). Portions are gargantuan, and it's not unusual for two semihungry people to share, say, one bowl of chowder and one clam plate, which comes with french fries and cole slaw. Total cost, with soft drinks, is less than $10 per person. You can get your food to take out, if you like.

WHAT TO DO: First thing every visitor does after arriving in Rockport is to take a stroll down **Bearskin Neck,** the narrow peninsula jutting into the water off Dock Square, the town's main square. Here you'll find lots of quaint shops and art galleries to draw your attention, and many good views of the water and of the town.

Other strolls in town are also rewarding, and local brochures will urge you to take a photograph of the red fisherman's shack called "Motif No. 1," apparently named for its popularity among the first picture painters who moved to Rockport. Actually it should now be named "Motif No. 2," as the original shack was swept away in the great storm of 1978 and a new one was built from scratch. In the interest of originality, I suggest that you try to be the first person to have visited Rockport *without* seeing this unimportant landmark. Take my word for it, the thing is now famous because it's famous.

Rather, spend your time looking at the local granite. It was cut at the town's Swan Quarry (now flooded), and shipped out, giving the town its name. Curbstones, markers, pavements, foundations, piers, even whole buildings were made of the durable stone during the town's quarrying heyday. Now, if "Motif No. 1" were a fisherman's shanty made of granite, that would be something to see!

For swimming, walk along Beach Street north to Front Beach and Back Beach, or wander (in your car or on your bike) north along the coast to **Pigeon Cove,** about two miles north (a half-hour walk).

You can go farther than Pigeon Cove by car or bike. In fact you can make a loop of Cape Ann on Rte. 127 via Pigeon Cove, Folly Cove, Plum Cove, Annisquam, and Lobster Cove, ending in Gloucester.

Halibut Point

Head north out of Rockport on Rte. 127, toward Lanesville and Annisquam, and after a few miles you'll see a sign pointing off to the right (north) to **Halibut Point State Park,** just before the Old Farm Inn. Drive to the parking lot, leave your car, and then follow the path through the forest for ten minutes, and you will come to an old granite quarry, now flooded with water. The park interpretive center, still being furnished at this writing, is in the building that dominates the quarry. Exhibits demonstrate the flora and fauna of the reservation, and how granite quarrying contributed to the culture and economy of the region. A weird World War II concrete observation tower has been grafted onto the building, a typical clapboard Cape Ann house. From the tower during the war, sharp eyes kept a lookout against enemy submarines. Entrance fee is $5.

Continue along the path to reach the Observation Point atop a cliff of granite quarry rubble. Far beneath, the Atlantic's waves roll in and crash on the smoothed granite bedrock below. You can make your way down to the water. Some people go swimming here, although it's not an ideal spot: the water is always chilly, the rocks difficult and slippery, the waves sometimes perilous.

Castle Hill

Not far from Rockport is Castle Hill, the fabulous hilltop mansion built by Richard Teller Crane, Jr., who made a fortune in plumbing and bathroom fixtures early in this century. The house, in a style from the time of King Charles II, is surrounded by extensive gardens and deer parks. You can take a tour of the house and grounds on certain Fridays and Saturdays during the summer; or you can visit for a crafts fair, concert, or theater performance and get a look at the estate that way. First thing to do is to find out what's scheduled, by contacting the Castle Hill Foundation, P.O. Box 283, Ipswich, MA 01938 (tel. 508/356-4070).

... AND THE SOUTH SHORE

1. PLYMOUTH
2. NEW BEDFORD
3. FALL RIVER

Of the many communities on the South Shore of Massachusetts Bay, Plymouth is easily the most famous. Crowds of visitors make the pilgrimage every summer to see one of the places where this country began. Due south of Boston on Buzzards Bay is New Bedford, one of the region's best-known towns during the whaling era, home of Melville's Captain Ahab of *Moby Dick* fame. The whaling museum and the ferry to Martha's Vineyard are the big attractions in New Bedford today. And in Fall River, on the border with Rhode Island, battleships and submarines are waiting to be visited and toured by nautical buffs, while everybody else goes shopping.

All of the South Shore towns covered in this chapter, including Plymouth, New Bedford, and Fall River, use the 508 telephone area code.

1. Plymouth

Plymouth is famous because of a small and rather unimpressive boulder. But when visitors come to look at Plymouth Rock, they are coming not because the rock is much to look at—its only notable features are a crack and the date "1620" engraved on it—but because Plymouth, as the landing-place of the Pilgrims, is a symbol for the ideal of religious freedom and the quest for a better life.

Besides the Rock, which will take you about five minutes to inspect, Plymouth has lots of other sights and exhibits dealing with Pilgrim and early American history: a collection of historic houses, a full-size replica of the Pilgrim ship *Mayflower,* an authentic re-creation of an entire Pilgrim village complete with living inhabitants, a wax museum, and still more. Many people make Plymouth a day trip, stopping here on their way from Boston to the Cape or vice-versa, but should you want to stay overnight in the Pilgrims' town, there are several attractive lodging possibilities.

GETTING THERE: Plymouth is served from Boston and Hyannis by buses of the Plymouth & Brockton Street Railway Company (tel. 617/773-9400). About two dozen buses a day run in each direction between Plymouth and Boston; about 16 buses a day run from Hyannis to Plymouth and back. In Boston, buses leave from either the Greyhound/Trailways Terminal at 10 St. James Ave. (tel. 617/423-

5810) or from the South Station Transportation Center (tel. 617/482-5510). On weekends, holidays, and after 6:30 p.m. weekdays, the Peter Pan Terminal at South Station is used. In Hyannis the P & B terminal (tel. 508/775-5524) is at Elm Street. In Plymouth, the P & B Terminal is at Industrial Park Road, Rte. 3, Exit 7, North Plymouth (tel. 508/746-0378), but buses stop downtown in Plymouth as well. The trip between Boston and Plymouth takes one hour and 20 minutes; between Hyannis and Plymouth, 40 minutes.

INFORMATION: The Town of Plymouth maintains an **Information Booth** (tel. 508/746-4779) and **Accommodations Service** on North Park Avenue. Samoset Street (Rte. 44) is the road you take east from the highway (Rte. 3), and Samoset turns into North Park after you cross Court Street (Rte. 3A). Look for the booth on your right just as the road jogs to the right. They'll help you find a room if you don't have a reservation or if you'd like to see what's available. They also have a current list of events and attractions for the area.

There is a **Regional Information Complex for Visitors** on Rte. 3 at Exit 5. For information, call 508/746-3377.

WHERE TO STAY: Most of your choices are among Plymouth's good selection of motels. But there are alternatives.

Guesthouses

You can find a room in a private home in Plymouth, "America's Home Town." Prices will be about $32 to $45 single, $40 to $65 double. Breakfast is included, of course.

Be Our Guest, P.O. Box 1333, Plymouth, MA 02360 (tel. 617/837-9867), will find you a room in or near Plymouth, Boston, and Cape Cod.

Call and see if there's a room at the **Hall's,** 3 Sagamore St., Plymouth, MA 02360 (tel. 508/746-2835), then head south along the waterfront from Plymouth Rock until you see the town green on your right. Turn up North Green Street, continue on Jefferson to Sagamore, and turn right. You'll see the Halls' tidy white clapboard house perched on the hillside at no. 3. There are two rooms here, sharing a bath, for $50 per room.

Motels

Right downtown are two motels with similar names and identical management, the **Governor Bradford** (tel. 508/746-6200), right on the waterfront street, and the **Governor Carver** (tel. 508/746-7100), on Summer Street at Town Square, Plymouth, MA 02360. Both are about the same distance—two blocks—from Plymouth Rock. The Governor Bradford has a little fish-shaped outdoor pool and two tiers of modern rooms, each having individual heat/air-conditioning units, two double beds, TV, and coffee makers. The Governor Carver is a three-story inn with 82 rooms, all with two double beds, a pool, and the other features of the Bradford, plus a restaurant and lounge. Rates at the two inns are similar and change depending on the view from your room. In season, rooms go for $97 to $108 single or double. Substantial reductions are offered outside the high summer months. Children under 14 stay in their parents' room for free. Package plans are available.

One of the better bargains is to be found at the **Cold Spring Motel,** 188 Court St. (which is Rte. 3A), Plymouth, MA 02360 (tel. 508/746-2222). Although a bit out of the center of town—it's about a half mile to the Rock—the surroundings of grass lawns and large trees make up for the small distance. Some 31 rooms and cottages, many paneled in pine, are for rent. All have air conditioning, electric heat, color TV, and parking at the door. A picnic area with fireplaces is provided for guests' use. Although there's no restaurant at the motel, there's one almost across the street in the small shopping plaza. The rate structure at present is quite complex because of the several types of accommodations (rooms with double beds, cottages with two bedrooms sleeping four). Single rates are $46; double, $51 to $65; two bedroom cottages, $63; $5 for each extra person, $5 extra per cot. These are the in-season rates: in April, May, and October, prices are $10 less. Note that the Cold Spring Motel *closes* in winter; exact dates vary from year to year.

The tiny **Blue Anchor Motel,** 7 Lincoln St., Plymouth, MA 02360 (tel. 508/746-9551), has only four units, and thus there's a good chance it'll be full in busy periods, but it's worth considering because it is on a quiet street next to Plymouth's town hall and only a short walk from the center of town. It's very much a ma-and-pa place, informal and friendly, with comfy rooms renting for $42 to $52, depending on the unit and the number in your party. Rates are about $5 less per room off-season. From the center of town, go south on Sandwich Street from the post office. The third street on the left is Lincoln.

Down near Plimoth Plantation, 2½ miles south of the center of Plymouth, is the **Pilgrim Sands Motel,** 150 Warren Ave. (Rte. 3A), Plymouth, MA 02360 (tel. 508/747-0900). The bonus here, besides proximity to Plimoth Plantation, is the beach, which you'd normally have to pay $3 to $5 ($3 weekdays, $5 weekends) to enjoy, but which is free for motel guests. There's an indoor and outdoor pool and spa as well, and all the modern amenities including air-conditioned rooms and all-tile bathrooms; some rooms have refrigerators. After a day's walking in the sun it's great to take a swim and then sit looking out to sea, before going to bed to be lulled by the sound of the surf. All rooms have two double or queen-size beds and cost $53 to $88 off-season, $85 to $108 in season (mid-June to Labor Day), the higher rates for oceanfront rooms. Open year round.

WHERE TO DINE: Plymouth has a number of snack places, sandwich shops, and restaurants, and although it's not noted for a wide range of culinary styles, the town will be able to fill your needs.

Among Plymouth's most popular restaurants is **Station One,** 51 Main St., at Middle Street (tel. 508/746-6001), in the commercial center of Plymouth, up the hill from the waterfront, open daily from 11:30 a.m. to 9:30 p.m. (10:30 p.m. on weekends). Station One started life as the town's Central Fire House in 1904, but has been utterly transformed into an elegant space paneled with mahogany and glistening with brass and crystal. Have lunch, dinner, or Sunday brunch either inside or on the patio out front. The menu is exhaustive, with something for any mood or taste, from crab bisque to ziti with chicken and broccoli. Prices are moderate: about $14 to $18 for lunch, $30 to $40 per person for a good dinner. Liquor is served.

For my money, the best way to sample Plymouth's seafood is to pick up lunch from one of the self-service places on the waterfront. You'll see them crowded together near Mayflower Seafood on the Town Wharf: Wood's, Souza's, the Lobster Hut.

My choice is the **Lobster Hut,** on the Town Wharf (tel. 508/746-2270). Open every day from 11 a.m. to 9 p.m., the Lobster Hut serves up steaming bowls of clam chowder, lobster bisque, fried clams, fish and chips, and lobsters, plus wine and beer (with your meal only). Order a huge portion of fish and chips, or fried clams, and with a soft drink you'll pay less than $10. Dine inside, or at one of the picnic tables overlooking the bay.

Just south of the turnoff to Plimoth Plantation, on Warren Avenue (Rte. 3A), is **Bert's Restaurant** (tel. 508/746-3422). Air conditioning keeps you cool and the view of the ocean, plus a decor accented with various pieces of ships' paraphernalia, make you think (almost) that you're out to sea. The menu features seafood but offers chicken and beef as well. Most entrees are in the range of $13 to $21, and full dinners (with appetizer, vegetable and potato, salad, dessert, and coffee) cost a few dollars more. Bert's is open for lunch and dinner daily, from 11:30 a.m. to 10 p.m.

WHAT TO SEE: Sightseeing in Plymouth means Pilgrim lore: what they looked like, how they dressed, how they lived from day to day. The many exhibits here make it possible to get a very clear picture of what arrival in America meant to these early pioneers.

Plymouth Rock

The Pilgrims have a special place in American history not only because they were very early settlers, but also because of their reasons for settling here. First they had left England for Holland, so that they could practice their beliefs and rites freely. However, noting the loss of their English character, they decided to seek another haven where cultural influences would not be so strong. Having received permission from London, they sailed for America in 1620. Actually, they had hoped to arrive at a point south of Plymouth, but after being blown off course they ran into Cape Cod; shortly after making Cape Cod, they sailed to the point where Plymouth stands today. The place where they debarked is marked by Plymouth Rock.

Today the Rock is sheltered by a monumental enclosure which stands in Plymouth Rock State Park (tel. 508/866-2580). Just as the Rock marks the beginning of the Pilgrims' adventure in America, so it can serve as the beginning point for your tour of Plymouth. Follow the road signs to find the Rock, and after your look at it, head for the attractions nearby.

Right next to Plymouth Rock is a replica of the sort of house the Pilgrims first built in the New World. Though there's not much to see inside, you can best imagine what it'd be like to live in so tiny a house when you're actually inside it. Remember that in the 1600s people were not as tall as average Americans today.

The Mayflower

The fact that the Pilgrims suffered to get to America will be brought home more forcefully when you tour the *Mayflower II* (tel. 508/746-1622), a replica of the original ship built in England in 1955 and sailed across the Atlantic to Plymouth in 1957. How, you are sure to ask yourself, was it possible for 102 people—even small ones—to fit themselves and all their baggage for setting up a new town into the tiny rooms and onto the tiny decks of this little ship? And how could they stay on it for 2½ months? The only answer that comes to mind is "by courage and dedication," and it's for that the Pilgrims are admired and remembered. Guides on the *Mayflower II* will tell you about the boat's workings and will answer questions; display panels on the dock and an excellent leaflet given to you as you enter will explain other details of nautical lore.

Mayflower II is only a few steps from Plymouth Rock, and is open April through November from 9 a.m. to 5 p.m.; in the busiest months of July and August the ship stays open until 6:30 p.m. every night. Admission is $5 for adults, $3.25 for children 5 to 12 (under 5, free); but *note:* a special combination ticket is good for the *Mayflower II* and Plimoth Plantation at $15 for adults, $10 for children.

Pilgrim Hall

Seeing how the Pilgrims lived in the earliest period of America's colonization is what Plymouth is all about. You can see exhibits like *Mayflower II* and the early huts to give you an idea, or you can see the actual Pilgrim furniture and huge oil paintings featured in Pilgrim Hall, 75 Court St. (tel. 508/746-1620), at the corner of Chilton and Court Streets. (Court Street, Main Street, and Sandwich Street are all different names for different sections of the same street.) The oldest historical museum in continuous service in the United States, Pilgrim Hall was built in 1824 to house artifacts the Pilgrims used, a library for research into Plymouth's early history, and galleries for the monumental paintings depicting important events in Pilgrim history. In the Lower Hall, the slide show puts the Pilgrim experience into the perspective of the times, surrounded by the exceptional furniture of Brewster and Bradford and the rest, and the arms and armor they brought with them. In the Main Hall above are the paintings, the relic of a 17th-century transatlantic ship, and the magnificent pewter, Delftware, and woodenware the Pilgrims and their descendants treasured, along with the tools and cookware of the Indians who lived beside the Pilgrims. Many of the items identified as *Mayflower* cargo, such as the wicker cradle of the first English child born in New England, are on display. Pilgrim Hall is open from 9:30 a.m. to 4:30 p.m. every day, all year, and costs $4 for adults, $3.50 for seniors and students, and $1.50 for children 6 to 15.

Plymouth National Wax Museum

Even more lifelike than Pilgrim Hall's paintings are the tableaux at the Plymouth National Wax Museum, 16 Carver St. (tel. 508/746-6468), at the top of the hill across the street from Plymouth Rock. The hill is Cole's Hill, where the first Pilgrim cemetery was established and where the first victims of the frigid New England winter were laid to rest. The museum's scenes trace the history of the Pilgrims from persecution in England through the move to Holland to the trip across the Atlantic and the foundation of the settlement at Plymouth. Soundtracks add to the vividness of the scenes. The Wax Museum is open from 9 a.m. to 5 p.m. in spring, summer, and fall, admission is $4 for adults, $2 for children.

Plimoth Plantation

Most lifelike of all the representations of early colonial life is Plimoth Plantation (tel. 508/746-1622), a living outdoor museum with inhabitants in period dress. Plimoth Plantation is "the living folk museum of 17th-century Plymouth," and represents a Pilgrim village as it may have looked in 1627. Historical research was done to determine every aspect of the village, and the result is as close as could be achieved: it's surrounded by a fortification (stockade), the small houses have thatched roofs and kitchen gardens, the women in period dress may be seen grinding corn, baking bread in an outdoor clay oven, or cooking on an open hearth, the men tending the fields or hewing logs to make planks. The animals here have been bred to resemble those of the 1600s! The people who "live" in Plimoth Plantation are known as "interpreters," and that's what they do for you: interpret the daily activities of a different era to make them comprehensible today. There is also a Wampanoag Indian Settlement with demonstrations of how they lived in 1627.

Plimoth Plantation is a nonprofit educational outdoor museum, open April through November from 9 a.m. to 5 p.m. every day; tickets are sold until 4 p.m. (it's hardly worth entering if you have less than an hour to look around). Admission costs $12 for adults, $8 for children 5 to 12 (under 5, free), but this includes free parking, films and slide shows at the theater, indoor exhibits on early life, gift shop and bookstore, a restaurant, and a picnic area.

The Forefathers' Monument

This is the sort of grand statue-and-pedestal one would expect to see on a central boulevard in a world capital, but instead it stands on Allerton Street, off Samoset (U.S. 44), in a small park—follow the signs on the road. Designed by Hammet Billings of Boston and dedicated in 1889, the monument (tel. 508/746-1790), is composed of a great granite statue of Faith, surrounded by smaller figures of Liberty, Law, Education, and Morality. The monument, 81 feet high, is impressive, and it's interesting to speculate about the times when it was erected, and the thoughts of those who planned and constructed it. The view from the little park, by the way, is very fine; a small cast-iron outline map near the base of the monument traces the outline of Cape Cod, which you can see on a clear day.

Plymouth's Old Houses

Of the antique houses in the town, several are of particular interest. The **Richard Sparrow House,** 42 Summer St., overlooking Town Brook Park (tel. 508/747-1240), is the oldest house in Plymouth, having been built in 1640. It's open from late May to Thanksgiving, daily except Wednesday from 10 a.m. to 5 p.m.; donation requested. There is also a craft gallery with pottery made on the premises.

The **Howland House,** 33 Sandwich St. (tel. 508/746-9590), dates from 1667, and is the only Plymouth house still standing which was known to have been occupied by Pilgrims. The parents of Jabez Howland, builder of the house, had come over on the *Mayflower,* and it's presumed that they spent their last years with their son. Hours are 10 a.m. to 5 p.m. (noon to 5 p.m. on Sunday), late May through mid-October. Admission costs $2.50 for adults, 50¢ for children.

Beams in the **Harlow Old Fort House,** 119 Sandwich St. (tel. 508/746-9697), are from the Pilgrims' log fort on Burial Hill. Built in 1677, the house is now occupied by costumed guides who demonstrate 17th-century crafts. It's open by appointment only. Admission costs $2.50 for adults, 50¢ for children.

The **Spooner House,** 27 North St. (tel. 508/746-9697), was built in 1749, and used to be the home of the Spooner family, famous through the Plymouth Cordage Company as the world's largest maker of rope and twine. James Spooner, last of the family to live here, died in 1954. It's open during June and from Labor Day to mid-September. Hours are weekends; 10 a.m. to 5 p.m. Thursday through Sunday. Adults pay $2.50; children, 50¢.

A handsome Federal-style structure is the **Antiquarian House,** 126 Water St. (tel. 508/746-9697), built by a wealthy shipowner in 1809 and furnished with precious objects brought home by his ships. The fully equipped 19th-century kitchen is a treat. Hours are 10 a.m. to 5 p.m. daily from late June to early September, weekends in June, and from mid-September to mid-October. Admission costs $2.50 for adults, 50¢ for children under 16, under 6 admitted free.

The **Mayflower Society Museum,** 4 Winslow St. (tel. 508/746-2590), was once the elegant home of Edward Winslow, part of which was built in 1754, and the other part in 1898. Besides the furnishings, the house's attraction is a daring, flying staircase which looks as though it really should fall down, but doesn't. It's double the size it was in 1754. The formal gardens are nice as well. The museum is open from late June through early September from 10 a.m. to 5 p.m. (from noon to 5 p.m. on Sunday), plus Fridays and weekends in June and till mid-October. It's open Thanksgiving weekend as well. Admission costs $2.50 for adults, 25¢ for kids.

Pilgrim Progress

At 5 p.m. on Friday in August a group of Plymouth citizens dressed as Pilgrims honor the memory of their ancestors by re-creating the procession to church. The number of persons, their sexes, and ages have been matched to the small group of Pilgrims who survived the first winter in the New World. When you see the procession you may be amazed at the small size of the group that started it all.

Cranberry World

Why do Americans have turkey with cranberry sauce for Thanksgiving? Because both are indigenous to New England. The Pilgrims found both turkeys and cranberries in abundance when they arrived, and made a fitting feast. Cranberry harvesting and processing is still a big industry in and around Plymouth, on Cape Cod, and on the islands. You can learn all about these tart, juicy berries, the bogs where they are grown, and the products made from them, by visiting Cranberry World Visitors Center, 225 Water St. (tel. 508/747-1000 or 747-2350), operated by Ocean Spray Cranberries, Inc. Admission is free, and you can sample free cranberry refreshments as well. From April 1 to November 30, hours are 9:30 a.m. to 5 p.m. daily, till 9 p.m. on weekdays in July and August.

2. New Bedford

New Bedford, like Fall River, owed part of its living to textiles, but its fame rests on its history as a whaling port. Herman Melville set his American classic, *Moby*

Dick, in New Bedford as the logical spot to begin a whaling epic, and so it was. During the heyday of whale-oil lamps, New Bedford had about 400 ships out scouting the seas for the monster denizens. A ship might be out at sea for several years, and when it returned to port it could have thousands of barrels of whale oil in its hold. The story of what whaling was all about—how the ships were manned and equipped, how the search went, how the men pursued and killed the whale, and then butchered and rendered it to make the oil—is all told in New Bedford's famous **Whaling Museum** on Johnny Cake Hill.

Today New Bedford's historic waterfront downtown section is undergoing extensive renovation and restoration. A pedestrian shopping mall complete with trees, benches, and music in the air—called **Melville Mall,** appropriately—has been completed and it does much for the town. East of the mall, going down to the water's edge, the **Custom House** and many merchants' buildings are being restored, cobbled streets are being uncovered or restored, and the center of the city is taking on an appearance much like it had during its 19th-century heyday.

INFORMATION: Right in the middle of the restoration area is the Bristol County Development Council's **Tourist Information Office,** 70 N. 2nd St., New Bedford, MA 02741 (tel. 508/997-1250); signs throughout town point the way. They're open from 9 a.m. to 5 p.m. Monday through Friday (Memorial Day weekend through Labor Day, also open on Saturday from 9 a.m. to 5 p.m. and 1 to 5 p.m. on Sunday), and are very helpful with maps, brochures, and touring suggestions.

Second Street is actually very important to visitors. Besides the Bristol County Development Council right next to the big parking garage, there is another source of information, the **City of New Bedford Visitor Center,** 47 N. 2nd St., New Bedford, MA 02741 (tel. 508/991-6200), open from 9 a.m. to 5 p.m. Monday through Saturday and 11 a.m. to 5 p.m. on Sunday. The Visitors Center is in a restored brick commercial building which now also houses numerous shops and eateries. The Visitor Center sponsors free one-hour walking tours every day in summer, departing at 11:30 a.m. and 2:30 p.m.; on Sunday there's one tour only, departing at 1 p.m.

In the same building at 47 N. 2nd St. are the offices of **Pineapple Hospitality** (see below under "Where to Stay").

Note that if you come to 2nd Street for information, you might want to plan a visit to the New Bedford Glass Museum at the same time, as it's right in between the two information offices.

WHERE TO STAY: There are several comfortable motels on I-195 west of downtown New Bedford. In the city proper is the **Durant Sail Loft Inn,** Merrill's Wharf, New Bedford, MA 02741 (tel. 508/999-2700), right in the waterfront district, which is half-commercial and half-industrial. The inn is in a fine old granite warehouse, now refurbished with 18 simple, comfortable, modern rooms, which rent for $62 with double bed or twin beds, $86 for a suite. The inn has its own restaurant. Finding the inn can be tricky. First find Union Street. Go south on Union, cross the expressway and turn right *just before* the gates of the New Bedford State Pier (don't enter the pier area). The inn is a short distance along this road.

New Bedford has its own bed-and-breakfast referral service, **Pineapple Hospitality,** 47 N. 2nd St., Suite 3A, New Bedford, MA 02740 (tel. 508/990-1696). They'll take your reservation and provide details on a local B & B anytime from 9 a.m. to 5 p.m. Monday through Friday. Actually they have listings for B & Bs throughout New England, but your most immediate need is here, now, in New Bedford. Room prices range from $30 to $95 single, $38 to $125 double (quite a range!). Many of the homes participating in the service welcome young children.

Why the pineapple, you ask? In New Bedford's nautical heyday, ships would bring this tropical delicacy back home at the end of a voyage. A pineapple set out in front of the house meant the occupants were at home, receiving visitors, celebrating the success of the voyage.

WHERE TO DINE: The most convenient eatery is **Johnny Cakes Restaurant, 1** Johnny Cake Hill (tel. 508/993-3326), just to the left of the Seamen's Bethel and only a few steps from the Whaling Museum. There's a light, cheery upstairs dining room or a sunny patio, and a menu of interesting lighter fare including seafood pie, vegetable stir-fry, various burgers, and a roast turkey sandwich. Lunch here should cost less than $10, all in. Hours are Tuesday through Saturday from 8 a.m. to 3 p.m.

WHAT TO SEE: You've come to see whaling memorabilia, of which New Bedford has lots. But there are other things to see as well, including the local glass museum, and a museum dedicated to firefighting.

The Whaling Museum

At 18 Johnny Cake Hill in the heart of the Historic Waterfront District, the museum complex (tel. 508/997-0046) of seven buildings covers the block between William and Union Streets. It's open from 9 a.m. to 5 p.m. Monday through Saturday and 1 to 5 p.m. on Sunday. Admission for adults is $3, $2.50 for seniors, $2 for kids 6 to 14. Inside, the first thing to confront you is the largest ship model in the world: a replica of the bark *Lagoda* made to exactly one-half the ship's original size. Rigging, tryworks, whaleboats, and other equipment are all in place, and you can walk about the model at will. The family who owned and operated the *Lagoda* donated the model, and the building to house it, to the museum. Around the walls of the museum are old photographs and drawings explaining the whaling industry, and many other rooms in the museum hold collections of other whaling lore: cooperage, chandlery, operation of the counting house, brokerage and banking, insurance, and articles of glass, china, and pewter brought home from whaling and trading voyages. A gallery exhibits dozens of paintings done on whaling themes. Perhaps the most beautiful exhibit besides the *Lagoda* is the scrimshaw, the delicate, intricate articles of carved whalebone and tooth which the whalesmen made to while away the long hours at sea. The artistry displayed is almost breathtaking, and the ingenuity very revealing of quick and sensitive minds. It wouldn't be far wrong to say that without understanding whaling, one couldn't understand 19th-century New England; and the place to find out about whaling is certainly New Bedford.

Seamen's Bethel

Across the street from the Whaling Museum is the Seamen's Bethel (tel. 508/992-3295), a chapel constructed in 1832 "for the moral improvement of sailors," and immortalized in *Moby Dick*. With a gratefully appreciated donation you can explore the Bethel. And several blocks away, at Pleasant and William, the **Public Library** has displays of whaling books and pamphlets. Open from 9 a.m. to 9 p.m. daily, May 1 through Columbus Day only.

New Bedford Glass Museum

The city of New Bedford has been producing glass continuously longer than any other town in New England, and an outstanding collection of its glass products is housed in a fine Federal mansion (1821) at 50 N. 2nd St. (tel. 508/994-0115). The museum's collection of almost 2,000 objects also includes many items of porcelain and silver, as well as drawings and paintings related to the crafting of glass. The museum costs $2.50 for adults, $2 for seniors, and 75¢ for children 6 to 12 to enter, and is open April through December Monday through Saturday from 10 a.m. to 5 p.m., on Sunday from 1 to 4 p.m.; January through March, the museum is open on Saturday, Sunday, and Monday only.

New Bedford Fire Museum

Anyone interested in the history of firefighting in America will want to take a look at the New Bedford Fire Museum, Bedford Street at 6th Street (tel. 508/992-2162). The museum's beginnings date back to 1890, and it is situated appropriately next to New Bedford's Fire Station No. 4, a building which dates from 1867 and is still in active use. Come from 9 a.m. to 5 p.m. any day in summer to see the restored antique fire trucks and other firefighting equipment, displays of old uniforms, working models of pumps and fire poles, and other memorabilia. Admission costs $2 for adults, half price for children.

Rotch-Jones-Duff House and Garden Museum

A beautiful example of Greek Revival architecture as practiced by New Bedford's wealthy whaling merchants, the Rotch-Jones-Duff House, 396 County St. (tel. 508/997-1401), dates from 1834. The lovely house and gardens are open to the public in April and May on Sunday from 1 to 4 p.m.; June through August, Tuesday through Friday from 10 a.m. to 4 p.m. and on Sunday from 1 to 4 p.m.; in September through November on Sunday from 1 to 4 p.m.

THE FERRY TO MARTHA'S VINEYARD: M/V *Schamonchi* carries passengers (no cars) from New Bedford to the island of Martha's Vineyard three or four times daily in summer for $7.50 one way, $13 round trip for adults; for kids under 12, $4.50 one way, $7 round trip. For schedules and information, call 508/997-1688 in New Bedford, or 508/693-2088 in the island town of **Vineyard Haven.**

---

3. Fall River

In the mid-19th century Fall River was a boom textile town. Because of its natural harbor, ample waterpower, and a moist climate ideal for working thread, it became a world textile-weaving center. Huge mills made from blocks of the local granite were built everywhere, making an awesome scene of industry and wealth. But in the 20th century the textile business began moving to the South, and Fall River's industry foundered.

Prosperity has returned to Fall River, and now many of the impressive granite mills produce finished apparel; others turn out rubber products, foods, and paper. The town's new Government Center, built on the airspace over I-195, is a symbol of Fall River's resurgence, and adds its impressive appearance to that of the great mills.

WHAT TO SEE: Most people pass through Fall River on their way from Providence to Cape Cod or from Boston to Newport, and when they do, the thing they stop to see is **Battleship Cove** (tel. 508/678-1100), permanent berth of a number of impressive craft. The U.S.S. *Joseph P. Kennedy, Jr.,* a World War II destroyer, is here, as is a wooden PT boat, and also the submarine U.S.S. *Lionfish.* But the star of the exhibit is the mighty U.S.S. *Massachusetts,* the battleship berthed here as a memorial to Massachusetts men and women who were killed in World War II. In the Fall River Heritage State Park Visitor Center are local history exhibits. From I-195, follow the signs for Battleship Cove (sometimes just the silhouette of the battleship is on the sign). The exhibits are open May to October, every day from 9 a.m. to 5 p.m.; November through April, every day from 9 a.m. to 4:30 p.m. There's a **Marine Museum** nearby at 70 Water St., Fall River (tel. 508/674-3533), which is open year round, Monday through Friday from 9 a.m. to 5 p.m., on Saturday and Sunday from 2 to 5 p.m.; open evenings in summer till 8 p.m. Tickets to all the ships and the museum cost $7 for adults, $3.50 for kids; active servicemen pay $5.50.

The combination ticket allows you to tour both above and below decks on all the ships. For lunch, you can have a meal or a snack in the wardroom of the U.S.S. *Massachusetts*. Other facilities at Battleship Cove, under the impressive I-195 bridge, are a snackbar, a Tourist Information Office with free hotel reservation assistance service, and toilets.

SHOPPING: Fall River is a mecca for those who love factory-outlet shopping, because the revival of apparel manufacture here has led to the opening of dozens of huge factory-outlet stores. Billboards on I-195 trumpet that it is the "largest factory outlet center in New England!" Signs lead you off the highway to the "Heart of Fall River's Factory Outlet District," with over 90 outlet stores. If you follow the signs will you really save money? Yes, a definitive yes!

I'm a skeptical shopper, and not a particularly enthusiastic one, but when I went to check out this factory-outlet district, even I was impressed. I ended up buying shirts, underwear, belts, and other items at very, very good prices. Quality can be either tops, or just under, or factory seconds, or worse. But in the store where I bought, quality was clearly marked, and prices were excellent on all of the different grades.

What can you find here? When it comes to clothing, *everything!* Shoes, sweaters, raincoats, accessories, designer labels, coats, handbags, jewelry, children's clothing, cosmetics, luggage. Branch out a bit and you'll find kitchenware, gifts, furniture, braided rugs, curtains, crystal, candy and nuts, greeting cards and gift-wrap, toys, towels, linens, baskets, brass—even wallpaper. This is definitely a town in which you can shop till you drop.

A NOTE ON LIZZIE: As for Fall River's other claim to fame, that's the celebrated Lizzie Borden murder trial in 1892, in which Lizzie, a young Fall River girl, was tried for chopping up her parents with an axe: it's good to remember that the poor girl was acquitted. The guilty party was never found.

CAPE COD

Cape Cod is a world of its own. This 70-mile-long arm of sand curled into the Atlantic was formed by glacial action and was given its name by an early (1602) visitor to the New World, Bartholomew Gosnold. The Pilgrims landed in the New World at Provincetown and drew up the Mayflower Compact before heading on to the mainland at what would become Plymouth.

Strictly speaking, Cape Cod is an island separated from the rest of Massachusetts by the Cape Cod Canal, a deep waterway built from north to south across the base of the cape in the early part of this century. Two graceful bridges span the canal, one at Bourne to the south (Rte. 28), one at Sagamore to the north (Rte. 6), and both are very busy in the warm months. Just before crossing either bridge, look for the little information sheds established by the Cape Cod Chamber of Commerce, open from 9 a.m. to 7 p.m. every day during the summer. Maps, booklets, motel brochures, and tabloid newspaper "current listings" are all yours for free, and if you need a room reservation, they'll help you get one.

The telephone area code for Cape Cod is 508.

1. Getting There

Cape Cod was once a seafarers' domain, and although it's still possible to get there by boat, the rail, bus, air, and road routes make it easy to get there any way you choose.

BY CAR: Coming from New York and Providence, take I-195 to Rte. 28 South and cross the Bourne Bridge if you're heading for Falmouth and Woods Hole; if you're going to Sandwich, Hyannis, or other Cape points, don't take the Bourne Bridge, but take U.S. 6 East just before the Bourne Bridge, and this will take you to the Sagamore Bridge, where you cross the canal. Coming from Boston, the Southeast Expressway (I-93) will take you right to Rte. 3 which goes straight to the Sagamore Bridge. If you're on your way to Falmouth and Woods Hole, stay on I-93 past the intersection with Rte. 3 and take Exit 66 for Rte. 24 South. This beautiful superhighway changes numbers and becomes Rte. 23, then Rte. 28, before taking you right over the Bourne Bridge.

BY RAIL: Cape Cod's first crowds of summer visitors came via rail from New York and Boston, and now you can come the same way.

Amtrak (tel. toll free 800/368-8725) in recent years has operated weekend service from New York City, Providence, and Boston to Hyannis, with trains departing New York on Friday and Saturday, and returning from Hyannis on Saturday and Sunday. One-way fare is currently $48. The railroad has arranged with Plymouth & Brockton St. Railway Co. for dedicated connecting bus service from Hyannis to Chatham, Dennisport, Eastham, Harwich, Orleans, South Yarmouth, Wellfleet, and Provincetown, which means that you can buy an Amtrak ticket in New York City for the trip all the way to the tip of the Cape. The service is funded in part by the Commonwealth of Massachusetts. Such special contracts are subject to governmental budgetary ups and downs, so you should definitely call Amtrak to see if the service is still running when you want it.

BY BUS: Bus service to the Cape from New York, Providence, and Boston is good, fast, and frequent. Here are the details:

From New York: Bonanza (Greyhound/Trailways ticket counter in Port Authority terminal; tel. 212/564-8484 or 212/594-2000) runs buses via two routes, along the coast or via Waterbury and Hartford. In high summer there are five buses a day from New York all the way to Provincetown at the tip of the Cape, and a good number of other buses going as far as Hyannis where you can transfer for other points.

From Providence/Newport: From Providence, catch the Bonanza bus (about six a day) to Hyannis, or the two a day going to Provincetown. The trip takes less than two hours to Hyannis. Bonanza's headquarters are at P.O. Box 1116, Annex Station, Providence, RI 02901 (tel. 401/751-8800).

From Boston: Plymouth & Brockton St. Railway Co. has buses which leave from the Greyhound Terminal (tel. 617/423-5810) and the South Station (Amtrak) Terminal (tel. 617/749-5067). The trip to Hyannis takes 1½ hours.

South Shore & Cape Cod Limo Service (tel. toll free 800/343-7540) makes four trips a day between Boston's Logan International Airport and Hyannis, with stops at Sagamore, Plymouth, and three other points. Reservations are strongly advised.

BY AIR: Business Express (tel. 203/222-1000, or toll free 800/345-3400), a Delta Connection carrier, provides service from Bridgeport, Conn., to Martha's Vineyard and Nantucket; also to Baltimore, Boston, Hyannis, New York (La Guardia), Philadelphia, and White Plains (N.Y.).

BY BOAT: Bay State Provincetown Steamship Company (tel. 617/723-7800 in Boston) operates the M/V *Provincetown II* on a run from Boston to P-town every day from late May through July and August until Labor Day; there's one daily sailing leaving Boston's Commonwealth Pier at 9:30 a.m., arriving P-town at about 12:30 p.m., and returning from P-town (at 3:30 p.m.) to Boston (arriving about 6:30 p.m.). A round-trip ticket for an adult costs $25, or $18 for Seniors and kids under 12; the one-way fare is $15; for seniors and kids, $13.

CAPE COD

TRANSPORTATION ON THE CAPE: Route 6, the Mid-Cape Hwy., is the fastest way to travel from the "Upper Cape" (the part you first come to by land) to the "Lower Cape" (the narrow portion north of Orleans to Provincetown). But Rte. 6 is not necessarily the prettiest way to go; if you have the time, travel one of the smaller, scenic roads instead.

Bus transportation on the Cape is provided by **Plymouth & Brockton St. Railway Co.,** Elm & Centre streets, Hyannis (tel. 508/775-5524). You can take a Plymouth & Brockton bus from Hyannis to Provincetown via Orleans, Eastham, and Wellfleet.

Transportation to the islands of Martha's Vineyard and Nantucket is covered in the sections on Woods Hole and Hyannis.

BED-AND-BREAKFAST RESERVATIONS: Bed & Breakfast Cape Cod, P.O. Box 341, West Hyannisport, MA 02672 (tel. 508/775-2772), will find you a room on Cape Cod for $36 to $60 single, $40 to $125 double, breakfast included. Write in plenty of time, and they'll send you a listing of homes that might interest you.

2. Falmouth and Woods Hole

Falmouth is a pretty town which has grown rapidly in recent years but which has managed to preserve a lot of the charm of a rural New England town. A city park next to the library, a well-preserved Village Green, and magnificent tall trees along Main Street make the downtown section attractive, and manicured lawns and white clapboard houses dress up the side streets. The town has a few pleasant historical inns, several good beaches, and daily ships to Martha's Vineyard.

A few miles past Falmouth to the south is Woods Hole, home of world-famous Woods Hole Oceanographic Institute; car-ferries depart from Woods Hole for Martha's Vineyard several times daily in summer.

TOURIST INFORMATION: The **Falmouth Chamber of Commerce,** P.O. Box 582, Falmouth, MA 02541 (tel. 508/548-8500), operates an Information Office downtown off Main Street in the Lawrence Academy building. Look for a short street called Academy Lane. If they can't answer your question, it's probably not about Falmouth.

WHERE TO STAY: Falmouth has dozens of motels, mostly expensive and somewhat sterile though modern and comfortable. For the true flavor of Falmouth, however, I'd recommend the moderately priced small inns and guesthouses. I've included descriptions of the best of the larger places as well. During off-season, when inquiring about room prices, be sure to ask about reductions for stays of a few days or more. A room costing $60 for one night may well cost $55 per night if you stay two or three days.

Guesthouses and Inns

Falmouth is rich in guesthouses, which is not surprising. The way to spend a week or two by the sea, at moderate cost, is to rent a room in a private home. Lots of houses in **Falmouth Heights,** southeast of the center of Falmouth proper, are devoted to renting rooms for about $40 to $45 double, with a shared bathroom. If you specifically request it, your room may have a view of the sea. You should also be aware that this is the most boisterous section of town. But before describing the guest-houses, you should know about two charming inns right downtown near Falmouth Green.

DOWNTOWN: A few steps from the Falmouth Historical Society is the **Palmer House Inn,** 81 Palmer Ave., Falmouth, MA 02540 (tel. 508/548-1230), very near the green and the center of town. Each of the eight guest rooms in this turn-of-the-century Victorian house has a private bath, and a wonderful haute-cuisine breakfast is included in the double-occupancy room price of $82 to $100. If the perfect location doesn't get you, the stained glass will.

Mostly Hall, 27 W. Main St., Falmouth, MA 02540 (tel. 508/548-3786), is only steps from Falmouth Green and the beginning of the bicycle path to Woods Hole. The plantation-style house was built in 1849 as a wedding present for the New Orleans bride of Capt. Albert Nye. These days you can stay in any of six guest rooms for $77 to $105 double with private bath; these rates include a full breakfast, the use of bicycles, and the inevitable tax. For getting the real flavor of Falmouth, Mostly Hall can't be beat.

ALONG GRAND AVENUE: The guesthouses on Grand Avenue in Falmouth Heights differ only slightly in price, accommodations, sea views, and charm. During the summer season your selection may well have to be made on the basis of availability.

Head down Falmouth Heights Road, which skirts the eastern side of Falmouth Harbor, and soon you'll see Grand Avenue bearing off to the right. It then makes a loop south and east, running along Falmouth Heights Beach before heading back to rejoin Falmouth Heights Road. Heading in this direction, house numbers go in descending order.

The **Grafton Inn,** 261 Grand Ave. South, Falmouth Heights, MA 02540 (tel. 508/540-8688), is right across the street from the main beach area, with snack stands and restaurants located conveniently nearby. All 11 rooms have private baths and rent for $72 to $94 double, year round. Rates include a fine buffet breakfast, an enclosed porch, sufficient parking, and a very comfortable, simple atmosphere. No smoking, no children, and no pets.

The **Gladstone Inn,** 219 Grand Ave. South, Falmouth Heights, MA 02540 (tel. 508/548-9851), is at the corner of Montgomery Avenue, across the street from the beach. A glassed-in veranda shares the sea view, and this is where you have your buffet breakfast or cool afternoon drink. All rooms share baths; singles go for $30, while doubles run $50. There is a newly renovated apartment over the garage behind the house, which rents for $66. Reservations are taken for two-night minimums only.

OUT OF THE CENTER: Located on Jones Road at the corner of Gifford Street are the venerable red farmhouse, barn, and sheds, which make up the **Coonamessett Inn,** (P.O. Box 707), Falmouth, MA 02540 (tel. 508/548-2300). After swiftly checking in at the hotel-like lobby, two people can move right into a sitting-room/bedroom combo for $127, a living-room/two-bedroom combo for $143 or a cottage for $154. Prices drop roughly 30% in the off-season. The rear of the property is landscaped beautifully, sloping gently down to a lake where a gaggle of geese make its home.

Moderately Priced Motels

My favorite in Falmouth is the **Elm Arch Inn,** off Main Street, Falmouth, MA 02540 (tel. 508/548-0133). Although originally a private house, the inn has been taking paying guests for over a century—more than 60 years under the present management. The location couldn't be better: right in the center of town, a few steps from the library park, and yet back off Main Street in peace and quiet. The inn's 24 rooms are furnished in colonial-style pieces, many handmade, and are just plain charming. Several have private baths; others have running water and share a bath down the hall. In Richardson House, the addition to the inn, there are private baths and air conditioning throughout. Rooms with a double or twin beds and bath cost $50 to $55 in season, $42 off-season. Rooms with running water cost $40. No meals are served, but the inn offers free coffee in the mornings, in season. Note that the inn rooms do not have air conditioning, but that a good crossbreeze usually makes it unnecessary anyway; the living room has a color TV. Although you're a 15-minute walk from the beach here, the inn has its own small pool, bordered by a lush lawn and large trees, and a big screened patio for summer evenings.

The **Shore Way Acres Motel** is more a resort than a motel, with two pools (indoor and outdoor), extensive grounds covered in lush grass, flowers, and trees. It's midway between downtown and the beach on Shore Street (tel. 508/540-3000, or toll free 800/352-7100 in Massachusetts)—you'll first come across its center-piece, the stately old white clapboard lodge, dripping with wisteria. Behind the lodge are several attractive buildings with rooms and the glassed-in pool building. Saunas and an exercise room are included among the facilities. The rates here are somewhat of a tangle, and depend on the building you stay in, the time of year you stay, the length of your stay, the number of beds you use, and whether or not your room has kitchen facilities. In general, double rooms with bath cost $83 to $138. In season and on holidays, the minimum reservation period on weekends is three nights.

WHERE TO DINE: Falmouth is not a culinary mecca, although it does have a few quite decent eateries, some good for breakfast or a light lunch, others for a more formal dinner. The **Town House Restaurant,** 275 Main St. (tel. 508/548-0285), across the street from the town library, has been serving for more than 40 years. One of the first things you'll notice as you enter is the wood wainscoting and barn boards that dress the walls, and the liberal use of brick that gives the restaurant a rustic but warm feeling. At lunchtime there are soup-and-sandwich specials, a bowl of the soup of the day plus a choice sandwich for under $5. In the evening, the Mariner Platter (sole, clams, scallops, shrimp, and onion rings) is $12. Broiled seafood and fresh boiled live lobsters are also offered. Be sure to inspect the seascape in watercolor painted by a local artist. Note that the Town House is open from late May to late October *only:* hours are weekdays from 7:30 a.m. to 10 p.m., weekends from 11:30 a.m. to 10 p.m.

Domingo's Olde Restaurant, on Rte. 28A, W. Falmouth (tel. 508/540-0575), serves excellent, moderately priced seafood (with Italian overtones) in an unassuming converted old home. Choose from lobster, swordfish, seafood kabob, or veal marsala. I had bouillabaisse chock-full of shrimp, haddock, oysters, scallops, and mussels, a side order of garlic bread, and a simple dessert for $28 (tax and tip included), but that's about as high as it goes, unless you order lobster. Check the daily specials for the freshest fish. Give Domingo's a day's notice and they can prepare a special request for you. The restaurant is open everyday from 4 to 11 p.m.; make reservations to be on the safe side.

For an earthy-crunchy, healthful lunch (from 11:30 a.m. to 3 p.m. any day), try **Peach Tree Circle,** on Old Palmer Avenue (tel. 508/548-2354). Take the Sippiwissett exit of Rte. 28 and keep to the left; it's worth the two-mile drive from the Village Green. In addition to selling flowers, fruit, cheeses, and other picnic fixings, they also serve fish chowder for $3.75 a cup, broccoli quiche for $3.50, and full chef's salads for $6. Enjoy a relaxing lunch out on the platform porch under the shade of old trees or inside amid natural stained paneling.

For quick and surprisingly light fried seafood, go where the locals go year round: **McMenamy's Fried Seafood,** on busy Rte. 28 heading toward Hyannis (tel. 508/540-2115). Eat on picnic tables behind the restaurant, inside with noisy families, or take it to the beach. For $5.50 try the fish 'n chips or splurge by these standards and get a shrimp or clam plate for $8.50. For an authentic taste add a dash of vinegar to the chips.

For Elegant Dinners

Falmouth's finest place to dine from late May through mid-September is undoubtedly **The Regatta** (tel. 508/548-5400), at the southern end of Scranton Avenue, overlooking the mouth of Falmouth's long harbor. Open only for dinner every evening from 5:30 to about 10 p.m., the Regatta offers classic French and American cuisine. You'll want to be dressed neatly, if informally, and you should bring $50 per person to dine, wine included. Start with Chesapeake Bay soft-shell crab pancetta, or grilled shrimp with three-mustard sauce; then proceed to the palette of two fish, each with its own sauce, or boneless rack of lamb en chemise, sauce Cabernet, and finish up with their chocolate seduction cake with raspberry sauce. Call for reservations.

On the same wavelength is the **Coonamessett Inn** dining room, on Jones Road at the corner of Gifford Street (tel. 508/548-2300); casual elegance, traditional New England cuisine, and service that's attentive yet not overbearing. Start with chilled oysters on the half shell or their popular quahog chowder, proceed to a delightful seafood Newburg in casserole, save room for a side of homemade fresh pasta of the day, and then linger over coffee and their deservedly famous Indian pudding. Expect to spend $35 (for one), including tax and tip, for that particular combination.

The dining room is open for lunch from 11:30 a.m. to 2:30 p.m. Monday to Saturday, noon to 3 p.m. Sunday; for dinner from 5:30 to 9 p.m. nightly. Eli's, a more casual alternative, serves the dining room lunch menu throughout the day; try a chicken club ($7) or shrimp scampi ($10). Before you leave check out the *Legend of the Mermaid* paintings that hang in the dining room.

WHAT TO SEE: Falmouth is a very pretty town, and walks through the beaches, the older sections of town, and along the Village Green are a must. For a detailed map, or for other information, send for the 68-page brochure from the **Falmouth Chamber of Commerce** (P.O. Box 582, Falmouth, MA 02541) (tel. 508/548-8500).

During the summer season the **Falmouth Historical Society** has offerings in its lovely old mansion on Palmer Street, just off the Village Green, open Monday through Friday from 2 to 5 p.m. Admission is $1 for adults, 50¢ for children. For the price of admission you get to see the house next door (Conant House), walk in the formal garden between the two, and view the memorial room to Katherine Bates, the poet who wrote "America the Beautiful," Falmouth's local-girl-made-good. The people at the historical society will be sure to point out that the white Congregational church on the green is equipped with a bell cast by Paul Revere.

One of America's—and the world's—most exciting experiments in ecological living is being carried out at the **New Alchemy Institute,** 237 Hatchville Rd., in Hatchville (East Falmouth), MA 02536 (tel. 508/564-6301). The latest, or sometimes the most ancient, cultivation methods are being researched and adapted to fit the world of the future. The success that the New Alchemists have had in growing nutritious vegetables and fruits year round, using solar energy, without chemical fertilizers or pesticides, is amazing. You have to see it all to believe it, and you can do it by dropping in any Wednesday through Sunday from mid-June through mid-September, for a guided tour at 1 p.m. Self-guided tours are possible daily year round. There is also a garden stand selling organically grown produce.

WHAT TO DO: A prime Falmouth activity is to rent bicycles and take the **bike path** down to Woods Hole (see below). The Bikeways Committee of the Falmouth

Chamber of Commerce publishes a pamphlet-map showing bike routes and beaches, and giving the addresses of shops that rent bicycles. Ask at the Information Office mentioned above, or call the chamber at 508/548-8500. By biking to a beach you avoid paying the several dollars for parking, and you can put the money saved toward the rental fee.

Besides bicycling down to Woods Hole, Falmouth's greatest outdoor attraction is its coastline. The **town beach** is down at the end of Shore Street (best to walk, as parking can be a problem). The water can be very chilly except in July and August, but otherwise the beach is fine, with a view of Martha's Vineyard in the distance.

Reputedly the best beach in Falmouth is called **Old Silver Beach,** several miles to the northwest of downtown Falmouth. If you have a bike, that's the way to go even though it's a distance, because it will cost you $6 to park when you get to Old Silver. In a way the parking fee is not so bad, for it helps the town keep the beach clean. A headland and several jetties set the beach off into sections; the town runs a **Clam Bar** which sells sandwiches, fried clams, and soft drinks, and offers changing rooms. The crowd at Old Silver is spirited, young, and sun-hungry.

The town of Falmouth sponsors free **band concerts** down at the Falmouth Marina on Thursday evenings during the months of July and August. Try to make it to at least one concert; it's a real oldtime event.

Falmouth also has its own summer theater, the **Falmouth Playhouse** (tel. 508/563-5922), with a playbill of musicals which begins June 2 and goes right through October. The playhouse has its own restaurant and lounge, and you get a cut on dinner-and-theater deals. Tickets are $12 Tuesday through Friday and Sunday, $14 on Saturday. Those with children will want to call and find out what's playing on the Children's Theater bill (Monday mornings and afternoons) as well, where all tickets cost $4.

ACROSS TO MARTHA'S VINEYARD: Falmouth's own *Island Queen,* Falmouth Heights Road (tel. 508/548-4800), built 1974, carries passengers and bicycles only (no cars) from Falmouth Harbor to Oak Bluffs on the island. It does not operate year round, but sails two times a day in each direction during early June and mid-September (four times a day on weekends), and seven times a day in each direction from mid-June through the first week in September. Adults pay $8 round trip ($4.25 one way); children under 13 pay $4 round trip. Bicycles are taken at a charge of $5 round trip. The voyage takes about a half hour, and is usually quite smooth and comfortable. A refreshment bar on board serves snacks, sandwiches, soft drinks, beer, and cocktails. There is even a moonlight cruise on Tuesday and Thursday evenings in July and August.

For car-ferries to the islands, you'll have to go to Woods Hole or Hyannis (see those sections for full particulars).

WOODS HOLE: When the Emperor of Japan visited the United States in 1976, one of the places he requested to visit was Woods Hole. Being a marine biologist himself, he was interested in seeing one of the world's great centers for the study of sea life, the **Woods Hole Oceanographic Institute** (WHOI). In a sense the institute is the town, for its buildings, and that of its sister establishments, take up most of the space at the tip of a tiny peninsula, leaving room for only a few streets of fine old houses, a few small boatyards, a restaurant or two, and the car-ferry docks to Martha's Vineyard and Nantucket islands.

The institute has no exhibits open to the public, but the U.S. Department of Commerce's National Marine Fisheries Service maintains an **aquarium** (tel. 548-5123), on Water Street (the town's main street) down at the end of the peninsula — follow Water Street through the town, and just after it turns right, the aquarium is on your left. It's open mid-June to mid-September from 10 a.m. to 4 p.m. daily; from 9 a.m. to 4 p.m. the rest of the year; admission is free.

Where to Stay

Staying overnight in Woods Hole is not particularly cheap, although it can be very pleasant. The **Sands of Time Motor Inn** (tel. 508/548-6300), just outside the downtown section on the main road to Falmouth, has a fine view of the harbor and is only a short walk from the ferry docks. A unit of motel rooms overlooks the water, while a huge old shingled house behind it serves as lodge. A small garden and swimming pool are fitted into the hillside between the two. In the motel rooms, prices are $93 to $105 double in season; all these rooms come with air conditioning, private bath, color TV, and two double beds (extra-person charge, $5). In the shingled "inn," rooms are lower in price, except the ones with working fireplaces and color TV, and all the inn rooms have a view of the water. The inn rooms are quite nice and flawlessly maintained, with crystal doorknobs, bright new paint, and sparkling bathrooms. A grandfather clock inhabits the pretty entranceway. Most of the rooms in the Sands of Time's several buildings have no air conditioning, but the breezes off the water usually render this unnecessary.

A few doors down from the motel you'll find eight more distinctive rooms and a cottage at the **Grey Whale Inn,** 565 Woods Hole Rd., Woods Hole, MA 02543 (tel. 508/548-7692). Two attic rooms share a bath, but the rest have private baths. Antique beds, immaculate rooms, a lovely view of Little Harbor, and complimentary bikes are included in the high-season room rate of $94 to $105 double. The inn is a half mile from the dock but the owners have been known to drive guests who have too much luggage to manage on their own.

Where to Dine

A few restaurants near the ferry docks specialize in big, rich seafood dinners at substantial prices—just what you don't want before taking a boat ride if there's any chance the water may be a bit rough, so I recommend that you have a light lunch at the **Fishmonger's Café,** on Woods Hole's main street just before the little bridge, on the left (official address, 56 Water St.; no phone). Lunch and dinner specials are written on the blackboard and sandwiches are available anytime. There are also many burgers and vegetarian entrees from which to choose. Fish and chips is $9.50; a good clam chowder is $3.15 a cup, $4.25 a bowl. Wine and beer are served with meals. The atmosphere is rustic, with rough wood tables, board floors, and sea breezes wafting in through the windows. Heavily patronized by local people and visitors to the institute, you may hear Japanese or Spanish being spoken as foreign biologists discuss their countries' marine problems and opportunities. Service is fast (there's a take-out window too), which is what you need if you have to catch a ferry. The Fishmonger's Café is open from 7 a.m. to 11 p.m. every day except Tuesday, when it opens at 11:30 a.m.

CAR FERRY TO THE ISLANDS: The **Woods Hole, Martha's Vineyard and Nantucket Steamship Authority,** P.O. Box 284, Woods Hole, MA 02543 (tel. 508/540-2022), operates car-carrying ferries between the points listed in their name, and also Hyannis. Schedules change several times a year, so it's best to call in advance for full current information. In fact, if you plan to ship your car, you *must* have a car reservation. You can get one by calling the number above. Ferries from Woods Hole to Vineyard Haven or Oak Bluffs on Martha's Vineyard Island leave about six times a day in winter, ten times a day in summer, on the 45-minute trip. Fares are $7.50 round trip for adults, half price for kids 5 to 15, free for kids under 5. Bikes go for $2.50 one way. Autos cost $26.50 one way in season. You can't get from Woods Hole or Falmouth to Nantucket, but you can from Hyannis (see "Hyannis").

It is possible to take your car from Woods Hole to Martha's Vineyard, and then, later, from the Vineyard to Nantucket, or vice-versa. Return to the mainland is to Hyannis only (see Section 4 on Hyannis).

Parking Fees at the Docks: If you don't plan to ferry your car over, and you don't ride a bike or take the bus to Woods Hole, figure on paying $6 to park your car for each *calendar* day ($12 if you leave your car overnight). It is virtually impossible to find a free, legal parking place in Woods Hole in summer or for overnight unless you stay at a motel and use its lot. The Steamship Authority has a dockside lot charging these fees, and also two large lots in Falmouth (if one is full they'll direct you to the other), with free shuttle-bus service to the Woods Hole docks. In late July and all of August you can often save yourself some time by planning to park in a Falmouth lot, because the dockside lot is almost always full.

The Woods Hole ferry docks are served by Plymouth & Brockton Street Railway buses to Boston and by Bonanza lines to Providence and New York. *Important note:* Although bus schedules leaving Woods Hole are designed to work in conjunction with ferry arrivals, connections are not guaranteed because weather can make the ferry late, and *the bus does not wait*. Do not take the last ferry of the day from the islands to Woods Hole (or to Hyannis) and count on getting the last bus out—you may in fact be able to do it, but it's not dependable. Take an earlier ferry.

---

3. Sandwich

Sandwich calls itself "the oldest town on the Cape" (incorporated 1639), and it is certainly one of the most beautiful and serene. Much of the vacation traffic to the Cape rushes past it on the way to Provincetown, leaving Sandwich to those few who appreciate it. The town holds its appeal both winter and summer, for although it has beaches, its antique stores and gracious old houses also draw visitors. Other attractions are Heritage Plantation, Dexter's Mill, and the Sandwich Glass Museum, which holds a fine collection of the interesting glassware once made here.

WHERE TO STAY: Sandwich has a good selection of guesthouses.

The prime bed-and-breakfast place in Sandwich has a perfect name: the **Summer House,** 158 Old Main St., Sandwich, MA 02563 (tel. 508/888-4991). Built around 1835 in the Greek Revival style popular at that time, the entire whimsical front of the house is set aside for guests. One double room, on the first floor, has a private bath ($66 to $77 double); the four bedrooms on the second floor share two baths ($55 to $66 double). Continental breakfast is included. You'll enjoy the porch, lawn, patio, and garden here.

The **Captain Ezra Nye House,** 152 Main St., Sandwich, MA 02563 (tel. 508/888-6142), is a lovely little place with six bedrooms, two of which share a bath and rent for $50 to $61 double, while the rooms with private bath rent for $72 to $83 double in season. From November to Memorial Day, they drop $10. Choose your bedroom according to color preference—green, yellow, blue, or calico—and admire the hand-stenciling upstairs on the floors and walls. An expanded continental breakfast is included in the rates.

The **Isaiah Jones Homestead,** 165 Main St., Sandwich, MA 02563 (tel. 508/888-9115), is a small bed and breakfast operated by the Catania family. The four rooms, all with private bath (one has a whirlpool), have a rather formal feel to them, but not uncomfortably so. Plush carpeting, chintz fabrics, alcove sitting areas, triple sheeting on the beds, and fresh flowers are all the norm here. A candlelit continental breakfast set at one long table and afternoon tea are included in the room rates of $88 to $110 double. Off-season, when Cape Cod is pleasantly devoid of traffic snarls, rates are $15 less per room.

WHERE TO DINE: Those watching their budgets and yet possessed of a great hunger will want to know about the **Sagamore Inn** (tel. 508/888-9707), on the Sandwich-Sagamore line on Rte. 6A (you come to the green-and-white inn after the

Sagamore Bridge, before the town of Sandwich). The decor is not fancy: wooden booths, a stamped-tin ceiling. The waitresses are all hometown women, the clientele local families, and the food is hearty, savory, and delicious, the portions huge, and the prices low. The cook's inspiration is Italian cuisine, and so you can find spaghetti dishes for $6.95 to $11.95, seafood for $9.50 to $14.95, sandwiches for $1.75 to $5.75, and such treats as a medium-size antipasto plate for $5. Everyone here is friendly and pleasant, and out to make you happy. Open from 11:30 a.m. to 9 p.m. Friday through Sunday and 4 to 9 p.m. on Monday, Wednesday, and Thursday in season.

Those not watching their budgets but who still value their dollar will want to know about the Conservatory at the **Daniel Webster Inn,** 149 Main St. (tel. 508/888-3622), right in the middle of town. The Catania family has been in the restaurant business for years, starting Hearth 'n Kettle restaurants and the Pewter Pot chain. The dining room here is a first-class establishment and serves all three meals. When you make dinner reservations (a must or be prepared for a wait) request the Conservatory—a grand solarium with high ceilings, views of the impeccable landscaping, potted indoor trees, servers in period costume, and beautifully presented dishes. The lighting for evening dinners is special. They offer a nice selection of beef and seafood. An early-evening special (you must be seated by 4:45 p.m.) will get you a complete dinner for $12.

WHAT TO SEE: Sandwich is an old-fashioned town true to its traditions, a very pleasant place to live or to visit. A walk downtown will give you clues to its character right away; backyard shops for artisans working in wood, leather, wrought iron, clay, or oil-on-canvas; graceful church steeples; small, well-groomed parks; comely old houses, many with the date of construction posted over the front door.

Sooner or later your walk will bring you by **Yesteryears Doll and Miniature Museum** at Main and River Streets, housed in what was once the First Parish Meetinghouse (tel. 508/888-1711). Literally hundreds of fascinating antique dolls, dollhouses, and toys as well as many other domestic articles are on display, and exhibits change from time to time. The museum is nonprofit, but charges admission to defray expenses: $2.50 per adult, $1.50 per child under 12, $2 for seniors. It's open mid-May through late October, Monday to Saturday from 10 a.m. to 4 p.m.

From Yesteryear's it's a short walk to the **Dexter Mill,** at the end of a lovely mill pond (complete with ducks), and next to a cool, splashing mill race and an old pump. The mill (1654) was fully restored in 1961, and is not just a picturesque attraction, although you can go in (daily from 10 a.m. to 5 p.m. till Labor Day) and see the wooden mechanisms at work. The mill actually grinds corn and you can buy bags of fresh meal the same day it's ground. Admission is $1.25 for adults, 75¢ for children 12 to 16.

Across from Sandwich's Greek Revival town hall on Rte. 130 is the **Sandwich Glass Museum** (tel. 508/888-0251), open daily from 9:30 a.m. to 4:30 p.m. April 1 through October 31, shorter hours in winter (closed January). Admission is $2.50 for adults and 50¢ for children between 6 and 12; special group rates and a year-round schedule are available. Sandwich was a major glass-producing town from 1825 to 1888, and although it specialized in the new process of pressing glass in a mold, it also produced blown, cut, etched, and enameled products as well. A brilliant collection of this American glassware is on display, and dioramas, videos, and pictures show how it was made. Glassmakers' tools and other articles of Sandwich memorabilia are also part of the museum's collection. The glass museum is the only one of its kind on the Cape. Special exhibits are installed each year.

Perhaps Sandwich's most famous attraction is the **Heritage Plantation of Sandwich** (tel. 508/888-3300), a mile from town on Grove Street. Another of the museums in which New England abounds, Heritage Plantation specializes not in any one era but has exhibits from all periods of American history. The automobile collection, 34 cars dating from 1899 to 1936, is one of the most popular things to see. Another collection is of firearms and military miniatures, and still others show American crafts and the tools used to perform them. The buildings and grounds of the plantation are an attraction in themselves: all are reproductions of early-style buildings set in gardens and nature areas covering 76 acres. The plantation is open daily from 10 a.m. to 5 p.m. mid-May through the end of October, and one ticket ($7 for adults, $6 for seniors, $3 for kids; 5 and under, free) admits a visitor to the grounds, all exhibits, and any of the periodically scheduled shows, concerts, and other activities.

Sandwich has several old houses open to the public for a fee, the best known of which is **Hoxie House,** on Rte. 130 along the shore of Shawme Pond (the mill pond). The house dates from the end of the 1600s, and has been restored and furnished with articles of that period. The house is open from 10 a.m. to 5 p.m. Monday through Saturday, 1 to 5 p.m. on Sunday, from mid-June through September. You can buy a $2 combination ticket good for admission here and at the Dexter Mill.

The town's beaches include **Town Beach,** the most westerly, and then, in order heading east, **Spring Hill Beach, East Sandwich Beach,** and over the line in Barnstable, **Sandy Neck Beach.** They all have toilets and places to park, and the bay side of the Cape has generally warmer swimming than the ocean side. Look for signs to the beaches on the side roads left (north) off Rte. 6A between Sandwich and Barnstable.

---

4. Hyannis

Hyannis gained national fame during the presidency of John F. Kennedy because of his summer home in nearby Hyannisport. Some of the town's growth and perhaps a good portion of its honky-tonk dates from that time, and although curious or devoted fans of the late president still stop to look at the town or to visit its memorial to JFK, the attractions in Hyannis these days are commercial. Should you need the services of an airline, department store, supermarket, or foreign auto parts warehouse while on the Cape, Hyannis is the place to come. If you don't need these things, there are many nicer places on the Cape to spend precious vacation time.

TRANSPORTATION: Specifics on schedules and routes are given above in this chapter's first section, "Getting There." Here's what you'll want to know about Hyannis's facilities:

Airport: The airport is right in town, a short taxi ride from the bus stations or downtown. Several companies offer small planes for charter.

Bus Stations: Greyhound/Bonanza and **Plymouth & Brockton buses** all use the same terminal at Elm and Centre Streets (tel. 508/775-5524). **Cape Cod Bus Lines** has its main terminal in Falmouth, and uses the Plymouth & Brockton terminal in Hyannis for its trips to Yarmouth, Dennis, Brewster, Orleans, Eastham, Wellfleet, Truro, and Provincetown. **Peter Pan Bus Lines,** which has routes from Hyannis to Amherst, Northampton, Holyoke, Springfield, and Worcester (daily in the summer but only on Friday and Sunday off-season) also uses the Plymouth & Brockton terminal.

Boat Docks: Hyannis has two main docks, at the foot of Ocean Street for fishing and cruise vessels, and at the foot of Pleasant Street for the passenger and car-ferries to Nantucket on the Steamship Authority's boats (tel. 508/771-4000). The docks are about five blocks from the bus stations. (Many buses connecting with ferries take passengers right to the dock.)

WHERE TO STAY: A choice area of motels and guesthouses is down Sea Street, off Main Street south toward Keyes Memorial Beach. One such place is just off Sea Street on Gosnold Street. The **Captain Gosnold Village,** P.O. Box 544, Hyannis, MA 02601 (tel. 508/775-9111), is a collection of different types of housing units spread through large and well-kept lawns and copses of trees. Guests have the use of a heated pool, children's playground, shuffleboard, and picnic tables. From late June until Labor Day, motel rooms cost $72 (suitable for two, three, or four people); efficiencies are $77; a one-bedroom cottage, $93 (other cottages higher); and $10 for an extra person. Also, discounts for longer stays (over a week) can save you money during off-season periods. Rooms are paneled, carpeted, equipped with a refrigerator, TV, and coffee maker, and all have private bath. The beach is a ten-minute walk away.

The **Sea Breeze Inn,** 397 Sea St., Hyannis, MA 02601 (tel. 508/771-7213), is very close to **Sea Street** Beach, and has 13 rooms and one efficiency cottage equipped with TV, private tile baths, and (in a few rooms) a view of the ocean. Rates vary with the size of the room, number of beds, and similar features, but a normal double costs $55 to $80 in season; breakfast is included.

Sea Street has at least six guesthouses varying from those with very simple rooms-only to those offering a bit of atmosphere and service. The **Sea Witch Inn,** 363 Sea St., Hyannis, MA 02601 (tel. 508/771-4261 or 775-3608), is one such guesthouse on the street, about equidistant from Main Street and Keyes Beach. The lawn is large and lush, shade trees rise here and there, and the inn is painted an appropriately nautical blue-and-white. Rooms here cost $30 to $65 per day for two people in a room; most rooms are in the $30 to $45 range. If you rent by the week there's a reduction, as there is if you come in months other than July and August. For longer stays, the Sea Witch has a studio apartment and a cottage for rent by the week.

What's in a name? Well, the turn-of-the century Victorian bed-and-breakfast **Elegance by the Sea,** 162 Sea St., Hyannis, MA 02601 (tel. 508/775-3595), would certainly answer "everything" to that question. With only six guest rooms in this huge house, bedrooms, common rooms, and even bathrooms are quite spacious. Upstairs are pineapple-post beds, other period antiques, and black-and-white tiled floors in the old-fashioned bathroom. All rooms rent for $80 double, but the room downstairs has a working fireplace; all include a hearty breakfast. If you come during the holidays, you'll be in for special treats.

One of my favorites is the **Inn on Sea Street,** at no. 358 Sea St., Hyannis, MA 02601 (tel. 508/775-8030). It's another small, elegant Victorian house, with flair and without pretense. Everything feels crisp, bright, neat, and useful. On the low end of the price scale ($55 double) is a white and wicker room that was fashioned from the sun porch; in fact, it's not rented on cool nights. The three highest-priced rooms ($80 double) have private baths, though for one of these access is down a private set of stairs. (It's unique and fun if you're in the mood.) Five small antique tables with lace cloths comprise the dining room where a delicious breakfast of fruits, cheese, and granola is served.

Bouchard's Tourist Homes and Apartments and Cottages, 83 School St., Hyannis, MA 02601 (tel. 508/775-0912), has several buildings and therefore a larger number of rooms at tourist-home prices, plus some apartments for long-term stays. Lowest price is for a room without running water which shares a tub-and-shower bathroom with one other room; cost is $35 single. For $40 two people can have a room with air conditioning; for $55 there are rooms with cable color TV, air conditioning, twin beds, private tub-and-shower bath, even a private entrance. Off-season rates for the rooms (after Labor Day until the last week in June) can go as low as $10 to $14 a day per person, double occupancy. The same woman has been running this place since 1935 and she'll only charge you $4 to keep your car here if you're heading to the islands.

WHERE TO DINE: Hyannis has a good number of restaurants, most of them serving the same things in the same surroundings at the same prices (with food of the same quality). All the national chains, from Burger King to Howard Johnson's, have representatives here, and while serviceable, these places are hardly atmospheric. If you've just landed in Hyannis from New York and you want to dive into New England's gustatory pleasures right away, seek out the following:

Follow your nose and the locals' toes to a newer place this season: **Up the Creek,** on Old Colony Road (tel. 508/771-7866). Turn left off Sea Street onto Gosnold Street and then take your first left (you can't miss the jammed parking lot). It's open for lunch weekdays and Saturdays from 11:30 a.m. to 2:30 p.m., brunch on Sunday (quite a bargain at $7.50), and dinner every night from 5 to 10 p.m. Reservations are recommended. Expect a cozy, tasteful, dark interior. Try a fish, chicken, or sirloin lunch for $5 to $6. For dinner choose from chicken Simone at $8.50 or a light sole Florentine at $9 or their special seafood strudel (lobster, shrimp, scallops, crab, and cheese wrapped in pastry) at $7.50.

In the mood to go where the pretty people go? Then head to the **Roadhouse Café** on South Street, right off Main Street (tel. 508/775-2386). It's as good for afternoon cocktails as it is for romantic dinner. The mood is evoked by hanging plants, a wraparound glassed-in porch with tables for two or four, lanterns on the stained exterior, and blue awnings. But what about the food? A standard variety of sandwiches and soups average $6. As for dinner, check the blackboard for daily specials in addition to these standbys: fettuccine primavera, baked stuffed cape scallops, beef burgundy, veal marsala, or chicken parmesan, offered for $12 to $15 each. Open year round, seven days a week from 11:30 a.m. to 10 p.m.

Right on Main Street, at no. 415, in the center of the shopping district, is the **Asa Bearse House Restaurant** (tel. 508/771-4131). The house's big old porch is a favorite Hyannis spot for cocktails; the crowd usually moves to the front-lawn terrace if the weather's fine. The luncheon menu lists lots of sandwiches, but the special lunch-of-the-day—something like a quiche or fish dish—is only $8, including salad and rolls. At dinner the menu turns exotic, to escargots, and familiar, to steaks; dinner costs about $35 to $45. Open daily from 11:30 a.m. to 10 p.m. for food, till 1 a.m. for drinks in season. The 1840 barn in back, opened in 1981, is quite handsome.

Harvard Square's **Wursthaus** (tel. 508/771-5000) has a branch in Hyannis, in the Cape Cod Mall. Boasting the "world's largest selection of foreign beers," the Wursthaus is the place to find Mexican Dos Equis and Israeli Gold Star as well as Löwenbräu and Beck's. A long list of sandwiches ($3 to $6), salad plates, side orders, and desserts keeps the light-lunch and late-night crowds happy, while for hungrier diners there are steaks ($8 to $14) and moderately priced fish. The Wursthaus specializes in Bavarian-style food and is open for lunch and then until midnight daily.

READER'S RESTAURANT SELECTION: "Whenever you find yourself on pricey Cape Cod looking for a restaurant that cuts down on the check and not on the quality of the food, go to **Gringo's,** on Main Street (tel. 508/771-8449). For about $10 you can wine and dine on Mexican food or delicious seafood. Have your meal outdoors by candlelight and observe the action on Hyannis's 'Sunset Strip'" (Eddy Verelst, Dendermonde, Belgium).

WHAT TO SEE: Many visitors to Hyannis stop to see the memorial to President Kennedy, a stone structure bearing the presidential seal and a small fountain, on Ocean Street right along the water. Hyannisport and the **"Kennedy compound,"** noted in news stories while the late president vacationed here, are not far from the monument. None of the buildings is open to the public.

Also along Ocean Street are **Kalmus Park** and **Veteran's Park,** with their respective beaches, bathhouses, and snackbars. Go down to the south end of Sea Street for none other than **Sea Street Beach.** Besides swimming facilities, Sea Street Beach has a little platform on top of a dune from which you can take a look at the sweep of the beach.

Big-name stars and bands are booked into the **Cape Cod Melody Tent,** at the West Main Street Rotary in Hyannis (tel. 508/775-9100). The season goes from late June through Labor Day, and runs the gamut—from Bob Hope and Tony Bennett all the way to Crystal Gayle. Tickets are priced differently depending on the show, but most run in the $16 to $30 range, with selected Tuesday and Thursday matinees and weeknight performances. Children's shows are Wednesday mornings at 11 a.m. Tickets can be charged by calling the box office.

FERRIES TO THE ISLANDS: Two firms operate ferries to the islands of Martha's Vineyard and Nantucket from Hyannis, each sailing from a different dock. Here are the details:

Woods Hole, Martha's Vineyard, and Nantucket Steamship Authority (tel. 508/540-2022 for car reservations; the number in Hyannis is 508/771-4000) runs car and passenger ferries from Hyannis's Pleasant Street docks (follow the signs in town). No direct service is run between Hyannis and Martha's Vineyard by this firm—you have to go via Nantucket or, preferably, direct from Woods Hole to Martha's Vineyard. The Steamship Authority's boats run six times daily to Nantucket in summer, less frequently off-season; the trip takes about 2½ hours and costs $8.50 for adults, half fare for kids 5 to 15, one way. Auto-ferry space must be reserved in advance; in high summer it costs $66.50 to ship a car one way from Hyannis to Nantucket. This includes fare for two adults and two children. Special round-trip excursions for stays of one to five days cost $84. In high summer, one passengers-only boat is run in each direction daily between Martha's Vineyard and Nantucket, taking about two hours and costing $8.30 per adult (kids pay half fare). The ferries are large, comfortable, and equipped with lunch counters and bars. Note that if you park in the dockside lots you'll have to pay $6 per calendar day for the privilege. *Special note:* When returning to Hyannis from Nantucket, don't plan on taking the last ferry of the day and meeting the bus to Boston or New York, for the ferries are often delayed and *the bus does not wait.* To be safe, catch a ferry well ahead of the last bus trip scheduled from Hyannis. If you find yourself in a jam because of ferry mix-ups, you can always take another line (see below) or fly.

The **Hy-Line** (tel. 508/778-2600) has several swift (two hours) passenger-only boats which depart from Hyannis's Ocean Street docks for Nantucket ($9.50 for adults, half price for a child) and Martha's Vineyard ($9.50 for adults, half price for kids). Round-trip rates of $20 and $9.50 apply, and although no cars are carried on the Hy-Line's boats, you can take your bicycle over for $4 one way. These boats operate May through October only. By the way, if you sign up for a same-day round trip, you'll have to tell them which boat you plan to return on, and they'll stamp your ticket with the boat's departure time. Reservations are accepted with an additional nominal charge (tel. 508/778-2602). Otherwise, parking is $6 to $8 per calendar day.

---

5. Barnstable, Yarmouth, and Dennis

The stretch of Rte. 6A between Sandwich and Dennis is a lush panorama of bogs and marshes, distant views of dunes and the sea, birds calling and fluttering, the winding road dotted with antique shops, craft shops, art galleries, and other businesses including lots and lots of real estate offices. The road leads through the villages of Barnstable, Cummaquid, Yarmouthport, Yarmouth, and Dennis before heading eastward to Brewster.

Visitors may be surprised to know that Barnstable, the largest incorporated town on the Cape, actually includes within its boundaries the busy commercial center of Hyannis, its airport, and several small historic villages on the wide salt marshes along the shores of Cape Cod Bay. The village of Barnstable proper is little more than a namesake for the much larger township.

Yarmouth is also a town with two natures. In the north, along Rte. 6A, it is hamlets of dignified old houses shaded by beautiful lofty trees. In the south, along Rte. 28, it is gaudy motels built chock-a-block along the crowded beaches.

The town of Dennis is much like Yarmouth, and Dennis can claim to be where the commercial cranberry-harvesting industry began, and salt works flourished for a period.

BARNSTABLE: As you wend your way eastward along Rte. 6A, the village of Barnstable offers several good choices for lodging.

Where to Stay

Though it only has four rooms (all with working fireplaces and private baths), the **Charles Hinckey House,** Old Kings Hwy. (P.O. Box 723), Barnstable Village, MA 02630 (tel. 508/362-9924), is very special and welcoming. This Federal Colonial house is a historic landmark and has been painstakingly renovated. Flowers from the profuse bank of wildflower gardens fill the interior. The innkeepers, while keeping their distance, will spoil you if you give them half a chance. Rooms rent for $108 to $149 and include a beautifully presented full breakfast.

A stay at **Ashley Manor,** 3660 Olde Kings Hwy. (P.O. Box 856), Barnstable, MA 02360 (tel. 508/362-8044), is a lesson in leisurely living. You'll undoubtedly linger over afternoon cocktails, evening conversations, and a full breakfast on the backyard brick terrace. The six spacious suites and guest rooms (all with private bath and all but one with working fireplace) in the main manor house range from $110 to $159 per room. A more private cottage with a wood-burning stove and efficiency kitchen rents for $899 a week.

Also on Olde Kings Hwy., at no. 2839 specifically is **Beechwood,** Barnstable, MA 02630 (tel. 508/362-6618). This Victorian house takes its name from the big old beech trees that shade the veranda. Don't let the staid parlor mislead you; it's not at all in keeping with the light and airy guest rooms. Period antiques, colored glass, marble-topped dressers, unique bathrooms, and tall shuttered windows make this place special. The Garret room in the attic is very private and has angled walls and eaves. A room with breakfast costs from $99 to $138.

YARMOUTHPORT: Yarmouthport has several fine inns and guesthouses, with good variety in prices and accommodations. It's a nice place to spend the night. Here's a description of the places as you'll encounter them going from west to east through the town on Rte. 6A.

Where to Stay

Yarmouth's best inns are actually bed-and-breakfast houses. The **Wedgewood Inn,** 83 Main St., Yarmouthport, MA 02675 (tel. 508/362-5157), is a gracious and comfortable place to relax. It's a charming place with period (1812) wallpaper, pencil-post beds, quilts, Oriental rugs, wide-board floors, and working fireplaces. Each of the six spacious rooms has a private bath; two have private screened porches. Doubles cost $105 to $160 (20% less in the off-season), and a full breakfast is, of course, included.

Atop Liberty Hill, set back from Rte. 6A (Main Street) at the corner of Willow Street, is the **Liberty Hill Inn,** 77 Main St., Yarmouthport, MA 02675 (tel. 508/362-3976). The classical pillars are a giveaway: Greek Revival architecture, built in 1825. The Liberty Hill is perhaps Yarmouthport's best bargain, as you get a double room (private bath) in the lovely house furnished with authentic Early American pieces, a continental breakfast, and a convenient location for $82 to $94 in season.

Despite its name, the **One Centre Street Inn** (tel. 508/362-8910) is on Main Street (Rte. 6A), also called the Old King's Highway. But the entrance is around to the side, on Centre Street, right in the middle of Yarmouthport. For simple good taste, the inn is first choice in this town. There are five guest rooms; baths are private or semiprivate; full breakfast is included in the price: $55 to $88. This is my favorite sort of hostelry: small, congenial, thoughtfully and finely furnished with taste but without pretension, walking distance to the activities of the town, friendly owners. Need I say more?

Where to Eat

The **Cranberry Moose,** 45 Main St., Yarmouthport, MA (tel. 508/362-3501), is one of the best restaurants on Cape Cod and the prices reflect the cuisine. The four white dining rooms are simple but elegant, with oak chairs and tables dotted with roses and carnations. Start with a goat cheese tart topped with thin slices of apples and move on to roast duck with a papaya and raspberry sauce. Save room for a rich crème brûlée with a caramelized sugar topping. For $35 to $40 per person (including tax and tip but no beverage) these artful presentations can be yours from 5:30 to 10 p.m. nightly in summer and Thursday to Monday from mid-October through mid-May.

What to See and Do

Across the street from the Old Yarmouth Inn is the **Parnassus Book Store,** in a building which started life as a church and later became the local incarnation of the A&P grocery chain. No charge for browsing.

Just down Rte. 6A from the inn, a minute's walk east, is the U.S. Post Office, and behind it are the **Nature Trails** of the Historical Society of Old Yarmouth. The trails are open during daylight hours seven days a week year round; 50¢ admission for adults, 25¢ for children. Note that these are not formal "botanical gardens," but rather trails through particularly beautiful wild areas of Yarmouth's land and marshes. Local flowers and trees, plants, and geological features are on view, and maps and trail booklets available at the gate house where you pay your admission will tell you all about what there is to see.

Near the Botanic Trails is the **Bangs Hallet House** (tel. 508/362-3021), built by a captain in the China trade. The house's history is as interesting as its Greek Revival façade. The devoted caretaker will fill you in on the confusing chronicle of the house's various owners and reconstructions. The house is open June 1 through Labor Day 2 to 4 p.m. Wednesday to Friday and Sunday. Admission is $1 adults, 25¢ for children. At other times of the year, call for an appointment to see it.

The **Winslow Crocker House** (tel. 508/227-3956), owned and maintained by the Society for the Preservation of New England Antiquities, is open June through mid-October on Tuesday, Thursday, Saturday, and Sunday from noon to 5 p.m. Admission is $2.50 for adults, $1.25 for children 5 to 12 years old. The rooms in this Georgian house are furnished with 17th- to 19th-century collections.

Yarmouth has a beach which is, by law, free and open to the public, as terms of the bequest that gave it to the town. It's **Grey's Beach** at the end of Centre Street (turn north off Rte. 6A), and as you go down to the beach, note the cemetery on your left with graves dating from 1639. Picnic tables, toilets, nice lawns, and parking facilities are all available at the beach, and a wooden walkway stretches a good distance out across the marshes, and is pleasant to stroll along even if you don't feel like a swim.

As you come into the center of Dennis, start looking for a cemetery and a white church, and as you come to them look for Old Bass River Road. Turn right onto this road and follow signs for eight-tenths of a mile to the **Scargo Hill Tower.** Park at the base of this stone structure surrounded by oak and pine, and climb the iron staircase inside to the top (not far) for a view that will tell you what the Cape is all about. On a clear day you can easily see Provincetown, the white blade of the Cape beaches cutting the deep blue of Cape Cod Bay. The Cape itself appears as a huge green scimitar, a sea of green trees with little white or silver-gray shingled houses poking through here and there. At the foot of the hill that holds the tower is Scargo Lake, and west is the outline of Barnstable Harbor. The tower was given to the town of Dennis in 1929 by the Tobey family, who had had ancestors living in Dennis since 1678. Follow the same road back to Rte. 6A.

DENNIS: More pretty scenes, including those cranberry bogs and salt marshes, await you in Dennis. If you get off of Rte. 6A to wander and explore, expect to get lost. This is a confusing, if beautiful, place. For instance, though the village of East Dennis is actually east of Dennis, the village of South Dennis is due north of West Dennis, and these two are due south of East Dennis . . . got it?

Where to Stay

The **Isaiah Hall B & B Inn,** 152 Whig St., Dennis, MA 02638 (tel. 508/385-9928), is a gem of a bed-and-breakfast. Good old-fashioned, homespun country comforts prevail in this 1857 Greek Revival farmhouse. The newly converted barn, with cathedral ceiling and white wicker, sports rooms with small balconies. The living room, dining room, and quilted guest rooms in the main house are filled with solid antiques and are very unpretentious. The house abuts a cranberry bog, is a ten minute walk to Corporation Beach, and is right behind the Cape Playhouse. Rates are quite reasonable in season: $44 to $77 for one, $51 to $88 for two; a tad less in the off-season.

Located across from Scargo Lake, the **Four Chimneys Inn,** 946 Main St. (Rte. 6A), Dennis, MA 02638 (tel. 508/385-6317), has some of the most spacious guest rooms on the entire Cape. Ceilings are high, floors painted, and common rooms (one with a VCR, one with a fireplace) relaxing. Seven of the nine impeccable rooms in this Victorian house have private bath; continental breakfast is served in the fireplaced dining room. Rates, for one or two people, are reasonable at $44 to $66 for a shared bath and $77 to $90 for a private. In the off-season they drop $5 to $20 per room; an additional person is $15 per night.

What to Do

The **Cape Playhouse,** on Rte. 6A in Dennis (tel. 508/385-3911), is the place to go on the Cape if you want to see a famous actor or actress in a well-known play. The plays (and actors) usually change every week, so call to see what's current. The season runs from early July through Labor Day, with performances each evening (except Sunday) at 8:30 p.m., plus matinees on Wednesday and Thursday at 2:30 p.m. Tickets are priced from $17 to $25. The playhouse has its own restaurant, open for lunch on matinee days, dinner, Sunday brunch, and after-theater snacks. Also here is the **Cape Cinema,** designed after the Congregational church in Centerville, home of the first-run movies and of a mammoth, 6,400-square-foot mural of the heavens by Rockwell Kent.

6. Brewster

Brewster is another of the picturesque little towns along Rte. 6A. A country store, several fine churches, and a Town Hall make it look like many other pleasant Cape towns, but Brewster's different in the number of noteworthy museums and exhibitions situated in the town or nearby. It also has one of the best French restaurants on the East Coast.

WHERE TO STAY: The **Old Sea Pines Inn,** 2553 Main St., Brewster, MA 02631 (tel. 508/896-6114), is a pleasant surprise. This converted girls' school has typically quaint rooms. The spacious, comfortable common rooms have hardwood floors and a working fireplace. Sit on green cane rockers or under the shade of oak trees on the wrap-around porch. Of their 14 rooms, the five smaller ones share baths and thus go for only $44. A double ranges from $66 to $93 (the $93 room has a fireplace and four-poster bed). The suite can accommodate two, three, or four people and thus costs either $93, $99, or $105. An additional cot can be arranged for $15. Off-season rates drop significantly. A full breakfast is included.

Just west of the intersection of Rtes. 6A and 124 South in Brewster is the **Old Manse Inn,** 1861 Main St. (P.O. Box 839), Brewster, MA 02631 (tel. 508/896-3149), a lovely old white building surrounded by tall trees. The nine guest rooms, all with private bath, in this former sea captain's house rent for $82 to $93 double during the high season (July and August), $71 in spring and fall, $66 in winter. Breakfast (included in the room price) and dinner are served in the inn's cozy sunroom or dining room, which is convenient if you just want to relax and not wander out for meals.

WHERE TO DINE: Chillingsworth, on Rte. 6A in Brewster (tel. 508/896-3640), is one of the loveliest restaurants on the Cape. The fare is contemporary French; the atmosphere is a delightful blend of modern and traditional, intimate and open. If you have a special celebration for a party of two to four, request the separate "library room." There are two seatings for the seven-course dinner: 6 to 6:30 p.m. and then again at 9 to 9:30 p.m. An evening for two will run close to $100. Lunch and dinner are served every night, except Monday, mid-May to mid-October. During those months only dinners are served on weekends. Reservations are a must.

The **Brewster Fish House,** also on Rte. 6A in Brewster (tel. 508/896-7867), is a nice place for an informal, leisurely lunch. Tables are set with paper placemats and servings are generous. A swordfish steak with fries and a small salad runs $9.50 at lunch, and the ever-popular fish sandwich is only $3.50. Open mid-April to mid-November, seven days a week during high summer season. Lunch ends at 3 p.m. and dinner begins at 5 p.m. but you can always get a filling bowl of soup between meals.

Back in the center of town, if you follow Main Street west from the Old Manse Inn, and then bear left onto Stony Brook Road, you'll soon come to Brewster's most captivating sight. Read on.

WHAT TO SEE: Brewster is proud of its **Old Grist Mill and Herring Run,** at the Stoney Brook Mill Sites, on Stony Brook Road near the intersection with Satucket and Run Hill Roads. The waterwheel, still in good working order, powers the grinding machinery inside the mill. You can watch the whole process at work, and buy freshly ground corn meal, from 2 to 5 p.m. on Wednesday, Friday, and Saturday afternoons in July and August. Upstairs there's a small museum with artifacts from the "Factory Village" which occupied this site over a hundred years ago.

The mill is now part of a park owned by the town of Brewster. Wander around the millpond, certainly one of the most romantic and picturesque locales on all of Cape Cod. If your visit falls during mid-April to early May, watch for the run of **alewives** (herring) which surges upstream from the ocean to freshwater spawning grounds.

Sealand of Cape Cod is right on Rte. 6A in West Brewster (tel. 508/385-9252). It's open year round and features a crew of performing dolphins as well as an aquarium with horseshoe crabs, loggerhead turtles, moray eels, otters, seals, sea lions, and any number of different fish. There are three large buildings and several outside pools set in a tree-filled park. The trick is to hit one of the performance times. Late June through Labor Day these are at 10 a.m., noon, and 1:30, 3, 4:30, and 6 p.m. In early and mid-June the times are 11 a.m. and 1, 3, and 5 p.m. In September, October, and May there are shows at 11 a.m. and 1 and 3 p.m. November through April regular shows are held on weekends at 11 a.m., and 1 and 3 p.m., on weekdays at 1 p.m. Tickets for adults are $6.95; children 5 to 11, $4.75; 4 years and under are free.

The **New England Fire and History Museum,** on Rte. 6A in Brewster (tel. 508/896-5711), has one of the world's largest (55 engines) and most varied collections of early firefighting equipment and memorabilia. Pieces date back to the 18th century and count among them the world's only 1929 Mercedes-Benz fire truck. Other exhibits include the Arthur Fiedler memorabilia collection, a historic apothecary and a blacksmith shop. Guided tours are given; related movies are shown. The museum is open daily Memorial Day weekend through Labor Day, weekends until Columbus Day, from 10 a.m. to 3 p.m. The entrance fee is $4 for adults, $2.50 for children ages 5 to 12; inquire about group rates.

Those interested in Cape Cod's flora, fauna, and ecology will want to visit the **Cape Cod Museum of Natural History,** on Rte. 6A (tel. 508/896-3867), open from 9:30 a.m. to 4:30 p.m. Monday through Saturday (plus 12:30 to 4:30 p.m. on Sunday during the summer). Closed Sunday and Monday from mid-October through April. The museum organization was founded in 1954 to preserve the wildlife and plant life in the area around Stony Brook and its marshes, to study this land, and to teach others about it. Nature walks, a lecture program, and children's classes are held the year round. Adults pay $2.50 and children 6 to 14 pay $1.50; under-6s are free.

---

7. Chatham

Chatham was once the railhead for Cape Cod, and the trains that brought vacationers in and took fish, salt, and shoes out also brought the opportunity for wealth. Chatham is therefore a graceful community with many big old houses and inns, an easy pace, friendly people, and pleasant vistas all around.

The town maintains an **Information Booth** on Main Street in the center of town (tel. 508/945-0342) during the summer season. It's run by citizens who know the town inside and out, and has available brochures on places to stay, copies of menus from local restaurants, and information on activities. Public rest rooms are next door, in the rear of the Town Hall.

WHERE TO STAY: Chatham seems to have at least one kind of every accommodation imaginable, so you should have little trouble finding a place you'll like by skimming down this list:

A Resort Hotel

The **Chatham Bars Inn,** at the corner of Chatham Bars Avenue and Shore Road, Chatham, MA 02633 (tel. 508/945-0096 or toll free 800/527-4884), is a true bit of old Chatham, a huge rambling, gracious 70-acre resort complex with 27 attractive cottages (no kitchens) on the property all operated on the Modified American Plan (rates include breakfast and dinner). Enter the inn by the motor entrance, bear to the right, and you'll enter the parlor, with its highly arched ceiling, lots of windows looking onto a shady veranda, and wicker furniture for cool sitting on warm summer days. The lobby is also grand, large, and spacious, and a stairway out the front door tumbles down the hillside to the road and beyond it to the inn's private beach. Swimming, tennis, and golf on the inn's own nine-hole course are other services offered. The staff is large, friendly, well trained, and soft-spoken. Of course, proper dress is required in the cocktail lounge and in the Main Dining Room in the evening: jacket and tie for men; summer cottons or cocktail dress for women. Both meals are included in these high season rates: $240 to $360 per couple per day, tax and service included, for a double with bath. If these figures look high, remember that, on the average, one pays around $100 for a luxury motel room, plus two breakfasts and two good dinners, which often brings a normal vacation day's expenses to about $220 per couple. The Chatham Bars Inn is a bit of history brought up to modern standards of comfort and service, and I doubt that you'd be disappointed here.

Inns

For my money, Chatham's most perfectly charming inn is the **Captain's House Inn,** 371 Old Harbor Rd., Chatham, MA 02633 (tel. 508/945-0127). Located a half mile from the center of town on Rte. 28 going toward Orleans, the Captain's House has plenty of space for green lawns and flower gardens. It was in fact built by a Capt. Hiram Harding in 1839, with various additions later. The 14 guest rooms in the house all have private bath and period furnishings, which include some wing chairs, canopy beds, and braided rugs. Three rooms have fireplaces. In the Cottage and the Carriage House are three bedrooms each, the best choice for large families or small groups. Rooms cost $95 to $150 double, continental breakfast included. This place is very nice indeed.

The **Queen Anne Inn,** 70 Queen Anne Rd., Chatham, MA 02633 (tel. 508/945-0394), is just a few blocks from the center of Chatham, and has been a favorite hostelry here for well over a century. The graceful shingled, gabled inn is authentic 19th-century Cape Cod, but with many of the amenities of a resort hotel: restaurant, tennis courts, bicycles, an indoor spa, boats for waterskiing, and excursions. Rooms, many with fireplaces and whirlpools, are priced from $99 to $199 double; some look onto the Oyster Pond.

In a town of sea captains' houses, the **Cyrus Kent House,** 63 Cross St., at Kent Place, Chatham, MA 02633 (tel. 508/945-9104), certainly stands out as a gem. It's not as old as many, dating "only" from 1877. But it was built by boatwrights from ship timber brought from Maine, and has been finely restored. Unencumbered by tons of Victoriana, the Kent House has an airy, sunny quality about it. Each of the eight guest rooms has a private bath, and rents in high season for $98 double, continental breakfast included. Here you're a mere block from the center of Chatham.

Near the downtown area—a five-minute walk—is the **Cranberry Inn,** 359 Main St., Chatham, MA 02633 (tel. 508/945-9232), very much like a large guesthouse in looks and atmosphere, but including a restaurant. All rooms have private baths, individual decoration, and prices of $107 double. The Cranberry Inn is open from mid-May to the end of October.

Another inn downtown is the **Chatham Town House Inn,** 11 Library Lane, off Main Street, Chatham, MA 02633 (tel. 508/945-2180). There are 24 rooms here with private bath, plus a new six-room lodge. All the rooms are decorated differently, but with great taste and thoughtfulness, even to using hand-hooked rugs rather than wall-to-wall carpeting so that the beautiful old floors can be seen. All the rooms have air conditioning, refrigerators, cable color TV, and individual thermostats. Rates in season are $100 to $155 for a double with bath, including a full breakfast. An extra person costs $25. A two-bedroom cottage rents for $1,400 per week in season. You can get a Scandinavian breakfast at the inn for $7 if you wish.

A Guesthouse

A nice cozy guesthouse out toward the water and also only a few minutes' walk from the center of town and a shopping center is the **Bow Roof House,** 59 Queen Anne Rd., Chatham, MA 02633 (tel. 508/945-1346), run by the Mazulis family. The main house is that of an old sea captain, and many rooms still have the fireplaces (not working now) that were installed to keep out the chill of those winter blasts that roll in off the water. A large living room with rough timbered ceiling and large fireplace is here for guests' use, and just through the door from it is a terrace with tables and umbrellas for a glass of wine (BYO) or tea in the evening. Rooms, based on three or more nights, cost about $42 to $48 double with private bath and continental breakfast. If you go in summer, the bank in front of the house will be a riot of wild-flowers, and the two yuccas by the door may be in bloom.

Motels

The **Bradford Inn and Motel**, 26 Cross St., Chatham, MA 02633 (tel. 508/945-1030 or toll free 800/562-4667), is right at the center of town. This newly renovated, extremely neat and tidy complex has 24 guest rooms, an outdoor heated swimming pool, a patio, and flowers everywhere. Rooms and suites come with a basket of amenities, cable color TV, private bath, air conditioning, and full breakfast; some have refrigerators and kitchen facilities. Prices are $116 to $178 double in high season; add $20 for each extra person in a room. This should be your first motel choice in Chatham. They also now serve lunch and Sunday brunch.

Accessible only by car is the **Pleasant Bay Village Resort Motel**, P.O. Box 772, Chatham, MA 02633 (tel. 508/945-1133), on Rte. 28 several miles north of town in the section called Chathamport. The motel is about as pleasant as you'll find, located on six acres of very carefully kept grounds, evergreen hedges, trees, bushes, and cascades of roses along the front rail fence. The motel's buildings are scattered through the grounds, and there's a heated pool, badminton, shuffleboard, and Ping-Pong, besides just lounging in the sun, to keep you occupied. The motel has a breakfast room (light lunches served as well). Rooms are modern with paneled walls, air conditioning, private bath, wall-to-wall carpeting, and cable color TV, and most have two double beds. In season (last week in June to Labor Day), motel rooms cost $80 for one double bed, $95 to $125 for rooms with two double beds of ever-increasing size and luxury.

Close to the downtown area without being right smack in the center is **The Moorings Motel and Motor Lodge**, 326 Main St., Chatham, MA 02633 (tel. 508/945-0848). The Moorings consists of a grand old Chatham house, its carriage house, with an annex of motel units. The complex once belonged to a retired admiral, and now serves well as a hostelry. Furnishings and styles of rooms vary with the building you stay in: the ones in the guesthouse are more traditional and Victorian; the ones in the modern motel annex are modern but decorated in the colonial style. Prices vary as well, the rooms on the upper floor of the carriage (or coach) house costing $66 to $83, those in the guesthouse and motel cost $83 to $94, including continental breakfast. Off-season rates are in effect during spring and fall.

WHERE TO DINE: Chatham has a good assortment of restaurants in different price ranges, each with its own ambience. It's easy to find one you like.

Best place to dine is at **Christian's**, 443 Main St. (tel. 508/945-3362). Lodged in an old Chatham house, Christian's has a cocktail bar and light menu served upstairs on a pretty deck (opens at 4 p.m.), and several dining rooms within the house itself. The dinner menu is original: crab buerrecks (flaky pastry filled with crabmeat and a bit of curry), seafood melange (lobster, shrimps, and scallops), or filet mignon prepared any of three ways. Dinner is served from 5 p.m. every day in summer. Expect to pay between $28 and $40 per person, all in. In the summer there is also nightly entertainment, while in the spring and fall it is reserved for weekends only.

The **Impudent Oyster**, on Chatham Bars Avenue just off Main Street (tel. 508/945-3545), has a long and eclectic menu perfect for those afternoons and evenings when you don't know what sort of cuisine to choose. Chinese, French, Italian, and Mexican-style dishes, each with a different local touch; sandwiches and elegant main courses; seafood and meats—all share the menu. The oysters, by the way, are freshly shucked. Plan to spend $30 to $40 per person for a nice dinner with wine. For lunch, anything on the menu can be yours for under $10. Dress neatly, but not formally, and call for dinner reservations. Hours are 11:30 a.m. to 10 p.m. every day in summer.

The young and golden and the young and hip have dinner at the **Chatham Squire Restaurant**, near the intersection of Main and Chatham Bars Avenue (tel.

508/945-0945) open every day from 11:30 a.m. to 11 p.m. The bar in the room to the left is semifunky, with license plates from a dozen states nailed to a huge rough ceiling beam; the dining room to the right is nicely furnished with Pennsylvania Dutch-style wooden benches and tables. It's a big place, attractive and well tended, and with an interesting menu: for lunch perhaps a "crock o' chowder" with crackers ($3.50) or a salad plate ($5 to $8); at dinnertime try any of the fresh fish specials. Dinner will cost $28 to $36; no reservations taken.

If you don't mind driving ten minutes from the center of town, head out to **Sea in the Rough,** on Rte. 28 in the direction of Harwich (tel. 508/945-1700). It's a good, hearty, informal, family place with red vinyl chairs, basic service, and generous servings. In nice weather, sit outside on the side patio under the shade of umbrellas. Open April through October, seven days a week from 11:30 a.m. to 10 p.m. (high season only); the entire menu is available all day. Dinner specials on the blackboard start at 5 p.m. and might be fresh salmon or tuna, or any number of chicken dishes, from $9.50 to $17. Regular seafood and steak entrees run $6.25 to $9.75.

Cafés

The **Garden Café** (tel. 508/945-4081) is in the Swinging Basket Mall, a small collection of shops at the intersection of Chatham Bars Avenue and Main Street. Set near numerous fascinating browsing places, the café is a fine place for a sip, a snack, or a supper (11:30 a.m. to 4 p.m. weekdays, to 8 p.m. on weekends, mid-June through August). For instance, their ploughman's lunch of cheeses, fresh fruit, and French bread costs $8; soups, salads, sandwiches, and wine and beer are served as well.

This season the place for ice cream seems to be **Cookie Manor,** 499 Main St. (tel. 508/945-1152). Don't let the noisy kids outside keep you away. Baked sweets, 18 flavors of ice cream, and "the best sandwiches in the state, no matter what state you're in" know no age limit. Whether it's a breakfast snack, baked ham sandwich ($3), or cookiewich (any two cookies with a scoop of ice cream in between; $1.85), you can be confident they're all done with expertise here. Open daily Memorial Day through Labor Day from 8 a.m. until 10 p.m., until 5 p.m. the rest of the year.

Nearby in Harwich Port

Café Elizabeth, 31 Sea St., Harwich Port (tel. 508/432-1147), is six miles from Chatham, south off Rte. 28. The atmosphere is that of an auberge, a French countryside inn. Marguerite, one of the owners, will greet you with a French accent and show you to a table in one of the small, intimate dining rooms. As for the food, well, try this: as an appetizer, shrimp quickly sautéed in butter, cayenne pepper, and fresh ground pepper, then flambéed with cognac. As a main course, try an assortment of four medallions: lobster with lobster sauce, veal with wild mushrooms, lamb with fresh tarragon, filet with béarnaise; as dessert, a special chocolate truffle. If you prefer a strawberry tarte, I'd suggest you put your name on one when you walk past the dessert tray; they seem to disappear rapidly. Expect to spend $40 to $50 per person for dinner here. Hours are 6 to 9 p.m. daily.

WHAT TO SEE: There's quite a lot to see and do in this venerable New England town.

The Light and the Fish Pier

The light is the first place to go in Chatham. Go east on Main Street and turn right (south) on Shore Road to the light. The lighthouse is right next to the Coast Guard Station; on the other side of the street is a place to park while you look at the view, some pay telescopes, and down below, a fine beach. The first light was erected on this point of land in 1808, and the present lighthouse dates from 1878, just over a century ago.

The view is very pleasant, looking out to sea across Nauset Beach (the sand bar, actually a peninsula, you see out in the water). The cool sea breeze in summer and the nautical blast in winter make one think it incredible that Rome is at almost exactly the same latitude (but 4,200 miles away) as Chatham. The pier (Main Street east to Shore Street, then left/north) is interesting in that it is operated by the town for licensed Chatham fishermen. Chatham is very proud of its fishing fleet of small boats, which the townspeople boast brings in the freshest fish around. The boast has some truth to it, for the use of little boats means that the catch must be brought home every day, whereas larger boats can stay out to sea for several days, refrigerating their catch on board.

The time to go down to the pier is between 3 and 6 p.m. (aim for 4). You'll see the fleet come in and unload, and you can buy the day's catch right after it comes off the boat. Those who'd like to do it themselves can rent a boat at Fish Pier for a day's hunting for bass, bluefish, and tuna out at sea.

Beaches

The town of Chatham has public beaches ($5 a day, $20 a week, $40 the season) at **Oyster Pond,** only a few blocks from the center of town south on State Harbor Road from Main Street; and a bit farther out at **Harding's Beach**—follow Main Street (Rte. 28) west from the center of town for about two miles, and turn left (south) on Barn Hill Road to Harding's Beach Road. Lifeguards and toilets are at both beaches, but no bathhouses.

The Bird and Wildlife Sanctuary

Chatham is a particularly good place for seeing birds, for **Monomoy Island,** south of the town, has been a National Wilderness Area since 1970. Over 300 different species of birds have been spotted on Monomoy. May is the best time to see birds in their mating plumage, and starting in late July many birds begin to be seen in winter plumage. The only way to get to Monomoy is by boat from Chatham. Full details on current offerings are available from the town's information booth on Main Street (tel. 508/945-0342). For wildlife-tour information, call 508/349-2615.

Band Concerts

One of the nicest things about Chatham in July and August is the schedule of band concerts (every Friday evening at 8 p.m.) in **Kate Gould Park,** just past the Wayside Inn on Main Street. Everybody comes to the concerts, and on a typical Friday evening the crowd may reach into the thousands. Most of the musicians in the town band are year-round residents of Chatham who live and work in the town and enjoy providing a little free entertainment for their fellow citizens and visitors once a week.

Theater

The **Monomoy Theater,** 776 Main Street, not far west of the intersection with Old Harbor Road (tel. 508/945-1589), is the summer-stock operation of Ohio University, and offers a different play each week during July and August. Performances are given Tuesday through Saturday (curtain rises at 8:30 p.m.), and the current play is advertised on flyers around town and in the local newspapers. Season tickets are available, should you be spending the summer in Chatham.

Historical Sites

Chatham has its share of antique buildings open to the public, each high-lighting a separate part of the town's interesting past. The **Atwood House and Museums** are run by the Chatham Historical Society (tel. 508/945-2493) and feature over 2,000 exhibits including an outstanding shell collection, a good number of pieces of Sandwich glass, and a crewel bedspread which took townspeople six years to make. Also on display at the house is a set of French lighthouse lenses used in the Chatham Light from 1923 until recently. Atwood House is open Monday, Wednesday, and Friday mid-June to mid-September from 2 to 5 p.m., except holidays. Admission is $1 for adults, 50¢ for students, free for children accompanied by adults.

Chatham's **Railroad Museum** is located in the old station on Depot Road (take Old Harbor Road north off Main Street, and Depot Street is a short distance up on the left). The station was built in 1887 by the Chatham Railroad Company, and turned into a museum in 1960. Among the railroading exhibits is a real caboose, once used by the New York Central until that company gave it to the museum. The museum is open Monday through Friday from 1:30 to 4:30 p.m. during late June, July, August, and early September. It's staffed with townspeople who act as volunteer guides, and admission is free.

Chatham also has an old **Grist Mill** open to the public daily except Tuesday, July and August only. Entrance is free, but donations are accepted. Sometimes corn is ground between the mill's stones if the wind is sufficient. To find it, take Cross Street south off Main Street to Shattuck Place, which winds down to the mill.

---

8. Orleans and Eastham

Orleans owes its name and its fame to French connections. Known as Nauset since its earliest settlement in 1644, the townspeople changed the name to Orleans in 1797 when the town was separated from neighboring Eastham and incorporated. The Duke of Orléans had made a visit to Cape Cod, and the town was named in the French nobleman's honor.

Orleans's other French connection was as close as can be without moving continents. In 1879 Orleans was physically connected by underwater telegraph cable with the town of Brest in France, almost 4,000 miles away. You can still see the telegraph station where the cable came ashore before continuing overland to New York.

In its day Orleans has made its living through fishing and shellfishing, clothing manufacture, agriculture, and production of salt from seawater, not to mention trade in contraband. During the Revolutionary War, Orleans sent men and supplies to aid the Revolutionary forces. In the War of 1812, the town refused to pay $1,000 "protection money" demanded by the British enemy. A landing force was sent ashore from H.M.S. *Newcastle,* and the town militia quickly convinced the Redcoats that it was probably a good idea to return to the ship, which they did. Needless to say, Orleans kept its $1,000. When a German submarine broke the surface off Nauset Beach during World War I, the townspeople again demonstrated their coolness in the face of danger. The sub released a few torpedos at some coal barges, and everybody turned out to watch the show.

Today Orleans is known as the midpoint between the Cape Cod Canal and Provincetown, a good place to stop for a meal or a night's rest.

WHERE TO STAY IN ORLEANS: You really have quite a choice of places to stay in Orleans, as motels and inns are the town's business.

Inns and Guesthouses

The **Nauset House Inn,** P.O. Box 774, East Orleans, MA 02643 (tel. 508/255-2195), is actually in East Orleans, nearer to the beach than to the Mid-Cape Hwy. Once you get on Beach Road in East Orleans, you'll come to the inn on the right-hand side as you head east. The setting is bucolic and relaxing, the inn nestled into lush surroundings, yet only a short distance from the beach. The 14 rooms range in price from $40 to $85 double, the higher priced rooms having such features as a balcony or sitting area or private bath. A single room rents for $40. Full breakfasts (for a few dollars each) are served every morning, to guests only. This is Orleans's most charming place to stay.

The **Ship's Knees Inn,** Beach Rd., P.O. Box 756, East Orleans, MA 02643 (tel. 508/255-1312), is a restored 150-year-old sea captain's house a mere ten-minute walk away from Nauset Beach. The inn has 19 rooms with shared bath done in a colonial decor, some with water views; the nearby Cove House has more rooms, each with private bath, color cable television and water view. Two rental cottages here are right at the water's edge, with private baths and color cable TV. Tennis court and swimming pool are on the grounds, and continental breakfast is included in the rates, which range from $55 to $99 for a double with shared bath or $94 to $105 double with private bath.

Though it's a bit off the beaten path, I still recommend the **Whalewalk Inn,** 169 Bridge Rd., Eastham, MA 02642 (tel. 508/255-0617), for those who want solitude after suntanning. Head toward Rock Harbor off the rotary out of Orleans and turn right onto Bridge Road. On 3½ acres, this restored 1830's whaling master's home offers a nice blend of modern updates and old-fashioned hospitality. A wide range of accommodations is available; all rates quoted are for high season. There are six double rooms with private baths at $95; a deluxe room with private entrance at $110; four suites with dining area, kitchen, and fireplace at $135 (an additional bedroom can be connected to either of these for $90); a studio cottage at $120. Off-season rates drop 10%.

Motels

The **Orleans Holiday Motel** is on Rte. 6A, Orleans, MA 02653 (tel. 508/255-1514, or toll free 800/451-1833, 800/451-1818 in Massachusetts), just past the intersection of 6A and 28 as you're driving northeast. The Orleans Holiday has contemporary motel rooms, all with tile bath and shower, cable color TV, air conditioning, picture windows, and a balcony-walkway. There's a fine large pool surrounded by lounge chairs and equipped with a slide and a backyard garden and picnic area. Most rooms have two double beds and rent for $84 double, $12 for an extra person, from late June through Labor Day. Several rooms in the unit behind Nick's Family Pub (open for breakfast, lunch, dinner, cocktails, and entertainment) are larger than normal, newer, and a bit more luxurious.

Another motel near the intersection of 6A and 28 is **The Cove,** on Rte. 28, Orleans, MA 02653 (tel. 508/255-1203). The rooms here are modern and soundproof (not that there's all that much noise in the Cove's area), the layout of the motel is quite beautiful, and it has its own heated pool. The rooms rent for $90 to $160 double in high summer, depending on whether you want one room, a two-room efficiency, or a water view. All rooms are air-conditioned.

WHERE TO DINE: Kadee's Lobster & Clam Bar (tel. 508/255-6184) is right next to the East Orleans Fish Market on Beach Road, and indeed these two establishments share the same telephone and management. That should tell you the fish, lobsters, and clams are fresh and moderately priced. What's left to say is that you dine in attractive rustic rooms or under a colorful umbrella on the pretty deck; or you dine wherever you like, having bought your chowder, fried fish, or boiled lobsters from the take-out window. The take-out is marvelously inexpensive, of course. But the dining room and deck are delightful: have kale soup, corn on the cob, steamers, fish, or order the full clambake ($22) of lobster, steamers, and corn on the cob. To find Kadee's, follow Beach Road east toward East Orleans, and watch for it on the left-hand side of the road. It's open from 11:30 a.m. to 9:30 p.m. every day.

Something less formal? The **Lobster Claw** (tel. 508/255-1800), right next to the Pancake Maid near the Orleans Holiday Motel on Rte. 6A, is open for lunch and dinner from April to October. Fish nets cover the restaurant's ceiling, and sea-blue booths and natural-wood tables and chairs crowd the floor. Upstairs is a lounge and raw bar. The menus are in the shape of lobster claws (why not?), and they list fish and seafood plates priced at $8 to $14, lobsters for about $15 to $20 (in season), and daily specials such as soft-shell crabs with french fries and cole slaw for $12. There's a special children's menu. The Lobster Claw is not very far from the big Orleans traffic circle, and is thus a good place to stop if you're just passing through. Open every day, April through November, from 11:30 a.m. to 9 p.m.

Serving creative cuisine in more eclectic surroundings is **The Arbor,** on Rte. 28 in Orleans (tel. 508/255-4847). This place combines just the right ingredients to make a person relax. Perhaps it's the yellow toy truck and the antique tins, or maybe it's the sincere service. At any rate, for starters you'll get homemade biscuits and an extensive assortment of vegetables and dips. Proceed to an overwhelming serving of pasta Lindsay: scallops, shrimp, and sea-crabmeat in a madeira-and-sherry cream sauce for $15. (There's also a wide range of veal, beef, fowl, and fish entrees, as well as gourmet pizza and Cajun specialties in the more casual Binnacle Tavern.) If you dine before 6:25 p.m. and pay cash, your dinner will be 15% less. The Arbor is open from 5 to 11:30 p.m. from May through October.

READER'S RESTAURANT SELECTION: "**Captain Cass,** in Rock Harbor, just north of Orleans off Rte. 6A (no phone), is your basic diner. It's right on the harbor and colorful buoys hang outside. Food is good and reliable; lobsters ($17 to $20) and lobster rolls ($9) being two house specialties. Its pleasant, informal atmosphere is popular with locals. Lunch is served from 11 a.m. to 2 p.m.; dinner, from 5 to 9 p.m. There is generally a 15- to 20-minute wait at dinner. It's not licensed but patrons can BYOB" (Andrew Effrat, Ontario, Canada).

WHAT TO SEE AND DO: Orleans has a rare sight: a museum in the building erected to house the American terminus of a transatlantic cable from Brest, France. Laid in 1879, the cable came to Orleans in 1891, and the **French Cable Station Museum** remains much as it was when the cable was still in use. Among other important messages, word of Lindbergh's arrival in Paris was transmitted via the cable; the cable was in use until 1959. Today the museum is open in July and August Tuesday through Saturday from 2 to 4 p.m., at $2 for adults, $1 for children 7 to 17 (7 and under free). It's located at Rte. 28 and Cove Road.

Several good beaches are a short distance from Orleans. Remember that Atlantic-side beaches will invariably be cooler for swimming than the beaches on Cape Cod Bay.

Nauset Beach, a stretch of sand ten miles long, is a town beach of Orleans and therefore is subject to a $5 ($10 on weekends and holidays) parking fee (use of bathhouse and other facilities included) per day; permits for a week or more also available at reduced prices. The surfing's not bad at Nauset, and a section of the beach is reserved for that activity.

Skaket Beach, on Cape Cod Bay, has less surf, but warmer water and a gently sloping beach. It's operated by the town, has lifeguards, parking places, and a bathhouse, and there's a $5 charge.

Pilgrim Lake is a freshwater swimming spot run by the town. A sand beach runs into the clear water, and a lifeguard is on duty during the summer season. No charge for use of the facilities.

A short detour to **Fort Point** off Rte. 6A will reveal a breathtaking view of the surrounding marshlands. There are also some nice trails you can take down to the Nauset Marsh.

Eastham

Eastham's main attraction is the Salt Pond Visitor Center of the Cape Cod National Seashore (see below). Right across the street from the Visitor Center is the quaint and attractive **Eastham Historical Society Museum.** Look for the curious gateway, made from the jawbones of a huge whale. The museum, once a schoolhouse, dates from 1869.

Just south of the Salt Pond Visitor Center on U.S. 6 is the oldest windmill on Cape Cod (1793), a favorite place to stop and take a photo. From the windmill, take a side trip west to **First Encounter Beach,** where the Pilgrims first met the Indian inhabitants of the Cape back in 1620. A plaque on a boulder up the hill just north of the parking lot commemorates the meeting which, apparently, was anything but cordial. You can visit the boulder plaque for free, but if you want to park and use the beach during the summer, you'll have to pay the town's beach-use parking fee ($5 daily, $10 weekly).

9. Cape Cod National Seashore

To preserve intact the particular wild beauty of Cape Cod, Congress established the Cape Cod National Seashore in 1961. It's administered by the National Park Service and includes something less than 27,000 acres of beach, dunes, marsh, forest, and glacial ponds. Acquisition of land for the Seashore is still going on, and therefore much private property is found in and around the Seashore. Within the Seashore, which stretches for 50 miles from the southern tip of Nauset Beach all the way to Provincetown, there are four developed areas for visitors:

NAUSET AREA: The **Salt Pond Visitor Center** is at Eastham on U.S. 6, and it's here you'll find interpretive exhibits and pamphlets, guide leaflets to the nature trails, an 8 p.m. evening program, rest rooms, picnic areas, and **Coast Guard Beach** and **Nauset Light Beach,** open for swimming. Parking is $3 at Nauset Light, but you must take a $3 shuttle bus to the Coast Guard Beach as parking is not allowed there. Several bicycle and bridle trails lead from the Visitor Center to the beaches through the pretty woods, marshes, and dunes. Be sure to enter the Visitor Center building and take in the picture-postcard view of Salt Pond, below.

MARCONI STATION AREA: The Seashore's headquarters is here near Wellfleet, and also an interpretive shelter at the site of Marconi's wireless station, the first in the United States; a nature trail; and Marconi Beach, open for swimming (parking is $3). The Great Island Trail is in a separate area southwest of the town of Wellfleet.

PILGRIM HEIGHTS AREA: Between North Truro and Provincetown, this area includes an interpretive shelter dealing with the Pilgrims and the Indians, nature trails, a picnic area, and, nearby, Head of the Meadow Beach, open for swimming.
You'll also see signs pointing the way to Highland Light, with its picturesque lighthouse and ocean observation point. On a nearby hill are several radar installations which look surprisingly like enormous golf balls. And then there's a golf course, right below.

PROVINCE LANDS AREA: A Visitor Center outside Provincetown on Race Point Road provides information and exhibits dealing with the Seashore and its natural treasures, with a schedule of programs at the amphitheater in the evening. Two beaches, a picnic area, a natural trail, and a bicycle trail are here as well. Parking costs $3 at Race Point and Herring Cove.

10. Wellfleet

Cooking lobsters and corn on the cob at a beach picnic, meeting friends downtown at the lunchcounter for a midmorning's lazy second cup of coffee, running errands barefoot or in rubber thongs—if you've enjoyed that sort of an easy summer atmosphere, Wellfleet will bring it back to you. Although a number of motels on U.S. 6 take in travelers heading for Provincetown, Wellfleet is mostly a town of "steadies," people who come every summer for all summer. But it does have a few inns and restaurants worth a look should you find it good to stop here.

WHERE TO STAY: Not far from the center of Wellfleet is the **Holden Inn,** P.O. Box 816, Wellfleet, MA 02667 (tel. 508/349-3450), open mid-April to Columbus Day. The inn consists of three buildings of very nicely kept rooms, all different, some with water views, and with double or twin beds. One room, for instance, is paneled all in cedar, and is very handsome. No meals are served, and rates vary with the plumbing: doubles with shared bath are $50; doubles with private bath are $60. Several of the rooms are furnished with some antique pieces. To find the Holden Inn, from Rte. 6 take a left at the Wellfleet Center sign, a left at the sign to the pier; the inn is on the right.

WHERE TO DINE: The **Wellfleet Oyster House** (tel. 508/349-2134) takes its name and its menu from the renowned Wellfleet oyster. It's just off Rte. 6 on East Main Street, the road into town, overlooking a small pond. The restaurant is in an early Cape house (built 1750) with wide-board floors and old paintings on the walls. Have oysters as an appetizer, or as a main course, broiled, in a stew, casino, or Rockefeller. The menu lists a dozen other seafood entrees, including seafood curries, paella, shrimp, sole, and lobster. For meat-eaters, there's prime rib, sirloin, and steak tartare. Most entrees are priced from $13 to $20, and as each includes relish tray, salad, vegetable, potato or rice, garlic bread, and coffee or tea, the entree price is virtually the dinner price (add 5.7% tax, tip, and cost of drinks). The restaurant is open each evening from 6 to 10 p.m., March through November (weekends only in off-season).

Try a restaurant called **Cielo** (pronounced "chello"), on East Main Street across from the Oyster House (tel. 508/349-2108), for a unique, romantic, five-course, evening-long dinner extravaganza. The two owners do it all: from gingerly cleaning fresh green beans to serving each course to washing the dishes afterward. As you can imagine, the set menu changes daily (if you're a vegetarian, don't dine there on a night they serve beef), and the restaurateurs can only keep up the consuming pace a few nights a week (Thursday through Saturday) Memorial Day through Labor Day. The set menu is about $40 per person. A sample evening's fare includes salad; pasta with a fresh, cool tomato-and-basil sauce; plum bisque; marinated and broiled boneless leg of lamb; rice and fresh vegetables; and an almond tarte with apricot glaze. The lovely, open dining room seats 16 or so, and the sole 8 p.m. seating is by reservation only.

For fine nouvelle New England cuisine, **Aesop's Table,** on Main Street (tel. 508/349-6450), is a must. The building is set high off the road and boasts a long history dating back to the early 1800s. Half the seating is conventional, half is art deco and all is in demand on summer nights, so call for reservations. Try their mussels anise poached in red zinfandel and "poulet d'art" (self-proclaimed artful variations of the classic chicken); finish with cappuccino chip cheesecake. Expect a full dinner for two to cost $75 with tax and tip, without wine. For a nice drink in relaxed surroundings, try the second-floor bar and lounge.

Down by the town dock is **Captain Higgins' Seafood Restaurant** (tel. 508/349-6027), with views of the pier and the harbor. In season, hours are noon to 9:30 p.m., and when last I visited, one could have a daily evening special of Wellfleet bluefish for $15. With a half dozen Wellfleet oysters on the half shell and a bottle of wine, two people can dine here for $55, wine, tax, and tip included. There is a children's menu.

The **Bayside Lobster Hutt** (tel. 508/349-6333) is hardly an exotic place— unless you come from far away. Wellfleet regulars and visitors come into this old oyster shack for a summer picnic-style self-service lobster dinner consisting of live boiled lobster—you pick 'em from the tanks—corn on the cob, steamed clams, and the like. A 1½-pound lobster, easily a huge meal for one person, with corn, costs about $12.50. Fish and chips is $8. Informal, fun, and good food. The Lobster Hutt, on Commercial Street, on the way to the town dock, is open for lunch and dinner daily from Memorial Day through September, noon to 10:30 p.m. Bring your own wine or beer.

Wellfleet's best place for a quick breakfast, good lunch, or inexpensive and tasty dinner is **The Lighthouse** (tel. 508/349-3681), on Main Street right in the center of town. It's Wellfleet's hometown eatery, and everybody meets everybody else here during the day, for brunch or for a cocktail out on the screened-in "deck." The atmosphere is very informal, the service by young local girls quick and friendly. Breakfast such as French toast, juice, and coffee is $3.75; at lunch, sandwiches such as turkey club or clam rolls are offered. Complete seafood dinners in the evening (till 9:30 p.m.) run $14 to $17; if you want the main-course plate only, it's a few dollars less. When you're searching for the Lighthouse, look for the little model of its namesake over the front door.

WHAT TO SEE: As most of Wellfleet's crowd is permanent for the summer, not as many things are available for the transient visitor. Note the town clock in the steeple of the First Congregational Church, which, Wellfleetans proudly say, is the only clock in the world that rings ship's time. The beaches are mostly reserved for permanent or all-summer residents (you need two different permits to swim there, and if you're passing through it's not worth getting them), but **White Crest Beach** and **Cahoon's Hollow Beach,** off U.S. 6 on the Atlantic coast, are open to day visitors for $10. And you can always go south on U.S. 6 a short distance from Wellfleet and turn left (east) to the **Marconi Beach** in the National Seashore. At the beach is an ocean overlook and an interpretive shelter explaining the activities of the Marconi Wireless Station, the first in the United States, which was on this site. The Atlantic White Cedar Swamp nature trail starts from here as well.

The Massachusetts Audubon Society operates the **Wellfleet Bay Wildlife Sanctuary** (P.O. Box 236, South Wellfleet, MA 02663; tel. 508/349-2615), 700 acres of woods and marshland which you can see on your own or by guided tour. The sanctuary is open all year long and interpretive walks are given in summer. There are also birding tours to Monomoy National Wildlife Refuge. Charge is $2 for adults, $1 for children. A natural history day camp for children operates in July and August, with trips and tours on and off the property. From July through September there's a field school for adults too.

A STOP IN TRURO: If you want to head straight to the beach, but you're starving from the long drive and don't want to deal with traffic in P-town, turn off Rte. 6A into downtown Truro for a quick stop. **Jams, Inc.** (tel. 508/349-1616), in addition to carrying standard grocery items, stocks an impressive assortment of pâtés, spreads, meats, cheeses, breads, imported crackers, and the like (even an authentic baklava). They keep long hours during high season.

---

11. Provincetown

Provincetown is a world unto itself, unlike any other place in all New England. Because it is separated from the rest of the Cape by sand, forest, and marsh, it has something of the ambience of an island, an ambience accentuated by the town's compact size. Out of season, the inhabitants are mostly fishermen, descendants of hardy Portuguese whaling men who came here for the whaling trade a century ago. In season Provincetown is a carnival constantly alive with all sorts of people from all around: New York, Boston, Montréal, Québec, and also Podunk. Artists and writers, the successful and the hopeful, college sophomores and sophisticates, dowagers and down-at-heels all mix and mingle in the evening along "P-town's" narrow streets. The town is at the same time quaint and sophisticated, elegant and tawdry, depending on where you look and how you see.

Of all things, the most important when planning a visit to P-town in late July and August is to *have a room reservation without fail*. It is just not possible to find a room in Provincetown for the six weeks of hectic high season unless you reserve ahead. If you have no reservation, it's best to plan to stay in Orleans, Wellfleet, or along U.S. 6 some distance from P-town and to drive up for the day.

Gay and Straight in P-town: Like San Francisco and Key West, Provincetown hosts a large gay community on vacation during the summer. The great majority of establishments—hotels, inns, guesthouses, restaurants, cafés, bars, and nightclubs—welcome all customers regardless of sexual preference, regardless of whether the proprietor is gay or straight. But in a few places you'll definitely feel out of place if your sexual preference doesn't match that of the proprietor and the majority of customers.

GETTING THERE: You can get to Provincetown by car, by bus direct from New York, Hartford, Providence, points in between, by sea, and by air. Here's the rundown:

By Car

U.S. 6 is divided highway all the way to P-town, where it ends and brings you face to face with a parking problem. *Don't* try to park right in the center of town. Get a space in one of the municipal lots (follow the signs) if you can.

By Bus

In summer, **Bonanza Bus Lines** will take you to Hyannis from New York (Port Authority Terminal, Greyhound counter; tel. 212/564-8484) or from Providence (Bonanza Terminal; tel. 401/751-8800 or 331-7500). In Hyannis, transfer to **Plymouth & Brockton** bus (tel. 508/775-5524). The trip takes eight hours from New York, 3¼ hours from Providence. Bonanza also runs buses from Albany and Springfield, Mass., to Hyannis, where you connect for P-town. In Hartford the terminal is at Union Station (tel. 203/547-1500). **Plymouth & Brockton** runs four buses daily in summer from Boston to Provincetown. Connections are arranged for buses coming from Montréal via Boston to the Cape (two buses daily in summer, with additional services on weekends). Note that the bus driver will drop you off near or right at your hotel, if it's out of the center of town, if you ask him to do so. This is a normal service, so feel free to ask.

By Sea

You can take a delightful cruise to Provincetown aboard the M/V *Provincetown II*, operated by **Bay State Provincetown Cruises**, 66 Long Wharf, Boston, MA 02110 (tel. 617/723-7800). The three-hour cruise costs $15 one way ($13 for seniors and children under 12), or $25 round trip ($18 for seniors and kids) if you make the round trip all in one day. The ship leaves from Boston's Commonwealth Pier: take the T (subway) Blue Line to Aquarium Station, or the Red Line to South Station, and then cross the Fort Point Channel. Ask for Northern Avenue, walk southeast along it for a few blocks, and Commonwealth Pier will be on your left. The walk from either subway stop takes about 15 minutes.

Here's the schedule: leave Commonwealth Pier at 9:30 a.m., arrive at P-town's MacMillan Wharf right in the middle of town at 12:30 p.m. The return trip leaves MacMillan Wharf at 3:30 p.m. to arrive at Commonwealth Pier by 6:30 p.m. Breakfast, lunch, snacks, cocktails, and refreshments are on sale aboard; a band provides music, and the captain describes the landmarks and sights in passing. The 1,100-passenger, 195-foot *Provincetown II* has three decks providing open, covered, and enclosed seating areas.

By the way, MacMillan Wharf is where intercity buses begin and end their runs, and where the Provincetown Chamber of Commerce operates its information office.

By Air

Pac Air (tel. toll free 800/359-7221) operates about seven daily flights by small Piper aircraft between Boston's Logan International Airport and Provincetown, a flight of less than half an hour.

INFORMATION: The **Provincetown Chamber of Commerce** operates an information office (tel. 508/487-3424) at 307 Commercial St. on the town wharf, called MacMillan Wharf. Boats from Boston arrive at this wharf, and the chamber's office is also the stop for intercity buses from New York, Providence, and Boston. Bus and boat schedules are posted here. You can also get information on the new shuttle bus that takes you to different points in P-town (50¢ for senior citizens, $1 for everyone else).

WHERE TO STAY: Provincetown's streets are lined with guesthouses and inns and motels, and in the six weeks from mid-July to Labor Day every room in every one will be rented. Outside of that time you have a chance of finding a room by arriving in town by late morning or early afternoon. A special note is in order concerning credit cards. Demand for services is so great here that very many hotels and restaurants *do not accept credit cards*. As they get all the business they want anyway, they choose not to bother with the extra expense, delay, and paperwork that cards entail. Also, most lodging places require some minimum stay during the peak season period, usually from three or four days (at least, on weekends) to a full week. And you won't be able to fudge it: you'll probably have to pay the full amount for your stay when you check in.

When you set out to hunt for accommodations, or to find your reserved room, remember that P-town is about three miles long from one end of Commercial Street (the main street) to the other.

P-town's ZIP Code is 02657, for reservations by mail.

West End Guesthouses and Inns

The quaint, picturesque character of Provincetown is best expressed in its small inns and guesthouses. The West End—west of MacMillan Wharf, that is—has the richest concentration of guesthouses. Many are really inns, carefully restored with lots of guest rooms, some luxury features, and moderate to high prices. Others are mom-and-pop establishments, simple and unpretentious, at very reasonable bargain rates. First I'll describe the nicer places, and then the West End bargain finds.

MODERATELY PRICED ROOMS: Start your room search by walking west along Commercial Street from MacMillan Wharf, with the street numbers descending as you go west.

The **Anchor Inn** is a gracious, expansive turn-of-the-century house at 175 Commercial St. (tel. 508/487-0432). As with most inns and guesthouses in P-town, every room is different, although most have a deck, balcony, or porch, and many have a sea view. Room size, view, and deck determine room price, and the date of your visit is an important factor as well. From Memorial Day through mid-September, expect to pay $88 to $116 for a double room, tax included. (During July Fourth and Labor Day weekends there's a seven-day minimum stay and a $10-per-room surcharge in effect.)

The **Captain and His Ship** (tel. 508/487-1850) sounds like the title of a Cape Cod novel, but in fact it's a handsome guesthouse at 164 Commercial St., corner of Central Street, just far enough from the heart of town to keep the noise level low.

PROVINCETOWN

Shipboard tidiness characterizes the house, its eight guest rooms, and its small front lawn complete with bench. Each room is different, furnished with fascinating Victoriana, and each has a different price: with private bath, rooms are $93 to $134; with shared bath, the double rooms are $72 to $104. The more expensive ones are those with water views, of course. Reductions of $15 to $20 are in effect anytime except mid-June through mid-September (the house is open all year); in high season, a four-night minimum stay is required if you plan to stay on a weekend or part of one.

Along Commercial Street, as you come to the Coast Guard Station on your left, note that Commercial Street bears left around the station. If you keep going straight you'll be on Tremont Street.

Past the Coast Guard Station, at 96 Commercial St., is the **Captain Lysander Inn** (tel. 508/487-2253). The ancestral home of Dr. Vannevar Bush, it was built by Capt. Lysander Paine in 1852. The rooms feature a blend of antique and traditional style furnishings. Rooms with private bath are $65 and those with shared baths are $60; the efficiency is $82. Each additional person pays $10 a day. Rates are about $10 to $15 less in the off-season. Enjoy a complimentary continental breakfast in the front parlor, or outside on the spacious front deck or sunporch. Parking is free. There is a four-night minimum over holidays and a three-night minimum for weekends.

Bright, cheerful, comfortable, and well equipped: that describes the **1807 House,** 54 Commercial St. (tel. 508/487-2173). The cedar-shingled main house faces the street, and behind it are several other buildings which hold rooms, studios, and apartments. Names say it all: the Master's Suite, the Artist's Studio, the Cottage Garden Apartment, the Cottage Studio Apartment, the Red Room, the Beige Room, etc. Each is tastefully, attractively done, many have kitchens, and all share the quiet location, free parking, and grassy lawns. The owners will be happy to describe each room for you, and will quote prices such as $38 single, $48 to $70 double—high-season rates. In fall, winter, and spring, prices are about $15 lower. Three-day minimum stays on Memorial, July Fourth, and Labor Day weekends.

The Masthead, 31–41 Commercial St. (tel. 508/487-0523), lists cottages, apartments, and motel rooms among its accommodations, but you must see the place to appreciate it. All these overnight possibilities are contained in a collection of cozy little cottages which look across flawless green lawn to a private boardwalk, a beach, and the water. Unless you can look in person, it's best to write ahead for a copy of the descriptive sheet detailing the 21 different types of accommodations, from modern rooms through efficiency studios to cottages for up to seven people. In high season (July through Labor Day), the cottages, suites, and efficiencies are rented by the week, anywhere from $798 to $1,211 for two people; a few motel rooms rent by the day for $53 to $127. Mid-September rates are a few dollars lower, but off-season rates (late September to early June) are substantially lower: most accommodations rent for $58 double, a few for more, a few for less. Holiday prices are somewhat higher. No pets.

BUDGET-PRICED ROOMS: Now let's do that same walk westward from MacMillan Wharf, this time looking for the lowest-priced rooms in P-town. While not fancy, these rooms are always comfortable; few have private bath, though.

Mrs. Helen Valentine is the lady who runs **Valentine House,** 88 Commercial St. (tel. 508/487-0839), a very tidy guesthouse with its own parking facilities and rooms that rent for $45 in season, $35 off-season, double. Quiet, fairly convenient —an excellent place to stay.

Corea's Guest House (tel. 508/487-0274) is at 5 Cottage St., off Commercial right behind Valentine House. A homey place run by a nice lady, it's comfy rather than classy or chic, but the prices are appealing: $25 single, $35 double (in a double bed), $40 for two in twin beds.

Nearby is the **O'Donnell Guest House,** 6 Atwood Ave., a little alley off Commercial (tel. 508/487-0103). John and Marian O'Donnell rent rooms which share a bath for $50 (twin or double bed), or $32.50 (single), plus a cottage (weekly for $400). It has a nice lawn, set back from the street, and free parking.

Tremont Street is parallel to Commercial Street and one block inland (in fact, if Commercial Street didn't jog around the Coast Guard Station, Tremont Street would be the natural continuation of Commercial—see the map). **Bob White's Rooms and Cottages,** 21 Tremont St. (tel. 508/487-0482), is actually operated by Mrs. Ethel White, who will show you a twin-bedded room with a TV, sharing a bath, for $35 or a room with private bath and color TV for $40; the cottage goes for $44 per day, double.

East End Guesthouses and Inns

The eastern reaches of Provincetown, along Commercial Street, Bradford Street, and the small cross streets between them, hold dozens of small inns and a few guesthouses. Generally speaking, these are more expensive than the majority of West End places. The location is roughly the same in terms of convenience. You may encounter a bit more noise here, though. Look your room over with this in mind.

The **Bradford Gardens Inn,** 178 Bradford St. near the corner of Miller Hill Road (tel. 508/487-1616), is certainly one of Provincetown's most charming and serene places to stay. Every room in the century-and-a-half-old inn is different, and each has a name rather than a number. All rooms have private bath and TV set (all color); six rooms have fireplaces as well, and these rent for $104 double in season; standard double rooms are $89. An extra person pays $15 sharing a room. Alternative arrangements include two apartments, a Swiss-chalet-type cottage, and a six- to eight-person lodge ($135 double, $15 for each additional person). Rates include a big breakfast and (for rooms with facilities to use it) firewood as well. And speaking of gardens, the Bradford has 'em, spreading around the house, set with benches, chairs, and even a garden swing.

The **White Horse Inn,** 500 Commercial St. (tel. 508/487-1790), is a neat and tidy place painted white, with blue shutters and a bright-yellow door. Inside, lots of quaint old pieces picked up in the area were used in decoration to keep the period feeling (the house is at least two centuries old), and every room seems to contain at least five original paintings. The beach is right across the street (guests have beach rights), and for after-swim, the inn's backyard lawn chairs hit the spot. Doubles with private bath go for $60; with shared bath, $50; studio apartments cost $550 weekly; single rooms are $30 to $35; and an extra person is charged $15. Off-season, the rates go down; just ask.

Asheton House (tel. 508/487-9966) is one of those immaculately restored, beautifully decorated guesthouses found in Provincetown. Each of the seven guest rooms is unique: one has a four-poster bed; another has a fireplace, dressing room, and private bath; yet another has a canopied bed. There's an apartment with bedroom, living room, and kitchen too. The smallest, simplest room with double bed and shared bath rents for $42; most others go for $58 to $65, although the suite (with the fireplace) costs $84. The apartment rents for $670 double per week, $10 per day or $70 per week for an additional person. All these prices are for summer, and all include the tax. Fall, winter, and spring prices are about 25% lower. Asheton House is at 3 Cook St., just off Commercial.

Motels

A nicely kept motel is the **Cape Colony Inn,** at 280 Bradford St. (tel. 508/487-1755). Here, besides clean and well-kept modern rooms, you have a big heated pool, volleyball, badminton, shuffleboard, and a coffeeshop. The Cape Colony has a policy of accepting reservations for a minimum of two nights (three on holidays). Rates for the rooms, all with two double beds (or one queen-size) air conditioning, room phones, refrigerator, and color TV, are $64 to $87 for two. There is a suite with two rooms and three double beds, with one bathroom to serve the two rooms, for $99 for up to four people. These in-season rates apply from the last week in July to Labor Day. Off-season, from April to closing, rates are lower.

The **Shamrock Motel & Cottages** is at 49 Bradford St., at the intersection with Shank Painter Road (tel. 508/487-1133). A cute little place with a swimming pool right near the center of town, it has accommodations of all different varieties: motel rooms, motel apartments large and small, and several cottages capable of sleeping from two to five people. In the motel rooms there are tile baths, wall-to-wall carpeting, and TV. The motel apartments are efficiency units with kitchen facilities. The rooms are $80 double in season, $60 off-season; motel apartments cost $75 for two, $85 for two to five; cottages range from $60 for a small studio capable of sleeping two or three, to a deluxe cottage which sleeps five, at $75 to $80 per night. These rates are cut by 40% off-season, and weekly rates both in season and off give you in effect one free night every week you stay.

The **Moors Motel** (tel. 508/487-1342), Bradford Street Extension (mail address: P.O. Box 661, Provincetown, MA 02657), is right at the tip of the Cape, at the very end of Bradford Street. It is, therefore, a bit out of the center of town, but this has its advantages. For one, the motel's 32 modern, bath-equipped rooms overlook the scenic moors of the National Seashore, and are very near the beach. The weathered wood of this two-decker motel is in the Cape Cod style, and on the second floor a walkway is good for sitting to look at the view. There's a small pool and color TV for those who tire of the view, and a good restaurant (Portuguese and American food) and cocktail lounge connected with the motel. Rates vary almost by the month, but at their highest they're $66 to $77 for two, going down to $34 to $37 in April and October. Note that every room sleeps three people (the third person pays an extra-person rate of $8). The higher prices in every case are for the second-floor rooms, which have balconies and the best views. Continental breakfast is included in the high-season rates. Stays of seven days in high season receive a 10% discount.

WHERE TO DINE: Provincetown has a bewildering array of restaurants, everything from classy places with sommeliers and an ocean view to hot-dog stands with a view of Commercial Street. Some general rules: All P-town restaurants specialize in seafood, often prepared Portuguese style. Most restaurants on the seaward side of Commercial Street, with sea views, are more expensive than those on the landward side. If this is your first experience dining on clams, oysters, or lobster, be sure to read "A Real New England Clambake" in Chapter I.

First I'll describe P-town's best all-round good, moderately priced establishments in the middle of town. Then I'll go on to some special, or elegant, or out-of-the-way places you might want to try.

Moderately Priced Restaurants

The **Grand Central Café** (tel. 508/487-9116) boasts that it was established in 1968. That might not seem a long run when compared to Boston's century-old Durgin-Park, but for Provincetown it's an eon. Why so long-lived? Because it's got the formula down: good food at moderate prices in attractive, cozy, even romantic surroundings. Stained-glass lamps, wrought-iron fancywork, plants everywhere, a variety of small dining rooms, and an outdoor garden provide the atmosphere, and the sea provides the main courses. Swordfish, lobster, fresh salmon, and scampi are at the high end ($14 to $21) along with the steaks and prime rib, but you can get sole Florentine or bluefish for $12, and that includes rice, potato or vegetable, salad, bread, and butter. There is a 10% discount on all dinners before 7 p.m. Wine and cocktails are served. Note that a 15% service charge will be added to your bill, so there's no need to tip. The café is at 5 Masonic Pl. (a little street that starts between 216 and 218 Commercial St.), open from Memorial Day to late September for dinner: early, leisurely, and late-night (till midnight).

Front Street, 230 Commercial St. (tel. 508/487-9715), is a very popular place for dinner these days. Through a trellis walkway and down into the basement of a 140-year-old house, you'll find entrees of duck, lamb, calamari, and soft-shell crab with tricolor pasta on the menu, each for about $16 or $18. Atmosphere is typical Cape Cod, with lots of wood and beams overhead. Call for reservations; they serve until 10:30 p.m. A complete dinner for two will cost $50 to $60.

Let's conjure up a mood now. It's the evening of a fine, adventurous day, and you want to have a good dinner at some small, very intimate candlelit spot with particularly interesting and delicious food at moderate prices. The place is **Sal's Place,** 99 Commercial St. past the Coast Guard Station in the West End (tel. 508/487-1279); the day is any day but Monday (closed); the time is 6 to 10 p.m. The food is Italian, and all cooked to order. Tiny wooden tables, chianti bottles hanging from the ceiling, and a small dining room both simple and romantic; there is also a new larger room on the water, and outdoor dining. First you order, say, fish soup or a shellfish appetizer, then perhaps spaghettini alla Foriana (with raisins, nuts, and anchovies), and then a main course of seafood or perhaps vitello saltimbocca or scaloppine con funghi. On Tuesday several veal dishes are featured; on Friday the specialty is calamari (squid). Appetizers, main courses, coffees, and wine for two at Sal's will bring the tab to about $50, all included. Call ahead for reservations.

Provincetown's most serviceable midrange restaurant is **Plain and Fancy,** at 334 Commercial St. (tel. 508/487-0147). It's open only for dinner, from 5 to 11 p.m., mid-May to mid-September. A highly polished floor matches the sheen on the wood tables, and charcoal drawings or watercolors of Provincetown scenes decorate each wall. The restaurant has three floors of dining, two bars, and air conditioning, but the big attraction is large portions of good food for reasonable prices: seafood dinners for $8 to $12 (but the daily special is always good and usually the best priced), meat entrees for a dollar or two more, Wellfleet oysters on the half shell for $6. A half-liter carafe of wine costs about the same. You can't go wrong here, as the prices quoted include entree, rice or potato, salad, vegetable, bread, and butter.

Out of Town, On the Moors

The **Moors Restaurant** (tel. 508/487-0840) takes its name from its location right at the end of Bradford Street Extension, at the junction with Rte. 6A, on the moors. The dining rooms are positively fraught with nautical paraphernalia, on the walls, on the ceiling, adorning the bar, but somehow it manages to be atmospheric rather than overwhelming. Lunch and dinner are served April through October, and the cuisine is pure Provincetown: seafood with Portuguese accents. At lunchtime you can eat for as little as $4 if you can be contented with a linguiça roll (linguiça is a mildly spicy Portuguese sausage) and a beer; or you can spend a few dollars more for sea-clam pie or something like broiled Cape scallops. Dinnertime main courses cost, in general, $11 to $15, but for the same price you can order the daily special dinner which includes soup, salad, and coffee. Besides the standard fresh fish and lobster casserole, you might find carangueijo vieira a moda de peniche (scallops and crabmeat in a casserole, made with wine, brandy, and tomato sauce; $14). On Sunday in July and August, come out to the Moors for a jazz brunch from noon to 3 p.m.: hot crêpes and cool live jazz, lots of fun.

The **Red Inn,** 15 Commercial St. (tel. 508/487-0050), is almost at the western end of the street, the town, and indeed the Cape. Perched on a grassy rise, it overlooks the harbor and takes full advantage of the view. A quaint old red Cape building, the Red Inn serves lunch and dinner every day of the year in its quiet location. The dining rooms are refined but not stuffy, with high-backed captain's chairs and nicely set tables. The menu is short, specializing in traditional dishes: broiled scallops, baked scrod, roast duckling, pork, lamb, and beef. The bill will come to $25 to $35 per person, all in.

An Outdoor Café

Want to sit at an outdoor café? The most obvious place to go is the **Café Blasé,**

328 Commercial St. (tel. 508/487-9465), just east of the center of town. Lots of tables shaded by umbrellas sit out in a courtyard surrounded by flower boxes. Should you want solid sustenance, try a portion of quiche Lorraine, mushroom and spinach, or crab ($6), a huge salad ($5.50 to $7.50), a Mexican snack, or the Blazing Blasé Burger made with fresh mushrooms, grilled cheese, and bacon for $7. The array of drinks offered is nothing short of astounding, with nonalcoholic specialties such as piña colada, orzata, grenadine, coco rico, guava and mango nectar. Imported and domestic beer, wine by the glass, half liter, or liter, or by the bottle satisfy stronger thirsts. The café is open for breakfast, lunch, cocktails, afternoon espresso, and dinner.

Another place to while away the day is the **Euro Island Grill,** 258 Commercial St. (tel. 508/497-2505), next to the Provincetown town hall. The outdoor café really does have a European ambience; breakfast, lunch, and supper (grilled burgers, pizza, a raw bar) are served. At 7 p.m. the indoor restaurant opens, with dining in a former church. The Euro is open from Memorial day through late October.

For Breakfast

Fresh coffee in the morning, yes, but also fresh bread and rolls: find the **Portuguese Bakery,** right down by MacMillan Wharf at 299 Commercial St.—follow the coffee and fresh-bread smells. Not only is breakfast the freshest here, it's the cheapest. Put it together yourself, take it out to the wharf to consume, and you can do it for $2.50 easily.

For a big breakfast on the quieter end of town, try **Pearl's Café,** 401½ Commercial St. (tel. 508/487-2114). The place itself is actually bustling: it's usually packed from 8 a.m. to noon. They serve a tasty granola concoction for $3, and a three-egg omelet with your choice of almost anything on it for $3.75.

For a Quick Fix

A real institution in P-town for do-it-yourself lunch or quick dinner is the **Cheese Market,** 225 Commercial St. (tel. 508/487-3032). They put together a multitude of different sandwiches, from large seafood sandwiches to large pastrami sandwiches ($5.50 to $7). Open from 9 a.m. to 11 p.m. daily from Memorial Day through October and until 7 p.m. the rest of the year.

WHAT TO SEE AND DO: Provincetown's an interesting small town to browse around. Although people-watching could keep one amused for days, here are some of P-town's other highlights. *Provincetown* magazine hits the streets every Thursday; it's free and will have plenty of suggestions for things to do.

Pilgrim Monument and Provincetown Museum

For a general view, the **Pilgrim Monument** and **Provincetown Museum,** on Town Hill off Winslow Street (tel. 508/487-1310), give you the best view of the town in both its physical and historical aspects. Both attractions are open during the same hours, and you pay one fee for the two: $2 per adult, $1 per child 4 through 12. The museum is an interesting potpourri of old fire fighting gear, costumes, a whaling ship captain's quarters on board, primitive portraits, World War I mementos, arctic lore, and a sequence of displays on the activities of the Pilgrims in Provincetown, for this is the first place they touched land in the New World. After seeing these you can continue with the Wedgwood, model of a Thai temple, antique dolls, etc. Then head for the tower.

The Pilgrim Monument is copied from the Torre del Mangia in Siena, Italy, and is all granite and 252½ feet high. The cornerstone was laid in 1907 with President Teddy Roosevelt in attendance, and the structure was completed three years later, when President Taft did the dedicating. You may think that there's an elevator in it. Well, there's not, and you'll have to c-l-i-m-b to the top, the equivalent of going up the steps in a 20-story building, to see the view. Most of the climb is on a ramp, not steps, and you can take your time and read the commemorative plaques from New England cities, towns, and civic groups which line the granite walls. The view is worth the climb: Provincetown and all Cape Cod spread out like the maps you've been following.

Both the monument and the museum are open at 9 a.m. The tower can't be climbed less than a half hour before closing, so get there before 4:30 p.m. From July through Labor Day, hours are extended to 9 p.m.

A Walk Around Town

Drop in at the chamber of commerce's information office down by the town wharf and pick up (25¢) the Provincetown Historical Society's pamphlet which tells you all the historic sights and houses in P-town. Check out the Pilgrims' first landing place, the monument commemorating the signing of the Mayflower Compact (America's first democratic "constitution"), and the 12-room Seth Nickerson House, the oldest house in town (1746), at 72 Commercial St., open June through October from 10 a.m. to 5 p.m. daily; $2 for adults, 50¢ for kids. The house is now the home of artist-photographer John W. Gregory and his wife, who will be happy to show you around and explain how it was built by a shipwright from heavy oak posts and beams salvaged from shipwrecks.

The **Provincetown Heritage Museum**—actually the municipal museum—at Commercial and Center Streets (tel. 508/487-0666), preserves the town's heritage in its wide-ranging displays. Relics of the fishing industry, Victoriana, and many other items capture Provincetown's history. Especially exciting for children are the antique fire engine, and the *Rose Dorothea*, the world's largest half-scale fishing schooner model. The museum is open from 10 a.m. to 6 p.m. daily from mid-June through mid-October. Adults pay $2; children under 12 free.

Galleries, Cinemas, and Theater

Latest schedules are published in the local sheet, the *Provincetown Advocate*. Galleries dot the downtown streets, often open until late in the evening. The **Provincetown Playhouse** (tel. 508/487-0955) is active all summer. Call for current information. The **New Art Cinema** (tel. 508/487-9222), across from the post office downtown at 212 Commercial St., plays both foreign and domestic first-run films. It's the newest cinema in P-town, blissfully air-conditioned. The **Metro Cinema** is right next to the Town Hall at Commercial and Ryder Streets.

Other Activities

Arnold's, at 329 Commercial St. (tel. 508/487-0855), and **Nelson's**, on Race Point Road (tel. 508/487-0034), rent **bicycles**, and you can use them in town or on the bike trails in the National Seashore. Drop in at the Seashore's Province Lands Visitor Center for a free guide pamphlet to the trails.

The **Provincetown Horse and Carriage Co.**, 27 W. Vine St. (tel. 508/487-1112), will rent you a riding horse for $20 per hour.

Several companies will take you through the dunes in a four-wheel-drive vehicle on a daylight or sunset tour for a reasonable price. Call **Drifting Sands Dune Tours** (tel. 508/349-9231) in North Truro for a reservation, or **Art's Sand Dune Taxi Tours,** at the corner of Standish and Commercial Streets (tel. 508/487-1950).

What about a sail on a schooner? Several boats make two-hour **cruises** through the waters around the tip of the Cape, giving you a very different view of the land and water. Try the *Hindu* (tel. 508/487-0659), or the *Olad* (tel. 508/487-9308); both have sunset cruises. It's best to reserve in advance. The price, like that for all the other activities here, is very reasonable, and won't set you back by even the price of a good dinner. Those who want more action on their cruise can go out with one of the two daily deep-sea fishing voyages that leave from MacMillan Wharf; whale-watching boats also leave from here, especially from mid-April to mid-June.

Should you want to do nothing more active than sit, you can have a local artist do your portrait in pastels while you're sitting. Shops are along Commercial Street and inside Whalers' Wharf near the town wharf, and prices start at $70 for a front view, $40 for the side, $40 and $20 if it's to be charcoal; frames and glass are extra and cost $35 and up. The portrait can be done, framed, and wrapped to take home in a surprisingly short time.

But biking, schooner sails, deep-sea fishing, and portrait-sitting can't equal the sense of freedom you get if you sail your own boat out onto Cape Cod Bay. You don't have to own a boat, of course, because Provincetown has **Flyer's Boat Rental,** 131A Commercial St., behind Gallerani's restaurant (tel. 508/487-0898). Little Sun Fish, larger (18- to 20-foot) sailboats, dinghies with outboard motors, and dinghies with just a pair of oars are all for rent. They'll even teach you how to sail if you don't already know.

Whale-Watching

Believe me, it's a great thrill when you see one of the monster denizens break the surface, spout, sport, and play. You can sight whales from the Coast Guard Station on Race Point Beach, and just with the naked eye you'll see their spouting and their backs roll. But to see them up close is something else, and for that you need to sign up for a whale-watching cruise. Several boats leave on morning and afternoon runs, and give you several hours in which to find and watch the whales. Call the **Dolphin Fleet** (tel. 508/255-3857, or toll free 800/826-9300), which by the way has a 99.7% sighting record; or **Portuguese Princess Excursions** (tel. 508/487-2651, or toll free 800/442-3188); or **Whale's Tales Tours** (tel. 508/497-2980, or toll free 800/942-5376); or the **Ranger V** (tel. 508/487-1582 or 487-3322, or toll free 800/992-9333) for times, prices, and reservations. Boats leave from the Town Wharf (MacMillan Wharf), and charge about $16 per person. By the way, the whales—which seem to perform expressly for the appreciative crowds on the boats —enjoy the trip as much as you do.

Nightlife

No one who visits Provincetown spends an evening without at least a few minutes' stroll along Commercial Street, for the main drag is P-town's greatest free-entertainment thrill, a circus in a straight line. But to get away from it all, try one of these things-to-do:

Lounges: After the dinner hour, many Provincetown restaurants will have entertainment in their lounges, perhaps a guitarist or pianist, even a violinist. Drop in at any one you see open in late evening, and see what's on. **Ciro and Sal's,** 41 Kiley Court (in the 400 block of Commercial Street), is a popular place; so is the **Terrace,** at the corner of Bradford and Standish Streets, as is the bar at the **Mews Restaurant,** 359 Commercial St.

Clubs: The Crown Club & Dance Bar, 247 Commercial St., is a veritable entertainment supermarket, with a disco at the rear of the parking lot named the Backroom; the front room ("Lobby Bar") on Commercial Street has live entertainment.

Speaking of revues, the **Madeira Room,** at 336 Commercial St. (tel. 508/487-0319), always has something going, usually on the decent side of raunchy, most often very funny. Pass by for a look at their signboard.

MARTHA'S VINEYARD AND NANTUCKET

These two islands are among the eastern seaboard's most attractive and visited resorts. There's something special about vacationing on an island, a particular feeling of isolation, of being apart from the schedules and worries of city life, and this is truly relaxing and therapeutic. Here is a detailed description of Massachusetts retreats in the Atlantic.

The telephone area code for both islands is 508.

MARTHA'S VINEYARD: To Bostonians and denizens of Cape Cod, it is simply "the Vineyard"; sometimes you'll see the name given as Martha's Vineyard Island, just so visitors know they're in a special place out to sea. The island got its odd name in the early 1600s, when mariner and explorer Bartholomew Gosnold stopped here. It's said he found wild grapes, and it's thought he had a daughter named Martha. *Voilà!* Today the island actually has a commercial vineyard and a winery producing fine vintages which you can sample and buy. But more of that later.

The Vineyard is not really a part of Cape Cod, and does not look upon itself as such. Vineyard residents are proud that the island is the County of Dukes County, not part of some mainland county, and they guard the anachronistic redundancy of that title very closely. For a long time the Vineyard had its own representative in the General Court (state legislature), and when redistricting made the island a part of the Cape Cod legislative district, the islanders threatened to secede from Massachusetts and become part of another state, one that would allow them their own representative.

Islanders get their exceptional sense of independence from a history of struggle with and mastery of the sea, from the days when whaling brought great wealth to an otherwise poor island. And just about the time the whaling industry declined, the tourist industry began, and Martha's Vineyard found its place in the modern world.

Today the big ferries that ply the waters of Vineyard Sound are packed with visitors every day in summer, and also very crowded on weekends in spring and fall.

A WARNING ABOUT RESERVATIONS: In high summer—July and August— you need reservations for everything: space for your car on the ferry, or for a rental car on the island, or for a hotel room, or for a weekend mainland-to-island flight. You can't reserve passenger space on the ferry, so the thing to do is get to the docks 15 or 20 minutes early, buy your ticket, and get in line. If the ferry's passenger capacity is reached, the remaining passengers in the line will have to wait for the next boat. If you don't have a room reservation in an island hotel, there's a direct-line telephone in the Steamship Authority ticket office in Woods Hole for island hotels; you'll have to wait in line to use it. On weekends in high season, chances for finding a room are not good; on weekdays you may find a room for a few nights because of a cancellation, or a gap between reservations. If all else fails, plan to visit the island for the day, returning to the mainland in the evening.

GETTING THERE: For ferries to Martha's Vineyard, see the information in the sections on Woods Hole, Falmouth, Hyannis (all in Chapter VII), and New Bedford (in Chapter VI). One ferry a day, between mid-June and mid-September, runs between the islands of Martha's Vineyard and Nantucket. Contact the **Hy-Line** ferry company (tel. 508/778-2600). When taking a ferry, note which island port—Oak Bluffs or Vineyard Haven—the ferry operates from or to.

Several regional and commuter airlines serve the islands. For details, see the beginning of Chapter VII, "Cape Cod."

GETTING AROUND THE ISLAND: There are lots of ways to get around: rental cars (which are best reserved in advance), buses, bikes, or motorbikes. Taxi service is also readily available.

Car Rentals

The big names are here: **Hertz** (tel. 508/627-4728) in Edgartown (closed Sunday) and at the airport (tel. 508/693-2402, open daily); **Budget** (tel. 508/693-1911) in Oak Bluffs and Vineyard Haven; and **National** (tel. 508/693-6454) at the airport and in Oak Bluffs (tel. 508/693-4059).

If these places produce no results or if you'd rather rent from a small local firm, try these numbers: **Adventure Rentals** of Martha's Vineyard (tel. 508/693-1959 and also a direct line from the Woods Hole Ferry Terminal) specializes in offbeat equipment such as dune buggies, vans, mopeds, four-wheel-drive vehicles, and trucks, but they do rent cars as well. Other firms are **Atlantic Auto Rentals** (tel. 508/693-0480) in Vineyard Haven and **All-Island Rent-a-Car** (tel. 508/693-6868) at the airport. Or try **Vineyard Rent-a-Car** (tel. 508/693-9780) on Water Street in Vineyard Haven.

Bikes and Motorbikes

Rental agencies abound, and you can barely descend from the ferry without coming across one. Prices are all competitive, and a three-speed bicycle should cost in the range of $8 to $12 for a day's rental (plus a $10 deposit); motorbikes and mopeds are a good deal more, in the range of $37 to $47, and entail greater responsibility, possible destination limitations, and more chance of breakdowns. I think the island and the bicycle were made for one another, and islanders have even helped this relationship along: there's a fine bike path between Oak Bluffs and Edgartown, right along the beaches. No need to reserve bikes in advance, for there are always plenty to go around.

Bus

Island Transport Bus Service (tel. 693-0058) operates school-bus-type vehicles between the Vineyard's various settlements every half hour or so, with stops

near the various ferry docks. (Trips to Gay Head from Vineyard Haven are much less frequent, though.) Prices vary according to distance traveled; round-trip tickets are always sold at a discount over the normal two-single-trip fare, so ask for a round-trip ticket if that's what suits your needs. The cheapest fare is Vineyard Haven to Oak Bluffs, and fares can be several dollars for longer trips. Don't plan on being in a hurry, as the buses frequently run behind schedule.

ORIENTATION: The island's three principal towns are **Vineyard Haven,** the commercial center where many of the mainland ferries dock; **Oak Bluffs,** a Victorian resort community of ornate "gingerbread" houses, a marina, and several grand old wooden hotels; and **Edgartown,** the county seat and main tourist attraction—clearly the prettiest town on the island. The more rural, less populated area is referred to as **Up Island;** these are the towns in the southwestern third of the island. I'll list the recommended hotels, restaurants, and things to do by town.

The **Martha's Vineyard Chamber of Commerce,** Beach Road, Vineyard Haven, MA 02568 (tel. 508/693-0085), is located a few doors down from the Tisbury Inn off Main Street. They publish a very helpful and complete visitor's guide, as well as a list of summer events. They can also help you with long-term accommodations.

You will undoubtedly learn it for yourself when you disembark from the boat, but let me be the first one to tell you. The best value on the Vineyard is a $1.55 homemade ice cream cone at **Mad Martha's.** Prime locales in Vineyard Haven, Oak Bluffs, and Edgartown will assure that no matter where you are, a Mad Martha's will never be very far. Keep your eyes peeled for their wild antique ambulance that zips between stores.

---

1. Vineyard Haven

Though the island's most popular vacation location is and always has been Edgartown, Vineyard Haven has been growing in popularity as a place to stay and to dine. Inns and motels are opening downtown, and guesthouses are springing up on the outskirts. The dining situation is both helped and hurt by Vineyard Haven's status as a "dry" town. You don't have the convenience of ordering wine with dinner, but if you remember to bring your own from Edgartown or the mainland, you'll save the normal (substantial) restaurant markup on beverages. Plan ahead and save.

WHERE TO STAY: The location of the **Lothrop Merry House,** at Owen Park, Vineyard Haven, MA 02568 (tel. 508/693-1646), makes it special. The lawn slopes gently down to a little beach on the quiet side of the harbor. The property is protected on both sides; it's a three-minute walk along the shoreline right to the boat dock. And if that's not enough, the sunrise sends reflections from the bay waters into most of the seven guest rooms. The tone in this 18th-century house is country comfortable, with braided rugs and uneven door frames. Bigger doubles with private baths on the first floor rent for $138 to $149 in season; smaller doubles, which all share a bath on the second floor, rent for $94 to $105 in season. While away the morning with the complimentary breakfast served on the patio overlooking the harbor. Ask about a sail on the innkeepers' 54-foot *Laissez Faire.*

The **Captain Dexter House,** 100 Main St., Vineyard Haven, MA 02568 (tel. 508/693-6564), is one of those rare finds: meticulously restored and exquisitely furnished in the colonial period, yet surprisingly unpretentious. Each of the eight rooms (one is actually a suite) has a private bath and some have working fireplaces and four-poster beds with white lace canopies. From the fresh flowers to the fresh-squeezed orange juice served with the "expanded" continental breakfast, you'll notice attention to detail which makes this one of the loveliest inns on the island. A bed and breakfast costs $110 to $160 double in season, $30 to $45 less per room off-season. If you're walking from the boat, it's two blocks away; if you have a car, there is private parking behind the house.

The **Vineyard Harbor Motel,** P.O. Box 1609, Vineyard Haven, MA 02568 (tel. 508/693-3334), near the edge of town on the coast road to Oak Bluffs, is modern and comfortable, with cable color TV, wall-to-wall carpeting, air conditioning, and a refrigerator in all rooms; some have kitchen facilities as well, and many have a fine oceanview. In-season rates are $100 for a harbor-view double room, $88 without the view. A two-room apartment is $110 for two people, and the penthouse, complete with view, waterbed, and private deck, is $121. An extra person pays $9 per day.

WHERE TO DINE: The finest place to dine in town, and one of the more expensive, is the **Black Dog Tavern** (tel. 508/693-9223), at the water end of Beach Street, right down next to the yacht marina. Its location and good food bring in the yachting crowd, and this keeps the quality high. A large screened porch overlooking the harbor and marina is the choice place to sit, and you must come early to get a seat there. No reservations are accepted, so get there by about 6 p.m. for dinner. I had island steamers, sautéed scallops primavera, and fresh-baked apple pie for dessert, and with coffee, tax, and tip the total was $32. The Black Dog is open May through October seven days a week from 6:30 a.m. to 11 a.m., 11:30 a.m. to 2:30 p.m., and 5 to 10 p.m. In the off-season it's closed Monday and Tuesday. Bring your own wine or beer, as Vineyard Haven is a dry town.

Walk up the street from the ferry, turn right, and soon you'll see the cobble-studded porch of **Le Grenier** on Main Street (tel. 508/693-4906). The menu, as you might guess, tends to classical French, but stresses local ingredients. Dinner (served nightly from 6 to 10 p.m.) will cost between $25 and $30. Try the stuffed mushrooms to start and the shrimp pernod flambé with cream sauce for a main course.

In the Tisbury Inn on Main Street is the **Tisbury Inn Café** (tel. 508/693-3416), where the specialty is new American cuisine with Cajun accents. The scrod jambalaya, for example, is a unique blending of New England and New Orleans. Dinner here goes for about $30; you bring your own wine.

Not quite a mile out on State Road toward Gay Head is **Louis' Tisbury Café** (tel. 508/693-3255). The name of the game here is pasta, great homemade pasta. Might I suggest a hot and spicy linguine shrimp diavolo for $13.75 or perhaps linguine with salmon, bluefish, scallops, and shrimp for $12.50. (Knock $2 off if you want it as an appetizer; everything on the menu is also available for take-out.) A low-key, casual atmosphere reigns here. Expect to wait if you don't arrive before 7 p.m.; no reservations are taken. Louis' enjoys a terrific following among the locals; they really pack 'em in here. Louis' is open Monday to Saturday from 11:30 a.m. to 4 p.m. and 5:30 to 9 p.m.; Sunday from 4 to 9 p.m.

---

2. Oak Bluffs

It's odd that this community, which began as a tent camp for summer meetings of the Methodist church, should be one of the two "wet" towns on Martha's Vineyard, but so it is. Although the camp meetings are still the most important part of the summer's activities here (your hotel will have a schedule), many other nighttime pleasures are available as well, including movies, penny arcades, and an antique merry-go-round called "The Flying Horses." During the daytime, stroll straight in from the ferry docks and along the shores of the marina for a view of the fantastically ornate Victorian "gingerbread houses" that face the marina. As you continue farther into the settlement the houses become even more wildly decorated.

WHERE TO STAY: The **Attleboro House,** at 11 Lake Ave. (P.O. Box 1564), Oak Bluffs, MA 02557 (tel. 508/693-4346), is in that marvelous row of gingerbread houses, next to the old Wesley, which faces the sheltered harbor. If you arrive by Hy-Line boat, you'll be able to spot Attleboro House even before you debark. The house's wide verandas are well furnished with rockers and fine views. Many rooms have porches overlooking the harbor. The eight rooms are spartan but tidy, and fully in the spirit of Oak Bluffs; in fact the house is on land owned by the Methodist Campmeeting Association, so guests must agree to refrain from "rude or loud behavior." Only a few rooms have washbasins; none has private bath; and though there are plenty of clean sheets and towels, maid service is strictly do-it-yourself. Single rooms cost $38; doubles are $50 to $66. Here, and at the Wesley (below), you're living right within Oak Bluffs' history.

You'll never see so much oak under one roof as at the **Oak House,** on the corner of Seaview and Pequot Avenues, Oak Bluffs, MA 02557 (tel. 508/693-4187), overlooking the water: oak ceilings, oak floors, oak paneling, oak furniture, oak bannisters, and even oak toilet seats. The living and dining rooms are dark and rich in contrast to the white, glass-enclosed sun porch. All ten bedrooms in this Victorian house have private bathrooms; three have private balconies; two are suites. Rooms rent for $93 to $143, more for the suites. There is a three-night minimum stay on summer weekends. In the spring and fall prices drop by 30% a room.

With 82 rooms, the **Wesley Hotel,** 1 Lake Ave. (P.O. Box 2370), Oak Bluffs, MA 02557 (tel. 508/693-6611), dominates the lodging market in town. From the Steamship Authority docks, walk straight inland toward the marina and the Wesley is a few blocks down on the left. This big, rambling wooden place has recently experienced a make-over. The lobby is country-formal and the hallways are papered with a pretty floral design. The rooms, while not in keeping with the gracious common area and dining room, are still clean and boast standard motel furnishings; most have televisions. A big plus here is the harbor view from the oldtime rocking chairs on the wrap-around porch. Rates, including continental breakfast, are $93 to $105 for a double with private bath, $49 for a double with a bath in the hall, $132 for a suite with private bath. An extra adult pays $20 in the summer but only half that in the spring and fall.

WHERE TO DINE: For some reason Vineyard Haven has a good number of good restaurants, and Edgartown has its share, but in Oak Bluffs the fare is less than inspired. Of course, resort towns always present problems to the visitor in search of a fine dinner: the crowds must be fed, and customers will continue to come whether the food is great or not, because they must eat. But you won't go to bed without your dinner (be it fashionable or filling) in Oak Bluffs.

The place that packs 'em in is **Giordano's,** at the corner of Circuit and Lake Avenues (tel. 508/693-0184). The large, modern, brightly lit dining room is full every night of high summer with the hungry and the thrifty filling themselves with the inexpensive Italian cuisine that's been offered here since 1930. Elegant it's not, and although it's a bit noisy, the service is efficient, the food is filling, and the price is reasonable: a full dinner special with chowder, potato, vegetable, coffee, and dessert can cost $9.50 (entree of veal cutlet or $12 sirloin steak). The à la carte items are also reasonably priced: the pizzas and spaghettis are in the $5 to $8 range. Cocktails, house wines sold by the half liter and liter, and bottled wines are available. There may well be a line of the value-minded waiting to get in, so it's good to arrive early. Open daily from 11:30 a.m. to 11:30 p.m.

For delicious breakfasts or lunchtime salads, soup, and sandwiches you can't beat **Linda Jean's,** Circuit Avenue (tel. 508/693-4093). It's nothing fancy, but is always full of folks who appreciate an honest meal at an honest price. Try L.J.'s omelet of three eggs, ham, tomato, broccoli, mushrooms, and cheese, plus home fries, toast, juice, and coffee for $5.50. At lunch order a bowl of tasty chowder for $2.50; a bacon cheeseburger goes for $3.15. The seafood platter of clams, scallops, shrimp, and haddock tops the menu at $11. Don't forget to leave room for a hefty slab of pie à la mode.

Very trendy and very upscale, that's the **Oyster Bar,** 162 Circuit Ave. (tel. 693-3300). The solitary strip of hot-pink neon, high on the back wall, sets the tone. General decor is pink and gray; lighting is soft, the ceiling high (it's tin so the noise level is a bit high, too), and the Doric pillars fake. The dinner menu (as well as the wine and dessert menu) is quite extensive: oysters galore from the raw bar or as a cooked appetizer, striped bass or mahi mahi, and a Belgian chocolate pâté with white and dark chocolate sauces, will run you about $33 per person without wine, tax, or tip. Dinner (6 to 10 p.m.) is served seven days a week from the end of May until Christmas. Reservations are advisable.

The **Ocean View** restaurant, a block from the northern end of the harbor on Chapman Avenue (tel. 508/693-2207), has a simple and basic New England dinner menu. A ten-ounce New York sirloin will run you $14, and a baked scrod topped with Ritz cracker crumbs will run you $12. The salad bar comes with the entree, but cooked vegetables are served à la carte. Check the board for fresh daily specials. This is a real neighborhood place, hardly intimate dining, but the food is certainly well prepared; ask to be seated to the left of the front entrance (it's less noisy). Open for dinner only from 6 to 10 p.m.

3. Edgartown

Undoubtedly the prettiest and most picturesque town on the island, Edgartown is the place most people want to stay when they come to Martha's Vineyard, and so the selection of rooms is fairly good. Whether your taste calls for a resort hotel with golf course, a modern motel with a sea view, or a colonial inn, Edgartown has what you want.

Besides being the residential center of the island, Edgartown has many good restaurants, most of the island's finer shops and art galleries, and street after street of attractive houses. Many of the houses were built by whaling captains with the profits of their voyages, and these same profits provided the funds to build the Methodist church (1843) on Main Street. In more recent times, Edgartown came to national prominence as the place where the movie *Jaws* and its first sequel were filmed, and many island residents made the daily stroll down to the harbor to look at the small mechanical shark in its special rack, covered by a canvas tarpaulin.

WHERE TO STAY: Edgartown has a place for any taste. Here's the rundown.

Inns Downtown
For many years visitors to Martha's Vineyard have been staying at the **Daggett House,** on North Water Street at Daggett Street (P.O. Box 1333), Edgartown, MA 02539 (tel. 508/627-4600). The rooms are tastefully furnished, several are of very good size, and some have good water views—the larger rooms and those with views are the more expensive ones. All rooms have king-size, queen-size canopy or four-posters, double, or twin beds, and private bath; some rooms, good for groups of friends or large families, are arranged in suites sharing a bath. There are even a few housekeeping rooms with kitchen, and a garden cottage with three double rooms down by the water. Prices for the 25 rooms in three different houses are $121 to $165 in summer; off-season, rates are $82 to $126. A full country breakfast is available. The original Daggett House has its own dock, and a "Chimney Room" said to be Edgartown's oldest tavern, now used for the breakfast service (ask them to show you the secret stairway here). The Cap'n Warren House is across the street, and is

equally nice, and guests at either house may use the lawns and beach. Needless to say, the Daggett House is a popular place to stay, and so it's best to write well in advance to get the type of room you desire.

Edgartown's most charming and elegant inn is the **Charlotte Inn,** South Summer Street (P.O. Box 1056), Edgartown, MA 02539 (tel. 508/627-4751), a unique hostelry combining the services of an inn, a fine art gallery, and a very good French restaurant called L'Étoile. Rooms here are all given a personal touch with furnishings—some antiques—selected by the owners, and thus the best way to select a room is to see several, although this is often difficult as many are sure to be occupied. The rates are in keeping with the elegant atmosphere: doubles run $137 to $368 in season (mid-June to mid-October); for a month on either side of high season, rates go down to $93 to $324 double; and during the winter they become $71 to $324 double. Continental breakfast is included every day but Sunday. Even if you decide not to stay at the Charlotte Inn, stroll by some evening to admire the graceful house, the very good gallery, and perhaps the garden-terrace dining at L'Étoile.

The **Edgartown Inn,** North Water Street (P.O. Box 1211), Edgartown, MA 02539 (tel. 508/627-4794), has been hosting famous guests for well over a century, including the likes of Daniel Webster, Nathaniel Hawthorne (who wrote *Twice Told Tales* here), and (Sen.) John F. Kennedy. The inn is thus a place of contrasts: in the rooms, 19th-century decor competes with the modern tile baths, and in the parlor, a portrait of Hawthorne hangs glowering at the color TV. There are 12 rooms in the inn proper, which cost $82 to $149 from May 25 to October 1, $50 to $94 off-season. In-season, for the main inn, they may not take reservations of less than five days.

Rooms in the "Captain's Quarters" out back do not have private bath, and rent for $55 in season; also, several rooms in the old barn attached to the inn are rented for $71 to $100. The Edgartown Inn serves country breakfasts in its quaint, cozy breakfast room, old-fashioned and neat as a pin: a deer head, a fine ship model, and the only "colonial" ceiling fans I've ever seen add to the decor. Whether a guest at the inn or not, you can have the full breakfast here for $5, or a continental breakfast of homemade cakes and breads baked every day for $3.50.

The **Colonial Inn,** 38 North Water Street (P.O. Box 68), Edgartown, MA 02539 (tel. 508/627-4711), looks like Edgartown's answer to the huge rambling Victorian hotels of Oak Bluffs and elsewhere, although to keep with tradition on North Water Street, this one is covered in cedar "shakes" (shingles) and many windows have shutters like those of the sea captains' houses. The advantages at the Colonial, besides its central location, recent renovations, and numerous rooms with sea views, are its large number of rooms and varied rates. Double rooms with private bath are the most expensive ($148 to $170), but if you choose a double with connecting bath—that is, shared with one other room—the price drops to $94. Children under 12 stay for free; an extra person pays $15 year round. Room rates off-season are $35 to $60 less per room. The Colonial has its own restaurant and pub, and is open from mid-April to mid-December.

Of the accommodations in Edgartown, the **Captain Henry Colt House,** 26 S. Summer St. (P.O. Box 302), Edgartown, MA 02539 (tel. 508/627-4084), is one of the nicest and most congenial. The proprietress, Mrs. Berube, is very helpful to her guests, and the street is quiet though very close to the center of town. The two apartments, each with a bedroom, living room, and kitchen, can accommodate four people. The apartment in front rents for $888 a week for four while the one in back rents for $100 less.

Inns on the Outskirts

As Edgartown is not that big a place, the outskirts in this case are only a few blocks from the center. These are on the way into town from Oak Bluffs, on Main Street near Cannonball Park.

The **Point Way Inn,** on Main Street at the corner of Pease's Point Way (P.O. Box 128), Edgartown, MA 02539 (tel. 508/627-8633), was once a 14-room whaling captain's house, but has been converted to a cozy, charming 15-room inn with a satisfying variety of accommodations. You'll know it's nice as you come through the garden, past the gazebo and croquet lawn, and into the house, which has a real family feel to it. There are small rooms, large rooms, 11 rooms with fireplace or deck, even a luxury two-room suite, all with private bath. Prices are $131 to $220 double, continental breakfast included.

Very near the junction of Main Street and Pease's Point Way is the **Dr. Shiverick House** (tel. 508/627-8497), P.O. Box 640, Edgartown, MA 02539. You'll spot the huge, substantial white house with mansard roof and rooftop observatory easily. Go in the mahogany front door, straight through the house, and you'll find a charming little patio garden. The interior is rich in period pieces; the bedrooms have private baths and appropriately sumptuous and frilly Victorian decor. Rooms cost $150 to $200 double per night, continental breakfast included. With fireplace and sitting room, suites, which sleep three, cost $265 double.

The **Governor Bradford Inn,** 128 Main St., Edgartown, MA 02539 (tel. 508/627-9510), is a handsome white clapboard New England Gothic house with high peaked roofs and bright windows. The feeling in the common rooms is one of restrained elegance rather than frilliness—a very satisfying feeling. Many of the 16 rooms have televisions; all have private baths and telephones. Rates include continental breakfast and afternoon tea: $105 to $170 double in season, $66 to $126 double off-season.

The **Jonathan Munroe House** (tel. 508/627-5536; P.O. Box 1165, Edgartown, MA 02539) is at 100 Main St. not too far from the center of town. It's a house converted to receive guests, which is exactly what it does, placing them in quaint and homey rooms, nicely done, and charging them $75 from the end of May to September. The six rooms share two upstairs baths. Guests share the use of a refrigerator; tea and coffee are offered free all day. Call for reservations.

WHERE TO DINE: Edgartown—and the island in general—can boast a large number of eateries, plain and fancy. I couldn't possibly list them all in the limited space here, and in fact an all-inclusive list would be more bewildering than helpful. Although I can heartily recommend the establishments below as delivering good value-for-money, you will no doubt want to do some exploration of your own.

Of Edgartown's restaurants, one of the most elegant and congenial is certainly **L'Étoile** (tel. 508/627-5187), in the garden and glassed-in terrace of the Charlotte Inn on South Summer Street. The white tables and chairs set out among the trees, vines, and flowers on a patio surrounded by trelliswork provide the perfect place for a warm-weather evening's repast; in bad weather the terrace room is just as good, with lots of windows and skylights. The menu reads like a list of ambrosias: roasted French pheasant with a sauce of oysters, mushrooms, warmed figs, thyme, and cognac; rack of lamb with warm goat cheese, balsamic vinaigrette, and herbed vegetable julienne; grilled swordfish steak with a trio of American caviars, champagne, and chive beurre blanc. Seven nights a week, dinner (6:30 to 9:45 p.m.) is set at $47, plus tax; Sunday brunch (10:30 a.m. to 12:30 p.m.), equally scrumptious sounding, is a more modest $22. They are closed New Year's Day through Valentine's Day.

As Edgartown is one of the Vineyard's two "wet" towns, you can order wine to accompany your meal. Call for reservations, and ask what the day's special will be.

After years of being Edgartown's prime fish market, **Lawry's,** on Main Street out of town toward Oak Bluffs (tel. 508/627-8857), added a modern dining room and became one of Edgartown's prime seafood restaurants as well. Formica tables and red padded benches make the atmosphere bright but simple, and while the restaurant serves sandwiches, the seafood is the thing. I recently filled myself with steamed clams (a huge portion that was sufficient for two), then a portion of broiled bluefish and one of fish-and-chips. The main courses came with cole slaw, potato, rolls, and butter, and the total bill was $19, tax, tip, and two glasses of beer included. All of Lawry's food can be taken out too. Lunch is served every day but Sunday from 11:30 a.m. to 2 p.m.; dinner is served nightly from 5 to 9 p.m.

The **Seafood Shanty,** on Dock Street at Kelley Street (tel. 508/627-8622), is a favorite with the younger crowd because of its atmosphere and its very reasonable seafood prices—not to mention a fine harbor view. At lunch (11:30 a.m. to 3 p.m.), something such as a seafood Newburgh crêpe is $11, but the fish-of-the-day is even less, and sandwiches a lot less. At dinner, fish main courses run $16 to $18, or you can have a steak, or chicken, or a huge salad if you prefer. Dinner is served daily from 5:30 to 10:30 p.m. seven days a week from Memorial Day through October.

Martha's Restaurant, across the street from Edgartown's Town Hall on Main Street (tel. 508/627-8316), has one dining room downstairs, another upstairs near the raw bar; this dining room spills onto an open terrace overlooking Main Street. The menu is interesting and varied, with everything from bluefish through fettuccine and Mexican dishes to sushi. Sunday brunch is a tradition. Prices are not bad, with many dinner entrees selling for $13 to $24, which means a full dinner with wine will cost anywhere from $22 to $45.

---

4. Up Island

The best place to get away from the crowds and to begin to feel the serenity of island living is to spend time "up island." This term refers to the towns and areas around West Tisbury, Chilmark, Menemsha, and Gay Head. The scenery here more closely resembles the English countryside; you'll find stone walls, forested roads, and plenty of space.

WHERE TO STAY: The **Captain Flanders House,** North Road (P.O. Box 384), Chilmark, MA 02535 (tel. 508/645-3123), enjoys 60 acres of rolling pastures and secluded woodlands; the house also overlooks the aptly named Bliss Pond. This renovated farmhouse built in the late 1700s offers only four modest rooms. A single with shared bath is $50 in season; a double with shared bath is $94; a double with private bath is $116. Off-season rates range from $36 to $66 with an expanded continental breakfast included.

At the other end of the spectrum is the **Beach Plum Inn and Restaurant,** North Road (P.O. Box 98), Menemsha, MA 02552 (tel. 508/645-9454). Immaculately kept formal gardens pave the way to a gracious, plush living-room with matching floral furniture. Rooms, located in the main house, private cottages, or farmhouse, range in price from $143 to $275 per couple with a full breakfast included. The restaurant is renowned, so you might rather choose rates which include a full dinner and late-afternoon cocktails and hors d'oeuvres (add $36 per person). For the ambitious, there is a pond stocked with bass and perch, as well as a tennis court. Chaise lounges on the shady lawn or their private ocean beach will satisfy other ambitions.

WHERE TO DINE: The restaurant at the **Beach Plum Inn** (tel. 508/645-9454) is unique on the island because dinners are cooked to order. You choose from five or six entree selections in advance. The fixed price is $40 per person, $45 for lobster. They serve nouvelle New England cuisine every night during high season. Two possible, good options are roast duck with a honey-curry sauce or filet mignon with a béarnaise sauce.

There's no better seafood platter (baked, broiled, or fried) on the island than at **Homeport,** Menemsha Harbor (tel. 508/645-2679). It's not an intimate place, but the sunset from here will bring out the romantic in anyone. At first, the main course price of $25 for swordfish or $21 for Vineyard scallops seems high, but further inspection tells you that the price includes an appetizer of your choice, salad, beverage, and dessert. Expect to spend $45 to $50 for two; bring your own wine. Call for reservations, for sure. Open nightly from 5 p.m.

5. What to See and Do on Martha's Vineyard

The most delightful thing about Martha's Vineyard is that it is its own entertainment, and one can often be fully satisfied just strolling along past picket-fence houses, swimming at the many beaches, or biking past the marshes, forests, and island heath. But should you wish a little directed, purposeful activity, you will not be at a loss. First thing to do is to find out what's on currently in the way of festivities and special events. There's an **Information Desk** in the Steamship Authority's dockside ticket office in Woods Hole, so you can find out some things even before getting to the island. But once on the Vineyard, pick up a copy of *This Week on Martha's Vineyard* (a pull-out section of the paper). Here you'll discover a list of the church-sponsored white elephant sales, musical concerts (many free), lectures, dances, movies, tournaments (kite-flying, fishing, table tennis), community sings, and the like. Two other free papers, *Island Light* and *Vineyard Summer,* can be picked up in most shops. The island's most important to-do is the annual **Regatta and Around-the-Island Race,** held on a weekend in late July (hotels are extra-full then).

TOURS: The **Gay Head Sightseeing Company** (tel. 508/693-1555) operates daily sightseeing bus tours of the island, including the Vineyard's six towns and two villages, the sea captains' houses (from the outside), and even a stop at the multicolored cliffs at Gay Head. The trip takes about 2 hours, covers 56 miles, and costs $7.50 for adults, $3.75 for children. Tours leave the ferry wharves after the arrival of the ship, and tickets may be purchased on board the ship or on the sightseeing bus.

THE THOMAS COOKE HOUSE: The Dukes County Historical Society (tel. 508/627-4441), at the corner of Cooke and School Streets in Edgartown, operates the island's most interesting museum in the former Thomas Cooke House (1760s). All the artifacts in the refurnished house came from Vineyard houses, including scrimshaw, china, glass, paintings, and nautical paraphernalia. In other buildings on the grounds, various types of boats that played a part in the island's history can be seen, and there's a special tower to hold the Paris-made lens (1854) that revolved in the Gay Head lighthouse from 1856 to 1952. A guided tour of the museum costs $2 for adults, 50¢ for children under 16. From mid-June to mid-September the museum is open from 10 a.m. to 4:30 p.m. daily except Sunday and Monday; in off-season, visits to the library can be made on Wednesday, Thursday, and Friday from 1 to 4 p.m., on Saturday from 10 a.m. to 4 p.m.

THE STATE LOBSTER HATCHERY: The Massachusetts State Lobster Hatchery (tel. 508/693-0060) is just outside Vineyard Haven on the road to Oak Bluffs, and is open Monday through Friday from 1 to 3 p.m., free of charge. Here thousands of tiny lobsters are raised on pieces of quahog (clam) meat to keep them from devouring one another until they are judged capable of fending for themselves in the chilly waters of the Atlantic.

A VINEYARD ON THE VINEYARD: Martha's Vineyard has its own real vineyard, and you can visit it. **Chicama Vineyards** (tel. 508/693-0309) is southwest of Vineyard Haven off State Road on Stoney Hill Road, in West Tisbury. The 33 acres are planted in vinifera varieties such as Cabernet, Chardonnay, Chenin Blanc, Pinot Noir, Riesling, Zinfandel, and others. It has been in operation since 1971. Visit daily May through September 11 a.m. to 5 p.m., Sunday from 1 to 5 p.m. The vineyard is closed on July 4 and Labor Day.

BEACHES AND BIKE TRIPS: The **State Beach** on the road between Oak Bluffs and Edgartown is probably the first beach you'll see. It's a fine long stretch of white sand, free and open to the public, with parking along the road. The **County Beach at Katama Bay,** also called **South Beach,** south of Edgartown has surf swimming, and is likewise free. The three major towns all have town beaches open to everyone, but the smaller towns and villages reserve their beaches for local property owners, or charge a beach-use fee.

Bicycle riding is fun anywhere on the island as the hills are few and gently sloped, but it's particularly good on the bike path between Oak Bluffs and Edgartown, and on the island of Chappaquiddick, reached by ferry (five-minute trip) from the docks in Edgartown. Wildlife preserves are dotted about Martha's Vineyard, particularly on Chappaquiddick and at Menemsha, Felix Neck, and Cedar Tree Neck. And the excursion to the strikingly beautiful cliffs at Gay Head is a must, but one must have a bit of stamina for this trip on a bike, and you should devote most of a day to it.

You can, of course, drive or take a tour to the **Gay Head Cliffs,** which is Martha's Vineyard's top "excursion." Don't expect a dramatic, towering wall of land staunchly resisting the thundering waves: the cliffs are dramatic only when one considers the more-or-less level terrain of the island. But the cliffs and their colors are pretty, and Gay Head is the perfect "goal" for what would otherwise be an aimless meander. You can view the cliffs for free (although you must pay to use the nearby public toilets).

In **Menemsha Harbor** there isn't exactly anything "to do" except stroll and loll away a couple hours. When you see this place, you'll wish you'd never used the word "picturesque" before. It's an authentic, small, working harbor, complete with seagulls, fishing nets, and aged bottles of whisky in the windows of boathouses. Turn right off South Road in Chilmark at Beetlebung Corner; the harbor is a mile or so down the way. If you arrive hungry try a lobster roll for $7 at the **Galley** (tel. 645-9819), a little snack shack with shaded picnic tables right on the edge of the harbor.

SAILING, CRUISING, AND SUCH: The **Harborside Inn,** on Lower Main Street (tel. 508/627-4321), will rent you a 15-foot Boston Whaler with a 25-hp outboard motor for $100 per day or a 17-foot Daysailer for $75 for 4 hours. The boatyard is open from 8:30 a.m. to 5 p.m. daily. If you don't understand the lingo or the techniques and can't tell a sheet from a painter, they'll even sell you lessons.

An even grander way to sail the seas is aboard the clipper schooner *Shenandoah* out of Vineyard Haven, commanded by Capt. Robert Douglas for the Coastwise Packet Company (tel. 508/693-1699). The *Shenandoah* is no small boat, measuring 108 feet along the rail, built at South Bristol, Me., in 1964. When she's going all out, the *Shenandoah* has all nine of her sails out in a classic square topsail rig, and can do better than 12 knots. You can sail aboard the ship for a week by paying $600 per person, which price pays not only for the adventure, but for food and lodging as well. Call for particulars.

The Vineyard's island sister, Nantucket, is even more of an ocean-going grande dame. More difficult of access (at least in terms of time and price), Nantucket draws an elite crowd. But the crowd is no smaller even though it's elite: prepare for your visit in advance, in high season, by booking reservations.

6. Nantucket

To its year-round inhabitants Nantucket is not just another resort island off Cape Cod, but a special sea-going world of its own. All the brochures and booklets handed out on the island seem to bear the legend "Thirty Miles at Sea." With its history of whaling, its choppy Indian name, and its people's reputation for hardiness, one might expect to find clusters of peasant dwellings and strong-armed shipwrights making rough island boats, but in fact the opposite is true: Nantucket's Main Street is lined with gracious buildings and towering elms, and the rest of the town boasts street after street of charming and dignified houses from the 18th and 19th centuries. And this is to be expected when you think of the money that whaling brought to Nantucket: before the oil sheiks there were the whale-oil magnates, for whale oil fired the lamps of all New England, whalebone provided the stays for the corsets then in style, and ambergris was the base for perfume, a luxury item.

In 1659 the first colonists came ashore to settle the island, already inhabited by four tribes of Indians. The **Jethro Coffin House,** the first fine house to be built, went up in 1686, almost 20 years after the first whale had been claimed off Nantucket's shores. By the time of the Revolution, Nantucket was already wealthy from the whale-oil trade and contributed greatly to the revolutionary cause, losing over 100 whaling ships and 2,000 Nantucketers in the war. Without time to recover fully, the War of 1812 came to the island and again interfered with its prosperity. In another 50 years the age of the sail-rigged whaling ship was at an end, but the same device which put an end to that era—the steamship—brought the beginning of a new era for Nantucket as a vacation destination. In summer, the cobblestones of Main Street are worn down by visitors from Boston, New York, and even farther away, and in winter the islanders go about their business getting ready for the next summer season.

GETTING THERE: Ferryboats carrying both cars and passengers run to Nantucket from Hyannis, Martha's Vineyard, and Woods Hole in summer. (See those sections in Chapter VII for details.)

By Air

Flights to Nantucket are operated by several national carriers and by various local air services. Except at the evening rush hour, or on weekends, you should be able to show up at Hyannis's Barnstable Municipal Airport or New Bedford Municipal Airport, buy a ticket, and be in the air, bound for Nantucket, within a half hour, even without advance reservations.

By the way, parking at the New Bedford airport is free of charge.

Business Express, a Delta Connection carrier, operates flights to Nantucket from New York (La Guardia) and Boston (Logan), with connections from many cities in the region, including points as far away as Albany, Baltimore, Burlington, Vt., Montréal, Philadelphia, Presque Isle, Me., Toronto, and Washington, D.C. For reservations and information, call toll free 800/345-3400.

Cape Cod Air, Chatham Municipal Airport, Chatham, Mass. (tel. toll free 800/553-2376), provides air-charter service from Chatham to Nantucket (20 minutes one way), or indeed to any point within flying distance.

Coastal Air Services, with offices at Groton–New London Airport, Groton, CT 06340 (tel. 203/448-1001), at Nantucket Memorial Airport (tel. 508/228-3350), and at Martha's Vineyard Airport (tel. 508/693-5942), provides air-charter and aircraft rentals. If you don't want to charter the entire plane, they'll help you put together an "Open Charter" whereby you fly with a few other people who want to travel to the same point at the same time.

Continental Express, a commuter operation of Continental Airlines (tel. toll free 800/525-0280), flies sturdy DC-3 and smaller craft on routes to Nantucket from Boston, Hyannis, Martha's Vineyard, New Bedford, and Provincetown.

Express Airlines (tel. 508/999-3231, or toll free 800/852-2332 in Massachusetts) flies a shuttle service in small planes between New Bedford and Nantucket, departing every two hours from 8:30 a.m. to 6:30 p.m. from New Bedford, 7:30

a.m. to 7:30 p.m. from Nantucket. The trip between New Bedford and Nantucket takes slightly over a half hour.

Nantucket Airlines, at Nantucket Memorial Airport (tel. 508/790-0300 or 228-6234, or toll free in Mass. 800/635-8787), flies daily shuttle service between Nantucket and Hyannis, departing about a dozen times a day from each place.

Nantucket Memorial Airport

Nantucket's one and only airport has a restaurant and bar called the Compass Rose, a gift shop, a photocopy machine, vending machines for soft drinks, and car-rental desks (Budget, Hertz, National). Note that during the summer there may not be any cars available for those who have not reserved them in advance. The airport is about 3 miles from the center of Nantucket town, about 5½ miles from 'Sconset.

GETTING AROUND: Nantucket's a small place without the need of a large bus service, but there are several buses run by the **Nantucket and 'Sconset Bus Line, Inc.** (tel. 508/228-0420 or 228-3118): five times daily in summer between Nantucket and 'Sconset, one bus a day to Wauwinet, to Jetties Beach (leaves every 30 minutes or so), and to other, more distant beaches. Buy tickets, get information, and board the bus at the bus stop on South Water Street at Chestnut Street, opposite the fire house.

Taxis abound and their rates are: $3 for one person within town limits, $1 for each additional person; between airport and town, $5 for one person, $1 for each additional person. Rates are higher at night. Other rates are established for trips to the beaches and sights, and are posted in the cab.

Bicycles and **mopeds** are for rent at over a half dozen shops in town. Rates for a bicycle are $8 to $12 a day, $24 to $36 for a moped, and these vehicles do well on this small island (except on the cobblestones of Main Street!). One can ride the seven miles to 'Sconset on a bike path in less than an hour—less than a half hour if you push it. Incidentally, almost any taxi driver will be glad to give you a tour of the island, with rates depending on how much ground you want to cover and time you want to spend.

INFORMATION AND RESERVATIONS: The Nantucket Chamber of Commerce (tel. 508/228-1700) and the Public Relations Committee have done a lot to organize the tourist industry on the island, and information about rooms, tours, and sights is surprisingly easy to get. The **Town Information Bureau** (tel. 508/228-0925 or 228-0926) is the place to go for a free copy of the *Nantucket Vacation Guide,* a summertime ads-and-information booklet; they'll also help you find a room for that day if you haven't already reserved one. But note that *they do not make advance reservations for you*—you must do that directly with the establishment concerned. The bureau is not far from Main Street and the ferry docks, at 25 Federal St., and it's open from 9 a.m. until the evening hours (usually 6:30 p.m.) during the summer (10 a.m. to 4 p.m. on Sunday), shorter hours off-season.

Reserve in Advance for Summer!

Rooms may be hard to find in July and August unless you reserve well in advance, and while you will have a chance of finding a room for a day or two during the week, on weekends it's sometimes impossible. If you plan to try to find a last-minute room in those two months, arrive on the island early in the day—fly over and beat the ferryboat crowds—and go straight to the Town Information Booth and ask them what's available in town.

Useful Facts

Nantucket Cottage Hospital, at South Prospect Street and Vesper Lane (tel. 508/228-1200), is a modern, accredited facility. You can contact the Massachusetts

State Police at their office on North Liberty Street (tel. 508/228-0706), and the Nantucket **Town Police** on East Chestnut Street (tel. 508/228-1212). The **emergency number** for police, firefighters, and ambulance service is 911.

Nantucket is well organized and governed, and local residents have various regulations which they want visitors to observe, such as not wearing bathing suits on Main Street, obeying all traffic rules when riding a bicycle, and not camping—whether in a vehicle or a tent or under the stars—anywhere on the island.

WHERE TO STAY: Nantucket Island harbors nearly 100 places to stay, but the real character of the place is best captured in the old whaling merchants' and ship captains' houses converted to inns and guesthouses. Many of these are carefully restored, luxuriously appointed, and staffed with professionals; others are run by one person or a couple and are modest but warm and friendly.

Notes on Reservations

Although some lodging establishments on Nantucket stay open all year, many operate only between May and October. Any place will give you an off-season discount on room rates if you come in spring or autumn, although the dates vary from one place to the next. In high season (roughly from mid-June to mid-September), you'll certainly have to send a substantial deposit to hold your room reservation. Minimum-stay requirements may also be imposed during the high season as well. Some lodging and dining places may not accept credit cards.

Here, then, are Nantucket's best guesthouses and inns, followed by a few recommendations for hotels.

The Top Inns

The **Jared Coffin House**, 29 Broad St., Nantucket, MA 02554 (tel. 508/228-2405), was the first three-story mansion to be built on the island. Its builder was a wealthy shipowner, and he put up the impressive Federal-style brick house in 1845, just before deciding to move to Boston. He and his family lived in the house for a matter of months, after which it became, and still is, a hotel.

Since its conversion to a hotel in 1846, additions have been built, and neighboring houses bought and converted to lodgings, so that the hotel now has 58 rooms in six different structures priced from $66 to $77 single, $121 to $192 double. In the Jared Coffin House proper are nine guest rooms with double or twin beds; the Eben Allen wing of the building has 16 rooms with single, twin, or double beds. The neighboring Swain House, dating from the 1700s, has three rooms, each with a queen-size canopy bed. Similar beds are in the six rooms of the Federal-style Henry Coffin House (1821), and also in the 12 rooms of the Greek Revival Harrison Gray House (1842). The Daniel Webster House (1964) is a recent building in a Federal-inspired style, with 12 rooms (canopy beds) and a conference room. No matter which building you choose, you will enjoy the elegant public rooms of the several buildings, and the hotel's two restaurants (see below).

Harbor House, P.O. Box 1048, Nantucket, MA 02554 (tel. 508/228-1500 for information, 228-5500 for reservations), is a modern hotel that looks just like a small group of old Nantucket houses. Set on their own private street amid groves of shade trees, the nine buildings of the Harbor House give you a choice between staying in the Townhouses, the six smaller places holding a total of 57 large and luxurious rooms, or in the main hotel, its neighboring Garden Cottage, or the Springfield House. All rooms are modern and have every comfort, but they are decorated in Federal-inspired style to harmonize with their location on Nantucket. The Townhouse rooms have twin double beds, and cost $247 double in high season; rooms in the main hotel have twin beds, two double beds, one queen- or one king-size bed, and cost $160 to $192 double. An additional person in a room costs $15.

Guests at the Harbor House can enjoy its outdoor swimming pool, with its own bar, and the hotel's main dining room, named The Hearth. There's a cocktail lounge as well. The location is good, walking distance from the center of town, and not far from Children's Beach and Brant Point.

The inn at **Seven Sea Street,** Nantucket, MA 02554 (tel. 508/228-3577), is among Nantucket's best small lodging places. Though built fairly recently, it follows the canon of post-and-beam construction, and is furnished in colonial style, so that you will feel Nantucket all around you. The eight guest rooms have queen-size canopy beds, exposed beams, and lots of colonial touches, but also cable color television sets, small refrigerators, and of course, modern private baths. The theme of modern comforts in colonial atmosphere continues in the public spaces. You can relax in a full-size, heated whirlpool bath, and then sit by the fireplace or go up to the widow's walk to take in the view. The location, just a few blocks from Steamboat Wharf and the center of town, couldn't be better. Rates include a good continental breakfast (served in bed if you wish), and range from $105 to $170 double, depending on when you visit. Two room suites for two people cost $137 to $220; an extra person in a suite pays $15. Sea Street is a short street, one block long, running between North Water Street and South Beach Street.

The Better Inns and Guesthouses

Nantucket is rich in charming small inns and guesthouses. Sometimes it's difficult to know whether a place should be called an inn or a guesthouse. I think of an inn as providing more services, such as meals and cocktails, and having more spacious public rooms and gardens. A guesthouse is more like someone's home, perhaps not as fancy as an inn, with few services but with a warm, family atmosphere. I'll start by describing some of the better inns, and then some more inns and guesthouses.

A trio of inns under the same management offer typical and charming Nantucket accommodations at moderate prices. The **Great Harbor Inn,** 31 India St., Nantucket, MA 02554 (tel. 508/228-6609), is an 18th-century sea captain's home now restored and furnished in 19th-century style with handmade patchwork quilts and four-poster or canopy beds. All rooms have 20th-century facilities, however, including private baths and color cable television sets. You can have your continental breakfast (included in the room price) served in your room, or in the parlor, or on the pretty terrace. Rates in high season are $110 to $154 double. The inn, located about five minutes' walk from the center, is open all year.

Another inn in this group is the **Brass Lantern Inn,** 11 N. Water St., Nantucket, MA 02554 (tel. 508/228-4064), only a few blocks from downtown on North Water Street. Here again there is a nice old Nantucket house, but besides the traditional rooms the inn has a more modern annex in which the rooms are larger and lighter, but still with traditional touches in the decor. There's a patio and a small grassy yard where you can have your breakfast. The Brass Lantern is open all year, charging $83 to $148 double in high season, continental breakfast included.

Fair Gardens (tel. 508/228-4258) is the description, as well as the name, of the guesthouse at 27 Fair St., Nantucket, MA 02554, in a quiet residential neighborhood. Behind the house is an English-style garden, complete with a Shakespearean herb plot, carefully tended flowers and lawns, and a patio for breakfast or an afternoon's cup of tea. The ten rooms are all unique, all have private bath, and there are two deluxe rooms in the Garden House. Rooms are priced between $105 and $148 double, with the lower prices in the old house, higher in the new Garden House; an extra person pays $15. All of these prices include breakfast with freshly baked bread, served in the garden in good weather.

The **House of Orange,** 25 Orange St., Nantucket, MA 02554 (tel. 508/228-9287), has seven rooms decorated with an artist's eye for color and harmony, as one of the house's owners is a painter. The rooms are as lovingly furnished and as carefully kept as is the little garden. Some rooms have fireplaces, although, as is often the case, local regulations prohibit guests from using them. Every room is different, from the small single with semiprivate bath at $45 through the doubles with semiprivate bath at $77 to $88. A double room with private bath is tops in price, at $99 to $121. The House of Orange is open year round.

Fair Street has its share of houses built by ship captains, but the **Ships Inn** (tel. 508/228-0040) is more a mansion than a house, its three stories looking over Fair Street from a position just opposite the Episcopal church. It was built in 1812 by Capt. Obed Starbuck and occupies the site that once held the birthplace of Lucretia Coffin Mott, the abolitionist and suffragist. The rooms are finished with period pieces and all, except two small singles, have private bath. Those little singles cost $45; otherwise, one person pays $90 for a room, two pay $100, with private bath. Off-season (November through mid-June), rates go down about 30%. The price of a room includes continental breakfast in season. The Captain's Table restaurant is in the basement of the Ships Inn.

The **Quaker House Inn,** 5 Chestnut St., Nantucket, MA 02554 (tel. 508/228-0400), at the corner of Centre Street, was built in 1847, and the huge tree out front may date from the same year, or even earlier. Located right in the heart of the historic district, just a few steps from shops and restaurants, the Quaker House is something of an anomaly in Nantucket. Because Caroline and Bob Taylor and their family do much of the work at the inn, and because they own the building, their costs are kept down, and so are yours. Their restaurant (see below) is justly famous for providing excellent dinners in attractive surroundings at moderate prices, and a similar level of quality is found in the inn's eight guest rooms. Each room is different: in one a brass bed, in another a carved four-poster. Dressers and wardrobes also echo the era when the inn was built, and tab curtains are a reminder of even earlier colonial days. Rooms are simple, but comfy and attractive, as befits an inn with a Quaker name. Each has private bath and queen-size bed. Rates are $85 to $110 double in high season.

Other Inns and Guesthouses

The **Anchor Inn,** 66 Centre St., Nantucket, MA 02554 (tel. 508/228-0072), is aptly named, considering that it was built (1806) by Archaelus Hammond, the first man to strike a whale in the Pacific Ocean. The location is good: close enough to the center to be convenient, far enough away to be quiet. Pass through the white picket fence and you'll find a sea captain's house which preserves many of its original features, from its old random-width floorboards to its working fireplaces. Outside is a shady garden. The ten guest rooms preserve the Federal period style, but have modern private baths and are priced at $85 to $115 double in season, continental breakfast included. Don't forget to add that ubiquitous 9.7% Massachusetts room tax. The Anchor Inn is open from April through December.

The **"While Away" Guest House** (tel. 508/228-1102) is of the oldtime guesthouse type, with a friendly proprietor (Mrs. Elise Link), a fine old house with bull's-eye windows and a widow's walk. A blossom-filled garden surrounding the house, a baby grand piano within, and a very good location across from the Jared Coffin House at the intersection of Gay, Centre, and Broad Streets (officially, 4 Gay St., Nantucket, MA 02554), makes the While Away a real find. Prices are low: $71 for two with shared bath, $82 for two with private bath, in spotless rooms. When looking for the While Away, try to spot the flagpole in the little park right next door —that will serve as a landmark.

After only a bit of wandering through Nantucket's shady streets, you will have passed **Le Languedoc Inn and Restaurant,** 24 Broad St. (P.O. Box 1829), Nantucket, MA 02554 (tel. 508/228-2552 or 228-4682). No doubt you have noticed the attractive restaurant; but it's not readily apparent that there are several nice guest rooms upstairs, and even more (and better) in nearby houses. In Le Languedoc proper are two tidy, homey rooms which share one bathroom, priced at $93 double; and one room with private bath, going for $110. Rooms at the 3 Hussey Street Guest House (tel. 508/228-4682 or 228-4298) are similar in comforts and price, with most sharing baths in this nice mid–19th-century building. However, accommodations at the Grey Lady Apartments (same phones) have recently been renovated and modernized, while keeping or adding many artistic and historical features. Rooms at the Grey Lady are light, attractive, and simple, each with one or two softly pretty modern paintings, and for contrast, one or two pieces of antique furniture, resulting in congenial decor without sensory overload. Each room has a modern private bath, and one room has a private deck, another a kitchenette with utensils. All rooms get to share the common living room, which has a color television set and refrigerator. A double with bath costs $115; with bath and kitchenette, $137; a suite for four with bath and kitchenette goes for $187 in high season.

The **Chestnut House,** 3 Chestnut St., Nantucket, MA 02554 (tel. 508/228-0049), between Centre and Federal, is Jeannette and Jerry Carl's home, which they open to visitors. There's a common room with television available to all guests. Rooms are furnished in the style of Nantucket's heyday, some with canopy beds, quilts, and interesting old pieces. Some rooms have private baths, and cost $85 double; others share baths, for $70 double. A neighboring cottage sleeps four, has a private bath, and costs $145. These prices are for high season, when a three-night minimum stay is required. The location, next to the Quaker House Inn on quiet Chestnut Street, is right in the midst of town.

A 10- or 15-minute walk northwest of the center of town is Cliff Road, so named because it follows the top of a ridge and offers fine views of the sea to several of its well-situated houses. It's in this quiet residential neighborhood that you'll find the **Century House,** 10 Cliff Rd., Nantucket, MA 02554 (tel. 508/228-0530), run by Jean Heron and Gerry Connick. The late Federal building has a wrap-around porch, a 19th-century parlor, and a custom of late-afternoon tea (which may also be early-evening cocktails). Furnishings follow the rules of Laura Ashley designs and canopy beds, and the double rooms have either private bath ($85 to $105) or shared bath ($75 to $95). The largest room, with a king-size bed, costs $95 to $130. These prices include your morning's continental breakfast, and snacks at tea/cocktail time. Jean and Gerry also rent a quaint cottage in 'Sconset.

Cliff Lodge, 9 Cliff Rd., Nantucket, MA 02554 (tel. 508/228-9480), has that marvelous Cliff Road view from its widow's walk, and many other views from its 14 guest rooms and two patios. The house was built in 1771 but has recently been redecorated in period style. All rooms have private baths, telephones, and TV sets, and some have king-size beds and fireplaces. Freshly made continental breakfasts, use of the pantry, refrigerator, and kitchen utensils, and towels for the beach are all included in the room prices of $50 to $60 single, $90 to $140 double. An apartment rents for $140 to $190 per night, $1,250 per week in high season. Other apartments are available at Cliff Lodge's sister facility, called Still Dock.

Run by the same family as the Roberts House, the **Periwinkle Guest House** is very close to the Whaling Museum, at 7 and 9 N. Water St., Nantucket, MA 02554 (tel. 508/228-9267). A nice old Nantucket house, the Periwinkle has 18 rooms of various shapes, sizes, sleeping capacities, and bath facilities: doubles with bath are $110 to $134 daily; doubles or twins with shared bath are $77 to $93. A few single rooms with shared bath are priced at $44. The Periwinkle—the name is that of a spiral-shaped saltwater snail—is open all year, and rates are 25% to 30% lower off-season. By the way, continental breakfast is included in all the above rates.

The **Bartlett House,** 14 Gardner St. (P.O. Box 1329), Nantucket, MA 02554 (tel. 508/228-1139), prides itself not merely on the attractiveness of the 150-year-old house and the coziness of its rooms, but on the quietness of its clientele. Only five rooms are for rent, at $55 to $85 per night, single or double, with a three-night minimum stay. Off-season rates are $5 to $15 lower. Two of the rooms share a bathroom, all the others have private facilities, although one room's shower is down the hall. Bartlett House has no living room for guests' use, but the garden is most people's first choice of a place to relax in any case. Room prices are among the best in town, and the silence, as they say, is golden.

The **House of the Seven Gables,** 32 Cliff Rd., Nantucket, MA 02554 (tel.

508/228-4706), was once the Victorian annex to an even larger old Victorian sea-side hotel. Actually, Seven Gables and a Tower would be an even more accurate de-scription of this good example of Victorian architectural enthusiasm. As it's not one of those small and quaint Nantucket houses, it has more rooms to offer—ten in all, with nine bathrooms. Continental breakfast is served year-round and rates run from $75 to $120 for a room with double bed and semiprivate bath, or a room with double bed and private bath, or a triple with private bath. Mid-September to mid-June these rates drop by about a third. The location is a ten-minute walk from Main Street, not as close into town as some other houses; but the area is a quiet residential one.

The **Cliff House,** 34 Cliff Rd., Nantucket, MA 02554 (tel. 508/228-2154 or 969-8293) was built as a cottage annex to the Seacliff Hotel, one of Nantucket's landmark Victorian resorts. The Seacliff is gone, but the Cliff House continues to lodge guests in its seven rooms (five with private baths). Four of the rooms have brass beds, another has a queen-size mahogany canopy bed, all have the appropriate Victorian furnishings, and several have views of the sea. The owners, Chris and Phil Cunningham, cook up a fancy continental breakfast each morning, and serve it out-side if the weather permits, as it often does. Rates in high season are $50 for a single room with shared bath, and $105 for a double with private bath.

Hotels

Nantucket still has a few of the rambling old Victorian wooden hotels that used to be found throughout New England, and indeed throughout North America, but which have been disappearing quickly since the advent of the automobile and the motel. Although there are a few motels on the island too, I'll describe an older hotel as it offers accommodations more in keeping with the island's traditions, at prices that are undeniably good value-for-money.

The **Folger Hotel,** at the corner of Cliff Road and Easton Street (P.O. Box 628), Nantucket, MA 02554 (tel. 508/228-0313), is just such an old rambling hotel, set on sunny lawns, well kept, but now easily informal whereas in earlier times everyone had to dress for dinner. Open only from mid-May to mid-October, the Folger charges $42 for a single room without private bath, $84 to $93 for a similar double; rooms with private bath cost $62 single, $94 to $103 double. In the annex, called the Captain's Corners (open April through December), rooms are $40 for a single with semiprivate bath, $67 to $76 for a similar double-bedded room; doubles with bath are $88 to $90. The hotel's restaurant, called the Whale, provides breakfast (in-cluded in the room price), and dinner too.

Budget Guesthouses

Almost all of Nantucket's budget guesthouses charge the same rates: $65 to $75 for a double room that shares a bath; $75 to $85 for a double with private bath. When you call for reservations, find out if breakfast is included, and if it's rolls-and-coffee or bacon-and-eggs. Ask if the room has a view, or is especially large. Every room is different, and you must know these things to get the most for your money.

The **Hungry Whale,** 8 Derrymore Rd., Nantucket, MA 02554 (tel. 508/228-0793), is exceptional in several ways. Mrs. Johnson, the smiling owner, charges sev-eral dollars *less* than most other houses, and includes a hearty breakfast to boot! The location is off North Liberty Avenue.

The **Nesbitt Inn,** 21 Broad St., Nantucket, MA 02554 (tel. 508/228-0156), despite its appellation and downtown location, is one of the island's lodging bar-gains, three blocks from the wharf, charging guesthouse prices for its rooms with shared baths.

The **Ivy Lodge & Cottages,** 2 Chester St., Nantucket, MA 02554 (tel. 508/228-0305, or toll free 800/626-8825), at North Water Street, is a homey, tidy place far enough from downtown to have reasonable prices, close enough to be very handy.

WHERE TO DINE: For a seafood lover, Nantucket is a dream come true. Look at it this way: all the dining tables are surrounded with waters full of fish, lobsters, crabs, clams, scallops, and squid! But visitors do not live by seafood alone. Island restaurants offer many wonderful dishes based on meat and fowl, as well as the occasional vegetarian platter. The range of cuisines includes French, Italian, New England, and new American, with the occasional Mexican entree. On weekends in July and August it may be good for you to have dinner reservations at the restaurant of your choice; otherwise, you may end up dining somewhere else—just as good perhaps, but not the place you had in mind.

I'll start by describing the best restaurants in Nantucket Town, then some of the good, dependable places there, and finally the dining opportunities in the village of 'Sconset.

Nantucket's Top Restaurants

Among Nantucket's most pleasant dining places is **Le Languedoc,** 24 Broad St. (tel. 508/228-2552), just up from Steamboat Wharf near the jared Coffin House. In good weather, most diners choose the umbrella-shaded tables in the pretty patio beside the house, though there are several simple but pleasant, small, airy dining rooms on the main floor of the inn. The cuisine at Le Languedoc offers very good French and new American food in attractive presentations, with cheerful and attentive service. Figure $50 per person for dinner (the only meal served), because you may want to try a glass or two of some interesting vintage available from their wine bar.

Obadiah's Native Seafood, 2 India St. (tel. 508/228-4430), near Federal, specializes in just that, and you can start your meal here with quahog pie (clams, salt pork, potatoes, and onions in a pastry shell), or scallop chowder, then go on to any of 20 main courses, including all the fresh seasonal fish, and things like broiled scallop brochettes. A full dinner might cost $35 to $45 per person. Dining areas include the cozy main dining room in the basement of the building, or the cool, shady patio behind it. Lunch and dinner are served every day, and on Sunday there's brunch from 11:30 a.m. to 3 p.m.

The famous Jared Coffin House at 29 Broad St. (tel. 508/228-2400), corner of Centre, has two restaurants worthy of consideration. First of these is **Jared's,** the main dining room. The menu lists such elegant and delectable items as sesame chicken and grilled duck. Service and surroundings here are more old-worldly, and prices for a full dinner range from $40 to $50 per person, all included.

Jared's informal counterpart is the Tap Room which, besides its 19th-century tavern, also has a wonderful verdant terrace shaded by lofty elms. The food is heartier and more traditional here, from baked sole Florentine to sirloin steak. Prices are lower, about $30 for dinner. Note that all three meals are served here daily (breakfast is on from 8 to 11 a.m.), and that there is entertainment most evenings in summer.

For northern Italian cuisine in the grand manner, head for **De Marco,** 9 India St. (tel. 508/228-1836), near Centre Street. The downstairs rooms of this old Nantucket house are furnished as simple but elegant dining rooms where diners nightly sample, among other treats, the linguine con vongole al pesto (the ever-popular pasta with Littleneck clams and basil-garlic sauce). A substantial part of the treat comes from the fact that all the pasta, baked goods, and desserts consumed in the restaurant are made right here, fresh daily. Seafood is prominent on the menu, but so are the classics, such as veal medallions and rack of lamb. If you have a light supper of an appetizer, a pasta plate, a dessert, and wine, with tax and tip your bill might come to $40. For a full dinner in the grand manner of Italian dining, figure $65 to $70 per person, all in. De Marco is open every day for dinner only from 6 to 10:30 p.m.

The **Company of the Cauldron,** 7 India St. (tel. 508/228-4016), serves only dinner, at one or two sittings (usually 7 and 9:15 p.m.)—and you *must* have a reservation. Then, the menu is completely table d'hôte, and fixed price: you have no choice, although if you've called for reservations (as you must), it's presumed you've asked what will be served, perhaps homemade fettuccine tossed with eggplant, capers, and olives, followed by an apple-and-watercress salad, and then medallions of veal rolled with spinach and mozzarella, served with a parfait of pimentos. In all, two dining together can expect to pay about $110 to $120 with wine, tax, and tip all in. The dining room is small, with kitchen and wine racks in the rear. A harpist plays at dinner. An antique-fancier's collection of old tubs, buckets, and cauldrons serves to show off a cascade of flowers. As you walk to the restaurant, don't look for a sign, but rather for the old copper tub (cauldron?) hanging above the entrance: that is the "sign."

Good Moderately Priced Restaurants

First place in this category must go to the **Quaker House Restaurant,** 31 Centre St. (tel. 508/228-9156), at the corner of Chestnut Street. Lunch is not served, but come for breakfast (8 to 11:30 a.m.), or drop in any evening for dinner (6 to 9 p.m.). The charming dining rooms have fireplaces, lace curtains, crisp tablecloths, antique accent pieces, and candlelight in the evening. At breakfast, try the baked apple pancakes, baked German pancakes, waffles or pancakes made with blueberries or pecans, fresh vegetable omelets, and fresh-squeezed orange juice. At dinnertime, order one of the seven main courses such as filet of sole, shrimp scampi, Bombay chicken, or beef burgundy, and you get Nantucket clam chowder, Portuguese bread and butter, a tossed garden salad, and a choice of dessert, all included in the price. And the price, for Nantucket, is truly surprising, as the most expensive dinner costs $22, plus drink, tax, and tip. Many dinners are priced at only $15. Beer, and wine by the glass, carafe, or bottle, are available at moderate prices. Note that the Quaker House has room for only 40 diners at a time, and does not accept reservations, so arrive early in order to be assured of finding a table.

If you find your way to **Vincent's Restaurant,** right across the street from the police station at 21 S. Water St. (tel. 508/228-0189), you'll find unpretentious food at prices that are very moderate for Nantucket: the Tourist Special plate of fish and chips is generous, and costs $9. A bowl of chowder and a fish filet sandwich costs even less, and Italian dishes such as chicken cacciatore and eggplant parmigiana cost $8 to $12. In good weather, you can even dine on Vincent's small outdoor terrace, or just have pizza and beer there.

During your shopping stroll on Old South Wharf, you can stop for a bite at the **Morning Glory Café** (tel. 228-2212), down near the water end of the wharf. Tables are set out on a brick patio beneath an awning. All three meals are served: breakfast omelets, French toast and pancakes from 7 to 11:30 a.m.; luncheon seafood chowder, sandwiches, salads, and pasta plates from 12:15 to 3 p.m. Dinner (6 to 10 p.m.) is fancier, but prices are still moderate and service is informal because all the utensils and plates here, except for the wine glasses, are disposable (the location on the wharf doesn't permit them to have a dishwasher). Cuisine is Italian, with spaghetti Sicilian style, fettuccine with fresh tomato and basil, or with shrimp and scallops, and penne rigate (tube pasta with sweet Italian sausage). Expect to spend $10 to $15 at lunch, $25 to $30 at dinner.

The **Captain's Table,** in the basement of the Ships Inn on Fair Street (tel. 508/228-0040), offers such things as lamb chops, and Nantucket scallops, for about $16 to $20. For dessert they may list chocolate mousse or cranberry sherbet with cassis. And don't let the "basement" dining room worry you. It is a supremely warm and cheerful place, with old oil paintings adding grace and beauty to the light-colored walls. The dining room is licensed, or you can have a drink in the Dory Bar. The restaurant is open every day from 7 a.m. to 10:30 p.m.

The **Mad Hatter Restaurant,** 72 Easton St. (tel. 508/228-9667), at South Beach Street, is a popular spot with people who own summer houses on Nantucket. Looking somewhat like a summer house itself, the restaurant is set in a green lawn, with shade trees and a small secluded patio café on the Easton Street side. Owners Jeanne and Richard Diamond have decorated the dining room in coral and green hues, and the ambience is that of an informal but proper yacht club. The dinner menu lists fettuccine Alfredo, baked stuffed shrimp, canneloni, and grilled salmon, as well as several meat and chicken dishes. The extensive wine list includes numerous American vintages. At dinnertime, a full meal, with wine, tax, and tip included, runs something like $25 to $35, but there is also a pub menu (4 to 9 p.m.) featuring sandwiches, pasta, soup, hamburgers, and salads, at considerably lower prices. The Mad Hatter is open daily mid-April through December for lunch from 11:30 a.m. to 2:30 p.m., for dinner from 5:30 to 9 p.m.; Sunday brunch is served from 11 a.m. to 2 p.m.

At **The Tavern,** on Straight Wharf at Harbor Square (tel. 508/228-1226), open daily, right by the marina, you may eat at tables set out in the picturesque brick-paved square, or on a second-floor balcony overlooking the marina and the activity on the street, or even in a little flèche-topped gazebo in the cobbled square. Drinks are served, as are salads, hamburgers, and sandwiches ($7 to $10) at lunch; dinnertime is 6 to 10 p.m., and then you can get fish and chips, scampi, or a London broil for $14 to $20. The food is okay here, but the situation is even better.

The **Gaslight Theatre Café,** on North Union Street just off Main Street (tel. 508/228-4479), is on the terrace of the Gaslight Theatre. The tiny patio is usually crowded with tables of diners having breakfast (8 to 11 a.m.), lunch (11:30 to 4) or dinner (5 to 10 p.m.), perhaps before attending the show, or perhaps just because of the excellent people-watching possibilities. Burgers, seafood kabobs, and fancier items such as grilled tuna steaks are offered. Lunch might set you back $6 to $10, dinner $15 to $25.

For Breakfast

The **Dory Restaurant,** 10 India St. (no phone), just off Centre Street, serves breakfast, brunch and light lunches only, from 6 a.m. to 1 p.m. daily. Being specialists at it, breakfast is good here, with a good selection of omelets, crêpes, croissants, pancakes, and bacon-and-eggs dishes. Sandwiches and burgers are added for lunch. Eat here, in true American lunch-counter atmosphere, or take out. You can spend anything from $2.50 to $5 or $6 at the Dory.

For Sandwiches

I'd recommend that everyone pick up a mammoth sandwich from **Henry's Sandwiches,** on Steamboat Wharf (tel. 508/228-0123), before they get on the boat. Henry's huge sandwiches are made in the best Italian sub/grinder/hoagie/po'boy tradition, and cost about $3 or $4. Soft drinks are available, and all can be wrapped to go or consumed post-haste at small tables on the premises. Remember Henry's if you're planning a picnic, or are down to your last $3 plus your ticket home.

Dining in 'Sconset

Most everyone who gets to Nantucket for a few days has a chance to ride a bike to 'Sconset on the other side of the island. You can go for dinner to the **Chanticleer Inn** (tel. 508/257-6231), which is noted for its elegant French cuisine and for the charm of its dining area which in summer is a courtyard surrounded by rose-covered trellises under which tables are set. Dinner prices are not low: the fixed-price menu is $50, plus wine, tax, and tip. Order à la carte to get roast duckling with a baked apple as a garnish, or delectable Nantucket-raised rabbit with mushrooms, white wine, and mustard sauce. There's a bar and lounge called the Chanty. This is 'Sconset's most elegant spot, and a meal here becomes a nice memory.

Right by the flagpole at the Siasconset traffic circle is **Claudette's** food-catering shop (tel. 508/257-6622), where you can sit at a tiny table on the wood deck and watch the easy activity of the square while drinking coffee, tea, or lemonade. Meanwhile, Claudette will be making you a delicious box lunch for your picnic or bike trip for $5; clam bakes are a specialty.

'Sconset's all-purpose eating place is the **Sconset Café**, Post Office Square (tel. 508/257-4008), open daily in summer for breakfast, lunch, and dinner. This light, pleasant eatery has pastel walls hung with local artists' works, and a tempting array of edibles such as breakfast pancakes made with blueberries and cranberries ($4.25), and a soup-and-salad special at lunch ($6). The fare at dinnertime (6 to 9:30 p.m.) is fancier, including Caesar salad, duck with lingonberry sauce, and a seafood mixed grill. Expect to pay $23 to $28 for dinner.

Just around the corner from the post office is the **Siasconset Market**, at which you can choose the makings of a sandwich or picnic lunch, and the clerk will put it all together for you so that all you have to do is the eating.

WHAT TO SEE AND DO: Once on Nantucket, your activity schedule will take care of itself. In good weather everyone takes off to the beaches, either by taxi, bus, or bike. For variety, the island offers tennis, golf, horseback riding, movies, antique stores, and art galleries. Sport fishermen should wander down to **Straight Wharf** to talk to one of the charter boat captains about a day's run for bluefish or striped bass. Those who just like being in a boat can rent a sailboat and take sailing lessons at one of the establishments on **Washington Street Extension** or **Steamboat Wharf**. The island's information office on Federal Street will be able to help you out with information on these.

Museums

Nantucket's history can keep one occupied for days as well. To run the full gamut, buy a special Visitor's Pass ($6) to the exhibits of the **Nantucket Historical Association** on Union Street (tel. 508/228-1894), which include the famous **Whaling Museum,** The Macy Warehouse (Nantucket history museum), the oldest house on the island, a windmill built in 1746 and still functioning, and seven other historical points of interest. To see them all, paying the individual admissions would cost much more, and the pass gives you the advantage of being able to browse in a museum for a while, go to the beach, and return to another museum later in the afternoon. You can get your pass at the Whaling Museum on Broad Street, or at any of the other Historical Association buildings.

The **Maria Mitchell Science Center** (tel. 508/228-0898 or 228-9198) is a group of buildings organized and maintained in honor of Nantucket's foremost astronomer, Maria Mitchell (1818–1889). Born on Nantucket of an astronomer father and teacher-librarian mother, Mitchell became interested in the stars at an early age. Out here on Nantucket, away from the pollution and haze of cities, she studied the heavens, and in 1847 discovered a hitherto uncharted comet. Her scientific feat earned her a gold medal from the king of Denmark and membership in the American Academy of Arts and Sciences (the only woman so honored at the time), and led to a distinguished career as a professor at Vassar College.

Founded in 1902, the Nantucket Maria Mitchell Association seeks to preserve a fitting memorial to the island's famous astronomer, and to make available science facilities to residents and visitors. The Science Center consists of its astronomical observatories, with lectures on Monday at 8 p.m. and stellar observations on Wednesday at 9 p.m. if the sky is clear; the Hinchman House at 7 Milk St., with its Museum of Natural Science, Thursday-evening (8 p.m.) lectures, birdwatching, wildflower, and nature walks, and children's nature classes; the Mitchell House at 1 Vestal St., birthplace of Maria Mitchell, with wildflower and herb gardens; the Science Library at 2 Vestal St.; and the aquarium at 28 Washington St. Check with the center for current activity schedules.

Tours

Tour buses of the various companies will meet your ferryboat at Steamboat Wharf or Straight Wharf, ready to take you on a 1¼-hour tour of the island. There's no better way to get your bearings, and the short time spent will help you better to organize the few precious days you'll have on the island.

Nantucket Island Tours, with offices on Straight Wharf (tel. 508/228-0334), offers six island tours daily in summer, charging $9 per adult, $4 for a child.

Barrett's Tours, 20 Federal St. (tel. 508/228-0174), the island's Gray Line company, operates six daily tours running on several different routes between Nantucket Town and 'Sconset. Their 1½-hour tour, the shortest, costs $7.50 for adults, $4.50 for children. Senior citizens get discounts on all tours departing from Barrett's office. Barrett's also operates a **surfside beach bus,** running to and from their downtown office to the beach six times daily.

Far and away the most romantic way to tour Nantucket Town is with the **Nantucket Carriage Company** (tel. 508/228-0313). For $15 per adult, $10 per child, you can enjoy a half-hour ride through town in a quaint horse-drawn carriage, with a driver in period dress. Rides depart from the Gordon Folger Hotel daily from noon to 3 p.m., and from 7 to 10 p.m.

Walking Tours of the Town

The Nantucket Historical Association, mentioned above, also publishes a number of detailed **walking-tour brochures,** available from the association's museum shop.

The Historical Association also sponsors a 1½-hour tour through the best of Nantucket's art and architecture. The tour begins at 8:30 a.m. Tuesday through Saturday, and departs the Thomas Macy Warehouse on Straight Wharf. Cost is $6 per person. Call 508/228-1894 Monday through Friday from 8 a.m. to 5 p.m. for a reservation, as the tour is limited to 15 people.

Music

In the past few years Nantucket has supported chamber music concerts at various times, particularly in the weeks of high summer. Ask at the Information Bureau, or look for notices of upcoming events.

Also, visiting and local bands often give free concerts in the gazebo near Straight Wharf (at the foot of Main Street). The *Weekly Vacation Guides,* available at the Information Bureau, will have listings of times and programs. There is also summer theater at the Folger Hotel.

'Sconset

The village of Siasconset is called nothing but 'Sconset by islanders—the contracted name is hallowed by tradition. The village consists of Post Office Square, a roundabout from which you can see the tennis courts, post office, Sconset Café, Claudette's, and various houses. To the right of Claudette's is the road to the beach, only 100 yards away.

The rest of 'Sconset is residential, with many typical Nantucket houses, but also a few streets of the small, low-roofed bungalows that sit squarely as though avoiding the violence of winter storms.

Though there are several daily buses to 'Sconset, in my opinion the best way to go is by bicycle along the bike path from Nantucket Town. The journey from the center of Nantucket Town to the center of 'Sconset is 7½ miles. If you make the trip in late July or early August, watch for the carpet of low-bush blueberries. Maybe you'll be in luck and find them full of tangy fruit, yours for the picking.

Once in 'Sconset, have something to eat, go to the beach, take a walk or bike ride around, and in the evening, drop in at the Siasconset Casino (on the opposite side of the tennis courts from Post Office Square) for a movie or a show. Just across the street from the casino is the Chanticleer Inn, founded in 1909, and still 'Sconset's prime spot for elegant dining (see above for details).

CENTRAL AND WESTERN MASSACHUSETTS

West of Boston spreads a landscape familiar to the early pioneers, a beautiful land of clear lakes and glacial ponds, cool forests and massive granite outcrops. Farming, forestry, and light industry occupy the people of central and western Massachusetts, not to mention the textile and paper mills dotted along its many rivers. Amid this bucolic scenery you'll also find several of America's finest colleges, posh 19th-century mountain resorts, and New England's premier summer music festival.

Wealthy vacationers of the 19th century who loved the sea would get away to Newport, Cape Cod, or Bar Harbor; those who loved the mountains would head for Saratoga Springs, N.Y., or for the storybook New England towns scattered through the low mountains known as the Berkshires in western Massachusetts. The grand residences and hotels of the wealthy remain in Stockbridge, Lenox, Williamstown, and other Berkshire communities, adding to the romance and interest of the area and serving a new purpose as hostelries for the new wave of vacationers. Today the lure of the Berkshires is enhanced by one of the country's major summer musical events, the Berkshire Music Festival at Tanglewood, near Lenox; another Berkshire town draws crowds because of its beauty and its educational opportunities, for Williamstown in the northern Berkshires has been the seat of Williams College since the school was chartered in 1785. Whatever your reason for going, you can't fail to enjoy the lush countryside, the picturesque towns with rows of fine houses, and the acres of manicured greenery.

The telephone area code for central Massachusetts is 508, for western Massachusetts, 413.

---

1. Getting There

BY CAR: From New York City, the Taconic State Parkway provides a very pleasant route to the Berkshires; from other points I-90 (the Massachusetts Turnpike) and I-91 can be used as the fastest routes to the area. There's convenient public transport as well.

BY BUS: Greyhound/Trailways (tel. 617/423-5810 in Boston or toll free 800/237-8211) provides direct service between Boston and Albany via Worcester, Sturbridge, Springfield, Lee, Lenox, and Pittsfield, Mass., with several buses a day. In addition, they have direct Toronto–New York services with stops in Albany, where transfer can be made to a Lenox-bound bus.

Vermont Transit (tel. 617/423-5810 in Boston) operates buses between Montréal and New York City, stopping in Albany at the Greyhound terminal, and from there one must transfer for the trip to Lenox. There are also direct buses between Montréal and Pittsfield, Mass., passing through Williamstown; in Pittsfield the transfer can be made for Lenox.

Englander Coach Lines (tel. 617/423-5810), operating from the Greyhound terminal in Boston, has several buses a day between Boston and Albany, stopping in Pittsfield; connecting services are also run between Boston and Providence.

Bonanza Bus Lines (tel. 212/971-6363 in New York City 617/423-5810 in Boston, or toll free 800/556-3815) has direct Providence–Albany service, with stops in Pittsfield, Lenox, and Lee, and also direct buses between New York City and Great Barrington, Stockbridge, Lee, Lenox, and Pittsfield. There is also direct service from Boston's Greyhound/Trailways terminal to Springfield, Pittsfield, Greenfield, North Adams, and Williamstown.

Peter Pan Bus Lines (tel. in Boston 617/426-7838 or in Springfield 413/781-3320) which operates from its terminal near Boston's South Station, provides service from Boston to Amherst, Northampton, Holyoke, South Hadley, Worcester, and Springfield, Mass., and thence to Pittsfield, Lee, and Lenox.

By taking a Greyhound/Trailways bus from Hartford or New York City to Springfield, you can connect with the Bonanza or Peter Pan buses to reach just about anywhere in Western Massachusetts.

Local buses connect Berkshire County towns and resorts with one another.

BY RAIL: Amtrak's *Lakeshore Limited* runs daily between New York/Boston and Chicago, one section leaving Boston (South Station) in midafternoon and another leaving New York City in early evening. The two sections link up in Albany-Rensselaer and continue on to Chicago. The section from Boston passes through Worcester and Springfield, and then Pittsfield, Mass., in the evening. The *Adirondack,* traveling between Montréal and New York City (Grand Central Terminal), passes through Albany-Rensselaer as well. From that point, arrangements would have to be made to get to your destination by bus.

In addition, Amtrak's Inland Route trains traveling between Boston and New York pass through Wellesley, Framingham, Worcester, and Springfield, Mass., as well as Hartford and New Haven, Conn. There are at least two trains daily on this route. Call Amtrak toll free 800/872-7245; in New York, 212/582-6875; in Boston, 617/482-3660.

2. Worcester

Massachusetts's second-largest city has much to recommend it, and only one serious drawback (which is not its own fault): Worcester is only an hour's drive west of Boston. What this means is that people consider Boston as the Massachusetts metropolis, and simply forget about her sister city so close at hand.

Worcester's claims to fame are considerable: it is the home of the American Antiquarian Society (founded in 1812), of the famed Worcester Art Museum, and of the Higgins Armory Museum. If you're searching for documents dating from America's early years, Edward Hicks's famous painting *The Peaceable Kingdom,* or rare suits of medieval armor, you've come to the right place.

PLANNING YOUR VISIT: What I'd suggest is this: get to Worcester, take a turn through the center of town, stopping at the fine Town Common and impressive city hall, and perhaps at the modern shopping, dining, and entertainment complex called the Galleria, then admire the massive auditorium named Mechanics Hall, 321 Main St., as you make your way to the Worcester Art Museum. Spend the morning at the museum and nearby sights, perhaps have a bite of lunch in the museum's restaurant, go on to the Higgins Armory, then head for Sturbridge (18 miles) to spend the night. Don't plan this tour for a Monday, as all of Worcester's museums are closed on that day. (The museum restaurant is open Tuesday through Saturday 11:30 a.m. to 2 p.m. for lunch, and 2 to 3 p.m. for dessert and beverages. Open Sunday, except in July and August, from 1 to 4 p.m. for dessert and beverages.)

SEEING THE SIGHTS: What you will see of Worcester is very pleasant. There are spacious parks and gardens, several academic institutions of note (Clark University, College of the Holy Cross, and Worcester Polytechnic Institute), and many attractive buildings. Such beauty must be paid for, and Worcester bought its share by being a very active manufacturing center during the mid-1800s. This city was the birthplace of ingenious machines which were the first to weave carpets, fold envelopes, and turn irregular shapes on a lathe. You can still see many of the old mill buildings in town. Some have been converted to office or retail centers, others lie abandoned, and many are still turning out products: men's and boys' clothing, raincoats, sportswear, winter coats, shoes, and dozens of other items. Worcester kept its spirit of Yankee ingenuity right into the 20th century. Dr. Robert Goddard, the father of modern rocketry, was a Worcester native.

Most of Worcester's products can be bought at a discount in the **factory outlets** sprinkled across the city—you'll see them. **Spag's,** at 193 Boston Turnpike (Rte. 9) in neighboring Shrewsbury, could be considered the L. L. Bean of discount houses. Vast quantities of discount merchandise are trucked in and sold out each day to a horde of loyal customers.

Worcester Art Museum

Worcester's famous art museum, at 55 Salisbury St., off Park Avenue and Main Street (tel. 508/799-4406), will surprise you. It's one of those smaller museums with an amazingly comprehensive collection, studded with masterpieces. Besides Hicks's *Peaceable Kingdom,* you'll see Paul Gauguin's famous *St. Bartholomew,* Rembrandt's *Brooding Woman,* and Mary Cassatt's *Woman Bathing.* The collection ranges from ancient Chinese, Egyptian, and Sumerian objects through Roman statuary and mosaics, pre-Columbian artifacts, Japanese *ukiyo-e* prints and European paintings by the great masters, to American primitives and works by the great American painters.

Hours are Tuesday through Friday from 10 a.m. to 4 p.m. on Saturday from 10 a.m. to 5 p.m., and on Sunday from 1 to 5 p.m.; closed Monday (also New Year's

Day, Independence Day, Thanksgiving, and Christmas). Admission is free on Saturday from 10 a.m. to noon, otherwise it is $3.50 for adults, $2 for students and senior citizens, free for youths under 18.

Worcester Historical Society

At 30 Elm St., just around the corner from the art museum is the historical society (tel. 508/753-8278), with a library and galleries dedicated to Worcester history and lore. You can visit Tuesday through Saturday from 10 a.m. to 4 p.m., Sunday from 1 to 4 p.m., for a voluntary contribution.

American Antiquarian Society

At 185 Salisbury St., only a few blocks from the art museum, the American Antiquarian Society (tel. 508/755-5221), is a research library of American printed materials dating from 1640 to 1877. The priceless archives are open only to scholars, but you can view displays of many documents important to American history Monday through Friday from 9 a.m. to 5 p.m. Free tours are given Wednesday at 2 p.m.

Higgins Armory Museum

That Worcester should have one of the world's great collections of medieval armor is not as odd as it may seem. The ingenious Yankees who lived here in the 1800s were fascinated by machinery, and thus deeply involved with metallurgy. John Woodman Higgins wanted to know how medieval armorers made such excellent steel, so he collected their work. Now over 100 magnificent suits, true works of art, are arranged in the museum, many in the Great Hall. You'll even see armor made for kids, and for dogs. Hours are Tuesday through Friday from 9 a.m. to 4 p.m., on weekends and holidays from noon to 4 p.m.; and on Monday from 9 a.m. to 4 p.m. in July and August. There's an admission fee of $4 for adults and $2.75 for Senior Citizens and children 5 to 12. The Higgins Armory Museum is at 100 Barber Ave., off Gold Star Boulevard (tel. 508/853-6015).

---

3. Sturbridge

The creators of Old Sturbridge Village couldn't have chosen a better spot for their "living museum." It's set in the beautiful hills of east-central Massachusetts right where the Massachusetts Turnpike (I-90) intersects with I-84, a major route to Hartford and New York City. Most people who tour New England would pass this junction sometime. Anyone who passes should certainly stop to see Old Sturbridge Village, and perhaps to spend the night.

WHERE TO STAY: Because of Old Sturbridge Village, and because the village of Sturbridge is very near the intersection of two major Interstate highways, motels abound in this town and nearby. Trade is brisk in summer, even brisker during the autumn foliage season, and briskest of all during the three annual Brimfield Flea Market weekends. Nearby Brimfield, eight miles west of Sturbridge on U.S. 20, is a normally sleepy place which springs to life in early May, mid-July, and mid-September. As Brimfield has few hotels and motels itself, those in Sturbridge—and even in Springfield, 35 miles away—are filled to overflowing. If you come at flea market time, have ironclad reservations. The flea markets are in May, July, and September.

During the normally slow months of January through March, several Sturbridge inns and motels band together to offer attractive discount "Winter Weekend" package plans. For details, contact the Publick House, described below.

You should note that the village of Sturbridge, a bona fide Massachusetts colonial-era town, and Old Sturbridge Village, a "living museum," are actually two different places in the same general area. They're only about a mile apart, but the village of Sturbridge's Town Common, or center, is on Rte. 131, while the entrance to Old Sturbridge Village is on Rte. 20.

With hotels, motels, and inns in the Berkshires packed to capacity on summer weekends, some visitors and music lovers actually plan to stay as far east as Sturbridge, where rooms are plentiful. Using Sturbridge as a base, a tour through the Berkshires, including a stop at Tanglewood, can be a day's outing.

Inns and Guesthouses

The **Publick House** on the Common, Sturbridge, MA 01566 (tel. 508/347-3313), is a local institution. Founded in 1771 by one Col. Ebenezer Crafts, the Publick House occupies the original building plus several large (but tasteful) additions, mostly furnished for dining. In the inn, there are 17 guest rooms, including several suites for three or four people. All rooms and suites have private bath, air conditioning, and direct-dial phone. In the adjoining Chamberlain House are four suites with queen-size beds, color TV, air conditioning, direct-dial phone, and living room area; each suite accommodates up to four people. Double rooms cost $88 to $100; suites are $130 to $135 for two.

The Publick House people also operate the **Colonel Ebenezer Crafts Inn,** Fiske Hill, Sturbridge, MA 01566 (tel. 508/347-3313), at the summit of Fiske Hill. The fine old house was built by David Fiske in 1786, and later converted to an inn. It's gracious, filled with antiques, and small, taking only about 20 people at one time. Rates are good for what you get: continental breakfast, a morning newspaper, and later on afternoon tea and sherry; and at bedtime you'll enter your room to find sweets by your bed. It's all included in the rates: $99 to $110 for a double room with private bath; a suite capable of sleeping four people costs $115 to $148. All the rooms are air-conditioned, and while they don't have TV, there's one in the library you can watch.

About two miles west of Old Sturbridge Village along U.S. 20 is the **Commonwealth Inn,** P.O. Box 60, Sturbridge, MA 01566 (tel. 508/347-7603), a nice big Victorian house now run as a bed-and-breakfast inn. The eight spacious guest rooms are decorated in period furniture, and five have private bath. Doubles cost $59, with a full breakfast included. The inn is on a quiet side street called Summit Avenue. Signs will direct you.

The **Maple Street Guest House,** Maple St., Sturbridge, MA 01566 (tel. 508/347-3746), owned by Mrs. Flora Farland, has only four rooms: a twin-bedded one with shower and private entrance; one with a double bed and two twins, plus full bath; one with a double bed and bath; and another with twins and a shower; the rate is $49 double. All are neat as a pin, and quiet—Maple is a dead-end street. To find it, leave U.S. 20 and turn onto Rte. 131, heading for the village of Sturbridge and the Publick House. About a quarter mile from U.S. 20, look for the Federated Church and the town library on your left. Turn left just before them—that's Maple Street, and the guesthouse is down a short way on the left. If you come to the Publick House, you've missed the Maple Street turn.

About 25 miles northwest of Sturbridge, at the junction of Rtes. 9 and 32, is the town of Ware, and the **Wildwood Inn,** 121 Church St., Ware, MA 01082 (tel. 413/967-7798). If you're headed for Amherst and would rather travel the scenic back roads than the turnpike, you'll find a friendly welcome here. Double rooms with shared baths and lovely handmade quilts are priced from $39 to $73, full breakfast included.

Motels

Prime among Sturbridge's modern hostelries and right across from Old Sturbridge Village is the **Sheraton Sturbridge Resort and Conference Center,** U.S. 20, Sturbridge, MA 01566 (tel. 508/347-7393, or toll free 800/325-3535).

This lavish 241-room spread on the shores of Cedar Lake has its own tennis and racquetball courts, health club, indoor swimming pool, and miniature golf course. Decor in the plush guest rooms is, of course, colonial. "Heritage Row," a special group of V.I.P. rooms, has its own private lounge and concierge services. Regular rooms go for $108 to $130 single, $123 to $141 double. Weekend packages that include some meals are available.

The **Old Sturbridge Village Motor Lodge** (tel. 508/347-3327), right next to Old Sturbridge Village, is owned by the Village. Guest rooms are clustered in a variety of buildings designed along colonial lines and positioned as though in an early American village. Besides the 47 modern, full-comfort rooms, the motel rents rooms in the Oliver Wight House (1789), a Revolutionary-era ten-room inn right next door. The modern rooms in the "village," Wight House suites, and cottage cost $72 to $94; each additional person pays $5 and children 12 and under stay free in their parents' room. Continental breakfast is included.

The **Sturbridge Coach Motor Lodge**, 408 Main St., Sturbridge, MA 01566 (tel. 508/347-7327), is on U.S. 20 almost opposite the entrance to Old Sturbridge, up on the hill. Although it's obviously a modern two-floor luxury motel, the inspiration for both design and decor is colonial. There's nothing colonial about the swimming pool, though, or the rooms, each equipped with color cable TV, air conditioning, and private bath with separate dressing room area. Rates in summer are $62 to $75 for two in a double bed, $66 to $81 for two in two beds.

The **Sturbridge Motor Inn** (tel. 508/347-3391) is on the service road parallel to I-84 a quarter mile north of I-84. (Take Exit 2 to Rte. 131.) With 34 rooms, the inn offers air conditioning, color TV, telephone, and an interesting swimming pool nestled among the pines. High-season prices (May through October) are $72 to $88, single or double. Each additional person is $5. By the way, the mail address here is P.O. Box 185, Sturbridge, MA 01566.

Right near the intersection of Rtes. 15, 20, and 131, the **Days Inn at Sturbridge** (P.O. Box 206, Sturbridge, MA 01566; tel. 508/347-9000) is a modern and attractive two- and three-floor brick and wood motel with a swimming pool. All the 100 rooms have air conditioning and color TV. Convenient, attractive, and comfortable, the rooms cost $70 single, $75 double in summer, continental breakfast included. From October to April rates are a few dollars more.

WHERE TO DINE: Sturbridge abounds in fast-food joints and snack shops, both for the hungry Old Sturbridge Village visitors and for highway passersby. But good places for a full meal do exist.

The **Publick House** (tel. 508/347-3313), mentioned above, is a Sturbridge favorite, located right on the Town Common on Rte. 131. It's big: the several dining rooms can handle a large number of diners at once, and yet the scale of an old New England inn has not been lost. The lunch menu lists a few sandwiches, but concentrates on hot main courses or cold meat or salad plates: omelets, chicken Cordon Bleu, and broiled fish are all priced about $10 to $12, but the price includes vegetable, potato, assorted relishes, and a bakery basket filled with freshly baked bread and rolls. Dinner is fancier, with main-course prices about $13 to $19; steaks are a few dollars higher. But for such a price you get almost a full meal, with all the extras that are given with a comparable luncheon plate plus salad. The Publick House's wine list is fairly short, diverse, and moderate-to-expensively priced.

The fare at the **Oxhead Tavern,** off U.S. 20 near the Sheraton Sturbridge Resort (tel. 508/347-9994), is designed with transients in mind. It's not an elegant restaurant, and doesn't try to be, but it succeeds beautifully in being a roadside tavern. Furnished in rustic colonial, an old-fashioned pub bar is at one end, a big stone fireplace at the other. The menu is well suited to what a roadhouse must provide: various meals at any time of day or evening. The fare includes New York sirloin for $12 and various meat and fish dishes for $7 to $10, and lots of sandwiches ($5) are cheaper and equally filling. And the ambience really is similar to what you might have found 100 years ago in this town, making allowances for modern dress and speech, of course. They serve from 11 a.m. to 11 p.m. Monday through Saturday and noon to 11 p.m. on Sunday.

A Sturbridge Institution

Rom's (tel. 508/347-3349), the Italian-American restaurant on Rte. 131 across from the shopping plaza, is an all-American success story. Started as a road-side sandwich-and-seafood stand, Rom's now seats up to 700 people in attractive, air-conditioned surroundings. What packs 'em in is Rom's unbeatable formula: good, plentiful food in pleasant dining rooms at low prices. A lunch of soup, broiled halibut steak, potato, vegetable, and cole slaw costs only $7.50; a four-course dinner need cost only $7 to $11.50, complete. The menu features Italian dishes, steaks, seafood, and traditional meals. Service is seven days a week from 11 a.m. to 9 p.m., on Saturday to 10 p.m.

The original dairy bar/lunchstand is still here, by the way. Food to go, including Italian dishes, is even lower in price.

WHAT TO SEE: Besides the obvious headline attraction in Sturbridge, you might want to have a picnic in **Wells State Park,** a few miles north of Sturbridge (take U.S. 20 east, then Rte. 49 north and follow the signs). Swimming and camping are available here as well.

Don't miss the chance to pore over trash and treasures at the **Brimfield Flea Market,** held three times a year (see the introduction to this section for details). If Brimfield is not in session, you can still do some browsing in the many shops on U.S. 20 west of Old Sturbridge Village.

Old Sturbridge Village

Old Sturbridge Village (tel. 508/347-3362) is one of the first of America's outdoor museums. It's a re-creation of a New England town of the early 1800s, but it's a re-creation formed with the artifacts: buildings and tools, machines and meth-ods of work were all collected and brought together in this beautiful part of the Mas-sachusetts hinterland so that Americans could see whence their ancestors had come. Like Plimoth Plantation and Mystic Seaport, Old Sturbridge Village is peopled with authentically dressed "interpreters," folks who perform the tasks of the village's dai-ly life, and explain to visitors how things are done and how things are made. Plan at least a few hours, or perhaps a full day, to get into village life.

When you pay your admission fee of $12 per adult, $5 per youth aged 6 to 15, you will receive a map and guide which will explain all about the exhibits in the Vil-lage. The Village is open throughout the year, closing only on Christmas, New Year's Day, and on Monday from November through March. Hours are 9 a.m. to 5 p.m. May through October and 10 a.m. to 4 p.m. Tuesday through Sunday from Novem-ber through April. Within the Village are several varied places to eat: a bake shop, the Pantry (serving soft drinks), a cafeteria, and the Tavern, which serves full meals, cocktails, and—from late May to late October—a luncheon buffet.

St. Anne Shrine

Those interested in Russian icons will want to stop at the St. Anne Shrine, a mile west of Old Sturbridge Village along U.S. 20, in Fiskdale (tel. 508/347-7338). As you drive through Fiskdale, watch for a sign on the right, just before the junction with Rte. 148, and turn right on Church Street up the steep hill.

The icons were collected by Msgr. Pie Neveu, an Assumptionist bishop who served in Russia from 1906 to 1936, and by other Assumptionist fathers who served as chaplains at the U.S. Embassy between 1934 and 1941. The collection of 60 treasured icons is rare, as they can no longer be exported from the Soviet Union. The exhibit, in a new building, is open every day from about 9 a.m. to 6 p.m. Admission is free, but donations are accepted.

---

4. Deerfield, Amherst, and Northampton

The Connecticut River cuts through western Massachusetts on its way through Hartford and Essex to Long Island Sound. In colonial times the river provided easy and cheap transport from the interior to the bustling markets of New York and Philadelphia. Today the river valley serves as pathway for Interstate 91, the modern equivalent of the ancient waterway.

Because of this easy access, pioneer farmers and settlers poured into Massachusetts's portion of the Connecticut River Valley very early in colonial times. The alluvial riverbed soil is rich, and white men were farming at Springfield as early as 1636. Remote from the colonial power centers, they suffered from attacks by the French and their Indian allies.

This early settlement gained the region its modern name: the Pioneer Valley. Although it is still a rich farming region, other interests now predominate: Springfield's industrial career started with the construction of an armory there in 1777, and Holyoke and Hadley benefited from abundant waterpower and fostered a paper industry. But to most of the world the towns of Amherst, Northampton, and South Hadley are famous for education. Here in this pastoral setting are five famous colleges and several smaller institutions: Amherst College, Smith College, Mount Holyoke College, Hampshire College, and the University of Massachusetts. To the north, Old Deerfield is one of the most gracious, best-preserved colonial and Federal towns in the country.

INFORMATION: The region has an area organization, the **Greater Springfield Convention and Visitors Bureau,** 56 Dwight St., Springfield, MA 01103 (tel. 413/787-1548). In addition, each town's chamber of commerce sponsors a visitor information office. In **Amherst,** there's an information booth right on the Town Common across the street from the bus depot, or you can look to the Amherst Chamber of Commerce, 51 E. Pleasant St., Amherst, MA 01002 (tel. 413/549-7555). For **Northampton** information, try the Greater Northampton Chamber of Commerce, on State Street (tel. 413/584-1900). In **South Hadley,** the chamber is at 362 N. Main St. (tel. 413/532-6451).

WHERE TO STAY: Accommodation in the area is very much geared to college life. Most visitors come on college business, and when big college events such as homecomings, graduations, and major football matches draw big crowds, rooms are scarce throughout the area. Try to plan and to reserve well in advance if you think you'll arrive in a busy time.

In Amherst

Every college town has its college inn, usually a gracious old place with a refined atmosphere and very comfortable—often plush—accommodations. Amherst is no exception, for right on the Town Common stands the **Lord Jeffrey Inn,** 30 Boltwood Ave., Amherst, MA 01002 (tel. 413/253-2576). Named for Lord Jeffrey Amherst, the Lord Jeff is cozy, colonial, and collegiate, but with all the conveniences: cable color TV, direct-dial phone, individual heating and air conditioning, and, of course, private bathroom. A tavern and dining room can provide food and refreshment from morning to night. In summer, the Lord Jeff charges $88 to $110 for a single room and $121 to $132 for a suite.

From the Town Common, head out North Pleasant Street and soon you'll see the **University Motor Lodge** at 345 N. Pleasant St., Amherst, MA 01002 (tel. 413/256-8111), on the right-hand side. Up on the hillside above the road, this is an attractive neocolonial place which charges $46 to $74 single, $57 to $74 double, for its newly renovated, fully equipped (right down to coffee in the room) motel rooms. The location is good, as you can walk in ten minutes either to Amherst or to U. Mass.

The University of Massachusetts ("U. Mass." for short) has its own major lodging facility for out-of-towners. Within the modern tower named the Murray D. Lincoln Campus Center is the **Campus Center Hotel** (tel. 413/549-6000), with over 100 rooms. Besides the standard luxuries such as air conditioning, color TV, telephone, and private bath, most rooms have wonderful, panoramic views of the campus, the town, and the surrounding farmland. Prices are $52 single, $62 double, $72 triple, tax included; suites are also available. To find the Campus Center, head north on North Pleasant Street, enter the U. Mass. campus, and follow signs to Campus Center Parking, an underground lot right next to the Campus Center.

Northampton Road is the highway (Rte. 9) between Amherst and Northampton. The road starts at the southern end of the Town Common, and exactly one mile later, after crossing the Amherst town line, it enters a commercial zone. A bit farther along Rte. 9 toward Northampton is the local **Howard Johnson Lodge,** 401 Russell St., Hadley, MA 01035 (tel. 413/586-0114, or toll free 800/654-2000). Although it's very close to Amherst—only a few miles from the Town Common—its mail address is Hadley. Rooms are of the high Hojo standard, some with cathedral ceilings and balconies, and in addition the lodge has a nice big outdoor pool and lots of deck chairs for sunning. All 59 rooms are newly renovated, have two double beds, and rent for $52 single, $63 to $94 double, tax included. V.I.P., handicapped, nonsmoking, and adjoining family rooms are also available. Children under 18 can stay in their parents' room for free.

In Deerfield, Buckland, and Ashfield

Deerfield, the 18th-century village that's virtually a museum, has an inn. Buckland, the picture-perfect New England village with the church, library, historical society, and beautiful 18th-century houses facing the village green, has a fine bed-and-breakfast which just happens to be one of those houses on the green. And Ashfield is yet another beautiful village, a leisurely 40-minute drive from Amherst or Northampton, in the foothills of the Berkshires.

Built in 1884, and modernized in 1981 after a disastrous fire, the **Deerfield Inn,** Main Street, Deerfield, MA 01342 (tel. 413/774-5587), now has 23 rooms which were inspired by the 18th-century, shall we say, but constructed with 20th-century materials and comforts. All the rooms have private bath and air conditioning, and they have been decorated with good replicas of period pieces to put you in the mood of two centuries ago. The inn has a good dining room, coffeeshop, bar, and lounge, and a very fine front porch with rocking chairs all set to take in the view of Main Street. The inn is open all year (except Christmas Day), and charges $133 single or double with breakfast, $205 with breakfast and dinner.

In Buckland, on the green, stands the **1797 House,** Charlemont Road, Buckland, MA 01338 (tel. 413/625-2975), run by a very hospitable lady named Janet Turley. The house (built guess when?) has three immaculate guest rooms, each with private bath, and also numerous fireplaces and interesting nooks and corners. Included in the price of your room is a full country breakfast; rates are $52 single, $63 to $75 double. Buckland is a few miles southwest of Shelburne Falls, just off Rte. 112. The inn is closed in November and December.

In Ashfield, overlooking Ashfield Lake, is the **Ashfield Inn,** Main Street (P.O. Box 129), Ashfield, MA 01330 (tel. 413/628-4571). The eight guest rooms that share four bathrooms in this Georgian mansion are all quite large and furnished to convey the elegance of the early 1900s. There's a living room (with a fireplace) in which to socialize, books to read, and VCR and TV to watch; there are tree swings and huge porches to enjoy the outdoors. Rates ($60 to $66 single, $82 to $93 double) include an expanded continental breakfast during the week and a full breakfast on the weekends. If the inn is not full, the innkeepers will make every effort to give you a private bathroom at no additional charge.

In Northampton

Closest thing in Northampton to the traditional college inn is the **Autumn Inn,** 259 Elm St., Northampton, MA 01060 (tel. 413/584-7660). From the street you see an attractive brick house, but behind the house are comfortable motel units and a small, very pretty swimming pool. Special attention is given to good-quality furnishings and equipment here; a lounge and dining room provide sustenance. Prices in summer are $50 to $60 single, $68 to $81 double, $12 for an extra person; children under 6, $6. Here on Elm Street you're right across the street from Smith College. By the way, Rte. 9 passes right along Elm Street as it makes its way through Northampton.

At the corner of Main and King streets, the grand **Hotel Northampton,** 36 King Street, Northampton, MA 01061 (tel. 413/584-3100) is the most prominent place to stay in town. After undergoing a substantial period of renovation, the rooms and suites have been furnished with classic pieces and Laura Ashely fabrics. Room rates are $77 single, $86 to $98 double, $125 for a suite. The various eateries within are popular meeting places for Northampton's young and old alike. Wiggins Tavern is a dark, colonial restaurant serving traditional American fare. The Coolidge Park Café dishes up lighter items and drinks; customers spill out onto the patio for dining in warmer months.

Budget Motels Farther Out

In the vicinity of Northampton are two members of the Susse Chalet budget motel chain that offer exceptional value. In the city of Holyoke on U.S. 5, there's a **Susse Chalet Inn,** 1515 Northampton, St., Holyoke, MA 01040 (tel. 413/536-1980, or toll free 800/258-1980, 800/572-1880 in New Hampshire). Look for the Susse Chalet on the right-hand side as you head south from Northampton, behind a Howard Johnson's restaurant. Susse Chalet Inn rooms are comfortably furnished with all the usual services, yet they cost a lot less than "standard" motel rooms: $45 single, $49 double, $53 for three, $56 for four persons. By the way, the exit to take from I-91 for this Susse Chalet Inn is Exit 17 or 17A.

At Chicopee, near Massachusetts Turnpike Exit 6, is a **Susse Chalet Motor Lodge,** Burnett Road, Chicopee, MA 01020 (tel. 413/592-5141, or toll free 800/258-1980, 800/572-1880 in New Hampshire). Susse Chalet Motor Lodges, almost as comfortable as the chain's inns, are a few dollars lower in price—and they still have all the conveniences, including TV, air conditioning, ice machine, coin-op laundry, direct-dial phone, even a swimming pool.

WHERE TO DINE: The area has a number of good restaurants. Here are my favorites.

In Amherst

Among the longtime favorites is **Judie's,** 51 N. Pleasant St. (tel. 253-3491), right on the main street in the center of town. The eclectic menu has something for everyone, from seafoods to salads, from quiche to beef. For lunch I had a cup of shrimp bisque, then a hamburger with cheddar, bacon, and onions, and with a soft drink the total bill, tax and tip included, was less than $10. Many people come just for a light meal of soup and a popover with apple butter (a specialty) for $5.50. Main courses at dinner cost between $10 and $15. You dine in one of several small, attractive dining rooms in this converted house or on the glassed-in streetside porch. Go early to get a porch table for lunch. Judie's opens at 11:30 a.m. every day, and closes at 11 p.m. (at midnight on Friday and Saturday). Liquor is served.

The **Lord Jeffrey Inn,** 30 Boltwood Ave. (tel. 253-2576), offers elegant colonial-style dining, serving breakfast (7:30 to 9:30 a.m.), lunch (noon to 2 p.m.), and dinner (6 to 9 p.m.), plus Sunday brunch (11:30 a.m. to 2:30 p.m.). Expect to spend $18 to $25 per person for a full dinner, less for a hearty lunch.

The **Top of the Campus Restaurant and Lounge** (tel. 545-0636) is in a unique position atop the Murray D. Lincoln Campus Center of the University of Massachusetts. Here the formula is decent food at decent prices, with that panoramic view as a bonus. Note the hours, though: lunch is served Monday through Friday from 11:30 a.m. to 2 p.m.; dinner is Tuesday through Saturday from 5 to 9 p.m. When college is not in session, more limited hours apply.

Bonducci's Café, 63 S. Pleasant St. (tel. 256-1390), right across from the little information kiosk on the green, opens at 7 a.m. (at 8 a.m. on Saturday and at 9 a.m. on Sunday), and stays open till 11 p.m. weeknights, 11:30 p.m. weekends. This is the place for morning croissant and coffee ($1.75), a bowl of soup and sandwich ($5), or a pick-me-up any time of day. In good weather, sidewalk tables authenticate its college-town café atmosphere. Bonducci's is also convenient if you're waiting for a bus. There is also a Bonducci's at 239 Main Street in Northampton (tel. 586-6370).

In Northampton

Not your average Chinese restaurant, **Sze's** (tel. 586-5708) on Main Street serves gourmet meals in a contemporary, stylish, and open (and thus rather noisy) dining room. All the old standbys are here—sweet and sour chicken, moo-shu pork, beef with pea pods—but they're done with flair. More exotic dishes include sesame game hen with a szechuan sauce or General Tso's chicken cooked in a spicy sauce with green and red peppers. Check the blackboard for daily specials; my favorite is the crispy orange chicken. Dishes fall between $6 and $14, but a full meal can be kept to $12 per person. Lunch is served Monday through Saturday from 11:30 a.m. to 3 p.m., dinner from 3 p.m. to 9:15 p.m. (till 10:45 p.m. on weekends). The Sunday brunch from 11:30 a.m. to 3 p.m. is always a good value, and the lounge is a nice place for a before- or after-dinner drink.

The place for breakfast and lunch (and I do mean breakfast *and* lunch—some devotees come with the newspaper at breakfast, do some shopping, and return for lunch) is **Curtis and Schwartz,** 116 Main Street (tel. 586-3278). There's much to love about this place: pecan waffles with fresh fruit, crème fraîche, and real maple syrup ($5.75), summer squash ravioli in a Parmesan cream sauce ($5.50), and a cheesy herb omelet ($4) served with a warm scone. Curtis greets and seats customers and Schwartz cooks. In a town with many breakfast places, this one reigns. There's always a line, but the wait never seems too long.

Good Mexican and Southwestern cooking in Northampton? You bet, at **La Cazuela,** 7 Old South St. (tel. 586-0400), off Main Street. The dining room accented with regional artwork is pleasant, but in the warmer months if the mosquitos aren't too fierce, I prefer eating outside on the terrace. A complimentary basket of corn chips and salsa was hastily dispatched before I settled into *pollo verde,* a breast of chicken baked with mild green chiles, cheese, tomatos, and cilantro for $9.50. Portions of food and drink are generous; a frosty margarita costs $3. Open for brunch on Saturday and Sunday from 11 a.m. to 3 p.m.; daily for dinner 5 to 9 p.m., until 10 p.m. on Saturday and Sunday.

On Northampton's main street is **Paul and Elizabeth's** (tel. 584-4832), a natural-foods restaurant. The main entrance is at 150 Main St., with a second entrance on Old South Street above Herrell's Ice Cream. In the pleasant dining room you'll see a cross-section of Northampton society dining on fresh fish, salads, tempura, fresh-baked breads, and desserts. Prices are quite moderate. For the fish lunch of the day, with salad, rice, and tea, you need pay less than $5. Wine and beer are served. Hours are 11:30 a.m. to 9:15 p.m. (to 9:30 p.m. on Friday and Saturday); closed Sunday.

A Coffeehouse Folk Club

The **Iron Horse Café**, 20 Center St. (tel. 584-0610), is just a few steps off Main Street right downtown. It's the real thing: a converted storefront with newspaper-readers, poets and proto-poets, and a full schedule of entertainment in the evenings, from the best in the Northeast to nationally known folk, jazz, rock, and blues artists. Drop by, pick up a schedule, and have one of a dozen coffees, or one of 52 beers. Full breakfasts, cheese boards, Greek salads, quiche, chocolate desserts, and fully licensed liquor bar are available from 8 a.m. to midnight daily (from 9 a.m. on weekends).

WHAT TO SEE: You'll want to take a tour of **Amherst College,** founded in 1821. The Information Booth on the Town Common in Amherst can furnish you with a handy map and guide. The college is all around you. Want more information? Contact Amherst College, Converse Hall (tel. 413/542-2000).

The sprawling campus of the **University of Massachusetts** takes more time to see, but there is a free PVTA bus line you can use, and an excellent campus map. Ask at the Information Booth on the Common, or at the Information Desk in the Campus Center (east end of second floor concourse; tel. 413/545-0111). U. Mass., by the way, was founded in 1863 as Massachusetts Agricultural College. Present enrollment on the Amherst campus is about 24,000—compare that to Amherst College's 1,500.

The roads between Amherst, Northampton, and South Hadley form a triangle and are some of the prettiest in the area. Rte. 116 between Amherst and South Hadley passes **Hampshire College,** the newest and most unconventional of the area's colleges. Farther along the road you may want to stop at **Atkins Fruit Bowl** (tel. 253-9528). Cider, pumpkins, apple-picking, maple sugar products, and locally grown produce are all here. Atkins has grown so large from its humble beginnings as a farm stand, that it now stays open daily, year round. Continuing along, you'll climb into the tiny Holyoke Mountain Range, the only range of mountains that runs east to west. Well-marked hiking trails lead in from the visitor's center here. Once over "the notch" you'll coast down toward South Hadley.

Mount Holyoke College in South Hadley bears the distinction of being the country's oldest women's college, founded in 1837. The lovely campus was originally designed by Frederick Law Olmsted, who fashioned so many beautiful parks and forests during the 19th century. The campus now boasts a new $9-million sports complex, an equestrian center, a Japanese tea house and meditation garden, and a unique handcrafted classical organ (one of the last designed by Charles B. Fisk) in the chapel. The College Art Museum is open year round to campus visitors, and the Summer Theatre offers plays in a tent on the green Tuesday through Saturday nights. The enrollment at Mount Holyoke is about 1,900 women. For a campus tour, call 413/538-2023.

On the way from South Hadley to Northampton on Rte. 47 (a gorgeous drive especially in the spring and fall), take a detour to **Skinner State Park** at the top of Mt. Holyoke (the mountain, not the college). On a clear day from the Summit House you'll have a great view of the winding Connecticut River, the fertile valley's patchwork of farmland, church and college steeples, and distant mountain ranges.

Also worthy of a stroll is the pretty campus of **Smith College** in Northampton, founded in 1871. You can arrange for a tour of the campus by contacting the Office of Admission, Garrison Hall, Northampton, MA 01063 (tel. 413/585-2500). But the handy Campus Guide folder available at the college switchboard in College Hall may well satisfy your needs. Smith's enrollment is about 2,700 women.

For a closer look at the Connecticut River, climb aboard the *Quinnetukut II* riverboat for a 12-mile, 1½-hour interpretive **boat cruise.** Geology, ecology, and history of the river are the featured subjects, but the scenery alone is worth the fee: $6 per adult, $2.50 per child; there's a $1 discount for seniors 55 and over. To check prices and schedules, call 413/659-3714. Call to make reservations so that you're sure to get the cruise you want. Buy your tickets at the Northfield Mountain Recreation and Environmental Center, on Rte. 63 to the north of Rte. 2, due east of Greenfield (take I-91 north to Exit 27, then Rte. 2 east, then Rte. 63 north).

OLD DEERFIELD: About 15 miles north of Northampton and Amherst on Rtes. 5 and 10 is **Historic Deerfield,** P.O. Box 321, Deerfield, MA 01342 (tel. 413/774-5581), a wide street lined with well-preserved 18th-century houses and shops. Unlike Old Sturbridge Village or Mystic Seaport, you pay nothing to stroll along the street and admire the nice old buildings and the setting, though there is an admission charge, which gives you two-day entry to all houses. Each of the houses has a guide or two who will give a 35-minute tour. Adults pay $7.50, children 6 to 17 pay $4. You can visit every day of the year (except Thanksgiving, Christmas Eve, and Christmas Day) from 9:30 a.m. to 4:30 p.m. Then head for the Hall Tavern Museum, across from the Deerfield Inn, for maps, brochures, information, and a short audio-visual show which gives you an overview of the village.

The **Wright House** (1824), beautiful in itself, holds collections of Chippendale and Federal furniture, American paintings, and Chinese export porcelain.

The **Flynt Textile Museum** (1872) houses a large collection of textiles, costumes, and needlework from America, England, and continental Europe.

The **Henry N. Flynt Silver and Metalwork Collection** (1814) holds the museum's collection of silver, pewter, and other base metals.

Allen House (1720) is furnished in items made in Boston and the Connecticut River Valley.

Stebbins House (1799–1810) is a wealthy landowner's house, with the rich period furnishings you might expect such a grandee to have.

Barnard Tavern (1740–95) is favorite with children because some of its rooms have exhibits that are okay to touch.

Wells-Thorn House (1717–51) has a series of period rooms extending from the frontier to the Federal periods.

Dwight-Barnard House (1725) was actually built in Springfield, and moved to Deerfield in 1950. Local furniture and a period doctor's office are the attractions.

The **Sheldon-Hawks House** (1743) was home for the same family during two centuries. Rich Deerfield farmers, the Sheldons were able to buy the best available at the time.

Ashley House (1730) was the minister's residence in old times, and by the look of it, this wasn't such a bad life.

One of the most fascinating exhibits is the **Ebenezer Hinsdale Williams House** (1816), which is open to view as a restoration-in-progress. You can take a tour which fills you in on the technical and historical work being done to re-create the house as it may have been between 1816 and 1838.

Besides the exhibits of Historic Deerfield, you should see the **Memorial Hall Museum,** at the corner of Memorial Street and U.S. 5 and 10 (tel. 413/774-7476). Open everyday May through October from 10 a.m. to 4:30 p.m. (from 12:30 to 4:30 p.m. on weekends). Admission costs $2.50 for adults, $1.50 for students, 75¢ for children 6 to 12.

Memorial Hall (1798) was the original home of famed Deerfield Academy, still one of New England's most prestigious private schools. Less than a century after its construction, the building became a historical museum of Pocumtuck Valley life, both Indian and Puritan. Local furniture, pewter, tools, textiles, decoration, and Indian artifacts, arranged in period rooms, make up the collection. There are special collections for carved and painted chests, local embroidery, musical instruments, and early (1880–1920) glass-plate photographs by the Allen sisters, Deerfield's talented early photographers.

But no exhibit brings life in old Deerfield closer than the **Indian House Door.** Deerfield suffered two Indian massacres in its early days, and numerous other battles. On February 29, 1704, during the French and Indian War, the Sheldon house (now gone) was attacked, its door suffering chops and bashes. The attackers finally hacked a hole in the center of the door, through which they got at the inhabitants. It's pretty dramatic.

---

5. Springfield

Springfield, Massachusetts's third-largest city, has a solid place in American history and life. The Springfield Armory produced weapons for use by American troops in the War of 1812, and by Union soldiers in the Civil War, including the famous Springfield rifle. The armory was a virtual cornucopia of small arms, many of which you can still see in its museum.

Yankee ingenuity and technical prowess were lavished on weapons, yes, but on other things as well. The monkey wrench was invented here, as were steel-bladed ice skates and the first American planetarium.

Elegant as these things may be, they were not Springfield's most elegant products. This honor is reserved for the Duryea and the Rolls-Royce. The Duryea brothers, Charles and Frank, built the first practical internal-combustion engine automobile (1894) on the top floor of the building at 41 Taylor St. And for a short time in the 1930s the world's most elegant auto, the Rolls-Royce, was assembled here in Springfield.

Among all its inventions, only one has brought real world fame to Springfield: basketball. Yes, this is the place where, in 1891, Dr. James Naismith, a physical education instructor at Springfield's YMCA college, originated the game. The city has a suitable memorial, the Basketball Hall of Fame, a new structure (1985) that's fascinating and fun even if you're not sports-minded.

SEEING SPRINGFIELD: Located at the junction of I-90 (Mass. Turnpike) and I-91, Springfield is a city most people know only through the car window. Even though you're headed for somewhere else, spend a few hours here. Exit from I-91 at State Street, go to Main Street and you'll find Court Square, Springfield's heart, surrounded by fine buildings including Symphony Hall, the First Congregational Church (1819), and the granite Hampden County Superior Courthouse, modeled somewhat on Venice's Palazzo Vecchio by H. H. Richardson. The statue in the square is of William Pynchon, who led the group of Puritans who settled here in 1636, and incorporated the town five years later.

Museum Quadrangle

Just northeast of Court Square is Springfield's quartet of museums, open from noon to 5 p.m. (closed Monday). Admission is free, unless otherwise noted, though donations are accepted.

At the entrance to the Quadrangle, in Merrick Park, is Augustus St. Gaudens's statue called *The Puritan.*

The **George Walter Vincent Smith Art Museum** (tel. 733-4214) houses the collection of its eponymous founder, who amassed a packet manufacturing carriages, and then spent it on works of art, everything from Japanese armor to Islamic carpets.

The **Museum of Fine Arts** (tel. 732-6092) continues the theme. Its collection is built on lesser masters, or lesser paintings of the great masters, but is a fine collection nonetheless. Pride of place—right above the main stairway—goes to Erastus Salisbury Field's *The Rise of the American Republic,* which can keep you busy for the better part of an hour. You'll see why.

Also in the Quadrangle is the **Springfield Science Museum** (tel. 733-1194), a good place to take the children. Besides the historic Seymour Planetarium, it has the largest freshwater aquarium in the Northeast, and displays on flora, fauna, and geology of the Connecticut Valley. Admission to the planetarium is $2 for adults, $1 for children; children under 6 are not admitted.

The **Connecticut Valley Historical Society Museum** (tel. 732-3080) holds one of America's oldest cars. This is where the pioneering Duryea brothers did some of their work.

Springfield Armory

The Springfield Armory National Historic Site is on Federal Street at State Street, a ten-minute walk from Museum Quadrangle. This was the place where, from 1795 to 1968, a good proportion of our national defense budget was spent. Springfield Technical Community College now occupies the gun factories and officers' quarters, except for the **Small Arms Museum** (tel. 413/734-8551), open daily from 10 a.m. to 5 p.m., on Sunday from 1 to 5 p.m., for free.

There's an awful lot of firepower here, not just the Springfields and Garands that were made in the armory, but even some weapons dating from the 1600s, and lots of Remingtons, Colts, Lugers, etc. It is thought to be the world's largest such collection of weaponry, and is mighty impressive. Don't miss the Organ of Rifles.

Basketball Hall of Fame

This is where you have some fun. Get to Union Street, south of State Street, and head west, passing under I-91, and you'll come smack up against the Basketball Hall of Fame. Hours are 9 a.m. to 6 p.m. daily July through Labor Day, 9 a.m. to 5 p.m. the rest of the year. Admission costs $5 for adults, $3 for kids 9 to 15.

The Hall of Fame is no stuffy museum, but a very active place. The light, spacious structure is decorated with elements relating to the sport: one whole wall is made of those tiny strips of hardwood used on courts. Video displays abound, telling the history of the sport and recalling its most exciting games and players. In a stand-up cinema, you're surrounded by giant movie screens synchronized to make it seem as though you are right in the middle of the frenzied action on the court. In another exhibit, you step onto a conveyor belt from which you can shoot balls at baskets which vary in height and distance from you. At the end of the belt, try your skill at jumping to touch one of the tapes hanging from the ceiling, suspended at heights from 7 to 11 feet. You can see and do a lot here in less than an hour, but you could also spend an entire morning.

Indian Motorcycle Museum

Here's an odd one. Do you know Indian motorcycles, those early motorized two-wheelers? If you have any interest whatsoever in motorized transport, call 413/737-2624 or 732-6029 to make sure it's open, then get on I-291 to the Page Boulevard exit, not far from the Mass. Pike interchange. Turn right (east) on Page Boulevard to an industrial complex and the small Indian Motorcycle Museum. If you're into motorized marvels at all, you've got to see this place. Admission is $2 for adults, $1 for children.

The Big "E"

Starting on the second or third Wednesday in September, for about 12 days, West Springfield hosts New England's largest country fair, "The Big E," located on the grounds of the Eastern States Exposition (tel. 413/737-2443). There's an admission fee to the grounds, but lots to do once you're inside. Call for exact dates and ticket information. The fairgrounds are on Rte. 147, near the Westfield River.

6. The Berkshires: Lenox and Lee

In the 1700s, pioneers spreading through the lands west of Boston came to settle among the fertile fields of the Berkshires. At first the settlement at Lenox was

called Yokuntown, after a local Indian chief, but the name was later changed to honor an English lord—Charles Lenox, Duke of Richmond—who was sympathetic to the American Revolutionary cause. Although small industries have at times appeared in the town, it has been predominantly rural and agricultural, and has remained unspoiled. In the 19th century business tycoons (including Andrew Carnegie) came to admire the tidy farms and streets of Lenox as the perfect place for a summer's retreat, and many farms were bought up by them for this purpose. The houses are still standing for visitors to admire.

If Lenox is the dowager aunt, pristine and correct in her beauty, neighboring Lee is the boisterous 20th-century daughter, lively and more modern, somewhat careless of her beauty.

BERKSHIRE INFORMATION: Granddaddy of Berkshire informational founts is the **Berkshire Visitors Bureau,** Berkshire Common, Pittsfield, MA 01201 (tel. 413/443-9186, or toll free 800/237-5747 in New England except Massachusetts), which can provide you with information on all of Berkshire County, covering the entire western end of Massachusetts.

The **Northern Berkshire Chamber of Commerce** is at 69 Main St., North Adams, MA 01247 (tel. 413/663-3735).

In Lenox, apply to the **Lenox Chamber of Commerce,** Lenox Academy Building, Main Street (P.O. Box 646), Lenox, MA 01240 (tel. 413/637-3646).

In Lee, the local chamber of commerce maintains an **information booth** (tel. 413/243-0852) right on U.S. 20 (Main Street) in the center of town by the park (officially 10 Park Pl., Lee, MA 01238).

Berkshire Bed and Breakfast, P.O. Box 211, Williamsburg, MA 01096 (tel. 413/268-7244) publishes a directory of homes scattered throughout the Berkshires. Write to them for a copy or call them between 1 and 7 p.m. weekdays.

WHERE TO STAY: The overnight lodging situation in Lenox is not the best. Proprietors of inns and motels bemoan the short season and the incredible press of traffic on Tanglewood weekends, which thins out to less-than-capacity during the week. For most lodging places, rooms are in great demand. Some Tanglewood travelers stay as far east as Springfield, and drive to the concert, then back to Springfield. In any case, have reservations for weekends.

As you begin the task of making reservations, you will discover that many inns require a three-night minimum stay on weekends, and full payment in advance; some inns do not accept credit cards, but will take personal checks with proper identification. Children under the age of 8, or even 12, may not be accepted; pets, almost certainly not.

During the off-season, though, all that's missing from Lenox is Tanglewood and the crowds. The same gorgeous rooms are still here, but at a fraction of the price. More and more travelers are realizing this value and making the Berkshires a year-round destination.

Lenox's Inns

Of the Berkshire inns, none is more dignified or luxurious than **Wheatleigh,** West Hawthorne Road (P.O. Box 824), Lenox, MA 01240 (tel. 413/637-0610). Center of the vast estate is the tawny brick mansion in the style of a 16th-century Florentine villa which once belonged to the American-born Contessa de Heredia. The gracious turn-of-the-century, top-of-the-heap lifestyle has been preserved in the airy public rooms, the 17 porticoed and balconied guest rooms and suites, and the sweeping lawns. There are Tiffany windows, tennis courts, and beautiful views in this, the Berkshires' best. Breakfast and dinner are served. Rates (18% service charge and 5.7% tax included) range from $295 to $527 on weekends during summer and fall foliage, $136 to $341 mid-week, and 50% less than that in winter. Full payment is required for a confirmed reservation. The restaurant compares to New York's finest; dinner is served nightly except Monday. Don't miss the unrestored clock tower-water tower-lookout down by the parking area. The contessa's poodles, all 20 of them, are buried nearby. To find Wheatleigh, start from the monument intersection in Lenox, go down the hill on Old Stockbridge Road, and turn right onto Hawthorne. At West Hawthorne Road, turn left and watch for signs.

Rather formal, the **Gateways Inn,** 71 Walker St., Lenox, MA 01240 (tel. 413/637-2532), is a fine place to stay, but an even finer place to dine. The Gateways is quite near the center of Lenox, a grand old white mansion built by Harley Proctor of Proctor and Gamble in 1912. In-season rates are $127 to $138 (weekdays) and $154 to $175 (weekends) for a double room with private bath and continental breakfast; from $239 to $327 for the cavernous Fiedler suite. With rooms as large as these it's no wonder there are only eight rooms in such a huge house. During July and August there's a three-night minimum stay if you plan to visit from Thursday to Sunday. The main courses at dinner are all fixed at $26 and may include medallions of beef or rack of lamb.

"Across the road from Tanglewood" is how the owners describe the **Apple Tree Inn and Restaurant,** 224 West St., Lenox, MA 01240 (tel. 413/637-1477). The name suits, as the century-old mansion is indeed in the midst of an apple orchard. Perched high on the hill directly opposite Tanglewood's West Street entrance, the gracious restaurant and public rooms, and many of the guest rooms, look out on a gorgeous panorama. Some rooms in the main house have a fireplace, most have private bath, all have air conditioning. There are also 20 modern rooms in the nearby guest lodge. The inn has its own heated swimming pool and clay tennis court, and in high season mid-week charges $90 to $230 for a double room, more for suites.

The **Birchwood Inn,** 7 Hubbard St., Lenox, MA 01240 (tel. 413/637-2600), was built in the 1700s as a private home, was converted to a tavern for a few years, became a private home again, and since 1954 has been an inn. If an inn can feel as welcoming as a private home, this is it! Across from the Church on the Hill, overlooking the village, the Birchwood has nine double rooms (some with canopied beds), a two-room suite, and a carriage house with two efficiency apartments, all in a very fine and convenient location. Rates range from $101 to $186 double; continental breakfast is included.

Across Greenwood Street from the Church on the Hill is the **Whistler's Inn,** 5 Greenwood St., Lenox, MA 01240 (tel. 413/637-0975), a half-timbered Tudor mansion built in 1820, now boasting 11 guest rooms (all with bath). Cozy, old worldly, and atmospheric, the house has seven fireplaces, seven acres of grounds, and a good location overlooking the village, just a short walk away. High-summer rates are $70 to $190 double, evening sherry and continental breakfast included.

Right downtown in Lenox is the **Village Inn,** 16 Church St., Lenox, MA 01240 (tel. 413/637-0020), a charming old landmark built in 1771 and furnished to match. All but three of the 29 rooms and suites have private bath, and prices range from $74 to $138 double in season. The restaurant serves breakfast, brunch on Sunday, afternoon tea, and full dinners nightly except Monday. There's also the congenial Village Tavern for drinks and light meals.

The **Garden Gables Inn** is very near the center of town at 141 Main St., Lenox, MA 01240 (tel. 413/637-0193), at the bottom of Church Hill down its own private road. The inn's name is appropriate, as you'll see when you drive or walk down the road through the gardens to the large white house with three sharply triangular gables set in its roof. The shape of the house gives you some idea of the rooms, for all are of different shapes and sizes, all have lots of interesting nooks, crannies, and angles. All are furnished differently. Downstairs there are two cozy low-ceilinged living rooms with rows of books and fireplaces. Rooms are $74 to $132 in July and

August, with a three-night minimum stay on weekends; the lowest price is for a mid-week small room, and the higher price for just the opposite: a large room with private bath on a weekend. The inn has its own 72-foot swimming pool out back. Breakfast is included in the rates. Rates November through May are dramatically lower. Guests are welcome year round.

Go down the hill from the monument intersection on Old Stockbridge Road, turn right onto Hawthorne Street, and at no. 15 is **Brook Farm Inn** (tel. 413/637-3013), about two blocks from the center of town. Brook Farm, run by Bob and Betty Jacob, has 12 guest rooms with private bath, a cozy, authentic Victorian atmosphere, a swimming pool, and prices of $69 to $143 double per night. Their brochure claims "there's poetry here" and there sure is: hundreds of volumes are carefully organized on shelves, renowned poets give readings, a poem-of-the-day is displayed, and guests, once they've learned to relax, have been known to spend an entire day pondering one or two poems. On a more somber note, there's that three-night minimum on summer weekends, as at most Lenox hostelries.

Walker House, 74 Walker St., Lenox, MA 01240 (tel. 413/637-1271), is right in the heart of town. Built in 1804, this spacious house has eight rooms, each with private bath and some with fireplace, many looking onto the three acres of lawn, gardens, and woods. Common rooms are decorated with modern art and attractive antiques, creating gracious eclectic spaces. Room prices of $100 to $144 double include breakfast, afternoon tea, and a small bottle of wine in your room.

Rookwood Inn, 19 Old Stockbridge Rd. (P.O. Box 1717), Lenox, MA 01240 (tel. 413/637-9750), is just a short walk down the hill from the monument intersection in Lenox. A charming Victorian place with a nice lawn and formal gardens, it can accommodate up to 35 guests in rooms with private baths. A full breakfast is included with rates of $106 to $132 double, in season, depending on which room you choose. A few have small screened-in porches, one has a multi-windowed turret.

Built in 1885, **The Gables Inn,** 103 Walker St., Lenox, MA 01240 (tel. 413/637-3416), is a Queen Anne–style Berkshire "cottage." Once owned by the family of Edith Wharton's husband, this was her home for two years while she waited for her own cottage, the Mount, to be built. The present innkeepers have re-created the famous eight-sided library where Mrs. Wharton wrote many short stories. To surround yourself with all this grace and history (as well as a swimming pool and tennis court) will cost $85 to $143 single or double, breakfast included.

The **Candlelight Inn** (tel. 413/637-1555) is best known for its restaurant (described below), but there are eight rooms with private bath for rent in the big and graceful old house at 53 Walker St., corner of Church, Lenox, MA 01240. Off-season, the rooms go for $53 to $85, but in July, August, and October the price rises to $70 to $164 double. The location is excellent, though. Call early for July, August, or October reservations.

The **Cliffwood Inn,** 25 Cliffwood St., Lenox, MA 01240 (tel. 413/637-3330), is a vast mansion set back from the street on its own crescent-shaped drive. As you pass through the curious split Dutch front door into the spacious foyer, you'll be surprised to learn there are only seven bedrooms (six with private bath, fireplace, and king-size bed) for rent—the huge place looks like it should hold many more. Evening wine and hors d'oeuvres and continental breakfast are included in the room price of $106 to $170 ($74 to $111 in winter) double. In five minutes you can walk into town from here.

A Lenox Guesthouse

The **Colonial Guest House,** 59 Walker St., Lenox, MA 01240 (tel. 413/637-0043), is right next door to the Candlelight Inn in downtown Lenox. A very fine old "summer cottage," it has spacious, airy rooms with simple, attractive furnishings which go with the houses and its era. In fact it's the only Lenox summer cottage that hasn't been substantially altered by the addition of private bathrooms, bars, large kitchens, and other modern "improvements." The huge front porch, right in the center of town, is wonderful for people-watching. Of the five rooms, two share an adjoining bathroom; the other three share baths in the hall. Prices are $74 double in summer. This place is really charming, but open only in July and August.

Inns in South Lee

The hamlet named South Lee is on Rte. 102, south of the Massachusetts Turnpike (I-90) and Lee proper. Right on Main Street is Charles Reynolds's elegant and authentic **Merrell Tavern Inn,** South Lee, MA 01260 (tel. 413/243-1794). Those two words describe it best, for this house, built in 1800, has been an inn since 1817. From 1947 to 1981 it belonged to the Society for the Preservation of New England Antiquities. Preservation of the inn's character, including a cage-like bar and authentic period furnishings, has obviously been paramount. In high season on weekends, prices (full breakfast included) are $68 to $127 per night; higher-priced rooms have fireplaces. During the week, prices drop to a very reasonable $55.

South Lee holds an inn famous for its cuisine as well as its rooms: the **Federal House,** Main Street, South Lee, MA 01260 (tel. 413/243-1824). Thomas O. Hurlbut had the brick Greek Revival mansion built in 1824 when he was head of the Owen and Hurlbut Paper Company here. Owned by the original family for 124 years, it was just recently converted to an inn. The seven guest rooms have many original Hurlbut touches and furnishings, but also modern private baths and air conditioning. Rates are $159 double in July and August, full breakfast included. Read on to find out about the restaurant.

Guesthouses in Lee

Lee has numerous guesthouses. They're not furnished in antiques like Lenox's inns, many don't have dining rooms, but they offer good lodging value in the Berkshires. Exactly what you pay depends on the particular room in the particular private home, but the price will easily be less than half that for a room in Lenox. As the rooms are scattered around town, the **Lee Chamber of Commerce** handles reservations. Contact them at 10 Park Pl., Lee, MA 01238 (tel. 413/243-0852), during business hours; an after-hours phone number is placed in the window of the information booth when it's closed.

A Motel

North of Lenox on Rtes. 7 and 20 (same road) are numerous motels, extending all the way to Pittsfield. One of the closest to Lenox proper is also one of the least expensive. The **Susse Chalet Motor Lodge** (tel. 413/637-3560, or toll free 800/258-1980, 800/572-1880 in New Hampshire) has all the standard motel facilities in an attractive hillside location priced at $68 for one or two. These are midweek rates; weekend rates are substantially higher. It's the best value in the Berkshires, but you must reserve early. There is a two-night minimum stay during Tanglewood season.

WHERE TO DINE: Lenox is not covered with restaurants, as many of the classy places to eat are out in the countryside. But for a snack or a good dinner in town, try one of these:

Very successful is the **Church Street Café,** "an American bistro" at 69 Church St. (tel. 637-2745). Lunch, dinner, and Sunday brunch are served daily in the small, cozy dining rooms or out on the pleasant covered decks. Service is personal and informal, and prices are quite moderate for Lenox. I had baked native goat cheese with minced greens to start; then charcoal-grilled Jamaican chicken. A lemon-almond tart and espresso finished up, and the bill—including tax, tip, and a half bottle of the California house wine—was $34. They make their own pasta here, and country pâté, too. Luncheon prices include $7 sandwiches and a few good southwestern items; dinner starts at $12.

Local restaurateur Jimmy De Mayo is at it again, this time with **Lenox 218** (tel.

637-4218) on Main Street slightly out of town. From the outside it doesn't look like much; conversely once you're inside don't be put off by the upscale, art deco interior. Chairs and tables are black, linens are white in the evening, and the ceilings are high. It's still a casual place though, and it can get rather loud. As for the food, try appetizers of fried zucchini in a tomato basil salsa or prosciutto and fresh fruit for lunch, followed by an all-meat pot pie or a California-style vegetable sandwich. Without a beverage lunch will cost $11 to $14, tax and tip included. Main courses at dinner run $10 (for grilled swordfish steak) to $19 (for French lamb chops grilled with mint conserves). The restaurant is open 11:30 a.m. to 2:30 p.m. and 5 to 10 p.m. every day.

The **Candlelight Inn,** 53 Walker St., at the corner of Church Street (tel. 637-1555), is right near the center of town, warm, friendly, and popular with locals and visitors alike. The menu lists a good number of appetizers and a selection of main courses, most of which are continental favorites like shrimp in a mustard-scampi sauce. Lunch at the Candlelight Inn is served daily from noon to 2:30 p.m. in the summer only; dinner is every day from 6 to 9:30 p.m. You don't have to dress up, but you'll feel better if you do. Expect to make reservations and to spend $25 to $35 per person here.

For Breakfast

It's easy to find kiwi-fruit–this and shiitake-mushroom–that in Lenox, but where do you find breakfast eggs and bacon, hash browns, and fresh coffee at 7:30 a.m., for $3.25? At **Cherry's,** 4 Franklin St., very near the town hall and police station, that's where. After 11:30 a.m. the menu switches to sandwiches and platters priced from $2 to $4. The eatery is run by the Desista School and many of its students are employed here in the school's culinary training program.

Dinner in South Lee

The aforementioned **Federal House** on Rte. 102 in South Lee (tel. 243-1824) is among the Berkshires' more acclaimed restaurants. Elegantly set tables are arranged in the mansion's original dining room, front parlor, and billiards room. To get a table on Friday or Saturday evening you must reserve well in advance for one of the two seatings. The fare is continental and classic, with innovative touches: flounder stuffed with scallops, roast duckling with brandied plums, or perhaps thinly sliced veal sautéed in Grand Marnier. The bill at dinner will come to around $38 per person, perhaps more if you get extravagant with the wine list. No lunch is served, but there's brunch on Sunday, with a smoked salmon omelet ($10). Good!

WHAT TO DO: The Number One activity in Lenox is, of course, the **Tanglewood Music Festival,** the summer season of the Boston Symphony Orchestra. Since 1934 the concerts have been held in July and August on the grounds of a fine estate called Tanglewood, about a mile from the center of Lenox out in the Berkshire hills. Seats in the Music Shed ($9 to $50) are difficult to come by, but general admission tickets to the grounds ($6) are easy to find at Tanglewood. All tickets can be bought by phone through TICKETMASTER. Bring a blanket and picnic lunch, and come early to get a good seat near the Music Shed. Grounds open two hours before concert time. Programs of the concert series are available from the information booth in Lenox, or contact Tanglewood, Lenox, MA 01240 (tel. 413/637-1600). In Boston you can reach the Tanglewood Ticket Office in Symphony Hall, 301 Massachusetts Ave., Boston, MA 02115 (tel. 617/266-1492).

When you call for information, be sure to ask about other happenings at Tanglewood, because the Music Festival concerts are not the only thing going on. Over 40 concerts take place during the Tanglewood season, not including the famous weekend BSO concerts. Performers are the young and extremely promising musicians who attend the Tanglewood Music Center for study and advanced training. Maestro Seiji Ozawa, now music director of the BSO, was once among this young up-and-coming elite. Chamber music, solo recitals, and full orchestra concerts are all on this 40-program list. For concert information, call 413/637-1666, July through August.

Tanglewood Tips

If you drive to Tanglewood for one of the BSO concerts, here are some tips to make things easier. First, expect heavy highway traffic. Plan to get to Tanglewood proper by 6 p.m. or earlier (the concert begins at 8:30 p.m.). Bring your picnic lunch — that's what everyone does, and that's why the parking lots fill up early, and that's why no one minds getting there three hours before the concert begins. Expect a tremendous jam of traffic when you leave at the end of the concert. The flood is ably directed by Tanglewood staff, but the exodus takes time nonetheless.

Other Concerts

Tanglewood has begun to sponsor a series of popular, folk, and rock concerts as well as the more lofty Tanglewood Music Festival series. When you call 413/637-1600, ask about what's coming up in the **Popular Artists' Series.**

South Mountain Concerts (tel. 413/442-2106), in nearby Pittsfield, specializes in chamber music, and concerts begin in August and last into October. South Mountain Concerts was started in 1918 in a lovely old hall located a mile south of Pittsfield on U.S. 7 and 20. For a printed schedule of concerts, drop a line to the South Mountain Association, P.O. Box 23, Pittsfield, MA 01202.

Shakespeare and Edith Wharton

What do the two have in common? **The Mount** (tel. 413/637-1899) is a house and gardens planned by the Pulitzer Prize–winning author. You can tour the house, and watch a salon drama based on Ms. Wharton's life and works, June through October, Tuesday through Friday from noon to 4 p.m., on weekends from 10 a.m. to 4 p.m.

On Tuesday through Sunday afternoons at 1 or 2 p.m. and evenings at 8 p.m., an outdoor stage at the Mount is the setting for Shakespearean plays staged by **Shakespeare & Company,** Lenox, MA 01240 (tel. 413/637-1197; box office at 413/637-3353). Shakespeare in the open air on a warm summer evening is definitely among the finer things in life, let me tell you!

The Mount is located just south of Lenox, at the junction of Rtes. 7 and 7A.

Sightseeing in Lenox

Lenox is home to the **Berkshire Scenic Railway Museum** (tel. 637-2210). Trains make two round-trip runs each Saturday in July and August, on a 15-mile route connecting Lenox, Lee, Stockbridge, and Great Barrington. Buy your round-trip ticket (adults pay $7; kids under 12, $4) from the conductor, hop off at one town, and catch a later train onward if you like. The 1920-vintage trains move at an amiable 10-mph pace, allowing leisurely sightseeing. Though the railroad's base is in Lenox, you can board in Stockbridge or Great Barrington as well.

In Lenox proper, be sure to walk to the top of the hill which is on Main Street (U.S. 7), north of the center of town, to see the "Church on the Hill," a very fine New England Congregational church building erected in 1805.

Otherwise, long walks or a drive around the "back streets" and lanes of Lenox can turn up unexpected sights: tremendous mansions, even small castles, nestled in fine parks and copses of trees, once occupied for a few months in summer by commercial and industrial magnates and their immediate families. Many of the mansions are still in private hands, enjoyed by an ever-widening circle of the descendants of the original builders. Most are not open to the public, except for tantalizing looks from the sidewalk.

For a beautiful hike through 1,000 acres of the Berkshire countryside, find your way to the **Pleasant Valley Sanctuary,** northwest of Lenox. Follow the signs, or take Rte. 7A north to West Dugway Road, then West Mountain Road. Pay the admission fee ($2 adults, $1 children 6 to 12) from dawn to dusk daily (closed Monday), and set out on the seven miles of nature trails to explore native Berkshire flora and fauna.

Sightseeing in Lee

The most notable sight in Lee is not in Lee at all, but in the tiny neighboring village of Tyringham, 5 miles south of Lee along the Tyringham Road. It's the **Gingerbread House,** a curious thatched cottage built as a studio by sculptor Henry Hudson Kitson at the turn of the century. Kitson's most famous statue is the one of Captain Parker *(The Minute Man)* on Lexington Green. Now an art gallery, you can look around the Gingerbread House for a fee of $2 for adults, $1 for children 6 to 12.

Jacob's Pillow Dance Festival

In Lee, a dilapidated barn served as the birthplace, in 1932, of a major American dance festival. Bought by Ted Shawn and renovated for performances, the barn and the festival grew larger and more important over the years, enlisting the talents of Alvin Ailey, Merce Cunningham, and similar lights.

The ten-week Jacob's Pillow season begins in June and runs through August. For a season brochure, contact Jacob's Pillow Dance Festival, P.O. Box 287, Lee, MA 01238 (tel. 413/243-0745). The performance center is eight miles east of downtown Lee, off U.S. 20. Performing groups change weekly and ticket prices range from $18 to $24.

---

7. Stockbridge

Any way you look at it, Stockbridge is a very beautiful town. Its wide Main Street is lined with grand houses and other buildings each set apart in its own lawns and gardens. Stately trees fill the skyline. Stockbridge is the center of many Berkshire activities, including the Berkshire Playhouse (details below) and also once the home of famed painter Norman Rockwell.

The town of **West Stockbridge** is a different municipality altogether, four miles west of Stockbridge and Lenox. The dilapidated town was bought up by developers some years ago and reconstructed, expanded, and spruced up as a real-life Disneyland for shoppers, browsers, and sightseers. Purists may say the town is now like a movie set, but many visitors enjoy their time here, meandering along the short streets, peering in windows and shops, having a meal or a cool refresher. It's all pretty commercial, it's true, but that's the attraction.

TOURIST INFORMATION: The Stockbridge Kiwanis Club maintains an **Information Booth** on the main street right in the center of town. They'll provide you with pamphlets and brochures, answer your questions, and even help you find an inexpensive room in a private home—but only if lodging conditions are tight. If the local motels are not full, they'll direct you to one of those, as the private-home rooms are more of an emergency measure.

WHERE TO STAY AND DINE: The **Red Lion Inn,** on Main Street in Stockbridge, MA 01262 (tel. 413/298-5545), is a town institution. The huge white frame hotel with a wide front porch was established as an inn in 1773. Always bustling with guests and diners in summer, the Red Lion charges its high-season rates on weekends from late May through October. Minimum weekend stay is two nights, at $86 (shared bath) or $118 to $144 (private bath) per night, double. On weekdays the rate drops to $68 or $89 to $107 for the same double with bath.

The Red Lion is also Stockbridge's premier place for dining. Besides the formal dining room, there's the Widow Bingham Tavern, a rough-hewn and woody place of colonial flavor. The Lion's Den, downstairs, is the cocktail lounge with a sandwich-and-salad menu. Plan to spend about $35 per person for a luxurious beef dinner in the dining room, about the same in the Widow Bingham Tavern. In summer there's dining in the pretty courtyard in back. By the way, the building dates from 1897 when it was constructed on the site of an earlier inn which was completely destroyed by fire.

In West Stockbridge

West Stockbridge harbors several establishments offering lodging and meals at lower rates than in Stockbridge proper. These are well worth a look.

So many places call themselves country inns these days, even though they have downtown locations, Muzak and cable color TV, bus tours, and whirlpools. The **Williamsville Inn** (tel. 413/274-6118) is a true country inn, however. It's out in the country, about four miles south of West Stockbridge on Rte. 41. Some of the 15 guest rooms have fireplaces, some have four-poster beds; all have private bath and fine old furnishings. Some are in the main house, while others are out back in a reno-vated barn and a cottage. The inn, built in 1797, has ten acres of grounds, a swim-ming pool, clay tennis court, and woodland trails. The dining room is well known and well regarded. June through October, rooms cost $106 to $138 double, and a three-day minimum is applied on summer and holiday weekends. The address is simply Rte. 41, West Stockbridge, MA 01266.

Over in West Stockbridge for the day, one of the very best things you can do is have a meal at the **Truc Orient Express,** on Harris Street (tel. 232-4204). Light and airy, with wicker furniture, it is an exceptionally attractive place, and a welcome change from the antique-packed dining rooms hereabouts. The "Orient" in the name is Vietnam: appetizers such as mien cua (crab and bean-thread soup) or ga nuong chanh (skewered lemon chicken), main courses of sautéed squid with bam-boo shoots or fresh flounder in a spicy sweet-and-sour sauce. For dessert, the cus-tomary lychee or not-so-customary flan finish up nicely. Such a dinner would cost $16 to $25, and if you choose carefully you might even squeeze a glass of sake or plum wine into the price. There are lots of vegetarian dishes too. Open for lunch and dinner. Don't miss it.

WHAT TO SEE AND DO: Stockbridge is rich in historical and cultural attrac-tions. You'll want to visit the **Norman Rockwell Museum,** in the Old Corner House (tel. 298-3822) in the center of Stockbridge, which has a large permanent collection of Norman Rockwell paintings. The famed American illustrator did many pictures for magazine covers and posters, and the originals of those paintings, or at least many of them, are housed in the Old Corner House. Admission is $5 for adults, $1 for children ages 5 to 16, and it's open from 10 a.m. to 5 p.m. every day; closed last two weeks in January.

Other old houses worth a visit are the **Mission House** (1739), on Main Street (tel. 298-3239), built by the Rev. John Sergeant to carry out his Christian mission to the Indians. The house is a National Historic Landmark owned by the Trustees of Reservations, and is furnished in American pieces all dating from 1740 or earlier. It's open from Memorial Day through Columbus Day, Tuesday through Sunday and holidays from 11 a.m. to 4 p.m. Admission is $3 for adults, $1 for children 14 and under. Guided tours.

Naumkeag, on Prospect Hill, was built by Stanford White for Joseph Choate, an American ambassador to Great Britain, in 1886. It's now owned by the Trustees of Reservations (tel. 298-3239). Many of the sumptuous furnishings are still in place, and there are extensive formal gardens. Take Pine Street from the Red Lion Inn, then turn onto Prospect Street to reach Naumkeag. The palatial house is open weekends and holidays only from 10 a.m. to 5 p.m., Memorial Day to late June and

Labor Day to Columbus Day. From late June through Labor Day it's open daily (except Monday) from 10 a.m. to 5 p.m., with the last tour at 4:15 p.m. Admission is several dollars.

Right near Naumkeag is another sumptuous estate reached by the same route via Pine Street and Prospect. From its beginning as an Indian mission in 1734, the estate atop Eden Hill in Stockbridge has seen many additions over the years. Having served as a mansion for the wealthy and as a private school, it is now a monastery for the **Marian Fathers,** and visitors are welcome to stroll the grounds and take in the impressive buildings and the views of the Berkshire Hills.

Chesterwood

Just a few miles from Stockbridge is Chesterwood (tel. 298-3579), the former summer estate of Daniel Chester French, sculptor of the statue of Lincoln that graces the Lincoln Memorial, and also of the *Minute Man* statue at Concord North Bridge. French (1850–1931) summered here from 1897 until 1931 and used the studio (built in 1898) near the house for his work. You can visit both the mansion and studio as well as an 1800s barn which has been converted to a gallery featuring exhibits on French's life and work. A lovely period garden, a nature walk laid out by French himself, a panoramic view of Monument Mountain, and a museum store are unexpected extras to a Chesterwood visit. Admission fees go toward the upkeep of the property, which is maintained by the National Trust for Historic Preservation. Adults pay $4.50; children 7 to 18 pay $1; children under six admitted for free. Chesterwood is open daily from 10 a.m. to 5 p.m. May through October. To get there, drive west on Rte. 102 from Stockbridge, and follow the signs.

Berkshire Theater Festival

In the **Berkshire Playhouse** (tel. 413/298-5536) and in a big red barn close by, the Berkshire Theater Festival hosts a series of performances now in its second half century. From late-June through August, plays are staged Monday through Saturday evenings, and on Thursday and Saturday afternoons. The classic plays with name performers are in the Playhouse proper. The Unicorn Theater Company puts on experimental and new plays in the barn, and throughout the summer special children's theater performances are held outside, under a tent, Thursday through Saturday at noon.

Hancock Shaker Village

Ten miles north of West Stockbridge along Rte. 41, then west on U.S. 20, will bring you to the outskirts of Pittsfield, Mass., and Hancock Shaker Village, one of the most fascinating sights in the Berkshires. Here lived—right up until 1960—members of a religious sect noted for their quiet, simple lives, hard work, and quality handcrafts.

"The United Society of Believers in Christ's Second Appearing," "The Millennial Church," more readily known as the Shakers, was a movement begun in 1747 in England as an offshoot of Quakerism. It gained momentum when Ann Lee, "Mother Ann," proclaimed that she had received the "mother element" of the spirit of Christ. Imprisoned for her zeal, Mother Ann and eight followers later (1774) immigrated to the American colony of New York and founded a settlement near Albany. By the time Mother Ann died in 1784, her followers were ready to spread out and found other Shaker communities based on the principles of communal possessions, celibacy, pacifism, open confession of sins, and equality of the sexes. Organization of the communities was into "families" of 30 to 90 people. Work was a consecrated act, which accounts for the high quality of workmanship and design in Shaker furniture and crafts: in effect, every product was a prayer.

Shakers, named for the trembling that came upon them from their religious zeal, believed that God had both a male and female nature. The male was embodied in Jesus, the female in Mother Ann. Though a convert devoted himself and all his possessions to the community, he was free to leave at any time. Celibacy, less than effective in the spreading of a people or a belief, and the onslaught of the 20th century's complex lifestyle, almost put an end to Shakerism after more than two centuries; there are only a handful of the faithful left now, living in small communities in Maine and New Hampshire.

One cannot help but admire a gentle fanaticism which feeds on kindliness and good hard work. Shaker products are still copied and admired, because these good people took daily tasks to the level of an art. Twenty of the original Shaker buildings at Hancock have been restored, furnished with artifacts of Shaker life, and staffed with men and women who can explain and demonstrate the Shakers and their lives to you. Hancock Shaker Village, P.O. Box 898, Pittsfield, MA 01202 (tel. 413/ 443-0188), is open Memorial Day weekend through October from 9:30 a.m. to 5 p.m. every day; shorter hours during the rest of the year. Admission is $7.50 per adult, $3.50 for children 6 to 12, $6.75 for seniors, $20 for a family (two adults and children under 18). Don't miss it.

Skiing

There are at least six well-known downhill ski areas in the Berkshires. Call to get information on ski conditions and year round activities: **Butternut** (tel. 413/528-2000), **Bosquet** (tel. 413/442-8316), **Catamount** (tel. 413/582-1262), **Brodie** (tel. 413/443-4752), **Berkshire East** (tel. 413/339-6617), **Jiminy Peak** (tel. 413/738-5500), and **Otis Ridge** (tel. 413/269-4444).

8. Great Barrington and Egremont

Although it is certainly not a city, Great Barrington is the largest town in the southern Berkshires, a major crossroads and commercial center. Supplies and services that you might not find in Stockbridge or Lenox will be available here.

Great Barrington was an important town even before the Revolution. The citizenry, angered at Britain's denial of the colonials' rights, prevented the king's judges from convening in the courthouse here in 1774. In the 19th century Mr. and Mrs. Edward Searles became the town's benefactors, establishing many public buildings and constructing for themselves an immense mansion in a 100-acre park which nudges right into the center of town.

INFORMATION: There's a little information kiosk in the center of town, by the Berkshire Motor Inn and Searles' Castle, on Main Street. It's operated by the **Southern Berkshire Chamber of Commerce,** 362 Main St., Great Barrington, MA 01230 (tel. 413/528-1510). They'll help you find a room if you need one. Donations are accepted to defray expenses.

WHERE TO STAY: A short ride from the center of Great Barrington on the way to South Egremont are two of the Berkshires' best lodging places.

Inns and Guesthouses

Jo and Ray Elling run **Elling's Guest House,** R.D. 3, Box 6, Great Barrington, MA 01230 (tel. 413/528-4103), which is one mile from the center of town southwest along Rte. 23. The house, which dates from 1746, is actually more like an inn. The six rooms are all pretty and quaint; those with private bath rent for $80, and those with shared bath for $55. An extra person in a room pays $15. The rates go down $10 in winter, but whatever the season, a good continental breakfast is included. No credit cards or children under 12 accepted, by the way, and there is a two-night minimum stay on weekends in season. Quiet, friendly, reasonably priced, this is the best of the Berkshires.

A bit farther along the same road, 2½ miles from the center of town, is the **Seekonk Pines Inn,** 142 Seekonk Cross Rd., Great Barrington, MA 01230 (tel. 413/528-4192). As you come from town, look for it on the right-hand side, behind the pines. Linda and Chris Best are your hosts here, and their inn features a nice swimming pool, a garden from which they will sell you fresh produce, bicycles for rent; and in winter, a fireplace in the large living room, besides the cozy rooms. It's clean, neat, the rooms decorated with antiques, old quilts, and Linda's watercolors, and moderately priced at $69 to $74 for a room with shared bath. For the suite with sitting area and room for four to sleep (perfect for a family or couple on a longer visit), and with private bath, the price for four is $122. An extra person pays $15. Discounts are given on stays of five days or more.

Motels

Besides these fine guesthouses, Great Barrington has motels. Numerous establishments are spread along U.S. 7 north of town, and one luxurious place is right in the center.

The **Berkshire Motor Inn,** at 372 Main St., Great Barrington, MA 02130 (tel. 413/528-3150), is right behind the town information booth and across the street from Searles Castle. The two-story building holds rooms with all comforts priced at $48 to $58 double Sunday through Thursday, $90 on Friday and Saturday nights in summer. An indoor pool, sauna, and central location are the bonuses.

If you have a car, try the **Lantern House Motel,** P.O. Box 97, Great Barrington, MA 01230 (tel. 413/528-2350), which is on U.S. 7 north of town, on the right. Accommodations are quite good (room phone, AAA approved, and cable TV), and prices are moderate for the Berkshires in high season: $49 to $58 on weekdays, $72 to $84 on weekends.

An Inn in Egremont

The first thing you must know is that Egremont actually consists of two towns. North Egremont is a tiny place on Rte. 71, due west of Great Barrington. It has a country store, an inn-restaurant, and a few houses. South Egremont is a much bigger place, with several inns and restaurants, shops, and churches, and more antique dealers than you've ever seen in one place before. South Egremont, on Rtes. 23 and 41, is four miles southwest of Great Barrington.

A block off the highway in South Egremont (follow the signs) is the **Egremont Inn,** Old Sheffield Road, South Egremont, MA 01258 (tel. 413/528-2111), sometimes called the 1780 Egremont Inn. A stagecoach inn since the early days of the republic, the inn's 22 guest rooms now are fitted out with private baths and air conditioning, besides the period furnishings. A swimming pool and tennis courts provide entertainment the stagecoachmen never had. All of the village is within walking distance. Rooms are rented with continental breakfast and dinner included for $155 double on July and August weekends (two-night minimum). Monday through Wednesday you can rent a room with continental breakfast for $65 single, $90 double.

Staying in Sheffield

Eight miles south of Great Barrington is the **Staveleigh House,** South Main St., Sheffield, MA 01257 (tel. 413/229-2129). It's a homey bed and breakfast, run by two women who enjoy the slower pace of life in this quiet corner of the state. And their comfortable living room and simple but lovely guest rooms reflect this. Antiques are used here, not doted over. The innkeepers enjoy chatting with the guests, suggesting outings, and making sure repeat guests aren't served the same breakfast twice. Doubles cost $64 to $90, singles $5 less. Only one room has a private bath.

WHERE TO EAT: In the center of town on Rtes. 23 and 41 is the **Old Mill** (tel. 528-1421), which in this case is indeed an old mill (1797) and blacksmith's shop.

The rustic interior has been faithfully preserved, and rings to the conversation of diners every evening of the week. Much of the talk is of antiques, and the Old Mill menu sticks appropriately to the classics, though with original touches. Dinner with wine costs about $30 per person. Lunch is served on Saturday and Sunday.

READER'S RESTAURANT RECOMMENDATION: "At **D & J's American Grill,** at the intersections of Rts. 23 and 7 north, Great Barrington (tel. 528-3201) you can get half a barbecued chicken for $7 or great barbecued ribs for $8 to $10. The place isn't fancy but it's an excellent grill" (Jenny Schmalz, Somerville, Mass.). [*Author's Note:* Located at 11 Stockbridge Road; open 11:30 a.m. to 9 p.m. every day but Wednesday.]

WHAT TO SEE AND DO: Great Barrington and South Egremont are the antiquer's towns par excellence. Everyone here, it seems, deals in antiques and old stuff. Browsing the shops is the daily passion, but several excursions out of town to nature spots provide an antidote to buy-and-sell.

Take U.S. 7 south from Great Barrington for about ten miles, and turn onto Rte. 7A for Ashley Falls. Your destination, a mile from Ashley Falls along Rannpo and Weatogue Roads, is **Bartholomew's Cobble,** bordering the Housatonic River. A "cobble" in this case is a high knoll of limestone, marble, or quartzite, 500 million years old, and covered with a rich and varied collection of native flora: trees, ferns, mosses, wildflowers. The nature reservation is owned by the Trustees of Reservations (tel. 229-8600), is open year round, and has six miles of hiking trails. A naturalist is on duty from mid-April to mid-October, Wednesday through Sunday from 9 a.m. to 5 p.m. to answer your questions and point out highlights.

Another pretty nature nook, good for a picnic, is **Bash Bish Falls,** 12 miles southwest of South Egremont, right on the New York state line. Take Rte. 41 south out of town, and turn right onto Mount Washington Road (signs for Catamount ski area). Follow signs to the falls, taking East Street, then West Street, and finally Bash Bish Falls Road, deep in the Mount Washington State Forest. You'll plunge into the valley carved by the Bash Bish Creek, and finally come to a parking area from which a steep trail leads to the falls. Stay on the road a bit farther and you'll come to another parking place, and an easier—but longer—trail. Stay on the road any longer and you'll end up in New York.

At the end of the trails, deep in the forest, is the 50-foot Bash Bish Falls, cascading into a chilly pool. A half hour's relaxation here on a hot summer's day is pretty close to Nirvana.

If mountain hiking is more to your taste, head north out of Great Barrington on U.S. 7, and after 4½ miles you'll see signs for **Monument Mountain.** There are two trails to the summit, one easier but slightly longer than the other. The hike to the top, a rest, and back down will take between two and three hours. The view at the summit is very fine.

9. Williamstown

The home of famous Williams College is also one of the prettiest towns in New England, a town of hills and dales and emerald greenswards. Besides the college, Williamstown has a noted theater festival and a fine art museum.

GETTING THERE: Most readers will be circulating throughout the Berkshires or southern Vermont, when they visit Williamstown. But if you are coming directly from Boston, contact **Bonanza Bus Lines** (tel. toll-free 800/556-3815 or 617/423-5810 in Boston). You may have to change buses in Springfield or Pittsfield.

WHERE TO STAY AND DINE: Far enough from Tanglewood to avoid the crush,

Williamstown is favored with a fine selection of small guesthouses and inns, moderately priced motels, and a full-service hotel. You should have little trouble finding the sort of room you want in this charming Berkshire town.

Small Inns and Guesthouses

My favorite place in all Williamstown is the **River Bend Farm,** 643 Simonds Rd., Williamstown, MA 01267 (tel. 413/458-5504 or 458-3121). This old roadside inn and tavern-turned-farmhouse is being restored lovingly by Dave and Judy Loomis. There are five rooms (sharing two baths) to rent to guests, at $53 double. True country-inn feeling without the commercial hype, River Bend Farm is just over one mile north of Williamstown's Information Booth, along U.S. 7; turn left onto the private drive immediately after crossing a bridge over the river. Open April through November.

Downtown next to the Williams Inn is **The House on Main Street,** 1120 Main St., Williamstown, MA 01267 (tel. 413/458-3031), a nice old Victorian recently renovated by Henny Poses and open in the warm months to provide "bed-and-breakfast for the carriage trade." Two of the guest rooms have private bath, the other two share 1½ baths. Because Williams College parents know about the House, you must reserve in advance. Prices are $55 single for a room with shared bath, $65 to $80 double, breakfast included.

A Motel

Right downtown in Williamstown, cheek by jowl with the Williams Inn, is the **Northside Inn Motel,** a few steps north of the junction of Rtes. 2 and 7, at 45 North St., Williamstown, MA 01267 (tel. 413/458-8107). The Northside is a neat little motel of one and two stories, with a small pool, and rooms equipped with individual thermostat, air conditioning, ceramic tile bath, cable color TV, and telephone. It's open all year, and charges $51 to $55 for a double room, the higher prices being for larger rooms with two double beds. For convenience, there's a motel coffeeshop for breakfast.

The Big One

Fanciest place to stay in Williamstown is the **Williams Inn,** right in the middle of town at the intersection of Rtes. 2 and 7, Williamstown, MA 01267 (tel. 413/458-9371). Although built only a few years ago, the feeling at the inn is like that at any other luxury hotel in a New England college town: full comfort, touches of elegance, colonial atmosphere. There are over 100 modern rooms, all air-conditioned and all equipped with shiny full baths and cable color TVs; an indoor swimming pool and sauna, and live entertainment in the lounge on weekends, are extra attractions. Perhaps the greatest attraction of all, though, is the inn's location within easy walking distance of everything—ideal when the town is just made for walking. Room prices are $69 to $79 single, $95 to $111 double. Remember that rooms in Williamstown are more difficult to find during special college functions such as reunions, graduation, and major football games.

A Restaurant

Williamstown has a small commercial district artfully hidden away on Spring Street (take Rte. 2 east—that's Main Street—from the intersection with U.S. 7, and look for Spring Street on the right). Here is where you'll find a tavern, a sandwich shop, and various stores. Follow Spring Street to its end, turn left onto Latham Street, and go down to the "T" at Water Street. Turn right and you'll see the **River House,** 123 Water St. (tel. 458-4820). Williamstown's most popular downtown restaurant, the River House is open Tuesday through Saturday from 4 p.m. to midnight, on Sunday and holidays from 4 to 10 p.m. Prices are moderate, the wine and spirits list is long, and the menu has something for everybody. Have spaghetti, roast turkey, or baked scrod for dinner, and you'll get a salad, garlic bread, and rice pilaf with it for less than $9. In the evening, complete dinners from soup to dessert are priced from $9 to $16: lots of beef entrees, chops, fish, and several Italian dishes are featured. Special platters for children under 12 and seniors (over 60) are a money-saving extra. Sandwiches and light meals served at all hours.

WHAT TO SEE AND DO: Take a walk around the **Williams College** campus. The college was founded in 1793, and named for Col. Ephraim Williams, a colonial soldier and early resident of the area. Although known as a private men's college, Williams has been coed for several years now.

For a small town in the Berkshires, Williamstown has a surprising number of cultural offerings. For instance, the **Clark Art Institute** (tel. 413/458-9545), on South Street, has a very fine collection of the impressionists, and also a good number of paintings by the old masters. The 19th-century French paintings are the strong point of the collection, but you may easily run into a Dürer, a work by Winslow Homer, or something by Memling. The Clark Art Institute is open all year, Tuesday through Sunday from 10 a.m. to 5 p.m. (closed Monday), and admission is free.

Williams College also has quite a **Museum of Art** (tel. 597-2429) in Lawrence Hall on Main Street, open Monday through Saturday from 10 a.m. to 5 p.m. and on Sunday from 1 to 5 p.m., admission free. Lawrence Hall is a Greek Revival building with a rotunda, easy to spot as you stroll along Main Street.

The **Williamstown Theatre Festival** (tel. 413/597-3400 for the box office) is staged during the summer months in the college's **Adams Memorial Theater** on Main Street. The festival has seen over three decades, with many famous performers (all are members of Actors Equity) taking the stage. Plays—over 45 per season—are on through July and August. During the college year the theater is used for collegiate productions which are also of a high caliber. For festival information, write to P.O. Box 517, Williamstown, MA 01267.

No matter if the weather is clear or cloudy, stroll over to the **Milham Planetarium** in the Hopkins Observatory Building on Main Street. The observatory itself is the oldest astronomical observatory in the United States. Mid-June through mid-August on two evenings each week the planetarium has free celestial shows; from October through May, when college is in session, shows are on Friday evenings.

RHODE ISLAND

1. PROVIDENCE
2. NEWPORT
3. NARRAGANSETT BAY
4. BLOCK ISLAND
5. WATCH HILL

Just because Rhode Island is the smallest state in the Union, many people assume that this in some way limits the variety of things one can see and do in this corner of New England. Not so. The state's beaches are famed throughout the region, sites and structures of historical importance abound, the cities are pleasant and of manageable size, and then there's Newport—a world apart. In fact, the only real effects the state's small size seem to have are to make the residents feel that they are a part of a very special place—which they are—and to make everything easily accessible to the visitor.

In the 1600s, when New England was being colonized by Europeans, the best solution to a community conflict was for the weaker of the conflicting parties to shove off into the wilderness and found and develop his own community. To save his skin and freely express his beliefs, Roger Williams left Puritan Salem in 1636 and came to Narragansett Bay, followed soon afterward by others who shared his views, or at least knew they would be allowed to disagree. Williams was way ahead of the times in his political, religious, and ethical thinking, and his contribution to the American democratic tradition is very important: in his new community of Providence, a man could think and say what he liked. In the years that followed the founding of Providence, Williams persuaded Parliament to include the settlements of Portsmouth and Newport on Rhode Island with his own Providence Plantation under the same charter—these towns had also been founded by dissenters who desired freedom of thought and speech thus securing to the colony as a whole the right of absolute liberty in matters of belief. The official name of the state to this day remains "Rhode Island and Providence Plantations."

Today Rhode Island is a manufacturing center, a maritime state, with a lot of rich agricultural land and several industries of importance. But the summer vacationers who come to Rhode Island—beginning with the very wealthy socialites who started the custom in the 19th century—are also an important part of the economy, and the state government does a lot to see that "Little Rhodie" retains the lure it had for those discriminating types who built palatial mansions in Newport, Watch Hill, and other coastal towns.

INFORMATION: You can get Rhode Island tourist information toll free by calling 800/556-2484 from any state between Maine and Virginia. By the way, the room tax in Rhode Island varies from only a few percent in Providence to a whopping 11% in Block Island and Watch Hill. The tax will be added to your hotel bill.

1. Providence

Providence is a pretty city. The downtown area is compact enough that a visitor can get off the train, or park the car, and walk to just about everything there is to see and do. The State Capitol, a pleasant and harmonious building of white Georgia marble, crowns a hilltop on the edge of the downtown section. College Hill rises from the east bank of the Providence River, which runs through downtown; Brown University, the Rhode Island School of Design, and a collection of exceptionally beautiful and interesting houses from the 17th, 18th, and 19th centuries give College Hill its character.

The city was founded in 1636 by Roger Williams (1603–83), who had been minister of the church at Salem, Mass., but whose free-thinking religious ideas had made the General Court banish him from Massachusetts Bay. (He held that the Massachusetts Bay charter was not legal, and that the Puritans should face the fact that they had really separated from the Church of England, whether they chose to admit it or not; and he said that in matters of conscience no civil authority had any power —no wonder the powers-that-be thought him a dangerous man!) Because of his own belief in free-thinking, he dedicated his new settlement of Providence to the proposition that all people should have freedom of conscience. A good number came from Massachusetts, and others came directly from England, to the new colony. Williams had bought the land for the town from the Narragansett Indians, and he remained on very good terms with them, even writing a book on their language which was published and sold in England.

Providence became the first colony to declare independence from England, in May 1776. After the Revolutionary War it took over from Newport the position as the state's most important seaport. It's still an important port, and its industries of textiles, machine tools, rubber, jewelry, and boatbuilding also contribute to its prosperity.

The telephone area code for all of Rhode Island is 401. The sales tax is 6%. Some municipalities levy a room tax of up to 11% as well.

GETTING THERE: Getting to Providence couldn't be easier, whether you're going by car or public transport.

By Car

I-95 goes right through the center of Providence on its way between New York and Boston; right downtown I-195 branches off to go through Fall River (turnoff for Newport), New Bedford, and then on to Cape Cod.

Note on Parking: Street parking in Providence is scarce, and meters are checked frequently. The center of town has lots of private pay lots, which it is best to use if you park downtown. Otherwise, park on a side street on College Hill, where there's plenty of shade and no time limit.

By Rail

The new, modern, white marble **Amtrak** railroad station (tel. 401/751-5416) in Providence is right at the base of the state capitol's southwest lawn, a five- or ten-minute walk from Kennedy Plaza. The old Union Station overlooking Kennedy Plaza is presently under restoration, but it will no longer be a railroad station. Ten trains a day in each direction pass through on their way between New York and Boston. Travel time from New York is less than four hours; from Boston, about an hour. You can, if you want, take an early-morning train from New York, get off in Providence and stroll around downtown and College Hill for several hours, have lunch, get back on the train, and be in Boston by four in the afternoon.

By Bus

The **Bonanza Bus Station** (tel. 401/751-8800) is a block from Kennedy Plaza. **(Greyhound/Trailways** uses this same terminal.) Bonanza and Greyhound run buses to Providence from New York City, Boston, Newport, Hartford, Cape Cod, Springfield (Mass.), and Albany. Travel time from New York is about four hours; from Boston it's one hour. A bus from Providence to Newport takes just over an hour; to Cape Cod (Hyannis) the trip takes an hour and a half.

By Air

Rhode Island is so compact that one airport handles all the important national flights: **T. F. Green State Airport** in Warwick, just a few miles south of Providence. From the airport you'll have to take a taxi to the center of Providence.

TOURIST INFORMATION: The people to ask are at the **Greater Providence Convention and Visitors Bureau,** 30 Exchange Terrace, Providence, RI 02903 (tel. 401/274-1636). Drop by, or telephone them, with any of your questions about the city.

WHERE TO STAY: Most people who visit Providence stay in motels on the outskirts of town as these offer the best value and the greatest selection, although staying out of the center entails driving and parking problems. Providence does have a choice place to stay right downtown, plus a few of the familiar and comfortable chain hotels.

Providence has a 4% room tax which, when added to the 6% state sales tax, increases the price of any Providence hotel room by 10%.

A Bed-and-Breakfast Inn

The **Old Court,** 144 Benefit St., Providence, RI 02903 (tel. 401/751-2002 or 351-0747), at the corner of North Court Street, is a handsome old three-story brick mansion only a short walk from downtown, on the slopes of College Hill. The house was built in 1863 as a rectory, but takes its name from the old Rhode Island Courthouse next door, which now houses the Rhode Island Historical Preservation Commission. The inn itself is a fine example of historic preservation, as all of its Italianate features such as 12-foot ceilings, plaster moldings, crystal chandeliers, brass sconces, and ornately carved marble mantelpieces, are in place. Furnishings in the spacious, airy guest rooms are true to the period, with wallpapers sporting large flowered patterns, antique-style telephones, and old-fashioned alarm clocks. But the full tiled baths attached to each room (often installed in what were formerly walk-in closets) are thoroughly modern in plumbing and fixtures. Some rooms have air conditioners. The price for a double room, including breakfast served in the pretty ground-floor breakfast room, is $117. This place is very nicely done, and quite charming.

Downtown Hotels

Right on Kennedy Plaza in the center of Providence is the **Omni Biltmore Hotel** (tel. 401/421-0700, or toll free 800/228-2121), Providence, RI 02903. The Biltmore was the most elegant hotel in Providence when it was built in 1922, and after a recent $14-million renovation, it's Providence's poshest place to stay once again Of the 289 rooms and suites, 120 have their own lounge areas; 14 are de-

signed especially for the handicapped. If you knew the Biltmore before, you'll hardly recognize it now, as much has been changed, although the outstanding features of 1920s elegance have been carefully preserved. Even the façade has seen a change, for now a glass-enclosed elevator starts from the hotel lobby, penetrates the three-story-high lobby ceiling, and glides up the side of the 18-floor hotel to the top. Rooms at the Biltmore cost $120 to $150 single, $140 to $170 double, with the highest prices going for the luxurious rooms. Ask about reduced weekend rates.

Another centrally located hotel is the downtown **Providence Holiday Inn,** at 21 Atwells Ave., Providence, RI 02903 (tel. 401/831-3900), right next to the Civic Center. The 13-story handicapped-accessible hotel has 274 rooms, a restaurant, a lounge with live entertainment, and an indoor pool. The bus and train stations are less than half a mile away. Rooms cost $100 to $105 single, $111 to $117 double; if a couple takes the higher-priced room (with two double beds), teenage children or younger can stay in the same room for free.

A Bed-and-Breakfast Service

Bed & Breakfast of Rhode Island, P.O. Box 3291, Newport, RI 02840 (tel. 401/941-0444), will find a room for you near Providence or any other Rhode Island town. Rates depend on the room, of course, but range from $45 to $90 single, $50 to $100 double.

On the Outskirts

Most of Providence's hotel capacity is on the outskirts of greater Providence, in the neighboring cities of Warwick near the airport to the south, Pawtucket to the north toward Boston on I-95, and Seekonk, Mass., on I-195, the road to Cape Cod. As most of these hotels and motels are right off the highway, it would be good to pick them according to your plans for *tomorrow:* if it's evening as you approach Providence, stay in Warwick and then see Providence the next day; if it's early in the day, tour through Providence and then head out I-95 to Pawtucket if your next stop is Boston, or I-195 to Seekonk if you're headed for Cape Cod. You can call for a reservation while you're seeing the sights in Providence.

Warwick has one of the five **Howard Johnson Motor Lodges** in the Providence area. This one is at 20 Jefferson Blvd., Warwick, RI 02888 (tel. 401/467-9800, or toll free 800/654-2000), which is at Exit 15 of I-95, near T. F. Green State Airport. There's a 24-hour restaurant, a lounge with entertainment, and a variety of package plans which can save you lots of money, particularly on weekends. Seniors get a discount; kids under 18 stay for free. Rates are $80 single, $91 double.

In Pawtucket your best bet is the local **Howard Johnson Motor Lodge,** a stone's throw off I-95 (Exit 27) at 2 George St., Pawtucket, RI 02860 (tel. 401/723-6700, or toll free 800/654-2000). The lodge charges $81 single, $92 double; an extra person is $10. Children under 18 can use their parents' room for free. The lodge has an indoor heated pool, a sauna, and an adjacent Hojo's restaurant open 24 hours a day.

In Seekonk, Mass., there are several good lodging possibilities. Note that you have a different telephone area code (508) to contend with if you're calling from Rhode Island. Take Exit 114A from I-195 for these.

Next best bet is the **Howard Johnson Motor Lodge** in Seekonk at the intersection of I-195 and Rte. 114A, 821 Fall River Ave., Seekonk, MA 02771 (tel. 508/336-7800, or toll free 800/654-2000). Facilities and rates are very similar to those in the Pawtucket Lodge mentioned above, but rooms with one bed (accommodating one or two people) are cheaper here: $64 single, $74 double. In the winter (November through April) special weekend package rates are offered. The lodge has no restaurant of its own, but there are several nearby.

There is also a **Ramada Inn** here, very close to the Howard Johnson at 940 Fall River Ave. (which is Rte. 114A), Seekonk, MA 02771 (tel. 508/336-7300, or toll free 800/228-2828). The Ramada is structured and priced very competitively, with pool, sauna, lounge with live entertainment, and a children's playground, all costing $85 single, $95 double; kids 18 and under stay free.

Budget Lodgings

A family-run set of motels in Seekonk, operated by the Darling family, are on U.S. 6 near the intersection of Alternate Rte. 114 (114-A), Seekonk, MA 02771. The **Esquire** and **Town 'n' Country Motels** are right across the highway from one another (tel. 508/336-9000) and share an outdoor pool, open during the warm months. Rooms are brightly painted and have individual air-conditioning units. The motels also share a putting green, coffeeshop, and cocktail lounge, as well as Eileen Darling's Restaurant. Rates for the rooms are $44 for one double bed, $49 for two double beds—one of the better bargains in the area.

WHERE TO DINE: Providence's sophisticated university crowd generates a need for good restaurants, and Providence has plenty. Not all of them are up on College Hill, however.

Downtown Restaurants

"The best of Paris in the heart of Providence" are the words used to describe the **Pot au Feu,** 44 Custom House St. (tel. 273-8953), off Weybosset Street, not far from Providence's famous Arcade. This is actually two restaurants in one. Upstairs is the Salon, an elegant dining room with high ceilings, gold chandelier, tall windows, spotless linen napery, fresh flowers, glistening crystal, and hushed, professional service. Downstairs is a dusky, brick-lined pub called Le Bistro. In the Salon, a sumptuously long menu of French classics and nouvelle cuisine dishes is presented for your delectation. There's salmon filet in lemon butter, poached in white wine with shallots, parsley, and essence of anchovies; and veal chops in a sauce of shiitake mushrooms, shallots, ginger, and heavy cream. One of the menu's best features is the provision whereby one can order a main course either à la carte or prix fixe. Ordering prix fixe costs somewhat more, but entitles you to choices from the other five courses at no additional cost. Thus you can have an appetizer, soup, salad, main course, dessert, and coffee for as little as $40 to $50 per person, tax, tip, and wine included. This is the perfect method if you are not ravenously hungry, for the prix-fixe portions of soup, salad, etc., are smaller than the normal à la carte portions.

In Le Bistro, the menu is just as long, and almost as elegant, but cheaper. Dinner downstairs might cost $25 to $35 per person, all in.

Lunch is served in the Salon from 11:30 a.m. to 2 p.m. Monday through Friday; dinner is on from 6 to 9 p.m. Tuesday through Thursday, till 10 p.m. on Friday and Saturday. The Salon is closed Sunday and Monday, but Le Bistro is open and serving brunch, lunch, and dinner seven days a week.

On the ground floor of the Omni Biltmore Hotel on Kennedy Plaza is **Stanford's** (tel. 272-6581), named for Stanford White, the famed architect who designed the Rhode Island State Capitol, the Newport and Narragansett casinos, and the original Madison Square Garden. Stanford's is "an American Bar and Grille," but both its food and decor are quite eclectic. This is a place where you can truly take your choice: take a seat in the modern café section, all bright colors, angles and split-levels, openness and coziness; or in the more formal salon; or even in the private dining room. Then choose from a long menu which includes prime rib, many steaks, and jumbo shrimp. Expect to spend $15 to $30, all included, for lunch or dinner here. Stanford's is open for breakfast, lunch, cocktails, and dinner, every day of the week.

Light Lunch, Downtown

The place to go if you're just interested in an informal bite is **The Arcade,** 65 Weybosset St. (tel. 456-5403). This National Historic Landmark was built in 1828, a Greek Revival shopping arcade running between Weybosset and Westminster

Streets, with three stories of shops surmounted by a glass canopy. The Arcade's ground floor is nothing but food shops, including the following: the China Inn, specializing in Chinese food to eat here or take out; the Grand Central Café, serving hot and cold beverages and pastries; Hot Dogs & More; the Providence Cookie Co.; Periwinkles, which has a very full sandwich menu; Villa Pizza; the Grog Boy Bar for stronger stuff; Natural Sweetness, a vegetarian restaurant; Great Soups, which serves just that; The Ritz, serving Middle Eastern pocket bread sandwiches; Le Greque, with a full menu of Greek dishes; Baby Watson, nationally famous for its cheesecake and other desserts; and Créme de la Créme, which may not have the right French accents, but has wonderful ice cream and candy nonetheless. It's difficult to spend more than $10 per person for lunch at the Arcade, and easy to fill up for $5 or $6.

Up on College Hill

Providence consumes almost as much succulent seafood as Newport, and a lot of the best seafood in Providence disappears at **Bluepoint**, an oyster bar and restaurant at 99 North Main St., corner of Elizabeth (tel. 272-6145), between Steeple and Meeting Streets. The one-room restaurant, with the oyster-and-spirits bar on the right as you enter, is usually filled with a classy young clientele talking but mostly eating. The clam chowder comes red Provençal (with tomatoes) or New England (with cream and potatoes) for $4.25. Oysters, a half dozen of any variety of your choice on the half shell, are $6.25 to $7.25; littleneck and cherrystone clams are a bit less. The list of main courses on the blackboard is very short because the daily specials are what most people order. The specials, whether they be squid, grilled prawns, swordfish, bluefish, or scallops, constitute the best and freshest seafood at the lowest price. Dinner will cost about $25 to $30 per person here, a bit more if you drink lots of wine or beer, a bit less if you order carefully. Bluepoint is an easy walk from downtown, and is open for dinner only, Sunday through Thursday from 6 to 11 p.m., to 11:30 p.m. on Friday and Saturday; the bar is open from 5 p.m. to 1 a.m. daily.

Another fine place for lunch or dinner is about ten blocks from Brown University. It's French in character and French in name: **Rue de L'Espoir,** at 99 Hope St. (tel. 751-8890), and it's open daily except Monday (Tuesday through Sunday from 11:30 a.m. to 2:30 p.m.; Saturday and Sunday brunch served). The menu offers perfect things for a light French-style lunch: several types of quiche, pasta, their own pâté, omelets, crêpes, vegetarian dishes, seafood, salads, and portions of cheese and bread—all in the $4 to $6 range. Fare at dinner includes filet mignon, brochettes, fish terrines, roast pork loins; prices are a bit higher, with several dinner plates priced at about $9 to $18. A full bar is available, and all desserts and pastries are made on the premises.

WHAT TO SEE: Preservation and urban redevelopment have done much to make Providence a delightful place to walk in today. The most interesting districts are small enough that you can make your way around on foot. For an expert look at Providence's historical treasures, consider the following:

Walking Tours

The **Providence Preservation Society,** 21 Meeting St. (tel. 401/831-7440), offers two audio cassettes and seven self-guided walking-tour booklets of historical areas in the city. Areas include Benefit Street, with its restored 18th- and 19th-century houses, the downtown section with its 19th- and 20th-century architecture, the waterfront, Brown University, and three Victorian neighborhoods named Armory District, Elmwood, and Broadway. Rent a cassette for $3.50 or buy the booklets for 80¢ each at the society's headquarters, Monday through Friday from 9 a.m. to 5 p.m. In spring and fall, society members lead guided walking tours of these and other areas. Call for details.

Seeing Providence, Old and New

The place to start touring Providence is **Kennedy Plaza,** in the center of town. Shady trees and benches make the plaza an oasis in the middle of the city, and an equestrian statue of Gen. Ambrose Burnside, the Civil War officer whose long side whiskers were the first "sideburns," watches over the eastern end of the plaza. **City Hall** is at the other end, an agreeable Second Empire building completed in 1878 (go inside to see a wall display of other entries in the competition for the city hall design).

From Kennedy Plaza to College Hill

Go one block southeast from the plaza to reach the **Westminster Mall,** a six-block section of Westminster Street closed to vehicles. The mall is a pleasant place to sit and people-watch, or to stroll down. Just past its eastern end, at 130 Westminster St., is the **Arcade,** which looks like an imaginative bit of urban renewal, but is in fact the creation of Russell Warren and James Bucklin, who designed the building in 1827. For a century and a half some of Providence's better shops have operated in the Arcade. There are three levels of shops topped by a roof of glass panes; one modern addition to the Arcade is an elevator to take shoppers to the upper floors. Besides restaurants, the Arcade has stores selling antiques, jewelry, rare books, fine tobaccos, cosmetics, and other luxury items. Decorative cast-iron balustrades and stairways remind one of the Arcade's early–19th-century construction. Look at both façades—on Westminster Street and on Weybosset—which clearly show that each architect had his own idea of how the façade should look. With two façades, each got his chance to do what he wanted.

Walk through the Arcade from Westminster Street to Weybosset Street, and turn right to get to Providence's historic **"Round Top" Church**—you'll see its golden dome in the distance. The church, officially known as the Beneficent Congregational Meeting House, got its name because of its dome, which is a departure from the usual New England church spire. Finished in 1810, it was influenced by the classical revival then going on in Europe. The interior is as pleasant to look at as the exterior: besides the gracious New England meetinghouse furnishings, the Round Top Church has a crystal chandelier consisting of almost 6,000 pieces. (Enter by the door on the side, around to the right.)

Now head northeast down Weybosset, past the Arcade, to the intersection of this street with Westminster and Exchange. Here in front of the Hospital Trust Bank activities and shows are held during the warm months, perhaps a Boy Scouts' display of fancy marching or a small (but highly amplified) jazz combo giving a lunch-hour concert.

College Hill

Walk two more blocks east and you will cross the Providence River to the foot of **College Hill.** The hill is the prettiest section of the city, its streets lined with 18th- and 19th-century houses, most of which have been well preserved or restored, many of which bear plaques put up by the Providence Preservation Society giving the builder's name and the date of construction. At the bottom of College Hill, on South Main Street between Thomas and Waterman Streets, take a stroll past the **First Baptist Meetinghouse.** Roger Williams founded the first Baptist congregation in the New World in 1638, but this building dates from 1775. The architect was Joseph Brown, and the steeple—designed from a plate in James Gibbs's *Book of Architecture* representing suggested steeples for St. Martin-in-the-Fields in London —rises to a height of 185 feet. It's one of the outstanding churches in New England, and a guide will take you through for free between the hours of 10 a.m. and 3 p.m. Monday through Friday, 10 a.m. to noon on Saturday, and at noon on Sunday following the weekly church service. Between November and March the church is open daily, but guides are available only by appointment. Call 751-2266 for an appointment. The front door of the church will probably be locked, so go around to the right to the side (office) door.

To the left of the church, at 7 Thomas St., is a fantastic old building with half-timbering and stucco bas-reliefs on its façade. This is **Sidney Burleigh's "Fleur de Lys" house,** built by this Providence artist in 1885 (the date is in the stucco). Thomas Street might be called "artists' row," because very near Burleigh's house is the Providence Art Club, at no. 11, which is open from 10 a.m. to 4 p.m. (3 to 5 p.m. on Sunday), with changing shows exhibited in its galleries. The Providence Watercolor Club is also on Thomas Street.

At the intersection of Waterman and Benefit Streets, turn right and go south on Benefit for a block to the **Museum of Art, Rhode Island School of Design,** at 224 Benefit St. (tel. 331-3511, ext. 360). RISD's museum is Providence's finest, and one of the best small museums in the country, with collections from Greece and Rome, China and Japan; paintings by Manet, Monet, Degas, Cézanne, Matisse, as well as by other masters; and a good collection of American painting, furniture, costumes, and modern works of art. Of the choicest pieces in this impressive collection, Rodin's famous statue of Balzac ranks high, as does Monet's *Bassin d'Argenteuil* and the collection of Townsend/Goddard furniture in Pendleton House, the museum's "American Wing." You can see all this for $1 for adults, 50¢ for senior citizens, 25¢ for children and youths (5 to 18), free for small children. The museum is always closed Monday. *Special note:* Admission is *free* on Saturday. Otherwise, hours are rather complicated. From mid-June through August, hours are noon to 5 p.m. Wednesday through Saturday; the rest of the year, the museum is open on Tuesday, Wednesday, Friday, and Saturday from 10:30 a.m. to 5 p.m., on Thursday from noon to 8 p.m., and on Sunday from 2 to 5 p.m.

The **Rhode Island School of Design** (RISD, known in Providence as *"riz-dee"*) is one of the country's best art, architecture, and design schools (founded in 1877), and it shares College Hill with Brown University (see below).

RISD has another attractive building besides its museum dedicated to the display of art. It's the **Woods-Gerry Mansion,** 62 Prospect St., which was built between 1860 and 1864 and now serves as RISD's administration building and gallery for students' works of art. Admission is free and the galleries are open Monday through Saturday from 11 a.m. to 4 p.m., on Sunday from 2 to 5 p.m. (except in summer when they're open weekdays only; closed all of August). The big old brick-and-brownstone mansion is empty of its plush furnishings now, but parquet floors and gorgeous marble fireplaces give an idea of what it must have been like, and the high-ceilinged rooms with large windows provide perfect space for exhibiting students' efforts: drawings, paintings, sculpture, or what-have-you, all guaranteed to be the most *avant* of the avant-garde. The grounds of the mansion are covered with grand shade trees and rhododendron bushes (which bloom in late June and early July), and dotted with pieces of sculpture and benches for a welcome rest. The museum is closed in August.

Another RISD building open to the public is the **Bayard Ewing Building,** 231 S. Main St., which houses RISD's architectural division. Exhibits here change frequently, and feature architectural and industrial design.

Also up here on College Hill is **Brown University** (tel. 863-1000), a member of the Ivy League, and the seventh-oldest university in the country. Founded in 1764, Brown's first building was University Hall, used as a barracks for Colonial and

French soldiers during the American Revolution. It's now a National Historic Landmark. To get to it, walk up the hill (east) on Waterman Street, cross Prospect Street, and turn into the gates on your right. Do you want a full, free tour of the beautiful and historic campus? Find your way to the College Admission Office, one block from University Hall at the corner of Prospect and Angell Streets. Tours depart from here at 10 and 11 a.m., and 1, 3, and 4 p.m.

Prospect Street is so named because it passes near **Prospect Terrace** (go north a block from Woods-Gerry House to Cushing Street and turn left). From the Terrace, a small park, you can see downtown Providence and the State Capitol, along with a famous but—pardon me—rather wooden statue of the founder, Roger Williams. His grave is here as well. Trees have grown up below and block a bit of the perspective, but the view is still panoramic and impressive.

College Hill has lots of other places to see including many historic houses. One of the fanciest of these is the **John Brown House,** 52 Power St. at Benefit Street (tel. 331-8575), a late-Georgian mansion constructed in 1786 and now owned and operated by the Rhode Island Historical Society. Proclaimed by John Quincy Adams to be "the most magnificent and elegant private mansion that I have seen on this continent," this restored house-museum reveals the prosperity of post-Revolutionary Providence and houses an outstanding collection of furnishings and decorative arts. John Brown was a merchant whose ships plied the seas both east and west out of Narragansett Bay and ultimately made him a wealthy man. The Brown family, by the way, had been prominent in Providence commerce and industry since the early 1700s. John's brother, Moses, joined with Samuel Slater to set up the first water-powered cotton mill in America in 1790, now known as Slater Mill (see below). One of his nephews, Nicholas Brown, was a graduate of Rhode Island College, which was later renamed Brown College (and later, University) in his honor. John Brown House is open Tuesday through Saturday from 11 a.m. to 4 p.m., on Sunday from 1 to 4 p.m.; closed holidays. Admission and guided tour costs $2.50 for adults, $1 for seniors and students. Combination tickets good for a visit to both the John Brown House and the Aldrich House (see below) are on sale as well.

The Rhode Island Historical Society (tel. 331-8575) also operates the **Museum of Rhode Island History,** in the Aldrich House, a Federal-style mansion (1822) at 110 Benevolent St. The museum holds changing exhibitions highlighting various aspects of Rhode Island, its history, and its citizens. Hours are Monday through Saturday from 11 a.m. to 4 p.m., and on Sunday from 1 to 4 p.m.; closed holidays. Adults pay $2 for admission; students and seniors pay $1; families pay a maximum of $5.

The State Capitol

Rhode Island government was conducted in the Old State House (1762), on North Main Street between North and South Court Streets, from 1762 to 1895 when the new State Capitol building was dedicated. The Capitol is a pleasant sight, its tall dome floating over the Providence skyline, its white Georgia marble gleaming in the sun. Whether it is "the most beautiful in the country," as the state's tourist brochures claim, might be disputed by admirers of 49 other such capitols, but certainly it is one of the more beautiful. Enter by the portal on Smith Street (Rte. 44) to see display cases filled with battle flags from the state's proud military units which served in the Civil War, Spanish-American War, and the World Wars. Here also is a cannon that was used in the Civil War and was hit right in the muzzle by another cannon's ball. When the crew tried to charge the cannon again, they put the powder and wad in and first they couldn't get the ball in; then they couldn't get the ball *out*. The gun was retired, but it was only in the 1960s, when the cannon had been here in the Capitol for decades, that someone remembered that the gunpowder charge was still in it! So after 100 years of having been loaded and ready, the Civil War charge was removed. Beyond the cannons is the rich, gleaming marble interior and hallways decorated with paintings of the founding fathers of Rhode Island and Providence Plantations. Free tours of the capitol are offered on weekdays from 9 a.m. to 4:30 p.m. (last tour at 3:30). It's worth seeing.

Sights on the Outskirts

Two more places to visit lie a few miles outside the center of town. **Roger Williams Park** is south of the city on Elmwood Avenue (Exit 17 from I-95), and boasts magnificently restored 19th-century Victorian buildings, the **Charles E. Smith Greenhouses,** a museum of natural history, zoo, and amusement area besides its 430 acres of beautifully kept lawns, copses, lakes, and paths. The park is open to the public for free, and special concerts and programs are scheduled throughout the summer—call 401/785-9450 for the latest information on these. The zoo, by the way, is open every day from 10 a.m. to 4 p.m.

Water-powered cotton and textile mills changed all of New England in the 19th century, and it all started in Pawtucket, a few miles from downtown Providence. In 1793 three enterprising men named Slater, Almy, and Brown set up the first water-powered cotton-spinning factory in America, on the Blackstone River. Today the early mills and the **Sylvanus Brown House** (1758), home of the skilled artisan, make up the **Slater Mill Historic Site.** The mills have many of their old machines in working order, and you can see them in action, such as the water wheel, shafts, and pulleys in **Wilkinson Mill** (1810). Earlier handcraft devices for doing the same jobs are also on display to show you what a breakthrough the machine-filled **Slater Mill** (1793) was. Besides the permanent exhibits, traveling and temporary displays are set up from time to time, and guided tours interpret the history of the textile industry, and the impact of factories on working conditions. Admission is $3 for adults, $2 for children 6 through 14. Group rates are available. It's open in summer, June 1 to Labor Day, Tuesday through Saturday from 10 a.m. to 5 p.m., on Sunday from 1 to 5 p.m.; in spring and fall it's open on weekends from 1 to 5 p.m., but closed in January and February. Call 401/725-8638 for information. To get there, take I-95 north from Providence, get off at Exit 28, and turn left (under the highway) onto School Street. Cross the Blackstone River and turn right into Roosevelt Avenue, and the site is on your right. From I-95 south take Exit 27 and follow signs to the mill.

---

2. Newport

Whatever glittering reports you've had of Newport, they're probably correct, because Newport is a fascinating, diverse place. Palatial mansions, the wealthy yachting set, major naval and Coast Guard installations, tennis tournaments, cocktails on marble terraces in the soft air of a summer's evening, or succulent seafood served in a waterfront restaurant—Newport is all of these.

Newport has enjoyed prominence during two periods in American history: in colonial times it was an important trade center, and so, like Salem, Mass., it has a lovely colonial section right downtown, much of which has been restored authentically in the styles of centuries ago; and in the mid–19th century it became a resort for the very wealthy, who built what are indeed palaces in another part of town. Newport preserves remembrances of this past while pursuing its future as one of New England's prime vacation destinations: people who own yachts and people who can only afford to look at yachts, people who play tennis and those who watch it, people who live in mansions and others who take guided tours through mansions —they all flock to Newport. Besides the visitors, Newport is home to tens of thousands of Rhode Islanders who take all the glamour and glitter for granted, and who live here year round.

Several things are important to remember when you're planning a visit to Newport. First, it is crowded in summer, particularly on weekends, and when the important tennis tournaments and yacht races are being held. Second, prices tend to go up on weekends and when the yachters are around. Third, Newport prides itself on having style, and many visitors will be dressed like movie stars; many restaurants, cocktail lounges, and hotels require "proper" dress at dinner, and perhaps even lunch: jacket, or jacket and tie for men, skirt and top or pants suit, or similar attire, for women.

HISTORY: Newport is at the southern tip of an island that the Indians called Aquidneck, and which the colonial settlers dubbed Rhode Island. As Providence was settled by Roger Williams, dissident from Salem, so Newport was founded by one William Coddington, who decided to strike out on his own from Providence in 1639. The new town soon became famous for shipbuilding, and as soon as the ships were built in sufficient numbers, for trade. The famous "triangle trade," from Newport to ports in the West Indies and Africa, would later bring great wealth to the town from the buying and selling of slaves, rum, molasses, and other goods. Because Providence and Newport were founded by dissidents, they became places of refuge for others wishing to worship as they pleased: Quakers from England, Jews from Portugal and Spain, and Baptists all came to Newport in the mid-1600s to find religious freedom. They brought talent and a gift for hard work, and the settlement prospered so that it became the colony's most important town, and one of the New World's busiest ports. The many beautiful colonial homes, the handsome Old Colony House (center of government), Touro Synagogue, and other landmarks attest to the wealth and prosperity of Newport at the time.

During the American Revolution the British occupied the town and its excellent harbor, and held it for three years. A British frigate, H.M.S. *Rose,* did much to hinder the transport of supplies to the Americans, and spurred them to found the U.S. Navy in retaliation. Despite a French naval blockade and an American siege, the British held onto Newport until 1779, and after this interruption in its social and economic life, Newport never regained its former status as Rhode Island's prime trade center.

Several decades later, however, it achieved prominence in another fashion. Drawn by the beautiful woods and dramatic coastline, wealthy merchants from New York and Philadelphia began to come to Newport to spend their summers. In the mid-1800s the first of Newport's famous mansions, Château-sur-Mer, was built, and others followed until Newport's Bellevue Avenue and Ocean Drive could boast the highest concentration of summer palaces—and they are *palaces*—anywhere in the world.

Today the city's symbol is the pineapple, a sign of welcome left from Newport's great commercial era when traders back from West Indies with this fruit would put a pineapple outside their warehouses to invite customers to come in and look over the stock. Newport is used to welcoming visitors, and with the hints and recommendations given below, you should have no trouble finding your way around and having a good time.

GETTING THERE: Newport is served by bus, boat, and air taxi service.

By Bus: Bonanza Bus Lines serves Newport, with a stop right downtown at Newport Gateway Center, 23 America's Cup Ave. (tel. 401/846-1820). Bonanza works in conjunction with Greyhound/Trailways Lines and the Rhode Island Public Transit Authority, and has frequent daily buses from Boston to Newport (2 hours), Providence to Newport (1 hour), and New York City to Newport (5½ hours).

By Boat: There are daily boats between Providence, Newport, and Block Island. See Section 4 on Block Island for details.

By Air: Several national and regional airlines fly into T. F. Green State Airport in Warwick, and from there you can take **Sakonnet Air Charter,** Newport State Airport, Middletown, RI 02840 (tel. 401/847-6948). Sakonnet will fly you one way in ten minutes for $33. They also offer shuttle service from Newport to Boston, Nantucket, Martha's Vineyard, and Block Island.

From Newport State Airport you'll have to take a taxi into town.

GETTING YOUR BEARINGS: On the island of Rhode Island there are three main towns: Portsmouth in the north, Newport at the southern end, and Middletown in between. Newport and Middletown are so close that many visitors to Newport stay in motels in Middletown and then drive the mile or two into Newport to see the sights. The two most important streets in Newport are **Thames Street** (pronounced "thaymz," *not* "temz"), center of the colonial section, the wharves, and of modern downtown; and **Bellevue Avenue,** parallel to Thames but south and east of it. Bellevue is the street with many of the old mansions on it. Maps and information are handed out by the **Newport County Chamber of Commerce** office, 10 America's Cup Ave. (P.O. Box 237TB), Newport, RI 02840 (tel. 401/847-1600). They're open from 9 a.m. to 5 p.m. every day in summer; weekends in winter from 9 a.m. to 4 p.m. Get help here if you're stuck without a reservation and can't find a room. America's Cup Avenue is parallel to Thames Street and runs right along the water downtown. If you'd like them to send you information on Newport, they're ready to do so.

WHERE TO STAY: Newport has several large, comfortable hotels, a good number of charming small inns, and numerous bed-and-breakfast houses. In neighboring Middletown are many inexpensive motels, and more guesthouses. No matter what sort of accommodation you choose, it's a good idea to have reservations in advance, particularly in summer and especially on weekends. If you arrive in Newport on Friday from mid-July through Labor Day, you may well have to spend hours searching for that last hotel or inn room. On summer weekdays there may be more rooms, but you may not be able to find your preferred facilities and price unless you reserve in advance. I'll start by describing some of Newport's fine inns, which are moderate in price but high in comfort and good looks, then go on to guesthouses (almost as charming, but cheaper), and hotels and motels.

The **Newport Chamber of Commerce** (tel. 401/847-1600) has a nice long list of bed-and-breakfast guesthouses and small inns. Send for it if you have the time; pick one up when you arrive if you don't; or call and ask for their help in locating a room. Note that Rhode Island has a 6% sales tax, and that a 3% Newport rooms tax is also applied to prices in establishments with ten or more rooms.

The **Guest House Association of Newport,** P.O. Box 981, Newport, RI 02840 (tel. 401/846-7666), will send you a list of its member establishments. If you call, they'll tell you where there are vacancies—but they won't make reservations for you. For that you must call the guesthouse directly. Members of the association tend to be the larger establishments with, say, 6 to 16 rooms.

Newport's Inns

For the full Newport experience, stay in a mansion right on Bellevue Avenue. **The Wayside,** Bellevue Avenue, Newport, RI 02840 (tel. 401/847-0302), is just that: a fine, huge, somewhat austere 1890s house of tawny brick set back from the avenue with its own little driveway and porte-cochère. The interior spaces are rich and elegant, but austere rather than fussy. The many parlors and bedrooms have been redone into comfortable accommodations with private baths which rent for $105 double. Continental breakfast is included in the rates. To find the Wayside, drive from the Newport Casino (International Tennis Hall of Fame) down Bellevue Avenue. Pass "The Elms" on the right, then the Oakwood Healthcare Center on the left. The next building on the left past the healthcare center is the Wayside. A small marble plaque with gilt letters, mounted on a post by the driveway, is the only marking.

The **Inn at Castle Hill,** Ocean Avenue, Newport, RI 02840 (tel. 401/849-

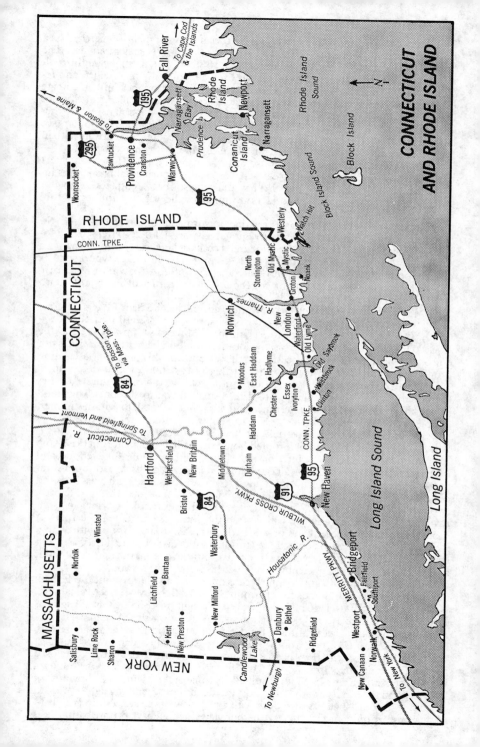

CONNECTICUT AND RHODE ISLAND

3800), is a Newport favorite, a marvelous Victorian summer mansion perched on a hill at the southwestern tip of Rhode Island, overlooking Narragansett Bay. The house was built in 1874 for Alexander Agassiz (1835–1910), naturalist, industrialist, and great benefactor of Harvard. It has been authentically maintained and restored, and is a fine example of a wealthy family's Victorian summer cottage extravaganza: dark wood, ornate fireplaces, large-flower-pattern wallpaper (different in each room, of course), Oriental carpets, a sunny solarium—it's all here. Whether you stay here or not, you can enjoy the house by coming for lunch or dinner (see below). If you choose to stay here, one of the six double rooms with private bath in the inn costs $180 in high summer; the three doubles with shared bath are $84. Rooms with shower in the Harbor House, an unobtrusive motel-style structure next to the inn and just above the pebble beach, cost $106. Continental breakfast is included in all these rates. The inn also has a number of beach cottages capable of lodging two to four people. The cottages are rented by the week in summer, and are booked very far in advance.

The **Yankee Peddler Inn** has a very fine downtown location at 113 Touro St. (between Spring Street and Bellevue Avenue), Newport, RI 02840 (tel. 401/846-1323). Though you get bed and (continental) breakfast here, you get more than in a simple B&B, as the Yankee Peddler is finely decorated in the old Newport style. A double room in the high season with shared bath is $65 to $70; with private bath, $85 to $95. Suites are more. Look for the inn at the corner of High and Touro streets in the center of Historic Hill.

"Where the past is present" is how innkeepers Rita and Sam Rogers describe their inn, the **Melville House**, 39 Clarke St., Newport, RI 02840 (tel. 401/847-0640). Only a few blocks up Historic Hill from America's Cup Avenue and the Brick Marketplace, on a quiet street, the location couldn't be better. The inn is not one of Newport's Victorian palaces, but rather a beautiful old colonial house dating from about 1750. The owners have been true to the period in their decorations, which recall colonial and Early American times, yet have catered to guests' desires for modern facilities by installing up-to-date, if small, private bathrooms. The mood here is one of antiques, good taste, quiet, and friendliness. You'll love it. In summer, double rooms with private bath cost $75 to $85; with shared bath, $65 to $75.

The **Inn of Jonathan Bowen**, 29 Pelham St., Newport, RI 02840 (tel. 401/846-3324), is a nice old gambrel-roofed house only a half block off America's Cup Avenue up Historic Hill. The interior of the house has been beautifully redone, and is as neat as a pin, with wall-to-wall carpeting and large modern tile bathrooms. But true to its historical heritage, the inn's guest rooms are furnished with brass beds and old oak wardrobes and dressers. There are nine rooms in all, six with private bath, two that share a bath. Room 7, one that shares a bath, is particularly bright and sunny. You'll enjoy relaxing in the parlor amid the antiques and Oriental carpets. A room with a queen-size bed and private bath costs $95; a larger room with a king-size bed and private bath costs $135. Continental breakfast is included, as is off-street parking in the inn's own lot. If you like antique charm, but can do without squeaky floorboards and ancient woodwork, this is the place for you.

Just slightly more than two long blocks off America's Cup Avenue, up Pelham Street on Historic Hill, stands the charming **Admiral Benbow Inn,** 93 Pelham St., Newport, RI 02840 (tel. 401/846-4256). It was built in 1855 by Capt. Augustus Littlefield to be used as a lodge for his guests, so it has always been an inn. The captain must have been a wealthy man, for the inn is a beautiful Victorian house with spacious rooms, lots of fine woodwork, and unusual arched windows. The guest rooms are furnished with brass beds and canopy beds, wing chairs, fireplaces (closed up), and pretty watercolors. Room 5 on the second floor in front is marvelous, a large space better termed a "junior suite." Its three arched windows allow lots of light to flood the room, and the large trees beside the house lend the light a pleasant green hue. Room 12 has its own deck with a fine view of the sea. But in fact all 14 rooms here are quite nice; some have harbor views, and all have private bath. Prices

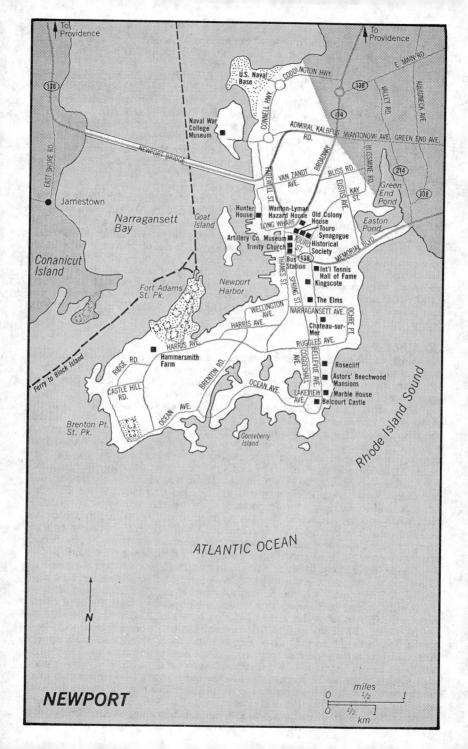

NEWPORT

are $75 to $100 double in summer. The inn also has an efficiency apartment for rent. This is a wonderful inn in a quiet, shady neighborhood (once Benedict Arnold's family farm), and you're sure to love staying here.

Very near Cliff Walk and the beach is the **Cliffside Inn,** 2 Seaview Ave., Newport, RI 02840 (tel. 401/847-1811), owned at one time by a painter named Beatrice Pasatorius Turner. Many of the antique furnishings date from the time when the house was built as a summer cottage for Governor Swann of Maryland in 1880, and the house exudes Victorian charm. Rooms have private shower and tub and rent for $89 to $111 in season (May through October). To get to the Cliffside, take America's Cup Avenue or Bellevue Avenue to Memorial Boulevard (Rte. 138A), follow Memorial east to Cliff Avenue, which is before you get to Newport Beach; turn right onto Cliff Avenue and go the two short blocks to Seaview Avenue. As you turn left onto Seaview, Cliffside is on your left.

For those who want to be very close to the beach, there's the **Cliff Walk Manor,** 82 Memorial Blvd., Newport, RI 02840 (tel. 401/847-1300), a striking mansion built in 1855, perched on a hill with a sweeping view of Newport Beach. The view of the beach from some of the guest rooms, and from the pleasant café deck, is panoramic. The guest rooms vary in price from $89 to $175 double in season, depending on view and amenities. At the lowest price are two rooms (one with an ocean view) that share a bath; at the highest price is a large ocean-view room with its own whirlpool bath. In between, ocean-view rooms with private bath are priced from $125 to $140. All rooms have television sets and air conditioning, and those in the mansion proper have Victorian furnishings, some of which are antiques. And yes, Cliff Walk begins right in front of the manor.

Guesthouses

Many of the lodging establishments listed below are similar in ambience and facilities to the inns listed above. These groupings of "inns" and "guesthouses," which are mine, are somewhat arbitrary. My feeling is that guesthouses have just a little more of that feeling you get when you stay in someone's home.

Ivy Lodge, 12 Clay St., Newport, RI 02840 (tel. 401/849-6865), is in the midst of the mansions, a block off Bellevue Avenue down Parker Avenue. Indeed, this huge shingled summer cottage with its gables and chimneys, its curving veranda with wicker furniture, and its tidy carriage house can stand proudly even in such an elegant neighborhood. When you enter the front door its elegance is even more pronounced, for there you are greeted by a lofty entrance hall done completely in glowing, artfully carved woodwork which rises all the way up to the third-floor roof. Staircases cascade down in front of you, and stained glass glows above. There's a fireplace, and to the right a formal parlor with etched-glass windows. To the left is the formal dining room, where breakfast is served. Guest rooms are similarly ornate and authentic. The hosts, Ed and Mariann Moy, will welcome you, and then leave you pretty much to enjoy yourself as you please. Rooms with shared or private bath and continental breakfast are priced at $95 to $111 double in high season. To find Ivy Lodge, drive along Bellevue Avenue and watch for the Oakwood Healthcare Center on the left; turn left onto Parker Avenue just before the center, then right onto Clay Street, and Ivy Lodge is a short distance along, on the left-hand side.

Of the several guesthouses downtown in Newport, perhaps the most convenient is the **Queen Anne Inn,** at 16 Clarke St., Newport, RI 02840 (tel. 401/846-5676), which is a half block off Touro Street at Washington Square, two blocks from the harbor, in the Historic District. Peg McCabe, the affable owner of the Queen Anne, advertises that you can "park your car in our lot and walk to everything," which is true of everything downtown, and even of the mansions if you're a good walker. One of the old Victorian town houses (rather than a wooden summer mansion), the Queen Anne has a dozen rooms furnished in a cheerful way with lots of nice little antique touches. Prices at present are $55 to $85 double, and there's one single at $37; seven baths are shared. Complimentary continental breakfast is served. The Queen Anne has its own patio and garden. You can't miss the place: headquarters of the Newport Artillery Company is right across the street. Open year round.

The **Covell House,** 43 Farewell St., Newport, RI 02840 (tel. 401/847-8872), was built in 1805, completely renovated in 1982, and has six antique-decorated guest rooms which rent for $69 to $85 double, depending on the bath situation and the season. Continental breakfast is included, of course. The neighborhood is a quiet residential one, but here you're still only a short walk from the bustling waterfront.

Aboard Commander's Quarters, 54 Dixon St., Newport, RI 02840 (tel. 401/849-8393), between Thames and Spring Streets, only a block from The Elms, is a welcoming guesthouse run by Commander (Dr.) Joseph F. Tracy, a psychologist, and his wife, Phyllis, a teacher. The 15-room, century-old house has two rooms and two suites, each with private bath, for summer guests. The rates, $70 to $80 double, include a continental breakfast; there's also free parking. The house is open from May through September only.

Hotels and Motels

Newport has several large downtown hotels with all the luxury services.

The **Sheraton Islander,** is on Goat Island, Newport, RI 02840 (tel. 401/849-2600, or toll free 800/325-3535), in the midst of the yachts, connected to the center of town by a causeway. The 200 rooms and suites come with all the amenities, and cost $150 to $178 double in high summer.

The **Newport Harbor Treadway Inn,** on America's Cup Avenue, Newport, RI 02840 (tel. 401/847-9000), has 133 rooms, all modern, some with fine sea views, all right in the very center of the action. Prices are $172 to $222 in season.

Among Newport's newest hotels is the **Newport Marriott,** 25 America's Cup Avenue, at Long Wharf, Newport, RI 02840 (tel. 401/849-1000 or toll free 800/228-9290). The hotel's amenities include an indoor-outdoor swimming pool, racquetball courts, health club, and four dining and drinking places. Many of the very comfortable rooms have water views. Rates in high summer are $195 to $240 double.

Besides these downtown hotels, there are many motels on the outskirts, in Middletown, particularly along West Main Road (Rte. 114). Prices are lower, but so are quality, convenience, and ambience.

WHERE TO DINE: Dining in Newport is anything you want to make it, from a seaside clambake on paper plates to an elegant dinner with candlelight, soft music, and polished service. There are two things you should know about Newport dining, however. First, if you plan to dine in one of the better restaurants, you may have to meet the requirements of a dress code. Many restaurants ask that their patrons meet jacket-and-tie/skirt-and-sleeved-blouse formality. Second, call for reservations when you plan to dine at one of the better places. Some restaurants are booked solid a week in advance for dinner on Saturday evenings in July and August.

Newport's Best Restaurants

The **White Horse Tavern,** at the corner of Marlborough and Farewell Streets (tel. 849-3600), boasts that it is America's oldest tavern building, and it is certainly a Newport institution, having been serving the hungry and thirsty since about 1687. One family, the Nichols, ran the tavern for almost two centuries. Rescued from a period of neglect by the Newport Preservation Society in the 1950s, it is again in private hands and in excellent condition.

The old tavern is authentic and totally charming, with large fireplaces, huge exposed beams, and old oil paintings. Staff are formal in black and white, soft classical music wafts through the air, and the menu lists dishes which are a fascinating blend of the old and new: duck is served with a cranberry sauce, beef Wellington with sauce périgourdine (Périgord is where they force-feed geese to produce foie gras), and sautéed lobster. Appetizers include poached salmon, and snails sautéed with ham. Desserts are rich and delicious. Expect the dinner check to cost $50 to $70 per person here, tax, tip, and wine included. Lunch is served from noon to 3 p.m. every day (on Sunday it's brunch); dinner is served daily from 6 to 10 p.m. Call for reservations, and come well dressed.

Of the waterfront redevelopment projects completed so far in Newport, the one at **Bannister's Wharf/Bowen's Wharf** is the most charming, and it has a selection of good restaurants. Bannister's Wharf is right next to the Treadway Inn, downtown on the waterfront, and would be West Pelham Street's extension if it were still a street. Poshest place on this very posh wharf is the **Clarke Cooke House** (tel. 849-2900), which has one of the most interesting French menus in Newport (not all frogs' legs and escargots) and two very different dining rooms. To your left at the top of the short flight of steps is the Dining Room, a very authentic-looking colonial room with rugged ceiling beams (original to the house, which is colonial), wood chairs and tables, gleaming crystal stemware, and tuxedoed waiters. To the right as you enter is the Candy Store Café, a light, airy, and open room overlooking the wharf and the water—about as different from the dusky colonial room as can be. Plan on spending about $40 to $55 per person on a full dinner here (served from 6 to 10 p.m.). In the café, a lunch or light supper will cost about $16.

The dining rooms at the **Inn at Castle Hill** (tel. 849-3800) are among Newport's most famous, partly for the cuisine, partly for the service, and partly for the marvelous ocean views. There are actually several dining rooms, and a wood-paneled bar with entertainment, on the ground floor of this imposing Victorian summer cottage on Ocean Drive (see above). One dining room is the solarium, all white; another is paneled in dark wood; yet another is lighter but still formal. Take your pick, then order lunch from among such dishes as chicken parmesan, stuffed sole Florentine, or a gargantuan club sandwich. The dinner menu is fancier, and more French, but stays in touch with traditional American tastes. Expect to spend $25 to $30 at lunchtime, twice that at dinner. Here are other details: lunch is served Tuesday through Saturday, Memorial Day through October; Sunday brunch is served April through November; dinner is served Monday through Saturday, June through October, and on Thursday, Friday, and Saturday in April and May; in November, it depends. No meals are served December through March, except continental breakfast to inn guests. In the dining rooms, men must wear jackets, and women must be similarly formal; no denim is allowed.

Best-Value Restaurants

Newport's well-established restaurant is the **Black Pearl** (tel. 846-5264), on Bowen's Wharf right next to the Clarke Cooke House. For lunch and dinner, on weekdays and weekends, the Black Pearl is crowded with the blonde and beautiful, the tanned and handsome. There are actually four places to dine here. In the Commodore's Room, dinner is served from 6 to 10 p.m., and a jacket is required for men and similarly suitable dress for women. This is not the busiest of the Pearl's eating places, but rather a refuge from the busy places. Table settings are quietly elegant and include a candle lantern on each table. The decor is subdued and not at all overdone or garish, which is characteristic of many waterfront restaurants. The menu is classic French, with all the familiar dishes of that tradition, and a full meal will cost about $50 per person with wine. Next to the Commodore's Room is the Tavern, where a jacket is not required, and happy, hungry yachting types press in for a drink, a "Pearlburger," omelets, or perhaps a daily special such as fresh bluefish with lemon-caper butter. Outdoors, next to the Black Pearl, are the outdoor bar, a sort of waterfront café, with white metal tables and chairs set out on a patch of white gravel, shaded by brightly colored umbrellas.

Also on Bowen's Wharf is **The Landing** (tel. 847-4514), which is the place to go if you like to sit by the water. There are lots of different places to do that here:

upstairs on the awning-shaded decks (one of which is the bar), in the glassed-in dining rooms, or on the open-air patios. The mood is yachting-informal and nautical, the menu is straightforward, with fish and chips, sandwiches, and numerous more substantial seafood plates. The Landing is open for lunch and dinner daily, and you can expect to spend from $15 to $24 here. Look for the Landing just down from Checkers Café, the café-club attached to the Newport Harbor Treadway hotel.

Those in the mood for beef should head for the **Chart House,** on Bowen's Wharf (tel. 849-7555), which is open daily for dinner only. Modern and attractive, it has only indoor dining rooms, but you get good views of all the activity through large windows. Tables are made with laminated nautical charts, and the menu lists steaks, prime rib, chops, and seafood in the traditional American manner. The daily specials are somewhat more inventive and adventurous. You can expect to spend $30 to $40 for a full dinner here.

The **Café Zelda,** 528 Thames St., corner of Dean Avenue (tel. 849-4002), adds the simple elegance of a French café atmosphere, plain furnishings of high quality in good taste. The luncheon standards—salads, burgers, quiche—are good and moderately priced, but it's the daily special plates, many featuring crab, that draw the crowds. A bowl of clam chowder, the fish of the day sautéed with almonds and wine, dessert, and a glass of wine could be served to you for $20 or less. Dinner is served till 10 p.m., except Monday.

After a hot morning's sightseeing in Newport, the **Brick Alley Pub and Restaurant** (tel. 849-6334 or 849-8291) has just what you want: a cool, shady, quiet place to sit down and have some refreshment. At 140 Thames St., it's right across the street from Brick Marketplace and right behind the block of shops housing the Newport Chamber of Commerce Information Office. Walk up the passage beside the restaurant and you'll come to a cool, shady courtyard with tables set out. The selection of sandwiches, burgers, salads, and omelets is enormous, all costing about $5 to $7 (for $3 more you can have soup and a whack at the salad bar). Open every day for lunch and dinner. There are indoor dining rooms as well.

Another good place for good, moderately priced fare is the **Rhumb Line,** 62 Bridge St. (tel. 849-6950), one block north of the new Gateway Information Center, in the Historic Point section. The menu here goes through the lighter selections and courses all the way to full-course dinners, and there's a full bar. Evenings on weekends there's live jazz (this draws a crowd). Expect to spend about $6 to $10 for lunch (served from 11:30 a.m. to 3 p.m. and until 5 p.m. on weekends), about $15 to $20 for dinner (from 5 to 10 or 11 p.m.). Sunday brunch is served from 11:30 a.m. to 4 p.m. What's a rhumb line? It's a line on a map or chart showing a constant compass direction straight to the destination. The principal advantage of a rhumb line is that it maintains a true direction, as does this establishment as an eatery.

The Ark, 548 Thames St., at the corner with Memorial Boulevard (tel. 849-3808), is Newport's restaurant for any taste, at any time. It has a prime location at Newport's busiest street corner, and the management uses it well by providing good, dependable food and competent, friendly service, a vast variety of dishes, moderate prices, and a full day's serving schedule. A sign outside advertises "Breakfast, Lunch, Cream Teas, Dinner, Raw Bar, Pub, Café," and it's all true. For instance, you can start the day with their English breakfast of eggs on fried bread with fried tomatoes and mushrooms, sausage, bacon, and coffee or tea for less than $7, all in— and it's a huge meal. Breakfast is served in July and August from 7 a.m. to noon. Lunch and dinner are served every day from 11 a.m. to 11 p.m. Come back and lunch on anything from tortellini to shepherd's pie, then dine on pasta primavera, veal medallions with sweetbreads, or blackened bluefish. Sit in the enclosed sidewalk café, or the gold-walled bar, or the cozy tavern with quiet booths, or in the upscale upstairs dining room. Dinner in any of the ground-floor rooms might cost $15 to $20; in the fancier upstairs dining room, it might be $25 to $40. The Ark is a Newport standard, and has been so for years, for good reasons.

Inexpensive Seafood

Newport has lots of places where you can get delicious seafood at very reasonable prices. Most of these are on upper Thames Street, across Memorial Boulevard from the center of town. Some restaurants allow you to bring your own wine or beer, which also helps to keep the price of a good seafood dinner in the reasonable range. You can pick up your favorite vintage or brew at **Thames Street Liquors,** 520 Thames St., or at one of several other stores in the area. The BYO restaurants can tell you how to find the nearest liquor store.

Dry Dock Seafood, 448 Thames St. (tel. 847-3974), seven very short blocks south of Memorial Boulevard on upper Thames Street, is an attractive, clean, and modern eatery with lots of bright, cheerful wood and tile, a lunch counter, and tables with bentwood chairs. Ceiling fans keep you cool, and hanging plants add a touch of greenery. Order New England clam chowder or clams casino, for starters, and then a sandwich of fish, meatballs, or chouriço (spicy Portuguese sausage) and peppers. Or you can order a main-course dinner such as fish and chips, or a fisherman's platter, or swordfish steak, or (as I did) broiled scallops. I got about a pound of succulent sea scallops perfectly broiled in a light coating of crumbs, with an immense mound of french fries and a paper thimble of cole slaw, for a mere $8.95. One of the things that keeps prices reasonable here is that you bring your own wine or beer. All in all, expect to spend as little as $6 or $8 for a cup of soup and a sandwich, or as much as $20 to $25 for a bowl of soup and a swordfish steak, tax and tip included. This place is great!

Shore dinners are an old New England custom. A shore dinner is a no-frills clambake, with clam chowder, steamed clams, boiled corn on the cob, steamed lobsters, and other simple but delicious dishes served on paper plates to diners seated at wooden picnic tables. Newport's most authentic shore dinner is served at the **Newport Shore Dinner Hall** in the Newport Harbor Marketplace, Waites Wharf, off upper Thames Street (tel. 848-5058). Here, a large open warehouse-type building has been nicely spruced up, painted and hung with colorful flags. Pick up wine or beer on your way here, or decide on soft drinks with your dinner, then order any of the aforementioned items, or lobster rolls, clam rolls, mussels, hot dogs, french fries, or clam cakes. Fish and chips costs $7, a large steaming plate of mussels is $6, and a steamed lobster over a pound in weight goes for less than $10 (depending on the season). The view, through large open doorways overlooking the bay, is among the best in Newport. The Shore Dinner Hall is operated by the S.S. *Newport* restaurant next door, and is open from 11 a.m. to 9 p.m. every day (till 10 p.m. Thursday through Sunday). There's plenty of free parking here. If you drive, turn right off Thames Street when you reach the high 400s of the street numbers; there's a small sign for the Shore Dinner Hall.

In the center of town is **Salas',** 341 Thames St. (tel. 846-8772), on lower Thames, a half block past the post office. Salas' actually consists of three establishments in one: a fish market and raw bar (open from 11 a.m. to 1 a.m.), a brasserie (open for lunch from 11:30 a.m. to 3 p.m.), and the dining room (open from 4 to 9:30 p.m. for dinner). Lunch could be breaded, fried fish strips with french fries and cole slaw, or any of numerous daily special plates priced from $6 to $9. For dinner there are several set-price meals which offer good value, such as the No. 1 Clambake, a one-pound lobster, clams, corn on the cob, sausage, clam broth, and so forth, for $21.

WHAT TO SEE: There is plenty to see in Newport, and therefore during the summer there are also plenty of people here to see it. Parking places are at a premium, although the situation is certainly not hopeless. But why bother? If you are among the readers of this book who live close enough to Newport to make it practicable, why not bring a bicycle, or rent one when you get here? You can't really see the mansions by car as you always have to keep moving (the car behind you will make sure you do), and Newport is small enough so that even an out-of-shape biker can see the town without much of a strain.

Several shops in Newport rent bikes, both three-speed (which is all you'll need), and ten-speed, among them **10 Speed Spokes,** 18 Elm St. (tel. 847-5609), at America's Cup Avenue, down the street from the chamber of commerce. You can rent a three-speed for $10 per day.

Tours

The Newport Historical Society sponsors **walking tours** of historic Newport on Friday and Saturday from mid-June through September, departing at 10 a.m. from the society's headquarters at 82 Touro St. (tel. 846-0813). The cost for an adult is $3; children under 12 can come along for free.

Should you want to get "the lay of the land" before heading out to see individual sights, take a bus tour of the town, Ocean Drive, Bellevue Avenue, and other districts. You don't necessarily have to take a tour that stops and goes through a mansion, although those are offered as well. **Viking Tours,** in the Brick Marketplace (tel. 847-6921), will take you on a 22-mile Newport tour for $9 (kids, $4.50); throw in another few bucks and they'll take you through one mansion. Viking also has one-hour Harbor Tours, from Goat Island for $5 (kids, $2.50).

Another way to tour Newport is to rent a cassette tape recorder complete with prerecorded taped tour commentary from **Art's Island Tours,** for rent at $7 through the chamber of commerce, 10 America's Cup Ave., right downtown on the water (tel. 847-1600). You put a deposit on the recorder, take their map, and walk or ride along the mapped route while listening to the commentary.

The Mansions

Newport boasts mansions of two types these days: those that are now, in effect, museums and are open to the public, and those that are still private summer residences and are most emphatically *not* open to the public. Believe it or not, many of these palatial houses are indeed still privately owned and maintained and lived in. In fact, the wealthy people who live in Newport mansions are also responsible for opening others to the public, for it was through the efforts of the Preservation Society of Newport County, to which many of them belong, that the marvelous houses were preserved. To think that The Elms, perhaps the most graceful and charming of the mansions, was to be torn down to make way for a housing development until the Preservation Society bought it, is nothing short of astounding.

Not all the mansions that are open to the public are owned by the Preservation Society, however. Several notable houses are privately maintained and open to visitors on terms similar to those of the society houses. When visiting the mansions, remember these two rules of thumb: first, figure on at least an hour per house to take it all in; second, don't try to see more than three, or at the most four, houses in one day unless you have a tremendous capacity for absorbing glitter and magnificence. More than three or four tours in one day will leave you dizzy and exhausted. Also, try to visit the mansions on a weekday when the crowds are smaller, saving Saturday and Sunday for Newport's other attractions. If you must go on Saturday, get there early.

PRESERVATION SOCIETY MANSIONS: The **Preservation Society of Newport County,** 118 Mill St. (tel. 847-1000), maintains six Newport mansions, plus **Hunter House** (a colonial house built in 1748), and **Green Animals** (a topiary garden with 80 sculptured trees and shrubs, many in the shapes of animals, in Portsmouth to the north of Newport).

A combination ticket covering all of these attractions is available for $25 per adult, $9 per child. Tickets for individual mansions cost $4.50 ($2 for children 6 through 11), but as you'll probably be seeing more than one mansion, buy a "strip ticket" good for two mansions ($8), three ($11), four ($14), five ($16), or six mansions ($19). Children's prices are less than half of these. Tickets are on sale at any of the society's mansions. During the summer (May to October) the mansions are open every day from 10 a.m. to 5 p.m. In the spring, in April the four fanciest mansions are open every day; the rest are open on Saturday and Sunday at the same times. Note that from July to Labor Day several mansions have late hours, and stay open until 6 p.m. Check which ones are currently open which evenings. During the winter, Marble House, The Elms, and Château-sur-Mer are open Saturday and Sunday from 10 a.m. to 4 p.m. They are decorated for the holiday season in December.

Admission to any mansion includes a very informative tour through the rooms, and the right to stroll about the grounds at your leisure. Tours are very frequent, and the guides are almost always charming and very well informed. Here is what you'll see:

The Breakers: Certainly the most grandiose of the mansions, and most popular with visitors, is The Breakers, an Italian Renaissance palace built for Cornelius Vanderbilt. It is nothing short of sumptuous, with lavish use of the finest marble. The marble columns in the two-story-high Great Hall have capitals carved of alabaster. Priceless tapestries, fine mosaic work, irreplaceable paintings, and ornate furniture testify to the wealth of The Breakers' owners and their desire to flaunt it. Hard to believe. The Breakers was built in only two years. It was designed by Richard Morris Hunt, who did a great many buildings in New England, especially in Newport.

Besides the mansion, there is a children's cottage on the grounds (included in the price of admission to the mansion).

The Elms: E. J. Berwind, son of a Philadelphia tradesman, got an appointment to the U.S. Naval Academy, and served in the navy until mustered out with high rank because of an injury. He soon made it big in the coal business, and secured the contract to supply all U.S. Navy ships with coal. With the profits he built The Elms, perhaps the most gracious and pleasant of the Newport mansions. Although it is grand, it is also supremely harmonious, having been modeled on a château in France. The sunken formal garden at the far end of the spacious lawn was designed by a French landscape artist. The Elms is the masterpiece of Philadelphia architect Horace Trumbauer. It was threatened with destruction when a land development firm bought it and planned to build a housing development on the site, but was saved by the zoning laws and the Preservation Society. Few of the original furnishings are left, but the mansion has been furnished with pieces from museum collections and private lenders.

Château-sur-Mer: The first stone mansion to go up on Bellevue Avenue was Château-sur-Mer (1852), built as a home for William S. Wetmore of New York. Wetmore's son, who met Richard Morris Hunt while on a tour of Europe, was responsible for bringing the American-born architect to Newport to rebuild his mansion, and later the mansions of others. (The senior Wetmore had lived in the mansion ten years before he died, and upon his death his son took it over.) The château is very rich Victorian Gothic, and to modern tastes it seems luxurious, but also dark and heavy. Château-sur-Mer has the feeling of being lived in and enjoyed— something that can't be said of some of the other mansions.

Marble House: Richard Morris Hunt threw himself into building this mansion for William K. Vanderbilt, finishing it in 1892. It was modeled on the palace at Versailles, and is therefore decorated pretty much in the style of Louis XIV which was, well, pretty grandiose—you'll see! As in The Breakers, the furnishings in Marble House are all original to the building. Get ready to see the Gold Room, a ballroom decorated with a king's ransom in gold, and the kitchen and the fascinating Chinese tea house.

Kingscote: Kingscote, built in 1839, is the type of "summer cottage" lived in by wealthy visitors to Newport before the great stone mansions were built. First built for G. N. Jones of Georgia by Richard Upjohn, it was later acquired by a merchant in the China trade called William H. King, who gave the house its name.

"Kingscote" is coined from "dovecote," so, by analogy, it means "Mr. King's Cottage." A cottage it isn't, for no peasant lived here; but rather a man who appreciated Tiffany glass and a gorgeous dining room.

Rosecliff: Another famous New England architect, Stanford White, built Rosecliff in 1902 for Mrs. Hermann Oelrichs, whose father had made a fortune in the California Gold Rush. The building is modeled on the Grand Trianon, the larger of the two châteaux in the park at Versailles, but was meant to be even more lavish in layout and decor. Its ballroom is the largest one in Newport, and the mansion is still used for summer entertainments as it has been for most of this century.

OTHER MANSIONS: Besides the mansions maintained by the Preservation Society, several others are open to the public. Grandest of these is **Belcourt Castle,** another creation of Richard Morris Hunt, done in 1891. Oliver Belmont and his wife, formerly Mrs. William Vanderbilt, had Hunt make them a castle in the style of Louis XIII (1610–43). Today the castle is filled with appropriate memorabilia: stained glass, armor, silver, carpets. It even boasts a golden coronation coach. Well-informed guides escort the visitor through the beautiful period rooms and explain the collection. Tea is then served. Belcourt Castle, on Bellevue Avenue, is open daily from 9 a.m. to 5 p.m. from mid-June through October 29. Admission is $4.50 for adults, $1.50 for children 6 to 15, $3.50 for senior citizens; a family admission costs $10. Special parties are arranged by calling 401/846-0669.

Beechwood, the house of William B. Astor, was built at 580 Bellevue Ave. in 1856. It was the home of *the* Astors. The "tour" here is quite a different experience from what you'll find at any other Newport mansion. Here, Beechwood Theater Company actors and actresses play the parts (tongue in cheek) of characters who might have lived in such a summer cottage during Newport's gilded age. It's all done in fun and with spirit, and it gives you quite another view of Newport life. Admission—which in this case is to a show as much as to a house—costs $5.25, $4 for seniors. For hours, call 401/846-7288.

Richard Morris Hunt's **Ochre Court,** a mansion built for Ogden Goelet, is styled after a French château. You can visit the mansion any weekday from 9 a.m. to 4 p.m., and admission is free. The **Edward King House,** in Aquidneck Park (which is bounded by Bowery, Spring, William, and King Streets) is now Newport's senior citizens' center. It was built in 1845 on the plan of an Italian villa. The architect was Richard Upjohn. The King House is open weekdays from 9 a.m. to 4:30 p.m. Admission is free.

Want to visit a summer White House? **Hammersmith Farm,** on Ocean Drive (tel. 846-0420), was built by John W. Auchincloss in 1887 as his family's 28-room summer "cottage." Jacqueline Bouvier, daughter of Mrs. Hugh Auchincloss, became Mrs. John F. Kennedy, and after the Newport wedding the reception was held at Hammersmith Farm. President Kennedy and his wife enjoyed visiting the farm when they could find the time, and no wonder. Beautiful rolling lawns and gardens, nature paths and copses of trees—not to mention the lovely old house itself—make the farm a seaside paradise. Mrs. Auchincloss sold Hammersmith Farm mansion in 1977, and it is now open to the public with many of the original furnishings. Guided tours are given daily: mid-April through mid-November and for "Christmas in Newport" from 10 a.m. to 5 p.m., in summer till 7 p.m. The charge is $5 per adult, $2 per child.

Newport's Other Sights

The mansions are on everyone's list of things to see in Newport, but there are lots of other things to do as well. Here's a rundown on some other possibilities:

A WALK IN WASHINGTON SQUARE: Right downtown between Thames and Spring Streets, next to the new Brick Market place shopping mall, is Washington Square, the center of colonial Newport. At the western tip of the square is the **Brick Market,**

a Newport landmark, built in 1762 and designed by Peter Harrison. (The name derives from its use as a market, and its brick construction—no bricks were sold!) Having served variously as a town hall, theater, and crafts center, as of this writing it is undergoing yet another metamorphosis to serve a new purpose. At the other end of the square from the Brick Market stands the **Old Colony House,** center of Newport governmental affairs for 160 years from its construction in 1739 until the Rhode Island General Assembly (which met in Newport in the summer) last used it in 1900. It was from the Colony (later State) House's balcony that the Declaration of Independence was read to Rhode Islanders. In the assembly room is Gilbert Stuart's famous portrait of George Washington. You can get a free tour of the building July through Labor Day daily from 9:30 a.m. to noon and 1 to 4 p.m. on weekdays, 9:30 a.m. to noon on Saturday and Sunday.

HISTORIC HOUSES OF WORSHIP: Because Rhode Island allowed so much religious freedom, many religious groups suffering persecution made their way here in early times. Thus Newport boasts a number of firsts. The **Touro Synagogue,** a half block from Washington Square up Touro Street, is the most famous of these. Designed by Peter Harrison (it resembles in some ways his King's Chapel in Boston) and built in 1763, the temple was the spiritual center of Congregation Yeshuat Israel, an Orthodox Sephardic congregation. The synagogue and congregation prospered along with Newport, but after the British occupation of the town during the Revolutionary War prosperity fled Newport and few of its erstwhile citizens returned. But in the late 19th century Newport came to life again. The temple reopened in 1883, and has been used for services ever since.

Touro Synagogue (the name may come from a 19th-century benefactor, Abraham Touro, son of the rabbi who presided at the synagogue's dedication) is open to visitors from late June to Labor Day Sunday through Friday from 10 a.m. to 5 p.m.; during other months it's open on Sunday from 2 to 4 p.m., and by special arrangement (call 847-4794). On Saturday you may come to attend services. Admission is free, though donations are accepted. During the summer, short tours are conducted. You can see a copy of George Washington's letter to the congregation, written while he was president in 1790.

The Newport Historical Society is housed today in another early house of worship, the **Seventh Day Baptist Meetinghouse** (1729), the first in America of that sect. The buildings are at 82 Touro St., a few steps from the Touro Synagogue; they're open Tuesday through Friday from 9:30 a.m. to 4:30 p.m., on Saturday to noon. Take a look at the meetinghouse and its famed pulpit, and also at the society's museum, which houses paintings, furniture, china, silver, and marine artifacts.

The **Quaker Meeting House,** at the corner of Marlborough and Farewell Streets, was built in 1699, but was greatly modified in the early 1700s and again in the early 1800s. The congregation, founded in 1657, is the oldest of the Society of Friends in this country. The meetinghouse has been restored to look as it did in the early 1800s. Admission is $2, and it's open from 10 a.m. to 5 p.m. Monday to Saturday from mid-June through August; other times by calling 846-0813.

Of course, Newport has a beautiful old pre-Revolutionary church, and this one, just restored, is a real gem. **Trinity Church** (1726), at the corner of Spring and Church Streets (tel. 846-0660), was built from plans by Sir Christopher Wren, and still has the "bishop's mitre" weathervane as it did before the Revolution. The church is full of history: Bishop George Berkeley gave the organ (1733), Washington was known to have worshiped here (pew no. 81), and its famous three-decker "wineglass" pulpit is widely admired. You can get in to see the church Monday through Saturday from 10 a.m. to 4 p.m. in summer (late June to Labor Day), the rest of the year on weekends from 1 to 4 p.m., or at Sunday services at 8 and 10 a.m. Other times, call 846-0660 and make an appointment. Donations accepted.

OTHER ATTRACTIONS: Army buffs will want to drop in at the **Artillery Company of**

Newport, 23 Clarke St., a few steps from Washington Square. The company got its charter in 1741, and since that time, besides defending Newport, has been collecting military uniforms. You can see this great collection on display June through September, afternoons Tuesday through Sunday from 1 to 5 p.m. At other times of the year it's open Saturday and Sunday afternoons only. Children are admitted free; adults are asked to give a donation.

   The International Tennis Hall of Fame and Tennis Museum is sure to be of interest to anyone obsessed with the game. It's in the Newport Casino building on Bellevue Avenue across from the shopping center. The Casino (1880) is the perfect location for a tennis museum, as it was here that the first national tennis tournaments were held. Major professional tournaments are played here during June, July, and August. The museum has on exhibit trophies, tennis fashions, and displays explaining the evolution of tennis equipment. The 13 grass courts (and 3 indoor courts) are open to the public for play, so bring your racquet and call 849-3990 to make arrangements. The Hall of Fame and Museum are open all year: daily from 10 a.m. to 5 p.m. April through November, and December through March on weekdays from 11 a.m. to 4 p.m. Admission costs $4 for adults, $2.50 for seniors, and $2 for children 6 to 18.

   Newport has a **Museum of Yachting** (tel. 847-1018), as you might imagine. It's in Fort Adams State Park on Ocean Avenue, a short drive along Ocean Avenue from the center of town. If you're at all interested in small wooden craft, boatbuilding, or yachting, you should make a visit. A new exhibit highlighting the singlehanded sailor is on the second floor. Hours are 10 a.m. to 5 p.m. Tuesday through Sunday, May through October.

   The **Newport Art Museum** (tel. 847-0179) has changing exhibits in a house (1862) designed by Richard Morris Hunt. Call for information on current shows, then visit between 10 a.m. and 5 p.m. Tuesday through Saturday, or 1 to 5 p.m. on Sunday. Admission is $2 for adults, $1 for seniors, free for those 18 and under. It's located at 76 Bellevue Ave.

WHAT TO DO: Here are several absolute musts while you're in Newport:

Ocean Drive and Cliff Walk

   Take a drive (or ride your bike, if you're in shape) along Newport's ten-mile **Ocean Drive.** The scenery is very beautiful, with low heath, evergreens, stretches of rugged coast, and several smooth grassy lawns maintained as state parks. **Brenton Point State Park** has parking, walking, and picnic areas, and there's a Public Fishing Area with parking nearby. Ocean Drive also gives you a look at some of the yachts sailing on Rhode Island Sound, and at the mansions dotted around the end of the island.

   For walkers, the pedestrian equivalent of Ocean Drive is **Cliff Walk,** a path which runs along the shore and along the edge of the "front yards" of the mansions on Bellevue Avenue. Official start of the hour-long walk is off Memorial Boulevard just before Newport Beach beneath the Cliff Walk Manor, but you can also get to the path by going east on one of the side streets off Bellevue Avenue. By the same token, you needn't take the entire walk, but can head back to Bellevue Avenue at various points along the way.

Fort Adams State Park

   On a peninsula jutting into Newport Harbor, this park (tel. 847-2400) offers several attractions. The park is open from 6 a.m. to 11 p.m. daily all year, and picnic and fishing sites are open to all. The fort itself, named after President John Adams, is open for guided-tours from 11:30 a.m. to 4:30 p.m. Wednesday through Sunday in the summer (for a fee). Boat-launching ramps, beach with lifeguard, picnic area, the Museum of Yachting (see above), and soccer fields are among the services. The fort's defenses are some of the most impressive in the country—so impressive, in fact, that it rarely came under fire. Views of the town and the harbor from hills in the park are well worth the short climb.

Beaches

Newport's beaches are of two types, public (open to everyone for a fee), and private (open to members only, "Keep Out—This Means You!"). Bailey's Beach, at the southern end of Bellevue Avenue, is definitely very private, but **Newport Beach,** also called "First Beach," is public and quite large. It's on the isthmus at the eastern reach of Memorial Boulevard. Second Beach is in Middletown, a bit farther along the same route where the street changes names to become Purgatory Road. Just around the corner from Second Beach is Third Beach, at the mouth of the Sakonnet River, facing east. It may be a bit chilly at any time except July and August.

Gooseberry Beach, on Ocean Drive, is an especially attrative beach, open to the public for a car-parking fee of $5 on weekdays, $1 for pedestrians and cyclists. It's framed by nice mansions on either side, and has interesting rock formations.

Jai Alai

An unusual spectator sport and game of chance in Newport is the fast-moving game of jai alai ("high-lie"), familiar to those who have traveled to Latin America and Florida. Because of a change in the law, minors (12 years and older) are now allowed if accompanied by an adult. The season is May 1 to October 13. The Newport Fronton is at 150 Admiral Kalbfus Rd., near the Newport end of the Newport Bridge. Seats cost $3 to $5 and general admission (standing room) is $2, $4 for the lounge and restaurant. Betting is on which player or team will win, and is parimutuel as it is at horse and dog tracks. The game is fast and exciting, and the ball (harder than a golf ball) moves at murderous speeds approaching 188 miles an hour. If you've never seen it before (or bet before), you can get a brochure at the door explaining it all. For seat reservations, call 849-5000 in Rhode Island, or out-of-state, toll free 800/556-6900. There are matinees Monday and Saturday, at which seniors are free; ladies, free Tuesday; closed Sunday. There's a moderately priced restaurant and a lounge which overlooks court action.

Festivals and Events

Newport seems to have a festival going, one or another, all summer long. For current information on exact dates and offerings, contact the **Newport County Chamber of Commerce,** 10 America's Cup Ave., Newport, RI 02840 (tel. 401/847-1600), or write for the State of Rhode Island's *Guide to Rhode Island* to: Rhode Island Department of Economic Development, Tourist Promotion Division, One Weybosset Hill, Providence, RI 02903. The *Guide,* a 50-page pamphlet, has a complete list of Rhode Island events and festivals for the current year.

One of the world's great yachting races, the **America's Cup Race,** held every three years or so, took place in the waters off Newport until 1983. Newporters hope to have the Cup "back home" some time soon.

The major festivals and approximate times are these:

Newport Music Festival: Perhaps the biggest annual event in the town, the Newport Music Festival attracts great crowds to the grand mansions for the many and varied concerts. There are performances morning, afternoon, and evening for two consecutive weekends and the weekdays in between in mid-July. As the capacity of all the mansions and halls is limited, it's best to write for tickets—and to make reservations for a hotel room—in advance. Write to the Newport Music Festival, P.O. Box 3300, Newport, RI 02840 (tel. 401/849-1133). They'll send you a list of all the concerts and performers, and the prices of tickets.

The **Kool Jazz Festival** in Newport is held on a weekend late in August, in Fort Adams State Park. Each day from noon to 6:30 p.m., top-name stars perform. The Viking Hotel (tel. 401/847-8100) is usually festival headquarters, where you can buy your tickets (general admission only).

May Breakfasts: May is officially celebrated as Heritage Month in Rhode Island, as "Little Rhody" was the first colony to declare independence from British rule (May 4, 1776). On May Day (May 1), or thereabouts, May Day Breakfasts are held by all sorts of church, civic, and fraternal organizations across the state, and the public is invited to most of them. These can be pretty lavish affairs, and you're sure to get your money's worth. Write to the Department of Economic Development (address above) for a full list of breakfasts throughout the state.

Outdoor Art Festival: The end of July, usually the last weekend, sees Newport's Outdoor Art Festival, when painters, sculptors, and craftspeople display their works downtown and in several parks throughout the city.

Fishing Tournaments: From June to October, tournaments are organized periodically to see who can make a record catch of one of the familiar fish in the waters off Newport. The chamber of commerce can tell you more.

Tennis: Championships are held at the Newport Casino (Tennis Hall of Fame) in July, hosting the top professional male stars. For tickets and information, contact the Hall of Fame, 194 Bellevue Ave., Newport, RI 02840 (tel. 401/849-3990).

---

3. Narragansett Bay

To get across Narragansett Bay from Newport, you will have to cross two bridges on Rte. 138: first, the Newport Bridge from Newport to Jamestown Island ($2, payable in both directions), and then the Jamestown Bridge from Jamestown Island to Saunderstown (free). The total fee therefore to cross from Newport to Saunderstown or vice-versa is $2. From Saunderstown, head south on Rte. 1A (Alternate U.S. 1).

NARRAGANSETT PIER: Route 1A skirts the southwestern shore of Narragansett Bay passing through this famous Victorian resort town, which is also the main town on the peninsula here. Although not quite so famous now, the town is still popular for the same reasons as in an earlier age: beautiful sea views, a fine waterfront promenade, and gracious old Victorian houses.

Where to Stay

The **Summer House Inn,** 87 Narragansett Ave., Narragansett, RI 02882 (tel. 401/783-0123), is just that: a bed-and-breakfast inn in a big summer house with 20 guest rooms that share baths. You can have breakfast (included in the room price) on the spacious porch while enjoying the mood of this charming bayside town. On weekends, a double room costs $54 double with shared bath, or $72 double with private bath; midweek prices are lower. By the way, children are welcome at the Summer House, something that cannot be said for all bed-and-breakfast places.

What to See

Passing through Narragansett on Ocean Road, you'll drive right under the last standing remnant of Stanford White's mammoth Narragansett casino, **"The Towers,"** built in 1882. The town's chamber of commerce maintains a Tourist Information Office in the base of the seaward tower—park on either side of the underpass arch and walk to the door.

The main beach in Narragansett is north of these hotels and the Towers, about a half mile distant. The parking fee is your admission fee, as usual.

FROM SAUNDERSTOWN TO POINT JUDITH: As you drive south along U.S. 1A to Saunderstown, look for signs off to the right (west) that point the way to the

Gilbert Stuart birthplace. Stuart (1755–1828) was America's most famous portrait painter after the Revolutionary era, and did no fewer than three portraits of George Washington from life, perhaps the most famous of which is the so-called *Athenaeum Head,* model for the portrait of Washington on the dollar bill. (Look for the original of this in the Museum of Fine Arts in Boston.) Stuart was the son of a snuff-maker, but his father had a comfortable living, judging from the house, and the son was able to go to London to study painting with Benjamin West. Period furnishings, water-wheel–powered snuff mill, and copies of Stuart's portraits adorn the house. Open daily except Friday from 11 a.m. to 5 p.m.; closed November through March. Admission is $1.50 for adults, 50¢ for children.

Ocean Road (U.S. 1A) also passes by the **Scarborough State Beach** facilities, very popular on hot summer days although never filled to capacity. Scarborough Beach, like all Rhode Island beaches, works on a system of parking/admission fees, charged *per car.*

Continuing along U.S. 1A south will bring you to Point Judith and the departure place for Block Island ferryboats.

POINT JUDITH/PORT GALILEE Jutting southeast into the Atlantic Ocean and dividing Block Island Sound from Rhode Island Sound is Point Judith. The peninsula of Narragansett's southern extremity offers several things to travelers: the car and passenger ferry docks for boats to Block Island, located at Port Galilee; camping and picnic facilities at Fishermen's Memorial State Park, only two miles from Port Galilee; and good sand beaches along the southern and eastern shores of the peninsula. Port Galilee exists for the ferries to Block Island, the Wheeler Memorial Beach, several small fisheries, and a Coast Guard station.

The Beach and the Ferry

First of all, be warned that Port Galilee has very few parking places on the street, and that these are usually taken up quickly by the people who work for the fishing companies. Parking for the beach is $2 a day ($3 on weekends and holidays) for Rhode Island residents, $4 a day ($6 on weekends and holidays) for out-of-state cars, but this includes the entry fee to the beach for everyone in your party, and is standard practice at all state beaches in Rhode Island. Whether you park next to George's of Galilee or at the large lots of the Wheeler Memorial Beach several hundred yards east, the rate and arrangement are the same.

For the ferry, parking fees are of the same order, and the lot is across the street and down a few yards from the ferry dock. Note that the restaurants and motel in Galilee have parking lots, but they also put out fierce signs that threaten to have your car towed if your intention is other than patronizing their establishments. It's best to take them at their word, especially if you're going away to Block Island for the day.

---

4. Block Island

In 1614 a man named Adriaen Block visited a small island off the coast of Rhode Island, but his visit did little more than give the island its name. Slightly over 20 years later a colonist was found in a boat near the island, presumed murdered by the local Pequot Indians, and this unhappy event precipitated a battle between Pequots and colonists which turned out to be very bloody.

A generation later, these events forgotten, settlers from the colony moved onto the island and the town of New Shoreham (incorporated in 1672) was built. For almost 200 years the people of Block Island lived their quiet lives, fishing in boats from the island's two natural harbors, growing what they could in the sandy and windswept soil. But in the mid-1800s the Age of Steam changed Block Island from a fishermen's outpost in the Atlantic to a summer excursion paradise, with regularly scheduled steamboats bringing residents of the sooty factory cities out for fresh air and bright sunshine. Late-19th-century frame hotels, huge and sprawling, went up to accommodate them, and the island's economy came to depend on tourism rather than fishing, and so it has remained. Most of the island's buildings—houses as well as hotels—date from the late 1800s or the turn of the century; the roads are rough and sandy (nobody has to be in a hurry to get quickly from one end of the island to the other—it's only seven miles); the pace is very relaxed; and the citizens of New Shoreham, which takes up all of the island, have a strong sense of community.

GETTING THERE: During the summer season from late June to early September, Block Island is very accessible, whether you're touring New England by car or by public transport. During spring, autumn, and winter, there's limited service to the island.

By Air

New England Airlines, Block Island's own airline, will fly you over from the State Airport, Westerly, RI 02891, on any of 14 daily flights year round. The $25 one way ($42 round trip) flight takes 15 minutes. You must have reservations, so call 401/596-2460, or toll free 800/243-2460 outside Rhode Island. If you're on Block Island, dial 466-5881. The airport is on Airport Road, Westerly, off Rte. 78.

Action Airlines (tel. 203/448-1646 or 448-1710 or toll free 800/243-8623) will fly you to Block Island from Groton/New London, Conn., or Madison, Conn., or Teterboro, N.J.

For details on flying to Block Island from Westchester County, N.Y., call the charter company **Westchester Air, Inc.,** at 914/279-5800.

By Boat

Boats leave for Block Island from four ports during the summer.

FROM PORT GALILEE: This is the port with the most frequent service, and there are at least six and at most nine daily sailings in each direction from mid-June to early September. The trip takes less than an hour and a quarter, and costs $5.20 per adult, one way, or $8.55 for a same-day round trip; children pay half price. It costs about $35 round trip for a car (driver not included), and you must have written for reservations in advance. The Port Galilee agent is the **Interstate Navigation Co.,** Galilee State Pier, Point Judith, RI 02882 (tel. 401/789-3502). Motorcycles and bikes are also carried. During spring, fall, and winter there are fewer trips, two daily in each direction in May and early June, and late September through October; in winter, there's one trip daily.

FROM NEW LONDON: In summer (mid-June to early September) there's one trip daily (plus an additional Friday evening boat) in each direction between New London and Block Island, leaving New London mid-morning, returning from Block Island midafternoon. The trip takes about two hours and costs $12 for adults ($16 for same-day round trip), and $8 for children over 5 ($10 for same-day round trip). A car costs $44 round trip. The fee for bikes is $6 round-trip. The boat leaves from Ferry Street, about one-eighth of a mile from the railroad station. Advance reservations for cars is a must. For more information, contact the **Nelseco Navigation Co.,** P.O. Box 482, New London, CT 06320 (tel. 203/442-7891 or 442-9553 during business hours). By the way, ferries from New London arrive at Old Harbor on Block Island, and you may have to take a taxi to reach hotel and restaurant choices.

FROM PROVIDENCE: The same people who operate the Port Galilee–Block Island ferry, the **Interstate Navigation Co.** (see above), run a daily passenger boat from Providence via Newport to Block Island. Departure from Providence's India Street dock is at 8:30 a.m., from Newport's Fort Adams dock at 10:30 a.m., arriving at Block Island around 12:30 p.m. The return trip leaves Block Island at 3:45 p.m., leaves Newport at 5:30 p.m., and arrives back in Providence at 7:45 p.m.

One-way fares between Providence and Block Island are $5.85 for an adult, $3.10 for a child. Bicycles and motorcycles can be transported, but no cars. Ask about special same-day round-trip fares.

FROM MONTAUK, L.I.: Another point of departure for Block Island is Montauk, N.Y., at the southeastern tip of Long Island. From here, the **Viking Fishing Fleet** (tel. 516/668-5700) operates a daily passenger boat (no cars) to Block Island at 10 a.m. The voyage takes 1½ hours, and same-day round-trip fare costs $25 for adults, $15 for kids ages 5 to 12.

MAIL/TELEPHONES: Block Island's ZIP Code is 02807; the telephone area code is 401, the exchange is 466.

ARRIVING IN OLD HARBOR: The boat trip is pleasant enough, plenty of room to sun on the top-deck benches, a small bar and snack counter on board. As you approach Block Island the character of the place becomes clear: dunes and white cliffs, low shrubs and grass with a few trees, ponds, and hillocks (highest point on the island is 211 feet above sea level). The big old hotels come right down to the harbor, most looking pretty weathered from the stiff breezes and salt air, not to mention the winter storms, that are the norm here. Several of the hotels have vans which will be waiting at the dock to pick up passengers who have reservations, or those who want a room but have not reserved.

WHERE TO STAY: Block Island is currently enjoying a tourist boom. Most of the large old Victorian hotels have been renovated and modernized, many small family guesthouses have been opened, and in general the lodging picture is good but pricey. Because demand for rooms is high, you should be sure to have reservations in advance during high season (from mid-July through Labor Day). You can save 10% to 20% on many lodging establishments by staying during the week (Monday through Thursday) instead of the weekend if your schedule allows for it.

Most hotels on Block Island serve breakfast to their guests at no additional charge. Breakfast may be anything from pastries and coffee to a full eat-all-you-can buffet. Also, all hotel prices are subject to the Rhode Island 11% tax on rooms, and some hotels levy a service charge (usually 4% to 6%) in place of your tips to the staff. These extra costs have been included in the prices given below, unless otherwise noted.

Reservations, Deposits, Refunds

Here are some general guidelines for lodging policies during high summer, which may vary slightly from hotel to hotel. Often there is a requirement that you stay at least two or three nights, perhaps even a week. All hotels require that you send a deposit (or give your credit-card number) to secure your reservation. Deposit refund policies vary, but may be something like this: your deposit will be returned, less a $10 to $25 processing fee, if you cancel more than 15 or 21 days prior to your planned arrival date. If you cancel closer to that date, your deposit may be refunded only if the hotel succeeds in renting your room to someone else. Most hotels require that you pay in full upon arrival for your reserved stay, by traveler's checks, credit card, or cash. Estimate the total cost of your stay, and make arrangements for payment.

Cancelled Flights

Several hotels caution guests that bad weather such as fog or storms may affect flights and ferryboats to the island; usually the flights are what's cancelled, and the ferries keep running. If you plan to fly, be aware that fog may cause cancellation of your flight, and you should plan your schedule so that in the event of fog you will still be able to catch a ferry and get to your hotel in time to claim your reserved room. If you don't make it, you will forfeit your deposit and your reservation.

Hotels

Without a doubt, Block Island's loveliest place to stay is the **Hotel Manisses,** Spring Street, Block Island, RI 02807 (tel. 401/466-2421 or 466-2063), operated by Block Island's premier hoteliers, the Abrams family. The Manisses was built in 1870 as a small Victorian resort hotel. Restored by the Abramses in 1972, it is at least as fine a hotel—probably better—than it was 100 years ago. The large-pattern floral wallpaper, white wicker and wrought-iron furniture, beveled mirrors, heavily carved and marble-trimmed parlor pieces, even the bubbling garden fountain, recall the best of a more gracious time. The 17 guest rooms have double, queen-size, or king-size beds; some have whirlpool baths and little refrigerators, and all have private baths, telephones, and period furnishings. The hotel's restaurant is the best on the island. Guest rooms at the Manisses, single or double, are priced at $138 to $275 in summer; these rates include 6% service charge, 11% tax, and a full buffet breakfast. The Manisses is open April through late October; its restaurant serves on weekends only from mid-April through late May, daily from late May through late October. (See my restaurant recommendations for details.) You'll love the Manisses.

Also operated by the Abramses is their original establishment, the **1661 Inn and Guest House,** Spring Street, Block Island, RI 02807 (tel. 401/466-2421 or 466-2063), just up the hill a short distance from the Manisses. A large white island house, the inn has been nicely adapted to hospitality, with many good-size guest rooms, pleasant public spaces, and decks with sweeping view of the Atlantic. As at the Manisses, guests at the 1661 Inn and its neighboring guesthouse (23 rooms in all) find all the little touches for which the Abramses are famous: a full buffet breakfast, beach towels, and a decanter of brandy and dish of hard candy in each room. Some rooms have private baths, refrigerators, and private decks with ocean views. Prices in high season are $94 to $146, single or double for rooms without private bath; $138 to $275, single or double, for rooms with private bath; 6% service charge and 11% tax are included in these prices. The buffet breakfast, which by the way is the only meal served in the 1661 Inn's dining room, is included in the summer rates. For other meals, by reservation, you can stroll down the hill to the Manisses. Though the Manisses and the 1661 Inn close from mid-November through March, the guesthouse stays open year round.

The **Inn at Old Harbour,** Water Street (P.O. Box 994), Block Island, RI 02807 (tel. 401/466-2212), stands on a rise overlooking the ferry docks. It's right on Water Street, Block Island's main street, and you'll spot it at once as you walk from the ferry to Water Street, turn left, and walk a half block. There, facing the statue of *Rebecca at the Well,* is this three-story gambrel-roofed Victorian inn dating from 1882. What was once the lobby is now occupied by shops, but the ten guest rooms upstairs have all been totally renovated, fitted with modern fixtures and carpeting, and half have been equipped with new private bathrooms. Each room is different, the decor being a blend of fresh decorator-modern style and Victorian accent pieces. The price for a room, single or double, is $117 to $150, continental breakfast included, during the summer. Prices are $20 less mid-week. The inn has its own eating establishment, the Water Street Café, and a Ben & Jerry's Ice Cream Parlour.

The **Water Street Inn,** Water Street (P.O. Box 580), Block Island, RI 02807 (tel. 401/466-2605), facing the ferry dock, is a blocky shingled building, just the opposite of Block Island's ornate Victorian gingerbread style. On the ground floor is the Block Island Broiler restaurant (see below). But if you walk down the right side of the building, go through the door and up the stairs, you'll find new, neat, and clean rooms totally refurbished, and now boasting wall-to-wall carpeting, bamboo furniture, color television sets, and private baths. The inn is a fine place to stay, cheery, comfortable, convenient, and well kept. Rooms with private bath and continental breakfast are priced at $122 to $144 double.

Just up Spring Street from the 1661 Inn is the **Spring House Hotel,** P.O. Box 902, Block Island, RI 02807 (tel. 401/466-2633 or 466-5844), a grand old clapboard Victorian hotel perched atop a hill with a magnificent view. Chairs for sunning and sipping are set out on the lawn and along the long veranda. In the spacious lobby, the Victorian ambience has been maintained, but brightened up and made a bit more plush to satisfy modern tastes. The guest rooms have been completely rebuilt, and are now very much like rooms in a modern luxury hotel. There is darkwood furniture with gleaming brass trim, including four-poster beds. Most of the 24 rooms are designed as "studio suites," with a sitting room, a bedroom, and a modern bathroom, all with baseboard heat. Not all rooms have ocean views, so ask for one with a view if you prefer it. The price list here is somewhat confusing. The least expensive accommodation is a "deluxe studio suite with ocean view," for $161 double in high summer, full breakfast and happy-hour cocktails included. Most expensive accommodation is the "superior three-room suite with ocean view," at $222 double, $20 each additional adult. Note that the Spring House is both a hotel and a condominium, so your neighbors may be newcomers or condo owners. The Spring House's dining room is gracious, and appeals to an older clientele.

The **Surf Hotel,** Dodge St., Block Island, RI 02807 (tel. 401/466-2241 or 466-5990) is another Victorian wood palace, rather homey as only a great Victorian wood palace can be homey: cranberry glass hanging lamps, wicker furniture, a great ornate iron stove, and a grandfather clock in the parlor, colonial wallpaper prints in the rooms. A good number of the rooms have fine beach views—the beach is just a few steps away down the hill—and the hotel is a mere block and a half from the Old Harbor ferry dock. All but three rooms do not have private bath, and during July and August reservations can be made by the week only. For a single with a shared bath the price is $50 per day, $310 per week; for a double, $60 to $66 per day, $400 to $440 per week (twin or double bed); there's no discount for children except for infants. Meals at the Surf Hotel cost $5.50 for breakfast ($33 a week). Cooking and service are home-style.

The **Harborside Inn,** P.O. Box F, Block Island, RI 02807 (tel. 401/466-5504), directly facing the ferry dock, is something of a social center in Block Island. Its terraced patio restaurant-café, right on Water Street, is popular with young and old, hotel guests and day-trippers alike. When it rains, the Harborside's spacious indoor bar, done with nautical motifs, is lively and jolly. As for the inn and its 36 guest rooms, it's an unpretentious Victorian beach hotel in which yet another coat of paint keeps things looking good. The large, simple rooms are popular with younger people and with families because they are clean and presentable, comfy, and located right in the midst of town. Doubles in summer, full breakfast included, cost $117 without private bath, $150 with private bath. An extra person in a room pays $20, and that price also includes a full breakfast.

The **National Hotel,** Water Street (P.O. Box 189), Block Island, RI 02807 (tel. 401/466-2901 or toll-free 800/225-2449), is a Block Island landmark, having been built in 1888 and renovated a short time ago. The renovations included the provision of telephone, color television set, radio, alarm clock, and new private bathrooms in all of the hotel's 45 rooms and suites, but each room also has several Victorian pieces as an echo of the hotel's golden age. Room prices in high season are $150 to $222; the standard ocean-view room with a queen-size bed is $183. Children under 12 can share their parents' room at no extra charge. Continental breakfast is included in the price. The National appeals to an upbeat crowd, who like the live, amplified entertainment at lunchtime on the porch, and at dinner in the lounge.

Guesthouses

The **Blue Dory Inn** (P.O. Box 488), Dodge Street, Block Island, RI 02807 (tel. 401/466-2254), right next to the Surf Hotel and the National Hotel, is actually a guesthouse and several cottages perched right at the tip of Crescent Beach. In the main building there are ten guest rooms, all with private bath and Victorian furnishings, and also a living room, and the kitchen, which serves as the breakfast room. The Cottage can sleep up to six, has kitchen facilities, and is perfect for a family or for two couples traveling together; it's priced at $272 (for four) per night. The Doll House ($155 double per night) is a one-room house good for couples who get along very well (it's tiny), and the Tea House ($189 per night) sleeps two, and has its own kitchen, plus a porch overlooking the beach and the sea. In the inn proper, double rooms with private bath cost $116 to $178 per night in summer. All these prices include 4% service charge, 11% tax, and continental breakfast. The inn notes that it does "not have facilities for children under 10."

The **Seacrest Inn**, High Street, Block Island, RI 02807 (tel. 401/466-2882), just a few steps from the statue of *Rebecca at the Well*, was renovated in 1982, and now holds very comfy, modern guest rooms with private bath which rent for $94 to $117 double in high summer. The inn has rooms for up to four people, renting for $155 (for four) per night. Free coffee, tea, cocoa, orange juice, and danish are available to inn guests each morning, and if I were you, I'd take a cup outside and sit in the cute little Victorian gazebo. The Seacrest is a family-owned and -operated inn which provides pleasant, comfortable lodging at moderate prices, with a smile and an honest welcome. It also has its own bicycle-rental shop, so you can be easily equipped for touring the island.

Lovers of family guesthouses will want to check out the **Gables Inn,** on Dodge Street (P.O. Box 516), Block Island, RI 02807 (tel. 401/466-2213), just around the corner from the Surf Hotel and behind the old National Hotel. The Gables is a traditional Block Island house converted to a guesthouse, and with its companion, the Gables II, it has a good variety of accommodations: single rooms are $50 daily; doubles are $73 to $100. Most of the rooms don't have running water, but there are bathrooms nearby. Now there are also efficiency apartments for $688 to $810 per week. The Gables has several advantages over other places on the island: its prices are low, it is open spring and fall, free coffee and tea are available throughout the day, and guests have the use of barbecues, picnic tables, a croquet set, and horseshoes for throwing, all in the back yard.

In New Harbor, one of the first hotels you'll see is the **Narragansett Inn,** New Harbor (P.O. Box 186), Block Island, RI 02807 (tel. 401/466-2626). The big advantages here are convenience to the New Harbor docks, and rooms a one-minute run across the lawn from the beach. The inn itself is a Victorian three-story house with several new additions. Prices are $105 to $139 double, depending on whether or not there is a private bath. The rates for the 54 rooms include breakfast.

WHERE TO DINE: I'm happy to say that there is good food on Block Island even though there are not all that many restaurants. You probably will have had breakfast at your hotel, so here are recommendations on where to have lunch and dinner.

As with lodging, the best place for dining is the **Hotel Manisses,** on Spring Street (tel. 466-2836). You can have lunch or dinner in the hotel's cozy dining room, or out on the awning-shaded deck by the bubbling fountain. Lunch is served from 2 to 5 p.m., and dinner is on from 6 p.m. For lunch, start with something elegant like gravlax (lightly salted cured salmon), and go on to something inventive, like "gourmet pizza," and your bill will be about $15 or $20, drink, tax, and tip included. At dinner there's fancier, more substantial fare such as two tournedos of beef with a sauce of two mustards, or quail, or bouillabaisse. The chef does not probe the exotic too deeply here, but neither does he ever bore your palate. Expect to spend $40 to $50 per person, all in, for dinner. In high season, especially on weekends, call ahead for dinner reservations, as the Manisses is small, and it does have the best situation and cuisine on the island.

The **Block Island Broiler,** Water Street (tel. 466-5811), in the Water Street Inn, faces the ferry dock. Those who approach its unassuming façade find inside a pleasant, upscale modern dining room done in blond wood, white walls, large windows, and enlarged photos of Block Island a century ago. There's a small bar for those awaiting tables, and a retail fish market, which shows that these people are serious about seafood. Have soft-shell crabs in blue cornmeal, or a tuna steak cut from a fresh fish just brought in by a charter fishing boat, or sautéed lobster with avocado. Your main course comes with a vegetable and potato or rice, which allows you to have an excellent dinner for only about $25 to $35, even less if you're satisfied with a sandwich and a salad. The restaurant's wine list offers a good selection, especially of California vintages. The restaurant is open nightly for dinner from 6 to 10:30 p.m. between Memorial Day and Columbus Day.

Block Island's most popular luncheon spot is definitely the front terrace café of the **Harborside Inn,** on Water Street facing the ferry dock (tel. 466-5504). Take in the sun, or duck beneath one of the shady café table umbrellas, and order something simple such as a hamburger or club sandwich, or something fancier, like baked stuffed clams, broiled scallops, or sirloin steak. Wine, beer, and cocktails are served, and lunch with a beer might cost $8 to $18. At dinnertime, fare is somewhat fancier but similar; and prices are still reasonable. Open daily.

WHAT TO DO: Most people coming to Block Island are looking for an easy schedule, quiet relaxation, time at the beach, bicycle trips, and seafood dinners. The island has a movie theater and a number of cocktail lounges, mostly in the hotels. A few small art galleries and craft shops are good for a browse. But beaching and bicycling are the two main activities.

Beaches

You can't miss **Crescent Beach,** to your right as you approach Old Harbor on the ferry. It stretches from the ferry dock for several miles north to the cliffs of Clay Head. It's simply beautiful, although the water is a bit brisk this far out in the Atlantic (it's warmest in late July and August, of course). Crescent Beach is divided into the State Beach, with a bathhouse, which is the section nearest the ferry dock, and Scotch Beach, which is the section farther north. Other beaches are over in the New Harbor area, several small ones on Great Salt Pond, and Charleston Beach facing west on the Atlantic.

Bicycle Touring

Block Island is too small to handle many cars, and so most visitors get around by bicycle. Rental places abound and rates are not expensive, about $5 per day for a three-speed, $10 for a ten-speed. The rental shop at the **Seacrest Inn,** High Street (tel. 466-2882), has good equipment and helpful personnel.

Mopeds are available for rent as well, but many local residents—especially those who belong to the medical rescue squad—advise visitors to rent a bike rather than a moped. If you are not an experienced motorcyclist, it's best to heed their advice. The medics respond to some six dozen moped accidents annually, some of them serious injuries. You'll get along better with the Block Islanders if you rent a bicycle.

A suitable Block Islandish goal for your bicycle outing is **Mohegan Bluffs,** and the nearby **Southeast Lighthouse,** about 1½ miles due south of town. Head out of town on Spring Street, which becomes Southeast Light Road which traces the heights of the bluffs.

About 2½ miles farther along, on Cherry Hill Road, lies **Rodman's Hollow,** a glacial ravine that's now protected as a wildlife refuge. Bring your binoculars if you plan to explore it.

Three miles north of town, on the eastern shore off Corn Neck Road, is the **Clayhead Nature Trail,** as well as a network of other trails on private land once known as the Maze. Take the nature trail east to the shore (less than a mile), then north all the way to Sandy Point, where you'll see the **North Lighthouse** and also

Settler's Rock. The granite lighthouse, now being considered for restoration, dates from 1867 and is no longer in use. Settler's Rock monument, erected in 1911, marks the spot where the island's first English settlers landed in 1661.

Only about a mile northwest of town along Ocean Road and West Side Road is the island's **cemetery,** with headstones dating from the 1600s and 1700s. It's a pretty spot, and interesting to anyone intrigued with Block Island's history.

Fishing

Several marinas on the island have fishing boats for hire, and surfcasting for striped bass and other delicacies is popular. Even if you're alone, the marina hands may be able to get together a party to go out, thereby reducing your costs greatly. For details, drop by any one of the marinas. All the boat-rental and sport-fishing businesses operate out of the New Harbor.

What Not to Do

Block Island and the town of New Shoreham are really one and the same, and so the local government of the island is the town council. While on the island the town's ordinances are the law, and these prohibit camping (except Scout groups and the like), sleeping overnight in cars or on beaches, riding motorcycles on the beaches, and shell-fishing without a license.

---

5. Watch Hill

Rhode Island is known for its beaches, and some of the finest are along the state's southwestern shore: wonderful Native American names such as Misquamicut, Weekapaug, and Quonochontaug identify the built-up areas along the strand. The buildings are usually private homes, or snackbars and restaurants, and much of the waterfront land is privately owned and fiercely guarded. But the state beaches dotted along the shore are open to all at a fee of $2 per car with Rhode Island plates, $4 per car with out-of-state plates during the week, a dollar more on weekends and holidays.

As a base for your day at the beach, you could choose no better place than Watch Hill, an old and genteel town at the end of a peninsula between the Atlantic Ocean and the Pawcatuck River. Watch Hill is a sort of Newport-in-miniature, with stately old homes (grand, but not palatial), yachts in the harbor (expensive, but not priceless), and a gentility still strongly felt if slightly faded. It's a quiet town, with fewer than a half dozen places to put up for a night or a week, unless, of course, you own a summer home.

WHERE TO STAY: Of Watch Hill's lodging places, the most comfortable and pleasant by far is the **Inn at Watch Hill,** Bay Street, Watch Hill, RI 02891 (tel. 401/596-0665). Don't expect a great old Victorian palace, for the inn here is actually a suite of motel-style rooms perched above a block of shops on the main street. You enter by going around to the rear, up the hill, where there is a large parking lot and a little office cabin. After check-in, you proceed along a wooden walkway to your room. Rooms 1 through 12 have the best harbor views; Rooms 14 and 15 have some water views; Rooms 16 and 17 see a bit of the harbor, but mostly shops. Whichever your room, the view is interesting and attractive. The rooms themselves are very good, new, neat, and tidy, each with a little refrigerator, microwave oven, and a small table for breakfast or snacks; all rooms have separate kitchen sinks. White brick walls, natural wood floors, and sliding glass doors opening onto little balconies overlooking the town make the rooms quite charming, and full private baths, air conditioning, and television sets add to the comforts. High-season summer prices are $114 to $131 double, depending on the size and comforts of the room, and whether you rent on a weekday or on the more expensive weekend. Weekly rentals offer reductions of 8% to 20%. An extra person pays $24 per night, but there's no charge for children, except if you need a cot or a crib. Call for reservations early, as this is the village's prime hostelry and it fills up early. Open May through October.

If you're pressed for lodgings, you might want to take a look at the **Harbour House,** on Bay Street, Watch Hill, RI 02891 (tel. 401/348-8998). Apartments, rooms, and suites rent for $67 to $72 double, but are often booked in advance by the week. Another possibility is **Hartley's Guest House,** Larkin Road, Watch Hill, RI 02891 (tel. 401/348-8253), up behind the Inn at Watch Hill, with simple, homey rooms renting for $61 to $72. Only one of the ten rooms has a private bath.

WHERE TO DINE: The most amusing place to dine in this pretty village is the **Olympia Tea Room,** Bay Street (tel. 348-8211), in a row of shops at the center of town, across from the little park and the police kiosk. The Olympia is an authentic early–20th-century seaside-resort soda-fountain café, with black-and-white checkerboard floor tiles, well-used wooden booths, a few sidewalk tables, and waitresses in black dresses with white aprons. The atmosphere is refreshingly real, not "re-created." As for the food, there's plenty of it, and it's more up-to-date: sautéed shrimp with feta cheese, clam stew, chicken fajitas with hot tortillas and guacamole, bouillabaisse, and of course, lots of seafood, from clams and sausages on linguine to boiled lobster. Lunch, served daily from noon to 5 p.m., might cost you $7 to $15. Dinner checks are usually $16 to $25, if you have a good, full meal. Breakfast is served daily as well. The Olympia is a wonderful bit of old New England, lovingly preserved for us all to enjoy.

WHAT TO DO: In Watch Hill, you spend time at the beach, you stroll along Bay Street and go window-shopping, you buy ice cream cones early and often.

Children will jump at the chance to ride (50¢) on the **1883 Carousel** at the end of Bay Street, one of the oldest merry-go-rounds in the nation.

In the little park across Bay Street from the Olympia Tea Room is a **statue of Ninigret,** Great Sachem of the Narragansett Indians, a noble man and friend of the local English colonists. The statue was erected in 1914.

Watch Hill is a place to start a romance, or to pursue one; to read and relax, or swim strenuously all day—to do as you please. There are no crowds, no neon signs, no plastic "lifestyles." Watch Hill is a bit of fading glory, which, luckily for those who go there, the rest of the world has already passed by.

CONNECTICUT

Connecticut's landscape is sprinkled liberally with lakes, rivers, and streams. But the state's namesake is the mighty Connecticut River, which springs from the Connecticut Lakes in northern New Hampshire, flows southward forming the boundary between New Hampshire and Vermont, cuts through Massachusetts and Connecticut, finally to empty into Long Island Sound. The great river is navigable as far north as Hartford, a significant fact that was not lost on the region's Native American inhabitants. They were the ones who gave it the name *Quinnehtukqut,* "the long tidal river."

Later inhabitants pasted different labels here. "The Nutmeg State" used to be a popular nickname, coming from the time when itinerant peddlers sold nutmeg from door to door. As often as not, the "nutmegs" were cleverly carved balls of wood. By the time a housewife discovered the fakery, the peddler was gone.

For obvious reasons, the people of Connecticut prefer the moniker "Constitution State," which reminds one and all that Connecticut was the first American colony to have a written constitution.

Almost three-quarters of the territory in Connecticut is woodland, and drives along the back roads through these forests reveal rich fields of corn, grain, vegetables, and tobacco, but the state's wealth comes not from agriculture, nor from tourism, but rather from insurance and manufacturing. The capital city of Hartford is laden with tremendous buildings which are headquarters for dozens of insurance companies. As for manufacturing, Charles Goodyear, Eli Whitney, Seth Thomas, and Mr. Fuller of Fuller Brush fame were all Connecticut Yankees. In the old days the state's production of buttons, pins, doodads, and kitchenwares gave rise to the breed of men known as Yankee peddlers, who traveled from town to town in horse and buggy, spreading the products of Connecticut's industry far and wide. Today the state's industries are a bit different: Sikorsky makes helicopters, General Dynamics makes atomic submarines, and the rubber companies turn out tires and products such as Naugahyde, the synthetic leather named after the Connecticut town of Naugatuck where it's made.

Although Connecticut has many historic houses and lovely New England villages, the places which are popular with tourists are mostly along the coast: New

Haven, home of Yale University; Essex, a fine old town at the mouth of the Connecticut River; Groton and New London, submarine capital of the world; and of course Mystic Seaport, the exciting and attractive re-creation of an old Connecticut maritime village. Hartford, although not what one would think of as a tourist mecca, is a pretty and interesting city well worth a short visit. Besides the attractions of the city itself, it can be used as a base for excursions into the lush farm and woodlands of Litchfield County, in the northwest corner of the state among the Litchfield Hills, Connecticut's "Berkshires."

The telephone area code for all Connecticut is 203.

The state tax on rooms and meals is 8%.

GETTING THERE: The capital and the southern coastal region are well served by public transport, most of which goes through or originates in the metropolis of New York.

By Air

The state is served by **Bradley International Airport** in Windsor Locks, 12 miles north of Hartford. There's direct one-plane service between Bradley and over 60 other North American airports, operated by Eastern, United, TWA, Delta, American, and USAir. Buses leave the terminal for downtown Hartford and for Springfield, Mass., periodically, and limousines shuttle from Bradley to most cities in Connecticut. By the way, the Connecticut Aeronautical Historical Association operates the **New England Air Museum** (tel. 203/623-3305) at the airport, with over 70 aircraft, plus engines, accessories, and memorabilia, on display. The collection is open to visitors all year from 10 a.m. to 5 p.m. every day. Admission for adults is $5; children (6 to 11), $2; children under 6, free.

By Rail

Amtrak runs trains daily from New York to Boston along both the coastal route (via New Haven, Old Saybrook, New London, Mystic, and Providence) and the inland route (via Hartford, Windsor Locks, and Springfield). Stopovers are allowed at no extra charge on most trains, so if you buy a ticket from New York to Boston, the stops in New Haven, New London, and Mystic, or New Haven and Hartford, need cost no more. It is usually possible to catch a train from New York in the morning, be in Mystic by noon, tour the Seaport thoroughly, catch another train around 5 p.m., arrive in Providence by about 6 p.m. and Boston by 8 p.m. The trip from New York to Hartford takes less than three hours; to New Haven, about 1½ hours; to New London, about 2¾ hours; to Mystic, about three hours.

Besides the Amtrak trains, there are frequent commuter runs operated on the Connecticut Department of Transportation's New Haven Line by Metro North. These trains depart New York's Grand Central Terminal hourly from about 7 a.m. until after midnight on weekdays, with even more frequent runs during rush hours. Service on Saturday, Sunday, and holidays is almost as frequent, with trains at least every two hours. The trip by Metro North takes one hour and 40 minutes. For exact schedule information, call toll free in Connecticut 800/223-6052 or in New York City 212/532-4900. The big advantages of the Metro North trains over Amtrak on the trip to New Haven are the convenience of Grand Central Terminal—midtown, right beneath the Pan Am Building—and the great frequency of trains.

By Bus

Greyhound/Trailways, Bonanza, and Vermont Transit all operate daily buses between New York City, New Haven, and Hartford. The trip to Hartford takes about 3 to 4¾ hours, depending on the line and the number of stops en route. Greyhound and Bonanza have services between New York and New London, and on to Providence and Cape Cod. From New York City to New London takes about 3 or 3½ hours, depending on stops. It's difficult to take a bus to Mystic Seaport—the train's the best way to get there.

From Hartford, **Bonanza** has buses to Providence and Hyannis; **Vermont Transit** operates buses to Vermont, New Hampshire, Montréal, and Québec City. All the large lines have buses between Hartford and Boston. In Hartford, the bus stations and the railroad station are all within a block of one another close to downtown. The terminal for Greyhound/Trailways, Vermont Transit, and Bonanza is at 409 Church St. (tel. 203/547-1500).

---

1. Ridgefield

Connecticut's extreme southwest corner is a busy maze of light industry, highways, and bedroom communities serving the metropolis of New York. But only a short drive to the north of the bustle along U.S. 7 lies Ridgefield, as tranquil and beautiful a town as one can find. Stately old trees shade the grassy lawns along its quiet streets, and huge old houses are well sited among the gentle rises and hollows of its topography.

To reach Ridgefield by car from the north, leave I-84 at Exit 3 near Danbury, and head south on U.S. 7. Coming from the south, leave I-95 or the Merritt Parkway near Norwalk, exiting to U.S. 7 North. From the west, you can exit from I-684 (the New York Thruway) at Katonah and head east on N.Y. 35, which becomes Conn. 35 at the state line, then leads straight into Ridgefield.

WHERE TO STAY AND EAT: Ridgefield has several gracious old inns. The grandest is the **West Lane Inn,** 22 West Lane, Ridgefield, CT 06877 (tel. 203/438-7323), set back from the street on a large lawn. Though the management advertises "colonial elegance," in fact the building dates not from colonial times but from the early 1800s, and was completely renovated as recently as 1978. You enter the fine old house to find a world of gleaming wood paneling, thick carpeting, wing-back chairs, fine old fireplaces, and a hushed quiet. In the guest rooms, furnishings are classic and comfortable, and facilities are right up-to-date. You'll find air conditioning, color television, radio, and telephone in each room, as well as a modern private bath. Rooms come with either one or two queen-size beds, and several have working fireplaces. Continental breakfast, including fresh-squeezed orange juice, muffins, and pastries, is included in the room prices of $100 single, $120 double, plus tax. Other services provided by the inn include babysitting, bicycle rental, laundry, and dry cleaning.

As for meals, the West Lane Inn serves light fare "from the pantry" such as sandwiches, desserts, and cold platters from noon till evening in the breakfast room or on the long, spacious front veranda furnished in wicker.

You'll find more formal, elegant dining next door at the **Inn at Ridgefield** (tel. 203/438-8282). The restaurant's entryway is paneled in ends from old whisky and wine crates, each printed with the shipper's trade name. Inside, a grand piano dominates the plush, understated dining room where waiters in black and white glide from table to table. One can start with a pâté aux trois poissons (pâté made from three different "fish:" salmon, sole, and lobster), flavored with fresh basil, and then go on to a sliced breast of duck in a sweet-and-sour sauce with green peppercorns. With pastry, and tea or coffee, this table d'hôte dinner is priced at $37; add the costs of wine, tax, and tip to get the final bill, which might be about $60. An à la carte dinner would cost more, but would also be well worth the money spent.

Another of Ridgefield's fine inns is the **Elms Inn,** 500 Main St., Ridgefield, CT 06877 (tel. 203/438-2541). It is in fact a colonial inn, having been built as a private residence in 1760, and converted to an inn in 1799. Since that year it has been an inn continuously, operated during almost two centuries by only five different families. Though colonial in decor, inn accommodations are quite modern in amenities and comforts, including private bath, color television, and telephone. Prices for double rooms range from $94 for a double bed, to $99 for twin double beds or a four-poster, to $120 for suites. Single travelers pay $10 less per room.

The restaurant is justly famous, as owners Robert and Violet Scala have mixed French, Italian, and new American cuisines on the long menu. Veal is a highlight, of course. Expect to pay about $50 for a good, full dinner with wine, tax, and tip.

An inn outside Ridgefield draws a loyal and appreciative clientele who love its situation off the main road, among the trees, right by a pretty little pond. It's called **Stonehenge,** on Stonehenge Road, off U.S. 7 (P.O. Box 667), Ridgefield, CT 06877 (tel. 203/438-6511). Don't expect a rocky, turreted castle. Rather, Stonehenge is a large, newly rebuilt farmhouse with six rooms in the main inn, filled with plush carpeting, some king-size beds, floral wallpapers, and brightly tiled private baths. In a nearby guest house and cottages are four more suites and six rooms. Furnishings in these are a mixture of antique pieces for proper ambience, and modern conveniences (color television, telephone, air conditioning) for comfort. The quiet of the country is yours for $97 to $157 double, more for one of the two suites. This includes a continental breakfast, which is brought to your room with the morning paper.

The dining room is justly famous as one of Connecticut's finest. The cuisine is French, sophisticated, artistic, sometimes rich, and always of a high order. Dinner is served nightly from 6 to 9:30 p.m.; expect to spend $55 per person, all in. The price for Sunday brunch is fixed at $23 per person.

WHAT TO SEE: Ridgefield's history dates from colonial times, when the town was a way station on the carriage road from New York to Boston. Carriage passengers need inns for sustenance and lodging, and Ridgefield provided them. One such inn is the **Keeler Tavern,** 132 Main St. (tel. 438-5485), at the junction of Rtes. 33 and 35. The tavern is now a museum, open (except January) on Wednesday, Saturday, and Sunday from 1 to 4 p.m. (last tour leaves at 3:20 p.m.). Pay the admission fee of $2 per adult, $1 per child, and guides in colonial garb will take you through the historic (1733) building with its late–18th-century furnishings, pointing out the tap room, guest quarters, dining room, kitchen, and parlor. Despite the careful preservation and reconstruction of the tavern's early life, its most famous feature was added by accident. During the Battle of Ridgefield (1777) in the Revolutionary War, a British gun sent a ball right into the Keeler's wall, where it remains to this day.

There is more to see in Ridgefield than cannonballs, however. The **Aldrich Museum of Contemporary Art,** 258 Main St. (tel. 203/438-4519), hosts changing exhibits of work by modern artists, even though the museum building itself is classic Ridgefield, having been built in 1783. The museum's sculpture garden is a fine place for a stroll or a few precious moments of peace, quiet, and beauty. Concerts, films, and lectures are offered from time to time. Plan your visit for Friday from 2:30 p.m. to 4:30; or on Saturday and Sunday from 1 to 5 p.m.; closed Monday through Thursday. Adults pay $2; seniors and children, half price.

---

2. New Haven

This is a town of spires and steeples, of Gothic towers and steel-and-glass towers, very much of the present and very much of the past. While New Haven was founded in 1638, the crucial year in its history was 1718, for in that year Connecticut's "Collegiate School" for the training of young men for the ministry decided to make its permanent and perpetual home in New Haven, ignoring the suits and blandishments of the other notable towns of Hartford and Saybrook. Perhaps the college came to New Haven because a local man offered a good deal of financial assistance, and in fact it was for this assistance that the school's name was changed to honor Elihu Yale.

New Haven has never been the same. Although today it is a town of business and industry—small arms, the telephone company, the county government—it is still more than anything the town where Yale is, and the presence of the great university dominates New Haven's social and cultural life.

INFORMATION: The **New Haven Convention & Visitors Bureau** maintains a year-round Information Center right in the center of town on the Green at 900 Chapel St., Suite 344 (tel. 203/787-8367), open Monday through Friday from 9 a.m. to 4 p.m. They also operate an information center off I-95 at Long Wharf Exit 4b, from mid-April to mid-October. At no cost, they will answer questions and give maps of the bus routes and streets, literature on the city's attractions including suggested walking tours, current material on recreational, educational, cultural, and special events in the area.

WHERE TO STAY: New Haven is short on those cozy, charming lodging places (inns and bed-and-breakfasts) which are found so densely scattered throughout the rest of New England. Most of the city's lodgings are to be found in modern hotels downtown, and motels on the outskirts.

Downtown Hotels

The prime downtown location is that held by the **Park Plaza Hotel,** 155 Temple St., New Haven, CT 06511 (tel. 203/772-1700), in the shopping and office complex facing the green. The Park Plaza has all those nice big-hotel services, such as an outdoor swimming pool, rooftop restaurant, a lounge with entertainment, and comfortable guest rooms with private bath, cable color television, and air conditioning. Rates for this convenient location are quite reasonable, at $79 single, $89 double.

The **Colony Inn,** 1157 Chapel St., New Haven, CT 06511 (tel. 203/776-1234), on Chapel between Park and York, is known to Yalies and their parents as a comfortable and convenient place to stay during campus visits. It's located just a block from the Yale Rep Theatre and the Yale Art Gallery, and only 3½ blocks west of the green, so you can't go wrong. The spacious rooms in this modern five-story building are done in contemporary style with colonial accents and reproduction pieces. All the comforts are here: free cable TV movies in your room, as well as telephone, air conditioning, and turn-down service. Other hotel services include indoor parking, a restaurant, and a lounge with live entertainment. Single travelers pay $82 to $84; two people pay $92 to $94; and an extra person pays $10. Suites are $150 to $400.

The **Holiday Inn–Downtown** is at 30 Whalley Ave., New Haven, CT 06511 (tel. 203/777-6221 or toll free 800/465-4329), very near Yale and only a five-minute walk from the center of town. The 160 rooms here are all equipped with color TV, and cost $69 to $96 single, $80 to $110 double. Teenage children can stay free with their parents. The hotel has its own "Café Sandalwood" restaurant and lounge, with foods from all over the world.

The downtown **Howard Johnson Motor Lodge–Long Wharf** is at 400 Sargent Dr., New Haven, CT 06511 (tel. 203/562-1111, or toll free 800/654-2000), near Long Wharf. Take Exit 46 from I-95. At this very comfortable, hotel-like lodge, you're very close to the Long Wharf Theatre and not far from the center of town. The rooms have king-size beds in some of them, but prices are $78 to $83 single, $85 to $91 double; an extra person pays $8, but kids under 18 stay free. Higher rates apply at graduation time. Senior citizens get a 15% discount.

The marvelous old **Hotel Duncan,** 1151 Chapel St., New Haven, CT 06511

(tel. 203/787-1273), boasts that it is "New Haven's oldest established hotel," and it is certainly well established, having stood solidly on Chapel Street between Park and York for at least half a century. To enter its Romanesque portal is to step back in time, right into a set for a black-and-white movie from the 1940s or 1950s. The Duncan's adventages are its location, just four blocks west of the green, and even fewer blocks from the Yale campus; its prices, which are $41 single, $56 double in a room; $50 single, $67 double in a suite; and the friendly, unpretentious, low-key staff and management. Don't expect up-to-the-minute comforts in these 100 rooms, for the Duncan is a true period piece. Expect basic, even worn, accommodations, but also basic cleanliness. The Duncan is a favorite with the young and the artistic, who love the fact that it is an honest, authentic echo of another time.

A Downtown Inn

The **Inn at Chapel West,** 1201 Chapel St., New Haven, CT 06511 (tel. 203/777-1201), is a well-located Victorian clapboard house that fills a gap in New Haven's lodging market. The ten rooms are elegant and sophisticated, catering largely to Yale parents, alumni, and dignitaries. All the rooms are, of course, uniquely decorated with a designer's flare: touches of lace, mahogany, brass fixtures, four-poster beds, and down pillows. Prices for all this luxury are $135 to $189 double; cots are available. A light breakfast is included; the innkeeper has it catered from a local restaurant.

Highway Motels

Your best bet for a good, moderately priced motel room is the cluster of hostelries near New Haven on the Wilbur Cross Parkway. The parkway is the scenic alternative to I-95. Passing several miles northeast of New Haven, the parkway provides access to the city at its Exits 57 (Conn. 34, Derby Avenue), 59 (Conn. 63, Whalley Avenue), and 60 (Conn. 10, Dixwell Avenue). Motels are grouped at each exit, but the best selection is at Exit 59, Whalley Avenue.

Staying at Exit 59 you'll be exactly 3½ miles from the greensward of Yale's Old Campus, the very center of the city. The "Amity Road" bus, no. B-1, will shuttle you between the motels and the center of town. A small shopping center and several restaurants are within walking distance of each motel.

The **Quality Inn,** 100 Pond Lily Ave., New Haven, CT 06525 (tel. 203/387-6651), boasts that it can accommodate 1,086 people at one time—and at moderate prices. The style here is what you might call "motel Georgian," handsome as well as functional. As you approach the motel (follow the signs from Exit 59), you'll think the place has about 18 rooms. But behind the main building (which is where you register) are several other large buildings boasting 125 rooms in all. You pay $58 single, $70 double (as always, tax included) to stay here. Swimming pools (one indoors), putting green, saunas, whirlpool baths, exercise room, and restaurant are all on site. The Quality Inn was once the city's prime place to stay. The motel was recently completely refurbished.

Farther north, at Exit 61 North (Exit 62 South) is a **Howard Johnson,** 2260 Whitney Ave., Hamden, CT 06518 (tel. 203/288-3831, or toll free 800/654-2000). The bonus here, as at many large nationally franchised motels, is that children up to 18 years old can stay with their parents for free. Rooms have color TVs, and cost $56 to $60 single, $60 to $68 double.

If you get off I-95 at Exit 55 coming from New Haven, turn right at the stop sign to pass underneath the highway and you'll come to the large **Branford Motor Inn and Conference Center,** P.O. Box 449, Branford, CT 06405 (tel. 203/488-8314). A U-shaped group of buildings faces U.S. 1 across a wide swath of lawn complete with swimming pool. Scores of guest rooms fill the two-story buildings, each room having air conditioning, direct-dial telephone, cable color TV and Home Box Office movies. Rooms in the newer annex are several dollars more expensive than those in the older main buildings, and the price structure is further complicated by the size, number of beds, and special features (waterbed, steambath, handicapped accessible, etc.). The cheapest single room goes for $50, the cheapest double for $67. The most luxurious, expensive mini-suite costs $108. Note that children aged 18 or under stay for free with their parents. You'll find a coffeeshop and restaurant right on the premises.

WHERE TO DINE: New Haven's restaurants are spread throughout the metropolitan area, with no particularly rich concentration right downtown such as one finds in Hartford or Boston. But if you are selective, it is not difficult to find the meal you're looking for, at the price you want to pay, within walking distance of the green. Part of the problem is that many New Havenites who enjoy dining out belong to private clubs (the famed Mory's is one of these), and thus tend not to patronize restaurants that are open to the general public.

Restaurants Near the Green

The chic brasserie and bar near the green is **Bruxelles,** 220 College St. (tel. 777-7752), at the corner of Crown Street, a block west of the green. Black bentwood chairs and tables are the main feature of the simple but elegant decor here. To the left as you enter is the well-stocked bar; to the right, the dining rooms, and huge vertical grills with spits loaded with chickens, ducks, and whole roasts of pork and beef. At dinner you can start with something like goat cheese on an herbed tomato, then order Texas barbecue chicken, or roast tuna steak au poivre, or roast duck with peach-raspberry sauce. There is good luncheon fare as well, but don't miss a roast in the evening. Dinner might cost $20 to $30, including a glass or two of some premium vintage or brew from the well-selected wine and beer lists. Bruxelles is open Sunday through Thursday from 11:30 a.m. to 11:30 p.m., on Friday and Saturday till 1:30 a.m., which makes it good for an after-theater drink and snack.

Perfect for elegant picnic supplies, that's **Soirée,** 230 College St. (tel. 562-0821), between Chapel and Crown Streets, a half block west of the green, and virtually next door to the Palace Theater. In this group of shops established in an old town house you can buy potato-leek soup, chicken salad, asparagus spears with wild-mushroom cream sauce, lobster salad, French cheeses and breads, and sandwiches. They will pack it all up to go, or you can sit at one of their little tables inside, or out front by the sidewalk, and dig in. You can easily spend $6 to $11 per person for restaurant-class fare. But for main courses such as grilled salmon or a braised lamb shank with goat cheese expect to pay upward of $19. The fancy desserts here are beautiful! The café is open every day from 11 a.m. to 3 p.m. and Tuesday to Thursday from 5 to 8 p.m., from 5 to 9 p.m. on Friday and Saturday. The shops are open every day, throughout the day.

Book lovers (and there are plenty of them in New Haven) congregate at the **Atticus Bookstore-Café,** 1082 Chapel St. (tel. 776-4040), right next to the entrance to the Yale Center for British Art. Sip tea and consume pastry while scanning the shelves from the comfort of your table, or browse through the store accompanied by the heavenly smell of coffee brewing. Come in the morning for croissants and coffee, in the afternoon for cakes and tea. Either repast might cost about $5, but perhaps you should add in the price of the book you'll discover, and buy. The store is open Monday through Friday from 8 a.m. to midnight, on Saturday from 9 a.m. to midnight, and on Sunday from 9 a.m. to 9 p.m.

An old standby for lunch or supper is the **Foundry Café,** 104 Audubon St. (tel. 776-5144), near the corner of Whitney Avenue and Audubon. The Foundry was just that, a machine foundry building, until it was recycled into a bookstore, shops, and the café. The one small café room has a bar/lunch counter, a blackboard menu, and some beautiful old inlaid wood chess tables as dining tables. Lunch and dinner are served Monday through Saturday from 11:30 a.m. to midnight. Fare is simple but tasty: a selection of sandwiches for $3 to $5, a seafood-salad platter for $6, cheesecake for less than $2. In the evening the Foundry Café is a bar and nightclub.

Happy hour, when the snacks are free, is every weekday evening from 4 to 7 p.m., and there's entertainment (usually jazz) on Wednesday through Sunday evenings.

Birthplace of the Hamburger

An audacious claim, to say that **Louis' Lunch**, 261 Crown St., at the corner of Chestnut Ridge Road (tel. 562-5507), was the "purveyor of the first hamburger in the U.S.A.," but so it is.

Louis' started in 1900, serving the first thinly sliced steak sandwich, and then developed the vertically grilled ground-beef sandwich. The beef is still ground fresh daily and grilled in the original antique vertical grills. Served on toast with tomato and onion, the hamburger ($1.70) is also available as a cheeseburger (introduced in 1931) for no extra charge. Threatened by downtown redevelopment some years ago, faithful Louis' fans saw to it that the brick structure was picked up and moved safely to its present location. Many—from all over the world—donated bricks for use in resettlement.

Louis' caters faithfully to New Haven's weekday lunch crowd from 9 a.m. to 11 a.m. and from 11:30 a.m. to 4:30 p.m., closed weekends. Coffee and soft drinks are available.

Restaurants near Wooster Square

About six blocks east of the green along Chapel Street lies Wooster Square, a lovely green park surrounded by some of this city's most interesting old houses. In this area, Chapel Street and Wooster Street (parallel, one block south) hold many restaurant choices, many of them featuring Italian cuisine.

My favorite here is **Tony & Lucille's Little Italy**, 150 Wooster St. (tel. 787-1621), near Crown and Chestnut Streets. It's actually a restaurant in two locations. At Wooster and Crown is a modern building meant to resemble an Italian villa inside, with a pleasant skylit courtyard and arcade that are sunny and cheery, but at the same time air-conditioned. An antique espresso machine shines gloriously beneath one arcade. Tables are clothed in red-and-white checks, waiters wear black and white, and the menu is pure Italian. I had a huge bowl of zuppadi mussels and clams on a bed of linguine—I couldn't finish it—with a salad that was in fact a small antipasto. With bread and butter, coffee, tax, and tip, I paid $13.50 at lunch. At dinner, top prices are for the fancy cuts of veal, but there are many pasta choices such as fettuccine, linguine, and some seafood dishes, so you can spend anywhere from $20 to $30 for a full meal.

The restaurant's other location, called the Annex, a block east at the corner of Wooster and Chestnut Streets, is a cozy storefront bistro serving simpler fare such as calzones for $4 to $6.

Hours for Tony & Lucille's are Tuesday through Thursday from noon to 10 p.m., on Friday to 11 p.m., on Saturday from 3 to 11 p.m., and on Sunday from 3 to 10 p.m.; closed Monday.

For pizza, New Haven's favorite is **Frank Pepe's**, on Wooster Street at Crown (tel. 865-5762), two storefronts in which you will find bare wooden booths, brick walls, little in the way of atmosphere, but fantastic pizza. People line up in front of the restaurant to receive the hot pizzas that issue from the huge ovens in the back. The assortment is bewildering, ranging from a small grated-cheese pizza for $3.50 to large pies at $10.50; large ones with chicken or fresh clams cost more, up to $15. Pepe's is open Monday, Wednesday, and Thursday from 4 to 10:30 p.m., Friday and Saturday from 11:30 a.m. to midnight, and Sunday from 2:30 to 10:30 p.m.; closed Tuesday.

WHAT TO SEE: The churches on the green have illustrious heritages of design, for Gothic-style Trinity Church is said to have been modeled somewhat on England's York Minster; Center Church and United Church are both said to have sprung from early plans for London's famous St. Martin's-in-the-Fields. Center Church, in Georgian style, is particularly interesting as it was built on an old burying ground, and today has a crypt under it where you can see over 100 of the early gravestones. Guided tours of the church are offered Tuesday through Sunday.

Three blocks northeast of the green is Grove Street Cemetery, a beautiful park-like sward, fitting final resting place for such eminent New Haven citizens as Eli Whitney, Noah Webster, and Charles Goodyear.

Yale University

New Haven's prime attraction is Yale, almost three centuries old, founded in 1701 and moved to New Haven in 1716. Daily, Yale sponsors free guided tours of the campus (tel. 432-2300) weekdays at 10:30 a.m. and 2 p.m., weekends at 1:30 p.m. Tours start at 344 College Street across from the green, at a place called Phelps Gateway (look for the inscription "Lux et Veritas"), where the university has its information office.

Yale's campus reminds one of England's Oxford, for it's much more American Collegiate Gothic than, say, Harvard, which is mostly Georgian and colonial in style. Yale's got lots of open, grassy courts, and flèched towers. Centerpiece of this English Gothic world is **Harkness Tower,** inscribed with the famous motto that has for generations admonished Yale students to move ever upward: "For God, For Country, and For Yale." Harkness Tower has a carillon, which is played daily throughout the academic year. You can also see the art galleries, the Beinecke Rare Book Library, the Georgian-style Connecticut Hall, and the Gothic-style Sterling Memorial Library.

The Peabody Museum

Yale's Peabody Museum of Natural History (tel. 432-5050 or 432-5799) is one of those fine, turn-of-the-century collections assembled when American scientists were venturing into all the corners of the world to bring back specimens of terra, flora, and fauna for study and observation by university students. Dinosaur bones, dioramas featuring exotic animals, mineral displays, and the like are all on show, although of course what the museum can show is only a fraction of its vast holdings. Besides the permanent exhibits, the museum sponsors special shows, lectures, and films. Admission is $2 per adult, $1 per child 5 to 15 (under 5, free). The museum, at 170 Whitney Ave. (on the corner of Sachem), is open from 9 a.m. to 4:45 p.m. Monday through Saturday, from 11 a.m. to 4:45 p.m. on Sunday. Free on Tuesday.

Galleries

Opened in April 1977, on the Yale campus is the **Yale Center for British Art,** 1080 Chapel St. near the corner of High Street (tel. 432-2800). The center has a fine collection of works by British artists, and also features regular special exhibitions, lectures, films, and concerts. Check *New Haven Info* or the *New Haven Register* listings for current offerings. You can visit and see what the center has to offer from 10 a.m. to 5 p.m. Tuesday through Saturday, from 2 to 5 p.m. on Sunday; closed Mondays. Admission is free.

Yale's major art collection is in the **Yale University Art Gallery,** on Chapel Street between High and York. The oldest university art museum in the western hemisphere, the Yale Gallery is justifiably proud of its Garvan Collection of American Furniture and Silver. Anyone interested in 18th-century American silver has got to see the Garvan—it's the best in the world. Along with Van Gogh's masterpiece *The Night Café,* there are paintings by Rubens, Hals, Manet, Picasso, and others. The university's collections form a substantial holding of European, African, pre-Columbian, American, and Asian art on view Tuesday through Saturday from 10 a.m. to 5 p.m., on Sunday from 2 to 5 p.m. There are also Thursday-evening hours from 5 to 8 p.m. during the academic year. Lectures, concerts, films, and special exhibits are always on when the university is in session; see the listings for current events.

Performing Arts

Because of Yale, New Haven has a surprisingly rich cultural life in music, dance, and drama. Each academic year sees concerts and performances by over a dozen excellent groups including the New Haven Symphony Orchestra, the Yale Concert Band, Yale Glee Club, Yale Jazz Ensemble, the Bach Society, the New Haven Civic Orchestra, and the Community Choir. The Yale Repertory Theater and the Long Wharf Theater (a proving-ground for New York–bound plays) get very good reviews each season, as does the Connecticut Ballet Company. New Haven also plays host to visits from the Boston Symphony Orchestra, major concert and popular performers, and groups. Several buildings in and around the campus are foci for these events. The listings recommended above have full information on the current season's performances. Most will be within a few blocks of the green. Long Wharf is a bit farther out, next to Howard Johnson's, in the wholesale market at 222 Sargent Dr. (Connecticut Turnpike Exit 46; tel. 787-4282).

Downtown theaters include the **Shubert** (tel. 624-1825) and the **Palace** (tel. 624-8497), across from one another on College Street between Chapel and Crown, a half block south of the green behind the Taft Apartments. The **Yale Rep** (tel. 432-1234) is in a former church building on Chapel Street, corner of York, two blocks west of the green.

Nightlife Notes

New Haven must retain its dignity as the seat of Yale University. But that doesn't mean things are dead at night. Try the **Foundry Café,** mentioned above under "Where to Dine," for live music.

Boppers, at the corner of College and Crown Streets (tel. 562-1957), is a re-created '50s diner, complete with half the body of a '56 Buick Special. Though you can dine here on burgers and pizza, the attraction is the '50s music (recorded) for dancing.

---

3. Connecticut River Valley

Strictly speaking, the Connecticut River Valley extends all the way from Long Island South to northern New Hampshire. It's the lower valley that we're interested in, though. Besides being particularly beautiful, the last 100 or so miles of the river's course has figured prominently in Connecticut history. The small towns retain the charm of a bygone era, and the river's banks are scattered with state parks and forests.

From New Haven, it's about 30 miles along I-95 to the mouth of the river. About midway you pass **Hammonassett Beach State Park,** which has facilities for camping and picnicking, hiking trails, and a fine beach for boating, swimming and scuba diving.

Before reaching the river's edge, the highway passes Westbrook, where there's a nice inn, and then Old Saybrook, a town with picturesque views. On the east bank of the river is Old Lyme, with several fine inns. Heading northwest up the river on Rte. 9 brings you to Essex, perhaps the busiest and most charming river town, with one of Connecticut's most acclaimed inns. Ivoryton, to the west, also has several fine inns, and an old steam railroad. Due north of Ivoryton lies Chester, a charming village with good possibilities for dining and lodging, and just across the river from it, by an antique car-ferry, is Hadlyme, with its own hilltop castle. North of Hadlyme, on the same (east) bank of the river is East Haddam, home of the famous Goodspeed Opera House, and several good inns. All of this is yours in a distance of 20 miles, from Westbrook to East Haddam.

WESTBROOK: In 1860, Capt. Elbert Stannard built a gracious mansion in Westbrook for his retirement years after a long career of commanding trading ships in the Orient. His home is now the **Captain Stannard House,** 138 S. Main St., Westbrook, CT 06498 (tel. 203/399-7565), a lovely old inn and antique shop. The house has been carefully restored and maintained, the guest rooms filled with nice old pieces of brass, wicker, and oak, including brass and four-poster beds, handmade textiles and crafts, and equipped with modern bathrooms and climate control. There's the antique shop for browsing, a lounge with TV, and a refrigerator with ice and soft drinks. The innkeepers, Arlene and Ed Amatrudo, are out to make your stay here an enjoyable and memorable one. Prices for the six guest rooms are $75 to $85 during the high summer season; the room with the canopy bed goes for $80 double. Two couples can share the Captain Stannard Suite of two rooms for $160 total. A light breakfast is included in these rates. To find the inn, take Exit 65 from I-95, to U.S. 1 East, then immediately left onto South Main Street. Follow this street to its end, where you'll see the grand house with a fan window above the door and a cupola perched on top.

OLD SAYBROOK: Old Saybrook is the gateway to scenic Saybrook Point, with its two lighthouses. If you have time for a pretty drive, come up from Westbrook on U.S. 1 East, then follow Rte. 154 through Knollwood, Fenwick (where Katharine Hepburn lives), and Saybrook Point to Old Saybrook. To cross the river to Old Lyme, you will have to leave all this tranquility and climb back onto I-95 eastbound.

OLD LYME: This village is a painter's paradise, and has been so for quite a while. During the early years of this century, Miss Florence Griswold opened the doors of her mansion on Lyme Street to painters, mostly American Impressionists, whom she admired, including Charles Ebert, Childe Hassam, Willard Metcalfe, Henry Ward Ranger, and Guy and Carleston Wiggins. Painters being painters, no matter how talented, they were sometimes unable to scrape together the month's rent for a room in the mansion, so instead they did what they could: they painted the door panels of the house with scenes from around Old Lyme. The house is now a museum, and one of your prime reasons for stopping here. The other reason is that Old Lyme has several fine inns, good for lodging and for dining.

Inns

The village's prime hostelry is the gracious and elegant **Old Lyme Inn,** Lyme Street, Old Lyme, CT 06371 (tel. 203/434-2600), a fine mansion dating from the 1850s. Innkeeper Diana Field Atwood has found period furnishings from many New England locales with which to do the rooms, and so you'll find canopy beds, marbletopped dressers and vanities, old steamer trunks, and antique mirrors. Nine of the guest rooms are in the new (1985) north wing which is designed to harmonize with the original mansion and other structures on historic Lyme Street. North Wing rooms are preferable because of their better size and quiet, though the five rooms in the original mansion are certainly charming. All rooms have air conditioning, private bath, telephone, and clock radio, and rent for $95 to $125 double. A continental breakfast is included in the rates.

The Old Lyme Inn's dining room is open for lunch daily except Monday from noon to 2 p.m., on Sunday for lunch from 11:30 a.m. to 4 p.m.; for dinner Tuesday through Saturday from 6 to 9 p.m., on Sunday from 4 to 9 p.m.; closed on Monday. Tapestries, gleaming silver, and a formal atmosphere greet you in the high-ceilinged dining room, renowned for its fine cuisine, especially local seafood and veal.

Bob and Penny Nelson's **Bee and Thistle Inn,** 100 Lyme St., Old Lyme, CT 06371 (tel. 203/434-1667), dates from colonial times (1756), with many later additions. Its situation, on its own estate of more than five shady acres bordering the Lieutenant River, is superb. The 11 guest rooms have furnishings reflecting the inn's long history: canopy, four-poster or spool beds, washstands, handmade quilts and afghans, wing chairs, but also private baths in most cases. The price for a room is $70 to $110 double. The dining room is open for lunch and dinner as well. Fare at lunch can be simple as a sandwich, but there are always daily special plates which are more elaborate. Dinner is full course, emphasizing seafood and game in elegant and ingenious preparations. The dining room is closed on Tuesday.

Museums

The **Florence Griswold Museum,** the late-Georgian mansion at 96 Lyme St. (tel. 434-5542), was built in 1817 and is now under the care of the Lyme Historical Society. Visit the first-floor rooms where Miss Florence's artist guests used to paint. Upstairs are galleries concentrating on the works of this "Lyme School" of American Impressionism, and on changing shows, including New England furnishings and decorative arts. Hours June through October are Tuesday through Saturday from 10 a.m. to 5 p.m., on Sunday from 1 to 5 p.m. (closed Monday); and November through May, Wednesday through Sunday from 1 to 5 p.m. Admission costs $2 for adults, and children under 12 can enter for free.

Lyme Street has a wealth of cultural offerings. The **Lyme Academy of Fine Arts,** 84 Lyme St. (tel. 434-5232), housed in another gracious building dating from 1817, has changing shows of modern and earlier painters. Hours are 9 a.m. to 4:30 p.m. Monday through Friday, or by appointment.

The **Lyme Art Association,** 70 Lyme St. (tel. 434-7802), has five major shows each summer, and asks only for a donation to see them. Call for news of the current exhibition, and viewing hours.

ESSEX: This was a shipbuilding and sea captain's town, founded in 1648. At first life in Essex was centered on farming, but within 100 years the shipbuilding industry grew and brought Essex much greater prosperity. The early name, by the way, was the Indian one of Potapaug, which served to identify the town until well into the 19th century.

Today Essex is one of the most picturesque towns in Connecticut, its old houses well kept, its boatyards and marina bobbing with sleek yachts and power boats.

Where to Stay and Eat

Essex's fine old **Griswold Inn** (tel. 203/767-1812) is famous throughout Connecticut for its location, food, and lodging. The rooms are quaint and old-fashioned, with low ceilings and exposed rough-hewn rafters, hooked rugs on the floors, perhaps a marble-topped vanity or a similar piece in one corner. All the rooms are air-conditioned, and all have private bath. Price for the rooms: $75 double (both double beds and twins are available). Continental breakfast is included in the rates. Note that in summer it may be necessary to reserve a weekend date two months in advance, so call or write to the Griswold Inn, Essex, CT 06426.

The Griswold's several dining rooms are well done and interesting. At lunch, have the Griswold's own brand of sausages for $5 or $6, or a sandwich for about the same. Luncheon plates are only $1 more. Dinner specialties are hearty, with seafood and steaks for $14 to $20. The wine list is quite good, the beer both domestic and imported, and the draft is the English lager named Courage.

The Griswold is known for its Sunday "Hunt Breakfasts," when for $12 (11 a.m. to 2:30 p.m.) you can help yourself to unlimited amounts of eggs, bacon, and ham, sausage, grits, fried potatoes, kippers, chicken, lamb kidneys, creamed chipped beef, smelts, or whatever else is offered for the day. For children 6 and under, breakfast is on the house.

One of the most elegant and delightful dining places in all southern Connecticut is a few minutes from Essex in nearby Ivoryton. It's the **Copper Beech Inn,** described a few paragraphs below—read on.

What to See and Do

From Essex Square (the intersection of Main, North Main, South Main, and

Pratt Streets), walk down Main Street past the Griswold Inn to the riverside end, known as the Foot of Main, where you'll come across the **Connecticut River Museum** (tel. 767-8269), a dockhouse for steamboats built in 1878 and recently restored. Ship models, paintings, photographs, and other exhibits recall life on the Connecticut River in years gone by. Kids will love the replica of the nation's first submarine, the *Turtle,* constructed in 1775. The museum is open year-round, Tuesday through Sunday from 10 a.m. to 5 p.m. Admission is $2.50. Call to verify winter hours.

Walk up Pratt Street for a look at the old houses, and then from Essex Square, take a drive out North Main Street to view the fine old mansions. This quick tour leaves out lots of interesting side streets, corners, and crannies of Essex, and if you have the time, you could do worse than to poke around town, turning up quaint vignettes and fine river views. To see the inside of an old Essex house, go to the **Pratt House** at 19 West Ave. (tel. 767-0861), west out of Essex Square on Methodist Hill, toward the highway, now owned by the Society for the Preservation of New England Antiquities. The house is a center-chimney colonial with an outstanding collection of American furnishings from earliest colonial times up through the last century. Except for a special exhibit at Christmastime, it's open from 1 to 4 p.m. only on Friday, Saturday, and Sunday from June through September. Admission costs $2.50 for adults, $1.50 for seniors, free for children under 12.

IVORYTON: Ivoryton is a part of Essex for municipal government purposes, but it has a character and history of its own. The name came from the ivory industry set up here by the Comstock family, and many of the ivory keys for America's pianos and organs were made here. The ivory industry is gone, but the company that makes Witch Hazel, that soothing and astringent distillate, is still going strong on the Essex/Ivoryton boundary.

Inns

The reason to go to Ivoryton is to dine at the **Copper Beech Inn,** on Main Street (tel. 767-0330). The inn was built as the home of a prosperous ivory merchant, and is now one of New England's most gracious places to dine: tables have fresh flowers and a full French service in silver. The Comstock Room has fine dark-wood paneling; the garden porch is mostly windows and plants, with a floor of quarry tiles and a unique pineapple chandelier. Behind the inn is the **Greenhouse,** a real one set with wicker chairs and small tables, and it's here that cocktails are served. The menu for dinner is among the best in New England: boned breast of pheasant, shrimp and scallops with tarragon cream and mushrooms, filet of beef Wellington with sauce périgourdine—and it goes on to 14 items, none common, all interesting. Entrees are mostly $22 to $25, with some less, some more. Appetizers such as clams roasted with garlic butter and Pernod, topped with hazelnuts, cost $8 to $13. The desserts offered (about $5) include the Copper Beech Inn's Sachertorte.

Dinner is served at the Copper Beech from 6 to 9 p.m. Tuesday through Thursday, to 10 p.m. on Friday and Saturday; Sunday dinner is from 1 to 9 p.m. The Copper Beech also has 13 fine guest rooms with air conditioning and private bath for $85 to $145 double, continental breakfast included.

On Main Street in Ivoryton is the **Ivoryton Inn,** Ivoryton, CT 06442 (tel. 203/767-0422). Once the favorite of ivory traders visiting the town, it's now a favorite with vacationers. You'll recognize the gray clapboard building with orange awnings a half mile west of the Copper Beech Inn, and just a few minutes' walk from the Ivoryton Playhouse. The 30 rooms here are quite simple and homey, but comfortable and sufficient, with private bath (except for two rooms). The price includes continental breakfast: $55 to $85 double. On the ground floor of the inn is the tavern, a world of mellow wood and Windsor chairs, and the fairly formal restaurant.

The Valley Railroad

On the way from Essex to Ivoryton, the road (Railroad Avenue) passes the station of the Valley Railroad (tel. 203/767-0103). You can ride the old steam train five miles upriver to Chester and back. At Deep River Station, if you wish, you can get off the train and onto the riverboat *Becky Thatcher* to motor farther upriver past Gillette Castle (see below). Trains leave four times a day in fall, two times a day during spring, and several times every day beginning at 10:30 a.m. in summer; they connect with the boat for a two-hour combination trip. The train ride alone costs $8 for adults, $4 for children under 11; with a one-hour cruise, the prices are $10 and $5. Call for the latest information on schedules and fares.

CHESTER: This is a picture-perfect little Connecticut riverside village, nestled in the valley of the Pattaconk Brook. Its buildings are of white clapboard, yellow brick, or somber granite, its fences of fieldstone. Little shops line the short main street, along with the general store, the post office, and the library. It is charming, scenic, small, and wealthy.

Indian deeds to the land once known as the district of Pattaconk date from the 1660s. Colonial settlers moved to the district from Saybrook in the early 1700s, and by 1836 the town was incorporated as Chester. During the colonial period Chester was an industrial town, with a grist mill and a sawmill, and shipyards. The ferry service across the Connecticut River to Hadlyme was inaugurated in 1769, and continues to this day.

There is little to do in Chester except to enjoy the place itself, to stroll its main street, to ride or walk through the surrounding countryside, to dine in one of its few restaurants, and to stay the night in its excellent inn.

Inns

The **Inn at Chester,** 318 W. Main St., Chester, CT 06412 (tel. 203/526-4961), is the town's prime place to stay. It is not right in the village proper, but almost five miles from the center. Follow Rte. 148 west from Rte. 9, and you'll find the inn just this side of the Killingham town line. Its full name is "The Inn at Chester at the John B. Parmalee House," and it is in fact a mini-resort of lush landscaped lawns and gardens with the clapboard farmhouse built during the Revolutionary War (1776–1778) at its center. State forests adjoin the inn's land, providing nature trails for walks and lakes for swimming or ice skating. The original farmhouse now serves as the inn's dining room, for elegant and fancy cuisine in an appropriate setting. The other inn buildings are modern, but inspired by the Parmalee house, with natural wood, brick, and fieldstone used throughout. The 48 guest rooms are furnished with a double, a queen-size, or twin beds, and cost $92 to $98, single or double. Each comfortable, modern room has a private bath, air conditioning, and television set, but also fresh flowers, antiques, replicas, and Oriental carpets to maintain the ambience of a country inn. It's a beautiful place in a fine setting, often selected by small business and social groups for country retreats.

Restaurants

Downtown Chester's prime dining spot is the **Restaurant du Village,** on the main street (tel. 526-5301), a former shop with a simple, even plain decor of white walls, white tablecloths, and fresh flowers. The food's the thing here, and the French country-inn menu includes among the appetizers various French soups, and also saucisson à l'ail (French garlic sausage), smoked salmon, terrines, and the traditional escargots. Main courses range from the delicate trout poached in Riesling, through duck with pistachios, to a braised shoulder of lamb with garlic and vegetables. In season (autumn) there's fresh game. Dinner, which might cost $40 to $50 per person, is served Wednesday through Sunday from 5:30 to 9 p.m. The restaurant is closed on Monday from Labor Day to Memorial Day (that is, in fall, winter, and spring).

A few doors down the main street is the **Pattaconk Inn** (tel. 526-9285), a good local eatery featuring lots of seafood, including shore dinners, twin lobsters, baked scrod, and filet of sole, but also Rhode Island duckling. A full dinner should cost $15 to $25 here. Lunch is served every day, and dinner is served every day but Monday.

Going on a picnic? Right next door to the Pattaconk Inn is the **Chester Bread Works,** a bakery providing fresh baked goods and soups for picnics.

HADLYME: If you're driving, the most enjoyable way to get from Chester to Hadlyme is to take the old **Chester–Hadlyme ferry,** which takes cars ($1 for car and driver) as well as pedestrians (25¢) at prices more antique than the fairly modern boat which makes the run. Although the boat is new, the history of the ferry run at this point goes back to 1769, when one Jonathan Warner would drag you across the river for a small fee. Today the ferry is run by the State of Connecticut, and it operates April 15 through November 15 from 7 a.m. to 6:45 p.m. every day. The trip across the river is made right in the shadow of Gillette Castle, and takes about five minutes, not counting the short waiting time.

Gillette Castle State Park

Shortly after the turn of the century, an actor named William Gillette realized a lifelong dream by building himself a castle to live in. His stage career, including a very successful period in the role of Sherlock Holmes, had brought him the wealth he needed, and so in 1914 he started. Over five years and a million dollars later, the result was a strange-looking mansion of fieldstone named "The Seventh Sister," complete with a commanding view of the Connecticut River and its own three-mile-long excursion railroad. Inside the castle, on River Road in East Haddam (tel. 526-2336), Gillette gave vent to his passion for detail and exotica, bringing furnishings from around the world and specifying in great detail the form that was to be given to the intricately carved oak trim and the ingenious wooden door latches. Today William Gillette's fantasy house is known as Gillette Castle, and it's a state park open to all and sundry. The narrow-gauge railroad is gone, but forest paths, picnic tables, and river vista spots have replaced it. Tours of the house itself are given daily Memorial Day to Columbus Day, and weekends through mid-December, from 10 a.m. to 5 p.m., at a charge of $1 for adults (children under 12, 50¢; 12 and over, $1). Gillette Castle is either Connecticut's most distinguished medieval castle, or the largest backyard barbecue ever constructed—you decide.

EAST HADDAM: From Hadlyme, drive northwest a few miles to East Haddam, where you'll come face to face with the wonderful old Goodspeed Opera House.

Goodspeed Opera House

The Goodspeed Opera House is a riverside Victorian gem built in 1876 and now carefully restored to serve as a venue for American musical theater. Its setting by the river and the bridge is so picturesque that it's worth the ride just to see the exterior, but if you have the time, take a tour of the interior (on Monday only, July through October 9, from 1 to 3 p.m.; $1.50 for adults, 75¢ for kids). Best of all, see a play; the specialty is the revival of early musicals and the production of new works. Eight Goodspeed shows have moved to Broadway. Three musicals are offered each season beginning in late April and continuing through early December with performances every day but Monday and Tuesday, and a matinee on Wednesday. Tickets cost $24.50 to $25.50 Friday through Sunday, $1 less on other days. For the latest information and ticket reservations, call 203/873-8668.

River Cruises

Across the river from East Haddam in the village of Haddam is the office of **Camelot Cruises, Inc.,** 1 Marine Park, Haddam, CT 06438 (tel. 203/345-4505). From March through Christmas, they will take you on board the M/V *Camelot* for a luncheon or dinner cruise along the placid river. There's no better way to enjoy the scenery, and you get a meal and live entertainment to boot. This is fairly formal dining, and you are expected to dress "appropriately," that is, suits or sport jackets for men, a dress, skirt and blouse, or a nice slacks outfit for women.

Cruises depart rain or shine; you board the boat at Haddam a half hour prior to cruising time. The luncheon cruise boards at 11:30 a.m. and departs daily at noon, returning at 2:30 p.m.; in October, November, and December, luncheon cruises are operated only on Saturday and Sunday. The evening dinner cruise boards at 6:30 p.m. and departs daily except Sunday and Monday at 7 p.m., returning at 10 p.m.; in October, November, and December, cruises are on Friday and Saturday only. The price, meal (but not tax and tips) included, is $20 per person for the luncheon cruise, $38 for the dinner cruise; $24 for the Sunday Brunch Cruise. Children under 12 pay half price on either cruise.

---

4. New London and Groton

Visitors to these navy towns are usually here to see the U.S. Coast Guard Academy, or the navy submarine base at Groton. But there are other things to see and do as well. New London has a state park and a beachfront amusement park, as well as car-ferry services to Block Island, R.I., Fishers Island, N.Y., and Orient Point, Long Island, N.Y. Groton has Fort Griswold State Park.

The big draw in this region is, of course, Mystic Seaport. Many visitors choose to stay near Mystic, and tour New London and Groton on a day trip. However, there are some lodging possibilities in New London, Groton, and the nearby towns of Niantic and East Lyme, to the west.

WHERE TO STAY: Lodging establishments in this area consist almost exclusively of highway motels. Many are geared to the tourist trade rather than to the business or armed forces traveler.

Motels in Niantic

Just off I-95, Exit 74, at the intersection with Rte. 161, north of the town of Niantic, is a collection of motels with similar facilities and fairly low prices.

The local incarnation of **Howard Johnson's,** P.O. Box 185, East Lyme, CT 06333 (tel. 203/739-6921, or toll free 800/654-2000), is a pretty good bargain at $50 to $75 single, $58 to $80 double, or for a family (in the higher-priced rooms) during the summer season (late June through Labor Day); April, May, the greater part of June, and September, rates are 20% lower. Two saunas, an indoor pool, and color TV in the rooms make it a fairly plush place for a reasonable price. Kids under 18 stay free, and there's a senior-citizen discount.

Motels in Groton

The **Windsor Motel,** 345 Gold Star Hwy., Groton, CT 06340 (tel. 203/445-7474), at the Rte. 184 exit from I-95, has a good choice of accommodations—some especially good for families—at reasonable prices. Of the 58 motel rooms, 33 come with complete kitchens; all have TV, refrigerator, and air conditioning. The price structure is to your advantage: use only one double bed and you pay only $40 to $52; use both double beds and the price is $55 to $65. Children of any age, when traveling with a parent, stay free, so the two-bed price is what a family of four would pay! All these prices are substantially lower off-season, or for longer stays (a week or more).

WHAT TO SEE IN NEW LONDON: The major tourist attraction in New London is the **U.S. Coast Guard Academy,** on Mogehan Avenue, New London, CT 06320 (tel. 203/444-8270), which opens its campus to visitors from 9 a.m. to sunset daily. Admission is free. Start your tour of the grounds at the Visitors' Pavilion (open from 9 a.m. to 5 p.m. from May 1 through October). The academy's museum is open from 9 a.m. to 4 p.m. weekdays year round, and from 9 a.m. to 5 p.m. weekends and holidays May through October. A special treat here is a visit to the Coast Guard's training barque, *Eagle,* generally in port at the academy in April and May (open to visitors on Friday, Saturday, and Sunday from noon to 5 p.m. when in port). If you miss the *Eagle,* perhaps you can catch the colorful dress review of the Corps of Cadets, usually held (weather permitting) in April, May, September, and October. For times and dates, contact the Public Affairs Office at the above number.

Ferry to the Islands

New London is a major ferryboat port, with frequent summer sailings to Block Island, Rhode Island, and Fishers Island and Orient Point, N.Y., on the tip of Long Island.

Block Island: See the Block Island section of Chapter X for full details. The pier in New London is north of the railroad station (tel. 203/442-7891 or 442-9553). Follow the red-and-white signs to the dock.

Fishers Island: Daily ferries go to this New York island a few miles off the Connecticut coast, departing from the dock on State Street. For fares and schedules, call 203/443-6851.

Orient Point, Long Island: The dock for these is on Ferry Street; details from the Cross Sound Ferry Service are available by calling 203/443-5281, 444-0783, 444-0482, or 443-5035; for reservations from Orient Point, call 516/323-2415, 323-2695, 323-2525, or 323-2743. Cars are carried ($25), and reservations for the 1½-hour cruise (adults, $9; kids, half price) are a must in high summer.

Ocean Beach Park

New London's major beach-and-amusement complex is at Ocean Beach Park, near Harkness Memorial State Park south of the city (Exit 75-76 from I-95; tel. 447-3031). Besides the beach, a boardwalk allows strolling to check out other members of the swimsuit set, miniature golf will test your reflexes, amusement rides provide a cheap thrill, and an Olympic-size pool is provided for diving and freshwater swimming. If amusement parks and commercial beaches are your thing, this is one of the best on the coast.

WHAT TO SEE IN GROTON: Groton, "The Submarine Capital of the World," makes its living from General Dynamics' Electric Boat Division and from Pfizer pharmaceuticals, besides the naval facilities at the navy submarine base. A warning is in order: rush-hour traffic (8 to 9 a.m. and 5 to 6 p.m.) in the Groton/New London area is extremely heavy, especially along I-95 and its feeder roads. Make your getaway before 5 p.m., or stay and have dinner till the roads empty out.

No one comes to Groton to see anything but submarines, and there are plenty to see. Your tour here should be an auto-cruise along **Submarine Drive,** the waterfront road along the eastern bank of the Thames River named Thames Street south of I-95, and Military Highway to the north. Take Exit 85 from I-95, and follow Bridge Street to Thames Street.

Near the point where Bridge Street runs into Thames, just south of the Gold Star (I-95) Bridge, is the **U.S.S. *Flasher* National Submarine Monument.** The conning tower of this World War II Angler-class sub has been established here as a memorial to the American submarine sailors who lost their lives during that war. The

Flasher sank more than 100,000 tons of enemy shipping during the war, and its crew was repeatedly cited by the president for their services.

South of the monument a short drive is the **U.S.S. *Croaker* Submarine Memorial** (tel. 203/448-1616), a World War II submarine built by the Electric Boat Company of Groton and commissioned in April of 1944. After service in the Pacific, at the end of the war the *Croaker* came back to Groton, and the sub is now moored next to its "birthplace" and is open to the public. You can visit the control room, the torpedo rooms, the conning tower, and the engine rooms. Admission to the sub costs $3 for adults, half price for children 12 and under, $2 for seniors. Members of the armed forces in uniform are admitted for free. Visit any day from 9 a.m. to 4:30 p.m. (to 3 p.m. in winter).

While you're down in Groton, see the **Fort Griswold State Park** (tel. 445-1729), at Monument and Park Streets (Monument runs parallel to Thames Street). The heroic, tragic story of the American force which defended the fort in 1781 against the British is told in the museum, open from Memorial Day to Columbus Day. The Memorial Tower (view from the top) was erected for the courageous defenders who fought until overpowered and then perished in the massacre by the victorious British. The state park is open all year, and both the park and the museum are free of charge.

North of the Gold Star (I-95) Bridge, Submarine Drive continues along the Military Hwy. Near the entrance to the U.S. Navy's Groton Submarine Base is the **U.S.S. *Nautilus* National Memorial** (tel. 449-3174 or 449-3558), featuring the world's first nuclear-powered submarine. Launched in Groton in January 1954, the *Nautilus* saw its finest hour when it passed beneath the ice cap at the geographic North Pole in 1958, the first ship ever to reach that geographically significant spot. Decommissioned after 25 years of service, the sub is now open for free to visitors daily (except Tuesday) from 9 a.m. to 5 p.m., till 3:30 p.m. in winter (mid-October through mid-April). Note that the sub is closed during the third week of March and September, the first week of June, the second full week of December, Thanksgiving, Christmas, and New Year's Day. Displays in the Submarine Force Library and Museum chronicle the history of the U.S. submarine force since the Revolutionary War. You can peer into working periscopes and ponder all the knobs and dials in an authentic control room, all at no charge.

5. Mystic and Stonington

Connecticut's maritime life, past and present, is all on view in the area comprising the open-air museum called Mystic Seaport, and the pretty old seaside town of Stonington. Mystic Seaport is one of the top tourist attractions in New England, drawing very large crowds every day of the summer. The huge open-air "museum" is big enough to handle the crowds, but the capacity of nearby motels is not, the motels are packed in July and August, and guests must prepay their entire stay.

You can avoid the hotel crush altogether by taking an Amtrak train through this area, getting off for the day at Mystic, where a bus will take you from the station to Mystic Seaport. After your day roaming around the ships, old buildings, and exhibits, board an afternoon train to Providence or Boston (or New Haven, or New York). There's no extra charge for the stopover if you buy a through ticket, and you obviate the need for a room.

INFORMATION: Each of the towns listed below has its own information booths and offices, which I'll mention as we go along. For general inquiries your best bet is the **Mystic and Shoreline Visitors Information Center,** Olde Mistick Village, Mystic, CT 06355 (tel. 203/536-1641). Olde Mistick Village is the new colonial-style shopping complex just south of I-95 on Rte. 27, very near Mystic Seaport. The

Information Center is in Building 1, and is open Monday through Friday from 9:30 a.m. to 5:30 p.m., to 6 p.m. on Saturday, and on Sunday from 10 a.m. to 5 p.m.

WHERE TO STAY: During much of the year, and especially in high summer, Mystic is crowded with visitors who've come to tour famous Mystic Seaport. Though there are lots of lodging places, most will be full in July and August, so advance reservations are good to have.

Lodgings in Mystic proper are mostly hotels and motels, with a few guesthouses. In the nearby quiet village of Noank, a few miles south and east along Rte. 215, are some quiet inns. And in the delightful village of Stonington, about five miles east of Mystic along U.S. 1 and U.S. 1A, are several bed-and-breakfast houses.

Mystic's Hotels and Motels

One of Mystic's longtime favorites is the expansive **Inn at Mystic,** at the junction of Rtes. 1 and 27, Mystic, CT 06335 (tel. 203/536-9604). This large complex has several different classes of accommodation in separate buildings, all set atop a hill overlooking the water. As you drive up, you first approach the tidy motel units in several large buildings. The office is here, and also the Flood-Tide Restaurant. Motel rooms are modern, clean, and attractive, with some colonial reproductions to put you in the proper mood for visiting old Mystic. All have television, air conditioning, and private bath, and are priced at $103 to $141 during high summer. Above the motel along a drive shaded by large trees is the inn, a fine old mansion at the summit of the hill. Green lawns complete with miniature waterfall surround the house, which has a number of fine guest rooms decorated with period furniture and replicas, including private baths, and renting for $151 to $189 double. The inn's wide veranda is a favored place to sit and take in the view. Beyond the inn is the Gatehouse, a smaller building, also very pretty. The inn has its own boat dock, tennis court, swimming pool and hot spa, and walking trail. Children can share their parents' room at no extra charge; a third or fourth adult in a room pays $10. This is a dependable favorite, and worthy of your consideration.

The **Mystic Hilton,** Coogan Boulevard, Mystic, CT 06355 (tel. 203/572-0731, or toll free 800/445-8667), across from the Mystic Marinelife Aquarium and Olde Mistick Village, is just off I-95 at Exit 90. All the modern conveniences, comforts, and luxuries are here, in the 187 guest rooms, in the indoor-outdoor swimming pool, and in The Moorings (the hotel restaurant) and Soundings (its lounge). The price for a room is $86 to $146 single, $101 to $162 double, but you should definitely ask about their package plans, which can be very attractive. Also, note that there is no charge for children, regardless of age, when they occupy the same room as their parents.

The cluster of motels at Exit 90, the Rte. 27 interchange on I-95 includes several branches of big chains, and several local establishments.

Best buy here is the **Howard Johnson,** P.O. Box 159, Mystic, CT 06355 (tel. 203/536-2654, or toll free 800/654-2000), where, besides their standard rooms with cable color TV, you can enjoy an indoor pool, sauna, and a lounge, with widescreen cable TV as well as live entertainment (although presumably not at the same time). Children up to 18 can stay free. Prices depend on when you go: off-season rates are lower, but mid-June through September, rates are $76 single, $87 double. An extra person pays $10.

At the 150-room **Ramada Inn,** I-95 at Rte. 27, Mystic, CT 06355 (tel. 203/536-4281, or toll free 800/228-2828), the facilities include a restaurant, sauna, indoor pool, live entertainment, and a playground too. The year-round rates are $103 single or double.

The **Taber Inn and Guest House,** 29 Williams Ave., on U.S. 1 east of Mystic, CT 06355 (tel. 203/536-4904), is more than a motel: besides its very tidy motel rooms, it can rent you a room in a restored inn (1829), a restored farmhouse, a two-bedroom cottage, or an efficiency apartment. All rooms have private bath, cable color TV, phone, and air conditioning. In high summer, rooms go for $92 double in the motel, about $15 less in the inn and farmhouse, free coffee included.

Only a few car lengths north of I-95 at Exit 90 is the **Days Inn**, Rte. 27, Mystic, CT 06355 (tel. 203/572-0574, or toll free 800/325-2525). The pleasant new two-story motel has 122 simple but clean rooms, each with two double beds, cable color television, wall-to-wall carpeting, direct-dial telephone, and air conditioning. Though prices are $76 to $82 single, $82 to $89 double, extra services such as a restaurant open for all three meals, an outdoor swimming pool, nonsmoking rooms, cots, cribs, and elevator service, are standard.

Guesthouses

Mystic has only a few guesthouses, but there may be more in the future, and the Information Office may be able to provide you with more names.

The **Harbour Inne & Cottage**, Edgemont Street (Rte. 1, Box 398), Mystic, CT 06355 (tel. 203/572-9253), is right next to the water in a part of town that is part residential and part industrial, but clean and quiet. The two small buildings of bright natural cedar, once a fisherman's house, are neat as a pin. In the guesthouse, the rooms are cozy and cheerful with that same honey-colored wood, private baths with shower stalls, television sets, and air conditioners. In the cottage next door are one bedroom, a kitchen and bath, and sofas that convert to beds so that the place can sleep up to six people. Rooms in the guesthouse cost $45 to $65 double; the cottage rents for $110 per night. Charley Lecouras, Jr., the smiling owner, will rent you a canoe or rowboat, and you can set out for a cruise right from the inn's own dock. To find it, first make your way to Mystic's Amtrak station. Take the dead-end street to the right of the station, then turn right onto Edgemont Street, also a dead end, and the guesthouse is down a ways, on the left.

Comolli's Guest House, 36 Bruggeman Pl., Mystic, CT 06355 (tel. 203/536-8723), is a tidy white house in a residential neighborhood very near Mystic Seaport, where your homey room has its own color television. Room prices range from $50 to $85, depending on the room, the privacy of the bath, and the season. Call Dorothy M. Comolli for reservations. Bruggeman Place is off Rte. 27 near Mystic Seaport, and the guesthouse is at the top of the hill, on the right-hand side.

An Inn in Noank

The **Palmer Inn**, 25 Church St., Noank, CT 06340 (tel. 203/572-9000), was once the home of local shipyard owners, who had the house built by their shipbuilding craftsmen. Approach the house through the high surrounding hedges, and through the lofty portico, and you enter a place of large spaces, fine materials, and careful detail work, though sparsely furnished with an eclectic assortment of pieces. On the second floor, Donald and Patricia Cornish rent four rooms with bath, named Oak, Mahogany, and Master, after themes in their decor or earlier function, for $124 to $162 double. On the third floor are the Brass, Balcony, and Wicker Rooms, which rent for $124 to $141 double, with private bath. Rates include a continental breakfast, and the innkeepers note that the inn does not accommodate children under 16 or pets. To find the inn, drive southwest from Mystic along Rte. 215. Turn left onto Noank village's main street, then left again onto Church Street. The village is so small that you can't possibly get lost for very long.

Bed-and-Breakfast in Stonington

The village of Stonington is five miles east of Mystic, on the water. It's a pretty, traditional New England seacoast village, just the place to stay if you want to escape the crowded highways and modern motels. Stonington's bed-and-breakfast guesthouse list is beginning to grow. If you can't get a room at the following places, drop by the **State of Connecticut Tourism Division Information Center** off I-95 southbound at North Stonington. They may be able to help.

Farnan House, 10 McGrath Court, Stonington, CT 06378 (tel. 203/535-

0634), is a large, nice old Stonington house which takes in travelers for the night. Originally a colonial homestead, it is now a guesthouse hosted by a nice lady, Ann Farnan. She has four guest rooms, one with a private half-bath ($65); the others share a bath ($63). Continental breakfast, served in the big country kitchen, is included.

Lasbury's, 24 Orchard St., Stonington, CT 06378 (tel. 203/535-2681), bills itself as "a quiet guesthouse" in the village of Stonington. Double rooms cost $72, and continental breakfast is included. To find Lasbury's, head into the village on Water Street, turn left onto Church Street, then left again onto Orchard.

WHERE TO DINE: The great number of Mystic's restaurants—and there are many of them—are connected to the many hotels and motels. There are exceptions, however. One quite good restaurant is on the grounds of Mystic Seaport, just outside the admission ticket office. Other good places to dine are in the town of Mystic, south of Mystic Seaport. Still better places to dine are found in Noank and Stonington. Here they all are:

At Mystic Seaport

The **Seamen's Inne,** 65 Greenmanville Ave. (tel. 536-9649), is right next to the main entrance to Mystic Seaport. The attractive building is actually three restaurants in one. Felicity's is the formal dining room, open daily for dinner from 5 to 9 p.m. (on Saturday till 10 p.m.), and for Sunday brunch from 11 a.m. to 2:30 p.m. Here the menu is fairly formal, and very appetizing: clams and oysters on the half shell, a smoked seafood platter, lobster pasta, a New England seafood stew, Long Island duckling, and New York sirloin are all offered, and a full dinner might cost $25 to $30 per person.

In the Inne's Atlantic Ocean Grill, you can dine in the Whaler's Room furnished in spindleback chairs and graceful brass lamps, or in the Tap Room paneled in rough boards, with a nice fireplace, or in the Tavern with a turn-of-the-century stamped-tin ceiling, bentwood chairs, a huge plant-filled bow window, and ceiling fans. The Grill is open every day from 11:30 a.m. to 9 p.m., offering oysters, nachos, soups, sandwiches, salads, and some fancier dishes such as sautéed soft-shell crabs. A light lunch here might cost $10 to $12; a full dinner, $20 to $30.

Finally, the Wine Bar is the place to go for drinks, snacks, and conversation, any day from 11:30 a.m. till closing.

Note that the Seamen's Inne is closed on Monday and Tuesday in January, February, and March.

In the center of the town of Mystic are several restaurants worthy of consideration. Head south on Rte. 27, then right onto Main Street, to reach the center of town. The restaurants are located in the commercial district, on the far side of the quaint old bascule bridge.

The Landing, 73 Steamboat Wharf (tel. 572-0549), behind some of Main Street's shops, has two nice dining areas. Downstairs is an informal dining room with lots of wood and nice views of the water through small windows. Upstairs is a café-restaurant with a bar—a tavern ambience—with small tables and views of the water. The long, eclectic menu lists onion soup next to buffalo wings and blackened swordfish steak, and is sure to have something for everyone. A full lunch need cost only $15; a full dinner, $18 to $28. Come to dine any day from 11 a.m. to 9 p.m. (till 10 p.m. on Friday and Saturday).

Giaco's Ships Lantern Restaurant, 21 W. Main St. (tel. 536-9821), always has an interesting blackboard menu out on the sidewalk. Last time I was there it listed fresh mako shark, fresh tuna steak, and a lobster dinner featuring a one-pound lobster with a pound of steamed clams, each priced at about $16. Nautical flotsam, jetsam, and memorabilia decorate the dining room, seafood fills the menu (along with prime rib and Italian specialties), and the dining hours are long, from 10:30 a.m. until 11 p.m. every day.

Looking for just a sandwich, a salad, or dessert? Head for the **2 Sisters Deli**, 4 Pearl St. (tel. 536-1244), just off Main. The sandwiches are fresh, and the menu is very long, listing 42 sandwiches, plus various soups, bagels, salads, salad plates, cakes, pies, brownies, and cookies. Come for breakfast, lunch, picnic, or an early supper, any day.

Lobsters in Noank

Here is something you *have* to do. If you love seafood, if you love shore dinners, if you love the real New England, follow Rte. 215 south to the village of Noank, go left on Main Street, then right on Pearl Street. Stop at the Universal Package Store here (open Monday through Saturday until 8 p.m.) to pick up wine or beer if you like, then continue along Pearl Street until you spot, on the left-hand side, **Abbott's Lobster in the Rough** (tel. 536-7719). Here you will find a parking lot, a large restaurant, and numerous seaside picnic tables. Approach the cashier's window and order what you like: clam chowder, steamed clams or mussels, oysters, shrimp in the shell, steamed lobster, a lobster or crab roll, cheesecake, carrot cake, and a soft drink (unless you prefer that wine or beer you brought). Pay the tab (about $14 to $25 per person), then take a table and wait for your number to be called. When it is, you get to enjoy some of the finest seafood in the region. It's not fancy, but it's fantastically delicious. The lobsters at Abbott's are steamed (the way I do them), not boiled, and I can personally attest to the difference. A steamed lobster is sweeter and more tender. Abbott's handy tabloid-newspaper-style menu bears full directions on how to eat a lobster. Besides, when lobster is this good, you learn fast. Abbott's is open every day, late April until Labor Day, from noon to 9 p.m. and Labor Day till late September every day except Wednesday from noon to 7 p.m.

Stonington Restaurants

Drive or walk down Stonington's main street, named Water Street, and you will pass several interesting restaurants. The best are all the way down on the southern part of the street near Cannon Square.

The **Harborview Restaurant**, 66 Water St., Cannon Square (tel. 535-2720), is among the best restaurants in the region. As you enter from Water Street, the darkish, cozy bar is to your right, and it features a special menu of lighter fare for lunches, snacks, and suppers. In the dining rooms, the atmosphere is nautical, with lots of ocean views, bentwood, and low lamps, but the service is polished and professional as well as friendly. The menu here is French and fairly classical, with appetizers such as brie en croûte (brie baked in puff pastry), French onion soup, and smoked salmon. Your main course might be beef tournedos with peppercorns, or escalope niçoise (veal cutlet with artichoke hearts, tomato, capers, and vermouth butter). There's plenty of seafood featured, of course. Come any day for lunch (11:30 a.m. to 4 p.m.) or supper in the bar, or brunch on Sunday from 11 a.m. to 4 p.m., and plan to spend about $15. For dinner (5 to 10 p.m. any day), expect to pay $30 to $40 per person, all in.

Behind the Harborview is its sister restaurant, the **Skipper's Dock,** 66 Water St. (tel. 535-2000), right by the docks and meant to be convenient to the yacht crews who tie up nearby. Open daily from 11:30 a.m. till late in the evening, the restaurant has nice waterside decks set with dining tables, as well as two indoor dining rooms fitted out with bentwood furniture. The air smells of the sea, the landward wall of the restaurant is hung with hundreds of salvaged lobster buoys, and the sound of bellbuoys wafts easily on the air. The menu here is simple: seafood, with the requisite token offerings of chicken and steak. Have a big bowl of steamed clams, or linguine with shrimp and clams, or broiled scallops, or an entire clambake with steamed lobster. Lunch, served from 11:30 a.m. to 4 p.m., can be yours for about $15; dinner, with drinks, tax, and tip, will cost $18 to $30.

Right in the center of Stonington's commercial district is **Noah's,** 115 Water St. (tel. 535-3925), an informal restaurant of two rooms with tin ceilings, booths sporting nice etched glass, and wood tables draped with cloths. Prints and paintings ornament the walls, and Noah's has a feeling of the authentically old-fashioned. You can come for breakfast from 7 to 11 a.m. (till noon on Sunday), when a tuck-in of the standard fare of eggs, pancakes, and muffins will be yours for $5 or less; or come for lunch, with a varied menu of light meals served from 11:15 a.m. (12:15 p.m. on Sunday) to 2:30 p.m.; or for dinner, when you can order seafood, filet mignon, or pork chops, and get vegetable, potato, salad, bread, and butter with your main course for $12 to $18 complete. Dinner is served from 6 to 9 p.m. (till 9:30 p.m. on Friday and Saturday). Noah's accepts no credit cards, and is closed on Monday.

WHAT TO SEE: The big draw here is, of course, Mystic Seaport Museum, but the area has other sights as well, including the Mystic Marinelife Aquarium, the shops in Olde Mistick Village, the Denison Nature Center, and the charming town of Stonington.

Mystic Seaport Museum

Mystic Seaport Museum (tel. 203/572-0711) is impressive. One could return again and again to see the various indoor exhibits, walk through the preserved 19th-century town, or climb aboard one of the venerable sailing ships moored and preserved here. (Foremost among these is the *Charles W. Morgan,* the last wooden whaling ship in the U.S.) Although it is technically a nonprofit museum, there is much more life to it than just rows of glass cases housing exhibits. While you will see scrimshaw, old tools, watches, clocks, chronometers, navigational instruments, and so on, most of your time will be taken walking through the village and watching the interpreters (staff) do their jobs and explain what they're doing. You will see a half dozen crew high in the rigging of the square-rigged ship *Joseph Conrad,* furling a sail in time to a chantey they sing, with one rope supporting all of them high above the deck.

To get the feel of the place, the management recommends that you stay at least three or four hours; if you've arrived late in the day, when you buy your ticket, have it validated for the next day for a small extra charge. With your ticket you'll be given a very handsome map of the village and its exhibits, plus a list of the daily events, from special lectures to sea chantey sings. Look at the list to get an idea what'll be in action for the hours you're in the village. The museum can be divided basically into three areas: the exhibits of various boats, instruments, figureheads, and the like, mostly near the Seamen's Inne entrance gate; the restored village and waterfront area; and the shipyard at the southern end of the grounds where the seaport cares for its ships.

Remember that the crowds are heavy in summer—although the museum seems large enough to absorb them all without too much crowding—and that traffic on the mile-long road from I-95 to Mystic Seaport may be pokey. At Mystic Seaport there's quite a lot of free parking.

Mystic Seaport Museum began in 1929 as the Marine Historical Association, founded by three citizens of Mystic who were interested in preserving aspects and objects from the town's maritime past. The site of the museum is the former shipyard of George Greenman and Company, which built wooden clipper ships in the 19th century.

The **Coastal Life Area** is the official name of Mystic's oldtime seaside village at the northern reaches of the museum, near the Seamen's Inne. The village includes the shops of a shipsmith, shipcarver, cooperage, model shop, bank, shipping office, grocery, hardware store, printer's, chapel, schoolhouse, pharmacy, rope walk, clock and nautical instrument shop, mast hoop shop, ship's chandlery, and tavern.

Indoor exhibits are housed in several buildings. In the three-story Stillman Building are ship models, paintings, scrimshaw, and an exhibit which traces the history of New England's maritime towns from their beginnings in the 1600s through their golden age in the 1800s. The Mallory Building is devoted to exhibits explaining the Victorian-era shipping business of the Mallory family, and also shipbuilding in Mystic. In the Wendell Building are collections of figureheads and other nautical woodcarvings. Changing exhibits of paintings, prints, and other artifacts are the specialty of the R. J. Schaefer Building.

Children are fascinated by the **Children's Museum,** a replica of the captain's quarters on a late–19th-century ship. Here the captain and his family would live, and kids can climb into the bunk, look through the porthole, and examine the toys and games used by seafaring children to ward off the boredom of a long sea voyage a hundred years ago.

The museum's shipyard is in the southern section. Today, the museum's **collection of old ships** includes the *Charles W. Morgan* (1841), the full-rigged training ship *Joseph Conrad* (1882), and the fishing schooner *L. A. Dunton* (1921). It also owns a steamboat called the *Sabino* (1908), which once plied the waters off Casco Bay in Maine, but which now takes museum visitors on half-hour cruises on the Mystic River during the period from mid-May to mid-October, for a small fee. In addition, the museum has a collection of 300 small craft, many of which can be seen in the Small Boat Exhibit and the North Boat Shed.

Besides these exhibits, the museum can boast of the **Henry B. duPont Preservation Shipyard,** fully equipped and staffed to perform repairs and to preserve wooden vessels; and the **Seaport Planetarium,** where shows explain the significance of stars in the night sky, and the importance of celestial navigation.

Mystic Seaport Museum is open every day of the year except Christmas Day. May through October, hours of admission are 9 a.m. to 5 p.m., and the grounds close at 6 p.m. November through April, hours are 9 a.m. to 4 p.m., and you must be off the grounds by 4 p.m. In winter, interpreted exhibits and craft demonstrations don't begin until 10 a.m. Admission costs $12.50 for adults, half price for children 5 through 15 years old. Museum members, armed forces personnel in uniform, and children under 5 are admitted for free.

Mystic Marinelife Aquarium

Near Exit 90 off I-95, on Coogan Boulevard, is the Mystic Marinelife Aquarium (tel. 203/536-3323), with 48 living maritime exhibits and over 6,000 sea creatures in the main aquarium. Marine mammal demonstrations are held every hour on the half hour, featuring Atlantic bottle-nosed dolphins, California sea lions, and beluga whales in the marine theater. An outdoor exhibit area called Seal Island lets you watch five species of seals and sea lions sport and play in re-creations of their natural habitat. There's a penguin exhibit as well. Admission hours are from 9 a.m. to 5:30 p.m. (but you can stay until 7 p.m.) daily in July and August, till 4:30 p.m. (but you can stay until 6 p.m.) the rest of the year. Admission costs $7 for adults, $4 for children ages five to 17.

Denison Homestead

On Pequotsepos Road is the Denison Homestead (tel. 536-9248), a restored 1717 house which has belonged to one family for 11 generations (open mid-May to mid-October from 1 to 5 p.m. daily except Monday; adults pay $2; kids, 75¢). Nearby is the **Denison Pequotsepos Nature Center** (tel. 536-1216), a 125-acre wildlife sanctuary with exhibits explaining the flora and fauna, and several miles of trails for nature walks. It's open April through October, Monday through Saturday from 9 a.m. to 5 p.m., on Sunday from 1 to 5 p.m.; November through March, Tuesday through Saturday from 10 a.m. to 4 p.m., on Sunday from 1 to 4 p.m.; closed Monday in winter. Adults pay $1; children 6 to 12, half price.

Stonington Sights

As you drive into Stonington, you will cross a bridge over the railroad tracks, turn left, and proceed down Water Street, the town's main street. Water Street holds many boutiques, antique shops, restaurants, and real estate offices. Beyond this commercial area is a residential one, ending in **Cannon Square.** The square is small, with two 18-pound cannons used in repelling a naval attack mounted by five English ships on August 10, 1814, during the War of 1812. The pretty square is surrounded by a neo-classical bank building, a fine old granite house, and several houses in Federal style.

Beyond Cannon Square, continue south along Water Street to visit the **Old Lighthouse Museum,** at 7 Water St. (tel. 535-1440), a fine old granite structure which was the first government lighthouse in Connecticut. Inside are displays of maritime gear from the days of wooden whaling and fishing craft, swords, firearms (some made right here in Stonington), local stoneware, toys, decoys, and 19th-century portraits. There's a special room for children's exhibits. The museum is open from May through October, daily except Monday from 11 a.m. to 4:30 p.m. Adults pay $1.50 admission; children 6 to 12 pay half price.

---

6. Hartford

Hartford is Connecticut's capital, a fairly small (pop. 150,000) and manageable city with an admirable range of attractive architectural styles and a businesslike spirit. It is and has been a city with a good amount of wealth, much of it generated by the tens of thousands of officeworkers who sit in the thousands of offices of Hartford's four dozen great insurance companies and banks. Insurance companies seem to have a penchant for expressing their wealth and prestige through skyscrapers: the Prudential Tower in Chicago, the John Hancock Tower in Boston, and others. Hartford has lots of insurance companies, and therefore lots of skyscrapers. The downtown area has been given a new attractiveness by redevelopment, which has left most of the buildings of great historical value intact.

The city was founded by Thomas Hooker, who left Newtown (Cambridge, Mass.) on foot with a band of followers in 1636 after a dispute with another clergyman over the strict rules that governed the colony of Massachusetts Bay. In 1639 Hooker and others drafted the Fundamental Orders as the legal constitution of their settlement, and it is upon this early document that Connecticut bases its claims as the first place in the world to have a written constitution. Every Connecticut auto license plate remembers Hooker when it proclaims Connecticut "The Constitution State."

TOURIST INFORMATION: The city maintains a Visitors' Information desk in the Old State House, 800 Main St., Hartford, CT 06103 (tel. 203/522-6766), in Old State House Square, right in the center of town. The desk is open Monday through Saturday from 10 a.m. to 5 p.m., on Sunday from noon to 5 p.m. There is no short-term parking convenient to the Old State House, so plan to park for the length of your visit in a downtown lot, and then walk to the Old State House to ask questions and pick up maps and brochures.

Another traffic note: Hartford is very much a commuters' town, and traffic is very heavy at rush hours. The best day to visit the city is Saturday, when most everything is open and parking is easily available. On Sunday a lot of things are closed.

WHERE TO STAY: As of this writing, Hartford has none of those wonderful little hotels and inns made from converted Victorian town houses, or from renovated farmhouses on the city's outskirts. The lodging stock here is large business-oriented downtown hotels and highway motels. Generally speaking, the hotels offer more convenient locations. Many of them are within a few minutes' walk of all the downtown sights. The motels, on the other hand, are not really very far out of the city, and they offer clean and comfortable accommodations at moderate, and even budget, prices. There are some bed-and-breakfast services which will find you a room in a

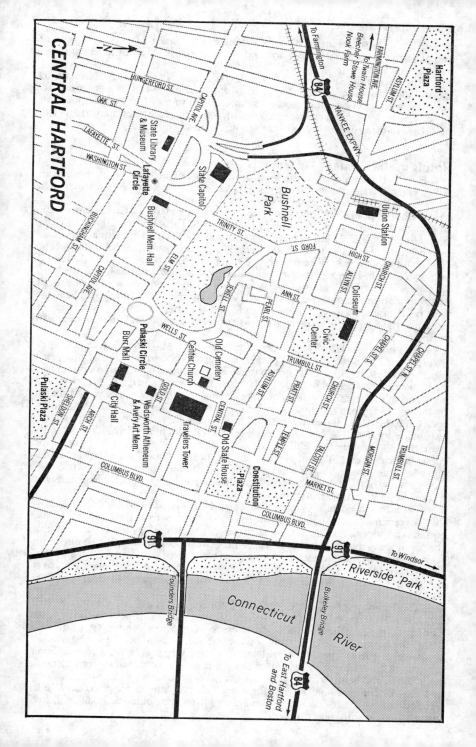

private home, as well. Finally, if you're willing to stay some distance out of the city and just drive in for the day, the surrounding countryside has some lovely old inns in quiet small towns.

When planning your visit to Hartford, you'd do well to make arrangements to stay in a downtown hotel on the weekend. Most of the hotels feature weekend package plans which can save you substantial amounts of money from regular rates. In any case, regular weekend rates are significantly lower than the rates charged on business days. In many cases, this rule holds for the highway motels also.

Hotels in the Center

Here is the rundown of the most convenient downtown hotels, those from which you can walk easily to all of the sights (except of course to Nook Farm, which is some distance from the center of town).

Without a doubt, the most convenient hotel to the Hartford Civic Center is the **Sheraton-Hartford,** 315 Trumbull St., Hartford, CT 06103 (tel. 203/728-5151 or toll free 800/325-3535). It features a pool and health club with sauna and conditioning equipment, a restaurant and lounge, a parking garage, and 55 shops. The bright and modern rooms rent for $108 to $143 single, $124 to $160 double. If you plan to be in Hartford over a weekend, take advantage of one of their weekend specials: a romantic "Champagne Classic" mini-vacation, which includes one-night accommodation, champagne, and breakfast for two for $110 complete. The Stage Café restaurant specializes in New England and continental favorites that range in price from $15 to $25 at dinner; an extensive breakfast buffet and full lunch are also served.

The **Parkview Hilton,** One Hilton Plaza, Hartford, CT 06103 (tel. 203/249-5611, or toll free 800/445-8667), on Ford Street at the corner with Asylum, just a block from the Civic Center, is aptly named. Many of its 410 modern rooms and 20 suites have views of Bushnell Park, of the twin towers of the Civil War memorial arch, and of the ornate Connecticut State Capitol. The benefit of the view is shared by the hotel's various restaurants, including the elegant Terrace on the Park dining room, and the Glass House coffeeshop. There's music for dancing most nights in the Esplanade lounge. The hotel has a full-service health club. With Hilton's family plan, there is no charge for children, regardless of age, when they occupy the same room as their parents. The hotel has several "executive floors" with extra amenities and concierge service. Singles here cost $97 to $148, and doubles are $112 to $164. Rooms at any of these prices have two double beds, making it possible for a family of four to stay for no more than the double rate.

The **Summit Hotel,** 5 Constitution Plaza, Hartford, CT 06103 (tel. 203/278-2000), is an independent 300-room hotel only a few steps from the Old State House and the shops of Main Street. Besides the hotel's comfortable regular guest rooms, the top floor is the "Concierge Floor" with extra amenities such as prompt room service, same-day valet service, bathrobes, and turn-down service; open bar and continental breakfast are included in the Concierge Floor rooms' higher rates. Rooms at the Summit, single or double, cost $129; those on the Concierge Floor are priced at $172.

The **Holiday Inn–Civic Center,** 50 Morgan St., Hartford, CT 06120 (tel. 203/549-2400, or toll free 800/465-4329), is about 2½ blocks from the Civic Center, on the northern side of I-84. Access to Main Street's shopping, to the Old State House, and to the Civic Center is quite good, and the hotel itself boasts 359 comfortable guest rooms, some with views of the river, all with free movies. Other services include babysitting, a game room, a gift shop, an outdoor swimming pool, restaurants, and kennels for your pet. A shuttle service runs to and from the hotel and Bradley International Airport for a small charge. Singles are priced at $96 to $107; doubles are $107 to $118. These rooms have two double beds, and children can stay for free with their parents.

The **Ramada Inn Capitol Hill,** 440 Asylum St., Hartford, CT 06103 (tel. 203/246-6591, or toll free 800/272-6232), is very near the Amtrak train station and the Greyhound bus station, just over a block from the Civic Center, facing Bushnell Park near the Civil War memorial arch. The location is very good, with some views of the Connecticut Capitol from the guest rooms and dining facilities. The hotel also has the advantage of being small, with 96 rooms, which allows for more personal service, and also quite moderately priced, considering its excellent location. The restaurant, Honiss' Oyster House, is one of the city's better seafood dining places. To stay here, one person pays $78, and two pay $89, plus tax.

Motels on the Outskirts

If you're visiting Hartford by car, these motels offer comfortable accommodations at truly moderate or budget prices, and none is more than a few minutes away from downtown Hartford by car.

The **Ramada Hartford (East Windsor),** 161 Bridge St., East Windsor, CT 06088 (tel. 203/623-9411 or toll free 800/272-6232), is at Warehouse Point, near Exit 45 off I-91, on the east bank of the Connecticut River. If you're coming down to Hartford from Boston, you'll see the hotel on your right as you approach Hartford along I-84. Rates are excellent, at $64 single, $71 double, for one of the 120 very comfortable rooms with one or two double beds, color television and radio, air conditioning, and some rooms even with their own steambaths. The hotel has its own outdoor pool, plus valet, laundry, and babysitting services. A hotel van will pick you up from Bradley Airport.

Another excellent value is Hartford's new **Courtyard by Marriott Hotel,** 1 Day Hill Rd., Windsor, CT 06095 (tel. 203/683-0022 or toll free 800/321-2211), seven miles south of Hartford at I-91 Exit 38 (Rte. 75, Poquonock Avenue). This new chain of Marriott hotels offers special amenities at moderate prices. For instance, there is an indoor swimming pool, and guest rooms have separate seating areas, full-size desk, king-size beds, and in-room coffee. Room prices are $66 to $72 on weekdays, $48 to $54 on weekends. The hotel has its own restaurant and lounge.

Those in search of budget lodgings will be happy to know that Hartford has numerous inexpensive motels, as well.

The **Super 8 Motel,** 57 W. Service Rd., Hartford, CT 06120 (tel. 203/246-8888, or toll free 800/843-1991), at I-91 Exit 33, north of the intersection with I-84, has 104 rooms with air conditioning and color television within a mile of the center of town, and includes a continental breakfast in these rates: $40 single, $46 double (in two double beds).

Hartford has a **Susse Chalet,** 185 Brainard Rd., Hartford, CT 06114 (tel. 203/525-9306), a 131-room motel at Exit 27 of I-91, with an outdoor swimming pool, and comfortable, television-equipped rooms going for $38 single, $42 double.

The 146-room **Motel 6,** 1341 Silas Deane Hwy., Wethersfield, CT 06109 (tel. 203/563-5900), is ten miles south of Hartford at the Silas Deane exit of I-91. Rooms have individual heating and air conditioning, television sets, full bath and shower, wall-to-wall carpeting, coin-operated laundry, and direct-dial phones with free local calls. There's a 24-hour restaurant adjacent to the motel. The price for a room is $36 single, $42 double.

Bed-and-Breakfast

For a bed-and-breakfast room priced from $30 to $55 single, $45 to $85 double, contact **Four Seasons International Bed & Breakfast,** 11 Bridlepath Rd., West Simsbury, CT 06092 (tel. 203/651-3045). Rates include full breakfast. Many of these B&Bs will be out in the country or in small towns near Hartford.

WHERE TO DINE: Though it's not a particularly large or cosmopolitan city, Hartford has an interesting selection of restaurants. You should find it easy to satisfy your appetite, your taste buds, and your budget, whatever they may be.

The Top Restaurants

Hartford's best dining place, by popular acclaim, is Chef Chris Pardue's restaurant called **L'Américain**, 146 Wyllys St., Hartford Square (tel. 522-6500), in a restored brick factory complex at the corner of Charter Oak Avenue and Wyllys Street, about a half mile from the Old State House. From the Old State House, follow Main Street south and turn left on Charter Oak Avenue, or from the Summit Hotel, follow Columbus Boulevard south and it becomes Wyllys Street. Hartford Square is a group of sedate old brick structures across the street from the Episcopal Church of the Good Shepherd. Enter beneath the name of the restaurant in gilt lettering above the door and you will find dining rooms remodeled with classical inspiration along clean, modern lines. Queen Anne chairs and heavy tablecloths add to the feeling of luxury. Prepare yourself for an elegant lunch or dinner, for the menu recently listed appetizers of duckling salad, veal pâté, or fresh fruit with liqueurs, or you might choose instead a clear lobster consommé. For a fish course, there was broiled Norwegian salmon filets in a sauce of white Zinfandel with roasted shallots and buttered spinach. Main courses ranged from hickory-smoked turkey through pork schnitzel and Moroccan chicken to a champagne, scallop, and pasta salad. A special effort is made to include on the menu dishes suitable for those wanting to eat less salt, fat, and cholesterol. Figure to spend about $25 for lunch (11:30 a.m. to 2 p.m. Monday through Friday), about twice that much for dinner (6 to 10 p.m. Monday through Saturday), per person, all in.

At least once during your stay in Hartford you must drop in at **Brown, Thomson & Company,** 942 Main St. (tel. 525-1600), just a few blocks' stroll north of the Old State House. The dark stone building which once housed the department store of that name was designed by Henry Hobson Richardson and built in 1877. It's a wonder of American Romanesque architecture with lots of Roman-arched windows, columns, and turrets. Much of the building is now occupied by shops and offices, but the southwest corner is the restaurant, and it preserves the original feeling of the building of a century ago: matchboard walls, glass that is beveled or etched or stained, stamped-metal ceilings, hanging plants, ceiling fans, a labyrinth of ascending staircases, and even a great old elk's head. The menu is just as interesting, listing everything from French onion soup and buffalo wings to broiled swordfish and prime rib of beef. There is pizza and huevos rancheros and fajitas and hot pepperoni. You might get intellectual indigestion if you read the entire menu carefully, but you are absolutely certain to find something that strikes your fancy. Equally copious are the dessert and drink offerings, from apple cobbler to chocolate-chip-cookie pie, and from frozen daiquiris (with or without alcohol) to Dom Pérignon (at the retail store price!). Needless to say, you can suit your budget as well as your appetite with such variety, spending anywhere from $10 to $35 for a meal. There's a special coloring-book menu for kids. Brown, Thomson opens every day at 11:30 a.m., and serves food most nights until midnight, till 1 a.m. on Friday and Saturday, till 10 p.m. on Sunday.

A View of the Park

For a drink or dining with a view of Bushnell Park, head for the **Metro Park Café,** 26 Trumbull St. (tel. 246-3355), facing Bushnell Park. Enter the big wooden doors, and the bar is to your right, the dining room to your left. The furniture is of bright bentwood with soft pastel upholstery, comfortable and elegant and modern. The menu lists many favorites of the new American cuisine, on which you can dine for about $25 to $35 per person while enjoying the view of the park (lunch is less). The restaurant opens at 11:30 a.m. Monday through Friday, and serves food until 10 p.m. Monday through Thursday, to 11 p.m. on Friday; Saturday hours are 5 to 11 p.m.; closed Sunday. The bar remains open for three hours after food service stops. Here you're only a short walk from either the Civic Center or the Old State House.

Civic Center Dining

To satisfy a pang of hunger at any time of the day or night, Hartford's citizens head for the Hartford Civic Center, which has its own collection of restaurants and fast-food shops, some operating 24 hours a day. If you enter from Asylum Street near the corner with Ann Street, you'll be on the Market Level. If you enter from Trumbull Street at the corner of Asylum Street, you'll be on Level One.

Perhaps the most famous of the eateries here is **Shelly's Downtown Deli** (tel. 278-1510), with a 300-item menu and breakfast served all the time. They'll even deliver an order to you anywhere downtown. Have chicken soup with matzoh balls ($2) if you wish, or a sandwich of Nova lox ($6.50). I had a good turkey sandwich on rye with bacon, lettuce, and tomato; the orange juice was watery, though.

George's Rotisserie & Bar, on the Market Level (tel. 527-3900), has another of those long and eclectic menus listing everything from chicken curry to seafood kebabs. A full sit-down meal here might come to $15 or $20. George's has a full bar. Lunch and dinner are served daily.

Buon Apetito, at Market Level (tel. 522-4635), is open Monday through Saturday serving seafood, salads, pasta, and those huge sandwiches called grinders in New England, for about $8 to $12.

Upstairs on Level One of the Civic Center are still more places to dine.

Your craving for a dinner of enchiladas, quesadillas, chili, and burritos can be satisfied at **Margaritaville** (tel. 724-3331), a Mexican restaurant and watering hole that opens at 4:30 p.m. every day and serves all sorts of Mexican food and drink until 10 p.m., till 11 p.m. on Friday and Saturday. Drinks include peach margaritas and banana-rum smoothies. The surroundings are as much fun as the food, with waiters in costume and lots of dark rough wood, stucco, and brightly colored Mexican craft items. You need spend only about $12 or $14 for a meal, but the price can go up if you order a second round of drinks.

Of the full restaurants in the Civic Center, the best is **Gaetano's** (tel. 249-1629), open for lunch (Monday through Saturday from 11:30 a.m. to 2:30 p.m.) and dinner (every day from 5 to 10:30 p.m.) The setting here is casual but stylish, the cuisine is continental, inspired particularly by French and northern Italian cooking. Start with bluepoint oysters topped with spinach and hollandaise sauce, or clams casino, and go on to tournedos Rossini or bistecchine (tenderloin tips). Of course there's pasta as well, everything from cavitelli bolognese through capellini angelica and fettuccine to lasagne. A full dinner will cost about $30 per person.

For Chinese Food

What about Chinese food? A long-standing Hartford favorite, indeed a veritable institution, is **Song Hays Restaurant,** 89 Asylum St. (tel. 525-6388), between the Old State House and the Civic Center. Song Hays is what you might call a "neighborhood Chinese place," complete with decor heavy in chinoiserie and a long menu listing heaping plates of Chinese delicacies for only a few dollars each. The luncheon special, for instance, comes in at less than $6; other main-course dishes are only $6 to $8.50. It's open seven days a week for lunch and dinner, and has a full bar.

A Curious Café

The **Russian Lady Café,** 191 Ann St. (tel. 525-3003), just a half block off Asylum (Ann Street is the western edge of the Civic Center), is right in the middle of things. It takes its name from the 1,600-pound solid-bronze statue group atop the building's façade. The statue, executed by the German sculptor Edwin Schulte, was the figurehead of the Rossia Insurance Company for many years, but when the building at Broad and Farmington was torn down to make way for the YWCA, the statue was saved and moved to its present perch. In fact, much of the Russian Lady's decor came from urban renewal: the lamps over the bar are from the ruins of the city's cathedral, which burned down some years ago; the stained-glass windows are from a former Russian Orthodox church. The menu includes the very best in Italian cuisine, with portions at reasonable prices, plus cocktails and draft beers. The Russian Lady Café is open Monday through Friday from 11 a.m. to 2 a.m., and on Saturday from 3 p.m. to 2 a.m. There's live entertainment three nights a week.

WHAT TO SEE: The **Greater Hartford Convention and Visitors Bureau** (tel. 203/728-6789) has organized all the sights in Hartford's downtown into what they call **The Walk,** and a free folder guiding you from point to point along the scenic stroll is available from them at One Civic Center Plaza, or from the Visitors' Information desk in the Old State House. Bushnell Park, the city's central park on the Walk, was laid out by the famous landscape architect Frederick Law Olmsted, the Hartford resident who also landscaped Central Park in New York, the Fenway parks in Boston, and Montréal's Mount Royal Park. Here are the highlights of the Walk:

The Old State House

Pure Bulfinch, the Old State House served as Connecticut's state capitol from 1796 to 1878. You can see the inside Monday through Saturday from 10 a.m. to 5 p.m., on Sunday from noon to 5 p.m.; admission is free. On the Main Street side, have a look at the statue of Hartford's founder, the Rev. Thomas Hooker (1586–1647). Compare this Bulfinch state house with the one in Boston, or with the Capitol in Washington, both Bulfinch achievements. Outdoor concerts are often held in the precincts of the Old State House, and three galleries inside hold exhibits which change frequently. Warm weather finds farm markets, festivals, and concerts outside on the large lawn. The Visitors Information Center and museum shop are open during regular hours.

The Cheney Building

North on Main Street a block from the Old State House is the mass of Connecticut brownstone built in 1877 by Henry Hobson Richardson for the Cheneys, a Connecticut family of silk manufacturers. It now houses the Brown, Thomson & Company restaurant (see above).

Constitution Plaza

Just east of the Old State House is this plaza, Hartford's triumph of urban renewal. The plaza has nice copses of trees (one of willows), a fountain designed not to splash or spray passersby in the wind, and the elliptical Phoenix Mutual Life building, perhaps Hartford's most striking building. Hartford is particularly rich in works by Alexander Calder, who had his home and workshop in the state. There's one of his mobiles suspended from the ceiling of the commercial banking room in the Connecticut Bank and Trust Company, on the Plaza.

The Travelers Tower

Between Main and Prospect Streets, right next to the Old State House, rises Hartford's tallest observation point, the Travelers Insurance Company Tower (tel. 277-2431). On weekdays in summer from 10:30 a.m. to 3:30 p.m. there are tours to the top of the building, leaving every half hour on the hour and half hour. In the 15 minutes spent at the top, you'll get the best possible view of the entire city, the suburbs, and the surrounding tobacco country. The Travelers Tower stands on the spot where there was once a tavern. It was in this tavern that Connecticut's royal charter disappeared during a dispute between colonials and royal officials, only to be hidden in the cavity of a nearby oak tree, the famous "Charter Oak" incident. Although the king's men ruled Connecticut illegally for a time (they could not find the charter and so destroy the legal instrument of Connecticut's self-rule), the charter survived, and is now on view at the State Library (see below).

By the way, there are 70 steps at the top of the tower which you must climb to get to the observation area. Also note that tours are run off-season, but you must call and make reservations.

Wadsworth Atheneum

This is Hartford's art museum, at 600 Main St. (tel. 278-2670), with a fine collection of over 40,000 items of painting, sculpture, primitive and modern art. Don't miss a visit. It's open Tuesday through Friday from 11 a.m. to 7 p.m. (the upstairs galleries close at 5 p.m.), on Saturday and Sunday from 11 a.m. to 5 p.m.; suggested donation is $3 for adults, half that for children under 13 and seniors. Free on Thursday. As you enter, ask for a guide leaflet to the collections.

Burr Mall

Between Wadsworth Atheneum and the attractive city executive office building, the Mall is a shady, fragrant spot with a fountain and a fine—if incongruously placed—stabile of Calder's called *Stegosaurus* (1971).

Across Prospect Street from Burr Mall, take a look at the interesting buildings: the **Masonic Temple** and the **Hartford Times Building**. The façade for the latter building was once the front of a church in New York, which explains its architecture, odd for a newspaper building!

Center Church and Ancient Burying Ground

Across Main Street from the Travelers Tower is the site of the first church in Hartford, whose pastor was Thomas Hooker (he's thought to be buried under the church). The present church dates from 1807. The gravestones in the cemetery date as far back as 1640.

Bushnell Park

The park has 500 trees of 150 varieties, and is an oasis in the middle of the busy city. The twin-towered Gothic gateway on Trinity Street is Hartford's memorial to its Civil War dead. Be sure to visit the park's **carousel,** one of the finest restored merry-go-rounds you'll ever see, complete with calliope and automatic drums and cymbals. Rides cost 10¢, and it is by no means only children who take advantage of this low price. It has three types of seating accommodation: "Lovers' Chariots" for the unadventurous, stationary wooden horses, and horses that move up and down. Remember to grab at the brass ring. Note that the carousel doesn't operate on Sunday, and you must see it with all the lights on and the music trilling to really get the feeling.

The Capitol and Lafayette Square

Richard M. Upjohn is the architect responsible for Hartford's great potpourri of architectural styles and periods—soldiers in Civil War uniforms standing in Gothic niches, etc. For all that, the capitol is fine to look at. Once it was topped by a statue of *The Genius of Connecticut,* a lady. You can see that statue inside the building, and also the battle flags and memorabilia preserved here. Across Capitol Avenue is the **State Library** and **Supreme Court,** a pretty building housing the paper treasures of Connecticut history, including the famous Royal Charter once hidden in an oak tree. Besides the documents, the library is now the repository of the Samuel Colt collection of firearms of more than 1,000 weapons. All together, the collections here make up the **Museum of Connecticut History,** and you can visit it Monday through Friday from 9 a.m. to 5 p.m., on Saturday to 1 p.m., closed Sunday; no charge for admission.

Near the Capitol and State Library, in Lafayette Square, is the **Bushnell Memorial Hall**, where many of the city's concerts, plays, and recitals are held. The interior is of the purest 1930s art deco, a style which has seen a resurgence in recent years. The Vienna Boys Choir or the Boston Symphony—you may find either on the playbill here depending on current schedules. For current information, call the Bushnell Memorial at 203/527-3123.

The Civic Center

This complex of several city blocks follows some of the best modernistic architecture, with fine shopping arcades, lots of open spaces, and mezzanines with hanging plants, small trees in pots growing up a story or two, and meeting rooms, restaurants, and clubs. The thing to do, especially on a hot summer day, is to enter its air-conditioned spaces and wander around enjoying the sights, perhaps stopping for a snack or a meal.

The Mark Twain and Harriet Beecher Stowe Houses (Nook Farm)

Hartford has a surprising number of palatial houses, most of them still occupied by wealthy families, and anyone interested in domestic architecture should take a drive through the residential sections northwest of downtown. For a look at two of the city's most impressive houses, drive out Asylum Street and Farmington Avenue about 15 blocks to the Mark Twain House, 77 Forest St. (tel. 525-9317). While you drive, look for the art deco steeple of Trinity Church—the Twain and Stowe houses are four blocks past that point, on the left. You can go by bus—catch any one of the following at the Old State House or along Asylum Street: E-1 ("Westgate–Health Center"), E-2 ("Unionville"), E-3 ("Bishops Corner"), or E-4 ("Corbins Corner").

The famous American author from Hannibal, Mo., settled in Hartford in the early 1870s. One of the wealthiest young men in town, Samuel Clemens (1835–1910) had this house designed by Edward Tuckerman Potter. It was finished in 1874 at a cost of $131,000, and is extremely rich in the sort of detail that makes Victorian architecture so much fun to inspect. Twain lived here for 17 years, only moving out after bad investments forced him to take a lecture tour of Europe to make some quick money. He loved this place for the best years of his life, and *Tom Sawyer, Huckleberry Finn, Life on the Mississippi, The Prince and the Pauper,* and *A Connecticut Yankee in King Arthur's Court* were all written while he lived here. To see the house you must take the tour, which is just as well for the guides have an encyclopedic knowledge of the house and its occupants.

In the same complex of buildings, known as Nook Farm, is a house once lived in by Harriet Beecher Stowe, who wrote *Uncle Tom's Cabin.* Although that work was written while Mrs. Stowe lived in Brunswick, Me., the author lived and wrote in this house from 1873 until she died in 1896. Lots of the original furnishings of the author's remain in this Victorian "cottage."

Both houses are open year round, Tuesday through Saturday from 9:30 a.m. to 4 p.m., Sunday from noon to 4 p.m. They are open on Monday from June 1 to the Columbus Day weekend, and in December; the houses are closed on Monday at other times, and closed on major holidays. A tour of both houses takes slightly over an hour and costs $6.50 for adults, $2.75 for children ages 6 through 16.

Outside Hartford

The region around Hartford has numerous other sights to see. In West Hartford is the birthplace of America's first great lexicographer, Noah Webster. And the colonial town of Old Wethersfield, about ten miles south of Hartford, has lots of interesting old houses.

Noah Webster (1758–1843) was born in a farmhouse on the outskirts of Hartford. He lived with his strict Calvinist parents and four siblings in this house, helping to work the land, until he was 16. Webster left home to attend Yale on the eve of the American Revolution, and was caught up in the intellectual ferment of the time.

He served with the American forces and afterward returned to Hartford to practice law. Webster saw it as his purpose in life to give Americans a new "national language" to go along with their new order of government and society. By 1828, working alone with pen and paper, he had completed his 70,000-word dictionary, which included 12,000 words never previously included in a dictionary. Sales of the dictionary were over 300,000 copies in some years. Along with his *Elementary Spelling Book* and grammar, it molded and standardized the distinctive spelling, pronunciation, and usage of Americans. His spelling book alone sold more than one million copies annually after 1850, and that was in a nation of only 23 million people! After Webster, Americans no longer had to use schoolbooks and dictionaries written and published in England for Englanders. To Webster we owe such simplified spellings as "honor" instead of the English "honour," and "neighborhood" instead of "neighbourhood."

The **Noah Webster House and Museum,** 227 S. Main St., West Hartford (tel. 521-5362), off I-84 at Exit 41, west of the center of Hartford, consists of Webster's boyhood home, a simple center-chimney colonial dwelling, and a modern museum. The house is furnished authentically in period style, and costumed guides give you a tour and explain what life was like in the America of almost two centuries ago. There is a typical garden of the period with herbs and dye plants. The house and museum are open from mid-June through September daily except Wednesday from 10 a.m. to 4 p.m., on Saturday and Sunday from 1 to 4 p.m.; from October through mid-June, hours are daily except Wednesday from 1 to 4 p.m. Admission costs $2 for adults, half price for children 6 to 12 years old, $1.50 for seniors.

The town of **Old Wethersfield** has a treasure trove for fanciers of old houses. Take I-91 south for about ten miles to Exit 26 and follow the signs to the town.

The **Buttolph-Williams House,** on Broad Street (tel. 529-0460 or 247-8996), is a mansion from the 1600s with excellent authentic period furnishings. The kitchen is especially good, and may be the most real-to-life of any extant in New England. Visiting season is mid-May to mid-October, Tuesday through Sunday from noon to 4 p.m. Adults pay $2, and children pay 75¢.

The **Isaac Stevens House,** 215 Main St. (tel. 529-0612), was a craftsman's home built in 1788, and it still has in it many of the family's original furnishings. Of particular interest are the collections of toys and ladies' bonnets. It's open all year, Tuesday through Saturday from 10 a.m. to 4 p.m., and also mid-May to mid-October on Sunday from 1 to 4 p.m. Admission fees are $2 for adults, 75¢ for children. A ticket good for this house, the Webb House and the Deane House costs $5 for adults, $2.25 for children.

The **Joseph Webb House,** 211 Main St. (tel. 529-0612), was the site of a strategy conference (1781) between the American commander-in-chief, Gen. George Washington, and his French ally, the Comte de Rochambeau. At the conference, Rochambeau outlined his plan to engage the British at Yorktown. It worked, and the battle ended the Revolutionary War. The house was built in 1752, and now contains period furniture, fabrics, porcelain, and silver. Hours and rates are the same as for the Isaac Stevens House described above.

The **Silas Deane House,** 203 Main St. (tel. 529-0612), was built in 1766 by a member (1774–1776) of the first Continental Congress and commissioner (ambassador) to France (1776). It's an elegant place for an elegant gentleman, with interesting architectural details. Deane, though a patriot, was ill-used by some of his American diplomatic colleagues, and he found himself condemned by Congress for profiteering. He lived out his life in exile, but in 1842 Congress made amends to his family and restored his good name and fortune.

If you've now become intrigued by Wethersfield's deep history, drop in at the **Wethersfield Historical Society,** 150 Main St. (tel. 529-7656), located in the Old Academy Museum, a fine Federal-style brick building dating from 1804. The society is in charge of the nearby William A. Keeny Cultural Center at 200 Main St., with permanent exhibits on Wethersfield, and also the Capt. James Francis House, 120

Hartford Ave. (enter from the Historical Society building). This house, dating from 1793, has exhibits which trace a single Wethersfield family through a history of 170 years.

---

7. Litchfield's Lakes and Hills

Northwest of Hartford is tobacco country. The Connecticut River Valley has very good conditions for growing a premium wrapper leaf for cigars, the famous Connecticut Valley shade-grown tobacco. The long barns next to the fields are for drying; and part of the year the crop will be covered with gauze enclosures to protect it from too much direct sun, hence the "shade-grown" name.

A pleasant morning or afternoon can be spent driving through part of the tobacco country on the way to Litchfield, the town from which Litchfield County takes its name. The county is all forest, rivers, and rolling hills, some of the prettiest country in this exceptionally pretty state, and the town of Litchfield itself is certainly among the most beautiful in New England.

Deeper into the northwest corner of the state you will come upon other charming towns, country inns, and resorts nestled in the Litchfield Hills (Connecticut's "Berkshires") and scattered on the shores of clear lakes. This is vacation country. In the charming old town of Salisbury, you're only four miles from the Massachusetts state line, 12 miles from the southern Berkshire town of South Egremont. (For the Berkshires, see Chapter IX.)

ON THE WAY: As you head west toward the Litchfield Hills, you might want to make several attractive detours. Head out of Hartford on U.S. 44, and soon you will be in Avon, where there is a nice hotel and restaurant. Farther along U.S. 44, just before Winsted, turn north for Riverton, the village where Hitchcock chairs are made and Seth Thomas clocks are sold.

Back on U.S. 44, just 8 miles west of Winsted, is the quiet ambience of Norfolk, where you'll find a lovely town green, three state parks, and Yale's Summer School of Music.

Avon

For decades, residents of Hartford have escaped to the country to find the **Avon Old Farms Hotel,** P.O. Box 961, Avon, CT 06001 (tel. 203/677-1651 or toll free outside Conn. 800/228-1651), at the intersection of U.S. 44 and Conn. 10, 10 miles west of Hartford (I-84 Exit 39). Escaping to the country does not mean giving up the city's comforts, for the spacious rooms at the hotel are furnished with king-size, queen-size, or twin double beds, antique reproduction lamps, mirrors, tables and chairs, color television, clock-radios, original paintings, and lots of little extras like shower caps, bath oil, and mending kits. You choose from several types of rooms here. Those in the hotel are larger and more modern, and open onto a corridor; they're priced at $107 to $129 single or double. The motel-style rooms are a bit smaller, and they open (as motel rooms do) to the outside; these are priced at $81 single or double. The registration lobby is elegantly done in Georgian style, with comfy sofas and a fine marble fireplace. Guests have the use of the hotel's exercise room and sauna, hair-styling salon, outdoor swimming pool, and tennis court.

The Avon Old Farms Inn was established in 1757, and a few rooms of the old inn now serve as charming dining rooms. The Forge Room is decorated with blacksmith's paraphernalia, and in chilly weather a fire in the hearth casts an appropriately mellow glow. Two other, smaller rooms near the front door are among the oldest in the inn, and are also charming. And a large dining room of more recent construction is decorated with Early Americana, dark-wood beams, old pine boards, and country curtains. The menu is American with continental touches: New England seafood,

roast beef with popovers, and several continental dishes which change frequently. On Sunday, brunch is an eat-all-you-like buffet. Expect to spend $35 to $40 per person for dinner, with wine, tax, and tip included. Lunch and dinner are served every day but Monday.

Riverton

A few miles west of the vast Barkhamsted Reservoir, in lovely wooded country (much of it state forest land) lies Riverton, a fine Connecticut hill village which looks much like it did in the 1800s. Driving or strolling along the village's main street, you pass the Grange Hall, the new Hitchcock Chair factory, the Village Sweet Shop, and other shops selling antiques, herbs, and contemporary crafts. The **Catnip Mouse Tearoom** (tel. 379-3745) will serve you lunch from 11 a.m. to 3 p.m., Monday through Saturday, and the **Riverton General Store** (tel. 379-0811) can provide all the raw ingredients for a marvelous picnic, including deli sandwiches, cheese, meat, other groceries, cold beer and hot coffee. The store also sells worms and crawlers if you happen to be interested. It's open seven days a week from 7 a.m. to 8 p.m.

At the **Hitchcock Chair Factory Store** (tel. 379-4826), look over the fine furniture in Lambert Hitchcock's original factory. Visiting hours are Tuesday through Saturday from 10 a.m. to 5 p.m., on Sunday from noon to 5 p.m., plus Thursday evenings until 9 p.m. (Closed Monday.)

Another place you won't want to miss is the **Thomaston Clock Discount Outlet** (tel. 379-1077), selling mantel, wall, travel, and grandfather clocks from some of America's best clockmakers. The store is open Tuesday through Sunday from 10 a.m. to 5 p.m.

Cross the Farmington River, and just across the bridge lies the **Old Riverton Inn**, P.O. Box 6, Riverton, CT 06065 (tel. 203/379-8678), on Rte. 20. Originally opened in 1796 by one Jesse Ives, the inn has seen many changes, modifications, and additions over the years, but it retains much of its early American charm, with heavy wood beams in the Colonial Dining Room, and grindstones from Nova Scotia providing the paving in the Grindstone Terrace. The 12 guest rooms are done in period style, with four-poster and canopy beds, country wallpaper, and some fireplaces. All have cable TV, private bath, and rent for $60 to $92 double; the single rate is $20 to $30 less on weekdays, but the same price on weekends. On the high end, a deluxe suite with a fireplace rents for $146.

Luncheon is served during the warm months from noon to 2:30 p.m.; dinner from 5 to 8:30 p.m. (till 9 p.m. on Saturday); Sunday from noon to 8 p.m.; closed Monday and Tuesday. At dinnertime expect to pay $17 for veal Française and a dollar more for broiled scallops.

Norfolk

In an area full of graceful homes-turned-bed-and-breakfast, the **Manor House,** Maple Ave. (P.O. Box 447), Norfolk, CT 06058 (tel. 203/542-5690), stands with the best. This stucco, timber, and stone inn, on five acres, was built in 1898 by Charles Spofford, the architect of London's underground; that helps explain the English overtones. A massive stone fireplace and authentic Tiffany windows set the tone for the common rooms. The eight guest rooms, most with private bath, have antique beds with down comforters; some rooms boast a fireplace or a private balcony. A full breakfast, with homemade harvested honey, is served in one of three places: in bed, in an elegant dining room, or on the sunlit porch. Prices are in range for the area: $70 to $156 single or double.

From Norfolk, you can continue west on U.S. 44 to Canaan, Salisbury, and Lakeville, or you can take U.S. 44 to Rte. 8 south through Torrington to U.S. 202 west, which will eventually bring you to Litchfield.

A TYPICAL 18TH-CENTURY TOWN: Connecticut's answer to the pretty Massachusetts towns in the Berkshires is Litchfield, a town which a National Park Service writer has called "probably New England's finest surviving example of a typical late 18th-century town." The town was incorporated in 1719, and in the following 100 years grew and prospered as a center for small industry and an important way station on the Hartford–Albany stagecoach route. With this prosperity came the urge, and the wherewithal, to build very fine, graceful houses, which is what the citizens did, making sure that the houses were set well back from the roadway. And while progress in the 19th century robbed Litchfield of much of its wealth—water-powered industry drove Litchfield's small-time craftsmen out of business, and the railroads bypassed the town—the town's decline may have been a blessing in disguise. Today Litchfield retains its late–18th-century beauty, unsullied by the workers' tenements and textile mills that have changed the face of so many other New England towns.

Where to Stay and Eat

As you see, Litchfield is an extremely beautiful town. It is also now home to numerous celebrated leaders in the arts, media, and business, who strive to keep it as beautiful and tranquil as it is. Thus you will find few services for visitors, and no lodging places in the town proper. But there is a fine place to stay just outside Litchfield.

Just over two miles northeast of the Village Green along U.S. 202 is the **Tollgate Hill Inn**, P.O. Box 1339, Litchfield, CT 06759 (tel. 203/567-4545), a farmhouse dating from 1745. Originally it stood on the Old East Litchfield Road, where in 1789 it became a tavern to feed, quench, and house travelers on the road between Litchfield and Hartford. But in 1923 it was moved to its present site on Tollgate Hill, where it continues its long tradition of offering fine food and lodging to travelers in the Litchfield Hills. Over the years the inn has been restored and renovated many times, the latest having been in 1983. The colonial spirit of the house was well preserved, and mated with recent improvements. You'll find a bar made of cherry to harmonize with the original paneling, a formal dining room with a fine fireplace, an arched corner cupboard, and a tavern dining room paneled in wide pine boards. In the Ballroom upstairs is a large fieldstone fireplace, lots of windows, brass chandeliers, and a fiddlers' loft from which music issues forth on Saturday nights.

The guest rooms are all different, as you might expect. Five rooms with colonial furnishings, private bath, and air conditioning rent for $97 double; three rooms with wood-burning fireplaces are priced at $108 double, with private bath and air conditioning; and two rooms go for $141 double, as one of these has a queen-size canopy bed, bar and refrigerator, cable television with VCR, and stereo tape cassette player, while the other is a small two-room suite with bedroom, sitting room, and color cable television with VCR. A continental breakfast, served in your room or on the patio (in good weather), is included in the rates.

If you're feeling in a less formal mood and you're in Litchfield at lunchtime on a sunny day, head over to the **Litchfield Food Company** (tel. 567-3113) on West Street. The white tile floor and built-in wooden shelves give the place an old-fashioned spiffy look. I ordered servings of very creamy pasta salad and chicken pesto, accompanied by blue corn chips and freshly brewed coffee, and my take-out tab came to about $6. Eat in at one of the few tables or cross the street, pull up a park bench, and enjoy the fine houses all around you. The store is open daily from 9:30 a.m. to 5 p.m.

What to See

At a tiny information booth on the Town Green, you can get a free booklet on the town's history, architecture, and activities, complete with a small map. The sightseeing is simple enough: drive down South Street just to get the feel of the gracious neighborhood. Stop at the **Tapping Reeve House** (1773), and take a look at the small, unprepossessing edifice beside it, which was the nation's first school of law, established here by Tapping Reeve in 1775 (the school moved into the one-room building in 1784). North Street is as attractive as South Street, and after a drive has given you the lay of the land, park at the green and stroll along either street to see the houses more closely. Tapping Reeve House and Law School is open mid-May to mid-October, Thursday through Monday from noon to 4 p.m.; adults pay $1.

The **Litchfield Historical Society** (tel. 567-4501) will give you a glimpse into the town's interesting past in many of its aspects, political, economic, industrial, decorative, and artistic. The society is on the green at the corner of South Street, and exhibits are open mid-April to mid-November, Tuesday through Saturday from 10 a.m. to 4 p.m.

The **White Memorial Conservation Center** (tel. 567-0015) is out on West Street (U.S. 202) heading toward Bantam, and is the state's largest nature center, with over 35 miles of trails for enjoying the flora and fauna, and several prime perches for birdwatching. Entry to the grounds is free, and they're open all year; the center's museum is open Tuesday through Saturday from 9 a.m. to 5 p.m., and also on Sunday from 11 a.m. to 5 p.m. Displays include dioramas, mounted specimens, live animals, a touch center, and a 4,000-volume nature library which includes a children's room. Admission to the museum costs $1 for adults and 50¢ for children 6 to 12.

Other Litchfield curiosities: **The Ethan Allen House,** thought to be the one in which the famous patriot and leader of Vermont's "Green Mountain Boys" was born, is at the southern end of South Street, in the road's fork. A **milestone** dating from 1787, which informed the traveler that it was "33 Miles to Hartford, 102 Miles to New York—J. Strong AD 1787," stands on West Street, northern side, just at the end of the Town Green. And the jail, right on the green at the beginning of North Street, is connected to the bank next door! Whether it's for the convenience of burglars who wish to escape or police who may nab burglars in the bank is not clear.

Litchfield's Winery

Just outside Litchfield is the **Haight Vineyard** (tel. 567-4045), on Chestnut Hill Road off Rte. 118 one mile east of town. This quaint but inviting place prides itself on being Connecticut's first farm winery (established 1975). Besides guided winery tours and wine tastings, you can take the Vineyard Walk, a self-guided tour of the vineyards during which you get to inspect the various types of grapes which make Haight wines.

Some of the favorite wines here are Covertside White, the table wines, a varietal Maréchal Foch, a chardonnay and a Johannisberg Riesling. They even make a sparkling wine made in the classic *méthode champenoise*. Prices are moderate.

The winery is open all year, Monday through Saturday from 10:30 a.m. to 5 p.m., on Sunday from noon to 5 p.m.

LAKE WARAMAUG: From Litchfield, drive along U.S. 202 south and west for 12 miles to New Preston. Then head north on Rte. 45, and you'll come to pretty Lake Waramaug. Attractive inns front the lake, as does a state park with picnic and camping facilities.

Lake Waramaug State Park, in New Preston, CT 06777 (tel. 868-0220), has 88 sites open May 15 through Labor Day. You can reserve in advance, but only by mail. Picnic grounds and swimming are here too.

The Inn on Lake Waramaug, off Rte. 45 on North Shore Road, New Preston, CT 06777 (tel. 203/868-0563, or toll free outside Connecticut 800/525-3466), is actually a mini-resort with all attractions. Indoor swimming pool, tennis court, air-conditioned rooms, restaurant and lounge, gift shop, and water sports (rowing, canoeing, sailing) are among the many offerings. There's even a small launch designed like an old "showboat" for tours of the lake. Even so, the inn retains an antique flavor. Of the 23 guest rooms, only five are in the original inn, while the others are in more modern but attractive guesthouses. All rooms have baths, and most have working fireplaces. Prices range from $182 to $232 per day for two people, breakfast, dinner, taxes, and tips included. The inn offers many special events, like old-fashioned ice harvesting and maple sugaring, which have become traditions over the years.

Not far from where the shore road rejoins Rte. 45, look for signs which point the way to the **Hopkins Inn,** New Preston, CT 06777 (tel. 203/868-7295). This graceful old mansion set on a hill above the lake is most famous for its restaurant, but ten rooms are for rent as well. If you share a bath, a double room will cost $49; with private bath, prices start at $57. Whether you stay or not, have a meal—but also, have reservations. This is a very popular dining spot, especially on Saturday evenings, when reservations are required. The blackboard menus change daily, but you can be sure of finding interesting, appetizing dishes. I had a difficult choice between clams casino and smoked salmon to start, and an even harder time choosing among backhendl with lingonberries, steamed lobster, wienerschnitzel, or live trout meunière (you can choose your own trout from the tank!). When it came to those Austrian desserts, the choice was impossible. Figure $25 to $30 per person for dinner, with wine. Note these short dining hours: lunch from noon to 2 p.m. and dinner from 5:30 to 9 p.m. (till 10 p.m. on Friday and Saturday), Sunday dinner from 12:30 to 8:30 p.m. The inn is open April through December every day except Monday; rooms are rented April through November. In warm weather you can dine on the shady patio outside, with a grand view of the lake.

A Visit to a Vineyard

Next door to the Hopkins Inn on Lake Waramaug is the **Hopkins Vineyard,** on Hopkins Road in Warren (tel. 203/868-7954). The quaint red barn winery is open for tours and tastings from 10 a.m. to 5 p.m. seven days a week from the beginning of May through the end of the year. January 2 through April 30, you can visit on Friday, Saturday, and Sunday only, from 10 a.m. to 5 p.m. The winery is closed Thanksgiving and Christmas Days.

Whoever heard of a vineyard in Connecticut? You'll be telling all your friends about vineyards in Connecticut once you taste Hopkins' fine, dry Seyval Blanc, perfect for a seafood meal at the inn across the street. Wine prices are moderate and quality is high. By the way, the vineyard is not affiliated with the Hopkins Inn, though the vineyard barn was obviously part of the same estate at one time.

NORTH TO SALISBURY: Back on Conn. 45, head north and you're on your way to **Cornwall Bridge,** which is famous for its picturesque covered bridge. **Housatonic Meadows State Park** (tel. 672-6772) is here with camping and picnic areas, north of town on U.S. 7.

You can head north on U.S. 7, then cross westward on Rte. 112 to pick up Rte. 41 north to Salisbury; or take Rte. 4 west from Cornwall Bridge to Sharon, then Rte. 41 north through Lakeville to Salisbury. The distance is about 16 or 18 miles.

Salisbury is an aristocratic, historic town on the edge of the Berkshires. Late in September there's a big flea market here, and at the height of the fall foliage color the Salisbury Antiques Fair is held in the Town Hall. Come any time of year, though. The town is pretty, tranquil, surrounded by gorgeous country, and only 20 miles from the heart of the Berkshires' summer and winter activities.

Where to Stay and Eat

Cornwall Bridge is famous for its picturesque covered bridge, and it also has a choice place to stay. The **Cornwall Inn and Motel,** on U.S. 7, Cornwall Bridge, CT 06754 (tel. 203/672-6884), is one mile south of the intersection with Conn. 45. The cozy old inn has a dining room, lounge, and five guest rooms ($95 double on weekends, $85 weekdays). These are supplemented by half a dozen tidy motel-style rooms. Constructed in red-barn style, the rooms have all the conveniences such as television and air conditioning, and cost $55 double on weekdays, $65 on weekends. There's a swimming pool. The location is good, out in the country where it's peaceful and quiet. Note that the dining room is closed on Monday and Tuesday.

You might put up at the **Ragamont Inn,** Salisbury, CT 06068 (tel. 203/435-2372), just off the Village Green on Rte. 44. You can't miss the inn's two Greek Revival façades with awning-covered dining patio between. The Ragamont rents rooms and suites, most with private bath, for $38 to $52 single, $63 to $74 double, $92 for the suite with a working fireplace. But the emphasis here is on dining as the owner happens also to be a Swiss-trained *chef de cuisine.* On a warm summer afternoon I lunched on vichyssoise, knackwurst Cordon Bleu (who could pass it up?), and pastry, for $15, all in. Fresh fish, the Swiss national dish of raclette, chef's salad, club sandwiches—all these and more were also offered. I caught a glance of the dinner menu (actually, a blackboard) and noted they were serving duck and veal Calvados (that's the apple brandy from France). I'd estimate about $33 for a full dinner with wine, per person.

A few miles down the road, you'll do well by dining at the **Wake Robin Inn,** Rte. 41, Lakeville, CT 06039 (tel. 203/435-2515). In the elegant French country dining room, start with a cassolette of snails with fresh mountain herbs or the soup of the day, and move on to medallions of veal simmered with herbs and walnuts or grilled swordfish with lemon butter. With a delectable dessert to top it off, the tab will come to roughly $38 per person, all in. Dinner is served in season Tuesday through Sunday from 5:30 to 9 p.m., until 8 p.m. on Sunday; Sunday brunch is 11:30 a.m. to 2:30 p.m. Rooms are expensive in this completely renovated former girl's school set on 15 acres, but if you're interested in staying here, they cost $146 to $173 double, more for a suite.

INTO THE BERKSHIRES: Up here in Connecticut's northwest corner, you're very close to one of America's oldest and finest resort areas, the Berkshire Mountains of Massachusetts. The towns of South Egremont, Great Barrington, Lee, and Lenox have great charm, good restaurants, fine old inns and guesthouses, a bewildering array of cultural activities, and more antique shops than you've ever seen before in one area at one time. For details on it all, see Chapter IX, "Central and Western Massachusetts."

NEW HAMPSHIRE

"**L**ive free or die" says the motto on every auto license plate in New Hampshire, echoing the stirring words of Gen. John Stark, victor at the momentous Battle of Bennington (1777) and a New Hampshire native. New Hampshire folk are still very patriotic in an old-fashioned way, and committed to material progress: modern facilities abound, and the road system is perhaps the best maintained in New England. On a vacation, "living free" in New Hampshire is a snap: mountains, beaches, lakes, amusements, special activities, and good restaurants are all available to the visitor.

On our tour through New Hampshire, we'll look first at the state's seacoast. Yes, New Hampshire has a seacoast! Next we'll visit the charming colonial town of Portsmouth on the border with Maine. Then we'll head north into the state's heart, passing through Manchester, the state's largest city, and Concord, its capital, on our way to Lake Winnipesaukee. From this veritable inland sea, we'll head north again into the White Mountains National Forest and the skiing/hiking center of North Conway, and then even farther north to Bretton Woods. Moving west, the next area we'll cover is that of Franconia Notch, North Woodstock, and Waterville Valley. Finally, we'll visit Lake Sunapee and then Hanover, the hometown of Dartmouth College.

By the way, throughout New Hampshire a rooms-and-meals tax of 7% will be added to your hotel, motel, or inn bill, and you'll also have to pay it every time you have a meal in a restaurant. For your convenience, except where noted, I've added this tax to the prices listed.

New Hampshire's telephone area code is 603.

GETTING THERE: New Hampshirites are committed to highway travel, and so air links and rail lines are played down in favor of bus and car. Amtrak, in fact, has no operations in New Hampshire proper, although it does run along the New Hampshire–Vermont border for a bit, stopping in Brattleboro, Bellows Falls, and White River Junction on the route between New York and Montréal.

By Limousine and Bus

Airport limousines run regularly from Boston's Logan Airport to many points in New Hampshire. **Hudson Bus Lines' Airporter Limousine Service** goes from Logan to Manchester, Concord, and other southern New Hampshire cities. Call toll free in New England, except New Hampshire 800/367-3885; in Manchester, call 603/883-4807.

C & J Trailways, runs hourly daily trips from Logan to New Hampshire's seacoast region and Portsmouth; call these numbers for schedules and reservations: toll free in New York and New England, 800/258-7111; in Portsmouth, 603/431-2424.

Concord Trailways, South Main Street, Concord, NH 03301 (tel. 603/228-3300, or toll free 800/852-3317 in New Hampshire, 800/258-3722 in other New England states), operates buses from Boston through Manchester and Concord to Laconia on Lake Winnipesaukee; from there the bus continues to Plymouth, North Woodstock, and through Franconia. Concord Trailways also has buses from Boston to Conway, North Conway, Glen, Jackson, Pinkham Notch A.M.C. Camp, Wildcat Mountain, and on to Berlin.

Vermont Transit, operating out of Boston's Greyhound terminal near the Park Plaza Hotel (tel. 617/423-5810), has routes from Portland, Me., to St. Johnsbury, Vt., via North Conway, Bretton Woods, and Bethlehem (near Franconia), N.H., besides running from Logan Airport in Boston to the cities of Manchester and Concord, and thence to Mount Sunapee and Hanover. Vermont Transit also runs buses from Montréal south into Vermont and a few points in New Hampshire, but Montréal visitors will have to transfer at least once to reach most of the vacation locations in the state. Vermont Transit buses depart from the Voyageur Terminal in Montréal (tel. 514/843-4231, or toll free 800/451-3292).

---

1. Hampton Beach

Many visitors to New England forget that Vermont is the only New England state without a seacoast, and that New Hampshire is in fact a maritime state, even though its coastline is only about 20 miles long. The 20 miles are almost all beach, with some rocky headlands and coves, and four state parks with their own uncommercial stretches of beach. **Hampton Beach State Park** is the most southerly, and the public parking and bathing facilities here are run in the clean, well-ordered way of state park management. But just north of the state park is the town of Hampton Beach, two streets wide (north along the waterfront, south along the inland street, as far as cars are concerned). Hampton Beach is a riot of closely packed motels and cottages, ice cream stands and hot dog stands, penny arcades, and watering places. Lights, glitter, and throbbing crowds of the young, tanned, and adventurous make it a nonstop circus, something out of a "beach party" movie, to revel in or abhor as your taste dictates.

FROM HAMPTON BEACH TO PORTSMOUTH: North of Hampton Beach, the state park beaches at **Rye Harbor** and **Wallis Sands** are not as bubbly with activity as Hampton, but to some tastes are all the more pleasant for that. At the state park beaches in New Hampshire, expect to pay a small parking fee, which includes use of all other facilities as well.

The drive along U.S. 1A north to Hampton Beach is very pretty, winding along the coast past a succession of ever more sumptuous and meticulously maintained

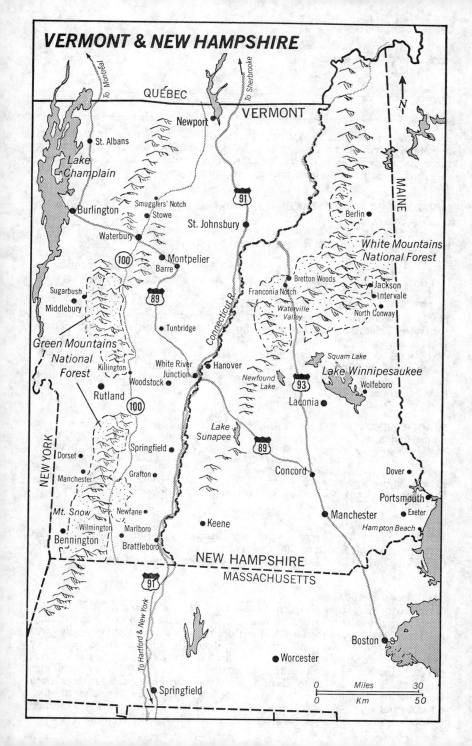

summer mansions, still inhabited by the wealthy and powerful of New Hampshire, Maine, and Boston.

2. Portsmouth

Of the gracious maritime towns along the New England coast, Portsmouth is one of the prettiest and most interesting. A morning or afternoon spent wandering through the town's restored historic side streets, perhaps with lunch, tea, or dinner in one of its restaurants, is both relaxing and entertaining.

WHERE TO STAY AND DINE: Portsmouth has a good place to stay and more than its share of good places to eat.

The **Sise Inn,** 40 Court Street, Portsmouth, NH 03801 (tel. 603/433-1200) has 34 rooms and suites all with rich carpeting, private bath, color cable TV, VCR, and telephone. This Queen Anne–style 1881 hotel caters to business people but off-the-road travelers won't feel out of place. Doubles are $94 to $106 depending on bed size, while suites start at $133 to $171. An ample continental breakfast is included in the price.

The **Library Restaurant,** in the Rockingham Hotel at 401 State St. (tel. 431-5202), is a good choice no matter what your culinary preference. The menu lists such varied delights as Long Island duckling, filet mignon, and veal and fish specials, along with more familiar fare and money-saving daily special plates. The old rooms of the hotel have been preserved without overdoing the decor; books line the walls. You might spend $20 to $28 for a good, full dinner with wine, tax, and tip, less than half that for lunch. Hours are 11:30 a.m. to 3 p.m. and 5 to 11 p.m., Sunday brunch from 11:30 a.m. to 4 p.m.

READER'S RESTAURANT RECOMMENDATION: "Every time I'm in Portsmouth, I eat at **Szechuan Taste.** It's a quirky place, different from Portsmouth's usual seafood restaurants; locals in-the-know always pack the place. It's family run, with good service. The simple, dimly lit restaurant is the kind of place you go with friends, the kind of place you might not venture into without a recommendation. There are many Thai or Szechuan choices on the menu for about $7" (Julia Regan, Dorchester, Mass.). [*Author's note:* Szechuan Taste is located at 54 Daniels Street (tel. 431-2226); open 11:30 a.m. to 10:45 p.m. weekdays, until 11:45 p.m. on weekends.]

WHAT TO SEE: The Greater Portsmouth Chamber of Commerce maintains a **Visitors Information Booth** at 500 Market St. (Exit 7 off I-95), Portsmouth, NH 03801 (tel. 603/436-1118), and also an information kiosk in Market Square.

Strawbery Banke

Portsmouth's jump from wilderness to settlement started in 1630, when a group of settlers sailed into the Piscataqua River's mouth in search of fresh water and good land. As they climbed up the rise from the shore they found not only good land and water but also wild strawberries, which delighted them so much they named the place Strawbery Banke. Today that name serves to identify the center of the city's historic restoration effort, a ten-acre section of 18th-century buildings brought back to life and peopled with craftspeople who are not here for show but in fact make their livelihoods right where you see them. The Strawbery Banke outdoor museum (tel. 603/433-1100) is open from 10 a.m. to 5 p.m. daily, May through October, at $7 for adults, $6 for seniors, $4 for children 6 to 16. For this price you can wander about, looking at the 42 houses and buildings, exhibits, period gardens, workshops, and artisans' galleries on display.

A walk through Strawbery Banke is educational as well as entertaining, for you'll see how chairs, tables, and cabinets were made besides seeing examples of the work itself; weaving and stoneware potting are explained, and early tools and architectural designs are spread out for your examination.

Finding the Strawbery Banke section is easy: just follow the directional signs, with arrows, posted throughout the town and on approach roads.

Strawbery Banke is the major part of Portsmouth's Old Harbour area, the cornerstone of which is **Prescott Park,** a waterfront park, dock, and amusement area donated to the city by the Prescott sisters in the 1930s and 1940s.

John Paul Jones's House

Of the other notable places in this pretty city, none is more notable than the National Historic Landmark house of John Paul Jones (1758), open mid-May through mid-October from 10 a.m. to 4 p.m. Monday through Saturday, and noon to 4 p.m. on Sunday in July and August. The stately house, at the corner of Middle and State Streets, was actually a rooming house when Jones stayed in it, a commander whose frigate, the famous *Ranger,* was still being built in a nearby shipyard. The house (tel. 436-8420) is now the headquarters of the Portsmouth Historical Society, and you can visit the house and museum on a one-hour guided tour at $3 for adults, $1 for children 6 to 12.

---

3. Manchester

Manchester borders the Merrimack River, and the cheap waterpower brought the city wealth in the textile boom of the mid and late 19th century. The very impressive **Amoskeag Mills** still border the river and the canals in the center of town, the brick facades stretching for almost a mile. The mills are used for various purposes today, including the manufacture of textiles and shoes (plenty of factory-outlet stores in town), and continued use preserves these monuments of American architectural and industrial history.

WHAT TO SEE: Although a business and manufacturing town, Manchester has two points of interest besides the giant mills. The **Currier Gallery of Art,** 192 Orange St. (tel. 669-6144), is a fine museum in a handsome building, open free to the public on Tuesday, Wednesday, Friday, and Saturday from 10 a.m. to 4 p.m., on Thursday to 10 p.m., and on Sunday from 2 to 5 p.m. The collection is strong in 19th- and 20th-century European and American glass, English and American silver and pewter, and colonial and Early American furniture. It also has a nice collection of paintings and sculpture from other parts of the world. Degas, Jan Gossaert, and a follower of Meliore are represented along with other masters. A beautiful new wing shows off the collections to best advantage. To find the museum, cross the Queen City or Amoskeag Bridge to downtown, and drive along Elm Street (Rte. 3) to Orange Street. Go east on Orange six blocks, and the museum is on your left.

About five miles south of Manchester, at Exit 11 of the Everett Turnpike, is the town of Merrimack, where you'll find **Anheuser-Busch Company's Merrimack Brewery** (tel. 595-1202). The company that brews Budweiser and Michelob is the largest brewer of beer in the world, with an annual capacity of about 80 million barrels at 12 breweries across the country.

In the warmer months (May through October), guided tours run continuously every day of the week from 9:30 a.m. to 3:30 p.m. (last tour). In winter, tours run Wednesday through Sunday only. Assemble in the special alpine-looking tour building.

After the tour there's sampling of the brew, of course, and perhaps a visit to the Clydesdale Hamlet, home for a dozen of the huge, majestic draft horses. You've probably seen them in eight-horse hitches pulling a brewer's wagon in advertisements or local parades.

WHERE TO STAY AND EAT: The newest, and the best value, is the **Susse Chalet Inn,** 860 S. Porter St., Manchester, NH 03103 (tel. 603/625-2020, or toll free 800/258-1980). The rooms, plainish but tidy and comfortable, are bargain priced at $43 single, $48 double, $51 for three, $54.50 for four. The Susse Chalet is at Exit 1 from I-293/Rte. 101.

Should you have to stay overnight on the road, I-293 at Manchester has several chain motels and one local one. The **Howard Johnson Hotel** is at the Queen City Bridge Exit (no. 4) from I-293 (tel. 603/668-2600, or toll free 800/654-2000), Manchester, NH 03102. King- and queen-size beds, satellite TV with HBO, an indoor pool, saunas, a lounge, and a restaurant (open from 6 a.m. to 2 a.m.) are offered with rooms ranging from $59 to $79 single, $63 to $97 double; children under 18 stay free in their parents' room.

At the **Holiday Inn West,** 21 Front St., Manchester, NH 03102 (tel. 603/669-2660), there is a restaurant, a lounge, an outdoor pool, and rooms for $70 to $80 double; children, including teenagers, stay free with their parents. Take the Amoskeag Bridge exit (Exit 6, Rte. 114) from I-293 for this one.

---

4. Concord

The capital of New Hampshire is a pleasant little city with an appropriate frontier-mountain feeling. First settled in 1725, the town was called Rumford for the first 40 years; the name later found its way into the title of Count Rumford, inventor of a certain sort of shallow fireplace. Since 1816 Concord has been the capital of the state. Granite, printing, electrical equipment, and leather goods, as well as a surprisingly small amount of state bureaucracy, keep the town going.

WHAT TO SEE: Mary Baker Eddy, founder of Christian Science, was born nearby in the village of Bow. Franklin Pierce, 14th president of the United States, was speaker of the New Hampshire General Court (legislature) as well as being among the town's prominent lawyers, and you can visit his house, which is now a National Historic Site, called the **Pierce Manse.** The Manse, at the farthest reaches of North Main Street, was saved from demolition by a civic-minded group named the Pierce Brigade, and it is open weekdays from June 12 through September 15 from 11 a.m. to 3 p.m. (closed Labor Day). Entrance costs $1.50 for adults, 50¢ for children and students. You might want to make an appointment by calling 224-9620.

The State Capitol, called the **State House,** was built in 1819 of—you guessed it—granite, and is the oldest capitol in which a legislature still occupies its original chambers. Inside are proudly displayed the state's battle flags and portraits of its notable military commanders. A statue of Daniel Webster, one of several native New Hampshire boys who made good on a national scale, stands before the building. The small size of the State House will surprise you; compared to the mammoth buildings in Providence, Hartford, and Boston, it seems barely big enough to hold just the governor's staff. But many of the tax-burdened citizens of other states are lured to New Hampshire every year by the low tax rate, kept low in part by keeping bureaucracy small.

Canterbury Shaker Village

Fifteen miles north of Concord on Rte. 106, on the way to Laconia, you can visit a restored village founded by the Shakers in 1792. Members of the United Society of Believers in Christ's Second Appearing were called Shakers because of the religious ecstasies they sometimes experienced. Their community at Hancock, Mass., in the Berkshires (see Chapter IX, Section 7, "Stockbridge") is the best known, but there were others, notably at Sabbathday Lake, Me., and here in Canterbury, NH (tel. 603/783-9511). These villages are still active Shaker communities.

Besides producing the much-admired Shaker furniture and craft items, the Canterbury Shaker community specialized in producing herbs and herbal medicines, which were sold throughout the country. You can still visit the 900-acre herb garden, as well as the original meetinghouse (1792), an apiary (bee house), a dwelling house, and a schoolhouse.

You can take a guided tour May through October, Monday through Saturday from 10 a.m. to 5 p.m.; the last tour is at 5 p.m. The cost is $6.75 adults, $3.50 for children 6 to 12.

All year on Thursday, Friday, and Saturday evenings you can also enjoy a traditional candlelight dinner here. There is one seating (family style at three long tables) at 7 p.m. sharp. The four-course meal (choose from a poultry, meat, or fish main dish) costs $32 per person. Recipes, ingredients, and cooking methods are all true to Shaker form and philosophy. After dinner has transported you to another era, you'll be guided through the village, or if it's off-season and the village is closed, you'll be treated to an evening of folk singing. You'll have an enjoyable evening either way.

5. Lake Winnipesaukee

The largest of the lakes in New Hampshire's Lakes Region is grand indeed: 28 miles long, close to 300 miles of shoreline, 72 square miles of water to swim in or boat on, and almost 300 islands. The name has been translated as "smile of the Great Spirit," and while the lake's irregular shoreline might suggest a wry grin rather than a sunny smile, the lake's large size would certainly do the Great Spirit justice. Summer is when the lake is busiest with swimmers, boaters, waterskiers, and the like, but winter snows draw crowds to the **Gunstock** and **Alpine Ridge** ski areas near the lake's shore.

LACONIA AND EAST: Laconia is Lake Winnipesaukee's largest town, and business and commercial center. Many of the companies with large shoe factories in the region have factory-outlet stores here where shoes sell at bargain prices. Downtown, the **Belknap** (pronounced *bell*-nap) **Mill,** a textile mill built in 1823, has been restored and you can tour it to see its machinery made of wood—gears, cogwheels, and all. Tours can be arranged in the late afternoon if you call ahead (tel. 524-8813). It's open from 9 a.m. to 5 p.m. Monday through Friday and 9 a.m. to 1 p.m. on Saturday all year.

Where to Stay

Coming to the lake for fun, people stay in the many motels and inns on portions of the lake's shore near Laconia, or in a small, pretty town such as Wolfeboro, due east of Laconia. Skiers stay at the inns located near the slopes or in a lakefront establishment with winterized cabins.

To get away from the hustle and bustle of the highway, drive along Rte. 11 and watch for signs pointing out a scenic shore road off to the left. Rte. 11 has been remade in recent years and is farther away from the lakeshore, while the motels are still along the old road which used to be Rte. 11. Most of the traffic uses the new road, leaving the old one much quieter.

Those looking for quiet, luxurious accommodations with all the conveniences, including color TV and air conditioning, will enjoy the **Belknap Point Motel,** R.F.D. 8, 107 Belknap Point Rd., Gilford, NH 03246 (tel. 603/293-7511). The Belknap Point has two sections: down on the shore of the lake, a number of modern efficiency units with kitchens and decks reach out almost over the water; and up the steep slope of the hill between the old road and the new (you can enter from either road) are a number of hotel rooms, all with ceramic tile bath, a little balcony, and gorgeous views of the lake. The owners have put a lot of thought into decorating the rooms nicely, and they work hard to make sure each guest is comfortable. The Belknap Point has its own swimming area and a grassy patio. Prices for the hotel rooms are $84 to $94 per day double, $21 a day less off-season (May, early June, September, and October). You can rent a room here for one or two days at $62 a day if there's an opening for that amount of time. The efficiencies down by the water rent by the week. An additional person in a room is $10; in an efficiency, $52.

The **Estate Motel and Cottages,** Scenic Drive (R.F.D. 4), Gilford, NH 03246 (tel. 603/293-7792), is another of the establishments along the scenic lakefront road. Here there are eight motel rooms and two efficiencies in white buildings. The rooms look out over a grassy lawn down to the lake; the lake boating and swimming dock are convenient. The Estate is secluded and quiet, and it's best to reserve in advance for one of its rooms: $64.25 double in a motel room, $107 double in one of the efficiency cottages, lower rates by the week. Rooms have two double beds, cable TV, shower, and refrigerator; the efficiencies have the same, plus a sink and stove, and kitchen utensils. Three cabins are rented by the week for $348 for one bedroom, $481 for two bedrooms.

What to Do

Ellacoya State Beach, on Rte. 11 southeast of Glendale, is one of the nicest beaches on the lake. The entrance fee is $2 for adults and children 12 and older, there's plenty of parking, and if you go early in the day you can get one of the picnic tables. A snackbar is in operation, and a lifeguard is on duty all the time the beach is open. The slope of the beach is very, very gradual, making it ideal for small children; for more experienced swimmers, a swimming dock floats in the water farther out.

Weirs Beach

Weirs Beach, on Rte. 11B near its intersection with U.S. 3, is a town beach with a similar admission charge, free parking at several lots in the town of Weirs Beach (look for the signs to the free lots—everything on the main street is metered). Weirs Beach is known more for its honky-tonk penny arcades, candlepin bowling alleys, pinball machines, fortune tellers, and fast-food stands than it is for the beauty of its beach. These amusements are open during the day and in the evening in summer, and give the town a character that differs greatly from what it once must have been: the grand old turn-of-the-century mansions seen here and there in the town are some of the finest of their genre, with lots of cupolas, turrets, gables, and all the other paraphernalia that make late-Victorian architecture so intricate. You can stay overnight at Weirs Beach in one of the hotels, motels, or guesthouses, although the low lakefront situation seems to lend a mustiness to most accommodations.

BOAT RIDES: A number of large boats make tours of the lake several times daily. Most famous is the M/S *Mount Washington* (tel. 603/366-5531), which runs cruises from Weirs Beach between May 20 and October 21, with the schedule varying depending on the time of year. The cruise around the lake takes 3¼ hours and costs $11 for adults, half price for children 5 to 12; under 5, free. Breakfast, luncheon buffet, a Sunday champagne brunch, and snacks are available on board. You can also pick up the boat in Wolfeboro every day at 11 a.m. The *Mount Washington* also leaves from Weirs Beach on moonlight cruises on Tuesday through Saturday evenings from July 1 through Labor Day weekend.

THE ALPINE SLIDE AND CHAIR LIFTS: During the summer, the ski areas at Gunstock and Alpine Ridge on Rte. 11A are busy with other things. Gunstock (tel. 603/293-4341) is turned into a giant 300-space camping area with a swimming pool and hiking trails; Alpine Ridge (tel. 293-0730) has an Alpine Slide, a sport imported from Germany, and now also an Aquaboggan Waterslide and two other water rides. The Alpine Slide is a sort of sled which runs along a concrete-fiberglass track down the side of the mountain. Each person has his or her own sled and can control the speed of descent. It's safe for people of all ages, children included, and has been used by people over 80 years old (over 70, you ride for free). The ski lift takes you to the top of Mount Rowe, where you get your sled for the ride down. Tickets are $5 for one ride, or $15 all day, for those ages 5 to 70; children under 7, and seniors over 70, ride free.

WOLFEBORO: Of the other towns on Lake Winnipesaukee, Wolfeboro is certainly the finest. The town escaped the blight that hit such textile-producing towns as Laconia because Wolfeboro never industrialized; and it has escaped the honky-tonk commercialism that has taken over some other lake towns, perhaps because of its "inconvenient" position at the southeastern tip of the lake. So today Wolfeboro is a fine, almost typical, New England town with the requisite historical society, white-steepled churches, gracious old houses, and some very good views of the lake.

There is less hustle and bustle in Wolfeboro than in some other lake towns, less to "see and do," but that makes it all the better for those who really want to relax. The M/V *Mount Washington* stops here to pick up and discharge passengers for its tours of the lake (see above under "Weirs Beach" for details); and a good number of the motels and resorts in town have their own stretches of beach. Wolfeboro is proud to call itself "the oldest summer resort in America," because in 1763 Gov. John Wentworth built what is thought to be the first summer house in the U.S. within the town's boundaries.

Where to Stay and Dine

Among the most serviceable of Wolfeboro's hostelries is the venerable **Wolfeboro Inn**, 44 N. Main St., Wolfeboro, NH 03894 (tel. 603/569-3016). The inn was built in 1812 (but recently extensively renovated and expanded), and prides itself on giving the "glitter-weary traveler" a comfortable and tasteful place to lodge or to dine. The 43 rooms have some antique pieces, and all have private bath. Doubles have air conditioning, color cable TV, and telephone, and cost $91 to $107 per night, continental breakfast included. As the inn is often full in high summer, it's best to reserve in advance. Suites are 25% to 50% higher.

The downstairs rooms of the inn are devoted to dining. The atmosphere is from the era of the inn's construction, with wooden chairs and tables and several fireplaces, including a large brick one in the main dining room. The menu offers a fairly standard selection of the popular beef, seafood, and fowl dishes, but the daily specials (available at both lunch and dinner) are the best values, and also the most interesting items: swordfish, lobster chunks, and frogs' legs on rice were offered when I was last there. Sandwiches at lunch are priced at $4.50 to $6; at dinner, entrees with side dishes cost $15 to $21, while the daily specials are usually nearer the lower end of that range. You can get something to eat, either in the dining room or the less formal tavern, from 11:30 a.m. to 11:30 p.m.

Staying on the Outskirts

Wolfeboro is surrounded by motels and inns on the outskirts, many of them very nice indeed. Herewith my favorites:

The **Pick Point Lodge**, 4½ miles north of Wolfeboro off Rte. 109 (mail address: P.O. Box 220D, Mirror Lake, NH 03853; tel. 603/569-1338), is truly unique. It was formerly a wealthy family's summer estate, and has been converted to accommodate a small number of guests in ten large cottages (up to four bedrooms) and in two rooms in the main lodge. It would be possible to fill pages with the good points of the Pick Point Lodge, but a quick list will give you the idea: cottages are all very comfy and tastefully done, with fireplaces, porches, full kitchens, and, in the larger ones, two bathrooms; the estate is on a 112-acre tract of forest, with several nature trails plotted for guests' use; guests can enjoy a full half mile of lake frontage, indoor and outdoor tennis courts, a private beach and jetty, indoor and outdoor games, and special cookouts, cocktail parties and such, which are "on the house," and which you can join or ignore as you wish. The hosts, the Newcomb family, are very gracious and solicitous of their guests' well-being and privacy, and couldn't be nicer. Rates for such quality are not low, but are reasonable for what you get; prices given below include the 7% tax. From late June to Labor Day rentals are by the week only, unless there is a cancellation or the like which leaves a cottage or room open for several days. Cottages range in price from $630 for a one-bedroom to $1,700 for a four-bedroom for one week from mid-July through Labor Day weekend; prices for May, June, September, and October are in the range of $630 to $850 for a cottage. In the main lodge, rooms cost $90 to $105 double, light breakfast included. This could easily be the finest place on Winnipesaukee.

Just about a mile north of town at 120 North Main Street is the **Lakeview Inn,** P.O. Box 713, Wolfeboro, NH 03894 (tel. 603/569-1335). The simple rooms, with one or two double beds, are primarily in the motor lodge; some of these have kitchenettes. Three of the 14 guest rooms are upstairs in the old inn. Regardless of location all have TV, private bath, and telephone. Summer rates, which include a self-service continental breakfast set up in the lounge, are $80 single, $80 to $91 double. Lunch is served weekdays from noon and 2 p.m.; dinner is served nightly from 5:30 p.m. The menu includes such selections as roast duckling and a veritable sea of scallops, crabmeat, langostines, and lobster. A full meal will total about $25 per person with tax and tip, but lighter fare is always available for about a third of the price.

What to Do in Wolfeboro

Several activities in Wolfeboro are worth a special mention.

Dr. Henry F. Libby, a Boston dentist who was born and raised near the shores of Winnipesaukee, devoted the latter part of his life to the study and collection of natural history specimens: fish, animals, and birds. Other interests of his included early Native American lore of the region, and artifacts from the times of early settlers. All these diverse exhibits are brought together in the **Libby Museum** on Rte. 109 north/west, open from 10 a.m. to 4 p.m. daily except Monday during the summer. Donation is $1 for adults, 50¢ for children. The museum is about three miles north of the town on Rte. 109.

Around the turn of the century Thomas Gustav Plant decided to build himself a retreat in the New Hampshire wilderness. While he was not alone in this—lots of rich men were building lavish estates in the region—his accomplishment is certainly among the grandest. Lucknow, as the estate was named, cost millions of dollars to build; the name comes from a castle in Scotland, and ultimately from a city in India, although the mansion has distinctly Central European touches to it. Today Lucknow is called **Castle in the Clouds,** on Rte. 171 in Moultonboro (tel. 603/476-2352), and is open to visitors who pay $7.50 per adult, $5.50 for children from 6 through 12. The grounds are very beautiful, and the view of the mountains and lakes is nothing short of spectacular. Horseback trail rides are available. Castle in the Clouds is open weekends in May and June from 9 a.m. to 6 p.m., daily during July and August to September 10 from 9 a.m. to 8 p.m. To get there, take Rte. 109 north from Wolfeboro for 17 miles, turn right (east) onto Rte. 171, and go three miles to the entrance.

MOUNT WASHINGTON VALLEY

The area along Rte. 16 between North Conway and Gorham, including the town of Bartlett on U.S. 302, is organized for tourist reasons as the Mount Washington Valley. The towns of North Conway and Jackson are centers for summer hiking, camping, and biking trips, and for winter skiing at the ski areas of Attitash, Mount Cranmore, Black Mountain, and Wildcat Mountain. The **Mount Washington Valley Visitors Center** (tel. 603/356-3171) has its main information office on Main Street in the center of North Conway, open during business hours and on weekends. They will be glad to help you with room reservations if you've had trouble finding a place to stay, and are in general very helpful indeed.

In addition, **North Country Tours,** P.O. Box 747, North Conway, NH 03860 (tel. 603/356-3212, or toll free 800/334-7378), will help you to make reservations at condos, inns, resorts, and motels throughout the White Mountain area, at no charge for the service.

---

6. North Conway

On the edge of the White Mountain National Forest and at the end of Mount Washington Valley, North Conway is the sports capital of the White Mountains. It's not a particularly large town, although the mile or two of motels and eateries along Rte. 16 south of town do seem to extend the boundaries. But basically one can walk to almost anything except this southern extension by parking downtown, somewhere near the antique railroad station.

North Conway has taken well to its role of mountain town, and the people talk hearty and look healthy. And while some of the businesses are oldtime mom-and-pop affairs, a lot of shops obviously have been citified to cater to the hiking and ski trades. But still the town has not been "taken over" by city people. Perhaps the character and charm of North Conway is best exhibited by the town library building on Main Street not far from the railroad station: although small, it's built of massive granite blocks and has a slate roof which will last forever; it's open to all and sundry on weekday afternoons and Wednesday mornings.

WHERE TO STAY AND EAT: North Conway has dozens of places to stay, including a good number of motels along the southern extension of Main Street (Rte. 16), but I'll concentrate mainly on the small inns in the town, and on those in the neighboring towns of Jackson and Glen, most of which have excellent dining rooms. Many of the lodging establishments listed here have mid-week and ski packages; be sure to inquire if you are planning an extended or active stay.

North Conway's Inns and Guesthouses

Perhaps the best inn to choose in North Conway, from the standpoint of price, convenience, and pleasantness, is the **Cranmore Inn,** North Conway, NH 03860 (tel. 603/356-5502), just off Main Street on the street leading to the Mount Cranmore ski area, and only a few blocks from the intercity bus stop. The inn is over a century old, with 23 guest rooms that reflect the charm of a Victorian country inn. Rooms come with private bath for $45 single, $56 double; with running water in the room and a bath down the hall, the price is $38 single, $48 double. Several two-bedroom suites (the two bedrooms share one bath) are available for families and friends traveling together, and can be rented at a price of $101 for three, or $104 for four persons. Meal service is family style. Although all this would make the Cranmore Inn well worth it, there are bonuses: a huge parlor with fireplace, a game room, and a TV room; nice big lawns suitable for games and Frisbee (in summer), and a swimming pool. From the inn you can walk to the slopes of Mount Cranmore in ten minutes, and the center of town in five or less. A five-minute walk will bring you to the Tennis and Health Club with full privileges. Note that in winter the rate structure is a bit different: breakfast and dinner are included in the price of the room, and rates vary depending on whether you come during the week or on the weekend.

On a quiet back street stands the **Sunny Side Inn,** Seavey Street, North Conway, NH 03860 (tel. 603/356-6239), an affordable and cozy bed-and-breakfast place with ten rooms and one efficiency unit. Rooms have shared or private bath, and rent for $27 to $59 single and $39 to $62 double, full breakfast included. There's a living room with fireplace and television, and also a reading nook you can use. To find the Sunny Side, turn onto Kearsarge Street at the traffic light, right again at the top of the hill, and it's on the left.

Another charming guesthouse, 1½ miles north of the center of North Conway, is named **Wildflowers,** North Main Street, North Conway, NH 03860 (tel. 603/356-2224). You'll see the sign on the left as you head north, and behind it the big white house with porch posts made of peeled and painted tree trunks. Homey, simple, convenient, friendly, the six bedrooms at Wildflowers (two with private bath, four with semiprivate) rent for $43 single, $64 to $86 double, continental breakfast included. Add $4 if you want a full breakfast.

The **Cranmore Mountain Lodge,** P.O. Box 1194, North Conway, NH 03860 (tel. 603/356-2044), is off the beaten path, which preserves a spirit of quiet and relaxation. A mile and a half from the center of town you'll come to the lodge, which consists of a nice old inn and a modernized barn loft. Rooms in the inn are the best bargains as they share several bathrooms; many rooms have sinks; prices are $60 to $67 for two, including breakfast. In the barn loft, rooms have private bath, color TV, air conditioning, one or two double beds—in short, all the comforts. Prices are commensurate with the degree of luxury, at $74 to $89 for two, again including breakfast. Cranmore Mountain Lodge has a 40-foot swimming pool, tennis and basketball courts, Jacuzzi spa bath, trout pond for fly angling, and outdoor barbecues. To find the lodge, turn east at the traffic light in North Conway onto Kearsarge Street; when you can go straight no longer, turn left. This is Kearsarge Road, and the lodge is a mile down.

The **Center Chimney,** P.O. Box 1220, North Conway, NH 03860 (tel. 603/356-6788), is just that: a big center-chimney Federal house built in 1787, now accepting guests. Rates are $38 single, $45 to $55 double, muffins and coffee included. (Extra bed for $10.) Look for the house north of town, just off Main Street, near the Saco River.

Hotels and Motels in North Conway

For decades the **Eastern Slope Inn,** Main Street, North Conway, NH 03860 (tel. 603/356-6321 or toll free in New England except New Hampshire 800/258-4709), was North Conway's posh place to stay, a stately white-pillared hotel with a genteel ambience. Swimming pool, clay tennis courts, a restaurant and pub, a summer theater next door, and a village center location are among the inn's advantages. Choose from rooms in the inn or in the motel-like Randall House nearby, suites, or efficiency suites, many of which are now condos. Rooms cost $92 to $214, single or double, depending on day of the week and season. Children of all ages can stay with their parents for free.

North Conway's snazziest hostelry, always in great demand, is the **Red Jacket Mountain View Motor Inn,** perched on a slope above South Main Street, North Conway, NH 03860 (tel. 603/356-5411). At the height of the season (summer or winter) its rooms go quickly because of its central location and its luxury accoutrements: a beautiful indoor pool covered by a dramatic wood roof, and an outdoor pool as well; saunas; a heated whirlpool; a game room with table tennis and electronic games; shuffleboard courts; tennis courts; dining room and cocktail lounge; many rooms with views and balconies, and some rooms with lofts so that a family can sleep more comfortably. Ceramic tile baths, two double beds to a room, color TV, air conditioning and heat, direct-dial telephones, and other luxury touches add to the draw, but it's the views and the convenience that convince many people to stay here. Rates are $98 to $150 double, and vary seasonally. Package plans are always available. À la carte evening meals in the dining room are in the $12 to $16 range. Lunch is now served in the Birchmont Tavern in the summer.

Staying in Intervale

A mile or two north of North Conway along Rtes. 16 and 16A are several inns and motels also worth considering. Although you won't be able to walk easily to town from here, these establishments have their own restaurants, and you're only a short drive from most of the hiking and ski points.

Off the main road, on scenic Rte. 16A (a short loop of a few miles) are several more lodging possibilities.

The **New England Inn and Resort,** Intervale, NH 03845 (tel. 603/356-5541), is the largest (35 rooms) of the establishments on Rte. 16A, comprising both the inn of that name and the Hampshire House across the road. It's quite a spread, with pools, four-hole golf course, clay tennis courts, and shuffleboard, besides rooms with or without bath in several buildings, costing $66 to $73 *per person;* a normal double room would thus cost about $140 total, per day, 7% tax and 15% service included. A big breakfast and dinner each evening are included in these rates. The one-room cottages for rent here have their own fireplaces and cost between $76 *per person* for up to four persons, meals included. Rates are 15% higher during foliage and ski season. Besides the inn's pine-paneled dining rooms, there's a lounge. The dining room, called Anna Martin's, is open to the public for all meals and specializes in Yankee cuisine with home-baked breads and desserts.

Just down the road from the New England Inn is the **Old Field House,** Intervale NH 03845 (tel. 603/356-5478), which is in a field, yes, but which is not old. It's hard to tell when you first see it whether this new and modern hostelry is an old building redone from top to bottom or a new building made to look good and last long. Despite its sturdy granite facade and gambrel-roofed wings, it is quite new, although meant to conjure up the romantic New Hampshire past. Rooms are all clean and shiny, with paneled walls, beamed ceilings, and colonial-style furniture. The bed arrangements are twins, one or two doubles, a queen-size, or a tremendous king-size. They also offer an efficiency apartment which overlooks the pool. The room prices are all for two people, including two continental breakfasts: $60 to $94. You get lots of extras at the Old Field House, such as a heated outdoor pool, tennis, laundry facilities, background music, cable TV, a game room, and shuffleboard. The entire place is air-conditioned.

Another place in Intervale is **The Forest, A Country Inn,** Rte. 16A (P.O. Box 37), Intervale, NH 03845 (tel. 603/356-9772), a large old house converted to take guests. There are 11 rooms in the inn itself and two in a nearby cottage, priced from $71 to $92 double, full breakfast included. For these prices you get a private bath, a nice living room (with fireplace) in which to meet new friends, a heated pool in summer, and cross-country skiing in winter on groomed trails, as well as summer hiking trails.

The **Riverside Inn,** Rte. 16A, Intervale, NH 03845 (tel. 603/356-9060) has it all: a quiet brook-side location, unpretentious guest rooms, lots of books spilling forth from the bookcases, creative country dining, and a small pleasant porch-side bar. Almost half of the seven rooms have private bath; these rent for $75 to $85, $10 more on the weekends. The other rooms never share a bath with more than one other room; these rent for $60 to $65, $5 more on weekends. A full breakfast is included, and as for dinner, you'd do well to stay put. When I was last there I had a hearty bowl of soup and lightly curried shrimp with candied ginger. My dinner bill was $28 including homemade Amaretto ice cream, tax, and tip.

Staying in Jackson

About 7 miles from North Conway going north on Rte. 16 is Jackson, right at the geographical center of the Mount Washington Valley, and the central point for cross-country skiing in the region. Besides being right in the middle of the downhill ski areas, Jackson has its own ski touring organization—but more of that below. It also has a collection of delightful inns open winter and summer. The **Jackson Resort Association** (P.O. Box 304, Jackson, NH 03846) will send you information, or you can contact the **Jackson/Glen Information Center** (tel. 603/383-9356). As the phone is only answered in peak season, it's better to write to the resort association for information.

At the center of Jackson is the **Village House,** Jackson, NH 03846 (tel. 603/383-6666), very near the covered bridge leading into the town from Rte. 16. The ten rooms here have all been redecorated, but the antique flavor of the house has been preserved. Eight rooms have private bath, and there's cable TV in the living room. Rates include use of the swimming pool, clay tennis court, and also a "deluxe" continental breakfast for each person. The basic charges for two are $75 to $86 double with bath.

The **Christmas Farm Inn,** Jackson, NH 03846 (tel. 603/383-4313), is just outside the center of Jackson village proper on the road up the hill to the Black Mountain Ski Area. Here the proprietors hold that "Hospitality makes the difference," but one must admit that the resort-style facilities help: the inn has its own pool and putting green (there are two professional golf courses near Jackson), a game room, sauna, lounge, living room, shuffleboard, and a dining room done in Early American. The Christmas Inn has no fewer than five separate places of accommodation, from the original inn (built in 1786) to a maple sugaring house converted into two modern rooms, with whirlpool, good for family accommodations. There are 35 rooms in all, priced at $166 to $190 for two persons, tax, service, breakfast, and dinner for each person included. Children under 12 sharing their parents' room are charged $36.

The **Inn at Thorn Hill,** Thorn Hill Rd., Jackson, NH 03846 (tel. 603/383-4242), is a huge old Victorian country house a short way outside Jackson which prides itself on several special features not often found. The baked goods are from its own ovens. As with several other Jackson inns, rooms here are in several buildings, including the inn itself, a nearby modernized carriage house, and three cottages. All rooms have private bath. In winter, breakfast and dinner come with the room at a price of $140 to $171 double.

Whitney's Inn, Rte. 16B (P.O. Box W), Jackson, NH 03846 (tel. 603/383-6886 or toll free 800/252-5622 in New England), has been serving a steady stream of families, skiers, and other loyal clientele since the early 1930s. The 35 rooms come in all shapes and sizes, from small singles to doubles complete with two double beds. The olive green farmhouse, with rambling additions, is one of the few places in the area that cater to children. There are nightly activities for them, as well as separate earlier dining. After a full breakfast of pancakes or eggs cooked any way you like them, simply ski out the back door and grab one of the four lifts to the top of Black Mountain. When the snow has melted there's swimming and tennis. Rates are high, with tax and service charge included, but worth it: $163 for a standard double, $55 per additional adult, $37 per additional child.

OLD-FASHIONED RESORTS IN JACKSON: Drive out of Jackson Village a mile or so, past a series of cascading waterfalls to find the **Eagle Mountain House,** Carter Notch Road, Jackson, NH 03846 (tel. 603/383-9111 or toll free 800/527-5022), one of the remaining premier grand old resorts in New England. Originally built in 1879 and completely rebuilt in 1986, the five-story white clapboard hotel commands a magnificent view of the surrounding mountains. Facilities include a heated outdoor pool, tennis courts, health club, a 9-hole golf course, and plenty of well-marked walking trails. The lobby is filled with rich leather sofas and the 84 guest rooms and suites with specially made furniture. Rates are reasonable: doubles range from $91 to $110, suites from $123 to $143; for an extra $28 per person per day, you can have breakfast and dinner daily. (Sunday brunch is particularly nice.) You'll enjoy staying here.

The **Wentworth Resort Hotel,** Jackson Village, NH 03846 (tel. 603/383-9700) is another turn-of-the-century hotel, complete with rambling frame main building, lounge, elegant dining rooms, various cottages and overnight rooms, 18-hole P.G.A. golf course, pool, and clay tennis courts. It's been redone from top to bottom, left to right, and all is shiny and bright. The hotel is definitely of a graceful, older time, though double room prices are a modern $80 to $134. Condominium units (rentable by the day, week, or month) have been added in clusters.

A MOTEL IN JACKSON: The village of Jackson is known for its country inns, and staying in one of these excellent places is a real treat. But—as you've seen—it is not an inexpensive proposition, especially when you add (as I have here for you) the 7% state room tax and the 15% "service charge," which is often found in the fine print.

For reasonable prices in this high-priced village, look to the **Covered Bridge Motor Lodge,** P.O. Box V, Jackson, NH 03846 (tel. 603/383-6630 or toll free 800/634-2911), an attractive hostelry right near the red covered bridge. The modern units here are designed not to clash with Jackson's forest mood, and prices are reasonable. For a standard comfortable double room with full bath you pay $58 to $68. Three efficiency apartments rent by the week, but another rents for $80 double per night with a two night minimum.

Mountain Hikers' Huts

The **Appalachian Mountain Club,** the organization that has done so much to preserve and maintain wilderness trails in New England, operates several lodging facilities in the White Mountains National Forest. At the **AMC's Pinkham Notch Camp,** Gorham, NH 03581 (tel. 603/466-2727), 11 miles north of Jackson on Rte. 16, people of all ages, whether AMC members or not, can find inexpensive bunkroom-type accommodations and simple but hearty meals. A bunk and breakfast costs $27.50 per adult; bed and supper is $31.50; bed, breakfast and supper is $36.50. Children under 12 receive a discount for the beds and meals, and as a convenience the kitchen will make up trail lunches for $3 per person. Note that you must have reservations, and they must be secured by a nonrefundable *per-person per-night* deposit. If you'd like a room alone, you will have to pay $19.50 extra for each unused bunk in the room, if others are turned away as a result. All these rules seem quite sensible. Note that the 7% tax is already included in these prices.

Besides the Pinkham Notch Camp, the AMC maintains a laudable system of mountain huts along its hiking trails in the mountains. Similar accommodations and meals are provided at similar prices, and with similar reservation arrangements. The huts are attended and trail meals prepared by "hutmen" and "hutwomen," a hearty breed of New England youth who pride themselves on being able to pack on their backs all the supplies needed in the huts—to a weight which would make a normal person stagger—and almost *run* up the mountains with the load several times a week. Guided hikes are featured throughout the summer. Write for details.

A Quiet Country Inn

Almost a century old, the **Bernerhof Inn,** on U.S. 302 several miles west of the town of Glen, NH 03838 (tel. 603/383-4414), has always been a way station for weary travelers along this major road. Today the owners, Ted and Sharon Wroblewski, concentrate on keeping the quality of the cuisine high and on entertaining their dinner guests, and sometimes diners here don't even know that rooms are for rent. They are, though, with full breakfast and at reasonable prices. Depending on the room's size, location, and plumbing, prices are $75 to $88 double.

WHAT TO DO: North Conway is the Mount Washington Valley center for winter sports, but even during the summer there's plenty to do.

Downhill Skiing

The Mount Washington Valley includes six alpine ski areas: Attitash, Black, Cranmore, King Pine, Tuckerman's Ravine, and Wildcat. Altogether there are 94 downhill trails and 21 lifts, and the slopes range from those for the beginner to those that present a challenge even to some experienced skiers. Many of the inns recommended above under "Where to Stay" offer special ski packages which include lift fees for all five areas.

You can get full free particulars on any or all of these areas by writing to the **Mount Washington Valley Chamber of Commerce,** P.O. Box 385, North Conway, NH 03860 (tel. 603/356-3171 or 356-5701).

Besides the five developed ski areas in the valley, it is possible to ski in the cirque at **Tuckerman's Ravine,** where the shadows protect the snow long past the time when the snow on other slopes has begun to melt. The special excitement at Tuckerman, besides the challenge of the *au naturel* slopes, comes from climbing the mountain you're going to ski down, for there are no lifts. This is oldtime skiing, with only a run or two a day, and only those with real stamina and strong legs should and will accept the challenge. But going back to the basics is exhilarating, everyone you meet here is your friend, and the fling down the mountain after the climb is a fitting way to end the season. Park in the Wildcat lot, recuperate in their cafeteria or lounge; follow the line of black dots up the mountain to the top.

Cross-Country Skiing

All of the alpine ski areas in the valley have some cross-country trails, some of which are very easy while others are only for experts. The center of the ski touring activity in the valley is Jackson, where the **Jackson Ski Touring Foundation,** (P.O. Box 216, Jackson, NH 03846) maintains and grooms over 150 km (90 miles) of cross-country trails. The foundation is a nonprofit village organization dedicated to encouraging ski touring in and around Jackson, and it has a small office in the center of the village (check here for passes, information, maps; tel. 603/383-9355). There is a nominal fee for the use of the trails. A season membership is available. Clinics, tours, and rentals are all available both in Jackson and in North Conway at the several ski shops.

Other Winter Sports

Because of the state parks, national forest, and private reserves in the valley, lots of other winter sports are popular here. Winter camping is possible, using a tent or the AMC huts, a few of which are open all winter. Note that many areas in the White Mountains have extremely severe weather—this writer has hiked into a blizzard, in a temperature of 14° and winds gusting to 100 mph on top of Mount Washington, on the last day of *August.* This does not mean you will hit impossible weather, but it does mean you should check with rangers and AMC personnel, and have good equipment and a knowledge of winter camping before you go in.

Snowmobiling is also pretty big in the valley, and rental places in North Conway will rent you a machine by the hour or the day. **Ice-skating rinks** are maintained by the towns of North Conway, Conway, and Jackson. Various ponds and lakes are not bad for **ice fishing**—the locals will be glad to give visitors tips on the most-visited ice-fishing spots.

Tennis clubs in Glen and North Conway now have indoor courts suitable for winter play, and guest memberships are available. Contact the Mount Cranmore Racquet Club (tel. 603/356-6301).

The Ski Areas in Summer

The three largest ski areas—Attitash, Mount Cranmore, and Wildcat Mountain—don't fully close down in summer. Indeed, they have developed full warm-weather recreation programs to keep the visitors coming and the bills paid. At **Attitash** (tel. 603/374-2368), the lifts keep working to take you up to the top of the Alpine Slide similar to the one described in the section on Alpine Ridge at Winnipesaukee. At Wildcat Mountain the cafeteria stays open for those wanting a snack before boarding the gondolas for the 25-minute round-trip ride up the mountainside (in operation late June to early September from 10 a.m. to 6 p.m. daily; from September 12 to October 11 it's open on weekends from 10 a.m. to 5 p.m.) You can buy a four-hour ticket for $15 or single-ride tickets for $5 per adult, $4.50 per child. The area around Wildcat Mountain and its base camp are kept immaculate because they're within the national forest and subject to its regulation.

Mount Cranmore, right in North Conway, has the most activities, however. The Skimobile is in operation on Memorial Day weekend, and then daily from late June through October to take visitors up 1,500 feet on a wooden trestle from the base to the summit for $6 per adult, $4.50 for kids 6 to 12. Next to the parking lot are several picnic tables in a pine grove next to a clear, cold mountain brook.

Summer Activities

Besides hiking and camping in the state parks and national forests, the Mount Washington Valley offers many other activities.

Right in town is the romantic old station of the **Conway Scenic Railroad** (tel. 356-5251), built in 1874 and restored to its present condition in 1974. For $6 (adults) or $4 (kids 4 to 12) you can buy a ticket for the scenic ride through the mountain country; choose your seat from among those in the enclosed cars or the open-air "cinder collectors." Two steam locomotives and a 39-year-old and a 44-year-old diesel engine are on hand to provide the power, and if you go a little early you can visit the round-house to see where the locomotives are turned around. From early May to early June the trains run on weekends only; from mid-June through late October the trains run every day, rain or shine. Departure times are 11 a.m. and 1, 2:30, and 4 p.m. The trip takes about an hour. The "Sunset Special" at 7 p.m. runs Tuesday, Wednesday, Thursday, and Saturday in July and August.

The **Mount Washington Valley Theater Company,** North Conway, NH 03860 (tel. 603/356-5776), currently performs at the playhouse on Main Street in the Eastern Slope Inn complex. Late June through Labor Day they offer a season of four lively musicals. Of course, it's most fun to see the entire series, watching the various members of the company take on different roles every other week, but even if you can't afford to stay in North Conway the entire season, you'll enjoy taking in a play here. The box office opens daily at 11 a.m., and curtain time is 8 p.m. sharp. Tickets run $12 to $8. Group rates are available.

A considerable part of northern New Hampshire is included in **White Mountains National Forest,** which is not to be confused with a national *park*. The forest does have a number of developed sites, however. Camping areas ($6 per night, cold running water, and pit toilets only) are dotted here and there, as are very pretty picnic areas. A maze of trails, both very easy and not so easy, cover a lot of the forest's vast expanse. Signs by the roadside mark the trail's beginning, but don't wander in just for a 30-minute walk if you're not familiar with the area. Instead, buy detailed maps of the trails and a trail guide from the **Appalachian Mountain Club,** 5 Joy St., Boston, MA 02108, or from the club's camp at Pinkham Notch on Rte. 16 north of Jackson. The trail guide will tell you all about the trail: how difficult it is, how long it is, the vertical rise, the average walking time, reference points along the way, and what to see as you walk.

Canoeing: Rent a canoe for the day or the week from **Saco Bound/Northern Waters,** two miles east of Center Conway on Rte. 301 (tel. 447-2177). The Saco

River has lots of smooth and easy areas, and you can go on a Tuesday or Thursday day trip—lunch, guide, and transportation included—for $22 per person. Overnight trips and canoe pickup service are available, as well as daily canoe rental.

Heritage New Hampshire, on Rte. 16 in Glen (tel. 383-9776), has a variety of lifelike scenes and dioramas with talking figures which outline New Hampshire's history, from the docks of an English port town through the Industrial Revolution at the Amoskeag Mills in Manchester. You can walk at your own pace through the maze of displays, and costumed guides will answer any questions you may have about New Hampshire's history. The price is $6.50 adults, $4.50 for children 4 to 12, and it's open from 9 a.m. to 6 p.m. daily in July and August, and then to 5 p.m. in June, and from Labor Day until late October.

Right next to Heritage New Hampshire is **Story Land** (tel. 383-4293), a children's amusement park with rides, clowns, animals, and lots of other treats. Once you've paid the $11 admission fee, all the rides are free; children under 4 are admitted without charge. Open daily from Father's Day through Labor Day, and then weekends only until Columbus Day.

The **Grand Manor,** three miles north of North Conway on Rte. 16 in Glen (tel. 356-9366), is an antique and classic automobile museum with such treasures as a '27 Caddie Phaeton, '30 Packard boat-tail speedster, '35 Duesenberg, '33 Rolls Phantom II, '36 Auburn, and '56 Mercedes 300SL Gullwing. Cars range in vintage from 1908 to 1963. Hours are 9:30 a.m. to 5 p.m. daily in the summer and on the weekends in spring and fall. Admission is $5 for adults, $3 for children.

Two Scenic Drives

A private business, the **Mount Washington Summit Road Company,** Gorham, NH 03581 (tel. 603/466-2222 or 466-3988), operates an alpine toll road to the top of the highest peak in the Northeast, 6,288-foot Mount Washington. Start from Rte. 16 in Pinkham Notch. You can drive your own car (no trucks or campers) to the top of the mountain at $11 for car and driver, and $4 for each passenger (kids pay $3); vans operated by the company will take you to the top and back down again for $15 per person (kids 5 to 12, $10) if you'd rather not drive. Hours are 7:30 a.m. to 6 p.m. for the road, 8:30 a.m. to 4:30 p.m. for the guided van tour. The season is normally from mid-May to mid-October, but remember that Mount Washington's summit has the most severe weather in the Northeast, and it's altogether possible that the road might be temporarily closed because of snow even in June or September. This, by the way, is only one of three ways to reach the Mount Washington summit, the others being on foot following the Appalachian Mountain Club trails, or by cog railway, described a bit further on in this book.

Route 112 between Conway and Lincoln is known as the **Kancamagus Hwy.;** its 33-mile length exhibits some of the finest scenery in the White Mountains, including the view from the 2,860-foot Kancamagus Pass. Almost the entire length of the road is within the boundaries of the national forest, and is therefore protected from any development more civilized than a campground (there are six along the road) or a picnic area. The drive is a must: this is White Mountains beauty in its purest form.

7. Bretton Woods and Crawford Notch

North and east on U.S. 302 from Glen will take you through Crawford Notch to the **Crawford Notch State Park.** The park is a fine place for hiking and fishing, and you can see two impressive waterfalls—the Flume and the Silver Cascades—from the highway. Facilities include a 24-site campground, a picnic area, an information booth, and a shop featuring the products of New Hampshire artisans. The ruins of the **Willey House** hold a mystery and a story from the 1820s, when the road was being cut through Crawford Notch and the Willey family set up house in Crawford Notch to provide for the teams that would pass through the valley. In August 1826 one of the worst storms ever to hit the White Mountains wreaked havoc in the valley, with floods, landslides, wind, and rain which left the Willey House unharmed, but resulted in the death of every member of the household.

WHERE TO STAY: At the **Mount Washington Hotel & Resort,** U.S. 302, Bretton Woods, NH 03575, is a downhill and cross-country ski area, several condominium developments, and three lodging establishments, the new and modern **Lodge at Bretton Woods,** the inn-like **Bretton Arms,** and the venerable rambling palace known as the **Mount Washington Hotel** (tel. 603/278-1000, or toll free 800/258-0330). The mammoth hotel was the site of the famous Bretton Woods conference of 1944 which established the world monetary system for the postwar period. Although great old hotels of this sort, with their private golf courses, riding stables, clay tennis courts, indoor and outdoor pools, live nightly entertainment, playhouses, and the like are almost as rare as dinosaurs, it is heartening to see that this one is still thriving, its gracious service and accommodations open to both the tourist and the conventioneer. The lobby is immense, with a baronial fireplace and lots of color and activity; nearby is a semicircular Conservatory with a dome and many small stained-glass windows. The views of the mountains and the grounds are very fine. There are hundreds of rooms, and they rent with two meals included in the price. Nearly all rooms have private bath, and the cost for room and meals is about $182 to $342 double per day, tax and service included. If you stay six nights, the seventh is free. There are small fees for use of the golf course, horses from the stable, bicycles, and for nursery and babysitting services. If you prefer a smaller place, Bretton Arms is a recently restored house on the property. The 34 rooms rent for $107 to $134 double, with no meals included. Guests are granted access to the facilities at the Mount Washington Hotel.

The Lodge at Bretton Woods out on the highway (U.S. 302) is associated with the hotel, and although the hotel operates only from late May to mid-October, the lodge stays open both winter and summer. Here the prices are for lodging only, but all privileges open to guests at the hotel are extended to guests at the lodge: a double usually with two double beds and with bath is $64 to $102; children are free in the same room with their parents.

At Crawford Notch, one of the most spectacular sites on the East Coast, stands the **Notchland Inn,** Harts Location S.R., Bartlett, NH 03802 (tel. 603/374-6131). Also quite magnificent in its own right, the granite mansion set on 400 acres has 11 rooms and suites furnished with wing chairs, designer fabrics, fireplaces, and antiques. Rates are set up two ways here: with two meals a day a double room costs $111 to $145; with breakfast only, rooms are $91 double. Take the dinner option— the multi-course repast is served by candlelight. The owners, by the way, keep rare and endangered species in their sanctuary; don't be surprised to see a llama grazing in the front corral.

WHAT TO DO: Certainly the quaintest way to get to the top of Mount Washington is by the **Mount Washington Cog Railway** (tel. 603/846-5404, or toll free 800/922-8825). It's a 3½-mile track along a steep trestle up the mountainside. The locomotive (powered by steam) drives a cog wheel on its undercarriage which engages with pins between the rails to pull the locomotive and train up the slope. In operation since 1866, the three-hour round-trip excursion is a lot of fun besides being very scenic indeed. At the portion of the run known as Jacob's Ladder, the grade is a surprising 37%, but the little engine pulls along trustworthily despite the steepness. At the top the average summer temperature is 40° Fahrenheit, and there may be a stiff wind. Stroll to the new Visitor Center for a snack, drink, or souvenir, and then tour the mountaintop: see the displays highlighting the worst of Mount Washington's weather. If you pick a clear day to ascend to the 6,288-foot summit, it will seem as though you can see all the way to Europe!

The Base Station, where you board the train, is six miles off U.S. 302 east of Twin Mountain, N.H. The season is Memorial Day weekend through Columbus Day (Canadian Thanksgiving), with weekends-only runs until June 10, then daily starting at 8:30 a.m., and keeping as close to an hourly schedule as possible, with the last train leaving at 4:30 p.m. Have reservations, or try to take an early train—perhaps the 8:30 a.m.—to avoid having to wait in line. From Labor Day through mid-October there are trains daily if weather permits at 11:30 a.m. and 2:30 p.m., and as needed. Fares (round trip) are $32 per adult, kids under 8 free if sitting on a parent's lap, kids 8 and over $16. Remember to take a sweater or jacket, or both, for the cool weather at the top, no matter how warm it is at the bottom.

8. Waterville Valley

In 1829 a small settlement in a remote New Hampshire valley was incorporated as a town. A few farms, perhaps a small store, and a tiny library—even here in the remoteness of the White Mountains, the symbol of New England's cultural life —that was all there was to Waterville Valley. Today the tiny settlement is still there, deep within the White Mountains National Forest, but a developer with great taste and tact now owns the valley, and dictated what shape the new resort community in this beautiful spot took. The results so far are very encouraging, almost a marvel: hotels and condominium developments under different ownership, all of striking and interesting design, furnished in good taste and staffed with competent, concerned personnel. Two ski areas are handy, a golf course and lots of tennis courts await visitors, and hiking, bicycling, fishing, and snowshoeing are right at one's doorstep. This is a very fine resort indeed.

All the places in Waterville Valley have the same postal address—Waterville Valley, NH 03215—and there is a **Lodging Bureau,** which provides free reservations service: call toll free 800/468-2553 and 603/236-8371 locally. Or write to Waterville Valley Lodging Bureau, Waterville Valley, NH 03215, for information.

WHERE TO STAY: The setting of Waterville Valley, in the shadow of Mount Tecumseh, is very beautiful, and the hotels have been designed to fit in well with the town and the natural beauty. Of the six hotels, the majority are of moderate price, one is expensive, and another is very low-priced.

Queen of the valley's hostelries is the **Snowy Owl Inn,** on Village Road (P.O. Box 407; tel. 603/236-8383), a dramatic structure of weathered wood and shining windows which reflect the trees and mountains surrounding it. The interior, like the exterior, is all of natural wood, with a large stone fireplace for accent in the three-story-high lobby. The rooms are modern, luxurious, and decorated with taste that might have come right out of a design magazine. All have two double beds, and some have refrigerators and whirlpools. Many rooms have fine views of the valley and mountains, others of Snow's Brook, the stream which runs by the hotel. Even if you don't have a mountain view, you can get one by climbing the spiral staircase at the top of the lobby to the little observation tower. The Snowy Owl has its own heated outdoor pool, of course. Rooms cost $58 to $69 single or double, including the 8% "association service charge" (children under 12 free in their parents' room). These are the summer rates; in winter the rates are about 15% higher.

King of the valley's hostelries is the new **Golden Eagle Lodge** (tel. 603/236-4551 or toll free 800/468-2553). Fashioned in the style of 19th-century grand New England resorts, the Golden Eagle rises proudly to the occasion. It was designed by Graham Gund Architects, one of the most distinguished firms in the U.S. The crescent-shaped six-story building with green shutters and turrets is a mass of oversized windows, more than half of which look on to Corcoran Pond, the name-sake of the man who has so carefully developed much of this valley. The 139 condo-minium suites vary in size from 650 to 1,050 sq. ft., sleeping two to eight people, and are fully furnished with understated accoutrements. In the high summer season rates range from $79 to $98 double; in winter from $101 to $183 double. An extra person pays $25 per day, children 12 and under stay free in their parents' suite. Rates include use of the pool, sports center, and many other facilities in the Valley.

The **Valley Inn & Tavern** (tel. 603/236-8336 or toll free 800/343-0969) is also among the posh places to stay in Waterville Valley. Its attractive design adds to the scenery in the valley, and also provides some unexpected bonuses to guests. For instance, many rooms have small private patios overlooking the valley and moun-tains; others have small balconies over the forest and settlement. The swimming pool is indoor/outdoor: part is enclosed by the building, but a huge window comes down just to water level, and you can swim underneath it to the outdoor portion of the pool, winter or summer. Heated water makes it useful all year. The Valley Inn has other athletic goodies: a platform (or paddle) tennis club with two courts, free to guests; an exercise room; a sauna; a massage room. The rooms are large, with two double beds, air conditioning, TV, telephone, and of course, private bath. There are three types of rooms, differing in views mostly: an economy room is about $147 to $160 double, tax, tips, and two meals a day included; at the other end of the scale, a deluxe suite would cost $20 more per night. Children 12 and under stay free in their parents room.

Long-term Stays

Several of the condominium developments in the valley have long-term (by the month or the season) rental rates for those who want an apartment rather than a hotel room. Accommodations range from one-bedroom apartments for one or two people to three-bedroom apartments that can take eight to ten people. Each apart-ment is completely furnished, including kitchen utensils and dinner service, all linens, and cable color TV. The apartments also rent by the day (two-day minimum) for $270 to $540 for a weekend, or $345 to $655 for a five-night ski week. In sum-mer you'll pay $322 to $765 per week. There are various package and weekly plans, both for normal and holiday periods, and low-season specials are available. For more information, contact **Windsor Hill Condominiums,** Jennings Peak Road, Waterville Valley, NH 03215 (tel. 603/236-8321 or toll free 800/343-1286 in New York, New Jersey, and New England except New Hampshire).

WHAT TO DO IN SUMMER: It seems as if they've thought of everything here. First and foremost, the valley is deep within the national forest, so hiking and fishing are easy to find. For tennis, there are 18 clay courts and lessons by a professional staff. The golf course in the valley is nine holes, and not too far away at White Mountains Country Club is an 18-hole course. Guests at the Valley Inn & Tavern can use its paddle tennis courts for free; the general public can use them, day and night, for a fee. Bikes can be rented from the Golf and Tennis Club. And then of course there's shopping in the Town Square or a ride to the top of Mount Tecumseh on the "High Country Express," the fastest gondola in the east.

WHAT TO DO IN WINTER: Although snowshoeing, hiking, skating, and general taking of country-mountain air are all possible and enjoyable in Waterville Valley, most people come to ski the trails and slopes of Mount Tecumseh and Snow's Mountain. **Mount Tecumseh** is the larger and more elaborate of the two, with two triple chair lifts, five double-chair lifts, a T-bar, a J-bar, and a platter-pull lift. The vertical drop is over 2,000 feet, and there are 35 trails and slopes. Rentals and lessons are easily available, as is a quick meal at the base cafeteria. A Schuss bus takes guests from Waterville Valley hotels to Tecumseh and back. The other area, **Snow's Moun-tain,** is right in the valley near the hotels of the village, and has three intermediate and beginners' slopes. It's for first-timers and learners, with one double-chair lift and a vertical drop of less than 600 feet. To keep the crowds down, Mount Tecumseh and Snow's Mountain operate on a limited-ticket basis (no more than a 15-minute wait for the lift on average). For information about snow at both areas, call 236-4144.

Ski packages for two, three, five, or seven nights are offered, and all facilities in the valley participate. Depending on what you want, you can get a package which includes lodging, meals, lifts, lessons, even rental equipment. Prices depend on which hotel you choose, and what options you need to do the sort of skiing you're after. Options are also offered for ski touring (trail fees, lessons, equipment, and lodging) in the packages.

---

9. The Franconia Notch Area

Interstate 93 comes up from Manchester and Concord to pass through the White Mountains National Forest. The towns of North Woodstock and Lincoln form the center of the developed area within the forest, and it's here that most people come to look for a room, a meal, or any of the other services of civilization. At this point the Kancamagus Hwy. heads east through the most scenic 33-mile drive in the mountains; north of Lincoln and North Woodstock are several natural curiosities, including the famous **Old Man of the Mountains** at the narrow pass called Franconia Notch.

The area centered on North Woodstock and Lincoln is very rich in possibilities for outdoor activities, especially hiking, camping, picnicking, and skiing at Cannon Mountain and Mittersill in Franconia Notch itself, and Loon Mountain near Lincoln on the Kancamagus Highway.

The local **Visitor Center** is at the intersection of I-93 and the Kancamagus Hwy. (tel. 603/745-8720). It is run both by the Lincoln–North Woodstock Chamber of Commerce personnel and also by national forest rangers; hours of operation year round are 8:30 a.m. to 6 p.m. daily.

WHERE TO STAY: You can make your base at any of several places in the area. At the southern end of Franconia Notch State Park lies **North Woodstock,** at the junction of U.S. 3 and Rte. 112, a small and fairly attractive commercial center with a few inns. Just across the Pemigewasset River where I-93 Exit 32 meets the Kancamagus Hwy. is the town of **Lincoln,** basically a commercial strip with some motels and residences.

At the northern end of the state park, near I-93 Exit 38, are the towns of **Franconia** and **Sugar Hill,** with a good number of nice inns. Finally, at I-93 Exit 42, only a few miles from the Vermont state line, is the town of **Littleton,** the largest settlement in these parts. It has two nice old inns for you to consider.

Inns in North Woodstock

The **Woodstock Inn,** Main Street (U.S. 3; P.O. Box 118), North Woodstock, NH 03262 (tel. 603/745-3951), is a century-old Victorian that's been very nicely redone, and now has six guest rooms which share three baths. Decor is Victorian of course, except for the color TV sets and air conditioners in some rooms. Prices range from $70 to $73 double, full breakfast included. Downstairs in the inn is a full restaurant and lounge (see below). Mid-week rates are slightly lower.

The inn also operates a bed-and-breakfast house called the **Riverside,** right by the Pemigewasset River, where each of the eight rooms has its own bathroom, color TV, and air conditioner, and prices go from $80 to $85 double. You're right in the center of town at the Woodstock, though the Cascade swimming area in the river is within walking distance.

Budget-minded readers will want to consider staying at the **Mt. Adams Inn,** on U.S. 3 south of the center of North Woodstock, NH 03262 (tel. 603/745-2711). A room with full country breakfast can be had for as little as $48, double (share a bath) and the restaurant specializes in Polish and American home-cooked food. The inn is open all year round. They also have a homey public lounge with a fireplace and color TV.

Motels in Lincoln

Route 3 north of North Woodstock is absolutely packed with motels of every shape, size, and price range, and you're sure to find a room here. But not all of those places are wonderful, and not all of the best places are located in this strip. Here's the pick of the crop, starting with a motel right near Franconia Notch itself.

North of North Woodstock on U.S. 3, Lincoln, NH 03251, is **Woodward's Motor Inn** (tel. 603/745-8141), which describes itself as "a complete family resort open all the year." This is one of the better motels on this strip of motels and restaurants; its 80 rooms are in buildings set back from the roadway behind a scattering of tall pine trees and a small pond. The pool is heated and is a comfortable 30 by 65 feet; guests get to play tennis on the Woodward's own court; and the Open Hearth Steak House is open to motel guests and the public alike. All rooms are air-conditioned and have color TV and telephone; many have two double beds—the traveling family's boon—as well. Rates for high summer and foliage season are $78 to $94 double in the motel rooms, all of which have private bath. Ski-season rates are slightly lower than these rates. The restaurant, by the way, is open for breakfast and dinner, 7:30 to 10:30 a.m. and 5 to 9 p.m. in season, 8 to 10 a.m. and 5 to 8:30 p.m. off-season; the Open Hearth is open only for dinner.

The **Kancamagus Motor Lodge,** Lincoln, NH 03251 (tel. 603/745-3365), on the Kancamagus Hwy. one mile west of Loon Mountain ski area (take Exit 32 from I-93, then drive east on Rte. 112), is a modern motel with heated outdoor pool, new rooms in a modern style furnished with private steambaths, wall-to-wall carpeting, phone, and color TV. Its attraction is in its location, very close to Loon Mountain and not far at all from the attractions of Franconia Notch. Rates in summer are $60 to $69 for two in a room, fully air-conditioned. In winter, a double room is $41 to $48 Sunday through Thursday nights; on weekends it's $60 to $69. The Kancamagus has a dining and cocktail lounge.

In the town of Lincoln proper, on Rte. 112, the **Lincoln Motel,** at 5 Church St., Lincoln, NH 03251 (tel. 603/745-2780), is an unprepossessing two-story structure with rooms that constitute one of the best bargains in the area, especially for skiers. Rooms have private bath, air conditioning, and cable TV, and a small kitchenette (fully-equipped) is open to guests. Besides the nine rooms in the motel proper, a nearby house has been converted to take transient guests and thereby increases the chance a visitor on a budget may find a room here. Rates are $51 to $62 double (the higher price for a room with kitchenette). Good, if basic, rooms, low prices, and Loon Mountain less than two miles away. You'll see the Lincoln Motel from the Kancamagus Hwy., set back from the road a half block on the left-hand side as you go from North Woodstock east toward Loon Mountain.

Inns in Franconia and Sugar Hill

In the small town of Franconia, a reference point is the confluence of Rtes. 18 and 116. After coming from the south and meeting, the two routes head north to Littleton.

Just over two miles south of Franconia along Rte. 116 (Easton Road) is the **Franconia Inn,** Easton Road, Franconia, NH 03580 (tel. 603/823-5542), a nice old white clapboard place built in 1868. It still provides many of the services that once brought wealthy Bostonians here: riding horses, outdoor swimming pool, four clay tennis courts, a family-size hot tub, bicycle tours, and hiking trails. Several golf courses are nearby. Right across the road from the inn is Foxfire Aviation, Inc. (tel.

823-8881), which will take you up for sailplane (glider) rides. Besides all these things to do, there is the tranquility and beauty of the verdant Easton Valley, with fine views of Cannon Mountain, Mount Lafayette, and the Franconia and Kinsman mountain ranges.

There are 35 guest rooms at the inn, well maintained and somewhat old-fashioned, but with clean baths. Prices depend on view and room size, and range from $60 to $90 single, $65 to $110 double, with two-room family suites going for $105. An adult can have breakfast and dinner daily for $30; meal plans for children depend on their ages. Add taxes and tips. When you call, ask for a corner room, and also about package plans which may save you some money.

For rainy days and evenings there are movies, a game room with coin-operated games for the kids, a billiards room, an oak-paneled library with fireplace, and a screened porch set with wicker furniture. Downstairs, the Rathskeller Lounge has quiet entertainment many nights. The nice candlelit dining room adds considerably to the feeling that you've settled yourself into a huge old summer estate in Robert Frost country owned by one of your rich uncles. The "uncles" in this case are inn-keepers Richard and Alec Morris. It's comfy here. Ski season, by the way, is one of the inn's best times, with trails radiating from the inn throughout the valley.

The Franconia Inn is open most of the year, but closed for most of April and May.

Lovett's Inn, by Lafayette Brook, Franconia, NH 03580 (tel. 603/823-7761 or toll free outside NH 800/346-3802) is a rambling farmhouse (c. 1784) with 30 modern cottages set amid pine trees or around the backyard pool. The poolside cottages are larger, but all have a sleeping/living area and TV, while some have a fireplace and air conditioning. The seven rooms in the old inn are simple and authentic, nothing fancy. In the summer rooms rates are $125 to $136 for a private bath in the house or a cottage in the pines; poolside cottages are $5 more. For one of the few shared-bath rooms in the inn, doubles cost $88 to $98. When you consider that these rates include breakfast and dinner, it becomes a pretty good deal. There's a TV room with a library of movies for the VCR; in winter there are cross-country skis to rent. There is plenty of room and activities for kids here.

The **Horse & Hound Inn,** Wells Road, Franconia, NH (tel. 603/823-5501), is a real true-to-life country inn according to the old style. It is not plush and fancy, with priceless antiques everywhere, but rather simple, well kept, and attractive, run by the Larson family who give you an authentic country-family welcome. It is well off the main roads, and blissfully, perfectly quiet except for the crackle of a fire in the fireplace on a cool day, or the murmur of conversation in the lounge. Rooms with private bath cost $75 to $128 double, and come with a double, a queen-size, two doubles, or a king-size bed. Rooms sharing baths cost $70; some have bunks good for children. Continental breakfast is included in these prices. The inn's dining room serves good, hearty, honest food such as sirloin steaks and surf and turf; a full dinner might cost $25 to $30 per person, drinks, tax, and tip included. To find the inn, head south out of Franconia on Rte. 18. About 2½ miles south of town, watch for Wells Road, on the right; the inn has a sign here. Head down Wells Road for less than half a mile to reach the inn.

The village of Sugar Hill is a few miles east of Franconia along Rte. 117. Leaving Franconia, turn left off Rte. 116 onto Rte. 117, and less than a mile's drive will bring you to the **Sugar Hill Inn,** Rte. 117, Sugar Hill, Franconia, NH 03580 (tel. 603/823-5621), perched up on a hill and surrounded by grassy lawns. The original farmhouse was built in 1789, but I doubt that it had such a commodious and welcoming front porch. In any case, the house became an inn in 1929, still with its original fireplaces (some now fitted with Franklin stoves), old board floors, and wood beams. But now the rooms have very pretty country furnishings, knitted pieces, old paintings, rocking chairs, and hand-stenciled designs on the walls. Each of the 11 rooms has a private bath, and either twin beds, a double bed, a queen-size, or a king-size bed. Beside the inn are six small guest cottages with similar decor, private baths, carpeting, and television sets; they're open mid-May through October only. In season, a double room with full breakfast costs $98 to $115, all in. At peak times guests may be required to take dinner here, which would add about $15 or $20 per person to the tab. At other times dinner is served by reservation, and there's usually a choice of meat, fish, and chicken, along with various soups, appetizers, and desserts. Small, quiet, friendly, congenial, authentic—that's the Sugar Hill Inn. Jim and Barbara Quinn are your hosts.

Littleton Inns

White clapboard churches loft their graceful steeples above the solid, four-square brick façades of Main Street's commercial district: this is Littleton, N.H., a fine New England town. Not a quaint village, not an industrial town, but something in between, Littleton may be to New Hampshire what Lake Wobegon is to Minnesota.

The local chamber of commerce and historical society have put together a pamphlet which will take you on a guided tour of the town's landmarks, including the post office and Courthouse, Masonic Temple, the public library and Tilton's Opera building.

The **Beal House Inn,** 247 W. Main St., Littleton, NH 03561 (tel. 603/444-2661), is Littleton's prime place to stay, right at the confluence of Rtes. 18 and 302, on West Main Street. Once a farmhouse and barn (1833), the house is now the inn and the barn an antiques shop. The entire place is furnished in antiques and local crafts, and is charming and comfortable. Guest rooms range in price from $40 to $80 double, breakfast and afternoon refreshments included, and the price you pay depends on the size of the room and of its bed; larger rooms with larger beds (queen- or king-size) cost the most. A few rooms share baths, but most have private facilities. The continental breakfast is of freshly made delights such as homemade breads and popovers; if you want a full country breakfast of bacon and eggs, it's available at an extra charge. Behind the inn are lovely lawns and woods, with a deck for sitting and relaxing. Children over 8 are welcome here. By the way, you should know that the inn is actually furnished from the antique shop, and thus anything you fancy can be purchased; the price tag should be on the object.

Though it's actually in Vermont, the **Rabbit Hill Inn,** Lower Waterford, VT 05848 (tel. 802/748-5168), is connected to Littleton, N.H., by cultural and commercial ties. Established in 1795, the inn was bought by John and Maureen Magee in April 1987, and they now rent its 18 rooms, each with private bath and most with views of the mountains, for $146 to $218 double, full breakfast, dinner, tax, and service charges all included. By the way, those mountain views are significant, as the inn is set into the side of a hill with the magnificent panorama of the mountains and the Connecticut River Valley spread out before it. And the plan to have breakfast and dinner here makes sense, as Lower Waterford is a tiny hamlet with few other dining opportunities.

This inn is antique and elegant in its furnishings, but homey in its welcome. Beautiful antique furniture is in the two dining rooms, the book nook, and the lounge, as well as in the guest rooms. Across the road from the inn is the village church, built in 1859, and next to that the small library. Besides these public-service buildings, the village of Lower Waterford has fewer than a dozen houses. No doubt, the Rabbit Hill Inn sometimes accounts for fully half of the village's active population! It's idyllic and special here, "like Brigadoon," as John Magee says, and you'll love it.

WHERE TO EAT: Dining possibilities are not particularly rich in this neck of the woods, and you'd do well in most cases to dine at your inn if possible. If your inn or motel doesn't serve main meals, here are the places to look for them.

Perhaps the best full menu hereabouts is at the **Woodstock Inn,** on Main Street in North Woodstock (tel. 745-3951). For a light lunch or a drink before or after dinner there's the Woodstock Station, Lincoln's original railroad station moved to a site adjoining the inn. The favored place to sit for dinner in the inn is on the enclosed porch by one of the large windows looking out onto Main Street, but there are other attractive Victorian dining rooms as well. Prices are moderate, because the price of your main course includes your choice of appetizer or soup, garden salad, fresh bread, rice or potato, and homemade fresh-fruit sorbet. Main courses range from sole stuffed with crabmeat and tortellini scallops Alfredo (tortellini with mushrooms and Gruyère, sautéed with fresh scallops, sauce Alfredo), through roast duckling and chicken curry with coconut and pinenuts, to tournedos au poivre, tournedos Rossini, and steak Diane. You can dine sumptuously here for a mere $20, but your dinner bill will more likely be $26 to $35 per person when drinks, dessert, tax, and tip are included. As the Woodstock Inn provides some of the best dining in the area, it's a good idea to call for reservations.

In Littleton there's a real old diner, like an enlarged railroad dining car, black-and-white floor tiles, revolving counter stools and booths filled early and often by local people. It's the **Littleton Diner,** 170 Main St. (tel. 444-6994), a 1928 Worcester-style diner open Monday through Saturday from 6 a.m. to 8 p.m., on Sunday from 7 a.m. to 2 p.m. As in any truly good diner, breakfast is served all day, and the standard, called "Earl's Favorite," consists of two eggs, home-fries, sausage, juice, and toast, plus coffee and tip, for under $5. If you come for lunch or supper, have a slice of homemade pie for dessert. There will probably be a slightly used copy of the Manchester *Union Leader* around for your edification and amusement. A great place!

WHAT TO SEE AND DO: Franconia Notch State Park is surrounded by the White Mountains National Forest.

The natural wonders of the park are impressive indeed, including the "notch" (pass, or gorge) itself, the Flume, the Basin, several lakes, and the rock outcrop in the shape of a man's profile which has all but become the state symbol of New Hampshire, the famous Old Man of the Mountains. The state park offers a wealth of outdoor activities: Lafayette Campground, the Appalachian Mountain Club's system of trails and huts, swimming in the mountain lakes, a number of beautiful picnic sites, and two ski areas, one of them with an aerial tramway which operates winter and summer.

The Old Man

The Old Man of the Mountains, also called the Great Stone Face, is one of New Hampshire's most famous features. It was discovered by white settlers at the beginning of the 19th century after having been in the process of formation for thousands of years at least. The profile is formed by several ledges of granite, and in a cubist sort of way the resemblance is quite striking. But don't expect a mammoth face: the face is only about 40 feet high, and it's way up on a cliff 1,000 feet above the valley floor. Its grandeur comes not from its size, but rather from its fidelity and its impressive perch high in the sky, gazing out over the mountains. In recent years the state has spent a good deal of money preserving the face from the ravages of nature, for even granite formations crumble given enough wind, rain, and ice. From the highway parking lot, a path leads down to the shores of Profile Lake, and descriptive plaques tell you all about the Old Man.

South of the Old Man along U.S. 3, some people think that the undulant crest of Mount Liberty to the east resembles George Washington lying in state. Take a look, and feel free to concur or disagree!

The Basin and the Flume

South of the Old Man along U.S. 3, signs will point to a side road and the Basin, a huge glacial pothole in the native granite, 20 feet in diameter. The hole is at the foot of a waterfall, and was presumably made by the action of small rocks and stones whirled around by the force of the water. It's a cool spot, good for contemplation.

Four miles north of North Woodstock, but still south of the Basin, is the Flume, a natural gorge or cleft in the granite. A boardwalk has been erected along the 800-foot length of the Flume, and for $5 ($2.50 for children) you can walk through its cool depths, the granite walls rising to 60 or 70 feet above you, mosses and plants growing precariously in niches here and there. Signs explain how nature formed the Flume, and point out interesting sights along the way. Near the Flume is a covered bridge thought to be one of the oldest in the state, perhaps erected as early as the 1820s. There is a seasonal information office (tel. 745-8391) here, open when the Flume is, from mid-April to mid-October.

Cannon Mountain Aerial Tramway

An impressive view of the notch and the mountains is yours if you take the Cannon Mountain Aerial Tramway (U.S. 3, Franconia Notch; tel. 603/823-5563) to the top of the line. The tramway operates in the summer from the end of May to mid-October, 8:30 a.m. to 4:30 p.m., at a cost of $6.50 for adults, $3 for children 6 to 12, round trip. The tramway station is just off U.S. 3 north of the Old Man, and has its own parking lot. In the weathered shingled building at the base and the summit station are cafeterias, should you be in need of a light meal.

Robert Frost's Farm

Only a mile or two from the town of Franconia is the Frost Place, Bickford Hill Road (tel. 823-8038), the farm that the great poet bought in the early part of this century. He lived here with his wife and children during some of the most productive and inspired years of his life, and wrote many of his best and most famous poems to describe life on this farm and the scenery surrounding it. Among these are "The Road Less Taken" and "Stopping by Woods on a Snowy Evening."

Admission to the site costs $3 for adults, half price for children 6 through 15, $2 for seniors. It's open on Saturday and Sunday from 1 to 5 p.m. Memorial Day through June and Labor Day through Columbus Day weekend; in July and August, every day except Tuesday from 1 to 5 p.m.

The price of admission admits you to a 20-minute slide show in the barn behind the house. The show explains much about Frost's early life and work, and about the countryside here. The farmhouse has been kept as faithful to the period as possible, and there are numerous interesting exhibits of Frost memorabilia, though much of the furniture is from other places. It is spare and simple, as was the rural lifestyle at the time. Behind the house in the forest is a half-mile-long poetry-nature trail. Frost's poems are mounted on plaques in sites appropriate to the things they describe. In several places the plaques have been erected at the exact spots where Frost composed the poems. The various trees, shrubs, and flowers along the path are marked, though only some will be in bloom when you visit.

To get to the Frost Place, leave Franconia on Rte. 116 South, and after exactly a mile look for a sign on the right indicating Bickford Hill Road. Then turn left onto Ridge Road, a dirt road, and the Frost Place will be up a way on your right. You come to the parking lot before the house; obey the sign and park in the lot, and walk up the road to the house.

The Lost River

As you travel through New Hampshire, you'll see many bumper stickers proclaiming "I found the Lost River." You can find it too, 6 miles west of North Woodstock on Rte. 112 in Kinsman Notch. Explore the narrow gorge and caverns with the help of walkways, ladders, and bridges. Like most of the attractions in this neck of the woods, it's open mid-May to mid-October. There's a small entrance fee.

Clark's Trading Post

Clark's on Rte. 3 just north of Lincoln has been a traditional stop for families traveling in the White Mountains since 1928. In addition to an old-fashioned photo parlor, water bumper boats, magic house, narrow-gauge steam locomotive, and a gift shop selling moccasins, a family of native black bears performs daily. It's a bit on the campy side, but it's also part of many people's childhood.

Skiing

There are three notable ski resorts in the Franconia Notch area: Cannon Mountain and Mittersill near the Notch itself, and Loon Mountain in Lincoln at the western end of the Kancamagus Highway.

Cannon Mountain (tel. 603/823-5563): Besides the new aerial tramway, Cannon has one triple-chair and two double-chair lifts, two T-bars, and a pony lift, all with an hourly capacity of close to 7,000 skiers. There are 26 miles of trails and slopes, about a quarter of them novice, another quarter expert, and the remaining half intermediate. The vertical drop is 2,145 feet, and besides having snowmaking equipment for the snowless days, the slopes are positioned so that they naturally receive and retain more than the average amount of snow. Cannon Mountain is operated by the state as it is in a state park. Besides the three cafeterias and the base and lounges nearby, there is a ski school, a nursery, and a ski shop where you can rent equipment.

Mittersill (tel. 603/823-5511): This is the junior cousin to Cannon Mountain, with a vertical drop of 1,600 feet, and one double chair and one T-bar for lifts. It's open daily, north of Cannon Mountain, off U.S. 3 on Rte. 18.

Loon Mountain (tel. 603/745-8146); for snow information, 603/745-8100): Just two miles east of Lincoln along the Kancamagus Hwy. brings you to Loon Mountain, a modern ski area with a gondola (four-passenger cars), two triple-chair, and four double-chair lifts to take 9,600 skiers an hour up the mountain. The vertical drop is 2,100 feet, and the longest run is three miles. Loon has a limited-lift-lines policy (make reservations), and top-to-bottom snowmaking capacity. The Mountain Club on Loon has 240 rooms and a restaurant; other services at the base lodge include a cafeteria, lounge, nursery, ski shop, and rental shop. Lift fees are $32 on weekends, and slightly less on weekdays.

In summer and fall, Loon Mountain's gondolas operate from 9:30 a.m. to 5 p.m. daily to take visitors on the 7,100-foot trip (1,850-foot rise) to the summit, at $7 per adult, $3 per child, free for age 6 and under. There are cafeterias at both the base and summit stations.

Several ski areas offer package arrangements through the **Ski 93 Association,** named because the areas involved are all accessible by using Interstate 93. Bretton Woods, Cannon Mountain, Loon Mountain, Tenney Mountain, and Waterville Valley are among the members, and you can get three-day or five-day cut-price lift tickets. Midweek passes good at all five areas are a real bargain. The association will be glad to help with reservations at area hotels, lodges, and inns. Contact them at P.O. Box 176, N. Woodstock, NH 03262 (tel. 603/745-8101).

---

10. Lake Sunapee

Lake Sunapee is a pleasant regional vacation spot in southwestern New Hampshire, not all that far from the town of Hanover, which is home to Dartmouth College. Besides summer sports such as swimming, boating, and canoeing, the area around Lake Sunapee also has its own small ski area in Mount Sunapee State Park. On a trip to Vermont or north to Hanover for a visit to Dartmouth, the shores of Lake Sunapee are a fine place to stop for a night, or even a week.

Of the towns around the lake, Sunapee (sometimes called Sunapee Harbor) on the western shore is the nicest, with a good collection of inns, motels, and resorts. Although in its early days Sunapee held a tannery, grist mill, and several shops for woodworking industries, for many years now it has made its living from summer visitors; and in recent years skiers have brought business to the town in winter as well.

The town of Mount Sunapee, on the southwestern shore, is not really a town at all, regardless of what it may say on your road map. The intersection of Rtes. 103 and 103B, with a motel and the state park and state beach entrance, *is* the "town." Don't plan to get gas there!

INFORMATION: Contact the **Lake Sunapee Lodging Bureau,** P.O. Box 400, Sunapee, NH 03782 (tel. 603/763-2495, or toll free 800/258-3530).

WHERE TO STAY AND EAT: Though the Lake Sunapee region is perfect for vacationers, there is some spirit among the local people to limit touristic growth. Thus many of the inns here are of long standing, and are more like self-contained miniresorts. There are a few motels for those on a vagabond tour.

Dexter's Inn and Tennis Club, Stagecoach Road, Box F, Sunapee, NH 03782 (tel. 603/763-5571 or toll free 800/232-5571), is hidden away on a back road, but has a fine view of Lake Sunapee and its surrounding mountains. Built in 1801, the yellow clapboard house was renovated in the 1930s and converted to an inn in 1948. It's been owned and run by the Simpson family for well over a decade, and has that family feel about it that makes even first-time visitors comfortable. Some of the 18 rooms have antique pieces, including the beds, and other rooms have more modern furnishings. All have private baths. Breakfast and dinner each day come with your room, which may be priced at $142 to $191 double, tax and service included; breakfast will be delivered to your room if you like, and dinner is taken in the dining room.

Amusements include a well-equipped library and piano in the living room, a pretty outdoor swimming pool, and three professional-grade tennis courts (complete with pro and pro shop). Other games include shuffleboard, croquet, and horseshoes. Dexter's is open May through October. Off-season package plans offer good savings on a vacation here.

Right near the entrance to Mount Sunapee State Park is the very popular **Mount Sunapee Motel,** Rte. 103, Mount Sunapee, NH 03772 (tel. 603/763-5592). The Mount Sunapee Motel is modern: tile bathrooms, with tub-shower combinations, TV, and at least two beds in each room. Half of the motel consists of 11 two-room units, each with a kitchenette; the outdoor swimming pool is shared by all. Summer rates are $51 to $57 double in a motel room, $62 to $73 double in a two-room unit. Add 5% if you pay with a credit card.

Out of sight from Sunapee Harbor but only a few hundred feet from it is **Haus Edelweiss,** 13 Maple Street (P.O. Box 609), Sunapee, NH 03782 (tel. 603/763-2100), a nice and homey bed and breakfast with five rooms. Guests tend to gather in the living room where a TV, light snacks, and a drink are offered by the hosts. Rates are $27 single, $48 to $53 double, with your choice of a traditional Bavarian or Yankee breakfast.

Sunapee Harbor visitors have been going to the **Woodbine Cottage** (tel. 763-2222) for over 60 years, and at my last visit it was as popular as ever: several smallish, but bright and cheery rooms with lots of polished blond wood, with pewter vessels and an old rifle hung here and there for effect. Lots of windows provide plenty of light especially on a bright day. At lunchtime, the daily luncheons are priced between $10 and $14.50, but that's for a full three- or four-course meal. At dinner the prices are in the $14 to $20 range for such favorites as baked ham in raisin sauce, broiled lamb chops, or lobster Newburg. Remember that these prices include appetizer, vegetable and potato, salad, roll, dessert, and coffee, tea, or milk. The Woodbine is open from May 30 through mid-October. The restaurant is open Tuesday to Saturday for lunch and dinner and Sunday for brunch; closed Monday.

WHAT TO DO: To see Lake Sunapee, there is no better way than to catch the **M/V Mount Sunapee II** (tel. 603/763-4030), which leaves Sunapee Harbor marina at 10 a.m. and 2:30 p.m. on Saturday and Sunday from mid-May to mid-June for tours of the beautiful, very pure lake. From mid-June to Labor Day there are sailings at 10 a.m. and 2:30 p.m. And until mid-October they are on weekends at 2:30 p.m. Both tours last 1½ hours and cost $7 for adults. Kids under 12 pay $4; kids under 5 ride free. The *Mount Sunapee II* holds 150 people, and the tour is narrated by the amiable captain.

In the summer, Sunapee hosts very well-attended **flea markets** out on Rte. 103B at the blinking light (between Sunapee Harbor and Sunapee Lower Village). Both buyers and sellers flock to the intersection's roadsides, and everything from craftwork through antiques to junk is available.

The best **beach** in the area is down near the state park entrance. It's the state park beach, and the entrance fee covers use of changing rooms. Lake Sunapee is a Class A reservoir—the water is about as pure and unpolluted as you'll find anywhere.

Across the large traffic circle from the entrance road to the beach is the entrance to the state park and its gondola to the summit of **Mount Sunapee.** In summer the price is $5 for adults, $2 for children 6 to 12, for the round trip in the three-person gondolas. The trip takes you over 1¼ miles (1,450 feet higher up) to the summit at 2,743 feet. At the top there are walking trails (not difficult) to an overlook and to a glacial tarn named Lake Solitude. At the base of the mountain, near the gondola station, is a cafeteria, spacious lawns, hiking trails, and picnic areas, all open to the public at no charge.

Skiing

The Mount Sunapee area (tel. 603/763-4020; toll free 800/322-3300 for snow information) has five double-chair lifts, a T-bar, a J-bar, and a rope tow, with a capacity of 6,000 skiers an hour. The vertical drop is 1,500 feet on 23 slopes and trails; in addition, there are ten miles of free ski touring trails, novice and intermediate (tel. 603/763-2356 for information). Ski school, ski shop with rental equipment, a cafeteria, and (weekdays) a nursery are all available.

---

11. Hanover

This small town is the home of one of the country's oldest and most prestigious colleges. **Dartmouth** (named for the earl who was colonial secretary to King George III) was founded in 1769, and its charter gives a hint why it was located in such a remote place: it was meant primarily "for the education and instruction of Youth of the Indian Tribes," and only secondarily for the education of "English Youth and others." Today Dartmouth is more than a small undergraduate college; its graduate schools of medicine, engineering, and business administration are well respected, and the Hopkins Center for the Arts is the cultural focus of the entire region.

In many ways the college is the town and vice-versa. College buildings of exceptional beauty and grace are scattered or clustered throughout Hanover, and most are shaded by trees of a prodigious height and girth. Anyone out for a drive would enjoy a walk through the campus, perhaps on one of the guided college tours (free) that leave from the college information booth during the summer at 9 and 11 a.m. and 3 p.m., and from the Hopkins Center at 2 p.m. (no tours on Sunday); in winter, tours depart from McNutt Hall. To order tickets to performances, or to find out what's showing at the Hopkins Center, call 603/646-2422.

In winter, **Dartmouth's Winter Carnival** is the major fun and social event, with special art shows, drama and concerts, an ice sculpture contest, and other amusements.

WHERE TO STAY AND EAT: The prime place in Hanover is the **Hanover Inn,** Hanover, NH 03755 (tel. 603/643-4300, or toll free 800/443-7024 in New York and New England, except New Hampshire), right in the center of town. Some rooms have views of the lawns and buildings of the college. It fills up quickly at major college events such as matriculation, graduation, and the big football games played at home. Decor is colonial, to fit in with the rest of Hanover, but the shiny new bathrooms and color TVs show that modern comfort has been given great consideration. Most of the rooms have twin beds, but there are a few double beds. Singles and doubles cost $128 to $149; the higher prices are for the larger and slightly newer rooms in the west wing. Suites run from $177 for a single to $225 for a quad.

The Hanover Inn's formal dining room and new restaurant are supplemented by a lovely outdoor patio, under an awning, in summer. The feeling is very much that of an exclusive country club. At lunch, sandwiches are only about $5, but full luncheon meals (the daily specials) can be had for $8 to $10. The dinner menu offers a good and balanced selection of well-known meat, fish, and fowl dishes: start with Norwegian gravlax and then have anything from pan fried brook trout to native spring lamb, and the total bill will be about $35 per person. The waitresses in black uniforms with white trim are silent, efficient, and friendly, waiting attentively at their stations when all the diners have been served. Room service is available for all three meals.

An Inn in Lyme

If Hanover is the busy college town, Lyme, NH., 10 miles north of Hanover on Rte. 10, is the peaceful New England village. At the center of Lyme you'll see the high-pillared façade of the **Lyme Inn,** Lyme, NH 03768 (tel. 603/795-2222). Built in 1809, the inn has 14 rooms, most with bath or shower, all with antiques and authentic decor. Prices, depending on which room you choose, are $77 to $83 single, $128 to $150 double, breakfast and dinner included. You should know that the inn has its own tavern, very handy in this otherwise sleepy village.

Across the River in Norwich

Just across the Connecticut River from Hanover is the village of Norwich, Vt. Here you'll find the **Inn at Norwich,** Norwich, VT 05055 (tel. 802/649-1143), a nice 26-room hostelry known for its charm, dignity, and warm welcome as well as for the excellence of its dining room. As the inn has been here since 1797, its furnishings reflect its heritage, with brass and canopy beds in many rooms, but also television set, telephone, and private bath in all. The cheery lounge is called the Jasper Murdoch Tavern, after the man who opened the inn almost 200 years ago. The current innkeepers, by the way, are the Savidges. Rooms at the inn are priced at $136 double, $30 less in the motel units; these rates include breakfast and dinner in the pretty, formal dining rooms or on the porch. The cuisine is of a high order.

WHAT TO DO: Everyone takes a tour of Dartmouth College, but for a more offbeat view of the campus and surrounding area take a **hot air balloon ride.** At the Post Mills Airport (P.O. Box 51, Post Mills, VT 05058, tel. 802/333-9254) you can take a sunrise or sunset balloon ride with trained, professional balloonists who will float you up or down the Connecticut River Valley depending on the whim of the wind. After you've helped with the set-up process, you'll be airborne for 1 to 1½ hours, and finish with a champagne reception at the touch-down sight. Oh, and don't worry, they'll take you back to the airport to pick up your car if you want. They fly daily, weather and wind permitting. The cost for all this fun is $150 per person, with a minimum of two people. To reach the airport from Hanover, take Rte. 10 north, cross the bridge to Vermont, head south on Rte. 5 and west on Rte. 244.

MAINE

There is something quintessentially American about this rugged and sparsely populated state, the largest in New England. It's as though the vast forests of the north and the jagged coastline of "downeast" Maine are the last American frontier, rich in natural resources but waiting for people equally rugged to tame them.

Although there are still areas of wilderness in Maine, some of the state's potential was exploited long ago, soon after its discovery by Europeans. When the French and English came to these shores, they found miles and miles of virgin growth. The tremendous white pines have been replaced by other varieties, and lumber products again yield a good deal of the state's economy.

Besides her forests, Maine has great stores of granite for building, but they're mostly untapped as yet. Although agriculture is difficult because of the rocky soil and the short growing season, Maine potatoes are known and used throughout the eastern United States. Maine's fishermen yearly pull great quantities of fish, scallops, shrimp, and the famous lobsters from the freezing Atlantic waters. But the largest industry in Maine these days is the vacation trade: campers, hikers, and fishermen in the mountains and lakes, yachting and summer residents in the beautiful old coastal towns. Good food—especially the fresh seafood—and clean air draw the crowds from Boston, Montréal, and New York, and life in the southern coastal towns is lively and interesting from mid-June through Labor Day, after which the visitors become those looking for the quiet of Indian Summer and the autumn foliage season. Most resorts close up by the last week in October.

Of the vacation areas in Maine, certainly the most popular is the southern coast, where pretty towns such as Ogunquit, Kennebunkport, Boothbay Harbor, and Camden provide an atmosphere either restful or lively, cultural or natural, as you like it. Next in popularity comes the famous old resort of Bar Harbor, which is a good ways "downeast." The crowds these days come to commune with the rugged beauty of **Acadia National Park.** Finally, a smaller number of hardy souls head into the hinterland among the mountains, forests, and glacial lakes for a piece of the outdoor life.

Meals and rooms in Maine are taxed at a rate of 7%, so look for this tax to be added to your bill each night, and at mealtimes. The telephone area code for the entire state is 207.

GETTING THERE: Amtrak does not operate in Maine, but its trains do connect with buses at Boston's South Station that will take you north into the state. If you're driving, be aware that the Maine Turnpike (I-95) is a toll road. U.S. 1 or its scenic alternate route, U.S. 1A, parallels the Maine Turnpike all the way to Brunswick, and while it's a bit slower, it costs nothing. Besides, it's more scenic, and in my opinion no other highway in the entire country could possibly have as many flea markets, antique shops, and white elephant sales as does U.S. 1 in Maine, all the way from Kittery to Ellsworth. Weekends are the best times to catch them, but in July and August any day will do. *Note:* If you're heading for Ogunquit, take the exit from I-95 soon after you cross the state line at Kittery—follow the signs for U.S. 1 and the "shore" or "scenic" route through York, and this will save you a toll. And now for some tips on traveling by public transport.

By Bus
Greyhound/Trailways Lines operates buses from Boston all the way to St. Stephen, New Brunswick, stopping at Portsmouth, N.H., Ogunquit, Kennebunk, Portland, Brunswick, Bath, Wiscasset, Camden, Bangor, and Ellsworth (for Bar Harbor). Two buses daily make the trip all the way to St. Stephen; another goes as far as Ellsworth and then runs down to its final stop at Bar Harbor. There are direct buses along this route from New York with a rest stop in Boston. Greyhound/ Trailways also runs between Montréal and Bangor, and there are connecting buses between Ottawa, Toronto, and Montréal, and between Bangor and Bar Harbor. One can also change at Bangor to go south along the coast. The Montréal-Bangor/ Bar Harbor bus goes through Bethel, Me., but for now only on Saturday runs does it stop there. In conjunction with Autobus Fortin Poulin, Greyhound runs between Québec City and Portland, Me.

Vermont Transit works in conjunction with Greyhound/Trailways and Voyageur to operate on routes between Boston and Portland, and from Portland west to North Conway, N.H., Bretton Woods and Bethlehem, N.H., and St. Johnsbury, Barre, Montpelier, and Burlington, Vt.; in Burlington, connections are made to or from Montréal.

C & J Airport Limousine Service operates those long airport limousines between Boston's Logan International Airport and points along the Maine coast, including Ogunquit and Kennebunk. In Ogunquit their terminal is at the Dunaway Municipal Building right in the center of town; in Kennebunk it's at the Kennebunk Inn. Places in the limousines are best reserved in advance.

By Air
Bar Harbor Airlines (tel. toll free 800/327-8376), an Eastern Express carrier, one of the older and better commuter lines, flies to many points in Maine: Augusta, Bangor, Bar Harbor, Portland, Presque Isle, and also to Burlington, Vt., Boston, Worcester, Hartford/Springfield, Albany, and New York City (La Guardia).

---

1. Ogunquit

The Indian name means "beautiful place by the sea," and it holds true even today, because Ogunquit's town government has ensured that the town remains tidy and picturesque despite its tourism development. Visitors feel welcome in the town, whether they're strolling along Ogunquit's picturesque "Marginal Way," a path along the rocky coast; relaxing at the Ogunquit Beach; or dining in one of the many excellent restaurants. At Perkins Cove, a tiny peninsula is festooned with the quaint low waterfront shops and shacks from Ogunquit's fishing-village heyday. Right along U.S. 1 is the **Ogunquit Playhouse** (tel. 207/646-5511), presenting Broadway plays and musicals from late June through Labor Day. Ogunquit has been a summer resort for over a century, and it's no wonder that people come back year after year.

INFORMATION: The chamber of commerce maintains an **information office** on U.S. 1 (P.O. Box 2289, Ogunquit, ME 03907), south of the center of town, and as Main Street is U.S. 1, you will come to the office just south of the downtown area. It's open during business hours in the summer season (tel. 207/646-5533).

WHERE TO STAY: Having been a summer resort for so many years, Ogunquit today has a good selection of accommodations in all price ranges, from the extravagant to the inexpensive.

It seems as though every place in town rents rooms, from the gas station to the gift shoppe. Many are on U.S. 1, however, which is busy with traffic. If you don't find a vacancy among the following selections, search along Shore Road toward Perkins Cove, where it's quieter.

Inns and Guesthouses

Heading down Shore Road from the main crossroads, a few steps will bring you to the **Seafair Inn,** 24 Shore Rd. (P.O. Box 1221), Ogunquit, ME 03907 (tel. 207/646-2181), on the right-hand side. Pass the two millstones at the beginning of the path, walk up through the pretty garden, go through the sunny front porch with wicker furniture, and enter the formal parlor of this onetime Victorian summer house. You've already got a good idea of the inn's charm. Double rooms with shared bath cost $50 to $55; with private bath, $70 to $85. There are also several efficiency apartments. Continental breakfast is included.

Of Ogunquit's cozy Victorian seaside hotels, the **Colonial Inn Resort,** just south of Obed's Lane on Shore Road (P.O. Box 895), Ogunquit, ME 03907 (tel. 207/646-5191), is the notable survivor. These days it's brimming with life, having been renovated by Chet and Sheila Sawtelle. The hotel has 22 suites with kitchenettes ($135 for one to four people), plus some motel units with kitchenettes ($100 double), besides the 45 rooms in the inn. The inn rooms all have private bath, and go for $55 single, $70 to $90 double—the higher price is for the rooms with the best ocean views. From May to late June and after Labor Day until Columbus Day, rates are about 30% lower. The Colonial has a heated pool, whirlpool spa, a breakfast coffeeshop, an elevator, and more important, a spacious veranda in the turn-of-the-century fashion, the perfect place for sitting, viewing, reading, and napping.

Of the several guesthouses on Shore Road near the turnoff to Perkins Cove, my favorite is the **Hayes Guest House,** 133 Shore Rd. (RR1, Box 12), Ogunquit, ME 03907 (tel. 207/646-2277). Mrs. Elinor Hayes is very kind and friendly, and has decorated her five rooms and two apartments with interesting old pieces such as a rope-frame bed made in Maine (now with a box spring, of course!), old sea chests, and patchwork quilts. Both twin and double beds are available. With private bath, a room is $68 to $70 ($10 per extra person in the room) or $65 with semiprivate bath. Guests have use of a refrigerator and the coffee maker; all rooms have air conditioning and TV. There's a pretty swimming pool. It's a charming place, and she's a charming lady, and here you're within walking distance of Perkins Cove with its restaurants, shops, and galleries.

Motels

For over a century vacationers have been driving up to the top of Bald Head Cliff, a few miles southeast of Ogunquit, to stay at the **Cliff House** (P.O. Box 2274)

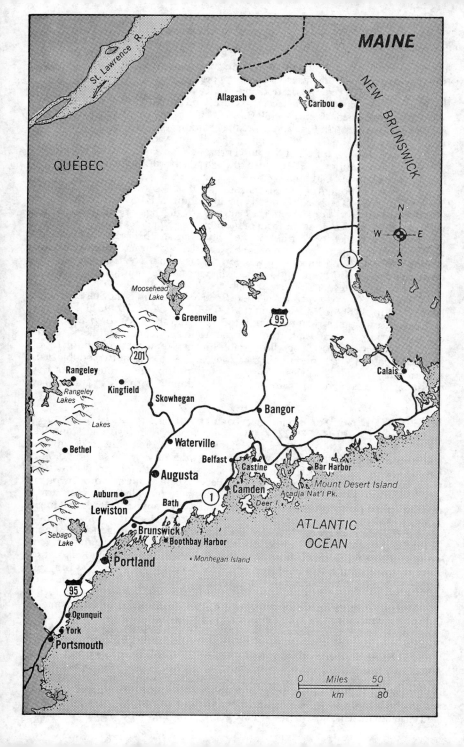

Ogunquit, ME 03907 (tel. 207/361-1000). Originally, one stayed in the large old house perched on the cliff, 90 feet above the surf, but now the house is overshadowed by several large and very modern motel units, all with a view of the sea. Extensive pine-covered grounds, a heated outdoor pool, and tennis courts add to the lure of the Cliff House's remote location and its view. The rooms are luxurious, with tub/shower combination bath in each, picture windows for the sea view, color TV; all are air-conditioned. From June 30 through Labor Day, they cost $110 to $120 double; in April through June and September through November the range is $65 to $86. Note that the Cliff House offers special mini-vacation package plans off-season (April through June and September through November). Cliff House provides free transportation in season into town, to the beach, and to other points of interest in and around Ogunquit.

Ogunquit's modern, "almost downtown" motel is the attractive **Country Squire Motel**, on U.S. 1 at Bourne's Lane, Ogunquit, ME 03907 (tel. 207/646-3162), just four blocks or so from the center of town. The inspiration is colonial, with an arched portico along the front of the motel, bay windows in each room, pots of plants, and colonial-style furniture. The facilities are another matter, however, for there's a swimming pool, and each room has a tiled tub/shower, heat and air conditioning, color TV, and uncolonial wall-to-wall carpeting. The Country Squire is open only from mid-May to mid-October, like most Ogunquit lodging places. In July and August, rates are $84 to $90 double.

Two blocks from downtown on Shore Road in Ogunquit is the **Sea Chambers Motor Lodge,** 37 Shore Rd., Ogunquit, ME 03907 (tel. 207/646-9311). The two-and three-story motel is right down near the water and also has its own heated pool and tennis court. You can walk from your room and get right on Marginal Way, the path along the rocky coast. The whole establishment is quite modern, and all rooms have bath, color TV, air conditioning, balcony, and twin beds or two double beds; most rooms have good sea views. In-season rates for late June through Labor Day, continental breakfast included, are $118 to $127 double, with an extra person paying $14.

WHERE TO DINE: For dinner in a country setting, try **Clay Hill Farm,** on Agamenticus Road (tel. 646-2272), two miles from downtown Ogunquit. The farmhouse has been converted into several large dining rooms with lots of windows and a very comfortable air. Start with clam chowder or vichyssoise and go on to broiled scallops or haddock, or perhaps a sole stuffed with lobster; with dessert, wine, tax, and tip, you'll pay $30 to $40 per person. Before and after dinner you can relax in the lounge and enjoy the piano entertainment provided. Clay Hill Farm is open in season (June to October) seven nights a week from 5:30 p.m. to midnight (kitchen closes at 10 p.m.), and for Sunday brunch from noon to 3 p.m.; in winter, you can have dinner here on Thursday, Friday, and Saturday during the same hours, or the Sunday brunch. Call for reservations, winter or summer. To get to the tavern, go south on Main Street (U.S. 1) from the blinker in the center of Ogunquit for three-tenths of a mile, to a blinker at a crossroads next to the Admiral's Inn; turn right—this is Agamenticus Road—and go 1.8 miles to the tavern, which will be on your right.

Perkins Cove, at the seaside end of Shore Road, has several good restaurants. In July and August it can be very difficult and expensive to park your car here, and you'd be well advised to take one of the "trolleys" (open buses) that run along Shore Road to the cove.

In Ogunquit, everybody goes to **Barnacle Billy's,** in Perkins Cove, and the reason is clear: good prices, good food, and good service as only you yourself could provide. The routine here is to enter, choose what you want from the blackboard menu, pay the cashier and get a slip, and submit the slip to the counterperson; then wander off into Barnacle Billy's waterfront dining room done all in pine with tables and chairs to match, and a hardwood fire going in the big stone fireplace if there's a chill in the air. The view of the marina and the cove is as good as the food: a 1¼-pound lobster for $9.50 (heavier ones for a dollar or two more), steamed clams, corn on the cob, salad, and garlic bread are all available. When the weather's fine, you can even order at a window on the flagstone terrace and have your meal while sitting in the sunshine, either on the terrace or on a deck a flight up, both terraces being right next to the Finestkind Boat Dock. Free parking for customers right across the street. Billy's is open May to mid-October daily from 11 a.m. to 11 p.m., more or less, depending on the crowds.

Right downtown in Ogunquit, one of the town's busiest dining spots is the **Old Village Inn,** 30 Main St. (tel. 646-7088). It's popular because of its location, and because of its several low-ceilinged dining rooms with their heavy beams barely six feet from the floor, all decorated with old crockery; if the weather's fine, you'll want to dine in the inn's glassed-in conservatory amid the flowers and plants. At dinner, have the delicious lobster bisque to start, then a seafood dish such as seafood imperial or perhaps roast duckling; the fish of the day is always a good choice; such a meal will cost about $30. At lunch/brunch, entrees are $8 to $10. Lunch/brunch is served from 10 a.m. to 3 p.m., and dinner from 6 to 10 p.m.; a small bar provides for the thirsty.

Ogunquit is prepared for New Yorkers who come north for the summer, or others in search of good corned beef, bagels, and the like. **Einstein's Deli,** at the corner of Shore Road and U.S. 1, has all these delights and lots more, besides several dining areas and a take-out service (tel. 646-5262). They're open till midnight, as a good deli should be. Note that even the clam chowder is New York style—with tomatoes.

WHAT TO DO: First thing to do is stop in at the town's information office and pick up a map, and then take off to walk **Marginal Way.** Start next to the Sachem Hotel and you'll come out right at Barnacle Billy's in Perkins Cove, a mile or so away. The Atlantic, the rocky coast, the gulls wheeling overhead, and the smiles of the other walkers you'll meet are all part of this Ogunquit institution, and all are a treat whether the sun is shining, or it's misty, or even if there's a gale coming.

Next thing to do is call the **Ogunquit Playhouse** (tel. 207/646-5511) to get seats for a performance, which will no doubt feature a star or two of national reputation.

As for **beaches,** Ogunquit is well equipped. The town's three beaches—Main Beach, Little Beach, and Fottbridge Beach—are ranged along a peninsula just a few minutes' walk from the center of town. Lifeguards are on duty from 8 a.m. to 5 p.m. daily in season.

Some lazy afternoon, be sure to leave time for a stroll around the shops and galleries of **Perkins Cove,** the picturesque old fishing-village section of town.

One can get to know the sea in Ogunquit by going down to Perkins Cove where, next to Barnacle Billy's, the dock of the **Finestkind boats** is located. Each hour during the day (except Sunday) the lobster boats set out to cruise the Maine coast, hauling in the lobster pots and the day's catch. You can go along and have the process of lobstering explained while you view the coastline and the fishing grounds, all at $6 for adults, $4 for children. Make reservations, if you like, by calling 646-5227, or just drop down to the docks for more information. They run cocktail, starlight, and lighthouse tour cruises as well.

Auto buffs can visit the **Wells Auto Museum** on U.S. 1 in Wells, just north of Ogunquit. From mid-June to mid-September, you can view the 1907 Stanley Steamer, a rare 1912 Pathfinder Roadster, a 1918 Pierce Arrow, and 75 other classics for $3 per adult, $1 for each child above the age of 6.

An Excursion to York

Just south of Ogunquit is York, or "The Yorks," as the town actually consists of old York, York Harbor, and York Beach.

York Harbor, at the mouth of the York River, is a summer resort much like Ogunquit. York Beach is more honky-tonk, with amusements and snack shops.

What you come to see is old **York Village,** first settled by Europeans in 1624. It received a royal charter in 1639, the first English town in the country to have this privilege.

Take a look at the **Old Gaol,** built as a jail in the 1700s, now a museum of colonial and Indian artifacts administered by the Old York Historical Society (tel. 363-4974). Hours are 10 a.m. to 4 p.m. Tuesday through Saturday late June through September.

Jefferds Tavern (1750) and the **Old School House** (1745) are next door to one another, providing an authentic glimpse of two aspects of life over two centuries ago. The **Emerson-Wilcox House** (1740) dates from the same era, and sheltered two presidents over the years; it's now a museum.

Down at the water's edge is the **John Hancock Warehouse and Wharf,** once owned by the great patriot, who signed the Declaration of Independence with a signature so large the king could read it without his glasses. It now holds exhibits on life in York during revolutionary times.

Near Sewall's Bridge on the York River is the **Elizabeth Perkins House,** built in 1730 but preserved with Victorian furnishings.

Finally, you may want to visit the **Old York Cemetery.** Besides having the standard collection of fascinating old New England tombstones, there is also a grave said to be that of a witch. Covered with a huge slab of stone to protect the townspeople from a reappearance, it's a real curiosity. One wonders what odd circumstances brought this poor soul such condemnation.

---

2. Kennebunkport

The several communities with similar names—Kennebunk, Kennebunkport, Kennebunk Beach—are clustered together on the Maine Coast and constitute one of the state's most popular vacation areas, particularly since they were put on the map by President Bush and his family.

Of the towns, Kennebunkport is perhaps the most interesting. As its name implies, Kennebunkport was the waterfront part of the Kennebunk area. It's been a resort for years, drawing both the well-to-do and the student crowd living on summer earnings. Prices for rooms and meals tend to be a bit high, but for most people the price is not so important so long as they can just find a room open in this delightful Maine town.

WHERE TO STAY: Kennebunkport has every sort of lodging. I've concentrated on inns, the quaint and charming places, with the occasional hotel or motel selected just in case that fits your mood.

Inns

Kennebunkport's inns come in all shapes and sizes, from the rambling old seaside "cottage" to the magnificently restored sea captain's mansion. Here are the best examples:

Jacques and Carol Gagnon's **Maine Stay Inn and Cottages,** Main Street (P.O. Box 500a-F), Kennebunkport, ME 04046 (tel. 207/967-2117), is a charming place, surrounded by gardens and lofty trees, but only a short walk from the center of town. Rates are $85 to $105 double in season. Though the rooms are equipped with all the modern conveniences, the spirit—and the welcome—are those of a cozy inn. A breakfast buffet is included, and tea is served to guests at 4 p.m.

At **The Breakwater,** Kennebunkport, ME 04046 (tel. 207/967-3118), the situation is excellent—the open sea is right next door. Prices are $91 to $134 double in season, the cheaper rooms being in the Breakwater building, the more expensive ones in the Riverside building, which is open year round and is more modern and, well, preferable. Off-season rates are 25% to 30% lower, from Columbus Day through mid-June. Continental breakfast is included in these prices. For dinner, the Breakwater has one of the best restaurants around (see below).

The **Captain Jefferds Inn,** Pearl Street (P.O. Box 691), Kennebunkport, ME 04046 (tel. 207/967-2311), is one of those old sea captains' houses so immaculately restored that it made the cover of *House Beautiful.* The house was beautiful, but the owners have improved upon it with unusual antiques, lots of them, and comfortable furnishings. Rooms cost $80 to $118, including tax and a country breakfast; there's a two-night minimum stay from July through October. Besides being everything a quaint inn should be, the Captain Jefferds Inn is just off Ocean Avenue, walking distance to everything in town.

Kennebunkport has a very special place to stay, and you should consider it. The **Captain Lord House,** P.O. Box 527, Kennebunkport, ME 04046 (tel. 207/967-3141), was built in 1812 by a naval captain whose sailors were blockaded in Kennebunk Harbor by the British. With nothing better for his men to do, Lord put them to work to build him a sumptuous mansion, and the master craftsmen who built his ships did an impressive job. Today, after years of benign neglect, the mansion has been meticulously restored. The Captain Lord Mansion is once again a luxurious house, with antiques everywhere, private baths all around, and working fireplaces in 19 of the 24 rooms, and you can stay here for $102 to $241 double (the highest-priced doubles are the ones with the fireplaces). A third person pays $25 in the same room. A full breakfast is included in these rates. If you've ever dreamed of staying in a work of art, a treasurehouse, or a National Historic Landmark, stay here, for the Lord Mansion is all three. Driving from Dock Square down Ocean Avenue, keep glancing to your left and soon you'll see the stately yellow mansion topped by its cupola/observatory at the back of a rich greensward a block long: Captain Lord meant this first sight of the mansion to be impressive, and it certainly is.

Guesthouses

You'll recognize the **Welby Inn,** P.O. Box 774, Kennebunkport, ME 04046 (tel. 207/967-4655), on Ocean Avenue across from the Nonantum, by its handsome handpainted tile signboard out front. One of the owners, Betsy Rogers-Knox, is the faïence artist who did the tiles for the sign, as well as those for all the bathrooms, and many of the paintings in this graceful old converted summer cottage. Five of the seven rooms have one of these private baths; prices are $70 to $91 double in season, breakfast included.

Of Kennebunkport's guesthouses, certainly the most pristine is the **Chetwynd House,** Kennebunkport, ME 04046 (tel. 207/967-2235), with only four rooms. The house is immaculately clean, which allows you to admire the fine wide-board floors of a rich honey color, and all the very decent furnishings, including many four-poster beds. Extra pleasures at the Chetwynd House include tea and cakes, and a full breakfast with your room; and here you're only two blocks from Dock Square and the center of town. Two rooms have private bath; the other two share a bath. Prices range from $90 to $134 double. Chetwynd House is on Chestnut Street, the second left off Ocean Avenue; the street is not marked, but Chetwynd House is a short distance up on the left, and is marked clearly by a sign.

Among the smaller and more modest inns, the **Green Heron,** on Ocean Drive (P.O. Drawer 151), Kennebunkport, ME 04046 (tel. 207/967-3315), has been a dependable Kennebunkport hostelry for years and years. This nice old house owned by Charles and Elizabeth Reid has been converted to hold ten guest rooms, and a cottage can hold an additional four people. Furnishings are simple but quite comfortable, and there's a cheery breakfast room with lots of big windows overlooking the water. These rates include a good breakfast: $56 to $80 double in season. All of the rooms have private baths, with tub and shower. The beaches are within walking distance.

Hotels

The **Nonantum Resort** (tel. 207/967-3338) is a very well-kept, classic 19th-century resort hotel, with comfortable and charming public rooms, lawns and a swimming pool, a waterfront location, and even a motel annex. The price, including tax, for a double with bath, is $85 to $150 double; $160 to $170 for an efficiency. This is a real slice of old Kennebunkport. Look for the Nonantum on Ocean Avenue, a half mile from town.

Those who want to be smack in the middle of town, right next to Dock Square, should consider **Austin's Inn-Town Hotel**, P.O. Box 609, Kennebunkport, ME 04046 (tel. 207/967-4241), right next to the Kennebunk River and the dock. The Inn-Town is a new and modern hostelry within an older-style building, and all rooms have private bath; it's possible to fit three, four, or even five people in several, which is good for traveling families to note. A room with a double bed is $69 to $99; for two double beds and a sofa the charge is $99 to $149. There's free parking for guests on the dock right next to the hotel.

WHERE TO DINE: Like any good resort town, Kennebunkport has a selection of restaurants in all price categories. Here are the ones I like best:

The Breakwater, not far from the Colony on Ocean Avenue (tel. 967-3118), is a restaurant and inn that is thought of highly by local people and visitors alike. The dining rooms are elegant without being overly formal, and from the sunporch—which is a dining room—one gets a beautiful view of the sea. It's difficult to know which facet of the Breakwater is the most enchanting: the decor and ambience, the staff, or the cuisine. Certainly the dinner menu is tempting, and the prices very sensible. Main courses come with baked potato, rice, or vegetable, salad, and a small loaf of bread. Thus you can order a beef kebab, or baked haddock; then there are broiled scallops. The delicacies proceed to swordfish and roast prime rib, with the lobster clambake priced according to the day's market. Soups and appetizers, vegetables, and beverages are all priced separately. A full dinner costs about $30 to $45. Have reservations, but be sympathetic when they tell you they can't reserve specific tables (the ones with the sea view are the hot ones). The dining room is open every day, for dinner only, from May through October 6 to 9 p.m. (5:30 to 10 p.m. in July and August).

The **White Barn Inn,** on Beach Street across from the Franciscan Monastery in Kennebunkport (tel. 967-2321), is a real barn converted to a restaurant. Everything that was found during the cleaning and renovation of the barn was hung on the many rafters and beams for effect, or so it seems. The menu includes snails, or chowder, or chicken livers wrapped in bacon, or baked stuffed lobster or shrimp, and marinated lamb kebab or veal piccata. Prices for entrees are generally $15 to $23, and this includes rice pilaf or potato, vegetable, and salad. Of the desserts, the homemade pie of the day or hot fudge puff would be my choice. Dinner is served every day at the White Barn from 5:30 to 9:30 p.m. (closed Monday off season). Beach Street (or Beach Avenue), by the way, is parallel to Ocean Avenue but across the inlet from it, to the south; if in doubt, ask for the St. Anthony Monastery, and the White Barn's very near, on the other side of the street.

Convenient to Dock Square, and good for a moderately priced supper, is the restaurant called **Arundel Wharf,** off Ocean Avenue a short distance from Dock Square (tel. 967-3444). Walking to the restaurant across its parking lot, the gulls will be squealing overhead; as you enter you'll see a modernistic back deck, a beamed ceiling, and several windows with water views, for the Arundel is indeed on a wharf by the Kennebunk River. The staff here are young and friendly. For lunch (11:30 a.m. to 3 p.m.) there are mostly sandwiches ($3 to $8) with a few platters offered, but for dinner (5 to 9 p.m.) you can have a boiled lobster, steak teriyaki, broiled haddock, or even lobster pie, for $10 to $14. A raw bar is open from 11:30 a.m. to 10 p.m.

The Arundel's name comes from the fact that Kennebunkport was once named Arundel after England's Earl of Arundel; in fact, it bore that name all through the better part of its maritime prominence, changing it only in 1821. Arundel Wharf is open daily from 11:30 a.m. to 3 p.m. and 5 to 9 p.m. (dinner served till 9 p.m.).

The **Olde Grist Mill,** on Mill Lane (tel. 967-4781), dates from 1749 and is listed in the National Register of Historic Places. Overlooking an inlet of the Kennebunk River, the restaurant is set back from the street on its own park-like grounds. Seafood is king, of course, but for a change of pace there's also baked stuffed shrimp macadamia and sirloin steak au poivre. Dinner (5:30 to 9 p.m.) will cost $30 to $40 per person, all in. To find the inn, from Dock Square ask for North Street; Mill Lane is a left turn a few blocks down.

Of course, the cheapest way to have a lobster dinner is to wander down to the lobster pound. Although many restaurants have appropriated the name "Lobster Pound," a real pound is simply the place where the live lobsters are kept in saltwater vats until a customer comes and buys them. Most lobster pounds these days have a few simple cooking facilities, and will boil up the lobsters for you if you wish, provide salad and french fries, butter and salt and a paper plate, and charge just a little above the price of a live lobster. There are several such lobster pounds in Kennebunkport, where a cooked lobster will cost between $8 and $12, depending on size and season.

WHAT TO DO: Shops and galleries around Dock Square draw lots of shoppers and window shoppers at all times, and one can spend some time browsing very pleasantly.

Gooch's Beach is right at the southern end of Beach Street, on the western shore of the Kennebunk River; **Kennebunk Beach** is west of Gooch's, along the coast. These fine, gradual beaches are good for swimming, especially on very hot days (the water tends to the chilly), for sunning on any sunny day, for walking, thinking, or jogging on almost any day.

Be sure to take a drive or a walk along **Maine Street** for a look at Kennebunkport's fine old mansions. For a look at the rocky coast, go south on Ocean Avenue to **Spouting Rock** to hear the crash of the surf.

A Trip to Cape Porpoise

Three miles northeast of Kennebunkport along Rte. 9, on the shore, is the village of Cape Porpoise. This charming little bit of Maine coastal life is a vacation haven for a small, knowledgeable few. Not fancy, not crowded, it has only a few craft shops, a few eateries, a few guesthouses, and a lot of Maine atmosphere. Drive out and head for the Pier, with its pretty views of the sea. A brass plaque on a rock atop the sand hill there bears this legend: "August 8, 1782, a British ship of 18 guns attacked a small force of inhabitants gathered on Goat Island and was driven away by severe musket fire, losing 17 men. James Burnham of this town was killed. This tablet erected by the Maine State Council, Daughters of the American Revolution, August 8, 1921."

Well, not an awful lot exciting has happened in Cape Porpoise since that signal victory, and it's just as well, for the quiet is what makes it nice.

Should you decide to stay here, Mr. and Mrs. Lyman P. Huff will rent you a room in their guesthouse, the **Old Garrison House,** Pier Road, Cape Porpoise, ME 04014 (tel. 207/967-3522), for $32 single or $50.25 twin (shared bath) or $53.50 (private bath) twin. You'll see the big yellow house on the left-hand side of the road at the head of the cove as you head for the Pier.

For real Maine lobster, try **Nunan's Lobster Hut** (tel. 967-4362), on Rte. 9 East. Nunan's is an unprepossessing low-roofed shack of a place, open from 11:30

a.m. to 2:30 p.m. and from 5 p.m. for dinner. They serve boiled lobster, steamed clams, salads, homemade pies, beer, and wine such that patrons return night after night. You need spend no more than $12 for dinner, though you may find yourself diving in and spending $16 or $20. Authenticity: that's Nunan's.

---

3. Portland

Cities in Maine have never had a reputation for chic or avant-garde ambience because Maine is a rural state, and it's the farmlands, woodlands, and coastal industries such as lobstering that count. But Portland, the state's largest city and its transportation hub and business center, may be changing all that. The **Civic Center** draws sports events, conventions, and big-name entertainers, and its revitalized waterfront area, known as the **Old Port Exchange,** is now even more attractive than it was in its Victorian heyday when the railroads, the huge sailing fleet, and the trade in lumber and fish made Portland what it is.

You can spend a day profitably in Portland, visiting the city's colonial, Early American, and Victorian landmarks, the **Portland Museum of Art,** or in taking a cruise in Portland Harbor or Casco Bay. Portland is also the American end of the Prince of Fundy Cruises, which will take you and your car to Yarmouth, Nova Scotia, on an eleven-hour, overnight cruise or on any one of a number of other cruises and tours (details below).

INFORMATION: The **Maine Publicity Bureau** in the **Greater Portland Chamber of Commerce,** 142 Free St., Portland, ME 04101 (tel. 207/772-2811), next to the Portland Museum of Art can fill you in on Portland life.

WHERE TO STAY: The city has a few lodging places downtown, but many visitors, especially those here on business, stay in motels near Exit 8 of the Maine Turnpike.

Downtown Hotels and Inns

The **Inn at Park Spring,** 135 Spring St., Portland, ME 04101 (tel. 207/774-1059), a few blocks west of the center, is a restored three-story brick town house with seven guest rooms, most with private bath but some with shared bath. As the house dates from 1935, a colonial or Victorian decor would be inappropriate, so instead the rooms are done in an assortment of nice old pieces and more modern furniture as well. All rooms have queen-size beds, and rent for $86 to $97 double, continental breakfast included.

Down in the Old Port stands the **Portland Regency,** 20 Milk St., Portland, ME 04101 (tel. 207/774-4200), a new hotel in a fine old waterfront building constructed in 1895 as an armory. Here you can walk to everything of interest in the port district, and you're only a few steps from the commercial center of town as well. The guest rooms are decorated in Early American reproductions, not exactly accurate to the hotel's age, but very nice nonetheless. There's a health club. A single room rents for $107, a double for $118.

If you visited Portland years ago, you remember the old Eastland Hotel. In its place stands the totally renovated **Sonesta Portland Hotel,** 157 High St., Portland, ME 04101 (tel. 207/775-5411, or toll free 800/343-7170). Still at the very heart of the city, the Sonesta provides all the up-to-date luxury hotel services at rates of $96 to $134 single, $113 to $150 double. Ask about the hotel's weekend packages when you call for reservations.

Holiday Inn has a downtown hotel in Portland, but out on the highway it's the **Portland-West Holiday Inn,** 81 Riverside St. (Exit 8 from the Turnpike), Portland, ME 04103 (tel. 207/774-5601 or toll free 800/465-4329). The 200 rooms here are all modern, with color TV, and are priced at $104 to $115 double in July and August, a few dollars less per room just on the other side of high season. There's live entertainment in the lounge most evenings in summer.

The **Howard Johnson Motor Lodge** is nearby at 155 Riverside St., Portland, ME 04103 (tel. 207/774-5861, or toll free 800/654-2000), and here the facilities include an indoor heated swimming pool and a sauna, a restaurant and lounge, and rooms with color TV. Special weekend minivacation packages are available, but normally the doubles rent for $97 to $102 in high season. If you're flying, a limo will bring you here from the airport, but you should call in advance.

The bargain place to stay, as ever, is the dependable **Susse Chalet Motor Lodge,** on Brighton Avenue, Portland, ME 04103 (tel. 207/774-6101 or toll free 800/258-1980), near the other motels mentioned. At the Susse Chalet, rooms are modern, heated, and air-conditioned, with bright new bathrooms and TV, plus all the other facilities you'd normally find in a modern motel, but the price is only $36 for one person, $41 for two, $43 for three, or $46 for four in a room with two double beds.

WHERE TO DINE: The renaissance of Portland's waterfront district has given rise to numerous restaurants in recent years, and a short walk through the tidy and picturesque restored blocks of Fore, Exchange, Middle, and Moulton Streets will reveal interesting and moderately priced places for a snack, a meal, or a relaxing drink.

The **Baker's Table,** 434 Fore St. (tel. 775-0303), is just that: the restaurant attached to the little Port Bakehouse at street level. For the restaurant, descend a flight of steps to the bright stuccoed walls and wooden beams in the dining rooms. An elegant cafeteria with bar adjoining, the system here is to pass through the line at lunchtime for, say, soup and salad, and after you're seated everything else you may need—more wine, coffee, or dessert—can be brought by a waiter or waitress. The salads are almost meals in themselves, but with a big bowl of fish chowder it'll fill you for sure. Such a lunch will cost less than $10 with fresh bread and beverage—that's a daily special. Lunch is from 11:30 a.m. to 5:30 p.m.; after that the heartier and more expensive dinner menu comes into play until 10 p.m. (to 10:30 on Friday and Saturday). There is full service at dinner, and you can have bouillabaisse, tournedos, or something like chicken provençale served amid linen tablecloths and sparkling stemware. The chef is getting quite a reputation. It's nice here for either meal: soft background music, paintings by local artists on the walls, an interesting crowd, well-stocked bar, and espresso machine. Dinner might cost $30 per person, all in.

For new American cuisine in an upbeat atmosphere, head for the **Café Always,** 47 Middle St. (tel. 774-9399), a colorful and stylish refuge of the designer set. The menu is as interesting as the clientele and the decor: lamb loin prepared with sun-dried tomatoes and fresh thyme, Korean-style hot-and-sour chicken, a fancy burrito, and a halibut filet with an orange-and-chive beurre blanc were all on the menu recently. The wine list is heavy with California vintages. Dinner, the only meal served, is on from 5 to 10 p.m. every day, and will cost about $45 per person, all in.

Go to the aforementioned Portland Regency Hotel, 20 Milk St. in the Old Port (tel. 774-4200), for a sumptuous Sunday brunch buffet, spread out from 10:30 a.m. to 2:30 p.m. The setting is the hotel's restaurant, called the **Armory,** a nice interior court complete with fountains and free-flowing champagne. Drink as many glasses as you like—the champagne is included in the price of the buffet, which is less than $20 once you add the tax.

Portland's choice for Chinese cuisine is **Hu Shang,** 7–13 Brown St. (tel. 774-0800), right downtown near the Civic Center. The cooking is drawn from Hunan, Szechuan, Shanghai, and Mandarin (Peking/Beijing) traditions: spring rolls, pan-fried dumplings, fried wonton, hot-and-sour or bean-curd soup are among the appetizers. Then lamb with ginger and scallions, chicken with cashews, moo shu beef, fresh scallops with peanuts and scallions—it's difficult not to order half a dozen entrees. But appetizer, entree, and lichee nut dessert will cost about $17, tea, tax, and tip included. Several people sharing just a few maincourse plates can dine very well for much less. This is one of the city's best restaurants, open every day for lunch and dinner from 11:30 a.m. to 9:30 p.m. (10:30 p.m. on weekends); no lunch on Sunday.

For Meeting People

The **Seamen's Club,** 375 Fore St., is a good place to meet Portlanders who work in or near the waterfront, particularly at lunchtime when the sandwiches (about $5) and the low-price table d'hôte ($7) draw a crowd. Sunday brunch is good too. At dinner the menu is filled with the popular classics, tried and proven: baked stuffed shrimp, roast duckling with orange sauce, filet mignon—solid and satisfying. Prices per main course may be anywhere from $13 to $20 (the higher end for the steaks, of course).

The **Old Port Tavern,** right across the street and down a short distance at 11 Moulton, is another popular watering spot where the people and the drink are as good, or better, than the food.

WHAT TO SEE AND DO: First thing to do is to ask at your hotel for a copy of the Greater Portland Chamber of Commerce's brochure called *The Portland History Trail,* which sets forth details and a walking tour (with map) of all the notable sights in the city. Here are some of the highlights:

Wadsworth-Longfellow House

The Wadsworth-Longfellow House was the boyhood home of poet Henry Wadsworth Longfellow. Built in 1785–86 by the poet's maternal grandfather, General Peleg Wadsworth, the house now holds furnishings that once belonged to the famous Wadsworths and Longfellows, as well as many other period pieces. There's a beautiful garden, and the Maine Historical Society, which received the bequest of the house in 1901, is located right next door. You can tour the house from June 1 through Columbus Day weekend, Tuesday through Saturday from 10 a.m. to 4 p.m., for $2.50 per adult, $1 per child under 12.

Tate House

The Maine forest was for a long time the prime source of masts for the British navy, and the man who managed the whole trade was one George Tate, who had this house built in 1755. The house is shown by guided tour from June 15 to September 15, Tuesday through Saturday from 11 a.m. to 5 p.m. and on Sunday from 1:30 to 5 p.m. To get to the house, at 1270 Westbrook St. in the Stroudwater section of Portland, go southwest on Congress Street for two miles, cross the stream, and turn left onto Westbrook Street, very near the Portland Jetport. The fee to get in is $2.50 for adults, $1 for kids under 12.

Victoria Mansion (Morse-Libby House)

Built between 1858 and 1860, the Victoria Mansion has fascinating Victorian decorations, and many original furnishings, all of which are on view Tuesday through Saturday from 10 a.m. to 4 p.m., on Sunday from 1 to 4 p.m., from June 1 through Labor Day (in September, hours are 10 a.m. to 1 p.m. Tuesday through Saturday and on Sunday from 1 to 4 p.m.). It's at 109 Danforth St. (tel. 772-4841), and costs $3 per adult, $1 per child under 18, to see.

Portland Museum of Art

Portland has a fine museum with a fine collection at 7 Congress Square (tel. 773-2787). Particularly strong are the collections of 19th- and 20th-century American art relating to Portland and to Maine, with paintings by Andrew Wyeth, Winslow Homer, and Edward Hopper. A gift of 17 Winslow Homer paintings is featured in the new building (done by I. M. Pei). Special exhibits change bimonthly.

The museum is open Tuesday through Sunday; admission is $3.50 for adults, $2.50 for students and seniors, $1 for kids under 18.

Boats and Cruises

Portland is the prime dock for Casco Bay and indeed northern New England, and you can climb aboard a boat with your car or without, for a few hours or overnight. Here are the major lines:

Casco Bay Lines, Custom House Wharf (tel. 207/774-7871), will take you (but *not* your car) over to Bailey's Island in summer. While on the four-hour cruise, you'll be told all about the island's history and its geologic features, plus lots of Portland and Casco Bay lore. On a sunny day, this is a very fine way to "take the air." The price for this cruise is $12 for adults, half price for children. Other cruises are a bit shorter and a bit cheaper, and leave all year: there's a sunset cruise to the islands (2½ hours), a cruise around Casco Bay (2½ hours), and the cruise on the U.S. Mail boat which goes to each of the Calendar Islands (three hours). The M/V *Longfellow,* 1 Long Wharf (tel. 774-3578), has a similar program.

Prince of Fundy Cruises to Nova Scotia

May through October on most days, the M/S *Scotia Prince* leaves Portland in the evening for Yarmouth, Nova Scotia, on an 11-hour overnight cruise. Return sailings from Yarmouth are in mid- or late morning. You can take your car with you, and duty-free shops are aboard. Current high-season (late June to late September) prices for the cruise are $65 (U.S. dollars) per adult, half price for children 5 to 14 accompanied by an adult; children under 5 go free. The fare for a car is normally $90. A cabin for two costs in the range of $32 to $95. A family of four can easily spend $350 one way. But there are several special fares which might suit your needs and which will save you money. Be sure to call Prince of Fundy Cruises for full particulars, latest fares, and schedules; credit cards now accepted for passage. In Portland, call 207/775-5616; elsewhere in Maine, call toll free 800/482-0955; in other states, call toll free 800/341-7540; in Nova Scotia, New Brunswick, and Prince Edward Island, call toll free 800/565-7900; in the rest of Canada, call 902/742-5164; and in Yarmouth, Nova Scotia, call 902/742-3411.

EXCURSIONS NORTH: Most people head east from Portland, aiming at Camden, Boothbay, Bar Harbor, or the Canadian border. But an excursion up Rtes. 302 and 26, deep into Maine's forested hinterland, will bring you right up against North Woods life.

Sebago Lake

Of Maine's hundreds of beautiful, clear lakes, Sebago Lake is one of the largest and most accessible. The eastern shore of the lake is somewhat developed with small villages, highway establishments, and the like; at the southern tip, the town of Sebago Lake is hardly more than a few dozen houses, two stores, and a gas station. But along the western shore in the area of the settlement called East Sebago there are a number of places which rent rooms and cabins, mingled among the larger private summer cabins and houses.

Although the roads that skirt the lake do have collections of cabins and houses here and there, it's hardly what you'd call thickly settled. You'll come across **Sebago Lake State Park** at the northern tip of the lake, where there's also a fine beach, picnic facilities, and a camping area. Although very busy in summer, the park is yours to enjoy with only a handful of others in early June or after Labor Day.

Sabbathday Lake

Thirty miles north of Portland along Rte. 26 is the settlement of Sabbathday Lake, the last living Shaker community in the country. Founded in the 1700s, the Sabbathday Lake community still has a handful of active members who continue to work and live in the Shaker tradition. A shop selling community products, a museum, and a welcome center are open to visitors, though most of the other buildings are not. For more on Shaker history and beliefs, see in Chapter IX on the Berkshires (Section 7, "Stockbridge") the description of Hancock Shaker Village.

The spare white buildings of the village are plain but extremely well kept. Most notable is the Brick Dwelling House. In the fields near the village are several small, simple cemeteries, each with only one monument, bearing the legend "Shakers" and the dates of interment.

Up the road a few miles is the village of **Poland Spring,** which gained fame in the 1800s when a man was miraculously cured by its waters. The water from the spring has been bottled and shipped throughout the country since that time. Several hotels here cater to those "taking the waters."

Continue north on Rte. 26 and you'll soon come to one of the prettiest towns in Maine, right at the edge of the White Mountains and a vast National Forest.

Bethel

Tucked away in the mountains on the western edge of Maine is the village of Bethel. Although the village is on U.S. 2, the highway that heads west to skirt the border of the White Mountains National Forest, there is little else that would bring travelers to the place were it not for two attractions: a well-known preparatory school called **Gould Academy** (founded 1836); and an excellent inn.

WHERE TO STAY: The inn referred to above is the **Bethel Inn,** on the Town Common, Bethel, ME 04217 (tel. 207/824-2175). A feeling of tastefulness and elegance is what you get as you drive to the inn's entrance through the greenswards in the center of the village. The main inn has a famous dining room, a large lounge with a fireplace to match, French doors leading out onto a terrace overlooking the mountains and the inn's manicured grounds. Special services include a swimming pool, tennis courts, a music room complete with Steinway, a library, a golf course, a boathouse (for boating and fishing) on a nearby pond, and entertainment and dancing in the evenings. The rooms are done with colonial accents (although the inn itself dates from 1913), and are priced to include breakfast, dinner, service, and tax at $140 to $238 double. The inn has rooms in the main building, and also in a number of old Bethel houses surrounding the Common, and so the selection of accommodations is very good.

Also on the green, but moderately priced, is the **Chapman Inn,** P.O. Box 206, Bethel, ME 04217 (tel. 207/824-2657), a bed-and-breakfast place since 1865. The cheery, homey rooms here are priced at $25 for a bed in the dormitory, $43 single, $59 double with shared bath, or $70 double with full bath; full breakfast is included. You get to use the game room, nearby pond, sauna, and hot tub as well.

As you drive into town on Rte. 26 from the south, you can't miss the **Four Seasons Inn,** Upper Main Street, Bethel, ME 04217 (tel. 207/824-2755). This huge, beautiful Victorian has porches, gables, and turrets to attract any eye. Inside, it's all angles, nooks, fireplaces, antique furnishings, and thoughtful touches such as tea or sherry in the afternoon and chocolates on your pillow. Room rates include a welcoming drink, continental breakfast, afternoon tea, and use of the Bethel Inn's recreational facilities: $54 single, $64 (shared bath) or $80 (private bath) double.

WHAT TO SEE: Should you have an hour to spend in Bethel, drop in at the **Dr. Moses Mason House,** 15 Broad St. (tel. 824-2908), on the Common, open in July and August, Tuesday through Sunday from 1 to 4 p.m., and by appointment (call during business hours) the rest of the year. Moses Mason was a congressman during the Jackson administration, and had this Federal house built in 1813. Today it's furnished in antiques of the period and also holds several murals attributed to Rufus Porter. Admission is $2 for adults, half price for children. There are research facilities, special exhibits, pictures, films, and a gift shop.

Otherwise, there's the great outdoors. North on Rte. 26 is **Grafton Notch State Park,** with a pretty waterfall named Screw Auger. West on U.S. 2 is the White Mountains National Forest. Between Gilead, ME., and Shelburne, N.H., the highway is lined with birch trees, the famous Shelburne birches. Most of us have never seen so many of these unusual, lovely trees in one spot. In autumn, when the birch leaves turn to brilliant yellow with dabs of red, they knock your eyes out.

For more on the national forest in New Hampshire, see Chapter XII.

---

4. Freeport, Brunswick, and Bath

North of Portland, the next major tourist destination is Boothbay Harbor. But you'll pass several interesting towns along the way, each with an attraction peculiar to Maine.

FREEPORT: This small Maine town, nothing special though nice enough, is known all over the country and throughout the world as the headquarters of **L. L. Bean** (tel. 207/865-3111), the company that sells equipment, clothing, and supplies for outdoor activities. L. L. Bean has been in Freeport for decades, but in recent years the store's popularity has burgeoned to epic proportions. A half dozen parking lots, administered by Bean employees, fill up quickly every day with cars bearing license plates from all over America and Canada. The large, attractive store is always mobbed during the day, and busy even at night, for Bean's is open all the time. It *never* closes.

Bean's reputation was built by selling sturdy, good-quality items at reasonable prices. The returns policy is absolute: if you find a Bean item unsatisfactory at any time, return it for a refund. Should you stop at Bean's, remember that the store carries dozens of items for which there is no room in the catalog, and that there's also a "factory store" for end-of-season and distressed merchandise. You should also know that Bean's will mail your packages home for you right from the store at no extra charge. Keep it in mind: if your trunk's too full, take the item you've just bought to the Customer Service counter, and they'll take care of the rest—for free.

The boom at Bean's has brought prosperity to Freeport, and a dozen other shops—Dansk, Anne Klein, Ralph Lauren, Hathaway, you name it—have opened in order to profit from the press of Bean buyers. In effect it's becoming Maine's town-size shopping mall.

BRUNSWICK: Surrounded by coastal resort towns, Brunswick is the cultural center of this part of Maine, for **Bowdoin College** is in Brunswick along with Maine's only professional music theater. The **Brunswick Music Theater** (tel. 207/725-8769) is on the Bowdoin campus, and presents musical productions from mid-June through Labor Day each summer.

Bowdoin's fame comes not from its theater, although that is certainly famous enough among summer visitors and residents, but rather from the distinguished alumni who have spent their time in Brunswick and then moved on to fame and glory: Longfellow, Hawthorne, and President Franklin Pierce were all Bowdoin graduates. The college is at Pine and College Streets, and free tours are available year round. While you're here, visit Bowdoin's **art museum** to see its collection of colonial works.

BATH: A ten-mile drive along U.S. 1 north from Brunswick brings you to Bath, another fine town of colonial and Federal houses built when Bath was a wealthy seaport and shipbuilding center. Take a drive along Washington Street to see what I mean.

While you're on Washington Street, stop at no. 243, the headquarters of Bath's famous **Maine Maritime Museum** (tel. 207/443-1316). One admission ticket ($5 for adults, half price for children six to 16, $15 for a family) admits you to the exhibit on the maritime history of Maine, the restored Percy and Small Shipyard and its buildings, the Apprentice Shop boat-building school, a lobstering exhibit, and, when she's in port, a 142-foot fishing schooner. Just about everything you'd associate with the sea is represented in these exhibits: early fishing methods, ship building, small boats, engines and steam yachts, navigation, ship models and paintings, sailors' memorabilia, and all sorts of coastal lore. There's even a play boat for children complete with crow's nest and a "cargo" of sand.

The museum complex is along the river, with plenty of space for picnickers. Wear outdoor clothing and good shoes. You'll need several hours to see everything; or you can have your ticket validated for the next day also, at no extra charge. For a few dollars more you can take a boat ride on the Kennebec River past nearby lighthouses and the Bath Iron Works. The museum is open daily from 10 a.m. to 5 p.m., except for major holidays.

WISCASSET: Billing itself "the prettiest village in Maine," Wiscasset might live up to its boast if Maine did not have such an abundance of pretty towns. It is pretty, though, and as you pass through the center on U.S. 1 you can confirm this. As you cross the Sheepscot River toward Damariscotta, look right (south) and note the two enormous hulks derelict in the water. The four-masted schooners *Hesperus* and *Luther Little* once carried cargoes along the Atlantic coast. But the many-masted schooners (a few were even built with six masts!) were the last of a proud breed, replaced by the more reliable steamboats. These two sad relics of a romantic age sit forlorn in the mud, awaiting restoration or final destruction.

---

5. Boothbay Harbor

North and east of Portland, the Maine coastline is a choppy succession of peninsulas, sea inlets, islands, and river outlets. The country here is beautiful, and vacation communities abound. Reaching many of these communities means driving down a peninsular road for quite a number of miles to the tip, and upon leaving one drives back up to U.S. 1 — few bridges or causeways span the inlets or rivers.

Boothbay Harbor is the principal town in a region of vacation settlements which include Boothbay, Boothbay Harbor, East Boothbay, Southport, and Ocean Point. I could write a book on this region alone, and so I've simplified by limiting my recommendations to Boothbay Harbor itself, which is the center of the action.

INFORMATION: As you drive down Rte. 27 from U.S. 1, several miles from town you'll come to a seasonal **information bureau,** on the right. If it's closed, don't worry for there's another one a bit farther along, right at the edge of town, and it's open year round. Or get in touch with the **Boothbay Harbor Region Chamber of Commerce,** P.O. Box 356, Boothbay Harbor, ME 04538 (tel. 207/633-2353).

WHERE TO STAY: As mentioned, Boothbay Harbor and the surrounding region have a plethora of vacation accommodations, hundreds of places in all. I've concentrated on the congenial places, like cozy guesthouses on a hilltop with a splendid view.

Admiral's Quarters, 103 Commercial St., Boothbay Harbor, ME 04538 (tel. 207/633-2474), is Jean and George Duffy's large old white-clapboard sea captain's house built around 1820 commanding marvelous views of the harbor from

McKown Hill. Upper and lower sundecks allow you to take in the view from each room. Seven comfortable modernized rooms with bath cost $65 to $75, single or double, morning coffee included.

Captain Sawyer's Place, 87 Commercial St., Boothbay Harbor, ME 04538 (tel. 207/633-2290), is a classic yellow-and-white Boothbay Harbor residence—complete with rooftop "observatory"—now run as a guest house by Jerry and Doreen Gibson. Rooms are tidy and bright, with some period furnishings, Martha Washington bedspreads, and very clean bathrooms with showers. A small patio overlooks the pedestrians on Main Street, and the house's long wraparound verandah overlooks everything. The location couldn't be any better, nor the welcome warmer. Rates are $75 to $120 for a double room with private bath, continental breakfast included.

Hilltop House, c/o The Mahrs, Boothbay Harbor, ME 04538 (tel. 207/633-2941 or 633-3839), is just that, right at the top of McKown Hill in town, next to Topside (see below). Mrs. Mahr, a real Maine native, will rent you a homey room in her house for $40 double with private bath, $30 with shared bath, $42 to $55 for a family unit. The porch, and its marvelous view, are yours to enjoy anytime you like. Homemade muffins and breads and coffee come with the price of the room.

Topside says it all about this charming hilltop house just two blocks from the center of Boothbay Harbor atop McKown Hill, Boothbay Harbor, ME 04538 (tel. 207/633-5404). Several fine old houses have been meticulously restored down to the marble fireplaces (in the living rooms) and stocked with antiques. All rooms have refrigerators. Several new motel rooms have been added, but in keeping with the architectural style of the house. And what a view! Many rooms have this view, and for variety you can sit in a lawn chair in the midst of Topside's lush green grass to take it all in as the cool breezes waft up from the harbor. Although there are other places on McKown Hill, Topside is smack at the top. Rates are $91 to $102, depending on the size of the room, its degree of comfort, and its exposure (all have private bath). As the number of rooms is limited, be sure to write or call well in advance for reservations. Open mid-May through November.

The **Oak Ledge,** 41 Oak St., Boothbay Harbor, ME 04538 (tel. 207/633-6640), may be the town's prettiest, most pristine bed-and-breakfast house. Located on the road into town, only 2½ blocks from the water, the rooms in this prim clapboard house have blond or honey-colored wood floors, stenciled borders on the walls, and craft items for decoration. Baths are shared; a double costs $50, continental breakfast included. It's great!

For something closer to a motel, check out the **Tugboat Inn,** 100 Commercial St., Boothbay Harbor, ME 04538 (tel. 207/633-4434), a few steps from the center of town, at the lower edge of McKown Hill. The inn has several lodging buildings and a good variety of accommodations, from simple but tidy inn rooms through efficiencies and motel-style rooms to luxury rooms and suites. Prices in high season range from $75 to $125 double; all rooms have private bath. You're right on the harbor here, with good views, handy to town, in an attractive and congenial establishment.

Outside Town

The **Ocean Point Motel,** Shore Road (P.O. Box 409), East Boothbay, ME 04544 (tel. 207/633-4200), couldn't have a better location. Way down at Ocean Point by the lighthouse, on the southern tip of a peninsula overlooking the harbor mouth, Ocean Point is all by itself except for a few houses. It's quiet here, and very serene. You stay in the motel, the inn, the lodge, or one of the cottages, and rates depend on which, though all rooms have private bath, electric heat, and color television. Least expensive rooms are in the inn ($70 to $80 double), but the other lodgings are not much more expensive ($70 to $96), though a few suites and cottages are higher in price. The Ocean Point has its own restaurant, as there's no other place to dine without driving into Boothbay Harbor.

The **Lawnmeer Inn and Motel,** Rte. 27, Southport, ME 04569 (tel. 207/ 633-2544), is a short drive from Boothbay Harbor, across the drawbridge in Southport. In a quiet country setting, the Lawnmeer offers motel-style rooms with private bath, television, and the other modern conveniences for $68 to $95 double. This is the place to go if you need to get away from it all.

The **Five Gables Inn,** Murray Hill Rd., East Boothbay, ME 04544 (tel. 207/ 633-4551), is a superbly restored old Maine coastal inn of 15 rooms, all with wonderful views of Linekin Bay and also with private baths; five rooms have working fireplaces. Innkeepers Ellen and Paul Morisette obviously love their work. After your buffet breakfast here (included in the rates), enjoy the view from the large verandah, or take the sun on the lawn, or cross the road for a swim. Bustling Boothbay Harbor is 3 miles away; here in East Boothbay, its much calmer and quieter. The Five Gables is open from mid May through mid November and charges $86 to $130 double.

Bed-and-Breakfast

I've chosen mostly establishments in town or in special locations outside. The Boothbay region does have a number of bed-and-breakfast houses, most off the beaten track. For information, check (or call) the information booth.

WHERE TO DINE: While Boothbay is no culinary Mecca swarming with gourmet Muhammeds, there are still a few places where you can find things besides fried foods or the infamous surf-and-turf.

For standard American seaside fare, try **Rocktide,** 45 Atlantic Ave. (tel. 633-4455), across the bay from downtown Boothbay Harbor (use the footbridge). Rocktide is a big place with four dining areas. On the Seadeck, in the Chart Room and Buoy Room, you can dress as you like, and no reservations are taken; in the Dockside and Harbor-side Rooms diners should observe "jacket" formality, and reservations are taken. The menu is old New England: fried Maine shrimp, ocean scallops, seafood casserole, finnan haddie, New England lobster pie, or a fisherman's platter. But there are unexpected items as well, such as a kabob of shrimp, scallops, lobster, and swordfish and sole Duxelleois and roast duck. Every main course comes with rights to the salad bar, a popover, and rice or potato. Dinner is served from 5:30 to 9 p.m. every evening. You can expect to spend $25 to $35 per person here.

A few steps from the center of Boothbay Harbor, down near the footbridge, is the **Chowder House** (tel. 633-5761), in a building called The Granary. Have a drink in the Loading Dock Lounge, a woody place filled with nautical paraphernalia, then move on to the dining room with its inside water-view room and outside terrace. The clam chowder and lobster stew are made fresh daily and served with freshly baked bread. A bowl of either would make a lunch in itself for only $8 to $10, or you might choose the lobster sandwich or seafood salad, but there's meat and fowl as well. Dinners are somewhat fancier and a bit more expensive, about $20 to $30 per person, all included. Popular choices are the native scallops sauteed with mushrooms and white wine in a light cream sauce, and the fried oysters. Come for breakfast, lunch, or dinner any day of the week.

Andrew's Harborside Restaurant, by the footbridge (tel. 633-4074), offers a lobster roll that's not gigantic but is positively stuffed with succulent lobster meat—no filler. With a soft drink, it'll cost you $10. Mako-shark burgers, chowders, and lots of other things fill the menu. Fresh flowers grace the tables covered in nautical blue-and-white cloths, and you have your choice of an indoor dining room with lots of windows or an awning-shaded terrace, both with fine views of the harbor. You can get draft beer or wine by the glass at lunch or dinner any day. For dessert, go downstairs to the Round Top Ice Cream booth beneath the terrace.

At **Gilchrist's East,** on Commercial Street just south of Fishermen's Wharf (tel. 633-5692), the boiled Maine lobster goes for $15 (whole dinner) or $12 (lobster only), which is reasonable; haddock, halibut, and scallops go for a bit less. But the most interesting item on the menu is the Candlelight Dinner, a succession of salads, vegetables, and fish dishes served on miniature china, for $16. The point is to give you various tastes without overfilling you. Otherwise, they serve coquilles St-Jacques, the scallops and mushrooms in shells. Liquor is served. You'll like it here. Open for lunch and dinner daily in season.

A place for lobster is the **Lobstermen's Co-op,** on Atlantic Avenue along the east side of the harbor (tel. 633-4900). The Co-op sells lobsters wholesale and retail (from 6 a.m. to 8 p.m.), and will cook up a live lobster, clams, and corn-on-the-cob while you wait, at the retail price. Select a few side dishes, a beverage, a hamburger for the one who can't stand seafood, and you're all set to munch lunch at one of their tables (from 11:30 a.m. to 8 p.m.). Cheap, fresh, good, authentic. Lobsters are priced from $8.50 to $16.

WHAT TO DO: In Boothbay Harbor, the sea comes first, as it always has. As the rocky, rugged coastline made travel overland virtually impossible until the day of the automobile and the modern highway, Boothbay Harbor was for centuries served from the sea.

Wander down to the shore in town, and you'll see lots of signboards and ticket kiosks for the boats that operate on cruises out of Boothbay Harbor. Ticket prices range from about $10 to $15, and may include a search for seals, water birds, whales, and other marine life, or perhaps a clambake or a chicken bake afloat. When the moon is near full, special moonlight cruises are arranged. Cruises can be anywhere from one to three hours in length. Ask around to find a style, length, and price that's right for you.

A Clambake on Cabbage Island

Go down to the Tugboat Inn on Main Street, look for the Boothbay Steamship Terminal (tel. 207/633-7166), and climb aboard the M/V *Islander* for a cruise out to Cabbage Island in Linekin Bay and a real Down East Maine-style clambake. Clams and lobsters are steamed amid seaweed the old-fashioned way and served up twice a day from Memorial Day through Labor Day. The *Islander* sails to the clambake Monday through Friday at 12:45 p.m. (returning by 4:35 p.m.) and 5:15 p.m. (returning before dark); on Sunday, departures are at 11 a.m. (returning by 2:45 p.m.) and 1 p.m. (returning by 5:45 p.m.). Total cost for the clambake is $30 per person, and that includes the delightful round-trip boat cruise, a cup of fish chowder, two lobsters, steamed clams, corn-on-the-cob, new Maine potatoes, and blueberry cake and coffee for dessert. The scenic island has games, paths, and sitting areas for you to enjoy, as well. Call 207/633-7200 for clambake reservations at least a half hour before sailing time.

To Monhegan Island

The *Balmy Days* is a sail-assisted motor craft that makes the run 16 miles out to sea to Monhegan Island, Maine's famous windswept resort-at-sea. One trip out, leaving in the morning, and one trip back from the island, leaving in midafternoon, are made daily. You cannot stay overnight on the island without previous hotel reservations, but the *Balmy Days*'s schedule allows you to have between three and four hours on the island if you go out and back in one day. Monhegan is noted for its interesting paths and walks, and that's mostly what there is to do. A one-way ticket to Monhegan Island is $14; a round trip is $23; children under 10 pay $14 roundtrip. While it's out at Monhegan, the *Balmy Days* makes one run around the island so you can see the rugged cliffs, and this costs $1 extra. By the way, you can easily hike all there is to hike (pretty much) in one four-hour stay on Monhegan. For detailed information, call 207/633-2284.

Other Activities

The Brick House, on Oak Street very near the central Town Square, is the present home of the **Boothbay Region Art Gallery** (tel. 633-2703), which arranges three shows of local artists each season. Paintings are on view daily from 11 a.m. to 5 p.m., on Sunday from noon to 5 p.m. The handsome old house was built in 1807 of bricks brought from England as ballast in ships which came to carry away Maine lumber—in such a forest-rich region, a brick house is a curiosity, as most houses would naturally be made from wood.

---

6. Camden

Picture a small Maine coastal town wedged between the salt waters of Penobscot Bay and a range of rocky hills, and that's Camden. With a population of barely 4,000 souls it's small, picturesque and manageable. Edna St. Vincent Millay came from these parts, but today Camden's chief claim to fame is that it is the home port for several two-masted schooners which take eager landlubbers for cruises along the Maine coast. The hills behind the town are included in the **Camden Hills State Park,** with campgrounds and picnic spots, and an auto road to the top of Mount Battie, the highest hill of the range.

TOURIST INFORMATION: The **Rockport-Camden-Lincolnville Chamber of Commerce,** P.O. Box 919, Camden, ME 04843 (tel. 207/236-4404), maintains an information booth on the public landing in Camden where you can get a directory of the area and also a brochure describing the walking and bike tours of Camden and Rockport outlined by the Camden Historical Society. The tours point up all the most historic places, and tell you much about the town, as well.

WHERE TO STAY: Camden is not packed with places to stay, and that's part of its charm. Many people stay at the motels scattered along both sides of U.S. 1, north and south of town. Here, I'll mention the best inns and guesthouses right in town, within walking distance of everything.

Inns

For almost a century, the **Whitehall Inn,** P.O. Box 558, Camden, ME 04843 (tel. 207/236-3391), has been Camden's prime place to stay. The graceful old inn, on U.S. 1 just north of the center, is easily recognizable by its pillared porches. Shortly after arriving, you'll learn that Camden's most famous daughter, Edna St. Vincent Millay, gave a reading here when just a girl. The decor is refined in both the public rooms and guest rooms, and the mood in the dining room is semiformal (jackets for dinner). During high summer, your room comes with breakfast and dinner, and costs $107 to $150 double, service and tax included. The inn also operates two bed-and-breakfast houses nearby. This is old Camden at its best.

The **Camden Harbour Inn,** atop the hill at the far end of Bay View Street (no. 83), Camden, ME 04843 (tel. 207/236-4200), stays open all year round. A nice big old inn (1874) with white clapboards and, from some guest rooms and from the dining room, beautiful views of Penobscot Bay, the Camden Harbour could be a model for the typical coastal Maine inn. Recent restorations have beautified the inn considerably and added to its authentic Victorian charm. There are 22 guest rooms, 20 of them with water views, 5 with fireplaces, 8 with private patios. You can have cocktails or dinner on the nice Victorian verandah, which also enjoys that fabulous view. Prices range from $115 to $182 double for rooms with private bath, full breakfast included; prices are lower off season, particularly on weekdays.

The towers and chimneys of **Norumbega,** 61 High St., Camden, ME 04843 (tel. 207/236-4646), will catch your eye as you drive north along U.S. 1 from the center of town. This vast stone fantasy of a Victorian summer cottage has nine guest rooms, some of them have fine views of Penobscot Bay, and all have private bath. The double rate, full breakfast included, is $175 to $195 per night. Children over seven are welcome.

Bed-and-Breakfast

The **Blue Harbor House,** 67 Elm St., Camden, ME 04843 (tel. 207/236-3196), is a friendly bed-and-breakfast guesthouse just a few blocks' walk south of the center of town, on U.S. 1. Two of the restored guest rooms share baths and are priced from $70 to $80 double; four rooms have private bath and cost $86 to $102 double. Full breakfast is served on the sunporch (for an additional charge). In the separate carriage house (built 1806) are three efficiency apartments for $495 per week, $95 to $105 nightly. A fine place!

Goodspeed's Guest House, 60 Mountain St., Camden, ME 04843 (tel. 207/236-8077), is on Rte. 52, a half mile up the hill west of the center. The house has been beautifully redone and furnished with antiques by its owners, who provide a warm welcome and rooms with shared bath for $43 to $47 single and $65 to $75 double. A tiny deck, set with umbrella-shaded tables and chairs, allows you to enjoy the quiet of this location. The suite, $99, sleeps four.

The Maine Stay, 22 High St., Camden, ME 04843 (tel. 207/236-9636), is a big white house built in 1813 with very charming rooms, some of which share baths and cost $40 single, $65 double, breakfast included. Two pretty living rooms and a deck overlooking the backyard are for guests' use. The Maine Stay is north of the center on U.S. 1, about a ten-minute walk to the commercial district.

Of the new, restored inns in Camden, among the most pristine is the **Hawthorn Inn,** 9 High St., Camden, ME 04843 (tel. 207/236-8842), just a few minutes' walk north of the commercial district on U.S. 1. The big Victorian house with a view of Camden Harbor has been carefully and lovingly restored, and the large, airy rooms furnished with antiques. Rooms come with shared bath at $70, with private bath with a fine harbor view at $80, or stay in a town-house apartment at $210 or a town-house suite at $100 to $132. Rates include a full breakfast.

The **Owl and the Turtle** (tel. 207/236-4769) is, perhaps, the strangest name for a guesthouse, but it is explained when one realizes that the building that houses the Owl and the Turtle Bookshop at 8 Bay View St., Camden, ME 04843, also houses a few very nice motel-type rooms, each with a marvelous view of the inner harbor. Prices for the rooms—while they last—are $70 to $75 for two, continental breakfast included, in summer. Believe me when I say the Owl's rooms are nice: Maine-made furniture, color TV, and private bath; but there are so few of them you *must* reserve in advance by phone or mail.

A short distance north from the center on U.S. 1 brings you to the **Edgecombe-Coles House,** 64 High St., Camden, ME 04843 (tel. 207/236-2336), another of those huge turn-of-the-century summer cottages which retains its earlier glory. Period furnishings fill the rooms, and the plumbing (all private baths) has been brought up-to-date. Cheapest double room here has a double bed with a private bath and a view of the garden, for $80 in summer; most expensive has a king-size bed, fireplace, private bath, and ocean view, for $130. A full breakfast is included.

In recent years the number of bed-and-breakfast houses in Camden has grown dramatically. During the summer high season, many of them will hang out the "No Vacancy" sign. Here's an additional list of places to check. Double-room prices range from $70 to $98, depending mostly on type of bath (shared or private), or breakfast (continental or full), and on view (water views cost more).

Windward House is at 6 High St., Camden, ME 04843 (tel. 207/236-9656), on U.S. 1 just a few steps from the center of town. A full delicious breakfast is included.

The **Swan House,** 49 Mountain St., Camden, ME 04843 (tel. 207/236-

8275), is on Rte. 52 four blocks from the center. The fine Victorian house dates from 1870, has six guest rooms, and specializes in generous full breakfasts.

WHERE TO DINE: Restaurants tend to open and close in Camden. Here are some that have managed to please customers well, and prosper.

The Waterfront, Harborside Square off Bay View Street (tel. 236-3747), is true to its name. It caters to the yachting bunch and those who sit longingly gazing at the tall ships, and because of its beautiful location and dockside tables, does a booming business. The restaurant is open from 11:30 a.m. to 10 p.m. every day of the week, with the full luncheon menu served from opening to 2:30 p.m., a light menu from 2:30 to 5 p.m., and dinner thereafter. While the dinner menu does carry always at least one steak and one chicken selection, seafood ($13 to $20) is what you'll want to eat if you dine here. The seafood brochette (scallops, gulf shrimp, sole filet, peppers, and mushrooms are skewered and broiled) is a favorite.

Cappy's Chowder House, right in the center of Camden at the intersection of Main, Bayview, and Commercial Streets (tel. 236-2254), has two dining levels (the upstairs one with a water view and raw bar), has a rich nautical decor, and an eclectic menu. The seafood—clam, fish, and lobster chowders, plates, salads—is excellent and moderately priced at $10 to $14 for lunch, $18 to $24 for dinner; and there are burgers, cajun specials, stir-fries, and steaks. A bar provides a social center and quick-lunch place; tables and booths are for serious diners. Liquor is served, and you are likely to run into a few local yacht crews. Cappy's is open from 7:30 a.m. to midnight daily, so you can get breakfast here as well.

The **Round Top Ice Cream Parlor,** Harbor Square, has delicious ice cream made on its own farm, plus the least expensive light fare in town. Go around to the "Galley" in back for $2.25 hamburgers, $5 lobster rolls, and similar treats. Take your purchases to the picnic tables overlooking the harbor (exclusively for Round Top customers), and you'll have some of the best restaurant seating in Camden at the lowest price.

Less than half a mile south of Camden on U.S. 1 is the **Spinnaker Restaurant** (tel. 596-6804), a trim gray clapboard place much favored by the locals. Chowder, main course, dessert, coffee, wine, tax, and tip will come to $20 to $25 at dinner-time. Come for lunch or dinner any day from 11:30 a.m. to 9 p.m. (11:30 a.m. to 2 p.m. and 4:30 to 8 p.m. off season).

WHAT TO SEE AND DO: If you have a car, drive north from town along U.S. 1 and follow the signs to the entrance to **Camden Hills State Park** and the auto road to the top of Mount Battie. Besides the town itself, the drive up will afford you a view of the rocky hills, the countryside beyond, and of blue, sparkling Penobscot Bay.

Camden's **Windjammer fleet** of schooners provides the adventurous with a very different vacation: dipping in and out of the myriad of small harbors and inlets along the Maine coast. Cruises usually leave on Monday and last a week; they cost about $360 to $400 per person, and space must be reserved in advance. The thing to do is to write to the chamber of commerce (see above) for current lists of who's sailing, and what the cost will be.

Go southeast along Bay View Street a ways and you'll come to **Laite Memorial Park and Beach,** with picnic areas and rest rooms as well as a nice, chilly Maine beach.

For the rest of your time in Camden, latch onto a copy of the walking tour brochure (mentioned above) put out by the Camden Historical Society, and stroll through the town to get the flavor of it.

Vinalhaven Island

From Rockland Ferry Terminal (tel. 207/596-2202), you can take a car-ferry to Vinalhaven Island, in Penobscot Bay, for a taste of island vacation life, cooled by sea breezes. The *Governor Curtis* (State Ferry Service, P.O. Box 645, Rockland, ME 04841) makes the 1¼ hour run to Vinalhaven three times a day, and the return trip is the same number of times. On Sunday there are two sailings in each direction.

7. Castine and Blue Hill

These little villages, set apart on a peninsula in the Penobscot Bay, are gems. Turn right onto Rte. 175 at Orland, east of Bucksport, and continue on Rtes. 166 and 166A to Castine. With only a few places to stay and to dine, these towns draw a steady crowd of summer regulars who come for the beauty, the seclusion, the quiet, the easy summer life.

CASTINE: No small part of Castine's charm is in its history. In the winter of 1613, Sieur Claude de Turgis de la Tour founded a small trading post here among the Tarrantine Indians, but it was not to remain in French hands for long. The struggle for North America's forest, natural, and maritime wealth was already beginning, and the Fort Pentagoët founded by Turgis de la Tour would be conquered by the English in 1628. Treaty returned Pentagoët to France in 1635, and during the tumultuous period until 1676, the place changed hands many times. The British took it and called it Penobscot Fort; the French retook it and built the formidable Fort Saint Peter. At one time the village was the capital of all French Acadia (the lands in what is now Atlantic Canada). Even the Dutch coveted the fort, and ruled here from 1674 to 1676. In the latter year Baron de Saint Castin recaptured the town for France, and opened a trading station. Fortifications were strengthened, and despite raids by the British, the family of Baron de Saint Castin ruled over the town (now called Bagaduce) even after the baron himself returned to France, a wealthy man, in 1703. By 1760, however, the fate of French North America was sealed, and Castin's Fort, or Bagaduce, was to be held by the British after that year.

English settlers brought new life to Bagaduce during the 1760s, and the dissatisfaction that boiled in the English colonies at this period didn't leave the town untouched. Some of the townspeople were loyal to the king, others sympathized—actively and passively—with the American revolutionaries. But in 1779 a British naval force came from Nova Scotia, intent on making the town safe for British Loyalists (and thereby influencing the negotiations that would determine the fledgling United States' northern border). The British built Fort George to defend the town.

The challenge to American sovereignty was taken up by the General Court (legislature) of Massachusetts, which governed the territory at the time, and the ill-fated Penobscot Expedition was outfitted and launched at an ultimate cost of $8 million (in those days!). Bad luck and bad commanding resulted in the destruction of most of the American force, almost bankrupting the Commonwealth of Massachusetts. Fort George was enlarged and strengthened over the years, and the town thrived until the border between the U.S. and Canada was determined. Unhappily for residents of Bagaduce, the boundary was to be the St. Stephen River (the present boundary), and not the Penobscot. Those loyal to the British Crown put their houses on boats and *sailed* them to sites along the coast of what is today New Brunswick, at St. Andrews, mainly. Some of the houses moved thus still stand in St. Andrews.

In 1796 the name of Bagaduce was changed to Castine, and although it was occupied by British forces during the War of 1812, there was never again to be much military action. But in the 350 years of Castine's history its forts—Fort Pentagoët, Fort George, and the American Fort Madison—saw a surprising amount of attack and defense.

You can visit Fort George and the sites of the other forts in Castine, but first, get a place to stay the night.

Where to Stay and Eat

As I mentioned, Castine has only a few places to put up for the night. Have advance reservations to be sure of a bed.

The **Pentagoët Inn,** P.O. Box 4B, Castine, ME 04421 (tel. 207/326-8616), a beautiful old gabled-and-turretted pale-yellow house with dark-green trim, is right in the center of the village. Interior decoration harkens back to Castine's fascinating Revolutionary period, although the inn building dates from Victoria's time, 1894. The comforts are modern, though, and a double room, with full breakfast and five-course evening meal, tax and service included, costs between $179 and $228. Drinks are served on the porch daily in the summer. The evening meal offers several choices, usually including Maine lobster. This is a charming place, and I recommend it for those who want a quiet getaway to a beautiful town. The Pentagoët's innkeepers, by the way, are Lindsey and Virginia Miller.

A perfectly delightful reason to go to Castine is to stay at the **Castine Inn,** Main St., Box 41, Castine, ME 04421 (tel. 207/326-4365), an elegant old village house stuffed with antiques, fireplaces, and shades of a gracious past. The cheerful innkeepers, Mark and Margaret Hodesh, have 20 rooms and 2 two-room suites on three floors, all with private bath. Dinner is served from 5:30 to 8:30 p.m. every night except Tuesday, before or after which many guests enjoy the big Victorian porch or the lovely gardens. Rates are surprisingly reasonable at $76 to $91 double, and include a full breakfast.

What to Do

Visit the sites for the forts: **Fort Pentagoët,** near the Wilson Museum on Perkins Road; **Fort George,** near the entrance to town; and **Fort Madison.** Fort George is now a State Memorial, kept up by the Bureau of Parks and Recreation.

Historical signboards placed around the village outline Castine's fascinating history. For a closer look, visit the **Wilson Museum,** on Perkins Street, three blocks from Main Street to the southwest. Open daily except Monday, late May through September, from 2 to 5 p.m. (admission free), the museum holds prehistoric artifacts from the Americas, concentrating on the growth of man's ability to fashion tools. Other exhibits explain the rich local history. On Sunday and Wednesday afternoons in July and August, you can also visit the museum's authentic, working blacksmith shop, see Castine's century-old hearses, and take a guided tour (for a nominal fee) of the John Perkins House (1763, 1783).

BLUE HILL: From Castine, it's about 20 miles to Blue Hill, due east across the peninsula. A town of lofty, majestic elm trees, prim white clapboard homes and churches, Blue Hill attracts visitors because it has no outstanding "attractions." Peace, quiet, and an easy pace are its greatest draw.

Blue Hill was settled in 1762 by settlers from Andover, Mass. By 1792 it was turning Maine's forest wealth into ships, and sending these ships around the world. In 1816 granite quarries were opened, and stonecutting complemented shipping. From 1879 to 1881 there was also a copper mine.

Today, if you're not coming to Blue Hill on vacation, you're probably coming to enroll your child in the George Stevens Academy (1803), a preparatory school. Or perhaps you've arrived to attend a concert in Kneisel Hall of the summer chamber music series.

Where to Stay

The **Blue Hill Inn,** Union St., P.O. Box 403, Blue Hill, ME 04614 (tel. 207/374-2844) has served as the town's prime hostelry since about 1840, and is an even better place to stay and dine since innkeepers Mary and Don Hartley took over in

1988. The inn's 11 rooms all have private baths, and 6 rooms have working fire-places and furnishings authentic to the period. Dinner is served by candlelight each evening in summer, and on weekends and holidays off season. From mid-June through mid-October, rates are $172 double with breakfast and dinner or $136 double for room and breakfast, 15% service charge and 7% tax included. Off-season rates are about 25% lower.

Two miles from the center of the village on Rte. 15 (turn at the Exxon station), **Blue Hill Farm,** P.O. Box 437, Blue Hill, ME 04614 (tel. 207/374-5126), is an authentic Maine farm now run as a bed-and-breakfast place by Jim and Marcia Schatz. It's quiet here, with ducks cruising serenely on the pond, and you'll think you're visiting some comfortably established country cousins. Rooms in the converted farmhouse and barn have private or semiprivate bath (two rooms to a bath), and go for $53 to $62 single, $62 to $72 double, breakfast included.

Arcady Down East, South Street, Blue Hill, ME 04614 (tel. 207/374-5576), is one mile from the village, south along Rtes. 172 and 175. As you drive up, you'll see a fantastic shingled castle of a place, looking as though it really belongs in Bar Harbor. If a summer cottage could be called "baronial," it would be this one run by Tommie and Andy Duncan. Lots of public rooms, views of Cadillac Mountain in the distance, and a great variety of guest rooms, one with a fireplace, all with private bath. A double room can cost anywhere from $60 to $108, full breakfast buffet, tax, and 13% service included.

Where to Dine

Locals rave about the **Firepond Restaurant,** on Main Street right in the center of Blue Hill (tel. 374-2135). The cozy dining room fills up quickly in the evenings, especially on weekends, as diners order such things as roast duckling with almonds and chutney, or veal sweetbreads sautéed with apples and calvados in a rich brown sauce. Dinner (the only meal served from 5 to 9:30 p.m.) might cost $25 to $35 per person here, all in.

At **Jonathan's,** on Main Street (tel. 374-5226), the fare is moderately priced and varied, including everything from new American cuisine to Szechuan stir-fried beef to braised rabbit dijonnaise. Dinner here may set you back only $20 or so.

What to Do

Visit the **Holt House** (1815), home of the Blue Hill Historical Society, open in July and August Tuesday through Friday from 1 to 4 p.m. The stocky but dignified four-chimney home is little changed from its Federal days. Take a look also at the pretty stained-glass windows in the First Congregational Church.

Those chamber music concerts in Kneisel Hall, performed by students and faculty of the summer music school here, are given twice weekly in July and August, at 8 p.m.

DEER ISLE: You can continue southward, taking Rte. 15 to Deer Isle and Stonington, its southernmost town. Just after you cross the humpback bridge onto Deer Isle proper, you'll see a little chamber of commerce **information booth,** open in summer. Shortly after passing the booth, you'll enter the village of Deer Isle.

Deer Isle's best hostelry is the **Pilgrim's Inn,** in the village of Deer Isle, ME 04627 (tel. 207/348-6615). The inn, dating from 1793, is furnished with many antiques, Laura Ashley fabrics, and nice country touches. Eight of the rooms have private bath, and rent for $180 to $192 double; with shared bath, the rate is $156 to $167. These prices include breakfast, dinner, 12% service, and tax. Each evening, hors d'oeuvres are served in the common room, with its eight-foot-wide fireplace, and dinner follows in the dining room, a converted barn. Innkeepers Jean and Dud Hendrick will lend you a bicycle so you can explore on your own, or will give you advice about local excursions, including to Isle au Haut, and to the Haystack School of arts and crafts.

Note that no smoking is allowed in guest rooms or in the dining room, that a two-night stay is encouraged, and that in August a three-night minimum stay is required. Should you want to stay for a full week, you can take advantage of special rates. No credit cards are accepted. The inn is open from late May through mid-October.

Stonington is a fishing village, summer resort, and former granite-quarrying town. Beyond Stonington is **Isle au Haut,** part of Acadia National Park. A mail boat (tel. 207/367-2468) will take you over to the island in less than an hour, and you can hike along the park trails.

---

8. Bar Harbor

When a Yankee talks about a "Downeaster," he's talking about somebody from Maine, but when somebody from Maine talks about a Downeaster, he means somebody from the region of Bar Harbor or even farther east. Most of the rest of us think of the Maine coastline as running its ragged way north, but a quick look at the map will show that Bar Harbor is at about the same longitude as San Juan, Puerto Rico, and that indeed the Maine coastline heads more directly east than it does north at this point. These are the wilder shores of Maine and the settlements are fewer, the vegetation not so lush, and the climate a bit harsher than in other parts of the state, but at the same time the scenery is more dramatic, the air is charged with life, and a sense of wild nature surrounds one.

The French influence was for a long time paramount in these parts, and many Downeasters today speak French as a second language—the French of Québec, the French brought to these shores by the great Champlain. In fact it was Samuel de Champlain who gave Mount Desert Island its name, in the form of "L'Île des Monts-Déserts," and even today the local pronunciation is dez-*zert* (like what you have after dinner, not like what's in Arabia), following the French style.

When steamships and railroads were opening up in America in the 1800s, they also opened up Downeast Maine, and by the end of the century Bar Harbor, a small town on rocky Mount Desert Island, boasted almost as many palatial summer homes as Newport, although the ones here were perhaps not quite so lavish—but pretty close. In any case, only a small number of the original dozens of mansions are still standing, for a great number were wiped out in the Great Fire of 1947.

Today Bar Harbor is a nice town with a wonderful collection of nice little inns; also lots of motels, most (luckily for the town) lining the roads into town from Ellsworth. The big attractions in the area, for which so much housing must be provided, are the town itself, the cruise boats to Yarmouth, Nova Scotia, and of course Acadia National Park. The park takes up something like half of the land of Mount Desert Island and much of that on the smaller surrounding islands, and is one of the few national parks in the eastern United States. It draws tremendous numbers of visitors every year.

INFORMATION: Bar Harbor's livelihood has been tourism for 100 years now, and so the townspeople know how to treat a guest. The chamber of commerce maintains an **information booth** at the *Bluenose* Ferry Terminal on Rte. 3 (tel. 207/288-3393; in winter, call the business office on Cottage Street at 207/288-5103). They'll help you out with information and with any questions you may have.

WHERE TO STAY: While the area draws thousands of visitors each year, there are plenty of rooms to handle the crowds. The problem is to get the room you want rather than one you're forced to take. Reservations are advisable in all recommended places, and as these are some of the choicer spots, I'd recommend that you reserve early.

Inns

Prime among Bar Harbor's elite places to stay is the **Bar Harbor Inn** (tel. 207/ 288-3351 or toll free 800/248-3351), set amid its own lush grounds on a point overlooking Frenchman's Bay, Bar Harbor, ME 04609. Once a large old private club, it has been converted, expanded, and completely renovated to take in summer visitors (now open year round), and the feeling is that of a very plush country club or a posh resort in the glittering 1920s. One dresses informally for dinner in the semicircular dining room overlooking the bay; white pillars frame the front porch; attendants pad quietly here and there. The inn's large heated swimming pool is next to a little copse of trees and only a few yards from the waters of the Atlantic, and here, as everywhere else at the inn, the views are magnificent. The rooms are not all oldfashioned, however, and all have private bath, color TV, and lots of windows looking either onto the bay or the inn's lush grounds. The poolside rooms are cheaper, of course, at $80 for two from mid-July to mid-September; in the same period, a room with a bay view will cost $152, suites more. The atmosphere is formal but friendly.

In 1900 a retired Boston publisher named Lewis Roberts built himself a "cottage" in Bar Harbor. The sumptuous result of his efforts has gone through several hands since then, lately having been owned by a former dean of Harvard Medical School. Today, however, it is among Bar Harbor's most desirable places to stay. It's called **Thornhedge Inn,** 47 Mount Desert St., Bar Harbor, ME 04609 (tel. 207/ 288-5398), and the aim of its owners is to "recapture the spirit of Bar Harbor at the turn of the century." This they have done by arranging to purchase many of the house's original furnishings, and so today the large, sunny, gracious master bedroom on the second floor is done in the turn-of-the-century style that suits it; adjoining is the original bathroom, which is a good deal larger than the standard motel *room* today. All rooms have a private bath and cable TV, and many rooms have working fireplaces, in which fire laws allow artificial logs to be burned. You can tell that I like Thornhedge, and when you stay there, you'll know why. The season is May 1 through October 20. In high summer, rooms range from $65 to $125, single or double; off-season rates are lower. There is also one cottage available at a lower rate. Morning coffee, juice, fruit, and muffins are included in these rates. As you're driving or walking along Mount Desert Street, you can't miss Thornhedge, for it's painted a bright, cheery yellow.

The **Stratford House Inn,** 45 Mount Desert St., Bar Harbor, ME 04609 (tel. 207/288-5189), is everything you could imagine in the way of Tudor domestic architecture. Gabled and half-timbered, it looks like Queen Elizabeth I's own summer cottage. Though built by a publishing magnate, Stratford House was the summer home of musical greats Fritz Kreisler and Jan Paderewski. Eight of the ten rooms have private bath (and some have fireplaces), and go for $80 to $125 double; those sharing a bath cost $65 to $75.

The **Manor House Inn,** 106 West St., Bar Harbor, ME 04609 (tel. 207/288-3759), is another huge Victorian "cottage" in which period furnishings fill the guest rooms, each of which has its own bathroom. The Chauffeur's Cottage, two guest cottages, and five gardens also occupy the acre of grounds. The Manor House is right across the street from the prestigious Bar Harbor Club, and Manor House guests can use club facilities for swimming and tennis, plus the reading room, lounge, and grounds. What does it cost to stay in a charming house, now listed in the National Register of Historic Places? Prices are $85 to $118 for rooms, $80 to $150 for suites, tax included, from June through late September. The inn is open mid-April through mid-November and the price includes a buffet breakfast which you can eat in the lovely garden.

The **Ledgelawn Inn,** 66 Mount Desert St., Bar Harbor, ME 04609 (tel. 207/ 288-4596), is a palatial mansion fully converted now to a luxurious and elegant inn.

Having escaped destruction in the Great Fire of 1947, the "cottage" built for Boston shoe magnate John Brigham now lives on. The public rooms are positively grand in scale, the lawns and trees elaborate, the guest rooms elegant. Many have working fireplaces and private baths, sauna-and-whirlpool baths, and prices are $90 to $170 per night double, depending on size, bath, view, fireplace, etc. The Ledgelawn has a widow's walk on top, open for the view or the warm rays of the sun until 6 p.m. There's a swimming pool, a hot tub, and access to the clay tennis courts and Olympic-size pool at the Bar Harbor Club for inn guests. By the way, a continental breakfast is included in the price of your room here.

The **Hearthside Inn,** 7 High St., Bar Harbor, ME 04609 (tel. 207/288-4533), run by Susan and Barry Schwartz, is on a quiet street not far from the center of town. The living room of the inn has a fireplace and other touches of past Bar Harbor elegance (re-created here) abound. Afternoon tea and evening wine and cheese are served. Most rooms have private baths, some have fireplaces or balconies; all come with an expanded continental breakfast baked at the inn, and cost $60 to $95 double. To find High Street, stay on Rte. 3 as it becomes Mount Desert Street and take the third left (High Street), a one-way street just before the Episcopal church.

Mount Desert Street is truly a street of inns. Among them is the **Mira Monte Inn,** 69 Mount Desert St., Bar Harbor, ME 04609 (tel. 207/288-4263), a fine old Victorian house (1864) lovingly restored and maintained by Bar Harbor native Marian Burns. All rooms come with private bath, color TV set, and period furnishings. Each room has something different: a canopy bed, brass bed, fireplace, porch, or bay window. Rates, continental breakfast included, are $80 to $125, single or double. Guests can use sports facilities at the Bar Harbor Club for a small extra fee.

The **Holbrook House,** 74 Mount Desert St., Bar Harbor, ME 04609 (tel. 207/288-4970), was built in 1880, its 19 rooms providing enough space for even the most enormous Victorian family. Now the family in residence—hardly of Victorian size—is that of Dorothy and Mike Chester, who will welcome you and rent a room for $75 to $95 double in peak season, all with private bath. A full breakfast and afternoon refreshments are included.

The **Central House,** 60 Cottage St., Bar Harbor, ME 04609 (tel. 207/288-4242), has what few other local inns have: its own restaurant. The chef is the innkeeper, and offers rooms with shared bath for $59 double, with private bath for $65 to $80 double, continental breakfast included. Some rooms have working fireplaces. And, yes, the inn is yet another of those lovely, huge old summer cottages, two blocks from the center of town.

Farther from the center of town, 500 yards from the *Bluenose* dock, up on a cliff, is the Jackson Family's **Cleftstone Manor,** Rte. 3 (Eden Street), Bar Harbor, ME 04609 (tel. 207/288-4951). What was it like to spend the summer in a 30-room cottage? You can get a taste of it here for $85 with shared bath or $90 to $175 with private bath, double. Breakfast of home-baked breads and pastries is included in the fee, as is high tea, evening refreshments, and car service between the Cleftstone and Bar Harbor Airport. There's also a new no-smoking policy at the manor. This is one of Bar Harbor's finest.

Bass Cottage in the Field, "in the field" behind the two banks on Main St., Bar Harbor, ME 04609 (tel. 207/288-3705), is one of the most centrally located and inexpensive, authentic cottages in Bar Harbor. Operated and run by sisters in the Bass and Maddocks family since it was built in 1885, the inn has 10 rooms, most with private bath and some with an ocean view. Breakfast is not included in the rate of $48 to $89 double (there are two singles for $32), but for that price you can walk to one of the many restaurants a block away. Relax on the wicker-furnished, glass-enclosed porch.

Guesthouses

Not as fancy or as grand as the Victorian summer cottages, Bar Harbor's guesthouses provide decent accommodations at budget prices. Here is an example.

The **McKay Cottages,** 243 Main St., Bar Harbor, ME 04609 (tel. 207/288-3531), are a mere 1½ blocks from the park and the center of town life. Rooms in the two yellow lodging cottages cost $30 double with shared bath, $36 to $45 double with private bath. No breakfast is served, but it's available nearby.

Motels

The **Golden Anchor Inn,** out on Granite Point off West Street near the Municipal Wharf, P.O. Box 46, Bar Harbor, ME 04609 (tel. 207/288-5033, or toll free 800/242-1231), is a luxurious motel with many sea-view rooms, all with little balconies over the water. The decor is a modern adaptation of Early American, and the luxury extras include a pool, direct-dial phones, color TV (the motel even has its own closed-circuit station), and docking facilities for your boat. The motel is open year round, and the highest prices are charged in July and August, to Labor Day: $75 to $125. The Golden Anchor is easily within walking distance of everything downtown.

On the other side of town is the **Villager Motel,** 207 Main St. (Rte. 3 heading south out of town), Bar Harbor, ME 04609 (tel. 207/288-3211 or 288-3011). The Villager is a very neat two-story motel of moderate size (63 units) and the usual comforts: a heated outdoor pool, modern rooms with private bath and TV, and a convenient location which still leaves you within walking distance of the sights, shops, and restaurants in town. All of these advantages, plus the moderate rates, assure that the Villager is often full, so it's good to make reservations in advance. From July 1 through August 31 the rates are $73 to $87, single or double; from September 1 to October 31 the rooms cost $47 to $59, and in May and June they're $38 to $50.

The **Anchorage Motel,** 51 Mount Desert St., Bar Harbor, ME 04609 (tel. 207/288-3959), is a tidy two-story motel set back from Mount Desert Street, the street with all the inns. Standard motel comforts are yours here for $77 double in high season.

Facing the park right in town is the small **Acadia Motel-Hotel,** 20 Mount Desert St., Bar Harbor, ME 04609 (tel. 207/288-5721). Rooms here are in the budget class, tidy but simple. All rooms have private bath and TV; some have air conditioners and private entrances (the "motel" rooms), while others are entered through the hall ("hotel"). The price is great: $42 double. Two rooms have two double beds and go for $48 to $59.

Budget Accommodations

Individual women travelers can stay at the **Mount Desert Island YWCA,** 36 Mount Desert St., Bar Harbor, ME 04609 (tel. 207/288-5008). Rooms rent by the night and by the week, and include clean bed linens, use of the laundry room, and kitchen privileges; there are no private baths. Nightly rates are $19 single, $32 double. Weekly rates are $73.50 single and $128.50 double. (Weekly rates are available only if paid in full at the beginning of your stay.) Upon arrival you will be charged a membership fee of $10 (for stays of a week or more) and a $25 returnable security deposit. Rooms are hard to come by in the summer so write ahead for reservations. Open year round.

WHERE TO DINE: Bar Harbor is well provided with restaurants to satisfy all appetites, but rather than beginning with the most deluxe, let's start with the one that's the most traditional and also the most fun.

Lobster Pounds

As you drive toward Bar Harbor from Ellsworth, the road is lined with little shacks and stores bearing the magic word LOBSTERS. Outside each is a strange arrangement of backyard barbecues in a row, with large pots or drums on them and stovepipes (in some cases very rickety ones) shooting up. These contraptions are used to prepare a traditional lobster clambake. The drums or kettles are filled with lobsters, clams, corn on the cob, and seaweed, and then salt water is poured in, the fire is started, and the whole business is cooked up and served to the droves of motorists who have been dreaming of such a feast, perhaps for days and for hundreds of miles. Some places have tables where you can sit to consume your feast, at others you take the goodies home with you, but in any case this is the way to get the most seafood for your dollar, and the eating couldn't be better! This is the real Maine experience, and shouldn't be missed.

How does one pick the right place to stop? Every single one seems to have a signboard out front giving the price-per-pound of lobster, and you can go by this to some degree. But the price and poundage depend on how the lobster is stored: the best places will store the live lobsters on ice, and *not* in seawater, as the seawater can add a great deal of weight to the lobster as it's put on the scale. In any case, make sure the lobster is alive, not dead and limp.

Restaurants

The Reading Room at the **Bar Harbor Inn** (tel. 288-3351) is certainly one of Bar Harbor's choice places to dine. The plush semicircular room is filled with brocade chairs and white-clothed tables, all of which share in the view of the bay. Open for dinner from 5:30 to 9:30 p.m. daily. I'd start off here with either the New England clam chowder or the lobster parfait, and go on to a swordfish dijonnaise, or the scallops en papillote (with mushrooms, ginger, snow peas, and soy sauce). By the way, there's a separate, short children's menu, and another for the long list of desserts. Expect to pay $40 to $50 per person for dinner here. Besides the rich atmosphere and good service that comes with the meal here, dinner guests have the pleasure of an evening's stroll around the inn's grounds. The Bar Harbor Inn Terrace serves lunch from 11:30 a.m. to 5 p.m. The menu features clam chowder ($3), burgers and sandwiches ($5.50 to $7), and seafood dishes such as grilled shrimp and scallop kebab ($12).

Whether or not seafood is your choice, the best, and perhaps most quietly elegant, meal in town can be found just off Main St., behind the First National Bank at **George's,** 7 Stephen's Lane (tel. 288-4505). You can dine outdoors in the back garden or inside the softly lit restaurant to the sound of piano music. Start with a seafood crepe of scallops, lobster, and mussels ($6.50), or my favorite baked goat cheese in crispy phyllo ($4.25). Move on to seared lamb ($16) or duck breast sautéed in honey, rum, and mango ($16.50). Dessert is not for the faint hearted; save room for a rich wedge of chocolate pecan pie or Mississippi mud cake ($4). Dinner is served nightly from 5:30 to midnight. George's is open June through October.

Opera aficionados and lovers of fine food will be delighted by the **Opera House,** 27 Cottage St. (tel. 288-3509). The restaurant is unique in many ways. Although the restaurant is open only for dinner from 5:30 to 11 p.m., the "listening room" is open throughout the day and everyone is invited to wander through the gallery and listen to a portion of the 90-minute taped program of the day while paying homage to the opera greats whose pictures grace the walls. A placard at the entrance advises Dining for Adults and You Are Welcome Dressed as You Are. The à la carte menu includes rainbow trout ($14) and seafood fettuccine ($15). The seven-course fixed-price menu features roast duck in cognac or cajun blackened halibut for $22. If you've dined elsewhere, at least have dessert and a cordial or coffee; the rich creme brûlée ($4) is a wonderful way to end an evening. Reservations are recommended.

Very near the town pier is the **Quarterdeck Restaurant** (tel. 288-5292), at the corner of Main and West Streets. Here you can start with sautéed mushrooms and then go on to boiled or broiled Maine lobster or lobster Fra Diavolo (lobster stuffed with Maine scallops, in a spicey tomato and mushroom sauce), and the price will be about $18 to $25 per person. There are a good number of other, cheaper selections as well, such as various spaghetti plates and omelets. The Quarterdeck is modern in decor, and the lights are kept fairly low in the evening so diners can take advantage of the views from the restaurant's many windows. Both lunch and dinner are served; open till 10 p.m.

The **Brick Oven Restaurant,** 21 Cottage St. (tel. 288-3708), is almost as proud of its decor as it is of its cuisine. Downstairs, the lights are low, lots of stained glass shines, and a turn-of-the-century atmosphere prevails. Upstairs is a Victorian Dining Car room, done up with real fixtures for authenticity. Another room has a cathedral ceiling hung with all sorts of flotsam and jetsam, including an ancient "Whizzer" motorbike. My meal of Maine clam chowder, a plate of fettuccine with scallops and parsley sauce and a salad came to less than $23, drink, tax, and tip included. Liquor is served.

The **Island Chowder House,** 38 Cottage St. (tel. 288-4905), is a half block off Main Street right downtown. Have a table in the attractive, woody dining room and order the shore dinner of clam chowder, steamed clams, lobster, french fries, and cole slaw, and the bill will be a reasonable $15, tax and tip included. Fish and chips is a third of that price. Lunch and dinner are served. Open from 11 a.m. to "late at night" seven days a week, May through October.

Bar Harbor now has a Mexican restaurant, called **Miguel's,** 51 Rodick St. (tel. 288-5117), behind the firehouse and down the street. The quaint, attractive store-front eatery offers delicious quesadillas, burritos, tacos, chilis rellenos, even mole poblano and carne asada. For an appetizer, try the chimitas for $3.25. You can have dinner from 5 to 9 p.m., for about $12 to $20 per person. Huge frozen margaritas (and other liquor) served. On summer evenings you can dine on the patio.

Another exotic dining possibility awaits you at **The Wok,** 30 Rodick St. (tel. 288-4060). The delicious Thai menu is the same for lunch or dinner, although lunch prices are discounted 10% to 40%. I recently dined on a full meal of golden crispy squid ($4.75), hot and sour fish soup ($2.75), and finished with the famous Pad Thai noodle dish with shrimp, egg, and bean sprouts ($6.25). There are enough choices to please any taste. Lunch is served from 11 a.m. to 4 p.m. Monday through Saturday. Dinner is served 4 p.m. to 9:30 p.m. Monday through Thursday, to 10:30 p.m. Friday and Saturday, and to 9 p.m. Sunday. Takeout is available.

For Meeting People

Bubba's, at 30 Cottage St. (tel. 288-5871), is a favorite sandwich-and-drinks place for many of the more interesting people in Bar Harbor on vacation. Soups, salads, and sandwiches ($3 to $8) make up the bill of fare all day, but sipping and socializing are what it's all about. The big bar and the bentwood make it all upbeat and enjoyable.

For a Bit of Nightlife

At **Geddy's,** on Main Street near the corner of West Street (tel. 288-5077), every night in summer is witness to some sort of live performance. Jazz, dixieland, pop, and rock all issue forth from its sidewalk windows. Check the playbill out front and then walk in. There's no cover or minimum, and beer is $1 or $2 (Miller's, for example) or a bit more (for Heineken and the like). Happy hour, from 3 to 7 p.m., sees all drinks reduced to about half price.

WHAT TO DO: As I mentioned above, Bar Harbor has been a resort for many years and town officials, along with the chamber of commerce, throw themselves into organizing activities and making sure there's lots to do.

Special Events

Special events are scheduled throughout the summer, and you should drop down to the information bureau on the town pier for a list of the latest ones. The **Bar Harbor Festival,** with concerts and similar goings-on, is held in July and August, and during the summer months free **band concerts** take place each Monday and Thursday evening on the Village Green.

Bicycling

Should you want to rent a bike for trips around town or into the national park, check with **Bar Harbor Bicycle Rentals** at 141 Cottage St. (tel. 288-3886), corner of Eden Street, Rte. 3 (Cottage Street is parallel to West Street but one block south of it, away from the water). Rates are $9 for up to four hours, $14 for up to 24 hours, plus deposit.

Cruises

The **Frenchman's Bay Boating Company** (tel. 288-3322) organizes sightseeing and fishing trips out into Frenchman's Bay, and you can take your choice of either one-hour trips for $7.50 (kids 5 to 12, $5), or two-hour trips ($9 for adults, $6 for kids 5 to 12). A half-day's fishing costs $19 to $25 (depending on the season), including rod, reel, and bait. Cruises are offered from mid-May to October, and all trips leave from the boat company's pier right next to the municipal (town) pier, from late May through mid-October.

You can also sail aboard Maine's only three-masted schooner the *Natalie Todd* or the smaller, but equally impressive two-masted *Janet May*. Both offer two-hour sails from the Bar Harbor Inn Pier for $16 per adult, $10 for children under 12. The *Natalie Todd* sails three times a day at 10 a.m., 2 p.m., and 6 p.m., and the *Janet May* sails twice a day at 11:30 a.m. and 3:30 p.m. Tickets are available at the pier or at the *Natalie Todd* Ticket Office at 27 Main St. (tel. 288-4585). For information in the off-season call 207/546-2927 or write Capt. Steven F. Pagels, P.O. Box 8, Cherry-field, ME 04622.

A Harbor-View Walk

If you're willing to walk for 30 to 45 minutes, you can enjoy one of Bar Harbor's nicest little hikes. Follow Main Street (Rte. 3) south out of town, past the park on the right, and about a mile down the road (15 to 25 minutes' walk) is a pull-off spot for cars (capacity: four vehicles). If you reach the Ocean Drive Motor Inn, you've come too far. Walk down the dirt road, closed by a chain, near the little metal sign marking the boundary of U.S. government land, posted on a tree. It's less than a ten-minute walk to Rocky Harbor along the dirt road through the fragrant forests. When you come to a fork, bear left with the road (a path goes off straight). When you reach the viewing-point, you'll find a grassy clearing furnished with litter barrels for picnickers (no tables). If you've brought a picnic, you can share it with the gulls and ducks. It's secluded, beautiful, quiet, and in walking distance from town—a fine place.

A Visit to Acadia National Park

The rugged terrain of Mount Desert Island has attracted lovers of natural beauty for over a century, and soon after summer visitors began to arrive here in numbers, preservation efforts were begun. By the end of World War II, Acadia National Park was well along to its present size of over 30,000 acres, or something like half the land on the island (the other half is still in private hands). Focal point of park activities is **Cadillac Mountain,** at 1,530 feet the highest point on America's Atlantic coast. The thing to do with Cadillac Mountain is to hike (or drive) to the top of it for the views. In fact local people have recognized that those who see the sun break forth on the horizon from Cadillac Mountain are the first people in the United States to greet the new day, and so there's a "Sunrise from Mount Cadillac Club." You can join by picking up a blank from the Bar Harbor Information Bureau, and filling it out with the help of your hotel manager the night *before* you plan to see the sunrise. Then, if you follow through, you get to be a member of this exclusive club.

Besides Cadillac Mountain, the first thing to do in the park is drive the Loop Road, a one-way scenic ocean drive which takes you past many of the most interesting scenic, topographic, and geologic features of the island. Admission to the park is

$5 per car; this pass is good for seven days. Stop at **Thunder Hole** when the surf's up to feel the bashing and pushing of the waves, or at **Sand Beach** for a chilly ocean swim. There's national park camping at **Black Woods** (follow the signs). This is the only campground where you can reserve ahead; call your local Ticketron outlet as early as the spring for reservations.

On the island's western peninsula, **Echo Lake** is the park's freshwater swimming area; there's a lookout tower atop **Beech Mountain**, and a park campground is down near the peninsula's southern tip at **Seawall**. And throughout the park are 100 miles of hiking trails (maps sold at park headquarters), and lots of "carriage roads" good for bike trips or horseback riding (horses can be rented in the park).

Not far from the town of Bar Harbor, in the park at Sieur des Monts Spring, is the **Abbe Museum of Stone Age Antiquities,** a wildflower garden, and a nature center. There's no admission charge to the park proper, but there are fees for various activities such as the campgrounds.

The beach at **Seal Harbor** is very fine, and open to the public for free. Park in the lot across the street. Seal Harbor, by the way, is one of Mount Desert Island's poshest summer resorts, with all sorts of famous and wealthy people inhabiting the big houses secluded along the forested streets of the village.

A visit to Acadia National Park wouldn't be complete without tea and popovers ($5) at the **Jordan House** (tel. 276-3116). A tradition for almost 100 years, the restaurant serves lunch on the porch from 11:30 a.m. to 2:30 p.m., afternoon tea on the lawn from 2:30 to 5:30 p.m., and dinner by the fireside from 5:30 to 9 p.m. You can get snacks and beverages on the overlook throughout the day from 9 a.m. to 6 p.m. Whether you dine or not you are invited to stroll around the gardens and spacious grounds; the view of the lake and mountains from the lawn is stunning. Open late May to late October.

Tours

National Park Tours (tel. 207/288-3327) runs two tours daily from Bar Harbor, beginning from Testa's Hotel, 53 Main St. The cost is $10 per adult, $5 per child under 12. The tour takes you through the town of Bar Harbor and stops at many of the mansions left from its heyday, and also past Cadillac Mountain, Sieur des Monts Spring, and Thunder Hole. Traditionally the tours have left at 10 a.m. and 2 p.m., but call in advance to check the times, and to make a reservation.

If you have a car, you can rent a cassette tape recorder with a prerecorded tour narration from **Sightseeing Tapes, Inc.** You pay the $10 rental fee for the tape and player ($7 if you only rent the tape), and start out to follow the description of many interesting points in the national park. The advantage here is that this tour is cheaper overall if you have several people in your car, and you can turn off the tape at any time should you want to spend a while at some point. Tapes and machines are for rent at the National Park Visitor Center (tel. 288-5262) at Hulls Cove, the first park entrance you come to when approaching Bar Harbor from the north on Rte. 3.

A Ferry to Nova Scotia

The Marine Atlantic ship M/V *Bluenose* sails from Bar Harbor to Yarmouth, Nova Scotia, and back again daily in summer between late June and late September. It's a car-ferry with room for 1,000 passengers and 250 cars, a sundeck, buffet, dining room, cafeteria, bar, casino, and duty-free shop. The *Bluenose* leaves Bar Harbor every morning in summer and returns from Yarmouth in late afternoon, arriving back in Bar Harbor at night. The trip takes about six hours each way, and costs $34 per adult, $17 per child 5 to 13 years; cars cost $63; trailers and campers cost $126 up to 30 feet long, with a summertime minimum charge of the normal car's fare. You can rent a day-use cabin for an extra $31. Off-season schedules are such that the ferry leaves Bar Harbor one day and returns the next; fares are about 25% lower. The vehicle fees do not include the driver's ticket, so a car-and-driver crossing in summer would pay almost $100. Note that *you must make reservations in advance*. Write to the Marine Atlantic Reservations Bureau, P.O. Box 250, North Sydney, NS B2A 3M3, Canada; or call these toll-free numbers: in Maine, 800/432-7344; in the continental U.S., 800/341-7981. The number in Bar Harbor is 207/288-3395. In Yarmouth call 902/742-3513.

ON TO CANADA: The coastal highway, U.S. 1, winds east and north from Ellsworth. You might want to wander south along Rte. 186 for views of the scenic **Schoodic Peninsula.** If not, head ever northeastward, toward the Canadian frontier.

When you get to Cobscook Bay, you will have reached the easternmost limits of the United States. Cobscook Bay can boast two state parks, **Cobscook Bay State Park** and **Quoddy Head State Park.** Another park is even more interesting, however.

Roosevelt Campobello International Park

A Canadian island with an Italian-sounding name on which an American president spent his summers? These little mysteries are not at all as difficult to solve as one might suppose. Campobello Island is officially part of Canada, even though the major access road comes from Lubec, Maine. And the "Italian" name is nothing more than the name of a former Nova Scotian governor, William Campbell, with two "o's" added for exotic flavor. When the island was granted to Capt. William Owen by Governor Campbell in 1767, it was still part of the Canadian province of Nova Scotia. (The province of New Brunswick was not formed until 1784, when large numbers of United Empire Loyalists fled New England to live in King George III's still-loyal dominions to the north.)

Franklin Delano Roosevelt's father, James, bought some land on the island in 1883, at a time when lots of important city people were building vast "summer cottages" at Bar Harbor, Passamaquoddy Bay, and other northern coastal locations. Young Franklin—to solve that last little mystery—came here long before he was president of the United States, and spent many a teenaged summer rowing, paddling, and sailing on the waters, and hiking through the woods.

In 1920 FDR ran for the vice-presidency—and lost. Taking on a banking job instead, he looked forward to a relaxing summer at Campobello in 1921. On August 10 of that year the first signs of illness showed, and two weeks later the doctors diagnosed the crippling disease as polio. When he left the island in September, he had no way of knowing that the few more times he would see the summer cottage and his Campobello friends would be brief weekend visits—as president of the United States.

The day-to-day lives of the great and powerful are fascinating to explore in detail, and a visit to the Roosevelt house on Campobello Island gives one a peek at the early years of this incredibly courageous man who went on to become governor of New York and president of the United States after having been crippled by polio. It is no less intriguing to see how a well-to-do family spent its summers at the turn of the century, with long and leisurely days filled by sports, games, and family fun. Servants saw to the chores, and even they must have enjoyed getting away from the city to such a beautiful spot.

The Roosevelt Cottage is now part of Roosevelt Campobello International Park, a joint American-Canadian effort open the Saturday prior to Memorial Day until Columbus Day from 9 a.m. to 5 p.m. Guides at the reception center will point out the path to the Roosevelt Cottage, show you movies about the island, and map out the various walks and drives in the 2,600-acre nature preserve.

Calais–St. Stephen

Residents of Maine and New Brunswick, while the best of friends, cling to memories of their ancestors' fervent support for, respectively, George Washington and George III. With the success of the American Revolution, United Empire Loyalists flocked across the frontier into Canada so as not to be disloyal to the monarch. The "Loyalist" and "Revolutionary" towns preserve this good-natured rivalry.

But things are different in Calais, Me. (pronounced like "callous"), and its sister city, St. Stephen, N.B. Folks in these two towns, cheek-by-jowl on the St. Croix River, make a point of telling visitors how they ignored the affinities of *both* sides during the War of 1812, and St. Stephen even supplied powder-poor Calais with gunpowder for its Fourth of July celebrations! In fact by the time the war came families in the twin towns were so closely intermarried that no one wanted to take the time to sort out who should be loyal to whom.

These days residents celebrate this unique plague-on-both-their-houses philosophy with an International Festival in the first week of August. The two bridges over the river between the towns are thronged with merrymakers moving back and forth —through the watchful but benevolent eye of Customs, of course—and Canadian and American flags fly everywhere.

Despite its interesting history, there's little to detain you in Calais, and soon you'll be heading onward, into Canada (see *Frommer's Canada*), or back down U.S. 1 to points south and west. When you return home, however, you'll know what the maritime forecasters mean when they predict weather for the coastline "from Eastport (on Cobscook Bay) to Block Island (Rhode Island)." And you'll be able to say that you've been at the easternmost point in the United States.

VERMONT

The Green Mountain State is one of the nation's most rural, with lots of trees and very few people—only about half a million (people, not trees) in the whole state. But the greenery is Vermont's glory, and green has even become the color of the state's auto license plates. To protect the sylvan beauty of their state, and to keep the roads from becoming cluttered with "off-site advertising," the state government has devised a plan whereby participating stores, restaurants, lodging places, and attractions put information on their establishments in a little book called the *Vermont Visitors' Handbook,* yours for free by writing to the Vermont Development Agency, Montpelier, VT 05602. The establishments in the handbook have numbers, and an attractive green sign out on the highway nearby will direct you to the store, restaurant, or motel, and will also bear its number.

Skiing is another of Vermont's glories, and resorts in this state are usually more winter than summer oriented. Heavy precipitation gives many ski areas a good, long season, and the mountain scenery and imported "alpine" architecture help get one into the spirit of winter fun. No Vermont lodge would think of opening without its fireplace stocked with logs to give the glow to an après-ski cocktail and conversation.

Although winter is its prime season, Vermont is very much open in summer. Room rates are lower, many ski resorts run their chair and gondola lifts for sightseers, and the state parks do a booming business with campers, hikers, and picnickers. And, winter or summer, most places in Vermont have the distinct advantage of being quite accessible, whether you plan to come by car, bus, train, or air.

The tax on rooms and meals is 6%, and the telephone area code for the entire state is 802.

INFORMATION: Vermont rates tourism as its second most important industry, and it's therefore out to tell you what you want to know. In New York City, ask them at the **New England Vacation Center,** 630 Fifth Ave., between 50th and 51st Streets, Rockefeller Center Concourse Shop No. 2 (tel. 212/307-5780). State information booths are maintained on the major access roads to the state; stop at one for a map and for the *Vermont Visitors' Handbook* mentioned above.

GETTING THERE: For being so rural, resorts and towns in Vermont are surprisingly accessible.

By Car

The fastest way to get anywhere by car is to take the Interstates: I-91 from New York City and Connecticut, I-93 to I-89 from Boston and Canada, 10 to 133 to I-89 if you're driving from Montréal. But the heart of Vermont is on and off Vermont's Rte. 100 which winds through the center of the state from north to south, linking most of the resort areas. By the way, Vermont has a law which prohibits skis from sticking out beyond the normal width of the car. Roads are very well maintained in Vermont in winter, but remember that the roads into the mountains are gradients, so it's best to have snowtires. Dry gas, to prevent your fuel lines from freezing, isn't a bad idea either.

By Air

Vermont's largest city, Burlington, is served by several major air carriers and their regional commuter subsidiaries such as Business Express (Delta Connection), Metro Airlines (Trans World Express), and Bar Harbor Airlines (Continental Express). In addition, USAir, United Airlines, and Continental Airlines have direct flights to Burlington in large aircraft. Direct flights go to Burlington from Atlanta, Boston, Buffalo, Chicago, Cleveland, New York City, Orlando, Philadelphia, Pittsburgh, and Washington, D.C.

By Rail

Two Amtrak trains serve Vermont, both running between New York City and Montréal. The *Montrealer* runs daily between Washington, D.C., via New York City to Montréal, stopping in Brattleboro (for Mount Snow), Bellows Falls, White River Junction (for Woodstock and Killington), Montpelier, Waterbury (for Stowe), Essex Junction (for Burlington), and St. Albans. Unfortunately, the *Montrealer* is the New York–Montréal night train.

The *Adirondack* runs daily between New York City and Montréal, skirting Vermont as it runs up the Hudson. Stops at Whitehall (for Rutland), Port Henry, and Port Kent (for Burlington) are the most convenient for reaching points in Vermont, although there are lots of other stops. The *Adirondack* is a day train.

By Bus

Luckily for visitors, Vermont has its own large bus line, **Vermont Transit Lines** (tel. 212/594-2000), which operates from New York (in conjunction with Greyhound/Trailways), Montréal (in conjunction with Voyageur), and Boston to virtually all points of interest in Vermont. Other services run from Portsmouth, N.H., Portland, ME., and Concord, N.H., to points in Vermont.

1. Brattleboro

The first town you are likely to encounter if you come from New York or Boston is Brattleboro, and in a way this is as it should be, for Brattleboro was the site of Vermont's first colonial settlement. In 1724 a small fortress was built at the spot now marked by a granite commemoration stone, and named Fort Dummer. There had been white settlers in the area before that, but the fort became the focal point of a community as well as its principal defense against the Indians.

Today Brattleboro is one of the state's larger towns, with a population around 13,000, and industries that range from printing and book manufacture to furniture making and the manufacture of optical products. As for famous sons, the great Mormon leader Brigham Young was born (1801) nearby in Windham County, and Rudyard Kipling married a Brattleboro girl in 1892, and they lived near the town for some time.

Brattleboro has some attractive residential sections and a decent collection of lodging places and dining places. The largest collection of motels is on U.S. 5 north of Brattleboro on the way to Putney (Exit 3N from I-95); another collection of places to stay and to dine is on Rte. 9 west of Brattleboro (I-95 Exit 2).

If you have an hour to spend in town before you rush off to the music festival at Marlboro, or the hiking and skiing at surrounding resorts, check out the **Brattleboro Museum & Art Center,** in the town's old Union Station down near the intersection of Rtes. 119, 142, and U.S. 5, only a few steps from the center of town. It's open Tuesday through Friday from noon to 4, on Saturday and Sunday from 1 to 4 p.m. Donations are accepted.

INFORMATION: The chamber of commerce **information office** is at 180 Main St., right in the center of town (tel. 802/254-4565), open during business hours.

WHERE TO STAY: Here's a look at the motels that line U.S. 5 (Putney Road) north of Brattleboro.

The best motel buy in town is, as always, the **Susse Chalet Motor Lodge,** near the Holiday Inn and the Lamplighter, Brattleboro, VT 05301 (tel. 802/254-6007, or toll free 800/258-1980). At the Susse Chalet you get a modern, air-conditioned motel room with shiny private bath, TV, and comfortable modern furnishings for the low prices of $33.70 for one, $37.70 for two, $40.70 for three, or $43.70 for four in a room. Prices stay the same year round. The motel even has a small outdoor pool.

WHERE TO DINE: Brattleboro's restaurants are found out in the countryside as well as downtown.

Common Ground (tel. 257-0855) is downtown Brattleboro's oldest natural-foods restaurant. The location also serves as a popular coffeehouse (live music on weekends) and gallery for local artists. It's at 25 Elliot St. (upstairs), and its second-floor location allows it to utilize a glassed-in patio terrace where diners may sit throughout the year. The menu is interesting and international, with Wednesday night set aside entirely for dishes from Italy, China, Mexico, the Middle East, India, the Caribbean, Japan, and the U.S.A., to name but a few. The prices are certainly reasonable (about $8 for lunch and $16 for dinner), the food delicious, and the staff friendly. Common Ground is open every day except Tuesday till 9 p.m.

Near Common Ground is Brattleboro's Italian restaurant, the **Via Condotti,** 69 Elliot St. (tel. 257-0094), just a block off Main in the center of town. Stucco walls give the place an old-country air, and copper kitchen utensils hung here and there add to the effect. The menu goes from grinders (the large sandwiches at $4.50) to calamari alla marinara (squid). Pasta dishes start at $5.95; baked manicotti is $5.75; the price range ascends slowly to a high of $10 for the veal parmigiana. In the restaurant's La Grotta lounge, wine is sold by the glass, half liter, or liter, beer by the mug or the pitcher, and all sorts of cocktails are available. The Via Condotti is open seven days a week, Monday through Saturday for lunch and dinner, on Sunday for dinner from 2 p.m.; the lounge is open from 4 p.m. to 1 a.m. daily, with food service until 10 p.m. on weekdays, to 11 p.m. on weekends.

Although Brattleboro is a nice city, it's the surrounding villages and resorts that draw the crowds. One of the most popular of these is Marlboro, home of the famous annual Marlboro Music Festival.

2. Marlboro and Wilmington

West of Brattleboro are some of Vermont's—and all New England's—loveliest unspoiled villages, worthy of a few days' stay, or at least a meal or a rest stop. Marlboro and Wilmington are on Rte. 9, west of Brattleboro, in the direction of Bennington.

MARLBORO: The town's name brings to mind immediately the summertime **Marlboro Music Festival,** directed by Rudolf Serkin for many years. The festival brings together dozens of the most talented musicians in the country, some famous and some soon to be famous, for two months' practice, consultation, and tutorial. On weekends from mid-July to mid-August the school is opened to concert audiences, most of whom have ordered their tickets weeks or months in advance and have also made early lodging reservations. The auditorium at Marlboro College seats fewer than 700 people, and to keep the spirit of the chamber music, demands for a larger hall are resisted by the directors and performers. If you're interested in attending weekend festival concerts, write early to: Marlboro College, Marlboro, VT 05344 (tel. 802/254-2394); this is the address to use from late June through mid-August. From September through mid-June, write to the Marlboro School of Music, 135 S. 18th St., Suite 101A, Philadelphia, PA 19103 (tel. 215/569-4690). Or you can phone the box office at tel. 802/254-2394, and ask for schedules, prices, and purchase forms. Then, when you've got your tickets, make a reservation either in Marlboro, or nearby Brattleboro, or even in Bennington—that city is only a 45-minute drive away through the forests of southern Vermont.

Where to Stay and Eat

Marlboro is a location more than a town, although when you drive to the dot on the map you will find a church, a small town office building, and several houses. But that's about all, and so for many products and services you must drive to Brattleboro. Several inns and restaurants in the area, however, provide well for year-round travelers as well as festival visitors.

The only lodging house right in Marlboro proper is the fine old **Whetstone Inn,** Marlboro, VT 05344 (tel. 802/254-2500). The Whetstone Inn has been an inn for close to two centuries: the upstairs was once a "ballroom" where the local gentry could stage their get-togethers; the downstairs was a tavern along the stage-coach route between Boston and Albany. In winter, cross-country ski trails start at the inn's back door. The inn's pond (the reservoir in case of fire) is right out back. As there's no great activity in the town, nothing will disturb you unless you take to your feet or your bicycle to go to the music festival, two miles away. Many rooms at the Whetstone Inn have private bathrooms; rates are $30 to $55 single, $55 to $75 double, the higher rates for rooms with a private bath or a kitchenette. During the Marlboro Music Festival a three-night weekend stay is required. Meals are not included, but you can get breakfast each morning (waffles, pancakes, popovers, and home-baked muffins and biscuits), dinners on concert nights during the summer and on weekends and certain weekdays at other times in the year.

Only a short drive from Marlboro College and the music festival is the **Longwood Inn,** P.O. Box 86, Marlboro, VT 05344 (tel. 802/257-1545), on Rte. 9, a fine old Vermont clapboard dwelling over two centuries old. Innkeepers Andrea and Douglas Sauer took over the inn a few years ago, and maintained a good reputation for warm hospitality and excellent cuisine. The inn's 15 rooms (all but two of them with private bath) are pretty and country-comfortable. It is the dining room, however, that is the center of inn life. The cuisine is up-to-date American Regional; the menu changes weekly. During the summer season when the music festival is running, and also during foliage season (till Columbus Day), the inn serves all three meals every day. At other times of the year, breakfast is provided for inn guests, and dinner is served to all Thursday through Sunday. Rates for the guest rooms are $113 to $165 double in high season, breakfast included. If you want breakfast and dinner (which may at times be required), rates are $155 to $214 double.

The **Skyline Restaurant** (tel. 464-5535) is just across Rte. 9 from a hilltop lookout. The restaurant is open daily in summer from 8 a.m. to 8 p.m.; winter hours are 8 a.m. to 3 p.m. on Monday and Tuesday, to 8 p.m. Wednesday through Sunday. Thus you can start the day here with a breakfast of griddle cakes and maple syrup for about $6. Luncheon special plates cost $6 to $10; entrees à la carte cost about $8 to $15. For dinner, pan-fried trout with almond butter is a good choice, or have baked stuffed sole, or fresh-cut filet mignon with sautéed mushrooms. The emphasis at the Skyline is obviously not on the expensive or exotic, but rather on traditional dishes made with care and with the best local ingredients. Rough wood furniture and accents make the decor, and fresh flowers cheer up every table in season. During the cold weather, the cheer is provided by a fireplace, and as always, by the friendliness of the staff and management.

Hogback Skiing

The Hogback area (tel. 802/464-5494) is small but pleasant, with four T-bars taking skiers to the top of a 500-foot vertical drop. It's a favorite with local people and with families, and has a cafeteria, equipment-rental shop, and plans for ski touring.

WILMINGTON: Almost equidistant between Brattleboro and Bennington is Wilmington, a crossroads town where Rte. 9 meets Rte. 100. Many people pass through Wilmington as they begin their journey northward along Vermont's central scenic artery, Rte. 100. There are many good inns here, partly because it's a crossroads and partly because it is close to the ski slopes of Mount Snow.

Where to Stay

What's in a name? Well, there's surely some reason why Jim McGovern named his place the **Hermitage Inn,** P.O. Box 457, Wilmington, VT 05363 (tel. 802/464-3511), on Coldbrook Road; follow Rte. 100 north for about 2½ miles, turn left onto Coldbrook Road, and the inn is about 3 miles along. When you see the inn, you'll understand: Jim raises his own game birds, makes his own maple syrup and jam, and has a vast and well-selected wine cellar. If he ever wanted to be a hermit, he'd be set for life. You can become a hermit in this plentiful hideaway, which was once the home of the editor of the *Social Register.* The main house is over a century old, has some of the original furnishings and many others from the same period, and

11 of the 15 guest rooms have working fireplaces; all have private bath. As you might expect from the bounty described above, the dining here is superb and exceptional, with lots of game fowl, trout, and fresh home-grown vegetables, plus wines from that venerable cellar which has been abuilding for almost three decades. The inn's other attractions include fine views of Haystack Mountain, lots of ski trails, a tennis court, trout pond, and a shop full of the local crafts and preserves. It's a real country experience, not a citified country inn. Rates are $220 to $244 double, breakfast and dinner included; lunch is sometimes served during the busy summer season, at an extra charge.

The **White House of Wilmington,** Rte. 9, Wilmington, VT 05363 (tel. 802/464-2136), could well be this area's most elegant and gracious inn. Housed in an imposing turn-of-the-century (1914) mansion with lofty porticoes and high-ceilinged public rooms with elegant furniture, it has a dozen charming, spacious guest rooms with private bath; five of them have fireplaces. The White House is a complete resort, really, with a 60-foot outdoor swimming pool, an indoor pool, sauna and health spa, whirlpool baths, a lovely rose garden complete with fountain, and lots of hiking and cross-country ski trails. The dining room is very well regarded, and serves breakfast and dinner daily. On Sunday, there's brunch, and in winter, a special skiers' lunch. Rooms are rented with breakfast and dinner included in the price, at $207 to $256 double.

And now for a special place. **Trail's End Lodge** (tel. 802/464-2727) is about five miles from Mount Snow, four miles north of Wilmington, VT 05363, off Rte. 100 on a side road (watch for small signs). Despite its woodland location, Trail's End is no backwoods establishment, for it has a swimming pool, tennis court, and trout pond, and a dining room in which remarkably delicious meals are the rule. The rates both summer and winter are usually based on room and two meals; $80 double for a small room with double bed and shower; a larger room with a queen-size bed costs $104 to $139 double. Service charge of 15% and a tax of 6% are included in these prices. Trail's End is certainly one of Mount Snow's most attractive, architecturally interesting, congenial places to stay.

Where to Dine

You can get good value at the **Roadhouse,** on Rte. 100 at Old Ark Road in Wilmington (tel. 464-5017 or 464-5694). For a full dinner of standard favorites, dessert and home-baked bread included, expect to pay only about $20 to $25. This is not a fancy place, just solid country-casual eating and full bar at a reasonable price. Open daily from 5 to 10 p.m.

---

3. Bennington

"Vermont's most historic area" is how the citizens of Bennington tout their town. The reason for this civic pride is that the Revolutionary War's Battle of Bennington was fought near here (the actual site is now in neighboring Walloomsac, N.Y.) in 1777. The battle is looked upon as a turning point in the war, since the British troops expected to encounter little resistance at Bennington and instead were forced to retreat after having lost a good number of casualties and prisoners to the Revolutionaries. Soon afterward, at the Battle of Saratoga, the British soldiers thus weakened were forced to surrender, giving the Americans their first great victory of the war.

Although the Battle of Bennington was certainly influential in the winning of the war, it is doubtless remembered so well today because of a 300-foot-high obelisk that was built in 1891 to commemorate it. Both the monument (which has an observation platform) and the well-known Bennington Museum's collection of Americana are open to visitors.

INFORMATION: The **Bennington Area Chamber of Commerce** is at Veteran's Memorial Drive (Rte. 7 North; tel. 802/447-3311 or 442-1162), about a mile from the intersection of Main and North/South Streets. Open during business hours, the chamber can give you a good, detailed map of the town and lots of information on both the town and the surrounding region.

WHERE TO STAY: Bennington has dozens of motels on the highways that approach it, but as is my custom I will concentrate most heavily on the establishments right in town. Several are within only a few blocks of the monument, the museum, and Old Bennington.

Motels

Try the **Best Western New Englander Motor Inn,** 220 Northside Dr. (Rte. Business 7A between Bennington and North Bennington), Bennington, VT 05201 (tel. 802/442-6311, or toll free 800/528-1234). The New Englander is a fairly large motel of over 50 rooms arranged around a central court with a swimming pool and the motel's restaurant, which helps block noise from the busy street. As this is Bennington, the rooms have been done with Early American inspiration, although all furnishings are modern. In the clutter and strip development of Northside Drive, the New Englander is a very pleasant oasis, complete unto itself, and rooms are moderately priced at $55 to $76 for a double-bedded room for two, $60 for a similar room equipped with a steambath, $46 to $69 for a room with one double and one twin bed (a slightly smaller room), and $5 for an extra person. Note that the New Englander's rooms have cable color TV, coffee makers, and air conditioning. It's a comfortable, pleasant place.

The **Kirkside Motor Lodge** is just that: right beside the handsome Gothic church, at 250 W. Main St., Bennington, VT 05201 (tel. 802/447-7596). Rates are $47 for a double bed, $55 for a queen-size bed, $60 for a king-size bed, all rooms for two people. Off-season, prices will be about one-third less, but during foliage season they're a few dollars higher. The rooms come with cable color TV and the usual motel comforts, only here they're shiny and new. There's little problem with street noise because of the motel's position and location. If you stay here, you'll be about equidistant from the center of town and the museum and monument.

The **Bennington Motor Inn** has the same location as the nearby expensive Paradise Motor Inn, but at much reduced prices. At 143 W. Main St., Bennington, VT 05201 (tel. 802/442-5479 or toll free 800/359-9900), the Bennington is smack up against the Paradise, its 16 little units right at the base of the hill holding the museum and monument. The little extras here include coffee makers in the rooms, color TV (with cable) individual thermostats, air conditioners, and direct-dial telephones. Some of the larger rooms, designated family units, can sleep up to six people, and these rooms also have little refrigerators for baby's bottle—or for papa's. In one queen bed two people pay $38 to $46, for two beds they pay $42 to $50, and an extra person pays $4. An extra bed is $4; foliage-season rates are higher.

A Guesthouse

Luckily, Bennington is particularly well endowed with fine guesthouses, those establishments which give you more warmth and home comfort than any other type of lodging place. One of the nicest and best located is in the grand old house at 226 W. Main St., Bennington, VT 05201, not far from the Bennington Museum. It's the **Mount Anthony House** (tel. 802/447-7396), a fine aristocratic dwelling with a large, almost wrap-around sunporch and cozy rooms which rent for $35 single, $40 double with shared bath, $50 with private bath. The house accepts guests all year round.

An Inn in Arlington

About 15 miles north of Bennington is the village of Arlington, which has a number of its own hostelries, in the town proper or on Rte. 7A between Bennington and Arlington.

The **Hill Farm Inn** is north of Bennington, and four miles north of Arlington, on Rte. 7A (R.R. 2, Box 2015), Arlington, VT 05250 (tel. 802/375-2269). Though the inn has been receiving guests since 1905, it was actually built as two farmhouses in the early 1800s. Of the 11 guest rooms and two suites, seven are in the inn proper, and six in the 1790 guesthouse next door. With shared bath, breakfast, and dinner, the double rate is $93, tax included; with private bath, it's $102.

WHERE TO EAT: A few restaurants in Bennington (besides those in the motels) provide plain and fancy cuisine for travelers and local folks. I'll start with the fancy places.

In Bennington there is a place called the Potters' Yard, a complex of shops and galleries in which local works of art and craft are displayed and sold, and in this same complex at School and County Streets is the **Brasserie in Potters' Yard** (tel. 447-7922). As the name might suggest, the Brasserie is fashioned on a French tavern restaurant, with beer and wine and delicious dishes such as the pâté maison with French bread or southern-style pickled shrimp. For lunch, have the Yard Special, a platter with Danish pâté, French bread, butter, and a Boston lettuce salad, for $9. A chef's salad or Greek salad, and a variety of sandwiches and omelets are about the same. The patio is the choice place to dine in good weather: it's paved in marble, and the little café tables all have marble or granite tops. Note that the Brasserie is open for lunch from noon to 4:30 p.m., for cocktails from 4:30 to 6 p.m., and for dinner from 6 to 8 p.m.; closed Tuesday and Wednesday in winter only. To get to the Brasserie and Potters' Yard, turn off Main Street by the Dunkin' Donuts (which is at 460 Main), and go straight down the street until it ends right at the Yard.

Bennington's purveyor of the daily fresh and delicious is **Alldays & Onions,** 519 Main St. (tel. 447-0043), a combination country store, delicatessen, gourmet food shop, restaurant and bistro, open from 7 a.m. to 6 p.m. Monday through Wednesday, till 8 p.m. Thursday through Saturday, and Sunday from 10 a.m. to 3 p.m. Drop by and join the assortment of locals and travelers, Bennington College students and professors for freshly baked morning muffins and Colombian coffee, a wonderful make-your-own sandwich, or a cool pasta salad. Evening suppers often feature enticing pasta dishes or fish. Expect to spend about $6 to $8 for lunch, $14 to $18 for supper here. They have a small but good eclectic wine list.

WHAT TO SEE: The historic sights of the town are mostly grouped along West Main Street, in the section called Old Bennington.

The Bennington Museum

The Bennington Museum, West Main Street (Rte. 9; tel. 447-1571), has a collection dominated by that for which the town was famous: its Revolutionary and early American history. Paintings, glass items (molded, blown, and pressed), American-made furniture and carvings, arms, toys, and costumes are all included, and there are considerable numbers of very attractive treasures. The Bennington pottery, for instance, is more like china with its gold or colored trim; it was made here for wealthy customers for over 100 years. Of the paintings, the most fascinating are the ones in the Grandma Moses collection. Anna Mary Moses (1860–1961) was a farm girl in nearby New York state, and later as a farmer's wife she did all the heavy, hard work that life on a farm demands, yet still found time to paint. After she was 70 years old and could no longer keep up with the heavy farm work, her paintings took on such a charming and primitive character, and such spirit, that one of her paintings now hangs in the Metropolitan in New York, and many others are here in the Bennington Museum. At the age of 100 she was still at work, and she died at 101. You can look back into what life was like for her in the exhibit called "And Life Is What You Make It" in the Grandma Moses Schoolhouse Museum, also in the Bennington Museum.

The Bennington Museum is open daily from 9 a.m. to 5 p.m., March through December; open weekends only January and February. Admission is $4.50 for adults, $3.50 for young people, ages 12 to 17 and seniors, free for children under 12, $10 per family.

The Bennington Battle Monument

You will want to know, first of all, that there is indeed an elevator in this 300-foot-high structure so that you needn't climb granite stairs to get to the observation deck. The stirring tale of the Battle of Bennington is outlined in a little leaflet which you can pick up as you pay the admission fee for the ride to the top. First, you will learn that the battle didn't take place here, but several miles west in what is today New York; but the storehouse of American arms that attracted Gentleman Johnny Burgoyne to divert his troops from their march to Saratoga was right where the monument now stands, and so the spot is, after all, a suitable place for a commemorative monument.

Should you want to visit the battlefield, go west on Rte. 67 from Bennington and just before Walloomsac, N.Y., is the Bennington Battlefield State Historic Site, open daily from 9 a.m. to 7 p.m. between Memorial Day weekend and Labor Day.

Park-McCullough Historic House Museum

Of Bennington's outstanding Victorian mansions, one is exceptionally well kept. The Park-McCullough House, at the corner of West and Park Streets in North Bennington (tel. 442-5441), is open for guided tours through the house daily, late May through October from 10 a.m. to 4 p.m. Adults pay $3; students and seniors, $2; children 11 and under accompanied by an adult, free. Besides the house, still stuffed with period furnishings and personal effects, there's a pint-size "manor" for a children's play house and a cupola-topped carriage house complete with century-old carriages.

While you're here in North Bennington, drive or walk through the campus of **Bennington College,** the unique loosely structured four-year college, which stresses artistic creation and an acquaintance with nature. The situation of the college is particularly beautiful and is particularly well adapted for the creative efforts of the students.

---

4. West Dover and Mount Snow

Because of its southern Vermont location within driving distance of the metropolitan centers of Boston, Hartford, Providence, and New York, Mount Snow is one of Vermont's most popular ski resorts. The ski resort encouraged the inn trade, and the inns began playing host to summer travelers, and now this area is as popular in the warm months as in the cold.

WHERE TO STAY: About 100 inns, lodges, hotels, and motels are clustered near the ski area, on the approach roads, or in the villages near Mount Snow. From this bewildering assortment of choices, several stand out prominently.

Perhaps the most famous inn in the area is the **Inn at Saw Mill Farm,** P.O. Box

367, West Dover, VT 05356 (tel. 802/464-8131). Innkeepers Rodney and Ione Williams, along with their son, Brill, and daughter-in-law, Luz, run the sort of inn that appears regularly in designer magazines with lavish spreads of photos showing the guest rooms—Victorian, Federal, turn-of-the-century—in the inn's various buildings. The dining rooms are particularly beautiful, providing the perfect ambience for cozy, romantic dinners of elegant, carefully prepared dishes from a positively sumptuous menu. On the inn's carefully tended grounds are a swimming pool, several fish ponds, and a tennis court. The inn proper, an old farmhouse and barn, houses 11 guest rooms, all with private bath. In addition, there are 10 rooms in other buildings, each with a fireplace and private bath. Rates are $268 to $317 double, breakfast and dinner included. Prices may be a bit higher in foliage season, and between Christmas and New Year's. Note that the inn has an annual closing from after Thanksgiving till mid-December, and that *no credit cards are accepted.* Children under 10 cannot be lodged at the inn. To find the Inn at Saw Mill Farm, get to West Dover on Rte. 100, and follow the signs.

Kitzhof, on Rte. 100 in West Dover, VT 05356 (tel. 802/464-8310), is a particularly nice alpine-style lodge set back from the highway, charging quite moderate prices. No two rooms are alike except in their comfort, sparkling cleanliness, and the presence of private baths. Knotty-pine boards and logs add rustic emphasis; a Finnish-style sauna and a whirlpool bath are added luxuries open to all guests. There's a BYOB bar with set-ups. *Per-person* weekend rates in ski season are $65 double, $70 double deluxe, $48 for four in a room. Reductions are in order for lots of things, such as 5½-day economy ski weeks, paying in cash (5%), coming early or late in the ski season. The Kitzhof takes bus tours in summer and can provide lodging for transient guests when there's room.

A short five-mile drive north on Route 100 from Mount Snow brings you to the village of West Wardsboro and the **Brush Hill Restaurant** (tel. 896-6100), a late 18th-century post-and-beam barn that's been restored and turned into a romantic dining spot. A 12-foot-long brick fireplace takes the chill off in foliage season; all diners enjoy it as there are less than a dozen tables. Chef Mike Sylva apprenticed at Jaspers in Boston, and while he's in the kitchen creating New American Cuisine treats, wife Lee acts as hostess (but she also makes the desserts). The menu changes daily, but recently dinner started with an unusual antipasto of grilled artichokes, shallots, red pepper, and smoked scamonza, and was followed by a rack of lamb with mint essence, grilled leeks, and garlic. Dessert may be the dieter's to-order-or-not dilemma, with pastry puffs filled with French vanilla ice cream topped by a chocolate rum sauce. Dinner, the only meal served (Wednesday through Sunday, 6 to 10 p.m.), will cost about $45 to $50 per person, wine, tax, and tip included.

SKIING MOUNT SNOW: The ski area is immense, with three different faces of the mountain covered with trails and lifts—13 lifts in all, including two enclosed, skis-on gondolas. The highest vertical drop is almost 2,000 feet, and you could take the same lift a dozen times and never come down the same trail or slope. It's crowded, yes, because it's close to the cities, and is a good mountain for beginners and intermediate skiers, but it's also got a lot of variety, and certainly a lot of activity. A resort this big has all the facilities: a "Pumpkin Patch" nursery for small children, a bar, a cafeteria, and equipment rentals, a ski school, and 40 miles of cross-country trails.

5. Newfane and Grafton

Two of Vermont's most picture-perfect towns, with tall old trees, white churches with high steeples, and gracious old houses designed with classical touches: that's Newfane and Grafton. Come early in spring when they're "sugaring off," and see town children tap the maple trees along village streets. Come in summer and explore for yard and antique sales. Come in autumn for the blazing color. Or come in winter to hide away in a comfy inn and dine each night from a superb menu.

NEWFANE: The best place to stay or dine in Newfane is the **Four Columns Inn,** P.O. Box 278, Newfane, VT 05345 (tel. 802/365-7713). Except for two weeks after Thanksgiving and three weeks in April, when the inn is closed, you can come for dinner any night Wednesday through Monday from 6 to 9 p.m. Find a table in the cozy dining room, which reminds one of a hunting lodge in Europe with its rough-hewn beams, large fireplace, and spindle-backed chairs. Then get ready for such delicacies as a cold salmon mousse, followed by venison or rack of lamb, duck, or steak, finishing up with fancy pastries. The wine list has vintages priced from $14 to $50, and a full dinner for two here might cost $80 to $125.

As for the guest rooms, they are as charming as the inn and the town, and rent for $85 to $130 double, with private bath, air conditioning, and breakfast included.

GRAFTON: Like Newfane, Grafton is a piece of old New England, but there is a nobility about this town—something like Woodstock—that makes it special. Carefully preserved houses and public buildings from a century or two ago are joined unobtrusively by more modern structures on the outskirts. Summer or winter, Grafton is a place bewitching in its beauty. Stop for a cup of coffee, a drink or a meal, or even for overnight. Be careful, though—one overnight easily leads to week-long stays here.

Grafton's hostelry, the **Old Tavern,** Grafton, VT 05146 (tel. 802/843-2231), is also a town landmark. It's been the center of Grafton's social life since it was built in 1801 as a way station on the stagecoach road. In its long history as a place to stay the night, the Old Tavern has played host to General Grant, Woodrow Wilson, Rudyard Kipling, and even woodsman-philosopher Henry David Thoreau. With its annexes, the inn can lodge about 100 people. Its rooms have private baths and modern conveniences, but the ambience is still old New England. Rates vary with the exact situation, size, and facilities, but range from $64 to $112, and that includes the 6% Vermont tax; no credit cards accepted. The Old Tavern is an authentic landmark, but it is not what one would call "quaint." Charming, hospitable, very comfortable —it is all these, though.

You have a choice of dining rooms. The jacket rule is in force each evening. For a drink before dinner, make your way to the Barn, with its own separate bar, several fireplaces, and a TV room. Lunch is served at the Old Tavern from noon to 2 p.m., and dinner from 6:30 to 9 p.m., by reservation. At dinner, main courses range from the raisin-stuffed veal steak at $18 to broiled filet mignon at $24, and these prices include soup, relish tray, potato, and vegetable.

What to Do

Grafton is perfect just for relaxing walks and sitting by the fireplace, but there are lots of other things to do as well. Start with a horse-and-carriage ride (in summer) around town. You'll see the driver, her steed, and her buggy at the stand in front of the Old Tavern daily except Sunday between mid-June and the end of October. The ride is not just for fun—you'll get a complete narrative tour of Grafton as you trot along.

Grafton harbors a number of antique shops, artists' galleries, a village store, and the **Grafton Village Cheese Company** (tel. 843-2221). The Cheese Company makes its own brand, Covered Bridge cheddar, and you can see it being made and buy samples or supplies by following the Townshend Road about a half mile south of the village. Hours are 8:30 a.m. to 4 p.m. weekdays all year, 10 a.m. to 4:30 p.m. on Saturday from June through October; closed Sunday all year.

By now no doubt you are completely enchanted with the town. To delve into its history, pay a visit to the **Grafton Historical Society Museum** (tel. 843-2584), on Main Street just down from the post office. The exhibits of Grafton memorabilia, old photographs, history, and genealogical files are open from 2:30 to 4:30 p.m. on Saturday from June through mid-October, on Sunday in July and August, and on holiday weekends and holiday Mondays.

---

6. Manchester and Dorset

MANCHESTER: The town of Manchester was once a summer resort on the order of the Berkshire towns. Settled before the Revolution, its wide main street and handsome houses retain the charm of the early Federal period.

As the county seat of Bennington County, Manchester was an important place long before Mount Equinox (3,800 feet), to the west, drew crowds of hikers and skiers. The sprawling Equinox Hotel right in the center of town has undergone an $18-million facelift.

In the modern town of Manchester Center, just a few miles north along U.S. 7, all is bustle and activity, with traffic lights, filling stations, shopping centers, supermarkets, restaurants, motels.

On U.S. 7 is Manchester's modern claim to fame: a beautifully restored house which holds the editorial offices of *Country Journal,* the magazine which has successfully combined city polish with country concerns.

Manchester is busy with locals in the summer, busier with skiers in the winter. Several inns and restaurants serve travelers year round.

Information

The **Manchester and the Mountains Chamber of Commerce** (tel. 802/ 362-2100) maintains an information office on U.S. 7 in Manchester Center for your convenience.

Where to Stay

The **Equinox Hotel, Resort, & Spa,** Manchester, VT 05254 (tel. 802/362-4700), saw its heyday in Victorian times, with four presidents as guests over the years. (It was almost five: Lincoln had reservations for 1864, but was assassinated.) As the inn's fame and clientele grew, wings and additions were added to the original building, making at last a vast, rambling wonder of a place. With its recent facelift, the Equinox is better than ever, and again ready to welcome the best. The 150 rooms here—the management boasts that no two are alike—cost $143 to $191 double. The Equinox has all the facilities of a luxury hotel, and then some: 18-hole golf course, heated swimming pool, five tennis courts, a health fitness center, lounge, restaurant, and Viennese-style bakery. When you get to the old village of Manchester (not the more modern Manchester Center), you can't miss the Equinox, for it dominates the Village Green.

Close by is the **Inn at Manchester,** P.O. Box 41, Manchester, VT 05254 (tel. 802/362-1793), a restored Vermont Victorian inn with plenty of room for guests in 14 rooms and suites in the inn, and four more in the restored carriage house. In the inn proper are six bedrooms with private bath ($94 to $106), five with shared bath ($70 to $82), two two-room family suites ($158), and a suite with king-size bed ($85). In the carriage house, the rooms ($75) all have private bath, and there's a separate lounge. The rooms bear the names of delightful mountain and meadow flowers such as primrose, black-eyed Susan, and blue phlox. Antiques are placed carefully in all the rooms, and each bedroom has a different style of coordinated linens and comforters. Old prints, paintings, and posters, picked up by innkeepers Stan and Harriet Rosenberg during their travels, are found on walls throughout the inn. A full breakfast is included in the rates, as are 10% service charge and 6% tax.

What to Do

In winter, this question is easy to answer: you ski. Big Bromley, Snow Valley, Magic Mountain, Stratton Mountain, and numerous ski touring centers are located within a few miles of Manchester Center. Right in Manchester is the ski-touring center at Hildene, more about which below.

In summer, you can play golf, swim, hike, or ride a bike. Rent a bike from **Battenkill Sports,** in the stone house 1.2 miles east of U.S. 7A along Rte. 11/30, Manchester Center (tel. 362-2734); or from the **Bicycle Shop** in Manchester Hardware, on Rte. 11/30 in Manchester Center (tel. 362-1625). Three-speed, ten-speed, men's, women's, and children's bikes are available.

At the Bromley ski area, an **Alpine Slide** (tel. 824-5522) draws downhill racers in summer. You pay the several dollars, take the lift to the top, and then hurtle along a twisty concrete trough on a small cart. The slide is open late May to mid-October from 9 a.m. to 5 p.m., if the weather's good. Bromley is six miles east of Manchester along Rte. 11. By the way, the slide is fun, but the chair-lift ride that takes you up over the verdant hills is equally enjoyable.

Take in a play at the **Dorset Playhouse** in nearby Dorset (see below for details).

Hildene

Abraham Lincoln had four sons, but only one of them lived to adulthood. When President Lincoln was assassinated in 1865, Robert Todd Lincoln was an officer serving under General Grant in the Union Army. Later a successful lawyer and businessman, Lincoln came to Manchester in 1902, bought 412 acres of land, and began construction of Hildene. The mansion was completed in 1904, and Lincoln spent the summers there until his death in 1926. The estate was inherited by his wife, and then his granddaughter, who left it to the Church of Christ, Scientist, in 1975. It's now owned and maintained by a nonprofit group, the Friends of Hildene (tel. 362-1788).

Robert Todd Lincoln built more than a house here. In all, Hildene includes 22 buildings: a dairy barn, horse barn, sugar house, greenhouse, even a small observatory. You can roam the grounds, tour the 22-room Georgian Revival mansion, inspect Lincoln family heirlooms, any day of the week, mid-May through October from 9:30 a.m. to 5:30 p.m. Admission costs $5 for adults, $2 for children. In winter, Hildene is the site of a ski touring center. To find it, go two miles south along U.S. 7A from the intersection with Rte. 11/30—the intersection is the main crossroads in Manchester Center.

DORSET: Settled in 1768, Dorset is one of the many villages in New England that is older than the American Republic. It's a gem of a village, having kept its rural spirit and fine buildings intact over the centuries, and any new structures were required to add to the harmony of the village and its setting.

For a number of years Dorset was an artists' and writers' summer resort, but these days it is usually only the successful in those fields who can afford to stay in one of Dorset's few charming old inns; rather, the village now caters to those who have become successful in the city, and who need to get away to the peace of the countryside for a few days or weeks.

In Dorset the sidewalks are marble, and so is a nice church with Gothic touches not far from the Town Green. There's a marble quarry about a mile south of town, and besides supplying the soft, easily cut stone for a myriad of uses in Dorset, the quarry supplied most of the marble for the New York Public Library building.

For recreation, Dorset has the **Dorset Playhouse** (tel. 802/867-5777), down past the church just past the end of the Town Green on Cheney Road. Plays are performed June through October. Also, the **J. K. Adams Company Factory Store,** on Rte. 30 a mile south of town, makes fine wood products—carving boards, butcher blocks, kitchen work tables, even kitchen organizers like a spice block that holds 16 glass jars and revolves on a lazy susan. All the items are available at a reduced price, and the "seconds" are sold at prices up to 40% off the norm.

Where to Stay and Dine

The **Dorset Inn,** right on the Town Green, Dorset, VT 05251 (tel. 802/867-5500 or 867-9392), claims to be Vermont's oldest continuously operated inn. The inn has several older rooms in the original building, and a larger number of rooms in an artfully disguised modern addition which blends in well with the older part. Room prices include breakfast and dinner, and are $183 double. Tax and 15% service are included in these figures. Dorset Inn guests enjoy privileges at the Field Club, which is virtually next door.

---

7. Woodstock and Plymouth

Woodstock was chartered in 1761, and within five years it had been designated the shire town (county seat) of Windsor County. The particular significance of these little facts is that they explain why the town is so beautiful today, and why so many lovely buildings survive, and why the town escaped the ravages (and riches) brought by 19th-century industry. The industry here was government, the only pollutant from which is hot air, and this rises out of sight at once.

Besides its fine buildings, Woodstock boasts no fewer than four church bells made by Paul Revere. Three are still in service, but one cracked after two centuries of use and is now on display on the south porch of the Congregational church.

Woodstock is particularly well situated, in a beautiful valley of the Ottaquechee River with mountains all around. In winter, skiers can put up in the town while they spend the day on the slopes of Mount Tom or Suicide Six.

INFORMATION: From late June through the foliage season, there is a town information booth in service on the Village Green. Go here for a free village map and list of town businesses.

WHERE TO STAY: Woodstock has a good variety of accommodations, grouped together here according to type:

Motels

The **Shire Motel** is east of the center of town along Rte. 4, at 46 Pleasant St., Woodstock, VT 05091 (tel. 802/457-2211). It is well kept and has the advantage of being within walking distance of the Village Green. A room with bath, TV, refrigerator, and air conditioning, and with one queen-size bed, costs $58 for two persons; a larger room with two double beds costs $70. I've found the proprietors at the Shire Motel to be particularly helpful and friendly.

East of town on Rte. 4 is the attractive **Braeside Motel,** P.O. Box 411, Woodstock, VT 05091 (tel. 802/457-1366), set up on the hillside away from road noise. You get the view from here, and also 12 modern wood-paneled rooms with wall-to-wall carpet, cable color TV, and Scottish touches. Prices at the Braeside are $68 to $83 single or double, continental breakfast included.

A Resort Hotel

Woodstock's top of the line is the **Woodstock Inn and Resort,** No. 14 on the Green, Woodstock, VT 05091 (tel. 802/457-1100), a very large and plush place which reminds me of a similar style hostelry found in college towns. The guest rooms are all quite new and modern, with color TV, air conditioning, and private baths, but the decorator has tried to keep to the Early American style by using beds, chairs, and papers for a 1700s effect.

Other facilities at the inn include ten tennis courts, two paddle-tennis courts, putting green (the Robert Trent Jones golf course is nearby), and a wading pool. As for food, the Woodstock Inn's "coffeeshop" is like many other restaurants, with full-course dinners. The restaurant, then, is super-elegant, and prices there for entrees go from $18 to $24, and you must have a reservation.

As for the rooms, prices are the same year round, and the ones quoted here include tax. Doubles cost $111 to $165; singles are just a few dollars less. No meals are included. You do much better if you avail yourself of a sports package plan—call for details.

WHERE TO DINE: Bentleys of Woodstock is at 3 Elm St. (tel. 457-3232), just a few steps and around the corner from the Village Green. Bentleys has captured the spirit of a Victorian tavern but without the heaviness: a pillared bar with potted palms, bentwood chairs, and lots of plants. The crowd is often young and spirited, the prices are moderate, and the food is good and simple or good and fancy. Lunch is burgers and sandwiches, light lunch plates, and omelets; for dinner, these same dishes are on order, or you can indulge in mustard chicken or veal Romanoff. For lunch, Bentleys is open from 11:30 a.m. till about 3 p.m.; for dinner, the hours are 5:30 to 9 or 10 p.m. Plan to spend around $40 per person for dinner here.

Very near Bentleys, and right beside the Woodstock Historical Society at 24 Elm St., is **The Prince and the Pauper** (tel. 457-1818), actually down an alley named Dana Lane which runs alongside the society's building. Low beamed ceilings, candle lanterns casting a golden aura onto the small tables, a worldly clientele, and good conversation are what make the mood here, but the exotic array of dishes and delicacies add to it: where else would you find calamari in beer batter as an appetizer, or main courses like salmon in pastry? Roast duckling is on the menu too. The menu changes frequently, of course, but the intimate atmosphere and the international flair remain. Expect to pay $35 to $45 per person for dinner, wine, tax and tip included. The Prince and the Pauper is open daily for dinner from 6 to 9:30 p.m.; the lounge opens at 5 p.m. Reservations are a good idea.

WHAT TO SEE: Two fine houses, both built in 1807, are open to visits. One is the Woodstock Historical Society's **Dana House,** on Elm Street (tel. 457-1822), just around the corner from the green, open daily from 10 a.m. to 5 p.m., on Sunday 2 to 5 p.m.; admission costs $2.50 for an adult, $1 for a senior citizen, 75¢ for a child. The collections here are of furniture and paintings, farm implements, and personal effects, and often the displays are as interestingly made as the objects they exhibit. The other house is also a museum, administered by the DAR Historical Society on the Village Green. The building was put up in 1807 to house the state legislature, and now contains exhibits of the museum's collection of Revolutionary-era furnishings. It's open Monday to Saturday from 2 to 4 p.m. in summer, for $1.50 admission.

In your walks around town, you might want to look for the three **covered bridges** across the Ottaquechee, including one built in 1969 and rebuilt five years later—Middle Bridge, just off the green in the middle of town.

On the far side of the Ottaquechee from the Town Green is a cemetery, and at the east edge of the cemetery is the beginning of a walking trail. The **Billings Park Trails** are maintained by the town, and are yours to enjoy for free.

Quechee Gorge

While in Woodstock, take a spin over to Quechee Gorge, 8 miles to the east. The highway bridge carries U.S. 4 right across the picturesque gorge; below, the

Ottaquechee River slips swiftly between boulders and jagged rock walls. The Grand Canyon it's not, but pretty? Definitely.

For the best view, follow the signs to the viewpoint north of the highway. Or enter Quechee State Park, on the east side of the gorge, and take the short hiking trail down to the edge of the gorge. The walk will take 15 minutes, one way. By the way, there's camping and picnicking at Quechee State Park.

SKIING AT WOODSTOCK: Woodstock was the site of the first ski tow in the United States—a rope on a pulley which pulled skiers up the slopes in a farmer's field. Today a well-known ski area is close by, called **Suicide Six.** In addition, the Woodstock Ski Touring Center, at the Woodstock Country Club, Rte. 106, Woodstock, VT 05091 (tel. 802/457-2114), has nearly 50 miles of marked trails, plus equipment rental, cross-country ski shop, restaurant and lounge, lessons, ski tours, and midweek ski-free plans with the Woodstock Inn. A new indoor sports center is located one mile away.

Suicide Six (despite the terrifying name) is a fine, mid-sized, family ski area with two double-chair lifts, and a free J-bar on the beginners' slope. Located on Rte. 12 three miles north of Woodstock, it also offers midweek ski-free plans with the Woodstock Inn. Package plans are available through the inn; there is 50% snow-making capability, and lessons and equipment can be had on the spot in a new base lodge which also houses a ski rental shop, restaurant, and lounge (tel. 802/457-1666).

You can stay in Woodstock and ski elsewhere, of course, and the Killington and Pico ski areas present all the challenge and facilities a skier could want. They're just a short drive away.

PLYMOUTH: Calvin Coolidge was born in this tiny Vermont hamlet not far from the intersection of Rtes. 100 and 100A, and you can visit the **Coolidge Homestead** and the **Calvin Coolidge Birthplace** (tel. 828-3226). The former president's early history is interesting, but the story of his "inauguration" is full of fascination. While he was vice-president, Mr. Coolidge came to Plymouth for a vacation in August 1923. Before he could even unwind, news came that President Harding was dead, and that he, Calvin Coolidge, was the 30th president of the United States. But he had to take the oath of office! The local notary public in the tiny town was none other than the new president's own father, Col. John Coolidge, and it was Colonel John who—as the only judicial official handy—administered the oath to his son by the light of a kerosene lamp at 2:47 a.m., August 3, 1923.

You can visit the Homestead, the Birthplace, the **Wilder Barn** (a farmers' museum), the village church, the cemetery where President Coolidge is buried, and **Wilder House,** which was once Coolidge's mother's house. Wilder House today holds a small restaurant and lunch counter.

The historic site is open daily Memorial Day through Columbus Day from 9:30 a.m. to 5:30 p.m. Admission for adults costs $2, children under 12 years of age enter for free, and a family ticket costs $6.

But don't miss Plymouth's outstanding attraction, the **Plymouth Cheese Company,** P.O. Box 1, Plymouth, VT 05056 (tel. 802/672-3650). The company's president, Mr. John Coolidge, is a scion of the famous village clan. Come to see the delicious Vermont granular curd cheese being made on weekdays from 11:30 a.m. to 1 p.m., or come to sample and purchase the cheese Monday through Saturday from 8 a.m. to 5:30 p.m., on Sunday from 9 a.m. to 5:30 p.m. Since the first time I tasted it, I've been hooked on Plymouth cheese. It comes cut to order by the ounce or the pound, or in three- and five-pound wheels, and it is aged 3, 6, or 12 months to produce mild, medium, or sharp cheddar. By the way, watching the cheese-making costs nothing; the cheese, last time I bought, was about $17 for the five-pound wheel (I get as much as I can carry).

8. Killington

With many skiers, Killington is the only word they have to hear before they begin thinking snow. The resort is one of Vermont's prime ski areas, and is especially noted for its progressive approach to development of its facilities (for instance, the addition of "gladed" ski trails which give one the feeling of skiing right in the forest) and its snow-making and grooming capabilities. But in recent years Killington has expanded its breadth of activities so that now you can go there for skiing in winter, organized backpacking and camping trips in summer, tennis practice and lessons, or for the summer Playhouse. The resort is booming, but it is laid out so well on the side of the mountain that there is plenty of room for all the activities and the visitors.

INFORMATION: The whole Killington area, which is part of the town of Sherburne, is organized with the **Killington Lodging Bureau** in charge of making room reservations for you. You can call or write to a lodge or motel directly, or you can call the Lodging Bureau to see what's available at 802/773-1330. The **Killington and Pico Areas Association,** P.O. Box 114, Killington, VT 05751 (tel. 802/775-7070), also maintains an information booth at the junction of U.S. 4 and Rte. 100 in Sherburne, at the Lothlorien Gift Shop; the booth is open during business hours.

WHERE TO STAY AND EAT: Killington is a well-organized resort community, and so virtually all activities here are organized around various package plans which are designed to save visitors money over the normal daily rates. A package would usually include lodging, meals, and the price of the activity: lift tickets, tennis lessons, horseback riding, backpacking trips. In ski season most inns operate on the Modified American Plan (MAP), in which you are required to take breakfast and dinner with your room. Call the Lodging Bureau at 802/773-1330 to ask about the package plans, or to make reservations; or send a card to Killington Ski Area, Killington, VT 05751, asking for information on ski, hiking, or tennis package plans.

Among my favorite places to dine in Killington is **Hemingway's Restaurant,** on Rte. 4 (tel. 422-3886). Established in a restored Vermont farmhouse, the restaurant has won several awards for its dishes. You might start dinner (the only meal served) by ordering hand-rolled fettuccine with smoked trout and scallions, or consommé of rabbit; then go on to shrimp with dark rum and currants, or grilled pheasant with beaujolais. The wine list is full and well balanced, everything from Château Lafitte-Rothschild ($150) to Sutter Home white zinfandel ($13). The restaurant is closed mid-April to mid-May. Expect to pay about $40 per person for dinner, all in. They also have a tasting menu which includes wine.

CONDOMINIUM RENTALS: Certainly the most comfortable and luxurious way of all to take a ski or summer vacation at Killington is to rent a fully furnished apartment unit complete with a full kitchen, all linens, a fireplace, perhaps even a dishwasher. A good number of these units, within a half mile or less of the Killington lifts, are up for rental both winter and summer. Rates vary by what sort of unit you want (a one-bedroom can sleep four, maximum; a two-bedroom does for up to six, a three-bedroom for eight), and also the exact week or weekend you want to rent: a normal Sunday to Friday ski-week rate in the middle of ski season would be $220 per person for a four-person one-bedroom unit. Summer rates run 50% less than the winter rates. For full information and very-necessary reservations, call **The Villages at Killington,** 118 Killington Rd., Killington, VT 05751 (tel. 802/422-3101 or 422-3613, or toll free 800/343-0762).

SKIING AT KILLINGTON AND PICO: Well, here you have it: one of the best-managed ski areas in the United States, with a good snow-making capability, a variety of trails, a well-organized ski school, a very accessible location, lots of parking, three lounges, quick food service or a nice restaurant, several bars, and a long skiing season—what more can I say? The vertical drop is over 3,000 feet, there are six chair lifts, a gondola said to be the longest in the world, and four Poma lifts, all with a total capacity of 10,000 skiers per hour. If that sounds like a mob scene, I must admit that it does get crowded, but also that it's a big mountain, and there does seem to be room for everyone.

The first thing to do when considering a weekend or week at Killington is to send for information on the package plans, for they will undoubtedly save you money. Even if you don't choose a package plan which includes room, meals, and lift tickets, Killington Resort has various packages just for the slopes, including special rates on lifts for two to seven days, or plans with which you get lifts and lessons for two to seven days at reduced rates, or all three—lifts, lessons, and equipment rentals —all for one price.

At Pico (pronounced *pie*-ko) Peak near Killington there are five chair lifts, two T-bars, a vertical drop of 2,000 feet, and plenty of easy parking. It's a good, challenging area in its own right, although today it is too often thought of as Killington's elder sister.

Vermont has two central ski report phones: 802/223-2957 and 223-2352. Call either one for weather and conditions reports at any Vermont ski resort.

SUMMER AT KILLINGTON: Everyone coming to the Killington area will want to take the **Killington Gondola,** on Rte. 4/100 north of West Bridgewater. The gondola is the longest such ski lift in North America, traveling 3½ miles up to the 4,241-foot summit. They say that this was the point from which the territory of "Verd-mont" ("green mountain") was christened in 1763. At the top you'll find the Killington Peak Restaurant and a self-guiding nature trail. In winter the gondola carries skiers; in summer it operates from early June to mid-October on Saturday and Sunday from 10 a.m. to 4 p.m. Tickets are $9 round trip for adults, $6 for children 6 to 12, free for those 5 and under.

Killington Playhouse is at the Snowshed Vacation Center, Killington, VT 05751 (tel. 802/422-3333), and has performances of Broadway musicals from the beginning of July through Labor Day, Tuesday through Sunday at 8 p.m. Tickets are $10 for adults; under 12 and over 65, $8. You can buy tickets at the door, but reservations are requested.

---

9. Middlebury

Like its more famous counterpart of Hanover, N.H., the town of Middlebury is replete with beautiful old Georgian and 19th-century buildings, a small college of high quality, and a pretty Town Green. Hanover has Dartmouth, and Middlebury has Middlebury College, but only Middlebury has the Vermont State Craft Center at Frog Hollow and the University of Vermont's Morgan Horse Farm—but more of that later.

INFORMATION: The local chamber of commerce has an **information office** just outside the center of town, on the right-hand side as you come into Middlebury from the south (on U.S. 7) or the east (Rte. 125). The office is open during business hours.

WHERE TO STAY AND EAT: You can't miss the **Middlebury Inn and Motel,** 20 Court House Square, Middlebury, VT 05753 (tel. 802/388-4961, or toll free

800/842-4666), as you enter the heart of town. The great old inn dominates the square even more than the red-brick courthouse just up the hill from it. The rooms, though, are all quite modern; most have private bath, TV set, and telephone, and rent for $81 to $119 double. Price is determined by the size and location (and thus the views) of the room. The modern motel rooms right next to the older inn are among the largest, and thus the most expensive. The inn has its own dining room, which serves breakfast, lunch, and dinner.

The **Addison County Chamber of Commerce,** 2 Court St., Middlebury, VT 05753 (tel. 802/388-7951), maintains a list of homeowners who rent rooms to visitors. When crowds of parents swell the town for graduation, or alums return for homecoming, the town's lodging places are always filled. The "Homeowners Listing" is a very useful service. Drop by the chamber's information office at the same address, or call.

Out of Town

The town of East Middlebury is east of Middlebury along Rte. 125, and it's here you'll find the **Waybury Inn,** East Middlebury, VT 05740 (tel. 802/388-4015). Rooms in the cozy, quaint (1810) inn have been refurbished in period style. Rooms, all with private bath and full breakfast, are $106 to $122 double, in summertime. The Waybury's dining room serves dinner and Sunday brunch at moderate prices. At dinnertime, a full-course meal of juice, main course, vegetables, potato, and bread made right in the inn, and dessert will cost between $25 and $30. There's also a fully licensed tavern.

WHAT TO DO: Once you've settled in and taken a stroll around this charming town, wander over to **Middlebury College** for a look at its exceptionally pretty campus and old granite buildings. Those in need of information about the college can get it by dropping in at the admissions office in Emma Willard House on Main Street (Rte. 30). Middlebury was founded by local people in the 19th century and went on to become a high-quality school. Robert Frost's participation in the Breadloaf Writers' Conference (held in Middlebury's mountain campus close to nearby Ripton) spread the college's reputation even farther.

Robert Frost wasn't the only person of renown to tramp the streets of Middlebury. A man named John Deere was an apprentice here from 1821 to 1825, after which he moved to Illinois and invented the world's first steel mold-board plow and his name became a household word in farms across the nation.

Deere's apprenticeship took place at Frog Hollow, which is down the hill from Court House Square, across the river bridge, and down Frog Hollow Lane on the right. The **Vermont State Craft Center at Frog Hollow** (tel. 802/388-3177) has fascinating craft exhibitions all year, not to mention craft classes and a gallery of Vermont crafts. Gallery hours are 9:30 a.m. to 5 p.m. Monday through Saturday year round, and noon to 5 p.m. on Sundays from July to mid-October.

To see the magnificent steeds at the University of Vermont's **Morgan Horse Farm** (tel. 388-2011), head west on Rte. 125 from Middlebury, turn right onto Rte. 23 (Weybridge Street), and follow signs to the farm for about 2½ miles. Admission to the farm is $2.50 per adult, $1 for teens (kids under 12 get in for free), 9 a.m. to 4 p.m. daily, May through October. Once into the farm, you'll get a guided tour of the stables, an audio-visual presentation about the farm and the Morgan horse, and the chance to roam the farm's spacious grounds and perhaps have a picnic at the picnic area.

10. Sugarbush, Warren, and Waitsfield

The area centered on Warren, Vt., along Rte. 100, can boast three well-known ski resorts: Sugarbush Valley, Mad River Glen, and Sugarbush North. Although much of the crowd here comes to stay in its own condominiums, a number of inns, motels, and guesthouses amply provide for the rest.

INFORMATION: The **Sugarbush Chamber of Commerce** will help you out with information regarding lodging, dining, events, and activities if you write to P.O. Box 173, Waitsfield, VT 05673, or if you call 802/496-3409.

WHERE TO STAY: The **Sugarbush Inn** (tel. 802/583-2301) is the area's posh resort inn. Its own pools (indoor and outdoor), batteries of tennis courts, golf course, and nature paths through the woods are all part of this complex on the Sugarbush Access Road, two miles west of Rte. 100. Rooms are tasteful and very comfy, and the inn gives off that quiet *something* that denotes class. Prices for double rooms run $111 to $160, and include free use of tennis courts and 18-hole golf course.

WHERE TO DINE: Right at Sugarbush Village is an eating place that can very easily fill all your alimentary needs:

The **Phoenix,** right in Sugarbush Village (tel. 583-2777), has a very fine, second-floor view of the Green Mountains through its large plate-glass windows. The rustic wood and heavy beams of the room contrast with the silver and linen on the tables, and a very impressive antique espresso coffee maker stands glittering to one side. The food is international, from fettuccine Alfredo to slices of veal cooked with chestnuts and cream. Highest-priced items on the menu are the sirloin steak with fresh peppercorns, and veal ($17 to $19). There's also a bar at the Phoenix, fashioned from—of all things!—a communion rail, and stained-glass windows above finish off the ecclesiastical effect. The Phoenix is closed Wednesday in summer, but any other day you can have dinner from 6 to 10 p.m., and reservations are suggested.

SUGARBUSH SKIING: Sugarbush has lots of opportunities for good skiing, and although the resort is not so highly ramified as those at Mount Snow, Killington, or Stowe, well, perhaps that's part of the charm here—an absence of big-time crowds. That doesn't mean you'll have no wait for the lift lines, though. Short lift lines these days are only at places with reserved-seat lift tickets, or at places not worth skiing, and Sugarbush, Sugarbush North, and Mad River Glen are not among these.

Sugarbush Valley

At Sugarbush proper, the slopes and trails come down almost 2,500 feet from top to bottom, and they're laid out so that close to half of them are rated as suitable for expert skiers. Lifts include a gondola almost two miles long, four chair lifts, and a Poma. Rentals, instruction, and cross-country ski trails are all part of the establishment. The ski school offers a ski-week "saturation skiing workshop" which claims to instruct students in centeredness and energy awareness as well as techniques on the slopes. Lots of package plans are up for grabs—call the information numbers given at the beginning of this section.

Mad River Glen

Mad River Glen is near Waitsfield, on Rte. 17, an easy drive from the hotel I've named above. It's a smaller area than Sugarbush, but still a good size, with four chair lifts all radiating out from one base station. The vertical drop is 2,000 feet, and the preponderance of trails (four-fifths of them) are for moderately well-trained or expert skiers. Mad River Glen has a rental shop, a ski school, and a nursery. For information contact Mad River Glen, Waitsfield, VT 05673 (tel. 802/496-3551).

Sugarbush North

Sugarbush North's trails and slopes descend 2,600 feet from top to bottom, and about half the runs are classed as good for the median-level skier. But a look at the mountain trail plan will show you that taking the no. 4 chair lift to the top of Mount Ellen will start you on some very long and pretty tricky runs. Sugarbush North has 36 trails and slopes in all, and usually a good amount of cover for a long season; there's not a lot in the way of snow-making equipment. For lodging information, call 802/583-2381 or toll free 800/451-5030. Equipment and lessons are yours at the base station for the appropriate fees.

SUMMER SOARING: The air currents around Sugarbush make it good for soaring or gliding, and the **Sugarbush Soaring Association,** P.O. Box 123, Warren, VT 05674 (tel. 802/496-2290), can fill you in on getting airborne. In fact, soaring is not the only aeronautical sport to be pursued here. Ballooning and powered flight are featured as well. Call or write for details. Just so you'll know: you can qualify for solo glider flight in less than two weeks of good, full daily lessons and flights.

A SIDE TRIP TO MONTPELIER AND BARRE: The reason to take a detour and visit the state capital of Vermont is to take a look at the capitol building, a comely classical structure modeled on the Grecian Temple of Theseus. It's made of granite from nearby Barre, of course, but the dome is of wood covered in copper and then gilded. The State House will surprise you: it's so small, but then you'll notice that the capital city, Montpelier, is pretty small too; and thus it is brought home to the visitor that he or she is in the midst of the most rural state in the Union, 48th in population (only about a half million Vermonters in all, spread through almost 10,000 square miles). It comes home to you that, as a Vermont schoolchild once wrote, in Vermont "the trees are close together and the people are far apart."

The first thing you must know about Barre is that its name is pronounced like the masculine name "Barry," and not like a drinking place. The next thing to know is that Barre is the granite capital of the world, having the world's largest quarry for the stone, and also a good number of the world's finest craftspeople to work it. Guided tours of the quarries and the workshops are offered daily, and prove a fascinating way to spend a few hours; but even more fascinating is a visit to the **Hope Cemetery,** eight-tenths of a mile north of the U.S. 302/Vt. 14 intersection, on Vt. 14. The cemetery has two gates, and is open until sunset. We speak of making "monuments to survive ourselves," and we usually mean something like a corporation, a law, a charitable institution, or a poem. In Barre the phrase is literal! Stonecutters here create the monument of their dreams for their own resting places. You'll see a balanced granite cube resting precariously on one corner, self-portraits and statues, a ponderous granite armchair (empty, of course!), even a relief of a man and his wife sitting up in bed, hands joined in eternal friendship. Hope Cemetery is more like a sculpture garden, a touching memorial to artisans and artists who came here from many parts of the world.

Details: The Rock of Ages quarry is open from the beginning of May through October, with tours every day from 8:30 a.m. to 5 p.m., free. You can take a quarry train ride from 10 a.m. to 3 p.m. Monday through Friday, June through September, for $2 per adult, half price for children.

---

11. Stowe

The lodges and inns around Stowe adopt alpine or Central European names, and although the terrain here is hardly "alpine," somehow the names make sense. The village is dominated by Vermont's highest mountain, Mount Mansfield (4,393 feet), certainly no Matterhorn; but there is definitely a European feeling in Stowe, the feeling one has in some tiny Austrian village amid emerald-green rolling hills, winding roads, and steep slopes. Perhaps it is the lushness (in summer) of the lawns, forests, and wildflowers, or perhaps it is the rain and mists—Lamoille County is said to have the greatest amount of precipitation in the state—which make everything so lush. Whatever, there is certainly an especially attractive air about Stowe.

The frequent rain is not a liability, either, for local people learn to plan on it, and the earth scents after the rain are part of the pleasure of Stowe. And besides, it's all this precipitation which makes Stowe one of the best skiing areas in the East, with plenty of deep cover and a long season.

Winter or summer, the narrow rocky mountain defile known as **Smuggler's Notch** is a dramatic place for a hike or a drive, and is just another one of those things that make Stowe special.

INFORMATION: Businesses in the area are organized in the **Stowe Area Association,** P.O. Box 1320, Stowe, VT 05672 (tel. 802/253-7321). The information office, in the center of Stowe very near the intersection of Rtes. 100 and 108 (the Mountain Road), is open daily in ski season from 9 a.m. to 6 p.m., to 5 p.m. the rest of the year. If you don't have a reservation when you arrive in Stowe, drop in here and they'll help you out.

For information on snow conditions in the area, call 802/253-8521 anytime or toll free 800/247-8693 in the winter.

WHERE TO STAY: Stowe has a good variety of lodging places. Posh or modest, dauntingly expensive or surprisingly cheap, it's here. In summer there is no problem finding exactly the room you want at the price you want to pay. But on busy winter weekends you'd be well advised to reserve in advance. Just give the Stowe Area Association a ring and they'll make the reservation for you. In winter the toll-free number is in operation; in summer, call on the regular line.

Most hostelries in Stowe require winter visitors to have breakfast and dinner; in the jargon this is called the Modified American Plan. Smaller places generally have BYOB bars or lounges, which helps greatly in reducing the expense of an after-ski glow. For supplies, trundle down to the Vermont State Liquor Store on Rte. 100 south of town, open from 9:15 a.m. to 6 p.m., till 8 p.m. on Friday; closed Sunday.

What follows is a selection of my favorite places to stay in Stowe, summer or winter. Bus service along Rte. 100 (the Mountain Road) connects the ski slopes to Stowe Village during the busy winter season.

Stowehof Inn, P.O. Box 1108, Stowe, VT 05672 (tel. 802/253-9722, or toll free 800/422-9722), about 3½ miles from Stowe village off the Mountain Road on Edson Hill Road, is a bold, unusual, and exciting place. The inn's inspiration is definitely alpine, and the public rooms give a sense of coziness and charm such as one might get in a small European *Schloss*. But architect Larry Hess's masterful planning of spaces—split levels, strange angles, nooks, crannies, high ceilings and low ceilings—has resulted in a truly delightful place to spend time. There's a sunken fireplace pit, a cardplayers' nook decorated with giant playing cards (a royal flush, no less), a library seating area, a living room with panoramic view of the valley, several dining rooms, and a downstairs pub. One motif used throughout the inn, from the main entrance to the dining and living rooms, is that of support "columns" of massive tree trunks stripped of bark and dried to a silvery, ringing hardness. All this sounds wild, but it's so well done that Stowehof is truly a delight to be in. Besides the main inn, Stowehof has lovely grounds, a heated swimming pool, tennis courts, shuffleboard, pitch-and-putt green, a sauna, a library, and a game room. Each of the 41 guest rooms is decorated differently, and each has a private bath and balcony or patio. Some "demi-suites" have extra Murphy beds, or fireplaces and kitchenettes. The dining room is among the area's best, with a full, wonderful dinner with wine costing about $120 for a couple. Rates for a room at Stowehof are $190 to $256 double, breakfast and dinner, tips and tax all included. Weekly rates and special package deals are available as well. This is my first choice in Stowe.

When I wrote of Stowe's having a European air about it, I must have been thinking particularly of the **Trapp Family Lodge** (tel. 802/253-8511), two miles along a side road up the mountain slope off Mountain Road, Stowe, VT 05672. The singing Trapp family of *Sound of Music* fame left the mountains of their native Austria before World War II and settled here in Stowe, later using this as home base for their worldwide concert tours. Members of the family still are involved in operating the resort.

The Main Lodge, destroyed by fire in 1980, has been rebuilt; there's also a Lower Lodge. All the rooms come with private bath, and many have a balcony as well. Prices, which include breakfast and dinner, range from $160 to $235 double.

To get to the Trapp Family Lodge, start up Rte. 108, Mountain Road, from the center of Stowe, and go two miles to a fork by a white church; Rte. 108 bears right, but you bear left and follow this side road up the mountain slope, following the signs to the lodge, for another two miles until you arrive.

The **Andersen Lodge**, R.R. 1, Box 1450, Stowe, VT 05672 (tel. 802/253-7336), is a small, friendly Tyrolean inn which has an authentic European ambience lent by its Austrian proprietors, Trude and Dietmar Heiss. Mr. Heiss is an Austrian-trained chef as well, and so the meals (which come with your room in ski season) are particularly hearty and 'alpine.' You can play tennis, the piano, or bumper pool, or just sit in front of the fire. Each room is equipped with color TV and air conditioner. Winter rates, with dinner and breakfast, are $76 to $104 double. Summer rates are $35 to $64 double, without meals. The Andersen is on Mountain Road, on the right-hand side as you're coming from Stowe.

The **Scandinavia Inn**, Stowe, VT 05672 (tel. 802/253-8555), keeps close to the spirit of its name. It's a dark-wood building with peaked gables and white trim, decked with Scandinavian flags, right on Mountain Road. In summer there are lounge chairs on the front porch and flower boxes provide splashes of color; in winter neat stacks of wood on the porch are a ready source of fuel for the living room fireplace. This inn has a surprising range of services, including a sauna, hot tub, swimming pool, whirlpool bath, game room, barbecue grills, and bicycles. In summer, rooms with shared bath are $56 for two, rooms with bath and color TV are $69 to $76 for two; and these rates include breakfast.

The **Ski Inn**, "on the lower slopes of Mount Mansfield," on Mountain Road (Rte. 108), Stowe, VT 05672 (tel. 802/253-4050), specializes in good food and good conversation. Very near the ski areas (both downhill and cross-country) the Ski Inn is a large white country inn with a big living room/BYOB lounge with a fireplace, a pine-paneled game room in the basement, and simple but bright and pleasing rooms rented with breakfast and dinner during ski season for $65 double without bath, $85 with bath. Mr. and Mrs. Heyer, who operate the Ski Inn, share their conversation, helpful hints, and friendly atmosphere with all their guests, and particularly lucky ones may even get some of Mrs. Heyer's wild berry preserves. In summer, the rooms rent without meals for $30 to $40.

Of the inns right in Stowe Village, I feel **The Yodler**, "first on Mountain Road," Stowe, VT 05672 (tel. 802/253-4836 or toll free 800/227-1108), is a good bet for price, facilities, comfort, service, and food. Besides the lovely old house that serves as the main part of the inn, there are a number of motel units next door, all done up in the white paint and black shutters that is a New England hallmark. Rooms are comfortable and traditional in the main lodge, but all have shower or bath, TV, and telephone; some are more modern in the addition to the lodge, and the motel-style rooms have combination tub/shower, cable TV, and two double beds or a king-size bed, the traveling family's boon. Winter ski-season rates include breakfast and dinner, and can range anywhere from $80 in a tiny "roomette" without private bath in the main lodge, to over $130 for a motel room; a normal lodge room with double or twin beds and either a bath or shower is $110. You can save several dollars per room if you stay five, six, or seven days, except during the holiday weeks, of course. Besides breakfast and dinner in the Yodler's well-known dining room, the rates include tea, cocoa, cookies, and canapés every afternoon and also set-ups for the BYOB bar. Although it's not absolutely required, the Yodler recommends that you submit to a 15% service charge rather than bother with tips. In summer, the Yodler's rates are for room only. Summertime prices are $20 to $110 single, $27 to $120 double, and some of these are housekeeping units. The swimming pool's open in the summer only, and there's a clay tennis court, hot tub, and free shuttle to the ski slopes.

You'll want to take a look at the homey, congenial **Gables Inn,** on the Mountain Road, Stowe, VT 05672 (tel. 802/253-7730), where you can get a room with bath in the inn proper for $70 to $82 double, a larger room with queen-size bed, fireplace, and hot tub for $100. The Gables has a swimming pool, picnic area, hot tub, and a front porch where you can have breakfast (till noon) while gazing at Mount Mansfield.

Motels

I've concentrated on ski lodges and inns as these places provide the most atmosphere and convenience for the money, but those who prefer a modern, well-run hotel will be happy to know that there are several good choices on the Mountain Road.

An attractive motel is the **Innsbruck Inn** on Mountain Road. (P.O. Box 1570), Stowe, VT 05672 (tel. 802/253-8582), a modern place with quite large rooms, each with a full bath plus an extra washbasin outside the bathroom, a color TV, AM-FM radio, refrigerator, two double beds or one queen-size and one double bed, outside and inside entrances, and with its own restaurant and bar downstairs. As the name implies, the Innsbruck's flavor is Austrian, with an Alpine dark-wood-and-white-stucco half-timbered effect, Austrian coats-of-arms and flags. The inn has an outdoor, heated pool, a whirlpool spa, a game room, and a sauna. The rooms are $42 to $64 double in summer, $52 to $78 double in winter, breakfast included.

Stowe's prime modern accommodations are at the **Golden Eagle Resort Motor Inn,** Mountain Rd., Stowe, VT 05672 (tel. 802/253-4811 or toll free 800/626-1010). You can bed down in a comfortable room, suite, efficiency unit, or vacation apartment; such amenities as fireplaces, balconies, refrigerators, and private whirlpool baths are available in some accommodations. The Golden Eagle has many facilities, including a hot tub, indoor and outdoor swimming pools, fitness room, sauna, whirlpool bath, tennis court, and even two stocked trout ponds for fishing buffs. There are three restaurants. Service here is friendly, experienced, and dependable. Rates vary greatly depending upon accommodation and season, but they range from $70 to $111 for luxury motel rooms, $84 to $180 for apartments; weekly and monthly rates can bring the apartment prices down somewhat. You can't go wrong here.

WHERE TO DINE: During ski season, of course, most people will want to eat at their inn, or will be obliged to do so. But for summer, or the odd day out, here are some other dining places to think about.

Look first at the recommendations (above) on Stowehof, the Golden Eagle, and the Yodler, for these are some of the preferred dining places in the valley. Almost every other inn serves meals as well.

An interesting, bright, well-run restaurant right in Stowe is the **Restaurant Swisspot,** right on Main Street just north of the intersection with Mountain Road (tel. 253-4622). The accent is on rusticity of course, with copper buckets hanging from the rough ceiling beams, butcher-block tables, a bar of very rough wood, and the flags of the cantons in the Swiss confederation decked on the walls; for summer supping, tables with umbrellas are set outside with a view of the road. I was not surprised to find on the Swisspot's menu a luncheon hamburger called the burger Verbier, which weighs a half pound and is covered in swiss cheese and curry sauce; you can get one with tomatoes and horseradish sauce for the same price, or you can pick from a dozen other burgers and just as many sandwiches. But there are appetizers, salads, fondues, quiches, daily fish and pasta specials, and main courses such as grilled veal sausages or a char-broiled sirloin, each entree coming with salad and rice or potato. Expect to pay $18 to $20 per person for dinner.

WHAT TO SEE AND DO: Much of the territory around Stowe is part of Vermont's **Mount Mansfield State Forest and Park,** and for summer visitors that means hiking trails (especially the Long Trail from Massachusetts to Canada), camping areas, and picnicking. Winter visitors will want to note the state ski area, and Spruce Peak ski area.

Skiing Stowe

The trails are down both Mount Mansfield and Spruce Peak, the mountains on either side of the Smuggler's Notch defile, and the variety of trails is such that there's plenty of adventure for everyone, no matter what your ability. In fact, the mountains, the staff in charge of trail maintenance, and especially the Sepp Ruschp Ski School have all worked hard over many years to earn for Stowe the high regard it has among skiers. The vertical drop is over 2,000 feet, and the lifts include five chairs, three T-bars, and a gondola with four-passenger cars. Beginners will want to start off at the Toll House Slopes, near the base of the toll road up Mount Mansfield; the next logical step is to Spruce Peak; and after you've mastered that, go on to the more difficult among the Mount Mansfield trails and slopes. Lessons and rentals are available, and there are restaurants at **Cliff House** (top of the Mansfield gondola) and **Octagon** (top of the toll road), as well as at the base camps.

A big event of the winter season at Stowe is the annual **Winter Carnival,** held during the second week in January, when special races, church suppers, square dances, hockey and skating matches, a snow sculpture contest, and even a Queen's Ball are held—hotel rates are not raised for this event. Check with the Stowe Area Association for a carnival schedule.

Summer at Stowe

Some of Stowe's pleasures are best appreciated during warm weather. The breathtaking ride to the top of Vermont's highest mountain in a gondola (tel. 253-7311) costs $8 round trip for adults, $4 for children. Or you can drive to the top of Mount Mansfield on the toll road, climbing even higher into the mist, past bunches of exotic wildflowers, feeling the air get cooler. The toll road base station is near the ski areas just south of Smuggler's Notch; you pay for your car and then proceed up the road, which is only paved for a quarter of a mile—the rest is stabilized dirt. (But the quarter of a mile at the bottom is so perfect for skateboarding that the management has had to erect a sign prohibiting the fast and fancy rollers from monopolizing this stretch of its land!) Both the gondola and the toll road are open daily from mid-June through mid-October, weather permitting.

It's hardly less exciting just to make the drive through Smuggler's Notch. You approach the mountains and the defile, and start turning the sharp bends in the road as you meet a sign saying "Shift to Low Gear Now"—and it *means* it. The road begins to twist among tremendous boulders fallen from the steep sides of the defile over the eons; the foliage gets very thick, the trees block much of the sun's light, and as you grind along up the switchback slope, a sense of wildness and excitement takes over. Just over the pass is a stopping place (you dare not stop unless you can pull off the road) with benches, toilets, a snack stand, and several impromptu trails which invite one to clamber—at least for a few hundred feet—into the rocks.

Cinema and Theater

Stowe now has a movie house, in the complex called **Stowe Center,** which is exactly a mile north of Stowe village along Mountain Road. Call 253-4678 to see what's playing. When you get there, you can choose a regular theater seat or a comfy corner of the Projection Room—a cocktail lounge—from which to see the film. What a good idea!

The **Green Mountain Guild of White River Junction** brings summer theater to Stowe during July and August, every week Tuesday through Saturday. Performances are at Stowe High School on Barrows Road. Contact the Stowe Area Association for current schedules, reservations, and prices.

Other Activities

It's no exaggeration to say that something's always happening here in June, July, and August. Antique car rallies, horse and dog shows, a craft fair, even a fiddlers' meeting, and a surprisingly authentic Oktoberfest (in October, natch) crowd into the schedule. English Leather hosts a tennis tournament at Topnotch at Stowe in August: the purse is a whopping $75,000, so it's no minor event. Speaking of **Topnotch,** that posh resort on Mountain Road near Mount Mansfield, this is the place to rent horses by the hour or for a trail ride: call 253-8585 and ask for the stables. The going rate is $12 per hour.

Stowe now has an **Alpine Slide,** operated by the Mount Mansfield Company (tel. 253-7311). You start by taking a cool and scenic ride up a chair lift. At the top, you mount a small sled and begin your descent along a concrete runway which weaves and turns like a bobsled run all the way to the bottom of the mountain slope. It's fun! The idea (and the Alpine Slide design) came from West Germany. The slide is open on weekends and holidays from Memorial Day to June 30, daily from July 1 through Labor Day, although it closes on days of rain. Rides cost $4 per adult, $3 per child, and five-ride ticket books are available. Take your slide-ride between 9:30 a.m. and 5 p.m., weather permitting. The Alpine Slide is six miles north of Stowe village on Rte. 108 at Spruce Peak.

The more familiar summer pastimes are well covered too. **Stowe Country Club** has an 18-hole golf course; tennis courts abound (many hotels and lodges have their own); hiking, bicycling, fishing, and photographing can fill whole weeks.

---

12. Burlington

The largest city in Vermont is a town of only about 50,000 population, but in this state small is beautiful. Burlington's situation on the shores of Lake Champlain brings it extra attractiveness and aquatic sports opportunities as well. The town is the seat of the University of Vermont, and student activities and cultural events add an extra dimension to Burlington's daily life. Of the city's native sons, the educator and philosopher John Dewey is the most famous, and Ethan Allen, while not born here, chose Burlington as his home in his later years. Today part of his farm is encompassed by Ethan Allen Park.

Besides being a college town, Burlington is industrial: weapons, data processing equipment, textiles, and consumer products are all made here, and Burlington's medical facilities serve the northern part of the state. Burlington is one of two termini for Lake Champlain ferryboat crossings (the other is Port Kent, N.Y.).

INFORMATION: The **Lake Champlain Regional Chamber of Commerce** is at 209 Battery St. (P.O. Box 453), Burlington, VT 05402 (tel. 802/863-3489). They'll offer a free area map and listing of summer events.

WHERE TO STAY: Most of Burlington's acceptable lodgings are a short way from the center of town, but there is one hotel right downtown.

Out at the intersection of U.S. 2 and I-89 is a 150-year-old **Sheraton-Burlington Inn** (tel. 802/862-6576, or toll free 800/325-3535). No, that's not a printer's error, there actually is a modern Sheraton Inn built around an old farm's barns and carriage shed. As much of the old structure as possible has been used for effect, but of course all the motel rooms are quite modern. The official address is 870 Williston Rd., Burlington, VT 05401, and there are 170 rooms, a restaurant, lounge with live entertainment, a new health spa, and indoor and outdoor swimming pool. Room prices in summer (July through October) are $73 to $105 single, $73 to $121 double. Higher prices are for the new additional wing rooms, connected to the main building by an authentic old Vermont covered bridge. At this location, you're only a mile from the airport.

The **Howard Johnson Motor Lodge,** P.O. Box 993, Burlington, VT 05402 (tel. 802/863-5541, or toll free 800/654-2000), is also here, at the intersection of U.S. 2 and I-89. Prices are on the order of the other chain hotels, but there are several advantages to staying at Hojo's, including indoor-outdoor pool, fitness room, hot tub, saunas, tennis courts, and cable color TV. Lots of rooms are equipped with two double beds, and the family plan allows kids under 18 to stay free with their parents. In the months from May to October, singles are $58 to $70, and doubles are $70 to $80.

Going down the price scale somewhat, **Econo Lodge** (tel. 802/863-1125, or toll free 800/446-6900) has an installation at the intersection of U.S. 2 and I-89, a quarter mile from Exit 14E, at 1076 Williston Rd., Burlington, VT 05403. At the Econo Lodge, in addition to a health spa you get the usual, expected motel comforts —rooms with one or two double beds, color TV, free HBO, full bath, even an outdoor swimming pool—but prices are very reasonable: $45 to $58 for one, $55 to $68 for two, $59 to $76 for three or four (usually a family, but nothing says two couples can't share a room).

Right downtown is the **Radisson Burlington Hotel,** at Burlington Square, Burlington, VT 05401 (tel. 802/658-6500, or toll free 800/333-3333). Many of the 200 rooms have gorgeous views of Lake Champlain, while others open onto the indoor swimming pool. The Radisson bills itself as "Vermont's most luxurious hotel," and although many other hotels may dispute the claim, there's no disputing the Radisson's luxury quality. Tropical plants bring freshness to an enclosed Garden Court next to the pool and whirlpool bath. The price is $102 to $141 for singles, and $118 to $141 for doubles; the more expensive rooms are those with a lake-and-mountain view, and the Plaza rooms with extra amenities. An extra person or bed is $20, but children under 18 stay with their folks for free. Parking is free too.

Of the many motels on U.S. 7 south of town, the **Colonial Motor Inn,** 462 Shelburne St., Burlington, VT 05401 (tel. 802/862-5754), is among the best. A substantial establishment, it boasts 40 modern rooms with air conditioning, color TV, telephones; an outdoor swimming pool is open in good weather. A shopping center with services and restaurants is a short walk away. For one double bed (single or double occupancy) the price is $38 to $45; for two double beds it's $40 to $56. From I-89 take Exit 13 to I-189; take I-189 to U.S. 7 and go north to the Colonial.

WHERE TO DINE: My choice is **Carbur's,** at 117 St. Paul St. facing City Hall Park (tel. 862-4106). Carbur's is done in heavy mod-Victoriana, and tends to the quietly outrageous: a sign in the window says "Famous Since 1974." The dining room has a tremendously high ceiling equipped with ceiling fans that spin slowly even on cool days, just for atmosphere. Soup and a large sandwich cost less than $10 at lunch, and salad plates go for only slightly more. The menu is a book 25 pages long, filled with sandwiches, soups, salad plates, almost all—with a few exceptions like the monster five-decker sandwich—for $10 or less. The menu, by the way, is laden with enough drawings and amusing patter to keep you entertained all through your meal.

WHAT TO DO: Much of Burlington's cultural life centers on the **University of Vermont** campus, and on the campuses of the other three colleges in the area: **St. Michael's, Trinity,** and **Champlain.** The university, of course, has a good museum on Colchester Avenue, called the **Fleming Museum,** open every day of the year and free to all visitors. Exhibits run the gamut: a Kang Hsi vase, Wei terracotta, a Cole painting, 17th-century Persian miniatures, early Roman glass, Coptic carvings, and a bona fide Egyptian mummy.

The University of Vermont also stages an annual summer **Champlain Shakespeare Festival,** held at the Royall Tyler Theatre (tel. 802/656-2094), on the Main Street side of the campus. A **Mozart Festival** is held in summer as well.

Much of the lakefront land in Burlington is encompassed by parks, including **Oak Ledge Park** and **Red Rocks Park** in South Burlington, **Battery Park** near Burlington's center and only five blocks from the ferries, and **Burlington Municipal Beach** on Institute Road north of the ferry dock along the lake shore. **Ethan Allen Park** is north of the center of town; take North Avenue (Rte. 127) starting at Battery Park.

Shelburne Museum

From mid-May to mid-October, visitors to Burlington must make a detour to the town of Shelburne, seven miles south of the city along U.S. 7, to see the Shelburne Museum, a gala festival of Americana collected into 37 historic buildings—a smoke house, a sawmill, an inn, a toy house, apothecary shop, and many historic houses—spread over 45 acres. Here you find yourself surrounded by the sights of a New England town of a century or more ago: the church complete with prayerbooks and woodburning stoves, the schoolhouse, the livery stable. Each building is filled with the artifacts of earlier American life, and the museum is said to have about the best and fullest collection of Americana ever assembled. Among the artifacts are "Old 220," a ten-wheeled steam locomotive, a 1920s carousel, a round dairy barn (1901), and even the huge 220-foot sidewheeler steamboat S.S. *Ticonderoga,* docked here after its last run on the lake. Three art galleries feature paintings and sculpture by European and American artists, and folk art both charming and authentic: quilts for instance, and decoys, and glassware, and furniture, plus the tools used to make these items.

The Shelburne Museum (tel. 985-3344) is open from 9 a.m. to 5 p.m. daily mid-May to mid-October; admission is $12 for adults, $4 for children 6 through 17, and free for under-6s. If you arrive late in the day, ask to have your ticket validated, which will allow you to return for a full day's visit the following day (you should allow at least several hours to tour the exhibit). The museum boasts a cafeteria, a bookshop, a museum gift shop, and free parking.

Lake Champlain Ferries

One of the favorite things to do in Burlington is to take the ferry over to Port Kent, N.Y., whether you're actually interested in getting to Port Kent or not. Ferries, leaving from the King Street Dock in Burlington, operate in spring, summer, and fall, leaving each terminus at about one-hour intervals from 8 or 9:20 a.m. to 5:30 or 6:30 p.m., a bit more frequently in summer, with 14 trips a day in each direction. You can take your car across if you're going somewhere: price for car and driver, one way, is $11.50; each extra adult pays $3 one way; children 6 through 12 pay $1. The trip, a marvelous way to get to know Lake Champlain, takes about an hour each way. This ferry doesn't run in winter, but ferries between Grand Isle, Vt., and Plattsburgh, N.Y., operate year round. You'll also find a ferry chugging between Charlotte, Vt., and Essex, N.Y., from early April through early January.

INDEX

Abbe Museum of Stone Age Antiquities (Bar Harbor, ME), 359
Abbot Hall (Marblehead, MA), 96–9
Adams (Fort) State Park, (Newport, RI), 241–2
Adams Memorial Theater (Williamstown, MA), 215
Air travel, 13–4, 16
  see also specific places
Aldrich Museum of Contemporary Art (Ridgefield, CT), 256
Allen (Ethan) House (Litchfield, CT), 292
Allen House (Old Deerfield, MA), 198
America's Cup Race (Newport, RI), 242
American Antiquarian Society (Worcester, MA), 189
Amherst (MA), 193–8
Amherst College (MA), 197
Amoskeag Mills (near Manchester, NH), 299
Anheuser-Busch Company's Merrimack Brewery (NH), 299–300
Antiquarian House (Plymouth, MA), 116
Aquariums:
  Boston (MA), 57
  Cape Cod (MA), 139–40
  Mystic (CT), 276–7
  Woods Hole (MA), 128
Archives and State House (Boston, MA), 26, 28, 50
Arnold Arboretum (Boston, MA), 57
Artillery Company of Newport, RI, 240–1
Art museums and galleries:
  Connecticut: Hartford, 285; New Haven, 262; Old Lyme, 265; Ridgefield, 256
  Maine: Boothbay Harbor, 345–6; Portland, 336, 338–9
  Massachusetts: Boston, 53–5; Cambridge, 78–9; Gloucester, 104; Springfield, 199; Stockbridge, 209; Williamstown, 215; Worcester, 188–9
  New Hampshire: Manchester, 299
  Rhode Island: Newport, 241
  Vermont: Bennington, 369–70
Ashfield (MA), 194–5
Ashley House (Old Deerfield, MA), 198
Athenaeum, Boston (MA), 57
Atkins Fruit Bowl (near Amherst, MA), 197
Atwood House and Museums (Chatham, MA), 144–5
Avon (CT), 288, 290

Back Bay (Boston, MA), 27, 28, 45
Back Bay Fens (Boston, MA), 28, 30
Bangs Hallet House (Yarmouth, MA), 137
Bar Harbor (ME), 352–61
  accommodations, 352–5
  restaurants, 355–7
  sights and attractions, 357–61
  tourist information, 352
Barnard Tavern (Old Deerfield, MA), 198
Barnstable (MA), 135, 136
Barre (VT), 382
Bartholomew's Cobble (near Ashley, MA), 213
Bash Bish Falls (near South Egremont, MA), 213
Basketball Hall of Fame (Springfield, MA), 200
Bath (ME), 341–2
Battleship Cove (Fall River, MA), 119
Bayard Ewing Building (Providence, RI), 224
Beacon Hill (Boston, MA), 26, 28, 43, 50

Bearskin Neck (Rockport, MA), 109
Beauport (Gloucester, MA), 104
Beechwood (Newport, RI), 239
Belcourt Castle (Newport, RI), 239
Bellevue Avenue (Newport, RI), 228
Bennington (VT), 367–70
Bennington Battle Monument (VT), 370
Bennington College (VT), 370
Bennington Museum (VT), 369–70
Berklee College of Music (Boston, MA), 63
Berkshire Music Festival (Lenox, MA), 63
Berkshires (MA), 200–8
  accommodations, 202–5
  map of, 201
  restaurants, 205–6
  sights and attractions, 206–8
  tourist information, 202
Berkshire Scenic Railway Museum (Lenox, MA), 207
Berkshire Theater Festival (Stockbridge, MA), 210
Bethel (ME), 340
Big "E" (Springfield, MA), 200
Black Heritage Trail (Boston, MA), 57
Block Island (RI), 244–51
  accommodations, 246–9
  getting there, 245–6
  restaurants, 249–50
  sights and attractions, 250–1
Blue Hill (ME), 350–1
Boating:
  Boston (MA), 31–2
  East Haddam (CT), 268–9
  Lake Winnipesaukee (NH), 302–3
  Martha's Vineyard (MA), 172
  Portland (ME), 339
Boothbay Harbor (ME), 342–6
Boothbay Regional Art Gallery (ME), 345–6
Boston, 20–67
  accommodations, 34–40; bed and breakfast, 35, 39; budget, 39–40; guesthouses, 40; luxury, 36–7; moderately priced, 38–9; outlying districts, 40; room rentals, 39; top hotels, 35–6; upper bracket, 37–8
  arrival and orientation, 21–3, 26, 28, 30–1
  getting there and around, 21–3, 32–4
  maps of, 82–3; Back Bay, 27; downtown, 29; environs, 82–3; the Freedom Trail, 49; Rapid Transit Lines, 33
  nightlife and entertainment, 60–6; cinema, 65–6; dance, 65; music, 64; nightclubs and singles bars, 61–2; opera and symphony, 62–4; theater, 64–5
  outlying districts, 30
  restaurants, 40–8; Back Bay: Newbury and Boylston Streets, 45; Beacon Hill, 43; budget, 47–8; Chinese dim sum, 46; Faneuil Hall Marketplace and the Waterfront, 43–4, 48; along the Freedom Trail, 48; Mexican, 47; moderately priced, 43–4; money-saving, 44–7; along Newbury Street, 45, 47; North End, 47–8; seafood, 45–6; Thai, 46–7; top, 41–3
  shopping, 58–69
  sights and attractions, 48–58; Arnold Arboretum, 57; the Athenaeum, 57; Boston Children's Museum, 56; Boston Tea Party Ship and Museum, 53; Christian Science Church Center, 57–8; Computer Museum,

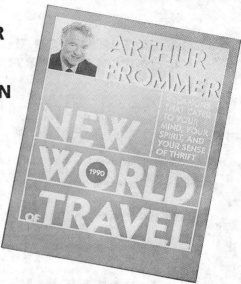

NOW, SAVE MONEY ON ALL YOUR TRAVELS!
Join Frommer's™ Dollarwise® Travel Club

Saving money while traveling is never a simple matter, which is why the **Dollarwise Travel Club** was formed 31 years ago. Developed in response to requests from Frommer Travel Guide readers, the Club provides cost-cutting travel strategies, up-to-date travel information, and a sense of community for value-conscious travelers from all over the world.

In keeping with the money-saving concept, the annual membership fee is low —$18 (U.S. residents) or $20 (residents of Canada, Mexico, and other countries)—and is immediately exceeded by the value of your benefits, which include:

1. Any TWO books listed on the following pages.
2. Plus any ONE Frommer City Guide.
3. A subscription to our quarterly newspaper, *The Dollarwise Traveler*.
4. A membership card that entitles you to purchase through the Club all Frommer publications for 33% to 50% off their retail price.

The eight-page *Dollarwise Traveler* tells you about the latest developments in good-value travel worldwide and includes the following columns: **Hospitality Exchange** (for those offering and seeking hospitality in cities all over the world); **Share-a-Trip** (for those looking for travel companions to share costs); and **Readers Ask . . . Readers Reply** (for those with travel questions that other members can answer).

Aside from the Frommer Guides, the Serious Shopper Guides, and the Gault Millau Guides, you can also choose from our Special Editions. These include such titles as **California with Kids** (a compendium of the best of California's accommodations, restaurants, and sightseeing attractions appropriate for those traveling with toddlers through teens); **Candy Apple: New York with Kids** (a spirited guide to the Big Apple by a savvy New York grandmother that's perfect for both visitors and residents); **Caribbean Hideaways** (the 100 most romantic places to stay in the Islands, all rated on ambience, food, sport opportunities, and price); **Honeymoon Destinations** (a guide to planning and choosing just the right destination from hundreds of possibilities in the U.S., Mexico, and the Caribbean); **Marilyn Wood's Wonderful Weekends** (a selection of the best mini-vacations within a 200-mile radius of New York City, including descriptions of country inns and other accommodations, restaurants, picnic spots, sights, and activities); and **Paris Rendez-Vous** (a delightful guide to the best places to meet in Paris whether for power breakfasts or dancing till dawn).

To join this Club, simply send the appropriate membership fee with your name and address to: Frommer's Dollarwise Travel Club, 15 Columbus Circle, New York, NY 10023. Remember to specify which single city guide and which two other guides you wish to receive in your initial package of member's benefits. Or tear out the next page, check off your choices, and send the page to us with your membership fee.

FROMMER BOOKS
PRENTICE HALL TRAVEL
15 COLUMBUS CIRCLE
NEW YORK, NY 10023
212-373-8125

Date_____

Friends:
Please send me the books checked below:

FROMMER™ GUIDES

(Guides to sightseeing and tourist accommodations and facilities from budget to deluxe, with emphasis on the medium-priced.)

☐ Alaska	$14.95	☐ Germany	$14.95
☐ Australia	$14.95	☐ Italy	$14.95
☐ Austria & Hungary	$14.95	☐ Japan & Hong Kong	$14.95
☐ Belgium, Holland & Luxembourg	$14.95	☐ Mid-Atlantic States	$14.95
☐ Bermuda & The Bahamas	$14.95	☐ New England	$14.95
☐ Brazil	$14.95	☐ New York State	$14.95
☐ Canada	$14.95	☐ Northwest	$14.95
☐ Caribbean	$14.95	☐ Portugal, Madeira & the Azores	$14.95
☐ Cruises (incl. Alaska, Carib, Mex, Hawaii, Panama, Canada & US)	$14.95	☐ Skiing Europe	$14.95
		☐ South Pacific	$14.95
☐ California & Las Vegas	$14.95	☐ Southeast Asia	$14.95
☐ Egypt	$14.95	☐ Southern Atlantic States	$14.95
☐ England & Scotland	$14.95	☐ Southwest	$14.95
☐ Florida	$14.95	☐ Switzerland & Liechtenstein	$14.95
☐ France	$14.95	☐ USA	$15.95

FROMMER $-A-DAY® GUIDES

(In-depth guides to sightseeing and low-cost tourist accommodations and facilities.)

☐ Europe on $40 a Day	$15.95	☐ New York on $60 a Day	$13.95
☐ Australia on $30 a Day	$12.95	☐ New Zealand on $45 a Day	$13.95
☐ Eastern Europe on $25 a Day	$13.95	☐ Scandinavia on $60 a Day	$13.95
☐ England on $50 a Day	$13.95	☐ Scotland & Wales on $40 a Day	$13.95
☐ Greece on $35 a Day	$13.95	☐ South America on $35 a Day	$13.95
☐ Hawaii on $60 a Day	$13.95	☐ Spain & Morocco on $40 a Day	$13.95
☐ India on $25 a Day	$12.95	☐ Turkey on $30 a Day	$13.95
☐ Ireland on $35 a Day	$13.95	☐ Washington, D.C. & Historic Va. on	
☐ Israel on $40 a Day	$13.95	$40 a Day	$13.95
☐ Mexico on $35 a Day	$13.95		

FROMMER TOURING GUIDES

(Color illustrated guides that include walking tours, cultural and historic sites, and other vital travel information.)

☐ Australia	$9.95	☐ Paris	$8.95
☐ Egypt	$8.95	☐ Scotland	$9.95
☐ Florence	$8.95	☐ Thailand	$9.95
☐ London	$8.95	☐ Venice	$8.95

TURN PAGE FOR ADDITONAL BOOKS AND ORDER FORM.

0190

FROMMER CITY GUIDES

(Pocket-size guides to sightseeing and tourist accommodations and facilities in all price ranges.)

☐ Amsterdam/Holland	$7.95	☐ Minneapolis/St. Paul	$7.95
☐ Athens	$7.95	☐ Montréal/Québec City	$7.95
☐ Atlantic City/Cape May	$7.95	☐ New Orleans	$7.95
☐ Barcelona*	$7.95	☐ New York	$7.95
☐ Belgium	$7.95	☐ Orlando/Disney World/EPCOT	$7.95
☐ Boston	$7.95	☐ Paris	$7.95
☐ Cancún/Cozumel/Yucatán	$7.95	☐ Philadelphia	$7.95
☐ Chicago	$7.95	☐ Rio	$7.95
☐ Denver/Boulder*	$7.95	☐ Rome	$7.95
☐ Dublin/Ireland	$7.95	☐ San Francisco	$7.95
☐ Hawaii	$7.95	☐ Santa Fe/Taos/Albuquerque	$7.95
☐ Hong Kong*	$7.95	☐ Seattle/Portland*	$7.95
☐ Las Vegas	$7.95	☐ Sydney	$7.95
☐ Lisbon/Madrid/Costa del Sol	$7.95	☐ Tokyo*	$7.95
☐ London	$7.95	☐ Vancouver/Victoria*	$7.95
☐ Los Angeles	$7.95	☐ Washington, D.C.	$7.95
☐ Mexico City/Acapulco	$7.95	*Available June, 1990	

SPECIAL EDITIONS

☐ A Shopper's Guide to the Caribbean	$12.95	☐ Manhattan's Outdoor Sculpture	$15.95
☐ Beat the High Cost of Travel	$6.95	☐ Motorist's Phrase Book (Fr/Ger/Sp)	$4.95
☐ Bed & Breakfast—N. America	$11.95	☐ Paris Rendez-Vous	$10.95
☐ California with Kids	$14.95	☐ Swap and Go (Home Exchanging)	$10.95
☐ Caribbean Hideaways	$14.95	☐ The Candy Apple (NY with Kids)	$12.95
☐ Honeymoon Destinations (US, Mex & Carib)	$12.95	☐ Travel Diary and Record Book	$5.95

☐ Where to Stay USA (Lodging from $3 to $30 a night) $10.95
☐ Marilyn Wood's Wonderful Weekends (Conn, Del, Mass, NH, NJ, NY, Pa, RI, VT) $11.95
☐ The New World of Travel (Annual sourcebook by Arthur Frommer for savvy travelers) $16.95

SERIOUS SHOPPER'S GUIDES

(Illustrated guides listing hundreds of stores, conveniently organized alphabetically by category.)

☐ Italy	$15.95	☐ Los Angeles	$14.95
☐ London	$15.95	☐ Paris	$15.95

GAULT MILLAU

(The only guides that distinguish the truly superlative from the merely overrated.)

☐ The Best of Chicago	$15.95	☐ The Best of Los Angeles	$14.95
☐ The Best of France	$16.95	☐ The Best of New England	$15.95
☐ The Best of Hong Kong	$16.95	☐ The Best of New York	$14.95
☐ The Best of Italy	$16.95	☐ The Best of Paris	$16.95
☐ The Best of London	$16.95	☐ The Best of San Francisco	$14.95

☐ The Best of Washington, D.C. $14.95

ORDER NOW!

In U.S. include $2 shipping UPS for 1st book; $1 ea. add'l book. Outside U.S. $3 and $1, respectively.
Allow four to six weeks for delivery in U.S., longer outside U.S.

Enclosed is my check or money order for $_____

NAME _____

ADDRESS _____

CITY _____ STATE _____ ZIP _____

0190

AMERICAN EXPRESS CAN DELIVER CASH
AND A REPLACEMENT CARD TO YOU WITHIN 24 HOURS,
AS LONG AS YOU'RE IN THIS GENERAL AREA.

No matter where you are in the world, if you lose your wallet, we can get a new American Express® Card and cash in your hands usually within 24 hours.*

If you're truly in the middle of nowhere, say the African Outback, it might take a little longer. Depending upon how many wandering hippos and fallen trees our local courier must contend with.

But more often than not, you'll have a new Card and cash the next day. Something you'd expect from American Express.

So carry the American Express Card. And no matter where on earth you go, you'll never leave civilization behind.

For assistance, call your nearest American Express office, or in the U.S. call our 24-hour number 1-800-252-3650; everywhere else call collect 602-954-1225. Don't leave home without it.*

MEMBERSHIP HAS ITS PRIVILEGES℠

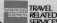 TRAVEL RELATED SERVICES *Delivery time may vary in some areas depending on transportation availability, existence of war or civil strife or other factors beyond our control. For U.S. Cardmembers only.